THREE & FOUR INGREDIENTS 500 RECIPES

THREE & FOUR INGREDIENTS 500 RECIPES

Delicious, no-fuss dishes using just four ingredients or less, from breakfasts and snacks to main courses and desserts, all shown in 500 fabulous photographs

JENNY WHITE

   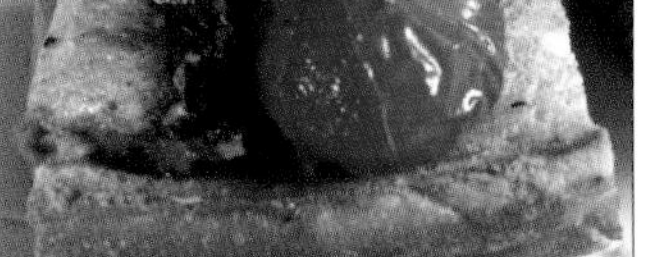 

This edition is published by Hermes House, an imprint of Anness Publishing Ltd, Blaby Road, Wigston, Leicestershire LE18 4SE
Email: info@anness.com
Web: www.hermeshouse.com; www.annesspublishing.com

If you like the images in this book and would like to investigate using them for publishing, promotions or advertising, please visit our website www.practicalpictures.com for more information.

Publisher: Joanna Lorenz
Editorial Director: Helen Sudell
Project Editor: Catherine Stuart
Copy-editor: Zoë Hughes Gough
Design: SMI and Diane Pullen
Jacket Design: Nigel Partridge
Production Controller: Don Campaniello

Notes

Bracketed terms are intended for American readers.

For all recipes, quantities are given in both metric and imperial measures and, where appropriate, in standard cups and spoons. Follow one set of measures, but not a mixture, because they are not interchangeable.

Standard spoon and cup measures are level.
1 tsp = 5ml, 1 tbsp = 15ml, 1 cup = 250ml/8fl oz.
Australian standard tablespoons are 20ml. Australian readers should use 3 tsp in place of 1 tbsp for measuring small quantities.

American pints are 16fl oz/2 cups. American readers should use 20fl oz/2.5 cups in place of 1 pint when measuring liquids.

Electric oven temperatures in this book are for conventional ovens. When using a fan oven, the temperature will probably need to be reduced by about 10–20°C/20–40°F.
Since ovens vary, you should check with your manufacturer's instruction book for guidance.

The nutritional analysis given for each recipe is calculated per portion (i.e. serving or item), unless otherwise stated. If the recipe gives a range, such as Serves 4–6, then the nutritional analysis will be for the smaller portion size, i.e. 6 servings. The analysis does not include optional ingredients, such as salt added to taste.

Medium (US large) eggs are used unless otherwise stated.

Main front cover image shows Roast Cod Wrapped in Prosciutto – for recipe, see page 72

Important: pregnant women, the elderly, the ill and very young children should avoid recipes using raw or lightly cooked eggs.

Contents

Introduction

When you're tired and stressed, the last thing you feel like doing is shopping for a long list of ingredients, then going home and preparing them all before finally cooking the meal. The temptation is to grab a ready-meal or to pick up a takeaway – but when you've had a hectic day, what you really need is to sit down with a tasty home-made meal. This book is devoted to helping you do just that.

The good news is that cooking doesn't need to be taxing. It's incredibly easy to make delicious dishes using just a few simple ingredients – the key to success lies in your choice of ingredients, and how you prepare and cook them.

The recipes in this book combine basic ingredients such as fruit, vegetables, meat, fish, herbs and spices, but they also make good use of ready-made or pre-prepared products such as curry pastes and pastry. Using these convenient products is a great way to save time without comprising the taste.

When buying ingredients, always try to buy the freshest, best quality ones you can to get the maximum flavour. Really fresh ingredients also have a higher nutritional content.

It is advisable to buy fruits and vegetables when they're in season. Although most are available all year round, you can really taste the difference between those that have been ripened naturally and those that have been forced. There are so many fabulous ingredients at their peak in their own season that you don't need to buy unseasonal ones. Why buy droopy asparagus in autumn when there are plenty of mushrooms, squashes and root vegetables around, which can be made into any number of delicious meals.

When buying pre-prepared or ready-made ingredients such as stocks for soups or custard to make ice cream, try to buy really good-quality varieties. When an ingredient is playing an intregral part in a dish, it needs to be well-flavoured with a good texture and consistency. If you use an inferior product, it will really show in the final dish.

Whether you're an experienced cook or an absolute beginner, you'll find the recipes in this book will suit you perfectly. There are dishes for every occasion: juices to quench your thirst; healthy breakfasts and light lunches to make when time is short. There are also fabulous meat, fish, vegetarian and side dishes to cook when you have more time on your hands or if you're entertaining guests. There is a selection of divine dishes to eat outside when the weather's sunny, and when you need a sweet treat, there are whole chapters devoted to cookies and cakes and sumptuous hot, cold and iced desserts. No matter what the occasion, how much time you have, how many people you need to feed – you are sure to find the perfect dish within these pages.

Every recipe has an ingredients list of four items or fewer, and the only other things you will need will come from the storecupboard (pantry): oil or butter to cook with and salt and freshly ground black pepper to season the food. In some cases flavoured oils such as garlic-, lemon-, or herb-infused olive oil are used for cooking or drizzling, so it's well worth keeping a small selection of these oils in the storecupboard. Occasionally, serving or garnishing suggestions are made, but these are optional extras.

Flavouring Methods

When cooking with a limited number of ingredients, the trick is to bring out the flavour of each one. The choice of cooking method is important because it can affect the flavour quite dramatically. Seasonings and aromatics complement and bring out the flavours of the main ingredients, while marinating or macerating help to intensify the relationship between the basic ingredient and the seasoning. The result is a full, rich flavour.

Above: Roasting vegetables in the oven really helps to bring out their sweet flavour as the natural sugars caramelize.

Above: Steaming is a delicate cooking method that is perfect for foods such as dumplings, vegetables and fish.

MAXIMIZING FLAVOUR

The way in which you cook food can make a real difference to the end result. For example, vegetables boiled for too long become soggy and insipid, devoid of nutrients and flavour. In contrast, lightly steaming vegetables, baking fish wrapped in paper or foil parcels, and dry-frying spices are simple techniques that trap and enhance the natural flavour of the food. Some methods also add other flavours during cooking: for example, sprinkling smoking chips on a barbecue gives the food an extra smoky flavour.

Cooking on a barbecue

Good-quality lumpwood charcoal will impart its characteristic smoky flavour to food. A variety of aromatics can also be added, including hickory, oak, mesquite or applewood chips; woody herbs, such as thyme or rosemary – just the stalks will do; or shells from almonds or walnuts. Soak nutshells in cold water for about 30 minutes before adding them to the barbecue to help them smoke.

Roasting

This is a good method for cooking meat, poultry, fish and vegetables. Long, slow roasting transforms sweet vegetables such as (bell) peppers and parsnips, bringing out a rich, caramelized flavour. A large, heavy roasting pan is essential for cooking big cuts of meat and vegetables; there must be room for heat to circulate.

Grilling/broiling

This method adds flavour by browning or charring the surface of the food. For good results the grill (broiler) must be pre-heated before cooking so that it is as hot as possible when the food is placed under the heat. A griddle pan can be used on the stove top to achieve similar results. Grilling is excellent for cheese, fish, poultry and lean meat, such as steak.

Dry-frying

Frying with no fat or oil is a useful technique for certain ingredients. Fatty meats such as bacon and pancetta release fat as they cook, providing fat in which to cook the meat and any other ingredients added to the pan. Dry-frying whole spices, such as coriander or cumin seeds, enhances their taste, taking the raw edge off their flavour while making it more intense and rounded. This technique is also known as roasting.

Shallow frying

Meat, poultry, fish and vegetables are all delicious pan-fried with a little oil or butter. They can be cooked quickly over a high heat to seal in the flavours, or more slowly over a low heat to achieve tender, juicy results.

Deep-frying

Meat, poultry, fish, vegetables and even fruit are delicious cooked in hot oil. It is a very quick method and gives rich results. The outside of the food is sealed almost as soon as it hits the hot oil, forming a crisp exterior that encloses the flavour and juices of the ingredients. Most foods need to be dipped in a protective coating such as batter or breadcrumbs first.

Steaming

This healthy cooking method is excellent for quick-cooking foods such as vegetables and fish. The natural flavours and nutrients of the food are retained, giving moist, tasty results. Few additional ingredients or flavourings are needed when steaming.

Microwaving

Vegetables, such as peas and green beans, can be cooked successfully in a microwave. The result is similar to steaming, trapping all the flavour and nutrients. Place the vegetables in a suitable covered container with a little added water, then cook on full power for a short time.

Baking in parcels

Traditionally known as cooking *en papillote*, this is a form of steaming. It is perfectly suited to foods such as fish and vegetables. The food is wrapped in baking parchment or foil to make a neat parcel, then baked. The steam and juices from the food are trapped within the parcel as it cooks, capturing the full flavour. Be sure to fold or crumple the edges of the parcel well to ensure that all the steam and juices are retained.

Above: Cooking vegetables, fish or meat over charcoal can help to give the food a wonderful, rich, smoky flavour.

Above: Deep-frying is a quick way of cooking that produces richly flavoured food with a crisp yet succulent texture.

Above: Fish, such as salmon, is delicious wrapped in a paper parcel with simple flavourings, then baked in the oven.

Above: To flavour a whole fish, stuff the cavity with slices of lemon and fresh herbs, season, then wrap in foil or baking parchment to cook.

Above: Rub spice mixtures into raw meat or poultry, then cook over a barbecue, grill, or bake until cooked through.

Above: Adding a drizzle of sesame oil to stir-fried vegetables gives them a wonderfully rich, smoky, nutty flavour.

INTRODUCING FLAVOUR

As well as selecting the cooking method best suited to the ingredients, there are several quick and easy ways to add flavour using herbs, spices and aromatics.

Flavours for fish

Classic seasonings used for flavouring fish and shellfish include lemon, lime, parsley, dill, fennel and bay leaves. These all have a fresh, intense quality that complements the delicate taste of fish and shellfish without overpowering it.

• To flavour whole fish, such as trout or mackerel, stuff the body cavity before cooking, then wrap in foil or baking parchment, ensuring the packet is well sealed. Place the fish in an ovenproof dish and bake until cooked through.

• To marinate chunky fillets of fish, such as cod or salmon, arrange the fish fillets in a single layer. Drizzle with olive oil, then sprinkle over a little crushed garlic and grated lime rind and squeeze over the lime juice. Cover the dish with clear film (plastic wrap) and leave to marinate in the refrigerator for at least 30 minutes. Grill lightly until just cooked through.

Pepping up meat and poultry

Meat and poultry suit both delicate and punchy seasonings. Dry rubs, marinades and sticky glazes are all perfect ways to introduce flavour. Marinating the tougher cuts of meat, such as stewing steak, also helps to tenderize them.

• To make a fragrant Cajun spice rub for pork chops, steaks and chicken, mix together 5ml/1 tsp each of dried thyme, dried oregano, finely crushed black peppercorns, salt, crushed cumin seeds and hot paprika.

• To marinate red meat, such as beef, lamb or venison, prepare a mixture of two-thirds red wine to one-third olive oil in a shallow non-metallic dish. Stir in some chopped garlic and bruised fresh rosemary sprigs. Add the meat and turn to coat it in the marinade. Cover and chill for at least 2 hours or overnight before cooking.

• To make a mild-spiced sticky mustard glaze for chicken, pork or red meat, mix 45ml/3 tbsp each of Dijon mustard, clear honey and demerara (raw) sugar, 2.5ml/½ tsp chilli powder, 1.5ml/¼ tsp ground cloves, and salt and freshly ground black pepper. Cook over the barbecue or under the grill and brush with the glaze about 10 minutes before the end of cooking time.

Vibrant vegetables

Most fresh vegetables have a subtle flavour that needs to be brought out. When using delicate cooking methods such as steaming and stir-frying, go for light, fresh flavourings that will enhance the taste of the vegetables. When using more robust cooking methods, such as roasting, choose richer flavours such as garlic and spices.

• To make fragrant, Asian-style steamed vegetables, add a bruised stalk of lemon grass and/or a few kaffir lime leaves to the steaming water, then cook vegetables such as pak choi (bok choy) over the water until just tender. Alternatively, place the aromatics in the steamer under the vegetables and steam.

• To add a rich flavour to stir-fried vegetables, add a splash of sesame oil (5ml/1 tsp maximum) just before the end of cooking time.

• To enhance the taste of naturally sweet vegetables, glaze them with honey and mustard before roasting. Mix together 30ml/2 tbsp wholegrain mustard and 45ml/3 tbsp clear honey, and season with salt and ground black pepper. Brush over the prepared vegetables to coat, then roast until sweet and tender.

Fragrant rice and grains

Classic accompaniments, such as rice and couscous, can be enhanced by the addition of simple flavourings. Adding herbs, spices and aromatics can help to perk up the rice and grains' subtle flavour. Choose flavourings that will complement the dish that the rice or grains will be served with.

• To make exotic fragrant rice to serve with stir-fries and braised dishes, add a whole star anise or a few cardamom pods to a pan of rice before cooking.

• To make zesty herb rice or couscous, heat a little chopped fresh tarragon and grated lemon rind in olive oil or melted butter until warm. When ready, drizzle the flavoured oil and herbs over freshly cooked rice or couscous.

Above: Glazing naturally sweet vegetables, such as parsnips and carrots, with a mixture of honey, mustard and oil enhances their natural flavour.

Above: Brush on sticky glazes towards the end of cooking time; if the glaze is cooked for too long, it will burn.

Above: Snipping fresh chives into a bowl of couscous not only adds flavour, but also adds a decorative finish to the side dish.

Cantaloupe Melon with Strawberries

If strawberries are slightly underripe, sprinkling them with a little sugar and grilling them will help bring out their flavour.

Serves 4
115g/4oz/1 cup strawberries
15ml/1 tbsp icing (confectioners') sugar
½ cantaloupe melon

1 Preheat the grill (broiler) to high. Hull the strawberries and cut in half. Arrange the fruit in a single layer, cut side up, on a baking sheet or ovenproof dish and dust with the icing sugar.

2 Grill (broil) the strawberries for 4–5 minutes, or until the sugar starts to bubble and turn golden.

3 Meanwhile, scoop out the seeds from the half melon using a spoon. Using a sharp knife, remove the skin, then cut the flesh into wedges and arrange on a serving plate with the grilled (broiled) strawberries. Serve immediately.

Papaya, Lime and Ginger Salad

This refreshing, fruity salad makes a lovely light breakfast. Choose really ripe, fragrant papayas for the best flavour.

Serves 4
2 large ripe papayas
juice of 1 fresh lime
2 pieces preserved stem ginger, finely sliced

1 Cut the papayas in half lengthways and scoop out the seeds. Using a sharp knife, cut the flesh into thin slices and arrange.

2 Squeeze the lime juice over the papayas and sprinkle with the sliced stem ginger. Serve immediately.

Variation
This summery salad is delicious made with 2 ripe peeled stoned (pitted) mangoes in place of the papayas.

Crunchy Oat Cereal

Serve this tasty crunchy cereal simply with milk or, for a real treat, with yogurt and fresh fruit such as raspberries or blueberries. There are so many variations on this theme you could have a different version every week.

Serves 6
200g/7oz/1¾ cups jumbo rolled oats
150g/5oz/1¼ cups pecan nuts, roughly chopped
90ml/6 tbsp maple syrup

From the storecupboard
75g/3oz/6 tbsp butter, melted

1 Preheat the oven to 160°C/325°F/Gas 3. Mix all the ingredients together and spread on to a large baking tray.

2 Bake for 30–35 minutes, or until golden and crunchy. Leave to cool, then break up into clumps and serve.

Cook's Tips
- *This crunchy oat cereal will keep in an airtight container for up to two weeks. Store in a cool, dry place.*
- *You can use the mixture to make Cranachan as a treat, adding Greek (US strained plain) yogurt and whatever soft fruit is in season.*

Variations
- *You can use other types of nuts if you prefer. Try roughly chopped almonds or hazelnuts instead of pecan nuts, or use a mixture of all three.*
- *Instead of maple syrup, which has a distinctive flavour, you could use golden (light corn) syrup or clear honey for a less intense taste.*
- *Add the juice and finely grated rind of half an orange or lemon to add a citrusy zing.*
- *Why not try this recipe with the addition of some dried fruit. You could simply use raisins or sultanas (golden raisins), or chop some ready-to-eat dried apricots or figs.*

Melon with Strawberries: Energy 46kcal/197kJ; Protein 1g; Carbohydrate 10.9g, of which sugars 10.9g; Fat 0.2g, of which saturates 0g; Cholesterol 0mg; Calcium 32mg; Fibre 1.6g; Sodium 12mg.
Papaya, Lime and Ginger: Energy 55kcal/233kJ; Protein 0.8g; Carbohydrate 13.4g, of which sugars 13.4g; Fat 0.2g, of which saturates 0g; Cholesterol 0mg; Calcium 35mg; Fibre 3.3g; Sodium 8mg.
Crunchy Oats: Energy 386kcal/1613kJ; Protein 5.8g; Carbohydrate 37.2g, of which sugars 12.6g; Fat 24.9g, of which saturates 7.5g; Cholesterol 27mg; Calcium 33mg; Fibre 3.1g; Sodium 128mg.

Muesli Smoothie

This divine drink has all the goodness of muesli, but without the lumpy texture.

Serves 2

50g/2oz/¼ cup ready-to-eat dried apricots
1 piece preserved stem ginger, plus 30ml/2 tbsp syrup from the ginger jar
40g/1½oz/scant ½ cup natural muesli (granola)
about 200ml/7fl oz/scant 1 cup semi-skimmed (low-fat) milk

1 Using a sharp knife, chop the dried apricots and preserved ginger into chunks. Put them in a blender or food processor and add the syrup from the ginger jar with the muesli and milk.

2 Process until smooth, adding more milk if necessary, to make a creamy drink. Serve in wide glasses.

Cranachan

This nutritious breakfast dish is a traditional Scottish recipe, and is delicious with a generous drizzle of heather honey. It is also wonderful served with fresh blueberries or blackberries in place of the raspberries.

Serves 4

75g/3oz crunchy oat cereal
600ml/1 pint/2½ cups Greek (US strained plain) yogurt
250g/9oz/1⅓ cups raspberries

1 Preheat the grill (broiler) to high. Spread the oat cereal on a baking sheet and place under the hot grill for 3–4 minutes, stirring regularly. Set aside to cool.

2 When the cereal has cooled completely, fold it into the Greek yogurt, then gently fold in 200g/7oz/generous 1 cup of the raspberries, being careful not to crush the berries too much.

3 Spoon the yogurt mixture into four serving glasses or dishes, top with the remaining raspberries and serve immediately.

Bananas with Yogurt and Honey

Baking bananas like this brings out their natural sweetness. If you are watching the calories, opt for low-fat Greek yogurt and leave out the nuts. Choose ripe bananas for maximum flavour.

Serves 4

2 ripe bananas, peeled
500ml/17fl oz/2¼ cups Greek (US strained plain) yogurt with honey
30ml/2 tbsp toasted hazelnuts, roughly chopped

1 Preheat the oven to 200°C/400°F/Gas 6. Wrap the bananas in foil and bake for 20 minutes. Leave the bananas to cool completely, then unwrap, place in a small bowl and mash roughly with a fork.

2 Pour the yogurt into a large bowl, add the mashed bananas and gently fold them into the yogurt. Sprinkle with the hazelnuts and serve.

Chocolate Brioche Sandwiches

This luxury sandwich is a twist on the classic pain au chocolat and beats a boring slice of toast any day. The pale green pistachio nuts work really well with the chocolate spread, adding a satisfying crunch as well as a lovely contrast in colour.

If you can't get hold of brioche, use an uncut white loaf and cut in thick slices.

Serves 4

8 thick brioche bread slices
120ml/8 tbsp chocolate spread
30ml/2 tbsp shelled pistachio nuts, finely chopped

1 Toast the brioche slices until golden on both sides. Spread four of the slices thickly with the chocolate spread and sprinkle over the chopped pistachio nuts in an even layer.

2 Place the remaining brioche slices on top of the chocolate and nuts and press down gently. Using a sharp knife, cut the sandwiches in half diagonally and serve immediately.

Muesli Smoothie: Energy 203kcal/862kJ; Protein 6.4g; Carbohydrate 40.1g, of which sugars 30.9g; Fat 3.2g, of which saturates 1.3g; Cholesterol 6mg; Calcium 163mg; Fibre 2.9g; Sodium 163mg.
Cranachan: Energy 276kcal/1152kJ; Protein 12.4g; Carbohydrate 17.2g, of which sugars 11.1g; Fat 19.7g, of which saturates 8.7g; Cholesterol 0mg; Calcium 255mg; Fibre 2.5g; Sodium 122mg.
Bananas with Yogurt: Energy 240kcal/999kJ; Protein 9.7g; Carbohydrate 14.6g, of which sugars 13.3g; Fat 17.7g, of which saturates 6.9g; Cholesterol 0mg; Calcium 201mg; Fibre 1.1g; Sodium 90mg.
Chocolate Brioche: Energy 512kcal/2149kJ; Protein 10.2g; Carbohydrate 70.5g, of which sugars 32.7g; Fat 22.9g, of which saturates 0.6g; Cholesterol 18mg; Calcium 118mg; Fibre 0.5g; Sodium 270mg.

Porridge

One of the oldest breakfast foods, porridge remains a favourite way to start the day, especially during the cold winter months. Porridge can also be a very healthy breakfast, especially if made simply with water, as oats are known to lower blood cholesterol levels and are a good source of fibre. For a treat at the weekend, brown sugar or honey can be added, and to spoil guests you could even add cream and a tot of whisky.

Serves 4

1 litre/1¾ pints/4 cups water
115g/4oz/1 cup pinhead oatmeal
splash of milk, to serve

From the storecupboard

good pinch of salt

1 Put the water, pinhead oatmeal and salt into a heavy pan and bring to the boil over a medium heat, stirring continuously with a wooden spatula. When the porridge is beginning to thicken, reduce the heat to a simmer.

2 Cook gently for about 25 minutes, stirring occasionally, until the oatmeal is cooked and the consistency smooth.

3 Serve hot with cold milk and extra salt, if required.

Cook's Tips

- *Use a whisk in place of a wooden spatula to make the porridge really smooth.*
- *Add the oatmeal in three batches to get a contrasting texture. The oats that have been cooked for the least amount of time remain slightly firm and have a nutty flavour.*

Variation

Rolled oats can be used in place of pinhead oatmeal for speed. The have slightly less flavour and lack some of the nutritional value, but cook quicker.

Eggy Bread Panettone

Panettone is a classic Italian bread made with butter and dried fruit. It can be found in most major supermarkets or Italian delicatessens. Thickly sliced stale white bread is usually used for eggy bread, but the slightly dry texture of panettone makes a great alternative. A light fruit bread could be used as a substitute. Serve with a selection of fresh summer fruits such as strawberries, raspberries and blueberries.

Serves 4

2 large (US extra large) eggs
4 large panettone slices
30ml/2 tbsp caster (superfine) sugar

From the storecupboard

50g/2oz/¼ cup butter or 30ml/2 tbsp sunflower oil

1 Break the eggs into a bowl and beat with a fork, then transfer them into a shallow dish.

2 Dip the panettone slices in the beaten egg, turning them to coat evenly.

3 Heat the butter or oil in a large non-stick frying pan and add the panettone slices. (You will probably have to do this in batches, depending on the size of the pan.) Fry the panettone slices over a medium heat for 2–3 minutes on each side, until golden brown.

4 Remove the panettone slices from the pan and drain on kitchen paper. Cut the slices in half diagonally and sprinkle with the sugar. Serve immediately.

Variations

- *For a more savoury twist why not serve the Eggy Bread Panettone with some sizzling crispy bacon.*
- *Alternatively, you could serve it with a spoonful of strawberry jam or any other fruit compote.*
- *You could even spice it up by adding some chopped chillies to the beaten egg mixture.*

Porridge: Energy 115kcal/488kJ; Protein 3.6g; Carbohydrate 20.9g, of which sugars 0g; Fat 2.5g, of which saturates 0g; Cholesterol 0mg; Calcium 16mg; Fibre 2g; Sodium 304mg.
Eggy Bread: Energy 344kcal/1442kJ; Protein 8.4g; Carbohydrate 39.5g, of which sugars 17g; Fat 18.1g, of which saturates 7.5g; Cholesterol 151mg; Calcium 89mg; Fibre 0g; Sodium 256mg.

Apricot Turnovers

These sweet and succulent pastries are delicious served with a big cup of milky coffee for a late breakfast or mid-morning treat.

Serves 4
225g/8oz ready-made puff pastry, thawed if frozen
60ml/4 tbsp apricot conserve
30ml/2 tbsp icing (confectioners') sugar

1 Preheat the oven to 190°C/375°F/Gas 5. Roll out the pastry on a lightly floured surface to a 25cm/10in square. Using a sharp knife, cut the pastry into four 13cm/5in squares.

2 Place a tablespoon of the apricot conserve in the middle of each square of pastry.

3 Using a pastry brush, brush the edges of the pastry with a little cold water and fold each square over to form a triangle. Gently press the edges together to seal.

4 Carefully transfer the turnovers to a baking sheet and bake for 15–20 minutes, or until risen and golden. Using a metal spatula, remove the pastries to a wire rack to cool, then dust generously with icing sugar and serve.

Variations

- *Use any other fruit conserve to ring the changes, for example, black cherry or damson would be delicious and give a gorgeous colour contrast, too.*
- *For a bitter-sweet alternative use a spoonful of marmalade instead of apricot conserve. A Bramley apple purée would make a comforting option.*
- *Try a coffee filling to complement your cup of milky coffee. Just pour 45ml/3 tbsp of near-boiling water over 30ml/2 tbsp of ground coffee and infuse for 4 minutes. Strain through a fine sieve. Cream 40g/1½oz/3 tbsp butter and 115g/4oz/½ cup caster (superfine) sugar together. Beat in 1 egg yolk, 115g/4oz/1 cup ground almonds and 15ml/1 tbsp of the infused coffee. Place a spoonful in the middle of each square of pastry.*

Pancakes with Caramelized Pears

If you can find them, use Williams pears for this recipe because they are juicier than most other varieties. For a really indulgent breakfast, top the pancakes with a generous spoonful of crème fraîche or fromage frais.

Serves 4
8 ready-made pancakes
4 ripe pears, peeled, cored and thickly sliced
30ml/2 tbsp light muscovado (brown) sugar

From the storecupboard
50g/2oz/¼ cup butter

1 Preheat the oven to 150°C/330°F/Gas 2. Tightly wrap the pancakes in foil and place in the oven to warm through.

2 Meanwhile, heat the butter in a large frying pan and add the pears. Fry for 2–3 minutes, until the undersides are golden. Turn the pears over and sprinkle with sugar. Cook for a further 2–3 minutes, or until the sugar dissolves and the pan juices become sticky.

3 Remove the pancakes from the oven and take them out of the foil. Divide the pears among the pancakes, placing them in one quarter. Fold each pancake in half over the filling, then into quarters. Place two folded pancakes on each plate. Drizzle over any remaining juices and serve immediately.

Cook's Tip

To make your own pancakes take 150ml/¼ pint/⅔ cup milk, top up with water to make 300ml/½ pint/1¼ cups. Sift 225g/8oz/2 cups plain (all-purpose) flour into a large bowl. Make a well in the centre and break 2 eggs into it. With a whisk, stir in the eggs, gradually adding the milk mixture to make a smooth pouring batter. Melt 25g/1oz/2 tbsp butter and stir in with the whisk. Leave to stand for 30 minutes and stir well before using. Preheat a heavy frying pan over a medium heat. Lightly butter and add a large spoonful of batter to make a pancake about 15–20cm/6–8in across. Cook for a minute or until the underside is golden brown. Repeat.

Apricot Turnovers: Energy 279kcal/1170kJ; Protein 3.3g; Carbohydrate 39.1g, of which sugars 19g; Fat 13.8g, of which saturates 0g; Cholesterol 0mg; Calcium 38mg; Fibre 0g; Sodium 182mg.
Pancakes with Pears: Energy 544kcal/2274kJ; Protein 7.7g; Carbohydrate 64.9g, of which sugars 42.4g; Fat 29.9g, of which saturates 6.5g; Cholesterol 27mg; Calcium 155mg; Fibre 4.3g; Sodium 144mg.

Sweet Breakfast Omelette

For a hearty start to a day when you know you're going to be too rushed to have much more than an apple for lunch, try this sweet version of a simple omelette, popular throughout the Middle East, with a spoonful of home-made jam or conserve.

Serves 1
3 eggs
10ml/2 tsp caster (superfine) sugar
5ml/1 tsp plain (all-purpose) flour
bread and jam, to serve

From the storecupboard
10g/¼oz/½ tbsp unsalted (sweet) butter

1 Break the eggs into a large bowl, add the sugar and flour and beat until really frothy.

2 Heat the butter in an omelette pan until it begins to bubble, then pour in the egg mixture and cook, without stirring, until it begins to set.

3 Run a wooden spatula around the edge of the omelette, then carefully turn it over and cook the second side for 1–2 minutes until golden. Serve hot or warm with thick slices of fresh bread and a bowlful of fruity jam.

Cook's Tip
Although this recipe is stated to serve one, it is substantial enough for two not-very-hungry people. Omelettes are best eaten the moment they emerge from the pan, so if you are cooking for a crowd, get each to make their own and eat in relays.

Variation
Continue the Middle Eastern theme when choosing a jam to serve with this omelette. Pick a conserve made from fruits such as fig or apricot. Alternatively, use raspberry or strawberry jam, which will be just as good.

Mushrooms on Spicy Toast

Dry-panning is a quick way of cooking mushrooms that makes the most of their flavour. The juices run when the mushrooms are heated, so they become really moist and tender.

Serves 4
8–12 large flat field (portabello) mushrooms
5ml/1 tsp curry paste
4 slices thickly-sliced white bread, toasted, to serve

From the storecupboard
50g/1oz/2 tbsp butter
salt

1 Preheat the oven to 200°C/400°F/Gas 6. Peel the mushrooms, if necessary, and remove the stalks. Heat a dry frying pan until very hot.

2 Place the mushrooms in the hot frying pan, with the gills on top. Using half the butter, add a piece the size of a hazelnut to each one, then sprinkle all the mushrooms lightly with salt. Cook over a medium heat until the butter begins to bubble and the mushrooms are juicy and tender.

3 Meanwhile, mix the remaining butter with the curry powder. Spread on the bread. Bake in the oven for 10 minutes, pile the mushrooms on top and serve.

Variations
Using a flavoured butter makes these mushrooms even more special. Try one of the following:
- *Herb butter: mix softened butter with chopped fresh herbs such as parsley and thyme, or marjoram and chopped chives.*
- *Olive butter: mix softened butter with diced green olives and spring onions (scallions).*
- *Tomato butter: mix softened butter with sun-dried tomato purée (paste).*
- *Garlic butter: mix softened butter with finely chopped garlic.*
- *Pepper and paprika butter: mix softened butter with 2.5ml/½ tsp paprika and 2.5ml/½ tsp black pepper.*

Omelette: Energy 351kcal/1465kJ; Protein 19.3g; Carbohydrate 14.4g, of which sugars 10.6g; Fat 24.9g, of which saturates 9.9g; Cholesterol 592mg; Calcium 100mg; Fibre 0.2g; Sodium 271mg.
Mushrooms on Toast: Energy 230kcal/966kJ; Protein 6.1g; Carbohydrate 25.1g, of which sugars 1.6g; Fat 12.5g, of which saturates 6.7g; Cholesterol 27mg; Calcium 63mg; Fibre 1.9g; Sodium 341mg

Boxty Potato Pancakes

Said to have originated during the Irish famine, these delicious pancakes use blended potatoes in the batter mix and can be made as thin or thick as you like. They are delicious served rolled around a hot savoury filling such as cooked cabbage and chopped bacon bound in a light mustard sauce.

Makes 4 pancakes
450g/1lb potatoes, peeled and chopped
50–75g/2–3oz/½–⅔ cup plain (all-purpose) flour
about 150ml/¼ pint/⅔ cup milk

From the storecupboard
knob (pat) of butter
salt to taste

1 Place the peeled and chopped potatoes in a blender or in the bowl of a food processor and process until the potato is thoroughly liquidized (blended).

2 Add the flour and enough milk to the processed potato to give a dropping consistency, and add salt to taste. The milk and flour can be adjusted, depending on how thin you like your pancake. Heat a little butter on a griddle or cast-iron frying pan.

3 Pour about a quarter of the mixture into the pan – if the consistency is right it will spread evenly over the base. Cook over a medium heat for about 5 minutes on each side, depending on the thickness of the pancake. Serve rolled with the hot filling of your choice.

Variations
The possibilities for Boxty Potato Pancake fillings are endless:
- *Field mushrooms fried with onions in a creamy sauce would make a perfect autumn breakfast, when mushrooms are widely available.*
- *There are any number of smoked fish options. Try smoked mackerel with wholegrain mustard, kippers (smoked herrings), or smoked salmon and chives.*
- *To break with tradition, why not try jam or conserve for a sweet filling.*

Potato Cakes

This is the traditional method of making potato cakes on a griddle or in a heavy frying pan. Commercial versions are available throughout Scotland as thin, pre-cooked potato cakes, which are fried to eat with a full breakfast or to enjoy with jam and butter.

Makes about 12
675g/1½lb potatoes, peeled
about 175g/6oz/1½ cups plain (all-purpose) flour
jam, to serve

From the storecupboard
25g/1oz/2 tbsp unsalted (sweet) butter
salt

1 Boil the potatoes in a large pan over a medium heat until tender, then drain thoroughly, replacing the pan with the drained poatoes over a low heat for a few minutes to allow any moisture to evaporate completely.

2 Mash the potatoes with plenty of salt, then mix in the butter and leave to cool.

3 Turn out on to a floured work surface and knead in about one-third of its volume in flour to make a pliable dough.

4 Roll out to about 1cm/½in thick and cut into triangles.

5 Heat a dry griddle or heavy frying pan over a low heat and cook the potato cakes on it for about 3 minutes on each side until browned. Serve hot with butter and jam.

Cook's Tip
Choose a floury variety of potato for excellent mashed potato. Maris Piper, Golden Wonder and Kerr's Pinks are all good choices, but make use of whatever varieties are available locally.

Variation
Serve with bacon rashers (strips) for a hearty start to the day.

Boxty Potato Pancakes: Energy 163kcal/689kJ; Protein 4.8g; Carbohydrate 30.9g, of which sugars 2.7g; Fat 3.1g, of which saturates 1.7g; Cholesterol 8mg; Calcium 69mg; Fibre 1.9g; Sodium 236mg.
Potato Cakes: Energy 1276kcal/5392kJ; Protein 30.4g; Carbohydrate 249.1g, of which sugars 6.7g; Fat 24.1g, of which saturates 13.4g; Cholesterol 53mg; Calcium 282mg; Fibre 14g; Sodium 203mg.

Fried Egg in Butter Sauce

So simple but so tasty, fried eggs are great when you need a treat. Use the freshest eggs you can. Cook in a heavy pan and make sure the butter is hot.

Serves 1
1 egg
dash balsamic vinegar

From the storecupboard
30ml/2 tbsp butter

1 Melt the butter until it begins to foam. Break the egg into it and cook for about 1 minute, until it begins to set.

2 Carefully turn the egg over. Cook for a few more seconds until the white has set. Remove the egg and keep warm. Return the pan to the heat and add rest of butter. When foaming, add a dash of balsamic vinegar. Cook for a few more seconds then pour over the egg.

Scrambled Eggs

Carefully cooked scrambled eggs are deliciously comforting. They cook best in a pan with a heavy base. Serve them on hot buttered toast or with bacon, sausages or smoked fish.

Serves 2
4 eggs

From the storecupboard
25g/1oz butter
salt and ground black pepper

1 Break the eggs into a bowl and beat lightly with a fork until well mixed. Season with salt and pepper.

2 Put a medium heavy pan over a medium heat and add half the butter. When the butter begins to foam, add the beaten eggs. Using a wooden spoon, stir the eggs constantly as they cook and thicken, making sure you get right into the angle of the pan to prevent the eggs sticking there and overcooking.

3 When the eggs are quite thick and beginning to set, but still creamy, remove the pan from the heat and stir in the remaining butter. The eggs will finish cooking gently in the residual heat of the pan as you keep stirring. When they are set to your liking, serve immediately.

Cook's Tip
To enrich this comforting dish, stir in 30ml/2 tbsp of double cream just before the eggs finish cooking; or add 45ml/3 tbsp of crème fraîche when you take the pan off the heat.

Variation
For a luxury breakfast you can't beat scrambled eggs with smoked salmon. For two portions, spread 2 slices of pumpernickel or wholemeal (whole-wheat) bread with butter and arrange 25g/1oz of smoked salmon on each slice. Cut in half and set aside while you make the scrambled eggs. When cooked, spoon the eggs on to the smoked salmon and garnish with a sprig of dill.

Poached Egg

Use only the freshest eggs for this delicate method of cooking. Use poaching rings in the water if you have them for a perfect shape.

Serves 2
2–4 eggs
muffins, to serve

1 Put a frying pan over a medium heat and add 5cm/2in of boiling water. Add the poaching rings if you have them.

2 When tiny bubbles begin to gather in the water and gently rise to the surface, break the eggs, one at a time, into a cup and slide them carefully into the hot water. Leave the pan on the heat for 1 minute as the water simmers very gently (on no account allow it to boil). Then remove from the heat and leave the eggs to stand, uncovered, in the hot water for 10 minutes.

3 Use a slotted spoon to lift the eggs out of the water and drain briefly on kitchen paper. Serve the poached eggs immediately with toasted muffins.

Scrambled Eggs: Energy 240kcal/995kJ; Protein 12.6g; Carbohydrate 0.1g, of which sugars 0.1g; Fat 21.4g, of which saturates 9.6g; Cholesterol 407mg; Calcium 60mg; Fibre 0g; Sodium 216mg.
Fried Egg: Energy 297kcal/1224kJ; Protein 6.4g; Carbohydrate 0.2g, of which sugars 0.2g; Fat 30.2g, of which saturates 17.2g; Cholesterol 254mg; Calcium 34mg; Fibre 0g; Sodium 252mg.
Poached Egg: Energy 74kcal/306kJ; Protein 6.3g; Carbohydrate 0g, of which sugars 0g; Fat 5.6g, of which saturates 1.6g; Cholesterol 190mg; Calcium 29mg; Fibre 0g; Sodium 70mg.

Coddled Eggs

This method of soft-cooking eggs became very popular in the Victorian era, and special decorative porcelain pots with lids were produced by Royal Worcester from the 1890s.

Serves 2
2 large (US extra large) eggs
60ml/4 tbsp single (light) cream
chopped fresh chives, to garnish

From the storecupboard
butter, for greasing

1 Butter two small ramekin dishes or cups and break an egg into each. Top with 2 spoonfuls of cream and a knob of butter. Cover with foil.

2 Put a wide, shallow pan over medium heat. Stand the dishes in the pan. Add boiling water to half way up the dishes. Heat until the water just comes to the boil, then cover the pan with a lid and simmer gently for 1 minute.

3 Remove from the heat and leave to stand, still covered, for 10 minutes. Serve sprinkled with chives.

Boiled Egg with Toast Soldiers

Boiled egg is one of the first eating experiences many people have. Eggs and toast are nutritious, warming and comforting. Toast soldiers have a smile-a-dip quality that is just unbeatable.

Serves 1
1 egg
4 thin slices bread

From the storecupboard
a little butter, for spreading
salt

1 Place the egg in a small pan and pour in hot, not boiling, water to cover. Bring to the boil and cook for 3 minutes for a very soft egg, 4 minutes for a soft yolk and firm white, or 8 minutes for a hard egg.

2 Meanwhile, toast the bread and cut it into fingers. Serve the freshly boiled egg with toast fingers, butter and salt to sprinkle.

Eggs Benedict

Use a good quality bought hollandaise sauce for this recipe because it will make all the difference to the end result. Eggs Benedict are delicious served on half a toasted English muffin. Always use organic eggs – they have a superior flavour to eggs from battery hens.

Serves 4
4 large (US extra large) eggs
4 lean ham slices
60ml/4 tbsp hollandaise sauce
English muffins, to serve

From the storecupboard
salt and ground black pepper

1 Pour cold water into a medium pan to a depth of about 5cm/2in and bring to a gentle simmer. Crack two eggs into the pan and bring back to the simmer. Simmer for 2–3 minutes, until the white is set, but the yolk is still soft.

2 Meanwhile, arrange the ham slices on four serving plates (or on top of four toasted, buttered muffin halves if using). Remove the eggs from the pan using a slotted spoon and place on top of the ham on two of the plates. Cook the remaining eggs in the same way.

3 Spoon the hollandaise sauce over the eggs, sprinkle with salt and pepper and serve immediately.

Cook's Tips
- *To make sure you don't break the yolk, crack the eggs into a cup before carefully adding them to the gently simmering water.*
- *Poaching pans are available with little cups for the eggs.*

Variation
If you prefer eggs cooked all the way through, scramble them instead of poaching. Then spoon over the ham and top with hollandaise sauce as before.

Coddled Eggs: Energy 92kcal/383kJ; Protein 6.3g; Carbohydrate 0g, of which sugars 0g; Fat 7.6g, of which saturates 2.9g; Cholesterol 196mg; Calcium 29mg; Fibre 0g; Sodium 85mg.
Boiled Egg: Energy 409kcal/1710kJ; Protein 12.5g; Carbohydrate 40.3g, of which sugars 2.8g; Fat 23.1g, of which saturates 12.3g; Cholesterol 235mg; Calcium 154mg; Fibre 2.5g; Sodium 556mg.
Eggs Benedict: Energy 553kcal/2304kJ; Protein 19.8g; Carbohydrate 31.6g, of which sugars 2.2g; Fat 39.7g, of which saturates 18.9g; Cholesterol 427mg; Calcium 148mg; Fibre 1.3g; Sodium 635mg.

Cinnamon Toast

This is an aromatic old-fashioned snack that is warming and comforting on a cold winter day. Cinnamon toast is perfect with a spicy hot chocolate drink or served with a few slices of fresh fruit, such as peaches, plums, nectarines or mango.

Serves 2
10ml/2 tsp ground cinnamon
30ml/2 tbsp caster (superfine) sugar, plus extra to serve
4 slices bread
prepared fresh fruit (optional)

From the storecupboard
75g/3oz/6 tbsp butter, softened

1 Place the softened butter in a bowl. Beat with a spoon until soft and creamy, then mix in the ground cinnamon and most of the sugar.

2 Toast the bread on both sides. Spread with the spiced butter and sprinkle with a little remaining sugar. Serve immediately, with pieces of fresh fruit, if you like.

Cook's Tips

- *Cinnamon is an effective detoxifier and cleanser, containing substances that kill bacteria and other micro-organisms.*
- *To round off this winter warmer, serve a quick cardamom hot chocolate with the cinnamon toast. Put 900ml/1½ pints/3¾ cups milk in a pan with two bruised cardamom pods and bring to the boil. Add 200g/7oz plain (semisweet) chocolate and whisk until melted. Using a slotted spoon, remove the cardamom pods just before serving.*

Variation

As an alternative to ground cinnamon, try using ground allspice, which is good for the digestive system. These small, dried berries of a tropical, South American tree have a sweet, warming flavour reminiscent of a blend of cloves, cinnamon and nutmeg. Although allspice is available ready-ground, it is best to buy the spice whole to retain its flavour, and grind just before use.

Welsh Rarebit

This has been a favourite snack for generations. Traditionally, the cheese is melted with butter, a little beer, mustard and seasoning, then spread on toast, but this is a quick and quirky version. It is best made with a good melting cheese, such as Cheddar, Monterey Jack or Caerphilly.

Serves 2
2 thick slices bread
10ml/2 tsp spicy or mild mustard
100g/3¾oz Cheddar cheese, sliced
pinch of paprika or cayenne pepper

From the storecupboard
butter, for spreading
ground black pepper

1 Preheat the grill (broiler) and lightly toast the bread on both sides. Spread with butter and mustard, then top with the cheese. Grill (broil) until the cheese melts and starts to brown.

2 Sprinkle a little paprika or cayenne on the cheese. Season with pepper.

Jammy Toast

The simplest snacks with minimal ingredients are often the treats that taste the best. Adding flavouring to the butter is not essential but makes a nice touch. You can use any jam on the toast, but a home-made one would taste excellent.

Serves 2
a little natural vanilla extract
grated rind of 1 lemon (optional)
4 slices bread
20ml/4 tsp jam (jelly)

From the storecupboard
75g/3oz/6 tbsp butter

1 Cream the butter with vanilla to taste until thoroughly combined. Mix in the lemon rind, if using.

2 Toast the bread on both sides. Serve piping hot or leave to cool on a rack until crisp, if preferred. Spread thickly with flavoured butter and jam, and eat immediately.

Cinnamon Toast: Energy 461kcal/1921kJ; Protein 4.7g; Carbohydrate 41.6g, of which sugars 17.3g; Fat 31.8g, of which saturates 19.6g; Cholesterol 80mg; Calcium 72mg; Fibre 0.8g; Sodium 499mg.
Welsh Rarebit: Energy 363kcal/1516kJ; Protein 17.3g; Carbohydrate 24.3g, of which sugars 1.6g; Fat 21.5g, of which saturates 13.7g; Cholesterol 59mg; Calcium 457mg; Fibre 1.1g; Sodium 687mg.
Jammy Toast: Energy 445kcal/1854kJ; Protein 4.4g; Carbohydrate 38.1g, of which sugars 13.1g; Fat 31.7g, of which saturates 19.8g; Cholesterol 80mg; Calcium 90mg; Fibre 1.7g; Sodium 475mg.

Smoked Salmon and Chive Omelette

Lightly beaten eggs, seasoned and fried to form a light omelette, provide a sustaining breakfast in about 3 minutes. The addition of a generous portion of chopped smoked salmon and some chives gives a really luxurious finish to this simple, classic dish. You can use this omelette recipe as the basis of endless variations. Simply replace the salmon and chives with any other ingredients you have handy.

Serves 2
4 eggs
15ml/1 tbsp chopped fresh chives
50g/2oz smoked salmon, roughly chopped

From the storecupboard
knob (pat) of butter
salt and ground black pepper

1 Beat the eggs until just combined, then stir in the chives and season with salt and pepper.

2 Heat the butter in a medium frying pan until foamy. Pour in the eggs and cook over a medium heat for about 3–4 minutes, drawing the cooked egg from around the edge into the centre of the pan from time to time.

3 At this stage, you can either leave the top of the omelette slightly soft or finish it off under the grill (broiler), depending on how you like your omelette. Top with the smoked salmon, fold the omelette over and cut in half to serve.

Variations
- *Try this breakfast omelette with chopped ham and parsley or grated Cheddar and torn basil leaves. These are just two of the endless permutations on the theme.*
- *You could also try making a souffléd omelette. Simply separate the whites from the yolks, whisk the whites until stiff, then fold into the beaten yolks until evenly blended. Heat the butter in the pan and spoon in the mixture, spreading it out evenly. Cook gently for 2–3 minutes, until it is golden and firm underneath and only just firm on top. Finish as you prefer.*

Quick Kedgeree

Kedgeree is a rice, lentil and onion dish that originally came from India. Fish and eggs were added by the British to make the breakfast dish that we know and love today. A garnish of fresh coriander leaves adds extra flavour and colour.

Serves 4
175g/6oz undyed smoked haddock fillet
4 large (US extra large) eggs
2 x 250g/9oz packets microwave pilau rice
coriander (cilantro), to garnish

From the storecupboard
salt and ground black pepper

1 Preheat the grill (broiler) to medium. Place the smoked haddock on a baking sheet and grill (broil) for about 10 minutes, or until cooked through.

2 Meanwhile, place the eggs in a pan of cold water and bring to the boil. Cook for 6–7 minutes (for soft yolks), then drain and place under cold running water until cool enough to handle.

3 While the eggs and haddock are cooking, cook the rice according to the instructions on the packet.

4 Shell the eggs and cut into halves or quarters. Flake the fish and gently mix into the rice, with the eggs, taking care not to break up the eggs too much. Spoon on to serving plates and serve immediately.

Cook's Tips
- *If you prefer your eggs soft, reduce the cooking time to 4½–5 minutes. Alternatively, if you like hard yolks increase the cooking time to 10–12 minutes.*
- *Shelling eggs can be tricky, especially if the eggs are very hot. These simple guidelines will make the process a lot easier. As soon as the eggs are boiled, remove them from the pan and place in a bowl of very cold water. When they are cool enough to handle, crack the shells evenly all over and start peeling at the rounded end. Remove the shell and membrane together.*

Salmon Omelette: Energy 221kcal/920kJ; Protein 19g; Carbohydrate 0.2g, of which sugars 0.2g; Fat 16.4g, of which saturates 5.9g; Cholesterol 400mg; Calcium 65mg; Fibre 0.1g; Sodium 641mg.
Quick Kedgeree: Energy 480kcal/2006kJ; Protein 23.5g; Carbohydrate 69.9g, of which sugars 0.1g; Fat 11.5g, of which saturates 4.9g; Cholesterol 224mg; Calcium 59mg; Fibre 0g; Sodium 536mg.

Kippers with Marmalade Toast

Kippers are plump herring that have been split, cleaned and soaked in brine for a few minutes, then smoked over an oak fire for 4–18 hours. Originally, freshly caught herrings were dried over smoking seaweed. Wonderful kippers are produced, where the herrings are still cured in traditional smokehouses. The smoky flavour of the kippers in this recipe is balanced by the sharp tang of the orange marmalade.

Serves 2

2 kippers (smoked herrings), preferably naturally smoked, whole or filleted
2 slices of bread
orange marmalade, for spreading

From the storecupboard

melted butter, for greasing
soft butter, for spreading

1 Preheat the grill (broiler). Line the grill pan with foil – to help prevent fishy smells from lingering in the pan – and brush the foil with melted butter to stop the fish sticking.

2 Using kitchen scissors, or a knife, cut the heads and tails off the kippers.

3 Lay the fish, skin side up, on the buttered foil. Put under the hot grill and cook for 1 minute. Turn the kippers over, brush the uppermost (fleshy) side with melted butter, put back under the grill and cook for 4–5 minutes.

4 Toast the bread and spread it first with butter and then with marmalade. Serve the sizzling hot kippers immediately with the marmalade toast.

Variation

Omit the marmalade and cook the kippers sprinkled with a little cayenne pepper. Serve with a knob of butter and plenty of lemon wedges for squeezing over.

Jugged Kippers

The demand for naturally smoked kippers, where split herring are hung from the rafters of traditional smokehouses over smouldering oak chips, is ever increasing. They are most popular for breakfast, served with scrambled eggs. Jugging is a traditional way to prepare kippers. It is a similar method of cooking to poaching, except that the only equipment needed is a jug and kettle. Serve with freshly made bread or toast and a wedge of lemon.

Serves 4

4 kippers (smoked herrings), preferably naturally smoked, whole or filleted
4 slices bread, to serve

From the storecupboard

25g/1oz/2 tbsp butter
ground black pepper

1 Select a jug (pitcher) tall enough for the kippers to be immersed when the water is added. If the heads are still on, remove them.

2 Put the fish into the jug, tails up, and then cover them with boiling water. Leave for about 5 minutes, until tender.

3 Drain well, dry with kitchen paper, and place on warmed plates with a knob (pat) of butter and a little black pepper on each kipper. Serve with slices of bread.

Cook's Tips

- *The best kippers have a silvery-golden colour, are plump and have an oily appearance.*
- *Always look for a good smoky smell.*
- *If possible, buy undyed kippers. Kippers are often dyed these days to give them the traditional golden colour. This is because curing times are getting ever shorter and the natural deep colour comes from long, slow curing over a smouldering fire.*
- *Bloaters are whole herring that have been cured and lightly smoked, but not split or gutted. They tend to look plumper than dry-cured fish.*

Kippers on Toast: Energy 518kcal/2155kJ; Protein 33.9g; Carbohydrate 17.6g, of which sugars 5.9g; Fat 35.1g, of which saturates 7.6g; Cholesterol 121mg; Calcium 126mg; Fibre 0.4g; Sodium 1640mg.
Jugged Kippers: Energy 248kcal/1025kJ; Protein 15.9g; Carbohydrate 0.1g, of which sugars 0.1g; Fat 20.4g, of which saturates 5.8g; Cholesterol 68mg; Calcium 49mg; Fibre 0g; Sodium 776mg.

Croque-monsieur

Gruyère is traditionally used in this classic French toastie, but you could use mild Cheddar instead. Prosciutto and Gorgonzola, served with a smear of mustard, also make a fabulous alternative to the classic combination.

Serves 4
8 white bread slices
4 large lean ham slices
175g/6oz Gruyère cheese, thinly sliced

From the storecupboard
a little softened butter
ground black pepper

1 Preheat the grill (broiler) and toast four slices on both sides and the other four slices on one side only.

2 Butter the slices of bread that have been toasted on both sides and top with the ham, then the cheese, and season with plenty of ground black pepper.

3 Lay the remaining slices on top of the cheese, with the untoasted side uppermost. Grill (broil) the tops of the sandwiches until golden brown, then cut in half and serve immediately.

Pancakes with Bacon and Syrup

Also known as drop scones, Scotch pancakes are available in most supermarkets. Raisin varieties can also be used.

Serves 4
8 ready-made Scotch pancakes
8 dry-cured smoked back (lean) bacon rashers (strips)
30ml/2 tbsp maple syrup

1 Preheat the oven to 150°C/330°F/Gas 2. Wrap the pancakes in a sheet of foil and place them in the oven to warm through.

2 Meanwhile, preheat the grill (broiler) and arrange the bacon on a grill pan. Grill (broil) for 3–4 minutes each side, until crisp.

3 Divide the pancakes between four warmed serving plates, top with the grilled bacon, drizzle with maple syrup and serve.

Smoked Haddock and Bacon

This classic combination is very much associated with Scotland. East coast haddock was first smoked over peat in the village of Findon, close to Aberdeen. The smokiness of the fish goes well with the rich flavour of the bacon – both are complemented by the creamy sauce.

Serves 4
4 undyed smoked haddock fillets
8 rashers (strips) lean back bacon
120ml/4fl oz/½ cup double (heavy) cream
chopped fresh chives, to garnish

From the storecupboard
25g/1oz/2 tbsp butter
ground black pepper

1 Preheat the grill (broiler) to medium. Over a gentle heat, melt the butter in a frying pan.

2 Add the haddock fillets, working in two batches if necessary, and cook gently, turning once, for about 3 minutes each side. When cooked, place in a large ovenproof dish and cover. Reserve the juices from the frying pan.

3 Grill (broil) the bacon, turning once, until just cooked through but not crispy. Leave the grill on.

4 Return the frying pan to the heat and pour in the cream and any reserved juices from the haddock. Bring to the boil, then simmer briefly, stirring occasionally. Season to taste with ground black pepper.

5 Meanwhile, place two bacon rashers over each haddock fillet and place the dish under the grill briefly. Then pour over the hot creamy sauce, garnish with chopped fresh chives and serve immediately.

Variation
Instead of topping the smoked haddock with bacon, use wilted spinach for a healthier, tasty option. Thoroughly wash a good handful of spinach for each person. Then plunge it into boiling water for 3 minutes, drain well and lay across each fillet.

Croque-monsieur: Energy 336kcal/1409kJ; Protein 20.3g; Carbohydrate 26.9g, of which sugars 1.7g; Fat 16.2g, of which saturates 9.8g; Cholesterol 57mg; Calcium 385mg; Fibre 0.8g; Sodium 897mg.
Pancakes with Bacon: Energy 324kcal/1358kJ; Protein 12.9g; Carbohydrate 33g, of which sugars 11.5g; Fat 16.5g, of which saturates 3.5g; Cholesterol 30mg; Calcium 79mg; Fibre 0.9g; Sodium 1153mg.
Haddock and Bacon: Energy 391kcal/1624kJ; Protein 28.8g; Carbohydrate 0.5g, of which sugars 0.5g; Fat 30.5g, of which saturates 16.5g; Cholesterol 119mg; Calcium 40mg; Fibre 0g; Sodium 1671mg.

Muffins with Bacon and Eggs

This luxury breakfast is ideal for birthdays, anniversaries or other days when you want to treat someone special. Remember to use eggs that are under a week old, as older eggs will not keep their shape when poached. For the best results use fresh organic eggs and break each one into a cup before using. The sauce is made in a blender or food processor, which turns it from a slightly difficult recipe into an easy option.

Serves 4
350g/12oz rindless back (lean) bacon rashers (strips)
dash of white wine vinegar
4 eggs
4 English muffins

From the storecupboard
butter, for spreading
salt and ground black pepper

For the hollandaise sauce (optional)
2 egg yolks
5ml/1 tsp white wine vinegar
75g/3oz/6 tbsp butter

1 Preheat the grill (broiler) and cook the bacon for 5–8 minutes, turning once, or until crisp on both sides.

2 Meanwhile, fill a large frying pan with water and bring to the boil. Add the vinegar and regulate the heat so that the water simmers. Crack the eggs into the water and poach them for 3–4 minutes, or slightly longer for firm eggs.

3 Split and toast the muffins while the eggs are cooking. Spread with butter and place on warmed plates.

4 To make the hollandaise sauce, process the egg yolks and white wine vinegar in a blender or food processor. Melt the butter. With the motor still running, very gradually add the hot melted butter through the feeder tube. The hot butter will cook the yolks to make a thick, glossy sauce. Switch off the machine as soon as all the butter has been added and the sauce has thickened. Season to taste.

5 Arrange the bacon on the muffins and add a poached egg to each. Top with a spoonful of sauce and grind over some black pepper. Serve immediately.

Oatmeal Pancakes with Bacon

These nutritious oaty pancakes have a special affinity with good bacon, making an interesting base for an alternative to the big traditional fry-up. Serve them with sausages, fried or poached eggs and cooked tomatoes. For a lighter and sweeter option, serve them drizzled simply with honey or maple syrup.

Makes 8 pancakes
115g/4oz/1 cup fine wholemeal (whole-wheat) flour
25g/1oz/¼ cup fine pinhead oatmeal
2 eggs
about 300ml/½ pint/1¼ cups buttermilk
8 bacon rashers (strips), to serve

From the storecupboard
butter or oil, for greasing
pinch of salt

1 Mix the flour, oatmeal and salt in a bowl or food processor, beat in the eggs and add enough buttermilk to make a creamy batter of the same consistency as ordinary pancakes.

2 Thoroughly heat a griddle, or cast-iron frying pan, over a medium-hot heat. When it is very hot, grease lightly with butter or oil.

3 Pour in the batter, about a ladleful at a time. Tilt the pan around to spread evenly and cook for about 2 minutes on the first side, or until set and the underside is browned. Turn over and cook for 1 minute until browned.

4 Once cooked, place the pancakes on a warm plate, cover with foil, and keep warm in a low oven, or over a pan of simmering water, while you cook the others. Fry the bacon. Roll the pancakes with a cooked rasher to serve.

Cook's Tip
When whole oats are chopped into pieces they are called pinhead or coarse oatmeal. They take longer to cook than rolled oats and have a chewier texture. However, they do retain a high proportion of their nutritional value.

Muffins with Bacon: Energy 612kcal/2549kJ; Protein 32.6g; Carbohydrate 30.2g, of which sugars 2.4g; Fat 41.1g, of which saturates 18.3g; Cholesterol 429mg; Calcium 143mg; Fibre 1.3g; Sodium 1880mg.
Pancakes with Bacon: Energy 202kcal/845kJ; Protein 11.9g; Carbohydrate 13.1g, of which sugars 2g; Fat 11.8g, of which saturates 4.8g; Cholesterol 87mg; Calcium 59mg; Fibre 1.5g; Sodium 654mg.

Laver Bread and Bacon Omelette

Laver bread is a tasty seaweed preparation commonly associated with Wales, but it has also been eaten in Scotland for centuries. Dried or canned versions are available and avoid the long preparation time, but if you prefer, use boiled spinach instead.

Makes 1 omelette
3 eggs
1 rasher (strip) lean back bacon, cooked and diced
25g/1oz prepared laver bread

From the storecupboard
oil, to prepare the pan
10ml/2 tsp butter
salt and ground black pepper

1 Heat a little oil in an omelette pan then leave for a few minutes to help season the pan. A non-stick or small curved-sided pan may also be used.

2 Break the eggs into a bowl large enough for whisking, season, then whisk until the yolks and whites are well combined but not frothy.

3 Pour the oil out of the pan and reheat. Add the butter, which should begin to sizzle straight away. If it does not, the pan is too cool; alternatively, if it burns, the pan is too hot. In either case, rinse it out, dry and try again.

4 Pour the whisked eggs into the pan and immediately, using the back of a fork or a suitable implement if using a non-stick pan, draw the mixture towards the middle of the pan, working from the outside and using quick circular movements going around the pan.

5 As the omelette is beginning to cook but is still not quite set, arrange the cooked, diced bacon and prepared laver bread evenly over one half of the omelette. Cook for another 30 seconds then remove from the heat.

6 Fold one half of the omelette over the half with the bacon and laver bread, leave for a minute or two, then turn out on to a warmed plate. Garnish with a herb of your choice and serve immediately while piping hot.

Sausage Loaf with Relish

This hearty breakfast dish will set you up for the day, whatever strenuous activities you have in store. Prepared simply in a loaf shape and chilled overnight, the sausage is then sliced before cooking. Accompanied by grilled tomatoes and a tangy relish, it is a delicious breakfast. Served with some creamy mashed potato, it would make a substantial meal.

Serves 4
900g/2lb minced (ground) beef
65g/2½oz/generous 1 cup stale white breadcrumbs
150g/5oz/scant 1 cup semolina
relish, to serve

From the storecupboard
5ml/1 tsp salt
ground black pepper

1 In a large mixing bowl, combine the beef, breadcrumbs, semolina and salt together thoroughly with a fork. Pour in 75ml/5 tbsp water, mix again and season to taste. Pass the mixture through a coarse mincer (grinder) and set aside.

2 Carefully line a 1.3kg/3lb loaf tin (pan) with clear film (plastic wrap).

3 Spoon the sausage mixture into the tin, pressing it in firmly with the back of a wooden spoon. Even out the surface and fold the clear film over the top. Chill overnight.

4 When ready to cook, preheat the grill (broiler). Turn the sausage out of the tin on to a chopping board and cut into 1cm/½in slices. Grill (broil) each slice until cooked through, turning once. Alternatively, fry until cooked through, again turning once. Serve hot with grilled tomatoes and relish.

Cook's Tip
For the best results, use standard minced (ground) beef for these sausages rather than lean minced steak, as the higher fat content is needed to bind the ingredients together.

Laver Bread: Energy 355kcal/1472kJ; Protein 23.6g; Carbohydrate 0.5g, of which sugars 0.4g; Fat 29.2g, of which saturates 11.4g; Cholesterol 605mg; Calcium 131mg; Fibre 0.5g; Sodium 691mg.
Sausage Loaf: Energy 691kcal/2886kJ; Protein 50.1g; Carbohydrate 40.7g, of which sugars 0.4g; Fat 37.4g, of which saturates 15.6g; Cholesterol 135mg; Calcium 47mg; Fibre 1.1g; Sodium 299mg.

Baba Ghanoush

Adjust the amount of aubergine, garlic and lemon juice in this richly flavoured Middle Eastern aubergine dip depending on how creamy, garlicky or tart you want it to be. The dip can be served with a garnish of chopped fresh coriander leaves, olives or pickled cucumbers. Hot pepper sauce or a little ground coriander can be added too, and a sprinkling of cayennne pepper to serve.

Serves 2–4
1 large or 2 medium aubergines (eggplant)
2–4 garlic cloves, chopped
90–150ml/6–10 tbsp tahini
juice of 1 lemon, or to taste

1 Place the aubergine(s) directly over the flame of a gas stove or on the coals of a barbecue. Turn the aubergine(s) fairly frequently until deflated and the skin is evenly charred. Remove from the heat with tongs. Alternatively, place under a hot grill (broiler), turning frequently, until charred.

2 Put the aubergine(s) in a plastic bag and seal the top tightly, or place in a bowl and cover with crumpled kitchen paper. Leave to cool for 30–60 minutes.

3 Peel off the blackened skin from the aubergine(s), reserving the juices. Chop the aubergine flesh, either by hand for a coarse texture or in a food processor for a smooth purée. Put the aubergine in a bowl and stir in the reserved juices.

4 Add the garlic and tahini to the aubergine and stir until smooth. Stir in the lemon juice. If the mixture becomes too thick, add 15–30ml/1–2 tbsp water. Spoon into a serving bowl. Serve at room temperature.

Cook's Tip
This creamy purée can be stored in an airtight container in the refrigerator for 3–4 days.

Hummus

This classic Middle Eastern chickpea dip is flavoured with garlic and tahini (sesame seed paste). It makes a surprisingly creamy blend and is delicious served with wedges of toasted pitta bread or crudités. You can add a handful of chopped black olives too. Enjoy it with drinks or as a snack while watching television.

Serves 4–6
400g/14oz can chickpeas, drained
60ml/4 tbsp tahini
2–3 garlic cloves, chopped
juice of ½–1 lemon

From the storecupboard
salt and ground black pepper

1 Using a potato masher or fork, coarsely mash the chickpeas in a mixing bowl. If you like a smoother purée, process the chickpeas in a food processor or blender until a smooth paste is formed.

2 Mix the tahini into the bowl of chickpeas, then stir in the chopped garlic cloves and lemon juice. Season to taste with salt and ground black pepper, and if needed, add a little water. Serve the hummus at room temperature.

Variation
A little ground cumin can also be added, and olive oil can be stirred in to enrich the hummus, if you like.

Cannellini Bean Pâté

Serve this simple pâté with Melba toast or toasted wholegrain bread as an appetizer or snack. A dusting of paprika gives an extra kick. You can also use other types of canned beans, such as borlotti or kidney beans. Other fresh herbs will be equally good; try chervil, thyme or oregano.

Serves 4
2 x 400g/14oz cans cannellini beans, drained and rinsed
50g/2oz mature (sharp) Cheddar cheese, finely grated
30ml/2 tbsp chopped fresh parsley

From the storecupboard
45ml/3 tbsp olive oil
salt and ground black pepper

1 Put the cannellini beans in a food processor with the olive oil, and process to a chunky paste.

2 Transfer to a bowl and stir in the cheese, parsley and some salt and pepper. Spoon into a serving dish and sprinkle a little paprika on top, if you like.

Cook's Tip
Canned beans are usually in a sugar, salt and water solution, so always drain and rinse them thoroughly before use – otherwise the finished pâté may be rather too salty.

Baba Ghanoush: Energy 91kcal/375kJ; Protein 1g; Carbohydrate 2.2g, of which sugars 1.5g; Fat 8.8g, of which saturates 1.4g; Cholesterol 8mg; Calcium 8mg; Fibre 1.4g; Sodium 52mg.
Hummus: Energy 190kcal/798kJ; Protein 8.4g; Carbohydrate 19.3g, of which sugars 1.4g; Fat 9.4g, of which saturates 1.3g; Cholesterol 0mg; Calcium 70mg; Fibre 4.1g; Sodium 19mg.
Cannellini Bean Pâté: Energy 155kcal/650kJ; Protein 7.4g; Carbohydrate 18.4g, of which sugars 3.9g; Fat 6.3g, of which saturates 0.9g; Cholesterol 0mg; Calcium 96mg; Fibre 6.9g; Sodium 394mg.

Garlic Dip

Two whole heads of garlic may seem like a lot, but roasting transforms the flesh to a tender, sweet and mellow pulp. Serve with crunchy breadsticks and crisps. For a low-fat version of this dip, use reduced-fat mayonnaise and low-fat natural yogurt.

Serves 4
2 whole garlic heads
60ml/4 tbsp mayonnaise
75ml/5 tbsp Greek (US strained plain) yogurt
5ml/1 tsp wholegrain mustard

From the storecupboard
15ml/1 tbsp olive oil
salt and ground black pepper

1 Preheat the oven to 200°C/400°F/Gas 6. Separate the garlic cloves and place them in a small roasting pan. Don't peel them at this stage.

2 Pour the olive oil over the garlic cloves and turn them with a spoon to coat them evenly. Roast them for 20–30 minutes, or until tender and softened. Don't be tempted to speed up this process as it is necessary to bring out the sweetness in the garlic. Leave to cool for 5 minutes.

3 Trim off the root end of each roasted garlic clove. Peel the cloves and discard the skins. Place the roasted garlic on a chopping board and sprinkle with salt. Mash with a fork until puréed.

4 Combine the garlic, mayonnaise, yogurt and mustard in a small bowl.

5 Check and adjust the seasoning, then spoon the dip into a bowl. Cover and chill until ready to serve. Sprinkle over some extra black pepper before serving.

Cook's Tip
If cooking the garlic on a barbecue, leave the heads whole and cook until tender, turning occasionally. Allow to cool, separate the cloves, peel and mash.

Artichoke and Cumin Dip

This easy-to-make dip is so tasty. Grilled artichokes bottled in oil can be used instead of canned ones and have a fabulous flavour. Try chilli powder in place of the cumin and add a handful of basil leaves to the artichokes before blending.

Serves 4
2 x 400g/14oz cans artichoke hearts, drained
2 garlic cloves, peeled
2.5ml/½ tsp ground cumin

From the storecupboard
olive oil
salt and ground black pepper

1 Put the artichoke hearts in a food processor with the garlic and ground cumin, and a generous drizzle of olive oil. Process to a smooth purée and season with plenty of salt and ground black pepper to taste.

2 Spoon the purée into a serving bowl and serve with an extra drizzle of olive oil and slices of warm pitta bread.

Peperonata

This richly flavoured spicy tomato and sweet red pepper dip is delicious served with crisp Italian-style breadsticks. It also makes a tasty relish served with grilled chicken and fish dishes. It is delicious served either hot, cold or at room temperature.

Serves 4
2 large red (bell) peppers, halved, seeded and sliced
pinch dried chilli flakes
400g/14oz can pomodorino tomatoes

From the storecupboard
60ml/4 tbsp garlic-infused olive oil
salt and ground black pepper

1 Heat the oil in a large pan over a low heat and add the peppers. Cook very gently, stirring occasionally, for 3–4 minutes.

2 Add the chilli flakes, cook for 1 minute, then pour in the tomatoes and season. Cook gently for 50 minutes to 1 hour, stirring occasionally.

Garlic Dip: Energy 155kcal/640kJ; Protein 1.7g; Carbohydrate 0.8g, of which sugars 0.7g; Fat 16.4g, of which saturates 3.1g; Cholesterol 11mg; Calcium 34mg; Fibre 0.2g; Sodium 142mg.
Artichoke and Cumin Dip: Energy 42kcal/172kJ; Protein 0.6g; Carbohydrate 1.2g, of which sugars 0.9g; Fat 3.9g, of which saturates 0.5g; Cholesterol 0mg; Calcium 41mg; Fibre 1.2g; Sodium 60mg.
Peperonata: Energy 66kcal/274kJ; Protein 1.1g; Carbohydrate 6.3g, of which sugars 6.1g; Fat 4.1g, of which saturates 0.7g; Cholesterol 0mg; Calcium 10mg; Fibre 1.7g; Sodium 9mg.

Blue Cheese Dip

This dip can be mixed up in next to no time and is delicious served with pears or with fresh vegetable crudités. This is a very thick dip to which you can add a little more yogurt for a smoother consistency. Add still more yogurt to make a great dressing.

Serves 4
150g/5oz blue cheese, such as Stilton or Danish blue
150g/5oz/⅔ cup soft cheese
75ml/5 tbsp Greek (US strained plain) yogurt

From the storecupboard
salt and ground black pepper, plus extra to garnish

1 Crumble the blue cheese into a bowl. Using a wooden spoon, beat the cheese to soften it.

2 Add the soft cheese and beat well to blend the two cheeses together.

3 Gradually beat in the Greek yogurt, adding enough to give you the consistency you prefer.

4 Season with lots of black pepper and a little salt. Chill the dip until you are ready to serve it.

Cook's Tip
Alternative blue cheeses that would work well in this dip are: the crumbly French Roquefort; the sharp yet creamy Italian Gorgonzola; the soft yet grainy Cabrales; and the spicy American Maytag Blue.

Variation
If you like, add a handful of finely chopped walnuts to this dip, because they go wonderfully well with the blue cheese, complementing its slightly spicy flavour. It is advisable to grind the nuts finely in a food processor to avoid the dip being too chunky in texture.

Quick Satay Sauce

There are many versions of this tasty peanut sauce. This one is very speedy and it tastes delicious drizzled over barbecued skewers of chicken. For parties, spear chunks of chicken with cocktail sticks and serve with a bowl of warm sauce.

Serves 4
200ml/7fl oz/scant 1 cup coconut cream
60ml/4 tbsp crunchy peanut butter
5ml/1 tsp Worcestershire sauce
Tabasco sauce, to taste
fresh coconut, to garnish (optional)

1 Pour the coconut cream into a small pan and heat it gently over a low heat for about 2 minutes.

2 Add the peanut butter and stir vigorously until it is blended into the coconut cream. Continue to heat until the mixture is warm but not boiling hot.

3 Add the Worcestershire sauce and a dash of Tabasco to taste. Pour into a serving bowl.

4 Use a potato peeler to shave thin curls from a piece of fresh coconut, if using. Sprinkle the coconut over the dish of your choice and serve immediately with the sauce.

Variation
Thick coconut milk can be substituted for coconut cream, but take care to buy an unsweetened variety for this recipe.

Cook's Tip
You could serve this satay sauce with skewers of pork fillet and pineapple. Cut the pork into 2.5cm/1in chunks, toss in a blended mixture of onion, garlic, soy sauce, lemon rind, ground cumin, ground coriander, ground turmeric and dark brown sugar. Thread the pork on to bamboo skewers alternating with chunks of pineapple. Cook on a medium-hot grill (broiler) for 10–12 minutes.

Blue Cheese Dip: Energy 206kcal/855kJ; Protein 12.1g; Carbohydrate 2.6g, of which sugars 2.6g; Fat 16.5g, of which saturates 10.7g; Cholesterol 44mg; Calcium 219mg; Fibre 0g; Sodium 473mg.
Quick Satay Sauce: Energy 108kcal/451kJ; Protein 3.6g; Carbohydrate 5.8g, of which sugars 4.9g; Fat 8g, of which saturates 2.1g; Cholesterol 0mg; Calcium 30mg; Fibre 0.8g; Sodium 150mg.

Sesame and Lemon Dip

This delightful little dip, originating from central Anatolia, in Turkey, is often served in outdoor cafés and restaurants as a meze dish on its own – a sort of whetting of the appetite while you wait for the assortment of exciting dishes to come. In Turkey, you will see groups of old men drinking raki or refeshing tea, sharing a plate of sesame and lemon dip, tahin tarama, while they play cards or backgammon. Sweet and tangy, it is good mopped up with chunks of crusty bread or toasted pitta bread.

Serves 2
45ml/3 tbsp light sesame paste (tahin)
juice of 1 lemon
15–30ml/1–2 tbsp clear honey
5–10ml/1–2 tsp dried mint
lemon wedges, to serve

1 Beat the sesame paste and lemon juice together in a bowl.

2 Add the honey and mint and beat again until thick and creamy, then spoon into a small dish.

3 Serve at room temperature, with lemon wedges for squeezing.

Cook's Tip
Tahin is made from sesame seeds that are ground to a fine, oily paste. This is used in several other traditional Turkish recipes, such as hummus and tahin pekmez.

Variation
Popular as a breakfast dish or as a sweet snack is tahin pekmez. To make it, combine 30–45ml/2–3 tbsp light sesame paste with 30ml/2 tbsp grape molasses (pekmez) to form a sweet paste, then scoop up with chunks of fresh bread. If you can't find pekmez, use date syrup from Middle Eastern and health food stores.

Chicken Liver and Brandy Pâté

This pâté really could not be simpler to make, and tastes so much better than anything you can buy ready-made in the supermarkets. Serve with crispy Melba toast for an elegant appetizer to enjoy with pre-dinner drinks or at a cocktail party.

Serves 4
350g/12oz chicken livers, trimmed and roughly chopped
30ml/2 tbsp brandy
30ml/2 tbsp double (heavy) cream

From the storecupboard
50g/2oz/¼ cup butter
salt and ground black pepper

1 Heat the butter in a large frying pan until foamy. Add the chicken livers and cook over a medium heat for 3–4 minutes, or until browned and cooked through.

2 Add the brandy and allow to bubble for a few minutes. Let the mixture cool slightly, then transfer into a food processor with the cream and some salt and pepper.

3 Process the mixture until smooth and spoon into small bowls. Level the surface and chill overnight to set. Serve garnished with sprigs of parsley to add a little colour.

Cook's Tip
Smooth patés freeze well for up to one month. They are best served sliced or scooped, as they can look slightly tired when presented in the dishes in which they were frozen. Home-made patés and spreads are excellent for topping canapés.

Variations
- *Varying the type of brandy will give a different nuance to the dish. Alternatively, port or madeira can be used instead of brandy.*
- *Use duck livers in place of the chicken livers and add 2.5ml/½ tsp grated orange rind.*

Sesame and Lemon: Energy 160kcal/664kJ; Protein 4.3g; Carbohydrate 6.4g, of which sugars 6.2g; Fat 13.3g, of which saturates 1.9g; Cholesterol 0mg; Calcium 155mg; Fibre 1.8g; Sodium 6mg.
Chicken Liver Pâté: Energy 227kcal/942kJ; Protein 15.7g; Carbohydrate 0.2g, of which sugars 0.2g; Fat 16.3g, of which saturates 9.6g; Cholesterol 369mg; Calcium 13mg; Fibre 0g; Sodium 144mg.

Sweet and Salty Vegetable Crisps

This delightfully simple snack is perfect to serve with pre-dinner drinks as an informal appetizer. Serve with a bowl of aioli or a creamy dip such as hummus, taramasalata or a blue cheese dip, and use the crisps to scoop it up. You can cook other sweet root vegetables, such as carrots, parsnips, celeriac and sweet potatoes, or even regular potatoes, in the same way. Prepare an attractive and appetizing snack by combining several different types of vegetable crisps, and then piling them together in a bowl. What could be more tempting than a pretty, colourful array of fresh, home-made vegetable crisps?

Serves 4
1 small fresh beetroot (beet)
caster (superfine) sugar

From the storecupboard
salt, for sprinkling
olive oil, for frying

1 Peel the beetroot and, using a mandolin or a vegetable peeler, cut it into very thin slices. Lay the slices on kitchen paper and sprinkle them with sugar and fine salt.

2 Heat 5cm/2in oil in a pan, until a bread cube dropped into the pan turns golden in 1 minute. Cook the slices, in batches, until they float to the surface and turn golden at the edge. Drain on kitchen paper and sprinkle with salt when cool.

Cook's Tip
Make sure that all the vegetable slices are separate before deep-frying. Place a handful at a time in hot oil and cook until they are crisp and golden.

Variation
Spiced plantain chips with hot chilli sauce make a tropical and flavoursome alternative to root vegetables.

Roasted Coconut Cashew Nuts

Serve these wok-fried hot and sweet cashew nuts in paper or cellophane cones at parties. Not only do they look enticing and taste terrific, but the cones help to keep your guests' clothes and hands clean and can simply be crumpled up and thrown away afterwards. Avoid serving these before a delicately flavoured meal.

Serves 6–8
30ml/2 tbsp clear honey
250g/9oz/2 cups cashew nuts
115g/4oz/1⅓ cups desiccated (dry shredded) coconut
2 small fresh red chillies, seeded and finely chopped

From the storecupboard
15ml/1 tbsp groundnut (peanut) oil
salt and ground black pepper

1 Heat the oil in a wok or large frying pan and then stir in the honey. After a few seconds add the nuts and coconut and stir-fry until both are golden brown.

2 Add the chillies, with salt and pepper to taste. Toss until all the ingredients are well mixed. Serve warm or cooled in paper cones or on saucers.

Cook's Tip
When preparing chillies, it is a good idea to wear rubber gloves to avoid getting capsaicin on your hands. This chemical, which is concentrated in chilli seeds and pith, is a strong irritant and will cause a burning sensation if it comes into contact with delicate skin. If you don't wear gloves, wash your hands with soap after handling chillies.

Variations
- *Whole almonds also work well if you cannot get hold of any cashews, but for a more economical snack, simply roast whole unsalted peanuts with chillies and coconut.*
- *Shelled pistachio and macademia nuts can also be substituted in this recipe.*

Sweet and Salty Crisps: Energy 155kcal/639kJ; Protein 0.3g; Carbohydrate 1.4g, of which sugars 1.3g; Fat 16.5g, of which saturates 2.4g; Cholesterol 0mg; Calcium 4mg; Fibre 0.4g; Sodium 12mg.
Roasted Cashews: Energy 301kcal/1247kJ; Protein 7.2g; Carbohydrate 9.7g, of which sugars 5.5g; Fat 26.2g, of which saturates 11.1g; Cholesterol 0mg; Calcium 14mg; Fibre 3g; Sodium 95mg.

Onion Cake

Serve this simple but delicious dish alone or with a salad accompaniment as an appetizer. It's particularly good alongside sausages, lamb chops or roast chicken as a more substantial meal. The cooking time will depend on the potatoes and how thinly they are sliced: use a food processor or mandolin (if you have one) to make paper-thin slices. The mound of potatoes will cook down to make a thick buttery cake.

Serves 6

900g/2lb new potatoes, peeled and thinly sliced
2 medium onions, very finely chopped

From the storecupboard

salt and ground black pepper
about 115g/4oz/½ cup butter

1 Preheat the oven to 190°C/375°F/Gas 5. Grease a 20cm/8in round cake tin (pan) with butter and line the base with a circle of baking parchment.

2 Arrange some of the potato slices evenly in the bottom of the tin and then sprinkle some of the onions over them. Season with salt and pepper. Reserve 25g/1oz/2 tbsp of the butter and dot the mixture with tiny pieces of the remaining butter.

3 Repeat these layers, using up all the ingredients and finishing with a layer of potatoes. Melt the reserved butter and brush it over the top.

4 Cover the potatoes with foil, put in the hot oven and cook for 1–1½ hours, until tender and golden. Remove from the oven and leave to stand, still covered, for 10–15 minutes.

5 Carefully turn out on to a warmed plate and serve.

Cook's Tip

If using old potatoes, cook and serve them in an earthenware or ovenproof glass dish. Remove the cover from the dish for the final 10–15 minutes to lightly brown the top.

Mushroom Caviar

The name mushroom caviar refers to the dark colour and texture of this dish of chopped mushrooms. Serve the mixture in individual serving dishes with toasted rye bread, or sourdough, rubbed with cut garlic cloves, to complement the rich earthy flavour of the mushrooms. Chopped hard-boiled egg, spring onion and parsley, the traditional garnishes for caviar, can be served as a garnish.

Serves 4

450g/1lb mushrooms, coarsely chopped
5–10 shallots, chopped
4 garlic cloves, chopped

From the storecupboard

45ml/3 tbsp olive or vegetable oil

1 Heat the oil in a large pan, add the mushrooms, shallots and garlic, and cook, stirring occasionally, until browned. Season with salt, then continue cooking until the mushrooms give up their liquor.

2 Continue cooking, stirring frequently, until the liquor has evaporated and the mushrooms are brown and dry.

3 Put the mixture in a food processor or blender and process briefly until a chunky paste is formed. Spoon the mushroom caviar into dishes and serve.

Cook's Tip

If garnishing with eggs, prevent black rings from forming around the egg yolks by cracking the shells all over as soon as the eggs are cooked, and cool quickly in cold water.

Variation

For a rich wild mushroom caviar, soak 10–15g/¼–½oz dried porcini in about 120ml/4fl oz/½ cup water for about 30 minutes. Add the porcini and their soaking liquid to the browned mushrooms in step 2. Continue as in the recipe. Serve with wedges of lemon, for their tangy juice.

Onion Cake: Energy 272kcal/1133kJ; Protein 3.5g; Carbohydrate 29.5g, of which sugars 5.8g; Fat 16.3g, of which saturates 10.1g; Cholesterol 41mg; Calcium 29mg; Fibre 2.4g; Sodium 135mg.
Mushroom Caviar: Energy 68kcal/283kJ; Protein 3.3g; Carbohydrate 6.4g, of which sugars 3.8g; Fat 3.5g, of which saturates 0.5g; Cholesterol 0mg; Calcium 24mg; Fibre 2.4g; Sodium 8mg.

Chopped Egg and Onions

This dish is one of the oldest dishes in Jewish culinary history. It is delicious served sprinkled with chopped parsley and onion rings on crackers, piled on toast, or used as a sandwich or bagel filling. Serve chopped egg and onion as part of a buffet with a selection of dips and toppings.

Serves 4–6
8–10 eggs
6–8 spring onions (scallions) and/or 1 yellow or white onion, very finely chopped, plus extra to garnish
60–90ml/4–6 tbsp mayonnaise or rendered chicken fat
mild French wholegrain mustard, to taste (optional if using mayonnaise)

1 Put the eggs in a large pan and cover with cold water. Bring the water to the boil and when it boils, reduce the heat and simmer over a low heat for 10 minutes.

2 Hold the boiled eggs under cold running water immediately (if too hot to handle, place the eggs in a strainer and hold under the running water). When cool, remove the shells from the eggs and discard. Dry the eggs and chop coarsely using a large knife with a lightly oiled blade.

3 Place the chopped eggs in a large bowl, add the onions, season generously with salt and black pepper and mix well. Add enough mayonnaise or chicken fat to bind the mixture together. Stir in the mustard, if using, and chill before serving.

Cook's Tip
The amount of rendered chicken fat or mayonnaise required will depend on how much onion you use in this dish.

Variation
For a tasty alternative, spread slices of toasted ciabatta with tapenade and top with the chopped egg mixture.

Cheese with Green Olives

In Israel, mild white cheeses spiked with seasonings, such as this one flavoured with piquant green olives, are served with little crackers or toast. It is also very good for brunch – spread thickly on chunks of fresh, crusty bread or bagels.

Serves 4
175–200g/6–7oz soft white (farmer's) cheese
65g/2½oz feta cheese, preferably sheep's milk, lightly crumbled
20–30 pitted green olives, some chopped, the rest halved or quartered
3–4 large pinches of fresh thyme

1 Stir the soft white cheese in a bowl with the back of a spoon or a fork until it is soft and smooth. Add the lightly crumbled feta cheese and stir the two cheeses together until they are well combined.

2 Add the olives and the pinches of fresh thyme to the cheese mixture and mix thoroughly. Spoon into a bowl, sprinkle with thyme and serve with crackers, toast, chunks of bread or bagels.

Marinated Feta with Oregano

Feta cheese is a salty, crumbly Greek cheese that is packed in brine. The longer the cheese is left to marinate, the better the flavour will be. Serve with tomato and red onion salad and some crisp flatbreads.

Serves 4
200g/7oz Greek feta cheese
1 lemon, cut into wedges
a handful of fresh oregano sprigs

From the storecupboard
300ml/½ pint/1¼ cups extra virgin olive oil

1 Drain the feta and pat dry with kitchen paper. Cut it into cubes and arrange in a non-metallic bowl or dish with the lemon wedges and oregano sprigs.

2 Pour the olive oil over the top and cover with clear film (plastic wrap). Chill for at least 3 hours, then serve with a selection of flatbreads and salads.

Egg and Onions: Energy 197kcal/816kJ; Protein 11g; Carbohydrate 0.7g, of which sugars 0.6g; Fat 17g, of which saturates 3.7g; Cholesterol 325mg; Calcium 69mg; Fibre 0.6g; Sodium 165mg.
Cheese and Olives: Energy 242kcal/1002kJ; Protein 13.8g; Carbohydrate 0.3g, of which sugars 0.3g; Fat 19.7g, of which saturates 12g; Cholesterol 54mg; Calcium 393mg; Fibre 0.6g; Sodium 972mg.
Feta with Oregano: Energy 165kcal/684kJ; Protein 9.3g; Carbohydrate 1.3g, of which sugars 0.9g; Fat 13.7g, of which saturates 8.3g; Cholesterol 41mg; Calcium 211mg; Fibre 0.1g; Sodium 841mg.

Celery Stuffed with Gorgonzola

These stuffed celery stalks are very easy to assemble. A delicious combination of creamy cheese and crisp celery, they go beautifully with salamis and and other cured meat but also make a tasty addition to a picnic.

Serves 4–6

12 crisp celery sticks, with leaves attached
75g/3oz/½ cup Gorgonzola
75g/3oz/½ cup cream cheese
fresh chives, to garnish

1 Wash and dry the celery sticks, then trim the root ends. Leave on the leaves for an attractive finish.

2 Place the Gorgonzola in a small bowl with the cream cheese and mash together until smooth.

3 Fill the celery sticks with the cheese mixture, using a spatula to smooth the top of the filling. Chill in the refrigerator for at least an hour.

4 To serve, arrange the chilled sticks decoratively on a serving platter and garnish the surface of the fillings with finely chopped chives. Serve immediately.

Cook's Tip
These crunchy sticks are also ideal to serve as nibbles with drinks, but guests will find them more manageable if they are sliced into bitesize pieces rather than served whole. Use the trimmed leaves as a garnish.

Variation
If you prefer a less tangy flavour for the filling, try using Dolcelatte, which is a mild version of Gorgonzola. Exceptionally creamy, Dolcelatte will blend easily with the cream cheese and still add enough flavour to the finished dish.

Crostini with Cheese

These cheese-topped treats will disappear in a flash!

Serves 6

4–6 slices day-old white or brown bread
75g/3oz thinly sliced cheese (Fontina or Gruyère)
anchovy fillets
strips of red (bell) pepper

From the storecupboard
ground black pepper
butter, for greasing

1 Cut the bread into small squares, triangles or circles. Preheat the oven to 190°C/375°F/Gas 5. Butter a baking sheet.

2 Top each slice of bread with cheese, cutting it to fit. Cut the anchovies and pepper strips into small shapes and place on top. Grind a little pepper over each. Transfer to the baking sheet and bake for 10 minutes, until the cheese has melted.

Walnut and Goat's Cheese Bruschetta

The combination of toasted walnuts and melting goat's cheese is lovely in this simple appetizer, served with a pile of salad leaves. Toasting the walnuts helps to enhance their flavour. Walnut bread is readily available in most large supermarkets and makes an interesting alternative to ordinary crusty bread, although this can be used if walnut bread is unavailable.

Serves 4

50g/2oz/½ cup walnut pieces
4 thick slices walnut bread
120ml/4fl oz/½ cup French dressing
200g/7oz chèvre or other semi-soft goat's cheese

1 Preheat the grill (broiler). Lightly toast the walnut pieces, then remove and set aside. Put the walnut bread on a foil-lined grill rack and toast on one side. Turn the slices over and drizzle each with 15ml/1 tbsp of the French dressing.

2 Cut the goat's cheese into 12 slices and place three on each piece of bread. Grill (broil) for about 3 minutes, until the cheese is melting and beginning to brown.

3 Transfer the bruschetta to serving plates, sprinkle with the toasted walnuts and drizzle with the remaining French dressing. Serve the bruschetta immediately with salad leaves.

Cook's Tip
Use walnut bread slices from a slender loaf, so that the portions are not too wide. If you can buy only a large loaf, cut the slices in half to make neat, chunky pieces.

Variation
This appetizer is delicious served with a beetroot salad. Take 2 beetroots (beets), peel and grate. Place in a bowl with sliced celery (1 stick) and 2 spring onions (scallions), chopped, toss with French dressing and cumin. Season and marinate for 1 hour.

Celery: Energy 154kcal/636kJ; Protein 4.8g; Carbohydrate 0.5g, of which sugars 0.5g; Fat 14.8g, of which saturates 9.4g; Cholesterol 33mg; Calcium 137mg; Fibre 0.7g; Sodium 327mg.
Crostini: Energy 151kcal/632kJ; Protein 8.7g; Carbohydrate 8.5g, of which sugars 0.7g; Fat 8.9g, of which saturates 5.6g; Cholesterol 26mg; Calcium 231mg; Fibre 0.7g; Sodium 387mg.
Bruschetta: Energy 558kcal/2321kJ; Protein 16.7g; Carbohydrate 25.6g, of which sugars 2.2g; Fat 37.2g, of which saturates 12.7g; Cholesterol 47mg; Calcium 137mg; Fibre 1.2g; Sodium 841mg.

Toasted Ciabatta with Cheese and Marjoram

In this very simple but tasty antipasto dish, marjoram flowers are used to give a distinctive flavour. The combination of cheese, tomato and marjoram is great, but lots of extras can be added, such as capers, olives, anchovies or slices of roasted peppers.

Serves 2
1 ciabatta loaf
4 tomatoes
115g/4oz mozzarella or Cheddar cheese
15ml/1 tbsp marjoram flowers

From the storecupboard
15ml/1 tbsp olive oil
salt and ground black pepper

1 Preheat the grill (broiler) to high. Cut the loaf in half lengthways and toast very lightly under the grill until it has turned a pale golden brown.

2 Meanwhile, skin the tomatoes: to loosen the skins, first plunge the tomatoes in boiling water for 30 seconds, then refresh them in cold water. Peel and cut the flesh into thick slices.

3 Slice or grate the mozzarella or Cheddar cheese. Lightly drizzle the olive oil over the toasted bread and top with the tomato slices and cheese. Season with salt and pepper and sprinkle the marjoram flowers over the top. Drizzle with a little more olive oil.

4 Place under the hot grill until the cheese bubbles and is just starting to brown. Serve immediately.

Cook's Tip
Add marjoram flowers to your favourite pizza topping. Sprinkle over 7.5–15ml/½–1 tbsp flowers or flowering tops and add a few of the leaves. The flavours are strong, so marjoram flowers should be used with care, especially if you haven't tried them before. The amount you use will depend on your own taste.

Devils on Horseback

This popular savoury, designed to be served at the end of a lavish dinner, also makes a good appetizer. The prunes are sometimes filled with pâté, olives, almonds or nuggets of cured meat. They may be served on crisp, fried bread instead of buttered toast.

Serves 4
16 pitted prunes
fruit chutney, such as mango
8 rindless rashers (strips) of streaky (fatty) bacon
8 small slices of bread

From the storecupboard
butter for spreading

1 Preheat the oven to 200°C/400°F/Gas 6. Carefully ease open the prunes and spoon a small amount of fruit chutney into each cavity.

2 Lay the bacon rashers on a board, slide the back of a knife along each one to stretch it and then cut in half crossways. Wrap a piece of bacon around each prune and lay them close together (if they touch each other, they are less likely to unroll during cooking) on a baking sheet.

3 Put into the hot oven for 8–10 minutes until the bacon is cooked through.

4 Meanwhile, toast the bread. Butter the hot toast and serve the bacon-wrapped prunes on top.

Variation
For a really luxurious appetizer why not make Angels on Horseback. This heavenly recipe employs oysters in place of prunes stuffed with chutney. You need 16 oysters, removed from their shells, and a squeeze of lemon juice. Preheat the oven to 200°C/400°F/Gas 6. Sprinkle the oysters with a little lemon juice. Wrap a piece of bacon around each oyster and secure with a cocktail stick (toothpick). Arrange on a baking sheet and place in the hot oven for 8–10 minutes. Meanwhile, toast and butter small slices of bread and serve the Angels on top.

Toasted Ciabatta: Energy 502kcal/2113kJ; Protein 22.3g; Carbohydrate 58.2g, of which sugars 9.3g; Fat 21.7g, of which saturates 9.5g; Cholesterol 33mg; Calcium 343mg; Fibre 4.3g; Sodium 783mg.
Devils on Horseback: Energy 309kcal/1303kJ; Protein 14.7g; Carbohydrate 41.7g, of which sugars 18.3g; Fat 10.4g, of which saturates 3.5g; Cholesterol 30mg; Calcium 75mg; Fibre 3.6g; Sodium 1132mg.

Brandade of Salt Cod

There are many versions of this creamy French salt cod purée: some contain mashed potatoes, others truffles. Serve the brandade with warmed crispbread or crusty bread for a tasty appetizer. You can omit the garlic, if you prefer, and serve toasted slices of French bread rubbed with garlic instead.

Serves 6
200g/7oz salt cod
4 garlic cloves, crushed
250ml/8fl oz/1 cup double (heavy) or whipping cream

From the storecupboard
250ml/8fl oz/1 cup extra virgin olive oil

1 Soak the fish in cold water for 24 hours, changing the water frequently. Drain the fish well. Cut the fish into pieces, place in a shallow pan and pour in enough cold water to cover. Heat the water until it is simmering and poach the fish for 8 minutes, until it is just cooked. Drain the fish, then remove the skin and bones.

2 Combine the extra virgin olive oil and crushed garlic cloves in a small pan and heat gently. In another pan, heat the double cream until it just starts to simmer.

3 Put the cod into a food processor, process it briefly, then gradually add alternate amounts of the garlic-flavoured olive oil and cream, while continuing to process the mixture. The aim is to create a purée with the consistency of mashed potato.

4 Season to taste with ground black pepper, then scoop the brandade into a serving bowl or on to individual serving plates and serve with crispbread or crusty bread.

Cook's Tip
The salting of cod harks back to a time before the introduction of freezers to fishing boats. Fishermen used to clean and gut the fish, adding layers of salt until the hold was full.

Sizzling Prawns

These richly flavoured prawns (shrimp) are a classic Spanish tapas dish, but they also make a perfect appetizer. Traditionally they are brought to the table in little individual earthenware dishes, sizzling frantically in the hot oil with garlic. The addition of fiery dried chillies gives them an extra kick, but if you prefer a milder appetizer, simply omit the chillies.

Serves 4
1–2 dried chillies (to taste)
3 garlic cloves, finely chopped
16 large raw prawns (shrimp), in the shell

From the storecupboard
60ml/4 tbsp olive oil

1 Split the chillies lengthways and discard the seeds. (Wash your hands with soap and water immediately.)

2 Heat the olive oil in a large frying pan and stir-fry the garlic and chillies for 1 minute, until the garlic begins to turn brown.

3 Add the whole prawns and stir-fry for 3–4 minutes, coating them well with the flavoured oil.

4 Remove the pan from the heat and divide the prawns among four dishes. Spoon over the flavoured oil and serve straight away.

Cook's Tip
Remember to provide a plate for the heads and shells, plus a fingerbowl and plenty of napkins.

Variation
Prawns are good simply fried in olive oil and served with a spicy tomato sauce.

Brandade of Cod: Energy 477kcal/1967kJ; Protein 11.6g; Carbohydrate 1.1g, of which sugars 0.6g; Fat 47.4g, of which saturates 15.4g; Cholesterol 65mg; Calcium 24mg; Fibre 0.1g; Sodium 141mg.
Sizzling Prawns: Energy 161kcal/668kJ; Protein 13.6g; Carbohydrate 0.8g, of which sugars 0.1g; Fat 11.5g, of which saturates 1.7g; Cholesterol 146mg; Calcium 60mg; Fibre 0.2g; Sodium 143mg.

Oysters on the Half-shell

The best native Irish oysters come from the Galway area on the west coast of Ireland and, every September, festivals are held there to celebrate the beginning of the new season. Dulse or dillisk, an edible seaweed, is an ideal garnish. Enjoy the oysters with freshly made brown soda bread thickly spread with butter, and a glass of Guinness.

Serves 2–4

24 Galway oysters, in the shell
crushed ice and dulse or dillisk (soaked if dried), to garnish
soda bread and butter, and lemon wedges, to serve

1 Use a blunt-ended oyster knife to shuck the oysters: insert the end of the knife between the shells near the hinge and work it until you cut through the muscle that holds the shells together. Catch the oyster liquid in a bowl.

2 When the oysters are all open, discard the flat shells. Divide the oysters, in the deep halves, among four serving plates lined with crushed ice and soaked dulse.

3 Strain the reserved liquid from the shells over the oysters. Serve with the lemon wedges and the buttered soda bread with a glass of Guinness.

Cook's Tips

- *Although they were once plentiful, Galway oysters are now a delicacy and eaten raw – buy them with their shells tightly clamped together, showing that they are still alive. The edible seaweed, dulse, or dillisk as it is also known, is an appropriate garnish for oysters.*
- *If you want oysters for a cooked dish, look for the widely cultivated, larger Pacific oysters, which are available all year round, unlike the native oyster which is found only when there's an 'r' in the month. Native oysters are named after their place of origin, such as the Irish Galway and the English Whitstable, Helford and Colchester, and in America the best known of the eastern and Atlantic oysters is the Blue Point.*

Grilled Oysters with Heather Honey

This salt-sweet way to serve oysters is quite unbeatable. Heather honey is very fragrant as the pollen is gathered by bees late in the season when heather is in full flower. Beekeepers take their hives up to the hills once the spring and early summer blossoms are over, to get an intense flavour.

Serves 4

1 bunch spring onions (scallions), washed
20ml/4 tsp heather honey
10ml/2 tsp soy sauce
16 fresh oysters
bread, to serve

1 Preheat the grill (broiler) to medium. Chop the spring onions finely, removing any coarser outer leaves.

2 Place the heather honey and soy sauce in a bowl and mix together. Then add the finely chopped spring onions and stir them in thoroughly.

3 Open the oysters with an oyster knife or a small, sharp knife, taking care to catch the liquid in a small bowl. Leave the oysters attached to one side of the shell. Strain the liquid to remove any pieces of broken shell, and set aside.

4 Place a large teaspoon of the honey, soy sauce and spring onion mixture on top of each oyster.

5 Place under the preheated grill until the mixture begins to bubble, which will take about 5 minutes. Take care when removing the oysters from the grill as the shells retain the heat. It is advisable to wear oven gloves or use a heatproof cloth to do this. Make sure that you don't lose any of the delicious sauce from inside the oyster shells. Arrange on a serving plate.

6 Allow the oysters to cool slightly before serving with slices of bread to soak up the mouthwatering juices. Either tip them straight into your mouth or lift them out of their shells with a spoon or fork.

Oysters on Half-shell: Energy 78kcal/330kJ; Protein 13g; Carbohydrate 3.3g, of which sugars 0g; Fat 1.6g, of which saturates 0.3g; Cholesterol 68mg; Calcium 168mg; Fibre 0g; Sodium 612mg.
Oysters with Honey: Energy 81kcal/343kJ; Protein 9.2g; Carbohydrate 9.1g, of which sugars 6.9g; Fat 1.2g, of which saturates 0.2g; Cholesterol 46mg; Calcium 121mg; Fibre 0.3g; Sodium 588mg.

Dublin Lawyer

This traditional dish used to be made with raw lobster, but it is now more usually lightly boiled first. The origins of the name are uncertain, but it is generally thought to refer to the fact that lawyers are more likely than most to be able to afford this luxurious dish.

Serves 2
1 large, (over 900g/2lb) lightly cooked lobster (see Cook's Tip)
75ml/2½fl oz/⅓ cup Irish whiskey
150ml/¼ pint/⅔ cup double (heavy) cream

From the storecupboard
175g/6oz/¾ cup butter
sea salt and ground black pepper

1 Tear off the claws from the cooked lobster. Split the body in half lengthways, with a sharp knife, just slightly to the right of the centre line to avoid cutting into the digestive tract. Remove the grey matter from the head of the shell and discard. Then remove the digestive tract right down the length of the body and discard. Lift the flesh from the tail – it usually comes out in one piece. Set the shells aside for serving and keep them warm.

2 Tear the two joints in the claw to separate them and, using a small knife, scoop out the flesh. With the back of a heavy knife, hit the claw near the pincers, rotating the claw and hitting until the claw opens. Remove the flesh and cut into bitesize pieces.

3 Melt the butter in a pan over a low heat. Add the lobster pieces and turn in the butter to warm through.

4 Warm the whiskey in a separate pan and pour it over the lobster. Carefully set it alight. Add the cream and heat gently without allowing the sauce to boil, then season to taste. Turn the hot mixture into the warm shells and serve immediately.

Cook's Tip
To cook, weigh the live lobster and put it into a pan of boiling salted water. Bring back to the boil and cook for 12 minutes per 450g/1lb for small lobsters, a little less if 900g/2lb or over. Remove the cooked lobster from the water and leave to cool.

Dressed Crab with Asparagus

Crab is the juiciest and most flavoursome seafood, possibly better even than lobster and certainly considerably cheaper. This dish is a combination of two paragons – crab as the king of seafood and asparagus as a prince among vegetables – a royal partnership.

Serves 4
24 asparagus spears
4 dressed crabs
30ml/2 tbsp mayonnaise
15ml/1 tbsp chopped fresh parsley

From the storecupboard
15g/½oz coarse salt

1 Wash and trim the asparagus spears to 10cm/4in lengths. Bring a pan of water to the boil, add coarse salt, then plunge in the asparagus. Cook for about 7 minutes, or until you can just spear a stem with a knife and the blade slips out easily. Drain when cooked and plunge the stems into iced water to stop them from cooking further. Drain them when cold and pat dry with kitchen paper.

2 Scoop out the white crab meat from the shells and claws and place it in a bowl. If you can't find fresh crabs, you can use the same amount of canned or frozen white crab meat.

3 Add the mayonnaise and chopped fresh parsley and combine with a fork. Place the mixture into the crab shells and add six asparagus spears per serving. Serve with crusty bread.

Cook's Tip
To dress a crab, first cook in a large pan of salted boiling water for 10–12 minutes. Then twist off the tail flap, both claws and the legs. Now insert a large knife between the body and the shell and twist to separate. Remove the gills on each side and the stomach sac behind the mouth. Cut the body into quarters and pick out the white meat with a skewer. With a teaspoon scoop out all the brown meat from the back shell and flaps. Crack open the claws and legs with a mallet and remove the claw meat in chunks. Scrape out any leg meat with a skewer.

Dublin Lawyer: Energy 1273kcal/5259kJ; Protein 37.8g; Carbohydrate 1.8g, of which sugars 1.8g; Fat 114.9g, of which saturates 71.1g; Cholesterol 469mg; Calcium 152mg; Fibre 0g; Sodium 1.08g.
Crab with Asparagus: Energy 207kcal/859kJ; Protein 19.5g; Carbohydrate 3g, of which sugars 2.8g; Fat 13g, of which saturates 1.9g; Cholesterol 72mg; Calcium 157mg; Fibre 2.6g; Sodium 540mg.

Rye and Caraway Seed Sticks

A great addition to the cheese board, these long sticks have crunchy caraway seeds inside and out.

Makes 18–20

90g/3½oz/¾ cup plain (all-purpose) flour
75g/3oz/⅔ cup rye flour
2.5ml/½ tsp baking powder
10ml/2 tsp caraway seeds

From the storecupboard

2.5ml/½ tsp salt
90g/3½oz/7 tbsp unsalted (sweet) butter, diced

1 Preheat the oven to 180°C/350°F/Gas 4. Mix the flours, salt and baking powder together. Rub in the butter until the mixture resembles fine breadcrumbs. Stir in 5ml/1 tsp of the caraway seeds. Add 60ml/4 tbsp boiling water and mix well to form a soft dough.

2 Divide into 18 equal pieces. With the tips of your fingers, gently roll each one out to 25cm/10in long. Place sticks on a non-stick baking sheet, sprinkle over remaining caraway seeds and bake for about 20 minutes until crisp. Remove from the oven and transfer carefully to a wire rack to cool.

Salted Almonds

Served with a glass of chilled dry sherry, these delicious salted nuts make a perfect tapas dish or pre-dinner snack.

Serves 4–6

1 egg white
200g/7oz/generous 1 cup shelled unblanched almonds

From the storecupboard

a good handful of flaked sea salt

1 Preheat the oven to 200°C/400°F/Gas 6. Whisk the egg white until it forms stiff peaks. Add the almonds and stir until thoroughly coated. Tip mixture on to a baking sheet and spread out evenly.

2 Sprinkle the salt over the almonds and bake for about 15 minutes, or until the egg white and salt are crusty. Leave to cool completely, then serve in bowls with a selection of nibbles.

Coconut Chips

Coconut chips are a tasty nibble to serve with drinks. The chips can be sliced ahead of time and frozen (without salt), on open trays. Once frozen, simply shake into plastic boxes. You can then take out as many as you wish for the party.

Serves 8

1 fresh coconut
salt

1 Preheat the oven to 160°C/325°F/Gas 3. First drain the coconut juice, either by piercing one of the coconut eyes with a sharp instrument or by breaking it carefully.

2 Lay the coconut on a board and hit the centre sharply with a hammer. The shell should break cleanly in two.

3 Having opened the coconut, use a broad-bladed knife to ease the flesh away from the hard outer shell. Taste a piece of the flesh just to make sure it is fresh. Peel away the brown skin with a potato peeler, if you like.

4 Slice the coconut flesh into wafer-thin shavings, using a food processor, mandolin or sharp knife. Sprinkle the shavings evenly all over one or two baking sheets and sprinkle with salt.

5 Bake for about 25–30 minutes or until crisp, turning them from time to time. Cool and serve. Any leftovers can be stored in airtight containers.

Cook's Tip

This is the kind of recipe where the slicing blade on a food processor comes into its own. It is worth preparing two or three coconuts at a time, and freezing surplus chips. The chips can be cooked from frozen, but will need to be spread out well on the baking sheets, before being salted. Allow a little longer for frozen chips to cook.

Rye and Caraway Sticks: Energy 65kcal/269kJ; Protein 0.9g; Carbohydrate 6.4g, of which sugars 0.1g; Fat 4.1g, of which saturates 2.4g; Cholesterol 10mg; Calcium 12mg; Fibre 0.6g; Sodium 77mg.
Salted Almonds: Energy 269kcal/1115kJ; Protein 9.6g; Carbohydrate 3g, of which sugars 1.8g; Fat 24.4g, of which saturates 1.9g; Cholesterol 0mg; Calcium 105mg; Fibre 3.2g; Sodium 259mg.
Coconut Chips: Energy 41kcal/178kJ; Protein 0.6g; Carbohydrate 9.2g, of which sugars 9.2g; Fat 0.6g, of which saturates 0.4g; Cholesterol 0mg; Calcium 54mg; Fibre 0g; Sodium 206mg.

Plantain Snacks

Sweet and crisp, deep-fried slices of plaintain are not only a great street snack, but also make excellent nibbles with drinks. The spice mixture used here – zahtar – is popular throughout North Africa and is also widely used in Turkey and Jordan. Its blend of sesame seeds, sumac and thyme is perfect with plantains, and the chilli adds a warm note.

Serves 2–4 as a snack
2 large ripe plantains
1 dried red chilli, roasted, seeded and chopped
15–30ml/1–2 tbsp zahtar

From the storecupboard
sunflower oil, for deep-frying
coarse salt

1 To peel the plantains, cut off their ends with a sharp knife and make two or three incisions in the skin from end to end, then peel off the skin. Cut the plantains into thick slices.

2 Heat the oil for deep-frying in a heavy pan to 180°C/350°F, or until a cube of bread browns in 30–45 seconds. Fry the plantain slices in batches until golden brown. Drain each batch on a double layer of kitchen paper.

3 While still warm, place them in a shallow bowl and sprinkle liberally with the dried chilli, zahtar and salt. Toss them thoroughly and eat immediately.

Cook's Tips
- *To roast the chilli, place it in a small, heavy frying pan and cook over a medium heat, stirring constantly, until the chilli darkens and gives off a peppery aroma.*
- *If you can't get hold of the Middle Eastern spice blend, zahtar, you can make your own by combining the following ingredients in a bowl: 15ml/1 tbsp dried thyme, 15ml/1 tbsp ground sumac, 15ml/1 tbsp roasted sesame seeds, a sprinkling of coarse salt. Store the mixture in an airtight jar.*

Polenta Chips

These tasty Parmesan-flavoured batons are best served warm from the oven with a spicy, tangy dip. A bowl of Thai chilli dipping sauce or a creamy, chilli-spiked guacamole are perfect for dipping into.

Makes about 80
375g/13oz/3¼ cups instant polenta
150g/5oz/1½ cups freshly grated Parmesan cheese

From the storecupboard
10ml/2 tsp salt, plus extra
90g/3½oz/7 tbsp butter
10ml/2 tsp cracked black pepper
olive oil, for brushing

1 Put 1.5 litres/2½ pints/6¼ cups water into a large heavy pan and bring to the boil. Reduce the heat, add the salt and pour in the polenta in a steady stream, stirring constantly with a wooden spoon. Cook over a low heat for about 5 minutes, stirring, until the mixture thickens and comes away from the sides of the pan.

2 Remove the pan from the heat and add the cheese and butter. Season to taste. Stir well until the mixture is smooth. Pour on to a smooth surface, such as a marble slab or a baking sheet.

3 Using a metal spatula, spread out the polenta to a thickness of 2cm/¾in and shape into a rectangle. Leave to stand for at least 30 minutes until cold. Meanwhile, preheat the oven to 200°C/400°F/Gas 6 and lightly oil two or three baking sheets.

4 Cut the polenta slab in half, then carefully cut into even strips. Bake for 40–50 minutes, or until dark golden brown and crunchy, turning from time to time. Serve warm.

Cook's Tip
The unbaked dough can be made a day ahead, then wrapped in clear film (plastic wrap) and kept in the refrigerator until ready to bake.

Plantain Snacks: Energy 334kcal/1408kJ; Protein 1.9g; Carbohydrate 59.4g, of which sugars 14.4g; Fat 11.5g, of which saturates 1.3g; Cholesterol 0mg; Calcium 8mg; Fibre 2.9g; Sodium 4mg.
Polenta Chips: Energy 34kcal/142kJ; Protein 1.2g; Carbohydrate 3.4g, of which sugars 0g; Fat 1.7g, of which saturates 1g; Cholesterol 4mg; Calcium 23mg; Fibre 0.1g; Sodium 76mg.

Parmesan Tuiles

These lacy tuiles look very impressive and make great nibbles for a party, but they couldn't be easier to make. Believe it or not, they use only a single ingredient – Parmesan cheese.

Makes 8–10
115g/4oz Parmesan cheese

1 Preheat the oven to 200°C/400°F/Gas 6. Line two baking sheets with baking parchment. Grate the cheese using a fine grater, pulling it down slowly to make long strands.

2 Spread the grated cheese out in 7.5–9cm/3–3½in rounds on the baking parchment, forking it into shape. Do not spread the cheese too thickly; it should just cover the parchment. Bake for 5–7 minutes, or until bubbling and golden brown.

3 Leave the tuiles on the baking sheet for about 30 seconds and then carefully transfer, using a metal spatula, to a wire rack to cool completely. Alternatively, drape over a rolling pin to make a curved shape.

Cook's Tip
Parmesan cheese will keep for months if stored properly. Wrap it in foil and store in a plastic box in the least cold part of the refrigerator, such as the salad drawer or one of the compartments in the door.

Variations
- *Tuiles can be made into little cup shapes by draping over an upturned egg cup. These little cups can be filled to make tasty treats to serve with drinks. Try a little ricotta cheese flavoured with herbs.*
- *Add ground black pepper, dried herbs or finely chopped nuts to the grated cheese before baking.*

Golden Gruyère and Basil Tortillas

These simple fried tortilla wedges – a variation on the Mexican quesadillas – are great for a crowd. Fill the tortillas in advance, for a party, and cook them at the last minute. They also make a tasty late-night snack with sweet chilli sauce.

Serves 2
2 soft flour tortillas
115g/4oz Gruyère cheese, thinly sliced
a handful of fresh basil leaves

From the storecupboard
15ml/1 tbsp olive oil
salt and ground black pepper

1 Heat the oil in a frying pan over a medium heat. Add one of the tortillas, arrange the Gruyère cheese slices and basil leaves on top and season with salt and pepper.

2 Place the remaining tortilla on top to make a sandwich and flip the whole thing over with a metal spatula. Cook for a few minutes, until the underneath is golden.

3 Slide the tortilla sandwich on to a chopping board or plate and cut into wedges. Serve immediately.

Cook's Tip
Gruyère cheese traditionally comes from Switzerland. It has a slightly grainy texture and a wonderful complexity of flavours. At first the taste is fruity, but then it reveals more earthy and nutty characteristics.

Variations
- *Instead of Gruyère you could use mild Cheddar, Monterey Jack or mozzarella. If you are using mozzarella cheese, make sure that it is drained thoroughly then patted dry and cut into thin strips. Cheddar or Monterey Jack can be thinly sliced or coarsely grated.*
- *If you have some ham or salami in the refrigerator you can add these to the tortillas too.*

Parmesan Tuiles: Energy 52kcal/216kJ; Protein 4.5g; Carbohydrate 0g, of which sugars 0g; Fat 3.8g, of which saturates 2.4g; Cholesterol 12mg; Calcium 138mg; Fibre 0g; Sodium 125mg.
Tortillas: Energy 354kcal/1474kJ; Protein 16.4g; Carbohydrate 15g, of which sugars 0.4g; Fat 24.6g, of which saturates 13.3g; Cholesterol 56mg; Calcium 453mg; Fibre 0.6g; Sodium 486mg.

Filo Cigars with Feta and Herbs

These Turkish cigar-shaped pastries are good as nibbles with drinks. The filo pastry can be folded into triangles, but cigars are the most usual shape. Here they are filled with cheese and herbs, but other popular fillings include aromatic minced meat, baked aubergine and cheese, or mashed pumpkin with cheese and dill.

Serves 3–4

225g/8 oz/1 cup feta cheese (mashed)
1 large (US extra large) egg
1 small bunch each of fresh flat leaf parsley, mint and dill, finely chopped
4–5 sheets of filo pastry
dill fronds, to garnish (optional)

From the storecupboard

sunflower oil, for deep-frying

1 Put the mashed feta in a bowl, beat in the egg and fold in the herbs.

2 Place the sheets of filo on a flat surface and cover with a damp dish towel to keep them moist. Working with one sheet at a time, cut the filo into strips about 10–13cm/4–5in wide, and pile them on top of each other. Keep the strips covered with another damp dish towel.

3 Lay one filo strip down in front of you and place a heaped teaspoon of the cheese filling along one of the short ends. Roll the end over the filling, quite tightly to keep it in place, then tuck in the sides to seal in the filling and continue to roll until you get to the other end.

4 As you reach the end, brush the tip with a little water to seal. Place the filled cigar, join-side down, on a plate and cover with another damp dish towel to keep it moist. Continue with the remaining sheets of filo and filling.

5 Heat enough oil for deep-frying in a wok or other deep-sided pan, and deep-fry the filo cigars in batches for 5–6 minutes until crisp and golden brown. Remove with a slotted spoon and drain on kitchen paper.

6 Serve immediately, garnished with dill fronds, if using.

Yogurt Cheese in Olive Oil

In Greece, sheep's yogurt is hung in muslin to drain off the whey before being patted into balls of soft cheese. Here the cheese is bottled in extra virgin olive oil with dried chillies and fresh herbs to make an aromatic appetizer or party nibble. It is delicious spread on thick slices of toast as a snack or a light lunch.

Fills two 450g/1lb jars

1 litre/1¾ pints/4 cups Greek sheep's (US strained plain) yogurt
10ml/2 tsp crushed dried chillies or chilli powder
30ml/2 tbsp chopped fresh herbs, such as rosemary, and thyme or oregano

From the storecupboard

about 300ml/½ pint/1¼ cups extra virgin olive oil, preferably garlic-flavoured
salt and ground black pepper

1 Sterilize a 30cm/12in square of muslin (cheesecloth) by soaking it in boiling water for several minutes. Drain and lay it over a large plate.

2 Season the yogurt with salt and transfer on to the centre of the muslin. Bring up the sides of the muslin and tie with string.

3 Hang the bag on a kitchen cupboard handle or a suitable position where it can be suspended over a bowl to catch the whey. Leave for 2–3 days until the yogurt stops dripping.

4 Sterilize two 450g/1lb glass preserving jars by heating them in the oven at 150°C/300°F/Gas 2 for 15 minutes.

5 Mix the crushed dried chillies and herbs. Take teaspoonfuls of the cheese one at a time and roll into balls with your hands. Put the cheese balls into the sterilized jars, sprinkling each layer with the herb mixture.

6 Pour the oil over the cheese and herbs until completely covered. Store in the refrigerator for up to 3 weeks. To serve, spoon the cheese out of the jars with a little of the flavoured olive oil and spread on slices of lightly toasted bread.

Filo with Feta: Energy 311kcal/1291kJ; Protein 12.4g; Carbohydrate 11.2g, of which sugars 1.6g; Fat 24.4g, of which saturates 9.5g; Cholesterol 92mg; Calcium 278mg; Fibre 1.6g; Sodium 838mg.
Yogurt Cheese: Energy 1331kcal/5488kJ; Protein 24g; Carbohydrate 7.5g, of which sugars 7.5g; Fat 138.2g, of which saturates 33.8g; Cholesterol 0mg; Calcium 563mg; Fibre 0g; Sodium 758mg.

Cheese Straws

Everyone loves these crisp, cheesy sticks and, fortunately, they are incredibly quick and easy to make. These cheesy pastries became popular when it was customary to serve a savoury at the end of the meal, but they are perfect for serving as party snacks or with pre-dinner drinks.

Makes about 10
75g/3oz/⅔ cup plain (all-purpose) flour
40g/1½ oz mature (sharp) hard cheese, such as Cheddar, finely grated
1 egg
5ml/1 tsp ready-made mustard

From the storecupboard
40g/1½ oz/3 tbsp butter, diced
salt and ground black pepper

1 Preheat the oven to 180°C/350°F/Gas 4. Line a baking sheet with baking parchment.

2 Sift the flour and seasoning and add the butter. Rub the butter into the flour until the mixture resembles fine crumbs. Stir in the cheese.

3 Lightly beat the egg with the mustard. Add half the egg to the flour, stirring in until the mixture can be gathered into a smooth ball of dough.

4 Roll the dough out to make a square measuring about 15cm/6in. Cut into ten lengths. Place on the baking sheet and brush with the remaining egg. Put into the hot oven and cook for about 12 minutes until golden brown. Transfer to a wire rack and serve warm.

Variations
- *Some or all of the cheese straws can be sprinkled with poppy, sunflower and/or sesame seeds before baking. A mixture of plain and coated straws make an attractive platter.*
- *You can use other types of cheese for making the pastry. Try Parmesan, Pecorino, Mahon or, for extra colour, red Leicester.*
- *Add a pinch of cayenne pepper with the cheese for warmth.*

Cucumber Sandwiches

Think of Edwardian England, and afternoon tea parties with dainty cucumber sandwiches come to mind. This traditional British sandwich makes a healthy children's tea party snack, and is just as appealing to adults. Why not serve them with a glass of chilled wine.

Make 24 fingers
½ cucumber
8 slices of white bread

From the storecupboard
soft unsalted (sweet) butter, for spreading
salt and ground black pepper

1 Peel the cucumber and cut it into thin slices. Sprinkle with salt, place in a colander and leave for about 20 minutes to drain. Butter the slices of bread on one side. Lay the cucumber over four slices of bread and sprinkle with pepper.

2 Top with the remaining bread. Press down lightly and trim off the crusts.

3 Cut the sandwiches into squares, fingers or diagonally into triangles. Serve immediately.

Cook's Tip
Cucumbers were first grown in English hothouses in the 16th century, just waiting for the sandwich to be invented 200 years later.

Variation
The possibilities for sophisticated sandwich fillings to be served are endless. Here are just a few to get you started: thinly sliced roast beef and English mustard; smoked salmon and black pepper with a squeeze of lemon; egg mayonnaise and watercress; grated cheese with thinly sliced apple or pear; and tuna with rocket (arugula). Try varying the types of bread you use to make an appealing platter of sandwiches.

Cheese Straws: Energy 49kcal/206kJ; Protein 1.5g; Carbohydrate 3.9g, of which sugars 0.1g; Fat 3.1g, of which saturates 1.9g; Cholesterol 13mg; Calcium 32mg; Fibre 0.2g; Sodium 39mg.
Cucumber Sandwiches: Energy 174kcal/735kJ; Protein 6.8g; Carbohydrate 29.2g, of which sugars 3.3g; Fat 4.2g, of which saturates 1.1g; Cholesterol 5mg; Calcium 92mg; Fibre 1g; Sodium 307mg.

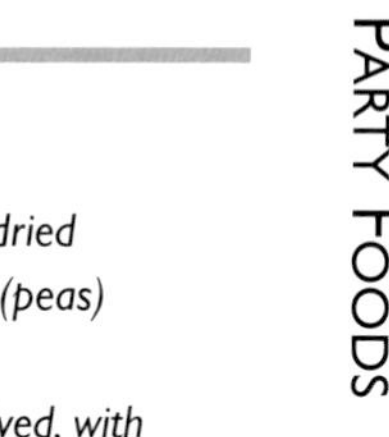

Eggs Mimosa

The name 'mimosa' describes the fine yellow and white grated egg in this dish, which looks very similar to the flower of the same name. The eggs taste delicious when garnished with black pepper and basil leaves. Grated egg yolk can also be used as a garnish for a variety of other savoury dishes, such as sauces, soups and rice dishes.

Makes 20
12 eggs, hard-boiled and peeled
2 ripe avocados, halved and stoned (pitted)
1 garlic clove, crushed
basil leaves, to garnish
a few drops of Tabasco sauce (optional)

From the storecupboard
15ml/1 tbsp olive oil
salt and ground black pepper

1 Reserve two of the hard-boiled eggs and halve the remainder. Carefully remove the yolks with a teaspoon and blend them with the avocados, garlic, oil and Tabasco sauce, if using, adding ground black pepper and salt to taste. Spoon or pipe the mixture into the halved egg whites using a piping (pastry) bag with a 1cm/½in or pipe star nozzle.

2 Sift the remaining egg whites, by pressing through firmly with the back of a spoon, and sprinkle over the filled eggs. Sift the yolks in the same way and sprinkle on top. Arrange the filled egg halves on a serving platter. Grind a little black pepper over the eggs, garnish with basil leaves and serve.

Cook's Tip
You can prepare the mimosa garnish in advance, but store the egg white and yolk separately, in small airtight containers, and keep chilled.

Variation
Mix 1 crushed garlic clove with 45ml/3 tbsp whipped cream and the egg yolks. Season, pipe into egg white cases and serve.

Akkras

These West African bean fritters are made in much the same way as Middle Eastern falafel. Slaves took the recipe to the Caribbean, where it remains very popular today.

Makes 20–24
225g/8oz/1¼ cups dried black-eyed beans (peas)
1 onion, chopped
1 fresh red chilli, halved, with seeds removed (optional)

From the storecupboard
vegetable oil, for deep-frying

1 Soak the black-eyed beans in plenty of cold water for 6–8 hours or overnight. Drain, then briskly rub the beans between the palms of your hands to remove the skins.

2 Return the beans to a bowl, top up with water and the skins will float to the surface. Discard the skins and soak the beans again for 2 hours.

3 Place the beans in a blender or food processor with the onion, chilli, if using, and a little water (about 150ml/¼ pint/⅔ cup). Process to make a thick paste. Pour the mixture into a large bowl and whisk for a few minutes.

4 Heat the oil in a large, heavy pan and fry spoonfuls of the mixture for 4 minutes, until golden brown. Drain on kitchen paper and then serve.

Variation
To make classic falafels, use white beans, red onion and a large garlic clove in place of black-eyed beans (peas), white onion and fresh red chilli. Prepare as for Akkras, except do not add water, instead add 45ml/3 tbsp finely chopped parsley, 5ml/1 tsp ground coriander, 5ml/1 tsp ground cumin and 7.5ml/1½ tsp baking powder before blending. Allow to stand at room temperature for 30 minutes. Then take walnut-sized pieces of the mixture and flatten into small patties. Set aside for another 15 minutes and deep-fry until golden brown.

Eggs Mimosa: Energy 79kcal/327kJ; Protein 4.1g; Carbohydrate 0.5g, of which sugars 0.2g; Fat 6.8g, of which saturates 1.6g; Cholesterol 114mg; Calcium 22mg; Fibre 0.6g; Sodium 43mg.
Akkras: Energy 238kcal/1004kJ; Protein 13.7g; Carbohydrate 33.4g, of which sugars 3.7g; Fat 6.5g, of which saturates 0.9g; Cholesterol 0mg; Calcium 55mg; Fibre 5.2g; Sodium 10mg.

Sweet and Sour Deep-fried Squid

This popular Asian dish is an example of Western influences coming into play – with tomato ketchup and Worcestershire sauce used alongside more traditional Eastern ingredients. Sweet and sour dipping sauces are available to buy in most large supermarkets.

Serves 4
900g/2lb fresh young, tender squid

From the storecupboard
vegetable oil, for deep-frying

For the marinade
60ml/4 tbsp light soy sauce
15ml/1 tbsp sugar

For the dipping sauce (optional)
30ml/2 tbsp tomato ketchup
15ml/1 tbsp Worcestershire sauce
15ml/1 tbsp light soy sauce
15ml/1 tbsp vegetable/sesame oil
sugar or honey, to sweeten
chilli oil, to taste

1 First prepare the squid. Hold the body in one hand and pull off the head with the other. Sever the tentacles and discard the rest. Remove the backbone and clean the body sac inside and out. Pat dry using kitchen paper and cut into rings.

2 In a bowl, mix the soy sauce with the sugar until it dissolves. Toss in the squid rings and tentacles and marinate for 1 hour.

3 Meanwhile prepare the sauce. Mix together the tomato ketchup, Worcestershire sauce, soy sauce and oil. Sweeten with sugar or honey to taste and a little chilli oil to give the sauce a bit of bite. Set aside.

4 Heat enough oil for deep-frying in a wok or heavy pan. Thoroughly drain the squid of any marinade, pat with kitchen paper to avoid spitting, and fry until golden and crispy. Pat dry on kitchen paper and serve immediately with the dipping sauce.

Cook's Tip
To avoid the spitting fat, lightly coat the squid in flour before deep-frying. Alternatively, fry in a deep-fat fryer with a lid or use a spatterproof cover on the wok or pan.

Potted Shrimps with Cayenne Pepper

Cayenne pepper adds a hint of spiciness to this traditional English seaside favourite. Serve with crusty bread or brown toast. The potted shrimps can be stored in the refrigerator for up to 3 days.

Serves 6
2 blades of mace
a pinch of cayenne pepper
600ml/1 pint/2½ cups peeled brown shrimps

From the storecupboard
115g/4oz/½ cup butter, plus extra for greasing
90ml/6 tbsp clarified butter

1 Put the butter, mace and cayenne pepper into a small pan and warm over a gentle heat until melted.

2 Add the peeled shrimps and stir gently until warmed through. Butter six small ramekin dishes.

3 Remove the mace from the shrimp mixture and divide the shrimps and butter evenly between the six ramekins, patting down gently with the back of a spoon. Chill until set.

4 When the butter in the shrimp mixture has set, put the clarified butter in a small pan and melt over a gentle heat. Pour a layer of clarified butter over the top of each ramekin to cover the shrimps and chill again to set.

Marinated Smoked Salmon with Lime and Coriander

If you want an elegant appetizer that is really quick to put together, then this is the one for you. The tangy lime juice and aromatic coriander leaves contrast perfectly with the delicate yet distinct flavour of the salmon. Serve with thinly sliced brown bread and butter.

Serves 6
200g/7oz smoked salmon
a handful of fresh coriander (cilantro) leaves
grated rind and juice of 1 lime

From the storecupboard
15ml/1 tbsp extra virgin olive oil
ground black pepper

1 Using a sharp knife or pair of kitchen scissors, cut the salmon into strips and arrange on a serving platter.

2 Sprinkle the coriander leaves and lime rind over the salmon and squeeze over the lime juice. Drizzle with the olive oil and season with black pepper. Cover with clear film (plastic wrap) and chill for 1 hour before serving.

Cook's Tip
You can make this dish up to 1 hour before serving. However, do not leave it for longer than this because the lime juice will discolour the salmon and spoil the look of the dish.

Sweet/Sour Squid: Energy 315kcal/1320kJ; Protein 35.2g; Carbohydrate 4.5g, of which sugars 1.7g; Fat 17.6g, of which saturates 2.5g; Cholesterol 506mg; Calcium 39mg; Fibre 0g; Sodium 1361mg.
Potted Shrimps: Energy 460kcal/1895kJ; Protein 9.6g; Carbohydrate 0.3g, of which sugars 0.3g; Fat 46.7g, of which saturates 29.4g; Cholesterol 193mg; Calcium 83mg; Fibre 0g; Sodium 555mg.
Marinated Salmon: Energy 67kcal/279kJ; Protein 8.7g; Carbohydrate 0.2g, of which sugars 0.2g; Fat 3.4g, of which saturates 0.5g; Cholesterol 12mg; Calcium 23mg; Fibre 0.4g; Sodium 630mg.

Marinated Anchovies

These tiny fish tend to lose their freshness very quickly so marinating them in garlic and lemon juice is the perfect way to enjoy them. It is probably the simplest way of preparing these fish, because it requires no cooking. Serve them sprinkled with parsley for a decorative finish.

Serves 4
225g/8oz fresh anchovies, heads and tails removed, and split open along the belly
juice of 3 lemons
2 garlic cloves, finely chopped
fresh parsley, chopped, to garnish

From the storecupboard
30ml/2 tbsp extra virgin olive oil
flaked sea salt

1 Turn the anchovies on to their bellies, and press down along their spine with your thumb.

2 Using the tip of a small knife, carefully remove the backbones from the fish, and arrange the anchovies skin side down in a single layer on a large plate.

3 Squeeze two-thirds of the lemon juice over the fish and sprinkle them with the salt. Cover and leave to stand for 1–24 hours, basting occasionally with the juices, until the flesh is white and no longer translucent.

4 Transfer the anchovies to a serving plate and drizzle with the olive oil and the remaining lemon juice. Sprinkle the fish with the chopped garlic, then cover with clear film (plastic wrap) and chill until ready to serve.

Variations
- *For a milder flavour, rinse the anchovies after marinating and then marinate in milk for a short time. Discard the milk and dress with olive oil, lemon juice and chopped parsley.*
- *Top a margherita pizza with these tasty little fish and serve in small slices.*
- *Serve the marinated anchovies with ripe tomatoes and slices of mozzarella drizzled with olive oil for a simple appetizer.*

Anchovy Toast

The Victorians loved anchovies in all kinds of dishes. In the late 19th century in England it became fashionable to serve anchovy butter in the French style – spread on fried bread and topped with Cornish clotted cream – but simple toast fingers are more suited to modern tastes.

Serves 4–6
50g/2oz can of anchovy fillets in olive oil, well drained
15ml/1 tbsp finely chopped fresh parsley
generous squeeze of lemon juice
4–6 slices of bread

From the storecupboard
75g/3oz/6 tbsp soft unsalted (sweet) butter
ground black pepper

1 Put all the ingredients into a food processor and blend to a smooth paste. Cover and chill until required.

2 Just before serving, toast the bread on both sides. Spread the anchovy butter over the hot toast, cut into fingers and serve immediately.

Blinis with Caviar and Crème Fraîche

Russian blinis, available in supermarkets, are made with buckwheat flour, which gives them a very distinctive taste. Caviar is costly, but a small amount goes a long way and the exquisite flavour is well worth it.

Serves 12
200g/7oz/scant 1 cup crème fraîche
12 ready-made blinis
60ml/4 tbsp caviar

From the storecupboard
salt and ground black pepper

1 Put the crème fraîche in a bowl and season with salt and ground black pepper to taste. Place a teaspoonful of the mixture on each blini.

2 Top each spoonful of crème fraîche with a teaspoon of caviar and serve immediately.

Marinated Anchovies: Energy 144kcal/597kJ; Protein 11.7g; Carbohydrate 0.1g, of which sugars 0.1g; Fat 10.7g, of which saturates 2.3g; Cholesterol 0mg; Calcium 55mg; Fibre 0.2g; Sodium 69mg.
Anchovy Toast: Energy 159kcal/661kJ; Protein 4g; Carbohydrate 10.4g, of which sugars 0.7g; Fat 11.5g, of which saturates 6.7g; Cholesterol 32mg; Calcium 55mg; Fibre 0.4g; Sodium 512mg.
Blinis with Caviar: Energy 109kcal/452kJ; Protein 2g; Carbohydrate 4.4g, of which sugars 1g; Fat 9.4g, of which saturates 4.6g; Cholesterol 33mg; Calcium 32mg; Fibre 0.1g; Sodium 135mg.

Salt Cod and Potato Fritters

These little fritters are extremely easy to make and taste delicious. Serve them simply on a cocktail stick with a bowl of garlic mayonnaise for dipping. Or create a simple appetizer with a wedge of fresh lemon and some watercress or green salad.

Makes about 24

450g/1lb salt cod fillets
500g/1¼lb floury potatoes, unpeeled
plain (all-purpose) flour, for coating

From the storecupboard

vegetable oil, for deep-frying
salt and ground black pepper

1 Put the salt cod in a bowl, pour over cold water and leave to soak for 24 hours, changing the water every 6–8 hours. Drain, rinse and place in a pan of cold water. Slowly bring to the boil and simmer for 5 minutes, then drain and cool. When cooled, remove any bones and skin and mash the fish with a fork.

2 Cook the potatoes in their skins in a pan of salted boiling water for 20–25 minutes, or until just tender. Peel and mash.

3 Add the fish to the potatoes and mix well. Season to taste with salt and pepper. Break off walnut-sized pieces of the mixture and roll into balls. Place on a floured plate, cover and chill for 20–30 minutes. Roll each ball lightly in flour, dusting off any excess.

4 Heat enough oil for deep-frying in a large pan and fry the balls for 5–6 minutes, or until golden. Remove with a slotted spoon and drain on kitchen paper. Serve hot or warm.

Cook's Tip

The traditional accompaniment to salt cod is aioli – a fiercely garlicky, olive oil mayonnaise. To make it, put 2 egg yolks, 2 peeled garlic cloves, 10ml/2 tsp lemon juice, 5ml/1 tsp Dijon mustard and some salt and ground black pepper in a food processor and blend. Drizzle in 350ml/12fl oz/1½ cups olive oil while blending until thick and pale. Serve in a bowl.

Chilli Prawn Skewers

Try to get the freshest prawns you can for this recipe. If you buy whole prawns, you will need to remove the heads and shells, leaving the tail section intact. Serve with extra lime wedges for squeezing.

Serves 4

16 giant raw prawns (shrimp), shelled, with the tail section left intact
1 lime, cut into 8 wedges
60ml/4 tbsp sweet chilli sauce

1 Place eight bamboo skewers in cold water and leave to soak for at least 10 minutes, then preheat the grill (broiler) to high.

2 Thread a prawn on to each skewer, then a lime wedge, then another prawn. Brush the sweet chilli sauce over the prawns and lime wedges.

3 Arrange the skewers on a baking sheet and grill (broil) for about 2 minutes, turning them once, until cooked through. Serve immediately with more chilli sauce for dipping.

Variation

For a more decorative way to serve the prawns (shrimp), try butterflying them. Using shelled prawns, with the heads removed but tails intact, make an incision down the curved back of each prawn with a sharp knife, just as you would when deveining. Use kitchen paper to wipe away the dark spinal vein. Mix 15ml/1 tbsp sunflower oil with a little coarse sea salt in a bowl. Add the prawns and toss to coat with the oil and salt. Thread the prawns on to pre-soaked wooden skewers, spearing them head first. Grill (broil), or barbecue, on a high heat for about 5 minutes, depending on the size, turning them over once. Serve hot with lime wedges and sweet chilli sauce.

Cook's Tip

Remember to provide your guests with fingerbowls and napkins. Also, lay out a few empty bowls for the discarded skewers and tails.

Salt Cod Fritters: Energy 92kcal/386kJ; Protein 6.8g; Carbohydrate 6.6g, of which sugars 0.3g; Fat 4.5g, of which saturates 0.6g; Cholesterol 11mg; Calcium 11mg; Fibre 0.3g; Sodium 77mg.
Prawn Skewers: Energy 59kcal/247kJ; Protein 11.3g; Carbohydrate 2.6g, of which sugars 2.5g; Fat 0.4g, of which saturates 0.1g; Cholesterol 122mg; Calcium 61mg; Fibre 0.1g; Sodium 242mg.

Crab and Water Chestnut Wontons

Serve these mouthwatering parcels as part of a dim sum selection or with a bowl of soy sauce for dipping as a first course for a Chinese meal. They are also perfect for serving as snacks with drinks at parties as they can be prepared in advance, then steamed at the last minute. Wonton wrappers are available in most Asian food stores and need to be soaked in cold water for a few minutes before use.

Serves 4
50g/2oz/⅓ cup drained, canned water chestnuts
115g/4oz/generous ½ cup fresh or canned white crab meat
12 wonton wrappers

From the storecupboard
salt and ground black pepper

1 Finely chop the water chestnuts, mix them with the crab meat and season with salt and pepper.

2 Place about a teaspoonful of the mixture along the centre of each wonton wrapper. Roll up the wontons, tucking in the sides as you go to form a neat parcel.

3 Fill the bottom part of a steamer with boiling water and place the wontons, seam down, in the steamer basket. Sit the basket on top of the water and cover with a tight-fitting lid. Steam for 5–8 minutes, or until the wonton wrappers are tender. Serve hot or warm.

Chilli-spiced Chicken Wings

These crispy chicken wings are always the perfect snack for parties and go incredibly well with cold beer. If you like your food spicy, use red hot cayenne pepper in place of the chilli powder. To make a milder version that will be a hit with kids, use sweet paprika in place of the chilli powder. Serve with a fresh tomato and onion salsa for dipping.

Serves 4
12 chicken wings
30ml/2 tbsp plain (all-purpose) flour
15ml/1 tbsp chilli powder

From the storecupboard
a pinch of salt
sunflower oil, for deep-frying

1 Pat the chicken wings dry with kitchen paper. Mix the flour, chilli powder and salt together and put into a large plastic bag. Add the chicken wings, seal the bag and shake well to coat the chicken wings in the seasoned flour.

2 Heat enough sunflower oil for deep-frying in a large pan and add the chicken wings, three or four at a time. Fry for 8–10 minutes, or until golden and cooked through.

3 Remove the chicken wings with a slotted spoon and drain on kitchen paper. Keep warm in a low oven. Repeat with the remaining chicken wings and serve hot.

Asian-style Crab Cakes

As well as making great party snacks, these little patties could be served as an appetizer for eight people. Use a mixture of white and brown crab meat, as the dark meat adds a depth of flavour and texture. Serve with sweet chilli sauce for dipping or a spicy Thai cucumber relish.

Makes 16
450g/1lb/2⅔ cups fresh crab meat, white and brown
15ml/1 tbsp grated fresh root ginger
15–30ml/1–2 tbsp plain (all-purpose) flour

From the storecupboard
60ml/4 tbsp sunflower oil
salt and ground black pepper

1 Put the crab meat in a bowl and add the grated ginger, some salt and ground black pepper, and the flour. Stir well until thoroughly mixed.

2 Using floured hands, divide the mixture into 16 equal pieces and shape roughly into patties.

3 Heat the sunflower oil in a frying pan and add the patties, four at a time. Cook for 2–3 minutes on each side, until golden. Remove with a metal spatula and leave to drain on kitchen paper for a few minutes.

4 Keep the cooked crab cakes warm while you cook the remaining patties in the same way. Serve immediately.

Cook's Tip
Serve these crispy little cakes with a red chilli and cucumber relish for an extra kick to the palate. To make it, shred 1 small cucumber with a mandolin, or chop finely. Transfer to a bowl and add 2 finely chopped shallots, and 2 small red chillies, seeded and finely chopped. Heat 25ml/1½ tbsp/ caster (superfine) sugar, 45ml/3 tbsp rice vinegar, 15ml/1 tbsp water together in a small pan, stirring occasionally, until the sugar has dissolved, then allow to cool. Pour the cooled liquid over the cucmber mixture and serve in saucers.

Crab Wontons: Energy 95kcal/404kJ; Protein 6.8g; Carbohydrate 14.7g, of which sugars 0.4g; Fat 1.9g, of which saturates 0.4g; Cholesterol 28mg; Calcium 34mg; Fibre 0.7g; Sodium 36mg.
Chicken Wings: Energy 350kcal/1455kJ; Protein 30.7g; Carbohydrate 2.6g, of which sugars 2.6g; Fat 24.1g, of which saturates 5.9g; Cholesterol 134mg; Calcium 11mg; Fibre 0.1g; Sodium 99mg.
Asian-style Crab Cakes: Energy 67kcal/280kJ; Protein 5.7g; Carbohydrate 1.5g, of which sugars 0g; Fat 4.3g, of which saturates 0.5g; Cholesterol 20mg; Calcium 3mg; Fibre 0.1g; Sodium 119mg.

Bacon-rolled Enokitake Mushrooms

The Japanese name for this dish is obimaki enoki: an obi (belt or sash) is made from bacon and wrapped around enokitake mushrooms before they are grilled. The strong, smoky flavour of the bacon complements the subtle flavour of mushrooms. Small heaps of ground white pepper can be offered with these savouries, if you like.

Makes 12
450g/1lb fresh enokitake mushrooms
6 rindless smoked streaky (fatty) bacon rashers (strips)
4 lemon wedges

1 Cut off the root part of each enokitake cluster 2cm/¾in from the end. Do not separate the stems. Cut the bacon rashers in half lengthways.

2 Divide the enokitake into 12 equal bunches. Take one bunch, then place the middle of the enokitake near the edge of one bacon rasher, with 2.5–4cm/1–1½in of enokitake protruding at each end.

3 Carefully roll up the bunch of enokitake in the bacon. Tuck any straying short stems into the bacon and slide the bacon slightly upwards at each roll to cover about 4cm/1½in of the enokitake. Secure the end of the bacon roll with a cocktail stick (toothpick). Repeat using the remaining enokitake and bacon to make 11 more rolls.

4 Preheat the grill (broiler) to high. Place the enokitake rolls on an oiled wire rack. Grill (broil) both sides until the bacon is crisp and the enokitake start to char. This takes 10–13 minutes.

5 Remove the enokitake rolls and place on a board. Using a fork and knife, chop each roll in half in the middle of the bacon belt. Arrange the top part of the enokitake roll standing upright, the bottom part lying down next to it. Add a wedge of lemon to each portion and serve.

Sausage Rolls

Small sausage rolls rank high in the league of popular teatime and party foods. They are delicious when home-made, particularly if good quality butcher's sausage meat is used to fill them. Serve them hot or cold. They also make an ideal addition to a picnic or packed lunch.

Makes about 16
175g/6oz/1½ cups plain (all-purpose) flour
250g/9oz pork sausage meat (bulk sausage)
beaten egg, to glaze

From the storecupboard
pinch of salt
40g/1½ oz/3 tbsp lard, diced
40g/1½ oz/3 tbsp butter, diced

1 To make the pastry, sift the flour and salt and add the lard and butter. Rub the fats into the flour until the mixture resembles fine crumbs. Stir in about 45ml/3 tbsp ice cold water until the mixture can be gathered into a smooth ball of dough. Wrap in clear film (plastic wrap) and chill for 30 minutes.

2 Preheat the oven to 190°C/375°F/Gas 5. Roll out the pastry on a lightly floured surface to make a rectangle about 30cm/12in long. Cut lengthways into two long strips.

3 Divide the sausage meat into two pieces and, on a lightly floured surface, shape each into a long roll the same length as the pastry. Lay a roll on each strip of pastry. Brush the pastry edges with water and fold them over the meat, pressing the edges together to seal them well.

4 Turn the rolls over and, with the seam side down, brush with beaten egg. Cut each roll into eight and place on a baking sheet. Bake in the hot oven for 30 minutes until crisp and golden brown. Cool on a wire rack.

Variation
Add 2.5ml/½ tsp English (hot) mustard powder to the dough mix for an extra little bite to your sausage rolls. Sift it into the bowl along with the flour.

Enokitake Mushrooms: Energy 84kcal/347kJ; Protein 6g; Carbohydrate 0.5g, of which sugars 0.2g; Fat 6.5g, of which saturates 2.2g; Cholesterol 16mg; Calcium 8mg; Fibre 1.2g; Sodium 321mg.
Sausage Rolls: Energy 125kcal/521kJ; Protein 2.5g; Carbohydrate 10.3g, of which sugars 0.5g; Fat 8.4g, of which saturates 3.9g; Cholesterol 14mg; Calcium 23mg; Fibre 0.4g; Sodium 142mg.

Vietnamese Spring Rolls with Pork

You will often find these little spring rolls, called 'rice paper rolls', on the menu in Vietnamese restaurants. Serve with a sweet chilli dipping sauce for an authentic taste of South-east Asia.

Serves 4
350g/12oz/1½ cups minced (ground) pork
30ml/2 tbsp oyster sauce
8 rice paper wrappers

From the storecupboard
15ml/1 tbsp sunflower oil
salt and ground black pepper

1 Heat the oil in a frying pan and add the pork. Fry for 5–6 minutes, or until browned. Season well with salt and pepper, stir in the oyster sauce and remove from the heat. Leave to cool.

2 Lay the rice paper wrappers on a clean work surface. Place one-eighth of the pork mixture down one edge of each wrapper. Roll up the wrappers, tucking in the ends as you go to form a roll, and then serve immediately.

Curried Lamb Samosas

Ready-made filo pastry is perfect for making samosas. Once you've mastered folding them, you'll be amazed how quick they are to make. Garnish the samosas with coriander (cilantro) leaves.

Makes 12 samosas
225g/8oz/1 cup minced (ground) lamb
30ml/2 tbsp mild curry paste
12 filo pastry sheets

From the storecupboard
25g/1oz/2 tbsp butter
salt and ground black pepper

1 Heat a little of the butter in a large pan and add the lamb. Fry for 5–6 minutes, stirring occasionally, until browned. Stir in the curry paste and cook for 1–2 minutes. Season and set aside. Preheat the oven to 190°C/375°F/Gas 5.

2 Melt the remaining butter in a pan. Cut the pastry sheets in half lengthways. Brush one strip of pastry with butter, then lay another strip on top and brush with more butter.

3 Place a spoonful of lamb in the corner of the strip and fold over to form a triangle at one end. Keep folding over in the same way to form a triangular package. Brush with butter and place on a baking sheet. Repeat using the remaining pastry. Bake for 15–20 minutes until golden. Serve hot.

Variation
Samosas can also be cooked by deep-frying. Heat the oil in a large deep-sided pan or wok and deep-fry the samosas, a few at a time, until golden and crisp. Remove with a slotted spoon and drain on kitchen paper. Samosas can be prepared in advance by frying until just cooked through and draining, then returning to hot oil for a few minutes to brown before serving.

Chicharrones

The Spanish eat everything that comes from the pig – even the humble rind that is used to make this delicious salted, piquant snack. The crispy, crunchy crackling is perfect with a glass of wine or bottle of San Miguel.

Serves 4
115g/4oz pork rind
paprika

From the storecupboard
vegetable oil, for frying
coarse sea salt, for sprinkling

1 Using a sharp knife, cut the pork rind into strips. There is no need to be too precise, but try to make the strips roughly 1cm/½in wide and 2.5cm/1in long.

2 Pour the vegetable oil to a depth of 2.5cm/1in in a deep heavy frying pan. Heat the oil and check that it has reached the correct temperature by immersing a cube of bread, which should brown in 1 minute.

3 Cook the strips of rind in the oil for 1–2 minutes, until they are puffed up and golden brown. Remove with a slotted spoon and drain on kitchen paper.

4 Sprinkle the chicharrones with paprika and salt to taste. Serve them hot or cold. Although they are at their best 1–2 days after cooking, they will keep reasonably well for up to 2 weeks in an airtight container.

Variations
- *Make these cracklings spicier, if you wish. Paprika is the pepper of Spain, and any kitchen may well have one sweet variety (our common paprika), as well as one smoked and one hot – hot chilli powder, cayenne and Tabasco sauce can all be substituted.*
- *Strips of streaky (fatty) belly can be used instead of pork rind. Cut the strips into the same lengths, removing any bones. Cook them until all the fat has run out, and they look like crisp honeycombs. These tasty morsels are known as torreznos.*

Spring Rolls: Energy 262kcal/1100kJ; Protein 19.3g; Carbohydrate 21.6g, of which sugars 2.5g; Fat 11.6g, of which saturates 3.5g; Cholesterol 58mg; Calcium 42mg; Fibre 0.9g; Sodium 181mg.
Curried Lamb Samosas: Energy 101kcal/423kJ; Protein 5g; Carbohydrate 10.4g, of which sugars 0.2g; Fat 4.6g, of which saturates 2.3g; Cholesterol 19mg; Calcium 37mg; Fibre 1g; Sodium 37mg.
Chicharrones: Energy 247kcal/1018kJ; Protein 4.1g; Carbohydrate 0g, of which sugars 0g; Fat 25g, of which saturates 6.4g; Cholesterol 28mg; Calcium 3mg; Fibre 0g; Sodium 20mg.

Chestnut and White Bean Soup

In the north of Portugal, this soup was once prepared during Lent, the weeks leading up to Easter during which Christians were forbidden to eat meat. It is quite substantial and was a good way of supplying energy to the workers. In order to have chestnuts available throughout the year, they were dried and, before use, were soaked for about 12 hours in just the same way as dried beans. They are now readily available peeled and frozen.

Serves 4

100g/3¾oz/½ cup dried haricot (navy) beans, soaked overnight in cold water and drained
90g/3½oz/generous ½ cup peeled chestnuts, thawed if frozen
1 bay leaf
1 onion, chopped

From the storecupboard

50ml/2fl oz/¼ cup olive oil
salt

1 Put the beans, chestnuts and bay leaf in a pan, pour in 1 litre/1¾ pints/4 cups of water and bring to the boil. Lower the heat and cook for about 1½ hours, until tender.

2 Meanwhile, heat the oil in a frying pan. Add the onion and cook over a low heat, stirring occasionally, for 5 minutes, until softened and translucent. Add it to the soup.

3 Season to taste with salt, remove and discard the bay leaf and mash the beans and chestnuts with a fork. Alternatively, pulse briefly with a hand blender. Serve immediately.

Cook's Tip

If using fresh chestnuts, do not store them for more than a week. The easiest way to shell them and remove their inner skins is to make a small cut in each one and par-boil or roast in the oven at 180°C/350°F/Gas 4 for about 5 minutes. Remove the shells and rub off the skins with a dish towel. Peeled frozen chestnuts are a simpler option.

Butter Bean, Sun-dried Tomato and Pesto Soup

This soup is so quick and easy to make: the key is to use a good-quality home-made or bought fresh stock for the best result. Using plenty of pesto and sun-dried tomato purée gives it a rich, minestrone flavour. As an alternative to butter beans, haricot or cannellini beans are good substitutes.

Serves 4

900ml/1½ pints/3¾ cups chicken or vegetable stock
2 x 400g/14oz cans butter (lima) beans, drained and rinsed
60ml/4 tbsp sun-dried tomato purée (paste)
75ml/5 tbsp pesto

1 Put the stock in a pan with the butter beans and bring just to the boil. Reduce the heat and stir in the tomato purée and pesto. Cook gently for 5 minutes.

2 Transfer six ladlefuls of the soup to a blender or food processor, scooping up plenty of the beans. Process until smooth, then return the purée to the pan.

3 Heat gently, stirring frequently, for 5 minutes. Ladle into four warmed soup bowls and serve with warm crusty bread or breadsticks.

Tuscan Bean Soup

Cavolo nero is a very dark green cabbage with a nutty flavour from Tuscany and southern Italy. It is ideal for this traditional recipe. It is available in most large supermarkets, but if you can't get it, use Savoy cabbage instead. Serve with ciabatta bread.

Serves 4

2 x 400g/14oz cans chopped tomatoes with herbs
250g/9oz cavolo nero leaves
400g/14oz can cannellini beans

From the storecupboard

60ml/4 tbsp extra virgin olive oil
salt and ground black pepper

1 Pour the tomatoes into a large pan and add a can of cold water. Season with salt and pepper and bring to the boil, then reduce the heat to a simmer.

2 Roughly shred the cabbage leaves and add them to the pan. Partially cover the pan and simmer gently for about 15 minutes, or until the cabbage is tender.

3 Drain and rinse the cannellini beans, add to the pan and warm through for a few minutes. Check and adjust the seasoning, then ladle into bowls and drizzle with a little olive oil.

Cook's Tip

Try to buy canned beans that do not have added salt or sugar.

Chestnut and Bean: Energy 184kcal/773kJ; Protein 6.2g; Carbohydrate 20.5g, of which sugars 3.1g; Fat 9.2g, of which saturates 1.4g; Cholesterol 0mg; Calcium 39mg; Fibre 5.1g; Sodium 8mg.
Butter Bean: Energy 264kcal/1109kJ; Protein 14.8g; Carbohydrate 27.4g, of which sugars 3.6g; Fat 11.3g, of which saturates 2.7g; Cholesterol 6mg; Calcium 109mg; Fibre 9.5g; Sodium 932mg.
Tuscan Bean: Energy 445kcal/1863kJ; Protein 18.9g; Carbohydrate 45.8g, of which sugars 9.3g; Fat 21.8g, of which saturates 6g; Cholesterol 19mg; Calcium 391mg; Fibre 9.1g; Sodium 707mg.

Avocado Soup

This delicious soup has a fresh, delicate flavour and a wonderful colour. For added zest, add a generous squeeze of lime juice or spoon 15ml/1 tbsp salsa into the soup just before serving. Choose ripe avocados for this soup – they should feel soft when gently pressed. Keep very firm avocados at room temperature for 3–4 days until they soften. To speed ripening, place in a brown paper bag.

Serves 4
2 large ripe avocados
300ml/½ pint/1¼ cups sour cream
1 litre/1¾ pints/4 cups well-flavoured chicken stock
small bunch of fresh coriander (cilantro)

From the storecupboard
ground black pepper

1 Cut the avocados in half, remove the peel and lift out the stones (pits). Chop the flesh coarsely and place it in a food processor with 45–60ml/3–4 tbsp of the sour cream. Process until smooth.

2 Heat the chicken stock in a pan. When it is hot, but still below simmering point, stir in the rest of the cream.

3 Gradually stir the avocado mixture into the hot stock. Heat but do not let the mixture approach boiling point.

4 Chop the coriander. Ladle the soup into individual heated bowls and sprinkle each portion with chopped coriander and black pepper. Serve immediately.

Cook's Tip
Once cut, avocados should be used immediately as they have a tendency to discolour. If you need to prepare avocados ahead of time, toss them in lemon or lime juice and store in an airtight container in the refrigerator.

Vichyssoise

This classic, chilled summer soup of leeks and potatoes was named after Vichy, France, the home of its creator. Sharpen the flavour with lemon juice, enrich with swirls of cream and garnish with chives.

Serves 4–6
600g/1lb 5oz leeks, white parts only, thinly sliced
250g/9oz floury potatoes (such as King Edward or Maris Piper), peeled and cut into chunks
1.5 litres/2½ pints/6¼ cups light chicken stock or half and half water and milk

From the storecupboard
50g/2oz/¼ cup unsalted (sweet) butter
salt and ground black pepper

1 Melt the unsalted butter in a heavy pan and cook the leeks, covered, for 15–20 minutes, until they are soft but not browned. Add the potato chunks and cook over a low heat, uncovered, for a few minutes.

2 Stir in the stock or water and milk, with salt and pepper to taste. Bring to the boil, then reduce the heat and partly cover the pan. Simmer for 15 minutes, or until the potatoes are soft.

3 Cool the soup then process it until smooth in a blender or food processor. Strain the soup into a bowl. Taste and adjust the seasoning and add a little iced water if the consistency of the soup seems too thick.

4 Chill the soup for at least 4 hours or until it is very cold. Taste the chilled soup for seasoning again before serving. Pour the soup into bowls and serve.

Variation
To make a fabulous chilled leek and sorrel or watercress soup, add about 50g/2oz/1 cup shredded sorrel to the soup at the end of cooking. Finish and chill as in the main recipe, then serve the soup garnished with a little pile of finely shredded sorrel. The same quantity of watercress can also be used.

Avocado Soup: Energy 407kcal/1676kJ; Protein 3.3g; Carbohydrate 3.4g, of which sugars 2.1g; Fat 42.2g, of which saturates 21.7g; Cholesterol 78mg; Calcium 73mg; Fibre 3.2g; Sodium 24mg.
Vichyssoise: Energy 362kcal/1494kJ; Protein 3g; Carbohydrate 11.1g, of which sugars 4g; Fat 34.2g, of which saturates 21.2g; Cholesterol 86mg; Calcium 51mg; Fibre 2.3g; Sodium 68mg.

Egg and Lemon Soup with Pasta

This light, nourishing soup, made with egg and lemon, has traditionally been a favourite throughout the Mediterranean. This Greek version contains orzo, tiny rice-shaped pasta, but you can use any small shape of pasta. Serve the soup with thin slices of lightly toasted bread and add a garnish of very thin lemon slices for a decorative appearance.

Serves 4–6

1.75 litres/3 pints/7½ cups chicken stock
115g/4oz/½ cup orzo pasta
3 eggs
juice of 1 large lemon

From the storecupboard

salt and ground black pepper

1 Pour the chicken stock into a large pan and bring to the boil. Add the orzo pasta or other small pasta shapes and cook for 5 minutes, or according to the packet instructions.

2 Beat the eggs until they are frothy, then add the lemon juice and a tablespoon of cold water. Slowly stir in a ladleful of the hot chicken stock, then add one or two more.

3 Remove the pan from the heat, then pour in the egg mixture and stir well. Season to taste with salt and ground black pepper and serve immediately.

Cook's Tip

Do not let the soup boil once the egg and lemon juice mixture has been added, or it will curdle. Take care when using a pan that retains heat because the soup may continue to simmer after the heat has been reduced.

Variation

Substitute orzo with other small pasta, such as stellette (stars) or orecchiette (little ears). The cooking time should be the same.

Simple Cream of Onion Soup

This wonderfully soothing soup has a deep, buttery flavour that is achieved with only a few ingredients and the minimum of fuss. It makes delicious comfort food on a cold day. Use home-made stock if you have it, or buy fresh stock for the best flavour. Crisp croûtons or chopped chives complement the smooth soup when sprinkled over just before serving.

Serves 4

1kg/2¼lb yellow onions, sliced
1 litre/1¾ pints/4 cups good chicken or vegetable stock
150ml/¼ pint/⅔ cup double (heavy) cream

From the storecupboard

115g/4oz/½ cup unsalted (sweet) butter
salt and ground black pepper

1 Melt 75g/3oz/6 tbsp of the unsalted butter in a large, heavy pan.

2 Set about 200g/7oz of the onions aside and add the rest to the pan. Stir to coat in the butter, then cover and cook very gently for about 30 minutes. The onions should be very soft and tender, but not browned.

3 Add the chicken or vegetable stock, 5ml/1 tsp salt and ground black pepper to taste. Bring to the boil, reduce the heat and simmer for 5 minutes, then remove from the heat.

4 Leave the soup to cool, then process it in a blender or food processor. Return the soup to the rinsed pan.

5 Meanwhile, melt the remaining butter in another pan and cook the remaining onions over a low heat, covered, until soft but not browned. Uncover and continue to cook the onions gently until they turn golden yellow.

6 Add the cream to the soup and reheat it gently until hot, but do not allow it to boil. Taste and adjust the seasoning. Add the buttery onions and stir for 1–2 minutes, then ladle the soup into bowls. Serve the soup immediately.

Egg and Lemon: Energy 107kcal/451kJ; Protein 5.7g; Carbohydrate 14.5g, of which sugars 0.8g; Fat 3.4g, of which saturates 0.8g; Cholesterol 95mg; Calcium 22mg; Fibre 0.6g; Sodium 307mg.
Onion: Energy 488kcal/2012kJ; Protein 3.8g; Carbohydrate 20.6g, of which sugars 14.8g; Fat 44.1g, of which saturates 27.4g; Cholesterol 112mg; Calcium 86mg; Fibre 3.5g; Sodium 189mg.

Pomegranate Broth

With its origins in Persia and Azerbaijan, this fresh-tasting delicate soup is perhaps the best way of eating sour pomegranates. Clear and refreshing, it is served as a palate cleanser between courses, or as a light appetizer. Sour pomegranates are available in Middle Eastern stores, but if you can only find sweet pomegranates, use them with the juice of a lemon.

Serves 4

1.2 litres/2 pints/5 cups clear chicken stock
150ml/¼ pint/⅔ cup sour pomegranate juice
seeds of 1 sweet pomegranate
fresh mint leaves, to garnish

From the storecupboard

salt and ground black pepper

1 Pour the stock into a pan and bring to the boil. Lower the heat, stir in the pomegranate juice, and lemon juice if using sweet pomegranates, then bring the stock back to the boil.

2 Lower the heat again and stir in half the pomegranate seeds, then season and turn off the heat.

3 Ladle the hot broth into warmed bowls. Sprinkle the remaining pomegranate seeds over the top and garnish with mint leaves.

Cook's Tips

- *The ruby-red grains of sweet pomegranates are eaten fresh, whereas the sour fruits are used in soups, marinades, dressings and syrups, and to make a cooling sherbet drink.*
- *Extracting pomegranate juice: for 150ml/¼ pint/⅔ cup juice, you will need 5–6 sour pomegranates. Cut the pomegranates in half crossways and squeeze them with a stainless steel, glass or wooden lemon squeezer to extract the juice. Do not use any metal other than stainless steel for squeezing or it will react with the astringent juice of the pomegranates, causing the juice to discolour and taste unpleasant.*

Potato and Roasted Garlic Broth

Roasted garlic takes on a mellow, sweet flavour that is subtle, not overpowering, in this delicious vegetarian soup. Choose floury potatoes for this soup, such as Maris Piper, Estima, Cara or King Edward – they will give the soup a delicious velvety texture. Serve the broth piping hot with melted Cheddar or Gruyère cheese on French bread, as the perfect winter warmer.

Serves 4

2 small or 1 large whole head of garlic (about 20 cloves)
4 medium potatoes (about 500g/1¼lb in total), diced
1.75 litres/3 pints/7½ cups good-quality hot vegetable stock
chopped flat leaf parsley, to garnish

1 Preheat the oven to 190°C/375°F/Gas 5. Place the unpeeled garlic bulbs or bulb in a small roasting pan and bake for 30 minutes until soft in the centre.

2 Meanwhile, par-boil the potatoes in a large pan of boiling water for 10 minutes.

3 Simmer the stock in another pan for 5 minutes. Drain the potatoes and add them to the stock.

4 Squeeze the garlic pulp into the soup, reserving a few whole cloves, and stir. Simmer for 15 minutes and serve topped with whole garlic cloves and parsley.

Cook's Tips

- *Hot herb bread, with lots of chopped fresh parsley and plenty of grated lemon rind, is delicious with this broth. Mix the parsley and lemon rind with butter and spread it between slices of French bread. Reshape the slices into a loaf and wrap in foil, then heat in the oven.*
- *Roast shallots with the garlic, or sauté some celery to add to the simmering soup about 10 minutes before serving.*

Pomegranate Broth: Energy 62kcal/260kJ; Protein 2g; Carbohydrate 3.9g, of which sugars 2.3g; Fat 4.4g, of which saturates 0.4g; Cholesterol 0mg; Calcium 14mg; Fibre 0.6g; Sodium 205mg.
Potato and Garlic Broth: Energy 75kcal/314kJ; Protein 1.6g; Carbohydrate 12.8g, of which sugars 4.8g; Fat 2.2g, of which saturates 0.4g; Cholesterol 0mg; Calcium 17mg; Fibre 1.6g; Sodium 12mg.

Winter Squash Soup with Salsa

Butternut squash makes excellent creamy soup with very few additional ingredients. Select a really good bought salsa for this soup and add a sprinkling of chopped fresh oregano or marjoram as a garnish.

Serves 4–5
1 butternut squash
2 onions, chopped
60–120ml/4–8 tbsp tomato salsa

From the storecupboard
75ml/5 tbsp garlic-flavoured olive oil

1 Preheat the oven to 220°C/425°F/Gas 7. Halve and seed the butternut squash, place it on a baking sheet and brush with some of the oil. Roast for 25 minutes. Reduce the temperature to 190°C/375°F/Gas 5 and cook for 20–25 minutes more, or until it is tender.

2 Heat the remaining oil in a large, heavy pan and cook the chopped onions over a low heat for about 10 minutes, or until softened.

3 Meanwhile, scoop the squash out of its skin, adding it to the pan. Pour in 1.2 litres/2 pints/5 cups water and stir in 5ml/1 tsp salt and plenty of black pepper. Bring to the boil, cover and simmer for 10 minutes.

4 Cool the soup slightly, then process in a blender to a smooth purée. Alternatively, press through a fine sieve (strainer) with the back of a spoon. Reheat without boiling, then ladle it into warmed bowls. Top each serving with a spoonful of salsa and serve.

Cook's Tip
To make your own salsa: roast 4 large ripe tomatoes, halved and seeded, 1 red (bell) pepper, seeded, 1 large red chilli, halved and seeded, in a fairly hot oven for 25 minutes. Allow to cool, then skin the pepper and chilli. Blend briefly in a food processor with tomatoes and 30ml/2 tbsp extra virgin olive oil. Stir in 15ml/1 tbsp balsamic vinegar and a pinch of caster (superfine) sugar. Season, then serve.

Pea Soup with Garlic

A great standby lunch dish or appetizer, if you keep peas in the freezer, you can rustle up this delicious soup in minutes. It has a sweet taste, smooth texture and vibrant colour and is great served with crusty bread and garnished with mint.

Serves 4
1 garlic clove, crushed
900g/2lb/8 cups frozen peas
1.2 litres/2 pints/5 cups chicken stock

From the storecupboard
25g/1oz/2 tbsp butter
salt and ground black pepper

1 Heat the butter in a large heavy pan until just foaming and add the garlic. Fry gently for 2–3 minutes, until softened, then add the frozen peas. Cook for 1–2 minutes more, then pour in the stock.

2 Bring the soup to the boil, then reduce the heat to a simmer. Cover the pan and cook for 5–6 minutes, until the peas are tender. Leave to cool slightly, then transfer the mixture to a food processor and process until smooth (you may have to do this in two batches).

3 Return the soup to the rinsed pan and heat through gently. Season with salt and pepper.

Variations
- *Ham stock makes a delicious base for pea soup. To complement the flavour, garnish the soup with diced cooked ham and a little finely shredded fresh sage.*
- *For a vegetarian version, use a good vegetable stock instead of chicken stock.*
- *Iced pea soup is food for hot summer days. Use frozen petit pois (baby peas) for a sweet flavour and add the grated rind and juice of 1 lime to the cold soup.*
- *Crisp cubes of pan-fried halloumi cheese are delicious in this plain pea soup. Have the pan hot, the soup ready in warm bowls and then cook cubes of cheese quickly until brown outside and soft inside. Float in the soup and serve.*

Winter Squash Soup: Energy 172kcal/712kJ; Protein 2.7g; Carbohydrate 12.6g, of which sugars 9.3g; Fat 12.6g, of which saturates 2g; Cholesterol 0mg; Calcium 86mg; Fibre 3.6g; Sodium 4mg.
Pea with Garlic: Energy 233kcal/965kJ; Protein 15.6g; Carbohydrate 25.5g, of which sugars 5.2g; Fat 8.5g, of which saturates 3.9g; Cholesterol 13mg; Calcium 49mg; Fibre 10.6g; Sodium 40mg.

Curried Cauliflower Soup

This spicy, velvety soup is perfect for lunch on a cold winter's day served with a large chunk of warm crusty bread and garnished with a sprinkling of fragrant fresh coriander.

Serves 4
750ml/1¼ pints/3 cups milk
1 large cauliflower
15ml/1 tbsp garam masala

From the storecupboard
salt and ground black pepper

1 Pour the milk into a large pan and place over a medium heat. Cut the cauliflower into florets and add to the milk with the garam masala. Season with salt and pepper.

2 Bring the milk to the boil, then reduce the heat, partially cover the pan with a lid and simmer for about 20 minutes, or until the cauliflower is tender.

3 Let the mixture cool for a few minutes, then transfer to a food processor and process until smooth (you may have to do this in two batches). Return the purée to the pan and heat through gently, checking and adjusting the seasoning. Serve immediately.

Cook's Tip
You can use all parts of the cauliflower to bring an excellent flavour to this soup. Just trim off any wilted or damaged leaves and the very tough stalk. Then cut off the florets, cut the stalks into a small dice and thinly slice the leaves.

Variations
- *Cauliflower lends itself wonderfully to mildy curried recipes, but you can also make broccoli soup in the same way, using the same weight of broccoli in place of the cauliflower.*
- *Parsnips are also complemented by curry flavours. Try this recipe with 4 large parsnips, peeled and chopped into large chunks and cooked until tender.*

Stilton and Watercress Soup

A good creamy Stilton and plenty of peppery watercress bring maximum flavour to this rich, smooth soup, which is superlative in small portions. Rocket can be used as an alternative to watercress – both leaves are an excellent source of iron. When choosing any salad leaves, look for crisp, fresh leaves and reject any wilted or discoloured greens.

Serves 4–6
600ml/1 pint/2½ cups chicken or vegetable stock
225g/8oz watercress
150g/5oz Stilton or other blue cheese
150ml/¼ pint/⅔ cup single (light) cream

1 Pour the stock into a pan and bring almost to the boil. Remove and discard any very large stalks from the watercress. Add the watercress to the pan and simmer gently for 2–3 minutes, until tender.

2 Crumble the cheese into the pan and simmer for 1 minute more, until the cheese has started to melt. Process the soup in a blender or food processor, in batches if necessary, until very smooth. Return the soup to the pan.

3 Stir in the cream and check the seasoning. The soup will probably not need any extra salt, as the blue cheese is already quite salty. Heat the soup gently, without boiling, then ladle it into warm bowls.

Cook's Tip
To make your vegetable stock put 900g/2lb chopped vegetables, including onions, leeks, tomatoes, carrots, parsnips and cabbage, in a large pan. Pour in 1.5 litres/2½ pints/6¼ cups water. Bring to the boil and simmer for 30 minutes. Strain into a container and discard the cooked vegetables. The stock can then be frozen for up to 3 months.

Stilton Soup: Energy 159kcal/659kJ; Protein 7.9g; Carbohydrate 0.7g, of which sugars 0.7g; Fat 13.7g, of which saturates 8.9g; Cholesterol 38mg; Calcium 168mg; Fibre 0.6g; Sodium 223mg.
Curried Cauliflower: Energy 151kcal/636kJ; Protein 12.9g; Carbohydrate 14.7g, of which sugars 13.2g; Fat 5g, of which saturates 2.4g; Cholesterol 11mg; Calcium 276mg; Fibre 3.7g; Sodium 107mg.

Wheat Noodles in Soya Bean Soup

Strands of thin wheat noodles taste great in a mild and deliciously nutty chilled soup. This is a perfect choice of satisfying soup for a warm summer's day. The iced broth is topped with succulent strips of cucumber and wedges of tomato, providing refreshing flavours to complement the tender noodles.

Serves 4
185g/6½oz/1 cup soya beans
30ml/2 tbsp sesame seeds
300g/11oz thin wheat noodles

From the storecupboard
salt

For the garnish (optional)
1 cucumber, cut into thin strips
1 tomato, cut into wedges

1 Soak the soya beans overnight. Rinse in cold water and then roll them between your palms to remove the skins.

2 Gently toast the sesame seeds in a dry pan until they are lightly browned. Place the peeled soya beans and the sesame seeds in a food processor or blender. Add 1 litre/1¾ pints/4 cups water and process until the beans and seeds are finely ground.

3 Strain the bean mixture through muslin (cheesecloth), collecting the liquid in a jug (pitcher) – this is soya and sesame milk. Chill the soya and sesame milk in the refrigerator.

4 Bring a pan of water to the boil and cook the noodles, then drain them and rinse in cold water.

5 Place a portion of noodles in each soup bowl, and pour over the chilled milk. Garnish with strips of cucumber and tomato wedges, then season with salt and serve.

Variation
For a quick and easy version, use 250ml/8fl oz/1 cup unsweetened soya milk rather than soaking and puréeing the soya beans. Simply add the ground sesame seeds to the soya milk and chill to make the soup.

Miso Broth with Mushrooms

This broth is so quick and simple to prepare, yet extremely delicious and nutritious too. Shiitake mushrooms give this soup superb flavour.

Serves 4
45ml/3 tbsp light miso paste
3 fresh shiitake mushrooms, sliced
115g/4oz tofu, diced
1 spring onion (scallion), green part only, sliced

1 Mix 1.2 litres/2 pints/5 cups boiling water and miso in a pan. Add the mushrooms and simmer for 5 minutes. Divide the tofu among four warmed soup bowls, ladle in the soup, sprinkle with sliced spring onions and serve.

Star-gazer Vegetable Soup

If you have the time, it is worth making your own stock for this recipe.

Serves 4
1 yellow (bell) pepper and 2 large courgettes (zucchini)
2 large carrots
900ml/1½ pints/3¾ cups well-flavoured vegetable stock
50g/2oz rice vermicelli

From the storecupboard
salt and ground black pepper

1 Cut the pepper into quarters, removing the seeds and core. Chop the courgettes and carrots lengthways into 5mm/¼in slices.

2 Using tiny pastry cutters, stamp out shapes from the vegetables or use a very sharp knife to cut the sliced vegetables into stars and other decorative shapes.

3 Place the vegetables and stock in a pan and simmer for 10 minutes, until the vegetables are tender. Season to taste with salt and pepper.

4 Meanwhile, place the vermicelli in a bowl, cover with boiling water and set aside for 4 minutes. Drain, then divide among four warmed soup bowls. Ladle over the soup and serve with fresh bread.

Wheat Noodles: Energy 268kcal/1121kJ; Protein 20.1g; Carbohydrate 17.9g, of which sugars 3.4g; Fat 13.3g, of which saturates 1.7g; Cholesterol 0mg; Calcium 174mg; Fibre 8.7g; Sodium 6mg.
Miso Broth: Energy 25kcal/103kJ; Protein 2.4g; Carbohydrate 2.6g, of which sugars 2.4g; Fat 0.6g, of which saturates 0.1g; Cholesterol 0mg; Calcium 107mg; Fibre 1.6g; Sodium 882mg.
Star-gazer Soup: Energy 96kcal/399kJ; Protein 3.4g; Carbohydrate 19.1g, of which sugars 8.9g; Fat 0.8g, of which saturates 0.2g; Cholesterol 0mg; Calcium 58mg; Fibre 3.1g; Sodium 20mg.

Cappelletti in Broth

This soup is traditionally served in northern Italy on St Stephen's Day (Boxing Day), the day after Christmas, and on New Year's Day as a welcome light change from all the rich celebration food. Cappelletti are little stuffed pasta shapes, usually filled with meat, that are said to resemble hats.

Serves 4

1.2 litres/2 pints/5 cups chicken stock
90–115g/3½–4oz/1 cup fresh or dried cappelletti
about 45ml/3 tbsp finely chopped fresh flat leaf parsley (optional)
about 30ml/2 tbsp freshly grated Parmesan cheese

From the storecupboard

salt and ground black pepper

1 Pour the chicken stock into a large pan and bring to the boil. Drop in the pasta.

2 Stir well and bring back to the boil. Lower the heat to a simmer and cook according to the instructions on the packet, until the pasta is *al dente*, that is, tender but still firm to the bite.

3 Swirl in the finely chopped fresh flat leaf parsley, if using, then taste and adjust the seasoning, if necessary. Ladle into four warmed soup plates, then sprinkle with the freshly grated Parmesan cheese and serve immediately.

Cook's Tip

This soup needs a well-flavoured stock as a base. If you don't have home-made stock, use two 300g/11oz cans of condensed beef consommé, adding water as instructed. Alternatively, buy chilled commercial stock.

Variation

Use other small filled pasta shapes such as tortellini, or for a very lightweight soup, simply use small, dried soup pasta.

Tiny Pasta in Broth

This wholesome Italian soup is ideal for a light supper served with ciabatta bread. It also makes a delicious first course for an *al fresco* supper. A wide variety of different types of pastina or soup pasta are available. Choose just one shape or use a combination of different varieties for an interesting result.

Serves 4

1.2 litres/2 pints/5 cups beef stock
75g/3oz/¾ cup dried tiny soup pasta
2 pieces bottled roasted red (bell) pepper, about 50g/2oz
coarsely shaved Parmesan cheese

1 Bring the beef stock to the boil in a large pan. Drop in the dried soup pasta. Stir well and bring the stock back to the boil.

2 Reduce the heat so that the soup simmers and cook for 7–8 minutes, or according to the packet instructions, until the pasta is *al dente*, that is, tender but still firm to the bite.

3 Drain the pieces of roasted pepper and dice them finely. Place them in the base of four warmed soup plates. Taste the soup for seasoning. Serve it immediately, topped with shavings of Parmesan.

Cook's Tip

There are many different pastini to choose from, including stellate (stars), anellini (tiny thick rounds), risoni (rice-shaped) and farfalline (little butterflies). You could also use the fine 'angel hair' pasta, capellini, broken into smaller pieces.

Variation

Use fresh (bell) peppers instead of bottled peppers. First roast them until charred, seal in a plastic bag to loosen the skins, then remove the skins and seeds and dice.

Cappelletti in Broth: Energy 111kcal/469kJ; Protein 5.8g; Carbohydrate 16.7g, of which sugars 0.8g; Fat 3g, of which saturates 1.6g; Cholesterol 8mg; Calcium 96mg; Fibre 0.7g; Sodium 228mg.
Tiny Pasta in Broth: Energy 104kcal/439kJ; Protein 5.6g; Carbohydrate 15.1g, of which sugars 1.8g; Fat 3g, of which saturates 1.7g; Cholesterol 8mg; Calcium 97mg; Fibre 0.9g; Sodium 265mg.

Baked Eggs with Creamy Leeks

This simple but elegant dish is perfect for last-minute entertaining or quick dining. Garnish the baked eggs with crisp, fried fresh sage leaves and serve with warm, crusty bread. Small to medium leeks (less than 2.5cm/1in in diameter) are best for this dish as they are so tender and only require a short cooking time.

Serves 4
225g/8oz small leeks, thinly sliced
75–90ml/5–6 tbsp whipping cream
4 small–medium (US medium–large) eggs

From the storecupboard
15g/½oz/1 tbsp butter, plus extra for greasing
salt and ground black pepper

1 Preheat the oven to 190°C/375°F/Gas 5. Generously butter the base and sides of four ramekins.

2 Melt the butter in a frying pan and cook the leeks over a medium heat, stirring frequently, for 3–5 minutes, until softened and translucent, but not browned.

3 Add 45ml/3 tbsp of the cream and cook over a low heat for 5 minutes, until the leeks are very soft and the cream has thickened a little. Season to taste.

4 Place the ramekins in a small roasting pan and divide the leeks among them. Break an egg into each dish, spoon over the remaining cream and season. Pour boiling water into the roasting pan to come about halfway up the sides of the ramekins. Transfer the pan to the oven and bake in the preheated oven for about 10 minutes, until just set. Serve piping hot.

Variation
For a stunning alternative, simply break large (US extra large) eggs into ramekin dishes, pour double (heavy) cream over, season and sprinkle generously with Parmesan cheese. Bake for 10 minutes at 160°C/325°F/Gas 3.

Pea and Mint Omelette

Serve this deliciously light omelette with crusty bread and a green salad for a fresh, tasty lunch. If you're making the omelette for a summer lunch when peas are in season, use freshly shelled peas instead of frozen ones.

Serves 2
50g/2oz/½ cup frozen peas
4 eggs
30ml/2 tbsp chopped fresh mint

From the storecupboard
knob (pat) of butter
salt and ground black pepper

1 Cook the peas in a large pan of salted boiling water for 3–4 minutes until tender. Drain well and set aside. Break the eggs into a large bowl and beat with a fork. Season well with salt and pepper, then stir in the peas and chopped mint.

2 Heat the butter in a medium frying pan until foamy. Pour in the egg mixture and cook over a medium heat for 3–4 minutes, drawing in the cooked egg from the edges from time to time, until the mixture is nearly set.

3 Finish off cooking the omelette under a hot grill (broiler) until set and golden. Carefully fold the omelette over, cut it in half and serve immediately.

Cook's Tip
Although special omelette pans are available, any heavy, medium non-stick frying pan will be sufficient.

Variations
- *This omelette can also be served cold and cut into wedges or fingers as an appetizer or to serve with drinks at a party.*
- *You could also try using lightly sautéed spinach or courgette (zucchini) instead of peas.*
- *Sun-dried tomatoes and onion with a pinch of thyme make a flavoursome alternative.*

Baked Eggs: Energy 149kcal/614kJ; Protein 4.4g; Carbohydrate 2.2g, of which sugars 1.8g; Fat 13.7g, of which saturates 7.5g; Cholesterol 123mg; Calcium 39mg; Fibre 1.3g; Sodium 64mg.
Omelette: Energy 205kcal/851kJ; Protein 14.3g; Carbohydrate 2.9g, of which sugars 0.6g; Fat 15.6g, of which saturates 5.8g; Cholesterol 391mg; Calcium 63mg; Fibre 1.2g; Sodium 171mg.

Fried Mozzarella Sandwich

This is reassuring snacking Italian style, with glorious melting mozzarella in crisp fried egg-soaked bread. The result is a delicious savoury sandwich guaranteed to lift the spirits.

Makes 2

115g/4oz/1 cup mozzarella cheese, thickly sliced
4 thick slices white bread
1 egg
30ml/2 tbsp milk

From the storecupboard
vegetable oil, for frying
salt and ground black pepper

1 Place the cheese on two slices of bread and season to taste. Top with the remaining bread to make two cheese sandwiches.

2 Beat the egg with the milk. Season with salt and pepper to taste and pour into a shallow dish.

3 Carefully dip the sandwiches into the egg and milk mixture until thoroughly coated. Leave to soak while heating the oil in a large, heavy frying pan.

4 Fry the sandwiches, in batches if necessary, until golden brown and crisp on both sides. Remove from the frying pan and drain well on kitchen paper.

Variation
Use any favourite cheese instead of mozzarella. Add some chopped spring onions (scallions) and sliced cooked ham or salami before sandwiching the bread together.

Toasted Sourdough with Goat's Cheese

The combination of sharp cheese with sweet and spicy chilli jam is truly delicious. Choose a good-quality, firm goat's cheese for this recipe because it needs to keep its shape during cooking. Serve with fresh rocket (arugula) leaves.

Serves 2

2 thick sourdough bread slices
30ml/2 tbsp chilli jam
2 firm goat's cheese slices, about 90g/3½oz each

From the storecupboard
30ml/2 tbsp garlic-infused olive oil
ground black pepper

1 Preheat the grill (broiler) to high. Brush the sourdough bread on both sides with the oil, and grill (broil) one side until golden. Spread the untoasted side of each slice with the chilli jam and top with the goat's cheese.

2 Return the bread to the grill and cook for 3–4 minutes, or until the cheese is beginning to melt and turn golden and bubbling. Season with ground black pepper and serve while hot.

Griddled Tomatoes on Soda Bread

Nothing could be easier than this simple dish, transformed into something really special by adding a drizzle of olive oil, balsamic vinegar and shavings of Parmesan cheese.

Serves 4

6 tomatoes, thickly sliced
4 thick slices soda bread
balsamic vinegar, for drizzling
shavings of Parmesan cheese, to serve

From the storecupboard
olive oil, for brushing and drizzling
salt and ground black pepper

1 Brush a griddle pan with olive oil and heat. Add the tomato slices and cook for 4–6 minutes, turning once, until softened and slightly blackened. Alternatively, heat a grill (broiler) to high and line the rack with foil. Grill (broil) the tomato slices for 4–6 minutes, turning once, until softened.

2 While the tomatoes are cooking, lightly toast the soda bread. Place the tomatoes on top of the toast and drizzle each portion with a little olive oil and vinegar. Season to taste and serve immediately with thin shavings of Parmesan.

Cook's Tip
Using a griddle pan reduces the amount of oil required for cooking the tomatoes and gives them a smoky barbecued flavour. The ridges on the pan brand the tomatoes with a stripy pattern, which looks very appealing. To make a cross-hatched pattern, turn the tomato slices 180 degrees halfway through the cooking time.

Variation
You could enhance this simple, yet flavoursome, dish further by using an infused oil, such as lemon oil, chilli oil, garlic oil or herb-infused oil. These are all available in supermarkets or can be made easily at home.

Fried Mozzarella: Energy 429kcal/1789kJ; Protein 18.9g; Carbohydrate 30.5g, of which sugars 2.7g; Fat 26.6g, of which saturates 10.4g; Cholesterol 129mg; Calcium 331mg; Fibre 1.9g; Sodium 539mg.
Toasted Sourdough: Energy 533kcal/2225kJ; Protein 23.4g; Carbohydrate 33g, of which sugars 9.5g; Fat 35.2g, of which saturates 17.7g; Cholesterol 84mg; Calcium 178mg; Fibre 1g; Sodium 826mg.
Tomatoes on Soda Bread: Energy 178kcal/751kJ; Protein 4.2g; Carbohydrate 26.3g, of which sugars 6.9g; Fat 7g, of which saturates 1g; Cholesterol 0mg; Calcium 66mg; Fibre 2.7g; Sodium 175mg.

Focaccia with Sardines and Tomatoes

Fresh sardines not only have a lovely flavour and texture, but they are also cheap to buy – so why not make an economical, yet utterly delicious, lunch. Small sardines have the best flavour.

Serves 4
20 cherry tomatoes
12 fresh sardine fillets
1 focaccia loaf

From the storecupboard
45ml/3 tbsp herb-infused olive oil
salt and ground black pepper

1 Preheat the oven to 190°C/375°F/Gas 5. Put the cherry tomatoes in a small roasting pan and drizzle 30ml/2 tbsp of the oil over the top. Season with salt and pepper and roast for 10–15 minutes, or until tender and slightly charred. Remove from the oven and set aside.

2 Preheat the grill (broiler) to high. Brush the sardine fillets with the remaining oil and lay them on a baking sheet. Grill (broil) for 4–5 minutes on each side, until cooked through.

3 Split the focaccia in half horizontally and cut each piece in half to give four equal pieces. Toast the cut side under the grill until golden.

4 Top with the sardines and tomatoes and an extra drizzle of oil. Season with black pepper, then serve.

Cook's Tip
Sardines are at their best in spring and early summer. Try to buy fish caught locally as they do not travel well.

Variation
Roast 2 garlic cloves, sliced, 1 red onion, cut into thin wedges, 12 black olives, pitted and coarsely chopped, and a handful of rosemary sprigs drizzled with olive oil for a potent alternative to the roasted cherry tomatoes.

Roasted Pepper and Hummus Wrap

Wraps make a tasty change from sandwiches and have the bonus that they can be made a few hours in advance without going soggy in the way that bread sandwiches often can. You can introduce all kinds of variation to this basic combination. Try using roasted aubergine in place of the red peppers, or guacamole in place of the hummus.

Serves 2
1 large red (bell) pepper, halved and seeded
60ml/4 tbsp hummus
2 soft flour tortillas

From the storecupboard
15ml/1 tbsp olive oil
salt and ground black pepper

1 Preheat the grill (broiler) to high. Brush the pepper halves with the oil and place cut side down on a baking sheet. Grill (broil) for 5 minutes, until charred. Put the pepper halves in a sealed plastic bag and leave to cool.

2 When cooled, remove the peppers from the bag and carefully peel away the charred skin and discard. Thinly slice the flesh using a sharp knife.

3 Spread the hummus over the tortillas in a thin, even layer and top with the roasted pepper slices. Season with salt and plenty of ground black pepper, then roll them up and cut in half to serve.

Smoked Salmon with Bagels and Cream Cheese

This sophisticated dish is perfect for a lunch on the go or brunch with friends. It's a deli classic that is quick and easy to make at home.

Serves 2
2 bagels
115–175g/4–6oz/½–¾ cup full-fat cream cheese
150g/5oz sliced best smoked salmon
lemon wedges, to serve

From the storecupboard
ground black pepper

1 Preheat the oven to 200°C/400°F/Gas 6. Put the bagels on a large baking sheet and warm them in the oven for 4–5 minutes.

2 Remove the bagels from the oven, split them in two and spread each half generously with cream cheese. Pile the salmon on top of the bases and grind over plenty of black pepper.

3 Squeeze over some lemon juice, then add the bagel tops.

4 Place on serving plates with the lemon wedges. If you have time, wrap each lemon wedge in a small square of muslin (cheesecloth), tie with fine string and put it on the plate.

Sardine Focaccia: Energy 301kcal/1262kJ; Protein 15.8g; Carbohydrate 27.6g, of which sugars 3.1g; Fat 15g, of which saturates 2.9g; Cholesterol 0mg; Calcium 106mg; Fibre 1.7g; Sodium 334mg.
Pepper Wrap: Energy 265kcal/1112kJ; Protein 6.8g; Carbohydrate 39g, of which sugars 6.5g; Fat 10.1g, of which saturates 0.9g; Cholesterol 0mg; Calcium 75mg; Fibre 3.3g; Sodium 345mg.
Salmon Bagels: Energy 375kcal/1571kJ; Protein 25g; Carbohydrate 28.9g, of which sugars 3.3g; Fat 18.6g, of which saturates 9.5g; Cholesterol 55mg; Calcium 44mg; Fibre 1.2g; Sodium 1775mg.

Crab and Cucumber Wraps

This dish is a modern twist on the ever-popular Chinese classic, crispy Peking duck with pancakes. In this quick and easy version, crisp, refreshing cucumber and full-flavoured dressed crab are delicious with spicy-sweet hoisin sauce in warm tortilla wraps. Serve the wraps as an appetizer for four people, or as a substantial lunch for two.

Serves 2
½ cucumber
1 medium dressed crab
4 small wheat tortillas
120ml/4fl oz/½ cup hoisin sauce

From the storecupboard
ground black pepper

1 Cut the cucumber into small even batons. Scoop the dressed crab into a small mixing bowl, add a little ground black pepper and mix lightly to combine.

2 Heat the tortillas gently, one at a time, in a heavy frying pan until they begin to colour on each side.

3 Spread a tortilla with 30ml/2 tbsp hoisin sauce, then sprinkle with one-quarter of the cucumber. Arrange one-quarter of the seasoned crab meat down the centre of each tortilla and roll up. Repeat with the remaining ingredients. Serve immediately.

Cook's Tip
Always buy shellfish from a reputable supplier who cooks fresh every day. If you're confident your dressed crab is really fresh, it will keep in the refrigerator for 2–3 days.

Variation
For a more spicy crab wrap, try adding a few drops of Tabasco sauce to the dressed crab and combine in your wrap with plenty of fresh rocket (arugula).

Fresh Crab Sandwiches

There's not much to beat the taste of freshly cooked crab, but if you can't face dealing with live crabs, buy fresh cooked ones. Serve the crab meat with a bowl of rocket and let everyone get in a mess cracking open the claws and making their own sandwiches.

Serves 6
3 live crabs, about 900g/2lb each
1 crusty wholegrain loaf, sliced
2 lemons, cut into quarters

From the storecupboard
butter, for spreading
salt and ground black pepper

1 Lower the live crabs into a pan of cold water, then slowly bring to the boil. (This method is considered more humane than plunging the crabs into boiling water.) Cook the crabs for 5–6 minutes per 450g/1lb, then remove from the pan and set aside to cool.

2 Break off the claws and legs, then use your thumbs to ease the body out of the shell. Remove and discard the grey gills from the body and put the white meat in a bowl. Scrape the brown meat from the shell and add to the white meat.

3 Serve the crab meat, and the claws and legs with crab crackers, with slices of brown bread, butter and lemon wedges and let everyone make their own sandwiches.

Cook's Tip
The most humane way to deal with a live crab is to chill it by submerging it in ice, or putting it in the freezer for 2–3 hours, until it is in a comatose state. When it is completely motionless, lay it on a chopping board, on its back, and look for a small hole, which you will find in a distinct groove if you lift up the tail flap. Drive a sturdy skewer or an awl into the hole. Then carefully position the skewer between the mouth plates, which are between the eyes, and drive the skewer in. The crab can now be plunged into a pan of boiling salted water.

Crab Wraps: Energy 484kcal/2046kJ; Protein 33.5g; Carbohydrate 74.8g, of which sugars 15.6g; Fat 7.6g, of which saturates 0.9g; Cholesterol 90mg; Calcium 162mg; Fibre 3.2g; Sodium 1559mg.
Crab Sandwiches: Energy 526kcal/2209kJ; Protein 30.1g; Carbohydrate 56g, of which sugars 2.6g; Fat 21.7g, of which saturates 9.1g; Cholesterol 85mg; Calcium 117mg; Fibre 7.7g; Sodium 1150mg.

Potato and Anchovy Temptation

This traditional Swedish gratin is utterly moreish. What could be more comforting on a cold wintry weekend afternoon than a steaming plate of creamy potatoes topped with sweet onions and anchovies?

Serves 4–6
900g/2lb potatoes
2 large, sweet onions, sliced
2 x 50g/2oz cans anchovies in olive oil, drained
450ml/¾ pint/scant 2 cups whipping cream or half and half double (heavy) and single (light) cream

1 Preheat the oven to 200°C/400°F/Gas 6. Cut the potatoes into thin slices, then cut the slices into matchstick strips. Sprinkle half of them in the base of a greased shallow 1.5 litre/2½ pint/ 6¼ cup baking dish.

2 Lay half of the onions on top of the potatoes, and season with black pepper. Lay the anchovies on top of the onions, then add the remaining onions and potatoes.

3 Mix the cream with 30ml/2 tbsp cold water and pour over the potatoes and onions. Cover with foil and bake for 1 hour, then reduce the oven temperature to 180°C/350°F/Gas 4 and uncover the dish. Bake for a further 40–50 minutes, or until the potatoes are golden and tender when tested with a knife.

Cook's Tips
• *If using salted anchovies, soak them in milk for a few hours prior to cooking to remove the extreme salty flavour.*
• *This dish is delicious served on its own or with a crispy green salad. It also work well as an accompaniment to cold meat. It is especially good with slices of home-cooked ham.*

Variation
For a twist on the traditional dish, try adding some chopped garlic and topping with breadcrumbs for a crunchy finish.

Crisp Fried Whitebait

This must be one of the simplest of all classic fish dishes and it is absolutely delicious served with lemon wedges and thinly sliced brown bread and butter. If you prefer, serve the whitebait with a simple lemon and herb dip.

Serves 4
150ml/¼ pint/⅔ cup milk
115g/4oz/1 cup plain (all-purpose) flour
450g/1lb whitebait

From the storecupboard
oil, for deep-frying

1 Heat the oil in a large pan or deep-fryer. Pour the milk into a shallow bowl and spoon the flour into a paper bag. Season the flour well with salt and pepper.

2 Dip a handful of the whitebait into the bowl of milk, drain them well, then put them into the paper bag. Shake to coat the fish evenly in the seasoned flour, then transfer to a plate. Repeat until all the fish have been coated. Don't add too many whitebait at once to the bag, or they will stick together.

3 Heat the oil for deep-frying to 190°C/375°F, or until a cube of stale bread, dropped into the oil, browns in about 20 seconds. Add a batch of whitebait, preferably in a frying basket, and deep-fry for 2–3 minutes, until crisp and golden brown.

4 Drain and keep hot while you cook the rest. Serve the whitebait piping hot.

Cook's Tips
• *Most whitebait are sold frozen. Always thaw them well before use and dry them thoroughly on kitchen paper before flouring.*
• *To make a delicious lemon and herb dip, mix 150ml/ ¼ pint/⅔ cup natural (plain) yogurt with the rind of one lemon and 45ml/3 tbsp chopped fresh herbs of your choice. Serve the dip chilled.*

Potato and Anchovy: Energy 509kcal/2111kJ; Protein 9.1g; Carbohydrate 31.5g, of which sugars 7.8g; Fat 39.3g, of which saturates 23.7g; Cholesterol 107mg; Calcium 121mg; Fibre 2.4g; Sodium 743mg.
Fried Whitebait: Energy 722kcal/2989kJ; Protein 26.8g; Carbohydrate 7.3g, of which sugars 0.2g; Fat 65.3g, of which saturates 0g; Cholesterol 0mg; Calcium 1183mg; Fibre 0.3g; Sodium 316mg.

Seared Tuna Niçoise

A traditional tuna Niçoise consists of tuna, olives, green beans, potatoes and eggs, but this modern version using fresh tuna is a simplified one – although just as tasty. Serve it with a green salad.

Serves 4
4 tuna steaks, about 150g/5oz each
30ml/2 tbsp sherry vinegar
2 eggs

From the storecupboard
45ml/3 tbsp garlic-infused olive oil
salt and ground black pepper

1 Put the tuna steaks in a shallow non-metallic dish ready for marinading. Mix the oil and vinegar together and season with salt and pepper.

2 Pour the mixture over the tuna steaks and turn them to coat in the marinade. Cover and chill for up to 1 hour.

3 Heat a griddle pan until smoking hot. Remove the tuna steaks from the marinade and lay them on the griddle pan. Cook for 2–3 minutes on each side, so that they are still pink in the centre. Remove from the pan and set aside.

4 Meanwhile, cook the eggs in a pan of boiling water for 5–6 minutes, then cool under cold running water. Shell the eggs and cut in half lengthways.

5 Pour the marinade on to the griddle pan and cook until it starts to bubble. Divide the tuna steaks among four serving plates and top each with half an egg. Drizzle the marinade over the top and serve immediately.

Marinated Courgette and Flageolet Bean Salad

Serve this healthy salad as a light lunch or as an accompaniment to meat and chicken dishes. It has a wonderful bright green colour and is perfect for summer dining. To give extra flavour to the salad add chopped fresh herbs before chilling. Basil and mint both have fresh, distinctive flavours that work well with the courgettes and beans.

Serves 4
2 courgettes (zucchini), halved lengthways and sliced
400g/14oz can flageolet or cannellini beans, drained and rinsed
grated rind and juice of 1 unwaxed lemon

From the storecupboard
45ml/3 tbsp garlic-infused olive oil
salt and ground black pepper

1 Cook the courgettes in boiling salted water for 2–3 minutes, or until just tender. Drain well and refresh under cold running water.

2 Transfer the drained courgettes to a bowl with the beans and stir in the oil, lemon rind and juice and some salt and pepper. Chill for 30 minutes before serving.

Baked Sweet Potatoes with Leeks and Gorgonzola

The smoky sweetness of the potatoes is perfectly balanced by the piquancy of the Gorgonzola cheese in this warming lunch dish. Not only does it taste wonderful, but it looks stunning too, if you use the vibrant orange-fleshed sweet potatoes.

Serves 4
4 large sweet potatoes, scrubbed
2 large leeks, washed and sliced
115g/4oz/1 cup Gorgonzola cheese, sliced

From the storecupboard
30ml/2 tbsp olive oil
salt and ground black pepper

1 Preheat the oven to 190°C/375°F/Gas 5. Dry the sweet potatoes with kitchen paper and rub them all over with 15ml/1 tbsp of the oil. Place them on a baking sheet and sprinkle with salt. Bake for 1 hour, or until tender.

2 Meanwhile, heat the remaining oil in a frying pan and add the sliced leeks. Cook for 3–4 minutes, or until softened and just beginning to turn golden.

3 Cut the potatoes in half lengthways and place them cut side up on the baking sheet. Top with the cooked leeks and season.

4 Lay the cheese slices on top and grill (broil) under a hot grill for 2–3 minutes, until the cheese is bubbling. Serve immediately.

Cook's Tip
Select evenly sized sweet potatoes with unblemished skins and wash them thoroughly before using. If the potatoes are cooked before you need them, wrap them in a warmed cloth.

Variation
Instead of the Italian Gorgonzola cheese you could use other blue cheeses, such as, Danish Blue, Roquefort or Stilton.

Seared Tuna: Energy 578kcal/2408kJ; Protein 46.4g; Carbohydrate 15g, of which sugars 10.6g; Fat 37.5g, of which saturates 7.1g; Cholesterol 235mg; Calcium 127mg; Fibre 4.7g; Sodium 585mg.
Courgette and Bean Salad: Energy 106kcal/444kJ; Protein 5.5g; Carbohydrate 11.9g, of which sugars 3.5g; Fat 4.4g, of which saturates 0.7g; Cholesterol 0mg; Calcium 62mg; Fibre 4.4g; Sodium 228mg.
Sweet Potatoes: Energy 338kcal/1425kJ; Protein 9.5g; Carbohydrate 44.8g, of which sugars 13.1g; Fat 14.8g, of which saturates 6.6g; Cholesterol 22mg; Calcium 206mg; Fibre 6.5g; Sodium 432mg.

Red Onion and Olive Pissaladière

For a taste of the Mediterranean, try this French-style pizza – it makes a delicious and easy-to-prepare lunch dish or a tasty snack. Cook the sliced red onions slowly until they are caramelized and sweet before piling them into the pastry cases.

Serves 6
500g/1¼lb small red onions, thinly sliced
500g/1¼lb puff pastry, thawed if frozen
75g/3oz/¾ cup small pitted black olives

From the storecupboard
75ml/5 tbsp extra virgin olive oil

1 Preheat the oven to 220°C/425°F/Gas 7. Heat the oil in a large, heavy frying pan and cook the onions gently, stirring frequently, for 15–20 minutes, until they are soft and golden. Season to taste.

2 Roll out the pastry thinly on a floured surface. Cut out a 33cm/13in round and carefully transfer it to a lightly dampened baking sheet.

3 Spread the onions over the pastry in an even layer to within 1cm/½in of the edge. Sprinkle the olives on top.

4 Bake the tart for 20–25 minutes, until the pastry is risen and a deep golden colour. Cut into wedges and serve warm.

Cook's Tip
To prepare the recipe in advance, pile the cooled onions on to the pastry round and chill the pissaladière until you are ready to bake it.

Variation
You can layer some thin slices of salami or chorizo sausage in with the caramelized onions for a change or, alternatively grate some Parmesan cheese on top.

Grilled Polenta with Gorgonzola

Golden squares of grilled polenta look and taste delicious. Serve spread with any flavourful soft cheese, preferably a blue cheese, or as an accompaniment to soups and salads.

Serves 6–8
350g/12oz/2½ cups quick-cook polenta
225g/8oz/1¼ cups Gorgonzola cheese, at room temperature

From the storecupboard
15ml/1 tbsp salt

1 Bring 1.5 litres/2½ pints/6¼ cups water to the boil in a large heavy pan. Add the salt. Reduce the heat to a simmer and gradually add the polenta in a fine, steady stream, whisking to incorporate. Change to a wooden spoon and cook, stirring, until the polenta comes away from the sides of the pan.

2 Sprinkle a work surface or large board with a little water. Spread the polenta out on to the surface in a layer 2cm/¾in thick. Allow to cool completely. Preheat the grill (broiler).

3 Cut the polenta into triangles. Grill (broil) on both sides, until hot and speckled with brown. Serve spread with the cheese.

Aubergine, Mint and Couscous Salad

Packets of flavoured couscous are available in most supermarkets – garlic and coriander is especially good for this recipe. Still, it is very simple to make your own flavoured couscous with a good stock and some fresh herbs. Serve with a crisp green salad.

Serves 2
1 large aubergine (eggplant)
115g/4oz packet garlic-and-coriander (cilantro) flavoured couscous
30ml/2 tbsp chopped fresh mint

From the storecupboard
30ml/2 tbsp olive oil
salt and ground black pepper

1 Preheat the grill (broiler) to high. Cut the aubergine into large chunky pieces and toss them with the olive oil. Season with salt and pepper to taste and spread the aubergine pieces on a non-stick baking sheet. Grill (broil) for 5–6 minutes, turning occasionally, until golden brown.

2 Meanwhile, prepare the couscous according to the instructions on the packet. Stir the grilled aubergine and chopped mint into the couscous, toss thoroughly and serve the dish immediately.

Cook's Tip
Although it looks like a grain, couscous is actually a form of pasta made by steaming and drying cracked durum wheat. The variety that is generally available in supermarkets is quick cooking. Simply place the couscous in a large bowl, add enough boiling water or stock to just cover it and leave covered for 10 minutes or until all the water has been absorbed. Fluff up the grains with a fork and season.

Pissaladière: Energy 436kcal/1815kJ; Protein 5.9g; Carbohydrate 37.4g, of which sugars 5.8g; Fat 31.1g, of which saturates 1.5g; Cholesterol 0mg; Calcium 77mg; Fibre 1.5g; Sodium 542mg.
Grilled Polenta: Energy 252kcal/1052kJ; Protein 8g; Carbohydrate 41.1g, of which sugars 0g; Fat 5.7g, of which saturates 2.5g; Cholesterol 10mg; Calcium 66mg; Fibre 1.2g; Sodium 160mg.
Aubergine Salad: Energy 251kcal/1044kJ; Protein 4.8g; Carbohydrate 32.5g, of which sugars 2g; Fat 12.1g, of which saturates 1.7g; Cholesterol 0mg; Calcium 53mg; Fibre 2g; Sodium 4mg.

Chicken Tikka Sandwich

Using cooked chicken tikka to fill a sandwich is a great way of enjoying the spiciness of Indian food without having to prepare or buy a whole meal.

Serves 1

1 chicken tikka breast (fillet)
2 thick slices wholemeal (whole-wheat) bread, buttered
mango chutney
watercress sprigs

1 Slice the chicken tikka thinly. Butter the bread and spread one slice with a little mango chutney.

2 Arrange the chicken on the bread and top with watercress sprigs. Cover with the second slice of bread and press down gently.

Chorizo and Spring Onion Hash

This quick and tasty lunchtime treat is a good way to use up leftover boiled potatoes. Fresh chorizo sausages are available from good butchers, Spanish delicatessens and most large supermarkets.

Serves 4

450g/1lb fresh chorizo sausages
450g/1lb cooked potatoes, diced
1 bunch of spring onions (scallions), sliced

From the storecupboard

15ml/1 tbsp olive oil
salt and ground black pepper

1 Heat a large frying pan over a medium heat and add the sausages. Cook for 8–10 minutes, turning occasionally, until cooked through. Remove from the pan and set aside.

2 Add the olive oil to the sausage fat in the pan and then add the potatoes. Cook over a low heat for 5–8 minutes, turning occasionally until golden. Meanwhile, cut the sausages into bitesize chunks and add to the pan.

3 Add the spring onions to the pan and cook for a couple more minutes, until they are piping hot. Season with salt and pepper, and serve immediately.

King Scallops with Bacon

This is the simplest of dishes, combining bacon and scallops with brown butter which has just begun to burn. The butter gives this recipe a lovely nutty smell, which is why the French call this dish 'noisette' – nutty.

Serves 4

12 rashers (strips) streaky (fatty) bacon
12 scallops
juice of 1 lemon
30ml/2 tbsp chopped fresh flat leaf parsley

From the storecupboard

225g/8oz/1 cup unsalted (sweet) butter
ground black pepper

1 Preheat the grill (broiler) to high. Wrap a rasher of bacon around each scallop so it goes over the top and not round the side.

2 Cut the butter into chunks and put it in a small pan over a low heat.

3 Meanwhile grill (broil) the scallops with the bacon facing up so it protects the meat. The bacon fat will help to cook the scallops. This will take only a few minutes; once they are cooked set aside and keep warm.

4 Allow the butter to turn a nutty brown colour, gently swirling it from time to time. Just as it is foaming and darkening, take off the heat and add the lemon juice. Be warned, it will bubble up quite dramatically.

5 Place the scallops on warmed plates, dress with plenty of chopped fresh parsley, season and pour the lemon butter over immediately.

Cook's Tip

Get the scallops on to warmed plates just as the butter is coming to the right colour, then add the lemon juice.

Chicken Tikka: Energy 360kcal/1525kJ; Protein 35.9g; Carbohydrate 43.3g, of which sugars 16.5g; Fat 6g, of which saturates 0.7g; Cholesterol 88mg; Calcium 139mg; Fibre 2.3g; Sodium 729mg.
Chorizo Hash: Energy 522kcal/2172kJ; Protein 14.4g; Carbohydrate 29.6g, of which sugars 3.7g; Fat 39.3g, of which saturates 14.3g; Cholesterol 53mg; Calcium 63mg; Fibre 2.1g; Sodium 869mg.
King Scallops: Energy 665kcal/2749kJ; Protein 24.4g; Carbohydrate 2.7g, of which sugars 0.6g; Fat 62g, of which saturates 34.7g; Cholesterol 189mg; Calcium 51mg; Fibre 0.5g; Sodium 1240mg.

Mussels in White Wine

This simple yet delicious dish is perfect for informal entertaining. Serve with a big bowl of French fries to share. To make a variation, cook the mussels in beer or cider instead of wine. You could also add some garlic and cream – they taste fantastic.

Serves 2
300ml/½ pint/1¼ cups dry white wine
1kg/2¼lb mussels, cleaned
45ml/3 tbsp chopped fresh parsley

From the storecupboard
25g/1oz/2 tbsp butter
salt and ground black pepper

1 Heat the butter in a large pan until foaming, then pour in the wine. Bring to the boil. Discard any open mussels that do not close when sharply tapped, and add the remaining ones to the pan. Cover with a tight-fitting lid and cook over a medium heat for 4–5 minutes, shaking the pan every now and then. By this time, all the mussels should have opened. Discard any that are still closed.

2 Line a large sieve (strainer) with kitchen paper and strain the mussels and their liquid through it. Transfer the mussels to warmed serving bowls. Pour the liquid into a small pan and bring to the boil. Season with salt and pepper and stir in the parsley. Pour over the mussels and serve immediately.

Cook's Tips
- *Mussels deteriorate rapidly, so you must ensure that they are alive when you cook them. When buying, look for ones that feel heavy for their size, indicating that they contain plenty of sea water. Do not buy any that have broken shells. They should be eaten within a day of purchase, but will keep briefly in the coldest part of the refrigerator.*
- *To clean mussels, first wash them in plenty of cold water, scrubbing them well. Scrape off any barnacles with a knife. Give any open mussels a sharp tap and discard any that fail to close as they will be dead. Finally pull out and discard the fibrous beard that sprouts between the two halves of the shell.*

Scallops with Fennel and Bacon

This dish is a delicious combination of succulent scallops and crispy bacon, served on a bed of tender fennel and melting mascarpone. If you can't get large scallops (known as king scallops), buy the smaller queen scallops and serve a dozen per person. If you buy scallops in the shell, wash and keep the pretty fan-shaped shells to serve a range of fish dishes in.

Serves 2
2 small fennel bulbs
130g/4½oz/generous ½ cup mascarpone cheese
8 large scallops, shelled
75g/3oz thin smoked streaky (fatty) bacon rashers (strips)

1 Trim, halve and slice the fennel, reserving and chopping any feathery tops. Blanch the slices in boiling water for about 3 minutes, until softened, then drain.

2 Preheat the grill (broiler) to moderate. Place the fennel in a shallow flameproof dish. Dot with the mascarpone and grill (broil) for about 5 minutes, until the cheese has melted and the fennel is lightly browned.

3 Meanwhile, pat the scallops dry on kitchen paper and season lightly. Cook the bacon in a large, heavy frying pan, until crisp and golden, turning once. Drain and keep warm. Fry the scallops in the bacon fat for 1–2 minutes on each side, until cooked through.

4 Transfer the fennel to serving plates and crumble or snip the bacon into bitesize pieces over the top. Pile the scallops on the bacon and sprinkle with any reserved fennel tops.

Variation
Instead of serving with fennel and mascarpone, cook the scallops and bacon with fresh sage and cider.

Mussels in Wine: Energy 189kcal/799kJ; Protein 26.4g; Carbohydrate 2.4g, of which sugars 1.9g; Fat 3.1g, of which saturates 0.5g; Cholesterol 60mg; Calcium 308mg; Fibre 0.4g; Sodium 319mg.
Scallops and Bacon: Energy 362kcal/1512kJ; Protein 36.9g; Carbohydrate 9g, of which sugars 5.4g; Fat 20.1g, of which saturates 9.4g; Cholesterol 99mg; Calcium 80mg; Fibre 4.8g; Sodium 675mg.

Scallops with Lime Butter

Chargrilling fennel releases its aniseed flavour, which tastes great with sweet and rich scallops. These wonderful shellfish are ideal for the barbecue because they have firm flesh that cooks quickly – simply toss in lime juice before cooking.

Serves 4
1 head fennel
2 limes
12 large scallops, cleaned
1 egg yolk

From the storecupboard
90ml/6 tbsp melted butter
olive oil for brushing
salt and ground black pepper

1 Trim any feathery leaves from the fennel and reserve them. Slice the rest lengthways into thin wedges.

2 Cut one lime into wedges. Finely grate the rind and squeeze the juice of the other lime and toss half the juice and rind on to the scallops. Season well with salt and ground black pepper.

3 Place the egg yolk and remaining lime rind and juice in a small bowl and whisk until pale and smooth.

4 Gradually whisk in the melted butter and continue whisking until thick and smooth. Finely chop the reserved fennel leaves and stir them in, with seasoning.

5 Prepare the barbecue. Position a lightly oiled grill rack over the hot coals. Brush the fennel wedges with olive oil and cook them over high heat for 3–4 minutes, turning once.

6 Add the scallops and cook for a further 3–4 minutes, turning once. Serve with the lime and fennel butter and the lime wedges.

Cook's Tips
- *When choosing fennel, look for bulbs that are white and firm.*
- *Thread small scallops on to flat skewers to make turning them easier.*

Prawn and New Potato Stew

New potatoes with plenty of flavour, such as Jersey Royals, Maris Piper or Nicola, are essential for this effortless stew. Use a good quality jar of tomato and chilli sauce; there are now plenty available in the supermarkets. For a really easy supper dish, serve with warm, crusty bread to mop up the delicious sauce, and a mixed green salad.

Serves 4
675g/1½lb small new potatoes, scrubbed
15g/½oz/½ cup fresh coriander (cilantro)
350g/12oz jar tomato and chilli sauce
300g/11oz cooked peeled prawns (shrimp), thawed and drained if frozen

1 Cook the potatoes in boiling water for 15 minutes, until tender. Drain and return to the pan.

2 Finely chop half the coriander and add to the pan with the tomato and chilli sauce and 90ml/6 tbsp water. Bring to the boil, reduce the heat, cover and simmer gently for 5 minutes.

3 Stir in the prawns and heat briefly until they are warmed through. Do not overheat the prawns or they will quickly shrivel, becoming tough and tasteless. Spoon into shallow bowls and serve sprinkled with the remaining coriander, torn into pieces.

Cook's Tip
Fresh prawns taste delicious, but are truly laborious to prepare. They must have their heads and tails removed, be peeled and 'deveined', removing the intestinal tract, before cooking.

Variation
To elevate this dish to dinner party status, try adding some cooked scallops and lobster meat with the prawns.

Scallops with Lime Butter: Energy 232kcal/961kJ; Protein 10g; Carbohydrate 2.2g, of which sugars 0.9g; Fat 20.5g, of which saturates 12.3g; Cholesterol 116mg; Calcium 31mg; Fibre 1.1g; Sodium 211mg.
Prawn Stew: Energy 218kcal/924kJ; Protein 16.9g; Carbohydrate 30.4g, of which sugars 5.4g; Fat 4.1g, of which saturates 0.7g; Cholesterol 146mg; Calcium 84mg; Fibre 2.9g; Sodium 171mg.

Fried Squid

In Greece, squid is generally rolled in flour and shallow-fried. There's an art to this, as the olive oil has to be at precisely the right temperature to keep the squid tender and moist. Fried squid can be served as a meze with salad or can accompany a soup or vegetable casserole.

Serves 4
900g/2lb medium squid, gutted
50g/2oz/½ cup plain (all-purpose) flour
large pinch of dried oregano
1 lemon, quartered, to serve

From the storecupboard
75ml/5 tbsp olive oil or sunflower oil, for frying
salt and ground black pepper

1 Having emptied the squid of all their innards, rinse the bodies thoroughly, inside and out, then drain well. Slice the bodies into 3–4cm/1¼–1½in wide rings.

2 Season the flour with salt and pepper and put it in a large plastic bag. Add the squid, keeping the rings and tentacles separate, and toss until evenly coated. Shake off any excess flour.

3 Heat the oil in a large heavy or non-stick frying pan over a medium heat. When it is sizzling, but not smoking, add a batch of squid rings. They should fill the pan but not touch each other.

4 Let the squid rings cook for 2–3 minutes or until pale golden, then use a fork to turn each piece over. This is a laborious process but worthwhile. Let each ring cook for 1–2 minutes more, until pale golden, then lift out with a slotted spoon and drain on a platter lined with kitchen paper.

5 Continue to cook the squid, leaving the floured tentacles to last, and take care, as they spit spitefully. The tentacles will need very little cooking as the oil will be quite hot and they will become crisp almost immediately. Turn them over after 1 minute and take them out as soon as they are golden all over.

6 Serve the fried squid on a large warmed platter and sprinkle dried oregano on top. Surround with the lemon wedges and invite guests to squeeze a little lemon juice over each portion.

Herrings with Mustard

This dish was inspired by a traditional Welsh recipe, where there is long history of fishing herring. Fillets were spread with mustard, rolled and cooked with potato, onion and apple. Both whole fish and fillets are delicious rolled in oats and then pan-fried in bacon fat, and served with a generous squeeze of lemon.

Serves 2
4–6 herrings, filleted
20–30ml/4–6 tsp wholegrain mustard
4–6 small young sage leaves
1 eating apple
wholemeal (whole-wheat) bread, to serve (optional)

1 Preheat the oven to 180°C/350°F/Gas 4. Rinse the herrings and dry inside and out with kitchen paper.

2 Open the fish and lay them, skin side down, on a board or work surface. Spread with 5ml/1 tsp mustard and tear one sage leaf over each one.

3 Quarter and core the apple and cut into thin wedges. Lay the wedges lengthways along one side of each fish, overlapping them as you go. Fold the other half of the fish over the apple.

4 Oil a baking tray (or line it with baking parchment) and carefully lift the filled herrings on to it.

5 Cook the herrings in the hot oven for 20 minutes, until they are cooked through and just beginning to brown on the edges. Serve, freshly cooked, with wholemeal bread, if using.

Cook's Tip
Herring is an oily fish, which must be cooked absolutely fresh otherwise it will taste rancid. An acidic sauce, such as gooseberry or mustard, counteracts the richness of the fish. Herring fillets are also made into rollmops or smoked to make kippers.

Fried Squid: Energy 349kcal/1464kJ; Protein 35.8g; Carbohydrate 12.4g, of which sugars 0.2g; Fat 17.7g, of which saturates 2.9g; Cholesterol 506mg; Calcium 47mg; Fibre 0.4g; Sodium 248mg.
Herrings: Energy 209kcal/870kJ; Protein 18.5g; Carbohydrate 3.5g, of which sugars 3.5g; Fat 13.5g, of which saturates 3.3g; Cholesterol 50mg; Calcium 102mg; Fibre 1.6g; Sodium 128mg.

Haddock with Fennel Butter

Fresh fish tastes fabulous cooked in a simple herb butter. Here the liquorice flavour of fennel complements the haddock beautifully to make a simple dish ideal for a dinner party. If you can buy only small haddock fillets, fold them in half before baking, or use cod as an alternative. Serve with tiny new potatoes and a herb salad to make a light, summery main course.

Serves 4
675g/1½lb haddock fillet, skinned and cut into 4 portions
1 lemon
45ml/3 tbsp coarsely chopped fennel leaves

From the storecupboard
50g/2oz/¼ cup butter
salt and ground black pepper

1 Preheat the oven to 220°C/425°F/Gas 7. Season the fish on both sides with salt and pepper. Melt one-quarter of the butter in a frying pan, preferably non-stick, and cook the fish over a medium heat briefly on both sides.

2 Transfer the fish to a shallow ovenproof dish. Cut four wafer-thin slices from the lemon and squeeze the juice from the remainder over the fish. Place the lemon slices on top and then bake for 15–20 minutes, or until the fish is cooked.

3 Meanwhile, melt the remaining butter in the frying pan and add the fennel and a little seasoning.

4 Transfer the cooked fish to plates and pour the cooking juices into the herb butter. Heat gently for a few seconds, then pour the herb butter over the fish. Serve immediately.

Cook's Tip
Flavoursome herb butters can be kept in the freezer. To make, simply chop the chosen herb finely, beat the butter until softened, then stir in the herbs to mix evenly. Chill and roll into a sausage shape, then wrap in clear film (plastic wrap) and freeze.

Baked Salmon with Caraway Seeds

This classic Czech way of cooking salmon is very easy and gives excellent results. The fish cooks in its own juices, taking on the lovely warm flavour of the caraway seeds. Serve sprinkled with flat leaf parsley and wedges of lemon for squeezing over the fish.

Serves 4
1.8kg/4lb whole salmon, cleaned
2.5–5ml/½–1 tsp caraway seeds
45ml/3 tbsp lemon juice

From the storecupboard
115g/4oz/½ cup butter, melted

1 Preheat the oven to 180°C/350°F/Gas 4. Scale the salmon, remove the head and tail and slice off the fins with a sharp knife, then cut the fish in half lengthways along the backbone.

2 Place the salmon, skin side down, in a lightly greased roasting pan. Brush with the melted butter. Season with salt and pepper, sprinkle over the caraway seeds and drizzle with lemon juice.

3 Cover the salmon loosely with foil and bake for 25 minutes. Remove it from the oven, lift off the foil and test the fish. (The flesh should be opaque and flake easily. Return to the oven if necessary.)

4 Remove the foil and carefully lift the fish on to a serving plate. Remove the bones. It may be served hot or cold.

Cook's Tip
Serve the baked salmon with a herb and lemon mayonnaise. To make: take 300ml/½ pint/1½ cups good quality mayonnaise, 30ml/2 tbsp natural (plain) yogurt or single (light) cream, finely grated rind of ½ lemon, 30ml/2 tbsp finely chopped fresh chives and 15ml/1 tbsp finely chopped fresh parsley. Place all the ingredients in a bowl and stir together, adding lemon juice to taste. Combined with a fragrant herby leaf salad, this would make an excellent lunch or supper dish, served with some wholemeal (whole-wheat) bread or new potatoes.

Haddock in Butter: Energy 231kcal/970kJ; Protein 32.3g; Carbohydrate 0.3g, of which sugars 0.3g; Fat 11.3g, of which saturates 6.7g; Cholesterol 87mg; Calcium 29mg; Fibre 0.3g; Sodium 190mg.
Baked Salmon: Energy 830kcal/3452kJ; Protein 69.5g; Carbohydrate 0.2g, of which sugars 0.2g; Fat 61.1g, of which saturates 22.3g; Cholesterol 233mg; Calcium 79mg; Fibre 0g; Sodium 328mg.

Baked Salmon with Green Sauce

When buying whole salmon, there are several points to consider – the skin should be shiny, the eyes bright and the tail should look fresh and moist. Baking the salmon in foil produces a moist result, similar to poaching. Garnish the fish with thin slices of cucumber and dill to conceal any flesh that may look ragged after skinning and serve with lemon wedges.

Serves 6–8

2–3kg/4½–6¾lb salmon, cleaned with head and tail left on
3–5 spring onions (scallions), thinly sliced
1 lemon, thinly sliced
600ml/1 pint/2½ cups watercress sauce or herb mayonnaise

From the storecupboard

salt and ground black pepper

1 Preheat the oven to 180°C/350°F/Gas 4. Rinse the salmon and lay it on a large piece of foil. Stuff the fish with the sliced spring onions and layer the lemon slices inside and around the fish, then sprinkle with plenty of salt and ground black pepper.

2 Loosely fold the foil around the fish and fold the edges over to seal. Bake for about 1 hour.

3 Remove the fish from the oven and leave to stand, still wrapped in the foil, for about 15 minutes, then unwrap the parcel and leave the fish to cool.

4 When the fish is cool, carefully lift it on to a large plate, retaining the lemon slices. Cover the fish tightly with clear film (plastic wrap) and chill for several hours.

5 Before serving, discard the lemon slices from around the fish. Using a blunt knife to lift up the edge of the skin, carefully peel the skin away from the flesh, avoiding tearing the flesh, and pull out any fins at the same time.

6 Chill the watercress sauce or herb mayonnaise before serving. Transfer the fish to a serving platter, garnish with thin cucumber slices if desired, and serve the sauce separately.

Pan-cooked Salmon with Sorrel Sauce

Sorrel leaves add their lovely lemony flavour to the sauce of this pan-cooked salmon dish. In its absence (because sorrel is at its best in spring and early summer) try using tender young spinach leaves or, better still, a tablespoon or two of laverbread, the Welsh delicacy made from boiled seaweed, with a squeeze of lemon juice added. Serve with some buttery new potatoes and lashings of freshly ground black pepper.

Serves 4

4 pieces salmon fillet, each weighing about 175g/6oz
large handful of fresh sorrel leaves (about 100g/3½oz), chopped
150ml/¼ pint/⅔ cup double (heavy) cream

From the storecupboard

15g/½oz/1 tbsp butter
10ml/2 tsp olive oil
salt and ground black pepper

1 Heat the butter and oil in a pan, add the salmon (flesh side down) and cook over medium heat for 3–5 minutes until golden brown.

2 Turn the fish over so that the skin side is down and continue cooking the second side for about 3 minutes until almost cooked through. Lift out and keep warm (the salmon will finish cooking while you make the sauce).

3 Add the sorrel to the hot pan and cook, stirring, until wilted and soft. If the sorrel gives off lots of liquid, bubble it gently until reduced to a tablespoonful or two.

4 Stir in the double cream, bring just to the boil and bubble gently for no more than 1 minute. Add seasoning to taste and serve with the salmon.

Variation

This recipe also works well with several other fish, such as sea trout, trout and sea bass.

Salmon with Sorrel: Energy 549kcal/2274kJ; Protein 36.7g; Carbohydrate 1.1g, of which sugars 1g; Fat 44.2g, of which saturates 18.1g; Cholesterol 147mg; Calcium 98mg; Fibre 0.5g; Sodium 145mg.
Baked Salmon: Energy 920kcal/3803kJ; Protein 41.7g; Carbohydrate 1.5g, of which sugars 1.2g; Fat 83g, of which saturates 13.3g; Cholesterol 166mg; Calcium 66mg; Fibre 0.1g; Sodium 556mg.

Teriyaki Salmon

Bottles of teriyaki sauce, a lovely rich Japanese glaze, are available in most large supermarkets and Asian stores. Serve the salmon with sticky rice or soba noodles.

Serves 4
4 salmon fillets, 150g/5oz each
75ml/5 tbsp teriyaki sauce
5cm/2in piece of fresh root ginger, peeled and cut into matchsticks

From the storecupboard
150ml/¼ pint/⅔ cup sunflower oil

1 Put the salmon in a shallow, non-metallic dish and pour over the teriyaki sauce. Cover and chill for 2 hours.

2 Meanwhile, heat the sunflower oil in a small pan and add the ginger. Fry for 1–2 minutes, or until golden and crisp. Remove with a slotted spoon and drain on kitchen paper.

3 Heat a griddle pan until smoking hot. Remove the salmon from the sauce and add, skin side down, to the pan. Cook for 2–3 minutes, then turn over and cook for a further 1–2 minutes, or until cooked through. Remove from the pan and divide among four serving plates. Top the salmon fillets with the crispy fried ginger.

4 Pour the sauce into the pan and cook for 1–2 minutes. Pour over the salmon and serve.

Cook's Tip
If you can't get hold of teriyaki sauce, or you just want to ring the changes, use the pungent Thai fish sauce instead to add a similar richness.

Variation
Thick juicy fillets of hake, halibut, hoki and fresh or undyed smoked haddock and cod can all be used for this Japanese teriyaki marinaded dish.

Sea Bass in a Salt Crust

Baking fish in a crust of sea salt seals in and enhances its flavour. Any firm fish can be cooked in this way. Decorate with a garnish of seaweed or blanched samphire and lemon slices, and break open the crust at the table to release the glorious aroma. Serve the fish with baby new potatoes roasted with olive oil and a sprinkling of dried rosemary, and steamed green vegetables such as broccoli or green beans.

Serves 4
1 sea bass, about 1kg/2¼lb, gutted, cleaned and scaled
1 sprig each of fresh fennel, rosemary and thyme

From the storecupboard
mixed peppercorns
2kg/4½lb coarse sea salt

1 Preheat the oven to 240°C/475°F/Gas 9. Fill the cavity of the fish with the sprigs of fresh fennel, rosemary and thyme, and grind over some of the mixed peppercorns.

2 Spread half the salt in the bottom of an ovenproof dish (ideally oval shaped) and lay the sea bass on it. Cover the fish all over with a 1cm/½in layer of salt, pressing it down firmly. Moisten the salt lightly by spraying with water from an atomizer. Bake the fish for 30–40 minutes, until the salt crust is just beginning to colour.

3 Bring the sea bass to the table in its salt crust. Use a sharp knife to break open the crust and cut into four portions.

Cook's Tip
Sea bass have very few small bones, which makes it suitable for serving whole at the table. You can leave the head on for this dish if you like. This firm-fleshed fish is almost unsurpassable for flavour, but good substitutes for this dish would be turbot or sole, or bluefish (very popular for this dish in Turkey).

Teriyaki Salmon: Energy 239kcal/995kJ; Protein 24.8g; Carbohydrate 2.1g, of which sugars 1.7g; Fat 13.3g, of which saturates 2.3g; Cholesterol 58mg; Calcium 93mg; Fibre 0.3g; Sodium 323mg.
Sea Bass in Salt Crust: Energy 83kcal/351kJ; Protein 16.1g; Carbohydrate 0g, of which sugars 0g; Fat 2.1g, of which saturates 0.3g; Cholesterol 67mg; Calcium 109mg; Fibre 0g; Sodium 2021mg.

Sea Bass with Fennel

The classic combination of sea bass and fennel works particularly well when the fish is cooked over charcoal. Fennel twigs are traditionally used inside the fish but this version of the recipe uses fennel seeds, which flavour the fish beautifully. Always make sure your barbecue coals are hot before you begin cooking.

Serves 6
1 sea bass, about 1.3–1.6kg/3–3½lb, cleaned and scaled
10ml/2 tsp fennel seeds
2 large fennel bulbs
60ml/4 tbsp Pernod

From the storecupboard
60ml/4 tbsp olive oil
salt and ground black pepper

1 Make four deep slashes in each side of the sea bass. Brush the fish with olive oil and season well with salt and ground black pepper. Sprinkle the fennel seeds in the cavity and slashes of the fish.

2 Trim and slice the fennel bulbs thinly, reserving any leafy fronds to use as a garnish.

3 Prepare the barbecue. Part the coals in the centre and position a drip tray. Position a lightly oiled grill rack over the hot coals. Put the fish inside a hinged wire grill or straight on to the grill rack over the drip tray. Cook over indirect medium heat using a cover, for 20 minutes, basting occasionally and turning once.

4 Meanwhile, brush the slices of fennel with olive oil and barbecue for about 8–10 minutes, turning the fennel occasionally, until tender. Remove the fish and fennel from the heat.

5 Sprinkle the fennel slices on a serving plate. Lay the fish on top and garnish with the reserved fennel fronds.

6 When ready for eating, heat the Pernod in a small pan on the side of the barbecue, light it and pour it, flaming, over the fish. Serve immediately.

Sea Bass with Parsley and Lime Butter

The delicate but firm, sweet flesh of sea bass goes beautifully with citrus flavours. Serve this summery dish with roast fennel and sautéed diced potatoes.

Serves 6
6 sea bass fillets, about 150g/5oz each
grated rind and juice of 1 large unwaxed lime
30ml/2 tbsp chopped fresh parsley

From the storecupboard
50g/2oz/¼ cup butter
salt and ground black pepper

1 Heat the butter in a large frying pan and add three of the sea bass fillets, skin side down. Cook for 3–4 minutes, or until the skin is crisp and golden. Flip the fish over and cook for a further 2–3 minutes, or until cooked through.

2 Remove the fillets from the pan with a metal spatula. Place each on a serving plate and keep them warm. Cook the remaining fish in the same way and transfer to serving plates.

3 Add the lime rind and juice to the pan with the parsley, and season with salt and black pepper. Allow to bubble for 1–2 minutes, then pour a little over each fish portion and serve immediately.

Variation
Try cooking sea bass in a variety of different flavoured butters. Here are a few classics that go with white fish. Take 115g/4oz softened butter, then, to make lemon butter: mix with the grated rind of 1 lemon and season; for herb butter, finely chop 50g/2oz fresh herbs, such as chives, tarragon, parsley, chervil or thyme, mix with butter and season; for garlic butter, mix 3 cloves of garlic, crushed, with the butter and season. These can all be stored in the freezer.

Sea Bass and Fennel: Energy 180kcal/750kJ; Protein 19.9g; Carbohydrate 1.2g, of which sugars 1.1g; Fat 8.1g, of which saturates 1.2g; Cholesterol 80mg; Calcium 146mg; Fibre 1.6g; Sodium 76mg.
Sea Bass and Parsley: Energy 214kcal/894kJ; Protein 29.2g; Carbohydrate 0.2g, of which sugars 0.2g; Fat 10.7g, of which saturates 4.9g; Cholesterol 138mg; Calcium 207mg; Fibre 0.3g; Sodium 156mg.

Grilled Hake with Lemon and Chilli

Choose firm hake fillets, as thick as possible. This is an ideal recipe if you are counting the calories, because it is low in fat. Serve with new potatoes and steamed fine green beans. Or, if you're not concerned about the calories, serve with creamy mashed potatoes with plenty of butter stirred in.

Serves 4
4 hake fillets, each 150g/5oz
finely grated rind and juice of 1 unwaxed lemon
15ml/1 tbsp crushed chilli flakes

From the storecupboard
30ml/2 tbsp olive oil
salt and ground black pepper

1 Preheat the grill (broiler) to high. Brush the hake fillets all over with the olive oil and place them skin side up on a baking sheet.

2 Grill (broil) the fish for 4–5 minutes, until the skin is crispy, then carefully turn them over using a metal spatula.

3 Sprinkle the fillets with the lemon rind and chilli flakes and season with salt and ground black pepper.

4 Grill the fillets for a further 2–3 minutes, or until the hake is cooked through. (Test using the point of a sharp knife; the flesh should flake.) Squeeze over the lemon juice just before serving.

Cook's Tip
Haddock or cod are less expensive substitutes for any hake recipe; hake are becoming quite scarce due to overfishing.

Variation
The classic Spanish way to serve hake is with a salsa verde – a spicy blend of green chillies, spring onions, garlic, capers, parsley, lemon, olive oil and green Tabasco.

Roast Mackerel with Spicy Chermoula Paste

Chermoula is a hot, tasty spice mix used widely in Moroccan and North African cooking. Many grilled fish and vegetable dishes benefit greatly from its distinct flavour. It is now readily available in most large supermarkets.

Serves 4
4 whole mackerel, cleaned and gutted
30–45ml/2–3 tbsp chermoula
2 red onions, sliced

From the storecupboard
75ml/5 tbsp olive oil
salt and ground black pepper

1 Preheat the oven to 190°C/375°F/Gas 5. Place each mackerel on a large sheet of baking parchment. Using a sharp knife, slash each fish several times.

2 In a small bowl, mix the chermoula with the olive oil, and spread over the mackerel, rubbing the mixture into the cuts.

3 Sprinkle the red onions over the mackerel and season with salt and pepper.

4 Scrunch the ends of the paper together to seal the fish and place on a baking tray. Bake for 20 minutes, until the mackerel is cooked through. Serve in the paper parcels, to be unwrapped at the table.

Cook's Tip
To make your own chermoula, take 2–3 garlic cloves, 5–10ml/1–2 tsp cumin, pinch of saffron (soaked in a little water), 60ml/4 tbsp olive oil, juice of 1 lemon, 1 hot red chilli, seeded and chopped and 5ml/1 tsp salt. Place all the ingredients in a mortar and pound with a pestle or process briefly in a food processor. Add a small bunch of finely chopped coriander (cilantro), and stir to combine. The quantities of herbs and spices can be varied to suit your preference, so be experimental!

Grilled Hake: Energy 188kcal/786kJ; Protein 27g; Carbohydrate 0.1g, of which sugars 0.1g; Fat 8.8g, of which saturates 1.2g; Cholesterol 35mg; Calcium 22mg; Fibre 0g; Sodium 150mg.
Roast Mackerel: Energy 422kcal/1753kJ; Protein 31.8g; Carbohydrate 1.9g, of which sugars 0.1g; Fat 31.9g, of which saturates 6g; Cholesterol 86mg; Calcium 51mg; Fibre 1.3g; Sodium 117mg.

Trout with Grilled Serrano Ham

Traditionally in this Spanish recipe, the trout would have come from mountain streams and been stuffed and wrapped in locally cured ham. One of the beauties of this method is that the skins come off in one piece, leaving the succulent, moist flesh to be eaten with the crisped, salt ham.

Serves 4
4 brown or rainbow trout, about 250g/9oz each, gutted
16 thin slices Serrano ham, about 200g/7oz
buttered potatoes, to serve (optional)

From the storecupboard
50g/2oz/¼ cup melted butter, plus extra for greasing
salt and ground black pepper

1 Wash the cavity of each fish thoroughly and pat dry with kitchen paper.

2 Extend the belly cavity of each trout, cutting up one side of the backbone. Slip a knife behind the rib bones to loosen them (sometimes just flexing the fish makes them pop up). Snip these off from both sides with kitchen scissors, and season the fish well inside.

3 Preheat the grill (broiler) to high, with a shelf in the top position. Line a baking tray with foil and butter it.

4 Working with the fish on the foil, fold a piece of ham into each belly. Use smaller or broken bits of ham for this, and reserve the eight best slices.

5 Brush each trout with a little butter, seasoning the outside lightly with salt and pepper. Wrap two ham slices round each one, crossways, tucking the ends into the belly. Grill (broil) the trout for 4 minutes, then carefully turn them over with a metal spatula, rolling them across on the belly so the ham doesn't come loose, and grill for a further 4 minutes.

6 Serve the trout very hot, with any spare butter spooned over the top. Diners should open the trout on their plates, and eat them from the inside, pushing the flesh off the skin.

Roast Cod Wrapped in Prosciutto

Wrapping chunky fillets of cod in wafer-thin slices of prosciutto keeps the fish succulent and moist, at the same time adding flavour and visual impact. Serve with baby new potatoes and a herb salad for a stylish supper or lunch dish.

Serves 4
2 thick skinless cod fillets, each weighing about 375g/13oz
75g/3oz prosciutto, thinly sliced
400g/14oz tomatoes, on the vine

From the storecupboard
75ml/5 tbsp extra virgin olive oil
salt and ground black pepper

1 Preheat the oven to 220°C/425°F/Gas 7. Wash the fish, pat dry on kitchen paper and remove any stray bones. Season with salt and pepper.

2 Place one fillet in an ovenproof dish and drizzle 15ml/1 tbsp of the oil over it. Cover with the second fillet, laying the thick end on top of the thin end of the lower fillet to create an even shape. Lay the ham over the fish, overlapping the slices to cover the fish in an even layer. Tuck the ends of the ham under the fish and tie it in place at intervals with fine string.

3 Using kitchen scissors, snip the vines into four portions and add to the dish. Drizzle the tomatoes and ham with the remaining oil and season lightly.

4 Roast for 35 minutes, until the tomatoes are lightly coloured and the fish is cooked through. Test the fish by piercing one end of the parcel with the tip of a knife to check that it flakes easily.

5 Slice the fish and transfer the portions to warm plates, adding the tomatoes. Spoon over the cooking juices from the dish and serve immediately.

Variation
Other firm-fleshed fish from the cod family, such as haddock or hake, can be used just as well for this recipe with equally sumptuous results.

Trout: Energy 369kcal/1546kJ; Protein 48g; Carbohydrate 0.6g, of which sugars 0.6g; Fat 19.4g, of which saturates 8.8g; Cholesterol 216mg; Calcium 66mg; Fibre 0g; Sodium 821mg.
Cod in Prosciutto: Energy 281kcal/1172kJ; Protein 32.8g; Carbohydrate 3.1g, of which sugars 3.1g; Fat 15.3g, of which saturates 2.3g; Cholesterol 81mg; Calcium 23mg; Fibre 1g; Sodium 116mg.

Tonno con Piselli

This Jewish Italian dish of fresh tuna and peas is especially enjoyed at Passover, which falls in spring. Before the days of the freezer, little peas were only eaten at this time of year when they were in season. At other times of the year chickpeas were used instead – they give a heartier result.

Serves 4
350g/12oz tuna steaks
600ml/1 pint/2½ cups fresh tomato sauce
350g/12oz/3 cups fresh shelled or frozen peas
45ml/3 tbsp chopped fresh flat leaf parsley

From the storecupboard
salt and ground black pepper

1 Preheat the oven to 190°C/375°F/Gas 5. Sprinkle the tuna steaks on each side with salt and plenty of ground black pepper and place in a shallow ovenproof dish, in a single layer.

2 Bring the tomato sauce to the boil, then add the fresh shelled or frozen peas and chopped fresh flat leaf parsley. Pour the sauce and peas evenly over the fish steaks in the ovenproof dish and bake in the preheated oven, uncovered, for about 20 minutes, or until the fish is tender. Serve the fish, sauce and peas immediately, straight from the dish.

Cook's Tip
To make a fresh tomato sauce, heat 15ml/1 tbsp olive oil in a pan, add 1 chopped onion and fry for 3–4 minutes until soft. Add 1 chopped garlic clove and cook for about 1 minute more. Pour in 400g/14oz chopped tomatoes and stir in 15ml/1 tbsp tomato purée (paste). Add 30ml/2 tbsp dried oregano and simmer for about 15 minutes, until thickened. Season with salt and pepper.

Variation
Try making this recipe with swordfish steaks instead of tuna.

Filo-wrapped Fish

Select a chunky variety of tomato sauce for this simple but delicious recipe. The choice of fish can be varied according to what is in season and what is freshest on the day of purchase. When working with filo pastry, keep it covered with clear film or a damp dish towel, as it dries out quickly once exposed to air and becomes difficult to handle.

Serves 3–4
450g/1lb salmon or cod steaks or fillets
130g/4½oz filo pastry (6–8 large sheets)
550ml/18fl oz/2½ cups tomato sauce

From the storecupboard
about 30ml/2 tbsp olive oil, for brushing

1 Preheat the oven to 200°C/400°F/Gas 6. Cut the fish into three or four even pieces, depending on how many people you are serving.

2 Take a sheet of filo pastry, brush with a little olive oil and cover with a second sheet of pastry. Place a piece of fish on top of the pastry, towards the bottom edge, then top with one or two spoonfuls of the tomato sauce, spreading it in an even layer.

3 Roll the fish in the pastry, taking care to enclose the filling completely, to make a little parcel. Brush with a little olive oil. Place on a baking sheet and repeat with the remaining fish and pastry. You should have about half the sauce left over, to serve with the fish.

4 Bake for 10–15 minutes, or until golden brown. Meanwhile, reheat the remaining tomato sauce. Serve immediately with the fish parcels.

Cook's Tip
Serve with a peppery rocket (arugula) salad for a heavenly lunch or superior supper.

Tonno con Piselli: Energy 339kcal/1411kJ; Protein 28.1g; Carbohydrate 15.4g, of which sugars 7.2g; Fat 16.7g, of which saturates 3g; Cholesterol 25mg; Calcium 49mg; Fibre 5.5g; Sodium 71mg.
Filo-wrapped Fish: Energy 233kcal/972kJ; Protein 18.4g; Carbohydrate 9.1g, of which sugars 2.2g; Fat 14g, of which saturates 8.2g; Cholesterol 84mg; Calcium 170mg; Fibre 1.7g; Sodium 213mg.

Pan-fried Skate Wings with Capers

This sophisticated way of serving skate, also known as skate with black butter, is perfect for a dinner party. Serve with a light, green salad and some new potatoes for an impressive main course.

Serves 6
6 small skate wings
grated rind and juice of 2 limes
30ml/2 tbsp salted capers, rinsed and drained

From the storecupboard
50g/2oz/¼ cup butter
salt and ground black pepper

1 Heat the butter in a large frying pan and add one of the skate wings. Fry for 4–5 minutes on each side, until golden and cooked through.

2 Using a fish slice or metal spatula, carefully transfer the cooked skate wing to a warmed serving plate and keep warm while you cook each of the remaining skate wings in the same way.

3 Return the pan to the heat and add the lime rind and juice, and the capers. Season with salt and ground black pepper to taste and allow to bubble for 1–2 minutes.

4 When cooked, spoon a little of the juices and the capers over each skate wing and serve immediately.

Cook's Tip
Skate wings are covered with a clear slime, which renews itself even after the fish is dead. To test skate for freshness, gently rub off the slime and ensure that it reappears. Even fresh skate has a faint smell of ammonia, which is perfectly normal. Wash the fish well in cold water prior to cooking in order to eliminate the smell. It will completely disappear during cooking.

Variation
Replace the capers with the same quantity of pitted black olives.

Poached Fish in Spicy Tomato Sauce

A selection of white fish fillets are used in this Middle Eastern dish – cod, haddock, hake or halibut are all good. Serve the fish with flatbreads, such as pitta, and a spicy tomato relish. It is also good with couscous or rice and a green salad with a refreshing lemon juice dressing.

Serves 8
600ml/1 pint/2½ cups fresh tomato sauce
2.5–5ml/½–1 tsp harissa
60ml/4 tbsp chopped fresh coriander (cilantro) leaves
1.5kg/3¼lb mixed white fish fillets, cut into chunks

From the storecupboard
salt and ground black pepper

1 Heat the tomato sauce with the harissa and coriander in a large pan. Add seasoning to taste and bring to the boil.

2 Remove the pan from the heat and add the fish to the hot sauce. Return to the heat and bring the sauce to the boil again.

3 Reduce the heat and simmer very gently for about 5 minutes, or until the fish is tender. (Test with a fork: if the flesh flakes easily, then it is cooked.)

4 Taste the sauce and adjust the seasoning, adding more harissa if necessary. Serve hot or warm.

Cook's Tip
Harissa is a chilli paste spiced with cumin, garlic and coriander. It is fiery and should be used with care at first. Start by adding a small amount and then add more after tasting the sauce.

Variation
Turn this dish into a tagine by frying some diced aubergine (eggplant) and courgette (zucchini), adding them to the tomato sauce and then adding 200ml/7fl oz/scant 1 cup fish stock and simmering for about 20 minutes before adding the fish.

Skate Wings: Energy 300kcal/1256kJ; Protein 26.4g; Carbohydrate 7g, of which sugars 6.7g; Fat 14.3g, of which saturates 8.8g; Cholesterol 36mg; Calcium 114mg; Fibre 1.2g; Sodium 272mg.
Fish in Tomato Sauce: Energy 219kcal/923kJ; Protein 36.2g; Carbohydrate 6.7g, of which sugars 3.2g; Fat 5.5g, of which saturates 1.5g; Cholesterol 94mg; Calcium 46mg; Fibre 1.4g; Sodium 370mg.

Fish with Tomato and Pine Nuts

Whole fish marinated in lemon juice and cooked with pine nuts in a spicy tomato sauce is a speciality of Jewish cooking. You can buy spicy tomato sauce in most supermarkets or make your own. The fish may be cooked and served with head and tail on, as here, or if you prefer, with these removed. A garnish of flat leaf parsley enhances this sumptuous dish.

Serves 6–8

1–1.5kg/2¼–3¼lb fish, such as snapper, cleaned, with head and tail left on
juice of 2 lemons
65g/2½oz/scant ¾ cup pine nuts, toasted
350ml/12fl oz/1½ cups spicy tomato sauce

From the storecupboard
salt and ground black pepper

1 Prick the fish all over with a fork and rub with 2.5ml/½ tsp salt. Put the fish in a roasting pan or large dish and pour over the lemon juice. Leave to stand for 2 hours.

2 Preheat the oven to 180°C/350°F/Gas 4. Sprinkle half of the pine nuts over the base of an ovenproof dish, pour over half of the spicy tomato sauce, then lay the fish on top and pour over its marinading juices. Add the remaining spicy tomato sauce and the remaining pine nuts.

3 Cover the ovenproof dish tightly with a lid or foil and bake in the preheated oven for 30 minutes, or until the fish is tender. Serve the fish immediately, straight from the dish.

Cook's Tip
To make a fresh spicy tomato sauce, heat 15ml/1 tbsp olive oil in a pan, add 1 chopped onion and fry for 3–4 minutes until soft. Add 1 chopped garlic clove and 1 red chilli, deseeded and chopped, and cook for about 1 minute more. Pour in 400g/14oz chopped tomatoes and stir in 15ml/1 tbsp tomato purée (paste). Add 30ml/2 tbsp dried oregano and simmer for about 15 minutes, until thickened. Season with salt and pepper.

Paprika-crusted Monkfish Kebabs

Such a chunky fish as monkfish is just perfect for skewering, as it is not likely to disintegrate before your eyes and fall between the grill bars as you cook. Monkfish can also take some strong flavours, such as this smoky paprika crust with chorizo. A cucumber and mint yogurt sauce is good on the side.

Serves 4

1 monkfish tail, about 1kg/2¼lb, trimmed and filleted
10ml/2 tsp smoked red paprika
2 red (bell) peppers, halved and seeded
16 thin slices of chorizo

From the storecupboard
15ml/1 tbsp extra virgin olive oil
salt and ground black pepper

1 Place both monkfish fillets in a flat dish. Rub them all over with 5ml/1 tsp salt, then cover and leave in a cool place for 20 minutes.

2 Prepare the barbecue. Rinse the salt off the pieces of monkfish and lightly pat them dry with kitchen paper. Mix the smoked red paprika with a pinch of salt and gently rub the mixture evenly over the fish. Slice each pepper into 12 long strips and cut each monkfish fillet into ten equal pieces. Thread six pieces of pepper and five pieces of fish on to each of four long skewers and brush one side with a little extra virgin olive oil.

3 Position a lightly oiled grill rack over the hot coals. Grill the skewered food, oiled side down, over medium-high heat, for about 3½ minutes. Lightly brush the top side with oil, turn over and cook for 3–4 minutes more. Remove the skewers from the heat and keep warm.

4 Grill the chorizo slices for a second or two until just warm. Thread one piece of chorizo on to the end of each skewer and serve the rest alongside on individual plates.

Cook's Tip
If it is easier, fry the chorizo on a hot griddle set on the grill rack for 30 seconds on each side.

Fish with Pine Nuts: Energy 215kcal/903kJ; Protein 25.5g; Carbohydrate 4.1g, of which sugars 2.1g; Fat 11g, of which saturates 1.7g; Cholesterol 48mg; Calcium 60mg; Fibre 0.8g; Sodium 260mg.
Monkfish Kebabs: Energy 375kcal/1572kJ; Protein 51.7g; Carbohydrate 7.1g, of which sugars 6.8g; Fat 15.9g, of which saturates 5.6g; Cholesterol 57mg; Calcium 115mg; Fibre 2.1g; Sodium 445mg.

Beef Patties with Onions and Peppers

This is a firm family favourite. It is easy to make and delicious, and it can be varied by adding other vegetables, such as sliced red peppers, broccoli or mushrooms. These patties are very versatile and can be served in a variety of ways – with chunky home-made French fries, with crusty bread, or with rice and a ready-made tomato sauce.

Serves 4
500g/1¼lb lean minced (ground) beef
4 onions, 1 finely chopped and 3 sliced
2–3 green (bell) peppers, seeded and sliced lengthways into strips

From the storecupboard
30ml/2 tbsp garlic-flavoured olive oil or olive oil
salt and ground black pepper

1 Place the minced beef, chopped onion and 15ml/1 tbsp garlic-flavoured oil in a bowl and mix well. Season well and form into four large or eight small patties.

2 Heat the remaining oil in a large non-stick pan, then add the patties and cook on both sides until browned. Sprinkle over 15ml/1 tbsp water and add a little seasoning.

3 Cover the patties with the sliced onions and peppers. Sprinkle in another 15ml/1 tbsp water and a little seasoning, then cover the pan. Reduce the heat to very low and braise for 20–30 minutes.

4 When the onions are turning golden brown, remove the pan from the heat. Serve with onions and peppers.

Cook's Tips
- *These satisfying patties are just as tasty made with minced (ground) lamb or pork. Try the lamb patties covered with red (bell) peppers and the pork patties with broccoli or greens.*
- *You can freeze these patties before cooking in an airtight container for 3–4 months. Place baking parchment between each one so that they can be easily separated.*

Steak with Warm Tomato Salsa

A refreshing, tangy salsa of tomatoes, spring onions and balsamic vinegar makes a colourful topping for chunky, pan-fried steaks. Choose rump, sirloin or fillet – whichever is your favourite – and if you do not have a non-stick pan, grill the steak instead for the same length of time. Serve with potato wedges and a mixed leaf salad with a mustard dressing.

Serves 2
2 steaks, about 2cm/¾in thick
4 large plum tomatoes
2 spring onions (scallions)
30ml/2 tbsp balsamic vinegar

From the storecupboard
salt and ground black pepper

1 Trim any excess fat from the steaks, then season on both sides with salt and pepper. Heat a non-stick frying pan and cook the steaks for about 3 minutes on each side for medium rare. Cook for a little longer if you like your steak well cooked.

2 Meanwhile, put the tomatoes in a heatproof bowl, cover with boiling water and leave for 1–2 minutes, until the skins start to split and loosen. Drain and peel the tomatoes, then halve them and scoop out the seeds. Dice the tomato flesh. Thinly slice the spring onions.

3 Transfer the steaks to plates and keep warm. Add the vegetables, balsamic vinegar, 30ml/2 tbsp water and a little seasoning to the cooking juices in the pan and stir briefly until warm, scraping up any meat residue. Spoon the salsa over the steaks to serve.

Cook's Tip
The cooking time depends on which cut of meat you choose and the thickness of the steaks. Press down with your finger to test how well done the steaks are. Rare meat will be soft, medium will be springy and well-done meat will be firm.

Beef Patties: Energy 431kcal/1789kJ; Protein 27.9g; Carbohydrate 21.1g, of which sugars 17.2g; Fat 26.6g, of which saturates 9.6g; Cholesterol 75mg; Calcium 60mg; Fibre 4.4g; Sodium 110mg.
Steak with Salsa: Energy 291kcal/1215kJ; Protein 35.3g; Carbohydrate 5g, of which sugars 5g; Fat 14.5g, of which saturates 5.9g; Cholesterol 87mg; Calcium 22mg; Fibre 1.7g; Sodium 110mg.

Pan-fried Gaelic Steaks

A good steak is always popular and top quality raw materials plus timing are the keys to success. Choose small, thick steaks rather than large, thin ones if you can. Traditional accompaniments include French fries, fried onions, mushrooms and peas.

Serves 4

4 x 225–350g/8–12oz sirloin steaks, at room temperature
50ml/2fl oz/¼ cup Irish whiskey
300ml/½ pint/1¼ cups double (heavy) cream

From the storecupboard

15g/½oz/1 tbsp butter
5ml/1 tsp oil
salt and ground black pepper

1 Season the steaks with pepper. Heat a heavy pan, over high heat. When it is hot, add the oil and butter. Add the steaks one at a time, to seal the meat quickly. Lower the heat to moderate. Allowing 3–4 minutes for rare, 4–5 minutes for medium or 5–6 minutes for well-done steaks, leave undisturbed for half of the specified cooking time; thick steaks will take longer than thin ones. Turn only once.

2 When the steaks are cooked to your liking, transfer them to warmed plates to keep warm. Pour off the fat from the pan and discard. Add the whiskey and stir to remove the sediment at the base of the pan. Allow the liquid to reduce a little, then add the cream and simmer over low heat for a few minutes, until the cream thickens. Season to taste, pour the sauce around or over the steaks, as preferred, and serve immediately.

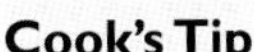

Cook's Tip

Trim the fat from around each steak to 5mm/¼in before cooking. Although a little fat gives a good flavour, the cooking time required for steak is not long enough to cook the fat. Then, using kitchen scissors, snip into the fat at 2.5cm/1in intervals to prevent the steak curling up during cooking. Pound the meat with a meat mallet (a heavy pan or rolling pin will do if you don't have one). This is important to break down the tissues, resulting in a more tender steak, especially if it is thick.

Beef Cooked in Red Wine

Shin of beef is traditionally quite a tough cut that needs long, slow cooking. Marinating the beef in red wine before cooking gives a tender result. When cooked, sprinkle the stew with rosemary and serve with mashed potatoes.

Serves 4–6

675g/1½lb boned and cubed shin of beef
3 large garlic cloves, finely chopped
1 bottle fruity red wine

From the storecupboard

salt and ground black pepper

1 Put the beef in a casserole dish with the garlic and some black pepper, and pour over the red wine. Stir to combine, then cover and chill for at least 12 hours.

2 Preheat the oven to 160°C/325°F/Gas 3. Cover the casserole with a tight-fitting lid and transfer to the oven. Cook for 2 hours, or until the beef is very tender. Season with salt and pepper to taste, and serve piping hot with creamy mashed potatoes and a deep green vegetable.

Cook's Tip

To make perfect creamy mashed potatoes, peel 675g/1½lb floury potatoes and cut into large chunks. Bring to the boil in a pan of salted water, then reduce the heat and simmer for 15–20 minutes, or until completely tender. Drain and return to the pan. Leave over a low heat for a couple of minutes, shaking the pan to get rid of excess moisture. Take the pan off the heat and, using a potato masher, mash the potatoes until smooth. Beat in 45–60ml/3–4 tbsp warm milk and a large knob (pat) of butter, then season with salt and ground pepper.

Variation

Beef also has an affinity with beer. Try replacing the wine in this recipe with 120ml/4fl oz/½ cup brown ale or stout and add 30ml/2 tbsp Worcestershire sauce before marinading.

Gaelic Steaks: Energy 738kcal/3062kJ; Protein 54.1g; Carbohydrate 1.3g, of which sugars 1.3g; Fat 54.2g, of which saturates 31.6g; Cholesterol 226mg; Calcium 49mg; Fibre 0g; Sodium 197mg.
Beef in Red Wine: Energy 287kcal/1196kJ; Protein 26.1g; Carbohydrate 1.1g, of which sugars 0.3g; Fat 10.5g, of which saturates 4.3g; Cholesterol 65mg; Calcium 15mg; Fibre 0.2g; Sodium 81mg.

Thai-style Rare Beef and Mango Salad

This simplified version of Thai beef salad is especially tasty served with little bowls of fresh coriander leaves, chopped spring onions and peanuts for sprinkling at the table.

Serves 4
450g/1lb sirloin steak
45ml/3 tbsp soy sauce
2 mangoes, peeled, stoned (pitted) and finely sliced

From the storecupboard
45ml/3 tbsp garlic-infused olive oil
ground black pepper

1 Put the steak in a shallow, non-metallic dish and pour over the oil and soy sauce. Season with pepper and turn the steaks to coat in the marinade. Cover and chill for 2 hours.

2 Heat a griddle pan until hot. Remove the steak from the marinade and place on the griddle pan. Cook for 3–5 minutes on each side, turning the steak 180 degrees halfway through if you want a criss-cross pattern.

3 Transfer the steak to a board and leave to rest for 5–10 minutes. Meanwhile, pour the marinade into the pan and cook for a few seconds, then remove from the heat. Thinly slice the steak and arrange on four serving plates with the mangoes. Drizzle over the pan juices to serve.

Cook's Tip
Serve with some sticky rice and a crunchy beansprout and mixed (bell) pepper salad, tossed in a lemon or lime dressing to awaken the tastebuds.

Variations
- *Why not set this dish alight with some fiery red or green chillies, deseeded and chopped.*
- *For an authentic Thai flavour, you could replace half the soy sauce with Thai fish sauce.*

Veal Chops with Basil Butter

Succulent veal chops from the loin are an expensive cut and are best cooked quickly and simply. The flavour of basil goes particularly well with veal, but other herbs can be used instead if you prefer. Serve with griddled vegetables, such as peppers and courgettes, or a salad.

Serves 2
15ml/1 tbsp Dijon mustard
15ml/1 tbsp chopped fresh basil
2 veal loin chops, 2.5cm/1in thick, about 225g/8oz each
fresh basil sprigs, to garnish

From the storecupboard
25g/1oz/2 tbsp butter, softened
olive oil, for brushing
salt and ground black pepper

1 To make the basil butter, cream the softened butter with the Dijon mustard and chopped fresh basil in a large mixing bowl, then season with plenty of ground black pepper.

2 Prepare the barbecue. Position a lightly oiled grill rack over the hot coals.

3 Brush both sides of each chop with olive oil and season with a little salt. Cook the chops over high heat for 7–10 minutes, basting with oil and turning once, until done to your liking.

4 Top each chop with basil butter and serve immediately, garnished with fresh basil.

Cook's Tip
Chilled herb butters make perfect impromptu sauces for cooked meats and fish. Basil butter is a firm favourite, but other fresh herbs such as chives, tarragon and parsley also work well.

Variation
If your budget doesn't stretch to veal, which can be expensive, you can make this dish with pork loin chops, or lamb chump chops, with equally flavoursome results.

Thai-style Beef: Energy 286kcal/1200kJ; Protein 27.4g; Carbohydrate 14.7g, of which sugars 14.4g; Fat 13.5g, of which saturates 3.5g; Cholesterol 57mg; Calcium 19mg; Fibre 2.6g; Sodium 615mg.
Veal Chops: Energy 718kcal/3017kJ; Protein 113.8g; Carbohydrate 0.3g, of which sugars 0.0g; Fat 29.13g, of which saturates 16.0g; Cholesterol 3135mg; Calcium 35mg; Fibre 0.3g; Sodium 448mg.

Irish Stew

Ireland's national dish was traditionally made with mature mutton, but lamb is now usual. There are long-standing arguments about the correct ingredients for an authentic Irish stew apart from the meat, and whether or not carrots are permitted. This is a modern variation using lamb chops.

Serves 4

1.3kg/3lb best end of neck (US shoulder or breast) of mutton or lamb chops
900g/2lb potatoes
small bunch each of parsley and thyme, chopped
450g/1lb onions, sliced

From the storecupboard

salt and ground black pepper

1 Trim all the fat, bone and gristle from the meat, and cut it into fairly large pieces. (See Variations if using chops.) Slice one-third of the potatoes and cut the rest into large chunks.

2 Arrange the potatoes in a casserole, add a sprinkling of herbs, then half the meat and finally half the onion, seasoning each layer. Repeat the layers, finishing with the potatoes.

3 Pour over 450ml/¾ pint/scant 2 cups water, and cover tightly; add a sheet of foil before putting on the lid if it is not a very close-fitting one. Simmer the stew very gently for about 2 hours, or cook in the oven at 120°C/250°F/Gas ½, if you prefer. Shake the casserole from time to time to prevent sticking.

4 Check the liquid level occasionally during the cooking time and add extra water if necessary; there should be enough cooking liquor to have made a gravy, thickened by the sliced potatoes.

Variations

- *Trimmed lamb or mutton chops can be arranged around the edge of the pan, with sliced onions and chopped potatoes, herbs and seasonings in the middle. Add the water and cook as above.*
- *Hogget – lamb over a year old – is available in the spring and early summer.*

Rosemary-scented Lamb

The bonus with this recipe is that all the work is done the night before. Ask your butcher to French trim the lamb racks to speed up the preparation time. Allow plenty of time for marinating, although the cooking time is quick, whether barbecueing or grilling.

Serves 4–8

2 x 8-chop racks of lamb, chined
8 large fresh rosemary sprigs
2 garlic cloves, thinly sliced
30ml/2 tbsp verjuice or red wine

From the storecupboard

90ml/6 tbsp extra virgin olive oil
salt and ground black pepper

1 Cut the chined racks into eight portions, each consisting of two linked chops, and tie a rosemary sprig to each one.

2 Lay the portions in a single layer in a bowl or wide dish. Mix the garlic, oil and verjuice or wine, and pour over the lamb. Cover and chill overnight, turning them as often as possible.

3 Bring the chops to room temperature 1 hour before cooking. Prepare the barbecue. Remove the lamb from the marinade and discard. Season the meat 15 minutes before cooking.

4 Position a lightly oiled grill rack over the hot coals. Stand the lamb chops upright on the rack over medium-high heat, propping them against each other. Cover with a lid or tented heavy-duty foil and grill for 2 minutes.

5 Carefully turn the chops on to one side, and grill for a further 4 minutes each side for rare meat or 5 minutes if you prefer lamb medium cooked.

6 Remove the chops from the grill, transfer to serving plates, cover and rest for 5–10 minutes before serving.

Cook's Tip

Allowing the hot chops to stand before serving will give the juices time to gather on the plate and create a light sauce.

Irish Stew: Energy 869kcal/3627kJ; Protein 69.1g; Carbohydrate 47.6g, of which sugars 7.7g; Fat 45.9g, of which saturates 20.8g; Cholesterol 244mg; Calcium 53mg; Fibre 4.5g; Sodium 218mg.
Rosemary Lamb: Energy 433kcal/1788kJ; Protein 23.4g; Carbohydrate 0g, of which sugars 0g; Fat 37.6g, of which saturates 16.4g; Cholesterol 101mg; Calcium 17mg; Fibre 0g; Sodium 83mg.

North African Lamb

This dish is full of contrasting flavours that create a rich, spicy and fruity main course. For best results, use lamb that still retains some fat, as this will help keep the meat moist and succulent during roasting. Serve the lamb with couscous or mixed white and wild rice, sprinkled with chopped coriander. Roasted chunks of red and yellow peppers, aubergine and courgettes, cooked in the oven with the lamb, complete the meal.

Serves 4

675g/1½lb lamb fillet or shoulder steaks, cut into chunky pieces
5 small onions
7.5ml/1½ tsp harissa
115g/4oz ready-to-eat pitted prunes, halved

1 Preheat the oven to 200°C/400°F/Gas 6. Heat a frying pan, preferably non-stick, and cook the lamb on all sides until beginning to brown. Transfer to a roasting pan, reserving any fat in the frying pan.

2 Peel the onions and cut each into six wedges. Toss with the lamb and roast for about 30–40 minutes, until the lamb is cooked through and the onions are deep golden brown.

3 Transfer the lamb and onions back into the frying pan. Mix the harissa with 250ml/8fl oz/1 cup boiling water and add to the roasting pan. Scrape up any residue in the pan and pour the mixture over the lamb and onions.

4 Stir in the prunes and heat until just simmering. Cover and simmer for 5 minutes, then serve with the accompaniment of your choice.

Cook's Tip

To prepare couscous, simply place in a large bowl, add enough boiling water or stock to just cover, seal with clear film (plastic wrap) and leave for 10 minutes. Fluff up with a fork and season.

Lamb Steaks with Redcurrant Glaze

This classic, simple dish is absolutely delicious and is an excellent, quick recipe for cooking on the barbecue. The tangy flavour of redcurrants, a traditional accompaniment, counters the richness of the lamb. It is good served with new potatoes and fresh garden peas tossed in butter.

Serves 4

4 large fresh rosemary sprigs
4 lamb leg steaks
75ml/5 tbsp redcurrant jelly
30ml/2 tbsp raspberry or red wine vinegar

From the storecupboard

salt and ground black pepper

1 Reserve the tips of the rosemary and chop the remaining leaves. Rub the chopped rosemary, salt and pepper all over the lamb.

2 Preheat the grill (broiler). Heat the redcurrant jelly gently in a small pan with 30ml/2 tbsp water. Stir in the vinegar.

3 Place the steaks on a foil-lined grill rack and brush with a little of the redcurrant glaze. Cook for about 5 minutes on each side, until deep golden, brushing with more glaze.

4 Transfer the lamb to warmed plates. Pour any juices from the foil into the remaining glaze and heat through. Pour the glaze over the lamb and serve, garnished with the reserved rosemary.

Cook's Tips

- *Serve this summery dish with some crushed new potatoes with parsley and lemon. Cook 675g/1½lb new potatoes in boiling salted water for 15–20 minutes, until tender. Drain and crush roughly, using a fork. Stir in 30ml/2 tbsp extra virgin olive oil, the grated rind and juice of 1 lemon and 30ml/2 tbsp chopped fresh flat leaf parsley. Season with ground black pepper to taste.*
- *Alternatively, try roasting new potatoes, cut in half, with some chopped garlic in olive oil.*

African Lamb: Energy 379kcal/1585kJ; Protein 35g; Carbohydrate 17.7g, of which sugars 15.4g; Fat 19.2g, of which saturates 8.8g; Cholesterol 128mg; Calcium 48mg; Fibre 3g; Sodium 151mg.
Lamb Steaks: Energy 362kcal/1518kJ; Protein 34.4g; Carbohydrate 12.9g, of which sugars 12.9g; Fat 19.6g, of which saturates 9.1g; Cholesterol 133mg; Calcium 16mg; Fibre 0g; Sodium 156mg.

Lamb Chops with a Mint Jelly Crust

Mint and lamb are classic partners, and the breadcrumbs used here add extra texture. Serve the chops with sweet potatoes baked in their skins and some steamed green vegetables, such as Kenyan green beans.

Serves 4
8 lamb chops, about 115g/4oz each
50g/2oz/1 cup fresh white breadcrumbs
30ml/2 tbsp mint jelly

From the storecupboard
salt and ground black pepper

1 Preheat the oven to 190°C/375°F/Gas 5. Place the lamb chops on a baking sheet and season with plenty of salt and ground black pepper.

2 Put the breadcrumbs and mint jelly in a bowl and mix together to combine. Spoon the breadcrumb mixture on top of the chops, pressing down firmly with the back of a spoon making sure they stick to the chops. Bake the chops for 20–30 minutes, or until they are just cooked through. Serve immediately.

Cook's Tip
This dish is extra special made with a home-made minted gooseberry jelly. To make, place 1.3kg/3lb/12 cups gooseberries, 1 bunch fresh mint and 750ml/1¼ pints/3 cups of cold water in a preserving pan. Bring to the boil, reduce the heat, cover and simmer for about 30 minutes, until the gooseberries are soft. Add 400ml/14fl oz/1⅔ cups white wine vinegar and simmer uncovered for 10 minutes. Pour the fruit and juices into a sterilized jelly bag suspended over a large bowl. Leave to drain for at least 3 hours, then measure the strained juices back into the cleaned pan. Add 450g/1lb/2¼ cups granulated (white) sugar for every 600ml/1 pint/2½ cups juice, then heat gently, stirring, until the sugar has dissolved. Bring to the boil and cook for 15 minutes, or to setting point. Remove the pan from heat. Skim, leave to cool, then stir in 45ml/3 tbsp chopped fresh mint. Pour into sterilized jars and seal.

Lamb with Oregano and Basil

Lamb leg steaks are chunky with a sweet flavour, which is complemented perfectly by the oregano and basil. However, you could also use finely chopped rosemary or thyme. Serve with flavoured couscous or flatbreads and spiced chutney.

Serves 4
4 large or 8 small lamb leg steaks
1 small bunch of fresh oregano, roughly chopped
1 small bunch of fresh basil, torn

From the storecupboard
60ml/4 tbsp garlic-infused olive oil
salt and ground black pepper

1 Put the lamb in a shallow, non-metallic dish. Mix 45ml/3 tbsp of the oil with the oregano, basil and some salt and pepper, reserving some of the herbs for garnish. Pour over the lamb and turn to coat in the marinade. Cover and chill for up to 8 hours.

2 Heat the remaining oil in a large frying pan. Remove the lamb from the marinade and fry for 5–6 minutes on each side, until slightly pink in the centre. Add the marinade and cook for 1–2 minutes until warmed through. Garnish with the reserved herbs and serve.

Cook's Tip
Couscous with roasted summer vegetables makes a good accompaniment to this herby lamb dish. Preheat the oven to 200°C/400°F/Gas 6. Arrange a selection of summer vegetables, such as red onion, courgette (zucchini), yellow (bell) pepper, aubergine (eggplant), leek, sweet potato and tomato, cut into similar size chunks in a roasting pan. Add plenty of crushed garlic, ginger and rosemary. Pour over plenty of olive oil, sprinkle with sugar or honey, season and roast for about 1 hour, or until tender and slightly caramelized. Baste with oil occasionally. When nearly cooked, put some couscous in a bowl with enough warm water to cover it and leave to stand for 10 minutes until absorbed. Rub in sunflower oil and break up any lumps, then transfer into an ovenproof dish, dot with butter, cover with foil and heat for about 20 minutes. Spoon vegetables on top and serve.

Lamb Chops: Energy 551kcal/2309kJ; Protein 64.1g; Carbohydrate 11.3g, of which sugars 2g; Fat 27.9g, of which saturates 13.3g; Cholesterol 248mg; Calcium 46mg; Fibre 0.3g; Sodium 316mg.
Lamb with Herbs: Energy 466kcal/1938kJ; Protein 40g; Carbohydrate 0.7g, of which sugars 0.6g; Fat 33.7g, of which saturates 12g; Cholesterol 152mg; Calcium 66mg; Fibre 1.3g; Sodium 180mg.

Roast Shoulder of Lamb with Whole Garlic Cloves

Long slow cooking on a rack gives a succulent result. The potatoes below catch the fat, giving garlicky, juicy results. Return the potatoes to the oven to keep warm while you leave the lamb to rest before carving. Serve with seasonal vegetables.

Serves 4–6

675g/1½lb waxy potatoes, peeled and cut into large dice
12 garlic cloves, unpeeled
1 whole shoulder of lamb

From the storecupboard

45ml/3 tbsp olive oil
salt and ground black pepper

1 Preheat the oven to 180°C/350°F/Gas 4. Put the potatoes and garlic cloves into a large roasting pan and season with salt and pepper. Pour over 30ml/2 tbsp of the oil and toss the potatoes and garlic to coat.

2 Place a rack over the roasting pan, so that it is not touching the potatoes. Place the lamb on the rack and drizzle over the remaining oil. Season with salt and pepper.

3 Roast the lamb and potatoes for 2–2½ hours, or until the lamb is cooked through. Halfway through the cooking time, carefully take the lamb and the rack off the roasting pan and turn the potatoes to ensure even cooking.

Cook's Tips

- *Remove the shoulder of lamb from the refrigerator about an hour before cooking and let it come to room temperature. This will result in a better flavour and make the meat more tender when cooked.*
- *Serve this sumptuous dish with some Kenyan green beans and baby carrots, or alternatively with a leafy green salad to soak up the garlicky juices.*
- *This is quite a rustic way to prepare lamb. However, to make the cooked lamb easier to carve, bone and roll the shoulder, tying the meat in place with string, before cooking.*

Roast Leg of Lamb with Rosemary and Garlic

This is a classic combination of flavours, and always popular. Serve as a traditional Sunday lunch with roast potatoes and vegetables. Leaving the lamb to rest before carving ensures a tender result.

Serves 4–6

1 leg of lamb, about 1.8kg/4lb
2 garlic cloves, finely sliced
leaves from 2 sprigs of fresh rosemary

From the storecupboard

30ml/2 tbsp olive oil
salt and ground black pepper

1 Preheat the oven to 190°C/375°F/Gas 5. Using a small sharp knife, make slits at 4cm/1½in intervals over the lamb, deep enough to hold a piece of garlic. Push the garlic and rosemary leaves into the slits.

2 Drizzle the olive oil over the top of the lamb and season with plenty of salt and ground black pepper. Roast for 25 minutes per 450g/1lb of lamb, plus another 25 minutes.

3 Remove the lamb from the oven and leave to rest for about 15 minutes before carving.

Cook's Tips

- *To carve a leg of lamb, start by cutting a wedge of meat from the top of the leg, towards the thin end, but not right at the end. Slice down through the meat as far as the bone. Carve slices, holding the joint firmly in place, starting from the cut you have made. These are prime slices of meat. Now turn over and cut small slices, across the grain, to remove remaining meat.*
- *Serve this classic roast with gravy. Remove the meat from the pan and spoon off most of the fat. Place over a low heat, add a splash of white or red wine, loosen any sediment from the pan, stir in 30ml/2 tbsp plain (all-purpose) flour and mix to a paste. Gradually pour in 450ml/¾ pint/scant 2 cups stock, stirring continuously. Bring to the boil and simmer until thickened.*

Shoulder of Lamb: Energy 668kcal/2775kJ; Protein 29.2g; Carbohydrate 20.8g, of which sugars 1.7g; Fat 52.6g, of which saturates 24.1g; Cholesterol 113mg; Calcium 22mg; Fibre 1.8g; Sodium 123mg.
Leg of Lamb: Energy 518kcal/2177kJ; Protein 61.3g; Carbohydrate 18.1g, of which sugars 1.5g; Fat 22.8g, of which saturates 8.2g; Cholesterol 200mg; Calcium 21mg; Fibre 1.1g; Sodium 138mg.

Roast Lamb with Figs

Lamb fillet is an expensive cut of meat, but because it is very lean there is little waste. To make a more economical version of this dish, use leg of lamb instead. It has a stronger flavour but is equally good. Serve with steamed green beans.

Serves 6
1kg/2¼lb lamb fillet
9 fresh figs
150ml/¼ pint/⅔ cup ruby port

From the storecupboard
30ml/2 tbsp olive oil
salt and ground black pepper

1 Preheat the oven to 190°/375°F/Gas 5. Heat the oil in a roasting pan over a medium heat. Add the lamb fillet and sear on all sides until evenly browned.

2 Cut the figs in half and arrange around the lamb. Season the lamb with salt and ground black pepper and roast for 30 minutes. Pour the port over the figs.

3 Return the lamb to the oven and roast for a further 30–45 minutes. The meat should still be slightly pink in the middle so be careful not to overcook.

4 Transfer the lamb to a board and leave to rest for about 5 minutes. Carve into slices and serve.

Sweet-and-sour Lamb

Buy lamb loin chops from your butcher and ask him to French trim them for you to save on preparation time. Serve with steamed carrots or green beans.

Serves 4
8 French-trimmed lamb loin chops
90ml/6 tbsp balsamic vinegar
30ml/2 tbsp caster (superfine) sugar

From the storecupboard
30ml/2 tbsp olive oil
salt and ground black pepper

1 Put the lamb chops in a shallow, non-metallic dish and drizzle over the balsamic vinegar. Sprinkle with the sugar and season with salt and black pepper. Turn the chops to coat in the mixture, then cover with clear film (plastic wrap) and chill for 20 minutes.

2 Heat the olive oil in a large frying pan and add the chops, reserving the marinade. Cook for 3–4 minutes on each side.

3 Pour the marinade into the pan and leave to bubble for about 2 minutes, or until reduced slightly. Remove from the pan and serve immediately.

Variation
You could make this marinated lamb dish equally well with red wine vinegar, or for a fruity flavour, a raspberry wine vinegar would fit the bill.

Roast Loin of Boar with Poitín-soaked Prunes

Farmed 'wild' boar is produced in Northern Ireland and is popular in restaurants throughout the country. Whiskey can replace the poitín. Suggested accompaniments include black pudding mash and cooked cabbage with some apple sauce.

Serves 4–6
8 pitted prunes
1 glass poitín or Irish whiskey
675g/1½lb boned loin of boar, any excess fat removed

From the storecupboard
salt and ground black pepper

1 Soak the prunes overnight in enough poitín or whiskey to cover.

2 Use a skewer to make a circular incision along the loin of boar and stuff with the prunes. Place a large square of foil on a flat surface. On top of the foil place a large square of clear film (plastic wrap). Place the loin on one end of the clear film and roll up tightly. Refrigerate for 2 hours.

3 Preheat the oven to 200°C/400°F/Gas 6. Remove the foil and clear film and cut the loin into tournedos (steaks). Preheat a heavy pan and sear the meat on both sides until brown. Season. Transfer to a roasting pan and cook in the oven for 7–10 minutes. Leave to rest before serving on heated plates.

Cook's Tips
- *To prepare the mash, add 225g/8oz cooked black pudding (blood sausage) to 1kg/2¼lb cooked mashed potatoes. Mash well with butter to taste. Stir in 15ml/1 tbsp mustard and season.*
- *To make an apple sauce, peel, core and slice 450g/1lb cooking apples and place in a pan. Add a splash of water, 15ml/1 tbsp caster (superfine) sugar and a few whole cloves. Cook gently over a low heat, stirring occasionally, until the fruit becomes pulpy.*

Lamb with Figs: Energy 527kcal/2213kJ; Protein 35.2g; Carbohydrate 39.5g, of which sugars 39.5g; Fat 23.5g, of which saturates 9.2g; Cholesterol 127mg; Calcium 187mg; Fibre 5.2g; Sodium 187mg.
Sweet-and-sour Lamb: Energy 258kcal/1077kJ; Protein 19.6g; Carbohydrate 7.9g, of which sugars 7.9g; Fat 16.7g, of which saturates 6g; Cholesterol 76mg; Calcium 12mg; Fibre 0g; Sodium 87mg.
Boar with Prunes: Energy 290kcal/1214kJ; Protein 36.6g; Carbohydrate 6.8g, of which sugars 6.8g; Fat 6.8g, of which saturates 2.4g; Cholesterol 106mg; Calcium 19mg; Fibre 1.2g; Sodium 120mg.

Basil and Pecorino Stuffed Pork

This Italian-inspired dish is very easy to make and looks extremely impressive. A great dish for entertaining, serve the pork, sliced, on a platter with sauteéd potatoes and seasonal vegetables, or with a chickpea and onion salad for a lighter dish.

Serves 6–8

2 pork fillet (tenderloins), each about 350g/12oz
40g/1½oz/1½ cups fresh basil leaves, chopped
50g/2oz Pecorino cheese, grated
2.5ml/½ tsp chilli flakes

From the storecupboard

45ml/3 tbsp olive oil
salt and ground black pepper

1 Make a 1cm/½in slit down the length of one of the pork fillets. Continue to slice, cutting along the fold of the meat, until you can open it out flat.

2 Lay the fillet between two sheets of baking parchment and pound with a rolling pin to an even thickness of about 1cm/½in. Lift off the top sheet and brush the meat with a little oil.

3 Press half the basil leaves on to the surface, then sprinkle over half the Pecorino cheese and chilli flakes. Add a little pepper.

4 Roll up lengthways to form a sausage shape and tie with kitchen string (twine). Repeat with the second fillet. Season both with salt.

5 Heat the remaining oil in a large frying pan and brown the fillets for 5 minutes, turning to sear on all sides. Transfer them to a roasting pan and cook in the oven for about 20 minutes, or until the pork is cooked through. Leave to stand for 10 minutes before slicing into rounds and serving.

Variation

The pork can be barbecued: first sear on all sides over hot coals, then cook over gentler heat until done, covering with a foil tent or lid, and moving the pork often to avoid burning.

Paprika Pork

This chunky, goulash-style dish is rich with peppers and paprika. Grilling the peppers before adding them to the meat really brings out their sweet, vibrant flavour. Rice or buttered boiled potatoes go particularly well with the rich pork.

Serves 4

2 red, 1 yellow and 1 green (bell) pepper, seeded
500g/1¼lb lean pork fillet (tenderloin)
45ml/3 tbsp paprika
300g/11oz jar or tub of tomato sauce with herbs or garlic

From the storecupboard

salt and ground black pepper

1 Preheat the grill (broiler). Cut the peppers into thick strips and sprinkle in a single layer on a foil-lined grill rack. Cook under the grill for 20–25 minutes, until the edges of the strips are lightly charred.

2 Meanwhile, cut the pork into chunks using a sharp knife. Season and cook in a frying pan for about 5 minutes, until beginning to brown.

3 Transfer the meat to a heavy pan and add the paprika, tomato sauce, 300ml/½ pint/1¼ cups water and a little seasoning. Bring to the boil, reduce the heat, cover and simmer gently for 30 minutes.

4 Add the grilled (broiled) peppers and cook for a further 10–15 minutes, until the meat is tender. Taste for seasoning and serve immediately.

Cook's Tip

To make a tomato sauce, heat 15ml/1 tbsp olive oil in a pan, add 1 chopped onion and fry for 3–4 minutes until soft. Add 1 chopped garlic clove and cook for about 1 minute more. Pour in 400g/14oz chopped tomatoes and stir in 15ml/1 tbsp tomato purée (paste). Add 30ml/2 tbsp dried oregano and simmer for about 15 minutes, until thickened. Season with salt and pepper.

Basil Stuffed Pork: Energy 174kcal/725kJ; Protein 21.3g; Carbohydrate 0.1g, of which sugars 0.1g; Fat 9.7g, of which saturates 3.1g; Cholesterol 61mg; Calcium 91mg; Fibre 0.3g; Sodium 131mg.
Paprika Pork: Energy 533kcal/2248kJ; Protein 50.1g; Carbohydrate 60.2g, of which sugars 17.8g; Fat 11.9g, of which saturates 3.3g; Cholesterol 110mg; Calcium 127mg; Fibre 10.7g; Sodium 659mg.

Pork Kebabs

The word kebab comes from Arabic and means on a skewer. Use pork fillet for these kebabs because it is lean and tender, and cooks very quickly. They are good served with rice, or stuffed into warmed pitta bread with some shredded lettuce leaves.

Serves 4

500g/1¼lb lean pork fillet (tenderloin)
8 large, thick spring onions (scallions), trimmed
120ml/4fl oz/½ cup barbecue sauce
1 lemon

1 Cut the pork into 2.5cm/1in cubes. Cut the spring onions into 2.5cm/1in long sticks.

2 Preheat the grill (broiler) to high. Oil the wire rack and spread out the pork cubes on it. Grill (broil) the pork until the juices drip, then dip the pieces in the barbecue sauce and put back on the grill.

3 Grill for 30 seconds on each side, repeating the dipping process twice more. Set aside and keep warm.

4 Gently grill the spring onions until soft and slightly brown outside. Do not dip in the barbecue sauce. Thread about four pieces of pork and three spring onion pieces on to each of eight bamboo skewers.

5 Arrange the pork and spring onion kebabs on a platter. Cut the lemon into wedges and squeeze a little lemon juice over each skewer. Serve immediately, offering the remaining lemon wedges separately.

Cook's Tip

If you are cooking the pork on a barbecue, soak wooden skewers overnight in water. This prevents them burning. Keep the skewer handles away from the fire and turn them frequently.

Pork with Juniper Berries and Bay

Juniper berries have a strong, pungent taste and are a great flavouring for rich, fatty meats such as pork, while bay leaves add a lovely aroma. Serve for Sunday lunch with roast potatoes and lightly cooked leafy green vegetables.

Serves 4–6

1kg/2¼lb boned leg of pork
5 fresh bay leaves
6 juniper berries

From the storecupboard

15ml/1 tbsp olive oil
salt and ground black pepper

1 Preheat the oven to 180°C/350°F/Gas 4. Open out the pork and season with plenty of salt and black pepper.

2 Lay the bay leaves on the pork and sprinkle over the juniper berries. Carefully roll up the pork to enclose the bay leaves and juniper berries and tie securely with fine string at several intervals along its length.

3 Rub the skin with the oil and then rub in plenty of salt. Roast the pork for 20 minutes per 450g/1lb, plus an extra 20 minutes.

4 Remove the pork from the oven and leave to rest for about 10 minutes before carving, then serve immediately.

Variations

- *Rather than cooking this dish as a joint, you could use pork leg steaks or escalopes (weighing about 200g/7oz each). Use one per person. Place the pork between two sheets of baking parchment or clear film (plastic wrap) and flatten with a meat mallet or rolling pin to 15 x 10cm/6 x 4in. Season, then add the filling, roll and tie with string.*
- *There are endless possibilities for fillings with which to stuff pork. A classic option is apple stuffing. To make, melt 25g/1oz/2 tbsp butter in the pan and gently fry 1 small chopped onion, add 50g/2oz/scant ½ cup breadcrumbs, 2 peeled and chopped apples, 50g/2oz/scant ½ cup raisins, finely grated rind 1 orange and a pinch of ground cloves, then season and stir thoroughly.*

Pork Kebabs: Energy 192kcal/806kJ; Protein 27.6g; Carbohydrate 9.2g, of which sugars 8.8g; Fat 5.1g, of which saturates 1.8g; Cholesterol 79mg; Calcium 21mg; Fibre 0.6g; Sodium 578mg.
Pork with Juniper: Energy 220kcal/921kJ; Protein 35.7g; Carbohydrate 0g, of which sugars 0g; Fat 8.5g, of which saturates 2.6g; Cholesterol 105mg; Calcium 12mg; Fibre 0g; Sodium 117mg.

Pan-fried Gammon with Cider

Gammon and cider are a delicious combination with the sweet, tangy flavour of cider complementing the gammon perfectly. Serve this dish with fluffy mustard mashed potatoes.

Serves 4
4 gammon steaks (smoked or cured ham), 225g/8oz each
150ml/¼ pint/⅔ cup dry (hard) cider
45ml/3 tbsp double (heavy) cream

From the storecupboard
30ml/2 tbsp sunflower oil
salt and ground black pepper

1 Heat the oil in a large frying pan until hot. Neatly snip the rind on the gammon steaks to stop them curling up and add them to the pan.

2 Cook the steaks for 3–4 minutes on each side, then pour in the cider. Allow to boil for a couple of minutes, then stir in the cream and cook for 1–2 minutes, or until thickened. Season with salt and pepper, and serve immediately.

Cook's Tip
To make mustard mashed potatoes, peel 675g/1½lb floury potatoes and cut into large chunks. Bring to the boil in a pan of salted water, then reduce the heat and simmer for 15–20 minutes, or until completely tender. Drain and return to the pan. Leave over a low heat for a couple of minutes, shaking the pan to get rid of excess moisture. Take the pan off the heat and, using a potato masher, mash the potatoes until smooth. Beat in 45–60ml/3–4 tbsp warm milk, 15–30ml/1–2 tbsp wholegrain mustard and a large knob (pat) of butter, then season with salt and ground pepper.

Variation
Add sliced dessert apple to the pan with the gammon.

Sticky Glazed Pork Ribs

These spare ribs have a lovely sweet-and-sour flavour and are always as popular with children as they are with adults, making them the perfect choice for a family meal. They're also great for cooking over a barbecue: make sure you leave them to marinate for at least 30 minutes before cooking. To enjoy sticky ribs at their best, you need to get stuck in and eat them with your fingers, so make sure you serve them with plenty of paper napkins.

Serves 4
900g/2lb pork spare ribs
75ml/5 tbsp clear honey
75ml/5 tbsp light soy sauce

From the storecupboard
salt and ground black pepper

1 Preheat the oven to 190°C/375°F/Gas 5. Put the spare ribs in a roasting pan and season well with plenty of salt and ground black pepper.

2 In a small bowl, mix together the honey and soy sauce and pour over the ribs. Turn the ribs several times, spooning over the mixture until thoroughly coated.

3 Bake the spare ribs for 30 minutes, then increase the oven temperature to 220°C/425°F/Gas 7 and cook for a further 10 minutes, or until the honey and soy sauce marinade turns into a thick, sticky glaze.

Fragrant Lemon Grass and Ginger Pork Patties

Lemon grass lends a fragrant citrus flavour to pork, enhanced by the fresh zing of ginger. Serve the patties in burger buns with thick slices of juicy tomato, crisp, refreshing lettuce and a splash of chilli sauce.

Serves 4
450g/1lb/2 cups minced (ground) pork
15ml/1 tbsp fresh root ginger, grated
1 lemon grass stalk

From the storecupboard
30ml/2 tbsp sunflower oil
salt and ground black pepper

1 Put the pork in a bowl and stir in the ginger. Season with salt and pepper.

2 Remove the tough outer layers from the lemon grass stalk and discard. Chop the centre part as finely as possible and mix into the pork. Shape into four patties and chill for about 20 minutes.

3 Heat the oil in a large, non-stick frying pan and add the patties. Fry for 3–4 minutes on each side over a gentle heat, until cooked through.

4 Remove from the pan with a metal spatula and drain on kitchen paper, then serve in burger buns.

Gammon with Cider: Energy 429kcal/1784kJ; Protein 39.6g; Carbohydrate 1.2g, of which sugars 1.2g; Fat 28.4g, of which saturates 10.1g; Cholesterol 67mg; Calcium 24mg; Fibre 0g; Sodium 1985mg.
Glazed Pork Ribs: Energy 358kcal/1509kJ; Protein 48.5g; Carbohydrate 21.8g, of which sugars 16.4g; Fat 9.1g, of which saturates 3.2g; Cholesterol 142mg; Calcium 25mg; Fibre 0.2g; Sodium 436mg.
Pork Patties: Energy 234kcal/974kJ; Protein 21.6g; Carbohydrate 0g, of which sugars 0g; Fat 16.4g, of which saturates 4.7g; Cholesterol 74mg; Calcium 8mg; Fibre 0g; Sodium 74mg.

Chinese Spiced Pork Chops

Five-spice powder is a fantastic ingredient for perking up dishes and adding a good depth of flavour. The five different spices – Sichuan pepper, cinnamon, cloves, fennel seeds and star anise – are perfectly balanced, with the aniseed flavour of star anise predominating. Serve the chops with lightly steamed pak choi and plain boiled rice.

Serves 4
4 large pork chops, about 200g/7oz each
15ml/1 tbsp Chinese five-spice powder
30ml/2 tbsp soy sauce

From the storecupboard
30ml/2 tbsp garlic-infused olive oil

1 Arrange the pork chops in a single layer in a non-metallic roasting pan or baking dish.

2 Sprinkle the five-spice powder over the chops, then drizzle over the soy sauce and garlic-infused oil. (Alternatively, mix together the garlic-infused olive oil, soy sauce and five-spice powder, and pour over the chops.)

3 Using your hands, rub the mixture into the meat. Cover the dish with clear film (plastic wrap) and chill for 2 hours.

4 Preheat the oven to 160°C/325°F/Gas 3. Uncover the dish and bake for 30–40 minutes, or until the pork is cooked through and tender. Serve immediately.

Variation
For an equally fragrant and flavoursome alternative, try a Cajun spice rub, popular in the Caribbean. Either buy a ready-made spice mix (available in most supermarkets), or mix together 5ml/1 tsp each dried thyme, oregano, finely crushed cumin seeds and hot paprika. Rub into the chops, then drizzle with olive oil.

Caramelized Onion and Sausage Tarte Tatin

Toulouse sausages have a garlicky flavour and meaty texture that is delicious with fried onions. Serve with a green salad of bitter leaves with mustard dressing.

Serves 4
450g/1lb Toulouse sausages
2 large onions, sliced
250g/9oz ready-made puff pastry, thawed if frozen

From the storecupboard
45ml/3 tbsp sunflower oil
salt and ground black pepper

1 Heat the oil in a 23cm/9in non-stick frying pan with an ovenproof handle, and add the sausages. Cook over a gentle heat, turning occasionally, for 7–10 minutes, or until golden and cooked through. Remove from the pan and set aside.

2 Preheat the oven to 190°C/375°F/Gas 5. Pour the remaining oil into the frying pan and add the onions. Season with salt and pepper and cook over a gentle heat for 10 minutes, stirring occasionally, until caramelized and tender.

3 Slice each sausage into four or five chunks and stir into the onions. Remove from the heat and set aside.

4 Roll out the puff pastry and cut out a circle slightly larger than the frying pan. Lay the pastry over the sausages and onions, tucking the edges in all the way around. Bake for 20 minutes, or until the pastry is risen and golden. Turn out on to a board, pastry side down, cut into wedges and serve.

Variation
You can make this recipe with any type of fresh sausage. Try Lincolnshire sausage, a British pork sausage flavoured with sage and thyme; Merguez sausage, a spicy Algerian sausage made of beef and mutton, flavoured with red (bell) pepper; or salchichas, a small Spanish sausage made with pork.

Chinese Chops: Energy 722kcal/2986kJ; Protein 32.6g; Carbohydrate 1.9g, of which sugars 0.6g; Fat 65g, of which saturates 22.5g; Cholesterol 144mg; Calcium 24mg; Fibre 0g; Sodium 647mg.
Tarte Tatin: Energy 765kcal/3176kJ; Protein 17g; Carbohydrate 43.7g, of which sugars 9.4g; Fat 59.9g, of which saturates 14.7g; Cholesterol 53mg; Calcium 114mg; Fibre 2.3g; Sodium 1053mg.

Mustard Baked Chicken

In this authentic Irish recipe, a mild, aromatic wholegrain mustard makes a tasty way of cooking chicken. Speciality mustards are now widely available in large supermarkets and delicatessens. Serve with new potatoes and peas or mangetouts.

Serves 4–6

8–12 chicken joints, or 1 medium chicken, about 1kg/2¼lb, jointed
juice of ½ lemon
15–30ml/2–3 tbsp whiskey (or wholegrain) mustard
10ml/2 tsp chopped fresh tarragon

From the storecupboard
sea salt and ground black pepper

1 Preheat the oven to 190°C/375°F/Gas 5. Put the chicken joints into a large shallow baking dish in a single layer and sprinkle the lemon juice over the chicken to flavour the skin. Season well with sea salt and black pepper.

2 Spread the mustard over the joints and sprinkle with the chopped tarragon. Bake in the preheated oven for 20–30 minutes, or until thoroughly cooked, depending on the size of the chicken pieces. Serve immediately.

Cook's Tip
With the right equipment it is quite straightforward to joint a chicken yourself. You need a large sharp knife and poultry shears. For eight pieces, remove the legs with a sharp knife and cut along the breast bone using poultry shears. Turn over and cut out the backbone. Cut each breast in half, leaving one portion attached to the wing. Cut off the wing tip at the first joint. Separate the legs into thighs and drumsticks.

Variation
A whole chicken can also be baked this way. Allow about 1½ hours in an oven preset to 180°C/350°F/Gas 4. When cooked, the juices will run clear without any trace of blood.

Tandoori Chicken

If you have time, prepare this dish when you get up in the morning and leave to marinate all day, so that it's ready to cook for supper. Serve with a red onion and cucumber salad and warmed naan bread.

Serves 4

4 skinless chicken breast fillets and 4 skinless chicken thigh fillets
200ml/7fl oz/scant 1 cup Greek (US strained plain) yogurt
45ml/3 tbsp tandoori curry paste

From the storecupboard
salt and ground black pepper

1 Using a sharp knife, slash the chicken breasts and thighs and place in a shallow, non-metallic dish.

2 Put the curry paste and yogurt in a bowl and mix together. Season with salt and pepper, then pour over the chicken and toss to coat well.

3 Cover the dish with clear film (plastic wrap) and chill for at least 8 hours.

4 Preheat the oven to 190°C/375°F/Gas 5. Remove the clear film from the chicken and transfer the dish to the oven. Bake for 20–30 minutes, or until the chicken is cooked through. Serve immediately.

Variation
To make your own spicy yogurt marinade, but without the distinctive red tandoori colour, dry-fry 5ml/1 tsp coriander seeds, 10ml/2 tsp cumin seeds, 6 cloves and 2 bay leaves in a large frying pan over a moderate heat, until the bay leaves are crispy. Allow the spice mixture to cool, then grind coarsely in a mortar and pestle. Finely mince (grind) 1 onion, quartered, 2 garlic cloves, and 5cm/2in piece of fresh root ginger, peeled and roughly chopped in a food processor or blender with the ground spices, 2.5ml/½ tsp chilli powder, 5ml/1 tsp turmeric and 150ml/¼ pint/⅔ cup natural (plain) yogurt. Pour over the chicken joints.

Mustard Chicken: Energy 426kcal/1768kJ; Protein 40.3g; Carbohydrate 0g, of which sugars 0g; Fat 29.3g, of which saturates 8.1g; Cholesterol 215mg; Calcium 13mg; Fibre 0g; Sodium 146mg.
Tandoori Chicken: Energy 592kcal/2479kJ; Protein 44g; Carbohydrate 77.5g, of which sugars 4.5g; Fat 11.4g, of which saturates 1.1g; Cholesterol 105mg; Calcium 54mg; Fibre 0.4g; Sodium 826mg.

Baked Chicken with Broad Bean Rice

This dish is a delightful combination of baked marinated chicken with juicy rice, broad beans and sausage. It should, ideally, be prepared with free-range chicken, which is much tastier and more tender. If the chicken is not free-range, reduce the cooking time by half.

Serves 6

1 free-range chicken, weighing about 1.8kg/4lb, cut into portions
2 garlic cloves, chopped
50ml/2fl oz/¼ cup white wine
sea salt

For the rice (optional)

800g/1¾lb/5⅔ cups shelled broad (fava) beans, thawed if frozen
105ml/7 tbsp olive oil
2 onions, chopped
1 sausage with little fat or salpicão
1 bay leaf
750ml/1¼ pints/3 cups chicken stock
250g/9oz/1¼ cups long grain rice

1 Season the chicken portions with salt and place in an ovenproof dish. Sprinkle with the garlic, pour over the wine and leave to marinate for 2 hours.

2 Preheat the oven to 160°C/325°F/Gas 3. Cover the dish of chicken portions and bake in the oven for about 1½ hours, until cooked through and tender. Meanwhile, pop the beans out of their skins by squeezing gently between your finger and thumb.

3 About 55 minutes before the end of the chicken's cooking time, heat the olive oil in a pan. Add the onions and cook over a low heat for 5 minutes, until softened. Add the sausage, bay leaf and 300ml/½ pint/1¼ cups of the stock and simmer for 30 minutes.

4 Remove the sausage and bay leaf from the pan. Discard the bay leaf, cut the sausage into small cubes and return it to the pan. Add the remaining stock and bring to the boil, then add the rice and cook for about 10 minutes.

5 Add the broad beans and cook for about 5 more minutes, until tender and still moist. Serve the chicken with the juicy rice handed round separately.

Chicken with Black Pudding and Sage

The combination of juicy roast chicken and black pudding is wonderful. Serve as part of a Sunday roast with roast potatoes and all the trimmings, or simply with a cucumber and tomato salad with plenty of fresh herbs and olive oil.

Serves 4

1 medium oven-ready chicken
115g/4oz black pudding (blood sausage), skinned
30ml/2 tbsp fresh sage leaves

From the storecupboard

25g/1oz/2 tbsp softened butter
salt and ground black pepper

1 Preheat the oven to 190°C/375°F/Gas 5. Carefully push your fingers between the skin and the flesh at the neck end of the bird to loosen it, making sure you don't tear the skin.

2 Shape the black pudding into a flat, roundish shape, to fit the space between the skin and the breast meat. Push it under the skin with half the sage leaves.

3 Smooth the skin back and tuck underneath. Tie the legs together and place the chicken in a roasting pan.

4 Spread the butter over the breast and thighs, and season. Sprinkle over the remaining sage leaves and roast for 1½ hours, or until the chicken is cooked through.

5 Remove to a board and leave to rest for 10 minutes before carving.

Cook's Tip

A traditional roast chicken dinner isn't complete without the stuffing. To make a herb stuffing, cook a finely chopped onion in 50g/2oz/4 tbsp butter in a large pan over a low heat until soft. Remove from the heat and stir in 150g/5oz/2½ cups fresh white breadcrumbs, 15ml/1 tbsp chopped fresh parsley, 15ml/1 tbsp chopped fresh thyme, juice and rind of ½ lemon, salt and pepper to season. Either spoon the stuffing into the neck cavity or roll into balls and bake for 20–30 minutes.

Chicken and Rice: Energy 823kcal/3429kJ; Protein 52.6g; Carbohydrate 50.9g, of which sugars 2.1g; Fat 45g, of which saturates 11.1g; Cholesterol 205mg; Calcium 104mg; Fibre 8.8g; Sodium 417mg.
Chicken with Black Pudding: Energy 549kcal/2280kJ; Protein 43.4g; Carbohydrate 4.3g, of which sugars 0g; Fat 39.8g, of which saturates 12.2g; Cholesterol 228mg; Calcium 26mg; Fibre 0g; Sodium 511mg.

Chicken Breasts Cooked in Butter

This simple and delicious way of cooking chicken makes the most of its light, delicate flavour and texture. It is ideal for midweek meals, when time is short, served with new potatoes and mangetouts.

Serves 4
4 small skinless chicken breast fillets
seasoned flour, for coating
fresh parsley sprigs, to garnish

From the storecupboard
75g/3oz/6 tbsp butter

1 Separate the two fillets of each breast. They come apart very easily: one is large, the other small. Pound the large fillets lightly, using a meat mallet or heavy rolling pin, to flatten them.

2 Dredge the chicken thoroughly in the seasoned flour, shaking off any excess.

3 Heat the butter gently in a large heavy frying pan until it bubbles. Place all the chicken fillets in the pan, in a single layer if possible. Cook over medium to high heat for 3–4 minutes, until they are golden brown on the underside.

4 Turn the chicken over. Reduce the heat to low to medium, and continue cooking until the fillets are cooked through but still springy to the touch – about 9–12 minutes in all. If the chicken begins to brown too much, cover the pan for the final minutes of cooking. Serve immediately, garnished with a sprigs of fresh parsley.

Cook's Tips
- *Make sure that the heat is not too high during the last part of the cooking process, otherwise the butter will burn and develop an acrid taste. Also, it is important that the chicken has a chance to cook through thoroughly, without the outer parts drying out and turning too brown.*
- *This chicken dish should be accompanied by delicately flavoured vegetables, such as mangetouts (snow peas) or fresh peas, so that its subtle taste is not overpowered.*

Star Anise Chicken

The pungent flavour of star anise penetrates the chicken fillets and adds a wonderful aniseedy kick to the smoky flavour contributed by the barbecue. Serve the chicken with a refreshing salad.

Serves 4
4 skinless chicken breast fillets
2 whole star anise
30ml/2 tbsp soy sauce

From the storecupboard
30ml/2 tbsp vegetable oil
ground black pepper

1 Lay the skinless chicken breast fillets side by side in a shallow, non-metallic dish and add both pieces of star anise, keeping them whole.

2 Place the soy sauce in a small bowl. Add the oil and whisk together with a fork until the mixture emulsifies. Season to taste with black pepper to make a simple marinade.

3 Pour the marinade over the chicken and stir to coat each breast fillet all over. Cover the dish with clear film (plastic wrap) and chill in the refrigerator for up to 8 hours.

4 Prepare a barbecue. Cook the chicken fillets over medium hot coals for 8–10 minutes on each side, spooning over the marinade from time to time, until the chicken is cooked through. Transfer to a platter and serve immediately.

Cook's Tip
With its aroma of liquorice, star anise is the chief component in Chinese five-spice powder. In China, the points of the star are sometimes snapped off and sucked as a breath freshener.

Variation
In wetter weather, this dish can be prepared indoors. Simply place the marinated chicken fillets under a grill (broiler) and cook, turning once, for the same amount of time.

Chicken in Butter: Energy 311kcal/1302kJ; Protein 36.5g; Carbohydrate 3g, of which sugars 0.2g; Fat 17.1g, of which saturates 10.2g; Cholesterol 145mg; Calcium 16mg; Fibre 0.1g; Sodium 204mg.
Star Anise Chicken: Energy 210kcal/884kJ; Protein 36.1g; Carbohydrate 0.3g, of which sugars 0.3g; Fat 7.2g, of which saturates 1.2g; Cholesterol 105mg; Calcium 8mg; Fibre 0g; Sodium 357mg.

Honey Mustard Chicken

Chicken thighs have a rich flavour, but for a low-fat option, use four chicken breast portions instead and cook for 5 minutes less. Serve with a chunky tomato and red onion salad.

Serves 4
8 chicken thighs
60ml/4 tbsp wholegrain mustard
60ml/4 tbsp clear honey

From the storecupboard
salt and ground black pepper

1 Preheat the oven to 190°C/375°F/Gas 5. Put the chicken thighs in a single layer in a roasting pan. Mix together the mustard and honey, season with salt and ground black pepper to taste and brush the mixture all over the chicken thighs.

2 Cook for 25–30 minutes, brushing the chicken with the pan juices occasionally, until cooked through.

Pan-roasted Chicken with Lemons

Roasting chicken and potatoes in this way gives an interesting variety of textures. The chicken and potatoes on the top crisp up, while underneath they stay soft and juicy. Serve with steamed carrots or curly kale.

Serves 4–6
675g/1½lb potatoes, unpeeled and cut into chunks
6–8 pieces of preserved lemon
1.3kg/3lb corn-fed chicken, jointed

From the storecupboard
30ml/2 tbsp olive oil
salt and ground black pepper

1 Preheat the oven to 190°C/375°F/Gas 5. Drizzle the olive oil into the bottom of a large roasting pan. Spread the chunks of potato in a single layer in the pan and tuck in the pieces of preserved lemon.

2 Pour about 1cm/½in of cold water into the roasting pan. Arrange the chicken pieces on top and season with plenty of salt and black pepper. Roast for 45 minutes–1 hour, or until the chicken is cooked through, and serve.

Soy-marinated Chicken

Two simple flavours, soy sauce and orange, combine to make this mouthwatering dish. Serving the chicken on a bed of asparagus turns the dish into a special treat. Wilted spinach or shredded greens work well as an everyday alternative. Boiled egg noodles or steamed white rice make a good accompaniment to this Asian dish.

Serves 4
4 skinless chicken breast fillets
1 large orange
30ml/2 tbsp dark soy sauce
400g/14oz medium asparagus spears

1 Slash each chicken portion several times diagonally and place them in a single layer in a shallow, ovenproof dish.

2 Halve the orange, squeeze the juice from one half and mix it with the soy sauce. Pour this over the chicken. Cut the remaining orange into wedges and place these on the chicken. Cover and leave to marinate for several hours.

3 Preheat the oven to 180°C/350°F/Gas 4. Turn the chicken over and bake, uncovered, for 20 minutes. Then turn the chicken over again and bake for a further 15 minutes, or until cooked through.

4 Meanwhile, cut off any tough ends from the asparagus and place in a frying pan. Pour in enough boiling water just to cover and cook gently for 3–4 minutes, until just tender. Drain and arrange on warmed plates.

5 Slice the chicken breasts across the width, then top with the chicken and orange wedges. Spoon over the cooking juices. Serve immediately.

Variation
Add 2 finely chopped garlic cloves and 15ml/1 tbsp clear honey to the marinade for a richer, more gutsy flavour. You could also replace the orange with lemon for more of a tang.

Mustard Chicken: Energy 287kcal/1205kJ; Protein 33.9g; Carbohydrate 12.1g, of which sugars 12.1g; Fat 11.8g, of which saturates 3g; Cholesterol 174mg; Calcium 30mg; Fibre 0.7g; Sodium 386mg.
Pan-roast Chicken: Energy 536kcal/2233kJ; Protein 28.3g; Carbohydrate 26.8g, of which sugars 2.2g; Fat 35.7g, of which saturates 8.4g; Cholesterol 133mg; Calcium 21mg; Fibre 1.7g; Sodium 123mg.
Soy Chicken: Energy 197kcal/833kJ; Protein 39.4g; Carbohydrate 5g, of which sugars 4.8g; Fat 2.3g, of which saturates 0.6g; Cholesterol 105mg; Calcium 50mg; Fibre 2.2g; Sodium 449mg.

Drunken Chicken

In this traditional Chinese dish, cooked chicken is marinated in sherry, fresh root ginger and spring onions for several days. Because of the lengthy preparation time, it is important to use a very fresh bird from a reputable supplier. Fresh herbs can be added as an additional garnish, if you like.

Serves 4–6
1 chicken, about 1.3kg/3lb
1cm/½in piece of fresh root ginger, thinly sliced
2 spring onions (scallions), trimmed, plus extra to garnish
300ml/½ pint/1¼ cups dry sherry

From the storecupboard
salt

1 Rinse and dry the chicken inside and out. Place the ginger and spring onions in the body cavity. Put the chicken in a large pan or flameproof casserole and just cover with water. Bring to the boil, skim off any scum and cook for 15 minutes.

2 Turn off the heat, cover the pan or casserole tightly and leave the chicken in the cooking liquid for 3–4 hours, by which time it will be cooked. Drain well, reserving the stock. Pour 300ml/½ pint/1¼ cups of the stock into a jug (pitcher).

3 Remove the skin and cut the chicken into neat pieces. Divide each leg into a drumstick and thigh. Make two more portions from the wings and some of the breast. Finally, cut away the remainder of the breast pieces (still on the bone) and divide each piece into two even portions.

4 Arrange the chicken portions in a shallow dish. Rub salt into the chicken and cover with clear film (plastic wrap). Leave in a cool place for several hours or overnight in the refrigerator.

5 Later, lift off any fat from the stock, add the sherry and pour over the chicken. Cover again and leave in the refrigerator to marinate for 2–3 days, turning occasionally.

6 When ready to serve, cut the chicken through the bone into chunky pieces and arrange on a large serving platter. Garnish the chicken with spring onion shreds.

Stir-fried Chicken with Thai Basil

Thai basil, sometimes called holy basil, has purple-tinged leaves and a more pronounced, slightly aniseedy flavour than the usual varieties. It is available in most Asian food stores but if you can't find any, use a handful of ordinary basil instead. Serve this fragrant stir-fry with plain steamed rice or boiled noodles and soy sauce on the side.

Serves 4
4 skinless chicken breast fillets, cut into strips
2 red (bell) peppers
1 small bunch of fresh Thai basil

From the storecupboard
30ml/2 tbsp garlic-infused olive oil
salt and ground black pepper

1 Using a sharp knife, slice the chicken breast fillets into strips. Halve the peppers, remove the seeds, then cut each piece of pepper into strips.

2 Heat the garlic-infused oil in a wok or large frying pan until it is smoking hot. Add the chicken and red peppers and stir-fry over a high heat for about 3 minutes, until the chicken is golden all over and cooked through. Season with salt and ground black pepper.

3 Roughly tear up the basil leaves, add to the chicken and peppers and toss briefly to combine. Serve immediately.

Coriander and Crème Fraîche Chicken

Boneless chicken thighs are used for this recipe but you can substitute breast portions if you like. Be generous with the coriander leaves, as they have a wonderful fragrant flavour, or use chopped parsley instead. Serve with creamy mashed potatoes. To make a lower fat version of this dish, use chicken breast portions and low-fat crème fraîche and serve with steamed rice.

Serves 4
6 skinless, boneless chicken thigh fillets
60ml/4 tbsp crème fraîche
1 small bunch of fresh coriander (cilantro), roughly chopped

From the storecupboard
15ml/1 tbsp sunflower oil
salt and ground black pepper

1 Using a sharp knife, cut each chicken thigh into three or four pieces. Heat the oil in a large frying pan, add the chicken and cook for about 6 minutes, turning occasionally, until it is cooked through.

2 Add the crème fraîche to the pan and stir until melted, then allow to bubble for 1–2 minutes.

3 Add the chopped coriander to the chicken and stir to combine. Season with salt and ground black pepper to taste, and serve immediately.

Drunken Chicken: Energy 608kcal/2552kJ; Protein 35.4g; Carbohydrate 52.7g, of which sugars 29g; Fat 17.6g, of which saturates 1.9g; Cholesterol 82mg; Calcium 107mg; Fibre 3.7g; Sodium 97mg.
Stir-fried Chicken: Energy 211kcal/892kJ; Protein 37.8g; Carbohydrate 6.9g, of which sugars 5.4g; Fat 3.7g, of which saturates 0.8g; Cholesterol 105mg; Calcium 67mg; Fibre 1.4g; Sodium 97mg.
Coriander Chicken: Energy 249kcal/1041kJ; Protein 32.1g; Carbohydrate 0.7g, of which sugars 0.6g; Fat 13.1g, of which saturates 5.6g; Cholesterol 174mg; Calcium 44mg; Fibre 0.6g; Sodium 143mg.

Chicken Escalopes with Lemon and Serrano Ham

Chicken escalopes are flattened chicken breast fillets – they cook quicker than normal breast portions and absorb flavours more readily. In this light summery dish, the chicken absorbs the delicious flavours of the ham and lemon. It can be assembled in advance, so is good for entertaining.

Serves 4
4 skinless chicken breast fillets
4 slices Serrano ham
1 lemon

From the storecupboard
40g/1½oz/3 tbsp butter, softened
salt and ground black pepper

1 Preheat the oven to 180°C/350°F/Gas 4. Beat the butter with plenty of ground black pepper and set aside.

2 Place the chicken fillets on a large sheet of clear film (plastic wrap) on a chopping board, spacing them well apart. Cover with a second sheet of clear film, then beat with a meat mallet or heavy rolling pin until the fillets are half their original thickness.

3 Transfer the chicken to a large, shallow ovenproof dish and crumple a slice of ham on top of each. Cut eight thin slices from the lemon and place two on each slice of ham.

4 Dot with the pepper butter and bake for about 30 minutes, until the chicken is cooked. Transfer to serving plates and spoon over any juices from the dish. Serve with a leafy green salad and some crusty bread to mop up the mouthwatering juices.

Variation
You can vary this dish with other types of cured ham, such as prosciutto, or alternatively use a cooked ham. The dish is also complemented by a sprinkling of freshly grated Parmesan cheese on top before baking.

Roast Chicken with Herb Cheese, Chilli and Lime Stuffing

Whether you are entertaining guests or cooking a family meal, a tasty chicken is a sure winner every time. This is a modern twist on the classic roast chicken – the stuffing is forced under the chicken skin, which helps to produce wonderfully flavoured, succulent flesh.

Serves 5–6
1.8kg/4lb chicken
1 lime
115g/4oz/½ cup cream cheese with herbs and garlic
1 mild fresh red chilli, seeded and finely chopped

1 Preheat the oven to 200°C/400°F/Gas 6. Using first the point of a knife and then your fingers, separate the skin from the meat across the chicken breast and over the tops of the legs. Use the knife to loosen the first piece of skin, then carefully run your fingers underneath, taking care not to tear the skin.

2 Grate the lime and beat the rind into the cream cheese together with the chopped chilli.

3 Pack the cream cheese stuffing under the skin, using a teaspoon, until fairly evenly distributed. Push the skin back into place, then smooth your hands over it to spread the stuffing in an even layer.

4 Put the chicken in a roasting pan and squeeze the juice from the lime over the top.

5 Roast for 1½ hours, or until the juices run clear when the thickest part of the thigh is pierced with a skewer. If necessary, cover the chicken with foil towards the end of cooking if the top starts to become too browned.

6 Carve the chicken and arrange on a warmed serving platter. Spoon the pan juices over it and serve immediately with some crispy roast potatoes and seasonal vegetables.

Chicken Escalopes: Energy 227kcal/952kJ; Protein 33.5g; Carbohydrate 0.3g, of which sugars 0.3g; Fat 10.2g, of which saturates 5.8g; Cholesterol 120mg; Calcium 9mg; Fibre 0g; Sodium 361mg.
Roast Chicken: Energy 512kcal/2120kJ; Protein 37.4g; Carbohydrate 0.1g, of which sugars 0.1g; Fat 40.1g, of which saturates 14.7g; Cholesterol 210mg; Calcium 36mg; Fibre 0g; Sodium 208mg.

Chicken in a Salt Crust

Cooking food in a casing of salt gives a deliciously moist, tender flavour that is, surprisingly, not too salty. The technique is used in Italy and France for whole fish, too.

Serves 6
1 chicken, about 1.8–2kg/4–4½lb

From the storecupboard
about 2.25kg/5lb coarse sea salt

1 Preheat the oven to 220°C/425°F/Gas 7. Choose a deep ovenproof dish into which the whole chicken will fit snugly. Line the dish with a double thickness of heavy foil, allowing plenty of excess foil to overhang the top edge of the ovenproof dish.

2 Truss the chicken tightly so that the salt cannot fall into the cavity. Sprinkle a thin layer of salt in the foil-lined dish, then place the chicken on top.

3 Pour the remaining salt all around and over the top of the chicken until it is completely encased. Sprinkle the top with a little water.

4 Cover tightly with the foil, then bake the chicken on the lower oven shelf for 1¾ hours, or until the chicken is cooked and tender.

5 To serve the chicken, open out the foil and ease it out of the dish. Place on a large serving platter. Crack open the salt crust on the chicken and brush away the salt before carving. Remove and discard the skin from the chicken and carve the meat into slices.

6 Serve with a selection of cooked fresh seasonal vegetables.

Cook's Tip
This recipe makes a really stunning main course when you want to serve something a little different. Take the salt-crusted chicken to the table garnished with plenty of mixed fresh herbs. Once you've scraped away the salt, transfer the chicken to a clean plate to carve it.

Turkey Patties

So much better than store-bought burgers, these light patties are delicious served hamburger-style in split and toasted buns with relish, salad leaves and chunky fries. They can also be made using minced chicken, lamb, pork or beef. If you are making them for children, shape the mixture into 12 equal rounds and serve in mini-rolls or in rounds stamped out from sliced bread.

Serves 6
675g/1½lb minced (ground) turkey
1 small red onion, finely chopped
small handful of fresh thyme leaves

From the storecupboard
30ml/2 tbsp lime-flavoured olive oil

1 Mix together the turkey, onion, thyme, 15ml/1 tbsp of the oil and seasoning. Cover and chill for up to 4 hours to let the flavours infuse (steep), then divide the mixture into six equal portions and shape into round patties.

2 Preheat a griddle pan. Brush the patties with half of the remaining lime-flavoured olive oil, then place them on the pan and cook for 10–12 minutes. Turn the patties over, brush with more oil, and cook for 10–12 minutes on the second side, or until cooked right through. Serve the patties immediately.

Cook's Tip
Make double the quantity and freeze half for use another time. Separate patties with sheets of baking parchment and place in a sealed bag. Freeze for up to 4 months.

Variation
Try sautéing the red onion before adding to the pattie mix for a sweeter flavour when cooked.

Chicken in a Salt Crust: Energy 133kcal/561kJ; Protein 30g; Carbohydrate 0g, of which sugars 0g; Fat 1.4g, of which saturates 0.4g; Cholesterol 88mg; Calcium 46mg; Fibre 0g; Sodium 75mg.
Turkey Patties: Energy 141kcal/596kJ; Protein 24.8g; Carbohydrate 0.8g, of which sugars 0.6g; Fat 4.4g, of which saturates 1.1g; Cholesterol 69mg; Calcium 15mg; Fibre 0.2g; Sodium 62mg.

Spatchcock Poussins with Herb Butter

Spatchcock is said to be a distortion of an 18th-century Irish expression 'dispatch cock' for providing an unexpected guest with a quick and simple meal. A young chicken was prepared without frills or fuss by being split, flattened and fried or grilled.

Serves 2
2 poussins, each weighing about 450g/1lb
2 garlic cloves, crushed
45ml/3 tbsp chopped mixed fresh herbs, such as flat leaf parsley, sage, rosemary and thyme

From the storecupboard
75g/3oz/6 tbsp butter, softened
salt and ground black pepper

1 To spatchcock a poussin, place it breast down on a chopping board and split it along the back. Open out the bird and turn it over, so that the breast side is uppermost. Press the bird as flat as possible, then thread two metal skewers through it, across the breast and thigh, to keep it flat. Repeat with the second poussin and place the skewered birds on a large grill (broiler) pan.

2 Add the crushed garlic and chopped mixed herbs to the butter with plenty of seasoning, and then beat well. Then dot the butter over the spatchcock poussins.

3 Preheat the grill to high and cook the poussins for 30 minutes, turning them over halfway through. Turn again and baste with the cooking juices, then cook for a further 5–7 minutes on each side.

Cook's Tip
Poussin is the French word for a young chicken, about four to six weeks old and weighing about 350–675g/12oz–1½lb. Each bird provides an individual portion. Poussins, which are sometimes called 'spring chicken', have a tender, delicate flavour. They can be cooked in various ways: roasting at 200°/400°/Gas 6 for 50–60 minutes (where they benefit from a moist stuffing), spatchcocking, grilling (broiling), pan-frying or barbecueing.

Chilli-spiced Spatchcock Poussin

When you are short of time these spicy poussins make a quick alternative to a traditional roast. Serve with a leafy salad and a rice pilaff.

Serves 4
2 poussins, 675g/1½lb each
15ml/1 tbsp chilli powder
15ml/1 tbsp ground cumin

From the storecupboard
45ml/3 tbsp olive oil
salt and ground black pepper

1 Spatchcock one poussin: remove the wishbone and split the bird along each side of the backbone and remove it. Press down on the breastbone to flatten the bird. Push a metal skewer through the wings and breast to keep the bird flat, then push a second skewer through the thighs and breast. Spatchcock the second poussin in the same way.

2 Combine the chilli, cumin, oil and seasoning. Brush over the poussins. Preheat the grill (broiler). Lay the birds, skin side down, on a grill rack and grill (broil) for 15 minutes. Turn over and grill for a further 15 minutes until cooked through.

3 Remove the skewers and split each bird in half along the breastbone. Serve drizzled with the pan juices.

Cook's Tip
Every cook has their preferred method of spatchcocking, but essentially it is a way to split and flatten a whole poussin so that it can be cooked more quickly.

Variation
Serve this dish with coriander (cilantro) and spring onion (scallion) rice. Cook 225g/8oz/generous 1 cup basmati rice in a large pan of salted water for about 10 minutes or until tender. Drain well and return to pan. Stir in 3 finely sliced spring onions and 1 bunch of fresh coriander, roughly chopped.

Spatchcock Poussins: Energy 621kcal/2583kJ; Protein 50.1g; Carbohydrate 0.3g, of which sugars 0.3g; Fat 46.8g, of which saturates 16.4g; Cholesterol 288mg; Calcium 21mg; Fibre 0g; Sodium 256mg.
Chilli-spiced Poussin: Energy 465kcal/1936kJ; Protein 36.6g; Carbohydrate 1.3g, of which sugars 0g; Fat 35.1g, of which saturates 8.4g; Cholesterol 189mg; Calcium 20mg; Fibre 0g; Sodium 131mg.

Quail with Apples

Nowadays, quail often appear on restaurant menus, and they are increasingly used by domestic cooks, too. As they are so tiny, the cooking time is very short.

Serves 2 as a main course
4 oven-ready quail
2 firm eating apples
4 slices white bread

From the storecupboard
120ml/4fl oz/½ cup olive oil
115g/4oz/½ cup butter
salt and ground black pepper

1 Preheat the oven to 220°C/425°F/Gas 7. Core the apples and slice them thickly (leave the peel on if it is attractive and not too tough).

2 Brush the quail with half the olive oil and roast them in a pan in the oven for 10 minutes, or until brown and tender.

3 Meanwhile, heat half the butter in a frying pan and sauté the apple slices for about 3 minutes until they are golden but not mushy. Season with pepper, cover and keep the fried apples warm until required.

4 Remove the crusts from the bread. Heat the remaining olive oil and the butter in a frying pan and fry the bread on both sides until brown and crisp.

5 Lay the fried bread on heated plates and place the quail on top. Arrange the fried apple slices around them, and serve immediately.

Cook's Tip
Quail are very small birds, native to the Middle East. They are available in game shops all year round. As they are so tiny, you will need to allow two whole birds per person for a main course and one bird per person if serving them as an appetizer or as a first course.

Guinea Fowl with Whisky Sauce

Served with creamy, sweet mashed potato and lightly boiled whole baby leeks, guinea fowl is magnificent with a rich, creamy whisky sauce. If you don't like the flavour of whisky, then substitute brandy, Madeira or Marsala. Or, to make a non-alcoholic version, use freshly squeezed orange juice instead. Garnish with sprigs of fresh thyme or fresh herbs of your choice.

Serves 4
2 guinea fowl, each weighing about 1kg/2¼lb
90ml/6 tbsp whisky
150ml/¼ pint/⅔ cup well-flavoured chicken stock
150ml/¼ pint/⅔ cup double (heavy) cream

From the storecupboard
salt and ground black pepper

1 Preheat the oven to 200°C/400°F/Gas 6. Brown the guinea fowl on all sides in a roasting pan on the hob (stovetop), then turn it breast uppermost and transfer the pan to the oven. Roast for about 1 hour, until the guinea fowl are golden and cooked through. Transfer the guinea fowl to a warmed serving dish, cover with foil and keep warm.

2 Pour off the excess fat from the pan, then heat the juices on the hob and stir in the whisky. Bring to the boil and cook until reduced. Add the stock and cream and simmer again until reduced slightly. Strain and season to taste.

3 Carve the guinea fowl and serve on individual plates, arranged around the chosen vegetable accompaniments. Sprinkle with plenty of ground black pepper. Spoon a little of the sauce over each portion of guinea fowl and serve the rest separately.

Cook's Tip
Guinea fowl are tender birds with slightly dry flesh, similar to pheasant. They do not have a distinctly gamey flavour, but lean more towards that flavour than chicken.

Quail with Apples: Energy 814kcal/3389kJ; Protein 53.3g; Carbohydrate 33.3g, of which sugars 10.5g; Fat 43.6g, of which saturates 23.4g; Cholesterol 69mg; Calcium 169mg; Fibre 2.4g; Sodium 644mg.
Guinea Fowl: Energy 854kcal/3568kJ; Protein 110.6g; Carbohydrate 0.6g, of which sugars 0.6g; Fat 41.7g, of which saturates 18g; Cholesterol 51mg; Calcium 159mg; Fibre 0g; Sodium 308mg.

Pheasant Cooked in Port with Mushrooms

This warming dish is delicious served with mashed root vegetables and shredded cabbage or leeks. Marinating the pheasant in port helps to moisten and tenderize the meat, which can often be slightly dry. If you prefer, marinate the pheasant in a full-bodied red wine and use button mushrooms.

Serves 4

2 pheasants, cut into portions
300ml/½ pint/1¼ cups port
300g/11oz chestnut mushrooms, halved if large

From the storecupboard

50g/2oz/¼ cup butter
salt and ground black pepper

1 Place the pheasant in a bowl and pour over the port. Cover and marinate for 3–4 hours or overnight, turning the portions occasionally.

2 Drain the meat thoroughly, reserving the marinade. Pat the portions dry on kitchen paper and season lightly with salt and pepper. Melt three-quarters of the butter in a frying pan and cook the pheasant portions on all sides for about 5 minutes, until deep golden. Drain well, transfer to a plate, then cook the mushrooms in the fat remaining in the pan for 3 minutes.

3 Return the pheasant to the pan and pour in the reserved marinade with 200ml/7fl oz/scant 1 cup water. Bring to the boil, reduce the heat and cover, then simmer gently for about 45 minutes, until the pheasant is tender.

4 Using a slotted spoon, carefully remove the pheasant portions and mushrooms from the frying pan and keep warm. Bring the cooking juices to the boil and boil vigorously for 3–5 minutes, until they are reduced and slightly thickened. Strain the juices through a fine sieve (strainer) and return them to the pan. Whisk in the remaining butter over a gentle heat until it has melted, season to taste, then pour the juices over the pheasant and mushrooms and serve.

Roast Pheasant with Sherry and Mustard Sauce

Use only young pheasants for roasting – older birds are too tough and only suitable for casseroles. Serve in winter with potatoes braised in wine with garlic and onions, Brussels sprouts and bread sauce.

Serves 4

2 young oven-ready pheasants
200ml/7fl oz/scant 1 cup sherry
15ml/1 tbsp Dijon mustard

From the storecupboard

50g/2oz/¼ cup softened butter
salt and ground black pepper

1 Preheat the oven to 200°C/400°F/Gas 6. Put the pheasants in a roasting pan and spread the butter all over both birds. Season with salt and pepper.

2 Roast the pheasants for 50 minutes, basting often to stop the birds from drying out. When the pheasants are cooked, take them out of the pan and leave to rest on a board, covered with foil.

3 Meanwhile, place the roasting pan over a medium heat. Add the sherry and season with salt and pepper. Simmer for 5 minutes, until the sherry has slightly reduced, then stir in the mustard. Carve the pheasants and serve with the sherry and mustard sauce.

Cook's Tips

- *Unfortunately, game birds, such as pheasant, are often sold with tiny balls of lead shot left in them. It is advisable to try and locate the shot and remove it from the birds before cooking, but remember to warn diners that there may be some remaining. Run your fingertips over the surface of the bird, feeling for any small hard lumps, and cut out any that you find with the point of a sharp knife.*
- *Pheasant are often sold in pairs, known as a brace, this consists of one male, the larger bird, and one female, smaller and more tender.*

Pheasant in Port: Energy 457kcal/1910kJ; Protein 46.2g; Carbohydrate 6.4g, of which sugars 4.5g; Fat 23.1g, of which saturates 6.1g; Cholesterol 9mg; Calcium 102mg; Fibre 2g; Sodium 483mg.
Roast Pheasant: Energy 692kcal/2897kJ; Protein 81.7g; Carbohydrate 1.2g, of which sugars 1.1g; Fat 34.2g, of which saturates 14.5g; Cholesterol 27mg; Calcium 133mg; Fibre 0g; Sodium 456mg.

Woodcock with Madeira

Woodcock is a small bird, weighing about 300g/11oz. It is sometimes hard to get hold of, but is much prized for its flavour. Unlike other game birds, the innards, known as the 'trail', are left intact apart from the gizzard – these are regarded as a great delicacy. This recipe gives ingredient quantities for each individual woodcock.

Serves 1

1 woodcock, or small pheasant
6 thin slices of lard
1 small onion, thinly sliced
50ml/2fl oz/¼ cup dry Madeira wine
fried bread and green beans, to serve

From the storecupboard

90g/3½oz/scant ½ cup butter
sea salt and ground black pepper

1 Clean the woodcock, rinse it and dispose of the gizzard. Season with salt and pepper and cover with the lard.

2 Place it in a pan with the onion and butter, and cook over a low heat for 30 minutes.

3 Remove the bird from the pan and remove the 'trail'. Mash it with the wine, then add to the sauce. Return the bird to the pan and cook for a further 10 minutes. Serve with fried bread and green beans.

Cook's Tips

• *Woodcock is a tiny bird with a plump meaty breast and a wonderful rich flavour. It is usual to serve one bird per person because of its size. The birds can be roasted, braised or grilled (broiled).*

• *A simple roasted game bird is excellent served with game chips, thinly sliced deep-fried potatoes, or roast parsnips, with a generous spoonful of fruit jelly on the side. Alternatively, serve with cumberland sauce, a fruity redcurrant jelly and red wine combination for pouring, or an old-fashioned bread sauce, spiced with freshly grated nutmeg.*

Roast Mallard

Wildfowl, such as mallard, teal and widgeon are in good supply from game stores during the late autumn and early winter. Traditional accompaniments include game chips, apple sauce or rowan jelly, and puréed Jerusalem artichokes. The roast mallard is especially tasty served on a potato cake bed.

Serves 2–3

1 oven-ready mallard
1 small onion studded with cloves
a few apple slices
5 streaky (fatty) bacon rashers (strips)

From the storecupboard

25g/1oz/2 tbsp butter, softened
salt and ground black pepper

1 Thoroughly wash the bird inside and out under cold running water and wipe dry on kitchen paper.

2 Weigh the mallard and calculate the cooking time at 15 minutes per 450g/1lb for rare meat, 20 minutes per 450g/1lb if you prefer the meat well done. Preheat the oven to 200°C/400°F/Gas 6.

3 Put the clove-studded onion and a few apple slices inside the bird. Spread the butter all over the skin, and season.

4 Cover with the bacon and put the duck into a roasting pan with 30ml/2 tbsp water. Roast in the preheated oven for the time estimated, removing the rashers for the last 10 minutes to allow the skin to brown. Keep the bacon rashers warm until you are ready to serve the mallard. Carve the meat, leaving the legs whole, and arrange on warmed plates.

Cook's Tip

Wildfowl from coastal areas can have a fishy flavour. To offset this, put the oven-ready bird into a pan of cold, salted water and bring to the boil; leave to simmer for 15–20 minutes, then remove the bird and wash and dry both inside and out before proceeding.

Woodcock with Madeira: Energy 1204kcal/4985kJ; Protein 58.6g; Carbohydrate 6.5g, of which sugars 6.5g; Fat 98.8g, of which saturates 55.3g; Cholesterol 652mg; Calcium 78mg; Fibre 0g; Sodium 683mg.
Roast Mallard: Energy 486kcal/2028kJ; Protein 49.6g; Carbohydrate 0.1g, of which sugars 0.1g; Fat 32g, of which saturates 14.1g; Cholesterol 278mg; Calcium 28mg; Fibre 0g; Sodium 1.08g

Marmalade and Soy Roast Duck

Sweet-and-sour flavours, such as marmalade and soy sauce, complement the rich, fatty taste of duck beautifully. Serve these duck breast portions with simple accompaniments such as steamed sticky rice and lightly cooked pak choi.

Serves 6
6 duck breast fillets
45ml/3 tbsp fine-cut marmalade
45ml/3 tbsp light soy sauce

From the storecupboard
salt and ground black pepper

1 Preheat the oven 190°C/375°F/Gas 5. Place the duck breasts skin side up on a grill (broiler) rack and place in the sink. Pour boiling water all over the duck. This shrinks the skin and helps it crisp during cooking. Pat the duck dry with kitchen paper and transfer to a roasting pan.

2 Combine the marmalade and soy sauce, and brush over the duck. Season with a little salt and some black pepper and roast for 20–25 minutes, basting occasionally with the marmalade mixture in the pan.

3 Remove the duck breasts from the oven and leave to rest for 5 minutes covered with foil.

4 Using a sharp knife, slice the duck breasts neatly across at an angle of about 45 degrees and serve drizzled with any juices left in the pan.

Cook's Tips
- *Duck is traditionally a bird with a high fat content. However, modern breeding and feeding methods have developed leaner ducks, which are widely available in supermarkets. These have a good proportion of breast meat and only a thin layer of fat under the skin. They are sold as whole birds, portions or breast fillets. Barbary and Aylesbury are popular breeds.*
- *Sharp fruits, such as, oranges, cranberries and sharp apples and cherries complement the rich meat.*

Duck with Plum Sauce

Sharp plums cut the rich flavour of duck wonderfully well in this updated version of an old English dish. Duck is often considered to be a fatty meat but nowadays, leaner ducks are widely available. For an easy dinner party main course, serve the duck with creamy mashed potatoes and celeriac and steamed broccoli or other steamed green vegetables.

Serves 4
4 duck quarters
1 large red onion, finely chopped
500g/1¼lb ripe plums, stoned (pitted) and quartered
30ml/2 tbsp redcurrant jelly

1 Prick the duck skin all over with a fork to release the fat during cooking and help give a crisp finish to the skin, then place the portions in a heavy frying pan, skin side down.

2 Cook the duck pieces for 10 minutes on each side, or until golden brown and cooked right through. Remove the duck from the frying pan, using a slotted spoon, and cover with foil to keep warm.

3 Pour off all but 30ml/2 tbsp of the duck fat, reserve and allow to cool, then keep in the refrigerator in an airtight container for future use. Now stir-fry the onion in the remaining fat for 5 minutes, or until golden. Add the plums and cook for 5 minutes, stirring frequently. Then add the jelly and mix well.

4 Replace the duck portions and cook for a further 5 minutes, or until thoroughly reheated. Serve immediately.

Cook's Tip
It is important that the plums used in this dish are very ripe, otherwise the mixture will be too dry and the sauce will be extremely sharp.

Marmalade and Soy Roast Duck: Energy 160kcal/672kJ; Protein 19.9g; Carbohydrate 5.8g, of which sugars 5.8g; Fat 6.5g, of which saturates 2g; Cholesterol 110mg; Calcium 16mg; Fibre 0.1g; Sodium 645mg.
Duck with Plum Sauce: Energy 608kcal/2515kJ; Protein 15.1g; Carbohydrate 17.4g, of which sugars 17g; Fat 53.5g, of which saturates 14.5g; Cholesterol 0mg; Calcium 35mg; Fibre 2.2g; Sodium 102mg.

Warm Penne with Fresh Tomatoes and Basil

This dish is fresh, healthy and ready in minutes. It is the perfect way to use up a glut of ripe summer tomatoes.

Serves 4
500g/1¼lb dried penne
5 very ripe plum tomatoes
1 small bunch of fresh basil

From the storecupboard
60ml/4 tbsp extra virgin olive oil
salt and ground black pepper

1 Cook the pasta in plenty of salted, boiling water according to the instructions on the packet.

2 Meanwhile, roughly chop the tomatoes, pull the basil leaves from their stems and tear up the leaves.

3 Drain the pasta thoroughly and toss with the tomatoes, basil and olive oil. Season with salt and ground black pepper and serve immediately.

Cook's Tip
If you cannot find ripe tomatoes, roast them to bring out their flavour. Put the tomatoes in a roasting pan, drizzle with oil and roast at 190°C/375°F/Gas 5 for 20 minutes, then mash roughly.

Variation
This simple dish works well with any type of dried pasta, but short pasta is preferable to the long strands, which work better with a smooth sauce rather than a chunky one. Try rigatoni, ridged hollow tubes, or farfalle, pretty butterfly or bow-tie shapes that are very popular with children. You could also use a stuffed pasta, such as tortellini. Always buy dried pasta made from 100 per cent durum wheat.

Broccoli and Chilli Spaghetti

The contrast between the hot chilli and the mild broccoli is delicious and goes perfectly with spaghetti. To add extra flavour and texture, sprinkle the spaghetti and broccoli with toasted pine nuts and grated or shaved Parmesan cheese just before serving.

Serves 4
350g/12oz dried spaghetti
450g/1lb broccoli, cut into small florets
1 fat red chilli, seeded and finely chopped

From the storecupboard
150ml/¼ pint/⅔ cup garlic-infused olive oil
salt and ground black pepper

1 Bring a large pan of lightly salted water to the boil. Add the spaghetti and broccoli and cook for 8–10 minutes, until both are tender. Drain thoroughly.

2 Using the back of a fork, crush the broccoli roughly, taking care not to mash the spaghetti strands at the same time.

3 Meanwhile, warm the oil and finely chopped chilli in a small pan over a low heat and cook very gently for 5 minutes.

4 Pour the chilli and oil over the spaghetti and broccoli and toss together to combine. Season to taste. Divide between four warmed bowls and serve immediately.

Cook's Tip
Cooking the spaghetti and broccoli in the same pan helps the pasta to absorb more of the vegetable's flavour and essential nutrients. To retain more of the nutrients, reserve a small amount of the cooking water and pour over the dish before tossing together all the ingredients.

Variation
Exclude the chilli for a tangy, but less spicy dish.

Penne with Tomatoes: Energy 552kcal/2336kJ; Protein 16.3g; Carbohydrate 96.9g, of which sugars 8.3g; Fat 13.8g, of which saturates 2g; Cholesterol 0mg; Calcium 65mg; Fibre 5.5g; Sodium 19mg.
Broccoli and Chilli Spaghetti: Energy 396kcal/1678kJ; Protein 17.3g; Carbohydrate 68.3g, of which sugars 6g; Fat 7.9g, of which saturates 0.8g; Cholesterol 0mg; Calcium 114mg; Fibre 5.6g; Sodium 24mg.

Minty Courgette Linguine

Sweet, mild courgettes and refreshing mint are a great combination and are delicious with pasta. Dried linguine has been used here but you can use any type of pasta you like. Couscous also works well in place of pasta, if you prefer.

Serves 4
450g/1lb dried linguine
4 small courgettes (zucchini), sliced
1 small bunch of fresh mint, roughly chopped

From the storecupboard
75ml/5 tbsp garlic-infused olive oil
salt and ground black pepper

1 Cook the linguine in plenty of salted, boiling water according to the instructions on the packet.

2 Meanwhile, heat 45ml/3 tbsp of the oil in a large frying pan and add the courgettes. Fry for 2–3 minutes, stirring occasionally, until they are tender and golden.

3 Drain the pasta well and toss with the courgettes and chopped mint. Season with salt and pepper, drizzle over the remaining oil and serve immediately.

Cook's Tip
To make garlic oil, add several whole cloves to a bottle of olive oil and leave to infuse (steep) for about 2 weeks before using.

Variations
- *For a more creamy version of this dish, add a few good spoons of crème fraîche, instead of the remaining oil, and put the pan back on a low heat for a couple of minutes to heat through, stirring gently.*
- *Alternatively, you can fry some finely chopped shallots with the courgettes (zucchini) in regular olive oil rather than garlic-infused oil. Varying the oil flavour can bring a new slant to this dish. Try lemon-infused oil for a more delicate flavour.*

Pasta with Roast Tomatoes and Goat's Cheese

Roasting tomatoes brings out their flavour and sweetness, which contrasts perfectly with the sharp taste and creamy texture of goat's cheese. Serve with a crisp green salad flavoured with herbs.

Serves 4
8 large ripe tomatoes
450g/1lb any dried pasta shapes
200g/7oz firm goat's cheese, crumbled

From the storecupboard
60ml/4 tbsp garlic-infused olive oil
salt and ground black pepper

1 Preheat the oven to 190°C/375°F/Gas 5. Place the tomatoes in a roasting pan and drizzle over 30ml/2 tbsp of the oil. Season well with salt and pepper and roast for 20–25 minutes, or until soft and slightly charred.

2 Meanwhile, cook the pasta in plenty of salted, boiling water, according to the instructions on the packet. Drain well and return to the pan.

3 Roughly mash the tomatoes with a fork, and stir the contents of the roasting pan into the pasta. Gently stir in the goat's cheese and the remaining oil and serve.

Cook's Tip
A good goat's milk cheese tastes as though it has absorbed the herby aromas of tarragon, thyme or marjoram. Include one or all of these herbs in a salad to accompany the dish, or sprinkle some of the chopped fresh herbs over the pasta dish to serve.

Variation
For a quick version of this dish, replace the roasted tomatoes with sun-dried tomatoes. Choose the ones preserved in olive oil and use their oil instead of garlic-infused oil.

Minty Courgette Linguine: Energy 536kcal/2261kJ; Protein 16.2g; Carbohydrate 86.3g, of which sugars 5.8g; Fat 16.4g, of which saturates 2.3g; Cholesterol 0mg; Calcium 86mg; Fibre 4.4g; Sodium 7mg.
Pasta with Tomatoes and Cheese: Energy 682kcal/2873kJ; Protein 25.6g; Carbohydrate 90.9g, of which sugars 11.2g; Fat 26.6g, of which saturates 11g; Cholesterol 47mg; Calcium 111mg; Fibre 5.5g; Sodium 324mg.

Home-made Potato Gnocchi

These classic Italian potato dumplings are very simple to make – it just requires a little patience when it comes to shaping them. Serve them as soon as they are cooked, tossed in melted butter and fresh sage leaves, sprinkled with grated Parmesan cheese and plenty of black pepper. They make a fabulous alternative to pasta.

Serves 2
900g/2lb floury potatoes, cut into large chunks
2 eggs, beaten
150–175g/5–6oz/1¼–1½ cups plain (all-purpose) flour

From the storecupboard
10ml/2 tsp salt

1 Cook the potatoes in salted, boiling water for 15 minutes, until tender. Drain well and return to the pan, set it over a low heat and dry the potatoes for 1–2 minutes.

2 Mash the potatoes until smooth, then gradually stir in the beaten eggs and salt. Slowly work in enough flour to form a soft dough.

3 Break off small pieces of the dough and roll into balls, using floured hands. Press the back of a fork into each ball to make indentations. Repeat until all the dough has been used.

4 Leave the gnocchi to rest for 15–20 minutes before cooking.

5 Bring a large pan of water to a gentle boil. Add the gnocchi, about ten at a time, and cook for 3–4 minutes, or until they float to the surface. Drain thoroughly and serve as soon as all the gnocchi have been cooked.

Variation
To make herb-flavoured gnocchi, add 45ml/3 tbsp chopped fresh herbs, such as basil, parsley and sage, to the potato and flour dough and combine well. Serve with butter and grated Parmesan.

Spaghetti with Butter and Herbs

This is a versatile recipe. You can use just one favourite herb or several – basil, flat leaf parsley, rosemary, thyme, marjoram or sage would all work well. Square-shaped spaghetti is traditional for this type of sauce, but you can use ordinary spaghetti or spaghettini, or even linguine.

Serves 4
400g/14oz fresh or dried spaghetti alla chitarra
2 good handfuls mixed fresh herbs, plus extra to garnish
freshly grated Parmesan cheese, to serve

From the storecupboard
115g/4oz/½ cup butter
salt and ground black pepper

1 Cook the pasta according to the instructions on the packet.

2 Chop the herbs roughly or finely, whichever you prefer.

3 When the pasta is almost *al dente*, melt the butter in a large skillet or pan. As soon as it sizzles, drain the pasta and add it to the pan, then sprinkle in the herbs and salt and pepper to taste.

4 Toss over a medium heat until the pasta is coated in the oil and herbs. Serve immediately in warmed bowls, sprinkled with extra herb leaves. Hand around freshly grated Parmesan at the table separately.

Variation
If you like the flavour of garlic with herbs, add 1–2 crushed garlic cloves when melting the butter.

Spaghetti with Garlic and Oil

Popular throughout Italy, this is one of the simplest and most satisfying pasta dishes of all. For the best flavour, it is essential to use a top quality extra virgin olive oil. Serve with freshly grated Parmesan cheese.

Serves 4
400g/14oz spaghetti
3 garlic cloves, chopped
60ml/4 tbsp chopped fresh parsley

From the storecupboard
90ml/6 tbsp extra virgin olive oil
salt and ground black pepper

1 Bring a large pan of lightly salted water to the boil and drop in the spaghetti.

2 Heat the oil in a large frying pan and gently sauté the garlic until it is barely golden. Do not let it brown or it will taste bitter. Stir in the parsley. Season with salt and pepper. Remove from the heat until the pasta is ready.

3 Drain the pasta when it is barely *al dente*. Add it to the pan with the oil and garlic and cook together for 2–3 minutes, stirring well to coat the spaghetti with the sauce. Serve immediately in a warmed serving bowl, with freshly grated Parmesan handed separately, if liked.

Gnocchi: Energy 687kcal/2916kJ; Protein 22.2g; Carbohydrate 140.5g, of which sugars 7.2g; Fat 8.1g, of which saturates 2.2g; Cholesterol 190mg; Calcium 179mg; Fibre 7.2g; Sodium 2087mg.
Herby Spaghetti: Energy 565kcal/2371kJ; Protein 12.9g; Carbohydrate 75g, of which sugars 4.1g; Fat 25.8g, of which saturates 15.2g; Cholesterol 61mg; Calcium 80mg; Fibre 4.2g; Sodium 186mg.
Garlic Spaghetti: Energy 549kcal/2315kJ; Protein 14.5g; Carbohydrate 86.7g, of which sugars 4.3g; Fat 18.9g, of which saturates 2.7g; Cholesterol 0mg; Calcium 55mg; Fibre 4.4g; Sodium 8mg.

Spaghettini with Roasted Garlic

If you have never tried roasting garlic, then this is the recipe that will convert you to its delicious mellowed sweetness. Spaghettini is the name given to very fine spaghetti, but any long thin pasta can be used in this dish – try spaghetti, linguine, tagliatelle or capellini. This simple pasta dish is very good served with a mixed leaf salad dressed with lemon juice and extra virgin olive oil.

Serves 4
1 whole head of garlic
400g/14oz fresh or dried spaghettini
coarsely shaved Parmesan cheese, to serve

From the storecupboard
120ml/4fl oz/½ cup extra virgin olive oil
salt and ground black pepper

1 Preheat the oven to 180°C/350°F/Gas 4. Place the garlic in an oiled roasting pan and roast it for 30 minutes.

2 Leave the garlic to cool, then lay it on its side and slice off the top one-third with a sharp knife.

3 Hold the garlic over a bowl and dig out the flesh from each clove with the point of the knife. When all the flesh has been added to the bowl, pour in the oil and add plenty of black pepper. Mix well.

4 Cook the pasta in a pan of salted, boiling water according to the instructions on the packet. Drain the pasta and return it to the clean pan. Pour in the oil and garlic mixture and toss the pasta vigorously over a medium heat until all the strands are thoroughly coated. Serve immediately, with shavings of Parmesan.

Cook's Tip
Garlic is recognized as one of the top foods for preventing cancer and these properties are unaffected by roasting.

Spaghetti with Lemon

This is the dish to make when you get home and find there's nothing to eat. If you keep spaghetti and olive oil in the storecupboard, and garlic and lemons in the vegetable rack, you can prepare this delicious meal in minutes. You can also add some freshly grated Parmesan cheese if you have some.

Serves 4
350g/12oz dried spaghetti
juice of 1 large lemon
2 garlic cloves, cut into very thin slivers

From the storecupboard
90ml/6 tbsp extra virgin olive oil
salt and ground black pepper

1 Cook the pasta in a pan of salted, boiling water according to the instructions on the packet, then drain thoroughly and return it to the pan.

2 Pour the olive oil and lemon juice over the cooked pasta, sprinkle in the slivers of garlic and add seasoning to taste. Toss the pasta over a medium to high heat for 1–2 minutes. Serve immediately in four warmed bowls.

Cook's Tip
Spaghetti is the best type of pasta for this recipe, because the olive oil and lemon juice cling to its long thin strands. If you are out of spaghetti, use another dried long pasta shape instead, such as spaghettini, linguine or tagliatelle.

Variation
If you have any other ingredients lurking in the storecupboard (pantry) or the refrigerator, they could be made use of here. Black olives, pitted and chopped, would complement this dish, or some rocket (arugula) leaves, either tossed into the pasta to wilt them, or as the basis for a nice leaf salad on the side. A sprinkling of chopped fresh herbs will add a touch of vibrance.

Garlic Spaghettini: Energy 545kcal/2296kJ; Protein 14.5g; Carbohydrate 84.9g, of which sugars 4.1g; Fat 18.7g, of which saturates 2.6g; Cholesterol 0mg; Calcium 55mg; Fibre 4.2g; Sodium 8mg.
Lemon Spaghetti: Energy 448kcal/1886kJ; Protein 10.5g; Carbohydrate 64.9g, of which sugars 3g; Fat 18.1g, of which saturates 2.5g; Cholesterol 0mg; Calcium 22mg; Fibre 2.6g; Sodium 3mg.

Vermicelli with Lemon

Fresh and tangy, this makes an excellent first course for a dinner party. It doesn't rely on fresh seasonal ingredients, so it is good at any time of year.

Serves 4
350g/12oz dried vermicelli
juice of 2 large lemons
200ml/7fl oz/scant 1 cup panna da cucina or double (heavy) cream
115g/4oz/1¼ cups freshly grated Parmesan cheese

From the storecupboard
50g/2oz/¼ cup butter
salt and ground black pepper

1 Bring a pan of lightly salted water to the boil, add the pasta and cook until *al dente*.

2 Meanwhile, pour the lemon juice into a medium pan. Stir in the butter and cream, then add salt and pepper to taste.

3 Bring to the boil, then lower the heat and simmer for about 4 minutes, stirring occasionally, until the cream reduces slightly.

4 Drain the pasta and return it to the pan it was cooked in. Add the grated Parmesan, then taste the sauce for seasoning and pour it over the pasta. Toss quickly over medium heat until the pasta is evenly coated with the sauce, then divide among four warmed bowls and serve immediately.

Cook's Tip
Lemons vary in the amount of juice they yield. On average, a large fresh lemon will yield 60–90ml/4–6 tbsp. The lemony flavour of this dish is supposed to be quite sharp – but you can use less juice, if you prefer.

Variation
For an even tangier taste, add a little grated lemon rind to the sauce when you add the butter and the cream in Step 2.

Fettuccine all'Alfredo

This simple recipe was invented by a Roman restaurateur called Alfredo, who became famous for serving it with a gold fork and spoon. Today's busy cooks will find cartons of long-life cream invaluable for this type of recipe. If you can't get fettucine, any long ribbon-like pasta can be used in this dish – try tagliatelle or the slightly wider pappardelle instead.

Serves 4
200ml/7fl oz/scant 1 cup double (heavy) cream
50g/2oz/⅔ cup freshly grated Parmesan cheese, plus extra to serve
350g/12oz fresh fettuccine

From the storecupboard
50g/2oz/¼ cup butter
salt and ground black pepper

1 Melt the butter in a large pan. Add the cream and bring it to the boil. Simmer for 5 minutes, stirring constantly, then add the Parmesan cheese, with salt and ground black pepper to taste, and turn off the heat under the pan.

2 Bring a large pan of salted water to the boil. Drop in the pasta all at once and quickly bring the water back to the boil, stirring occasionally. Cook the pasta for 2–3 minutes, or according to the instructions on the packet. Drain well.

3 Turn on the heat under the pan of cream to low, add the cooked pasta all at once and toss until it is well coated in the sauce. Taste the sauce for seasoning. Serve immediately, with extra grated Parmesan handed around separately.

Variation
For an even simpler version of this dish, which children adore, simply cook the pasta, drain, transfer into a warmed bowl, then add the butter and Parmesan a third at a time, tossing the pasta after each addition until it is evenly coated. Without the cream you will need to double up the amount of Parmesan. Season to taste, add more Parmesan if needed, and serve.

Vermicelli: Energy 706kcal/2934kJ; Protein 20.3g; Carbohydrate 70.4g, of which sugars 1.9g; Fat 37.9g, of which saturates 24.6g; Cholesterol 61mg; Calcium 406mg; Fibre 0.1g; Sodium 420mg.
Fettuccine: Energy 697kcal/2912kJ; Protein 16.3g; Carbohydrate 65.8g, of which sugars 3.8g; Fat 42.8g, of which saturates 26g; Cholesterol 108mg; Calcium 199mg; Fibre 2.6g; Sodium 226mg.

Pansotti with Walnut Sauce

Walnuts and cream make a rich and luscious sauce for stuffed pasta, particularly the types filled with cheese and herbs. Serve this indulgent dish with warm walnut bread and a light, fruity white wine.

Serves 4
90g/3½ oz/scant 1 cup shelled walnuts
120ml/4fl oz/½ cup double (heavy) cream
350g/12oz cheese and herb-filled pansotti or other stuffed pasta

From the storecupboard
60ml/4 tbsp garlic-flavoured olive oil
salt and ground black pepper

1 Put the walnuts and garlic oil in a food processor and process to a paste, adding up to 120ml/4fl oz/½ cup warm water through the feeder tube to slacken the consistency. Spoon the mixture into a large bowl and add the cream. Beat well to mix, then season to taste with salt and black pepper.

2 Cook the pansotti or stuffed pasta in a large pan of salted, boiling water for 4–5 minutes, or according to the instructions on the packet. Meanwhile, put the walnut sauce in a large warmed bowl and add a ladleful of the pasta cooking water to thin it a little.

3 Drain the pasta and transfer it into the bowl of walnut sauce. Toss well, then serve immediately.

Variation
Use pesto for an alternative nutty sauce that is an absolute classic. Jars of ready-made sauce are widely available, but it is quick and easy to make your own with the aid of a food processor. Blend 50g/2oz fresh basil leaves with 25g/1oz/¼ cup toasted pine nuts and 2 peeled garlic cloves. With the motor still running, drizzle in 120ml/4fl oz/½ cup extra virgin olive oil until the mixture forms a paste. Pour into a bowl and add 25g/1oz/⅓ cup freshly grated Parmesan. Season to taste.

Spaghetti with Fresh Tomato Sauce

This is the famous Neapolitan sauce that is made in summer when tomatoes are very ripe and sweet. It is very simple, so that nothing detracts from the flavour of the tomatoes themselves. It is served here with spaghetti, which is the traditional choice of pasta.

Serves 4
675g/1½lb ripe Italian plum tomatoes
1 onion, finely chopped
350g/12oz fresh or dried spaghetti
1 small handful fresh basil leaves
shaved Parmesan cheese, to serve

From the storecupboard
60ml/4 tbsp olive oil
salt and ground black pepper

1 With a sharp knife, cut a cross in the base of each tomato. Bring a medium pan of water to the boil and remove from the heat. Plunge a few of the tomatoes into the water, leave for 30 seconds or so, then lift them out with a slotted spoon. Repeat with the remaining tomatoes, then peel off the skins and roughly chop the flesh.

2 Heat the oil in a large pan, add the chopped onion and cook over low heat, stirring frequently, for about 5 minutes, until softened and lightly coloured. Add the tomatoes, with salt and pepper to taste, bring to a simmer, then turn the heat down to low and cover. Cook, stirring occasionally, for 30–40 minutes, until thick.

3 Meanwhile, bring a pan of lightly salted water to the boil, add the pasta and cook until *al dente*. Shred the basil leaves finely.

4 Remove the sauce from the heat, stir in the basil and taste for seasoning. Drain the pasta, turn it into a warmed serving bowl, pour the sauce over and toss well. Serve immediately, with coarsely shaved Parmesan handed separately.

Cook's Tip
The Italian plum tomatoes called San Marzano are the best variety to use. When fully ripe, their thin skins peel off easily.

Pansotti: Energy 702kcal/2931kJ; Protein 14.3g; Carbohydrate 66.1g, of which sugars 4g; Fat 44.1g, of which saturates 13g; Cholesterol 41mg; Calcium 58mg; Fibre 3.3g; Sodium 11mg.
Spaghetti: Energy 383kcal/1623kJ; Protein 11.9g; Carbohydrate 71.3g, of which sugars 9g; Fat 7.6g, of which saturates 1.1g; Cholesterol 0mg; Calcium 38mg; Fibre 4.4g; Sodium 18mg.

Tagliatelle with Vegetable Ribbons

Narrow strips of courgette and carrot mingle well with tagliatelle to resemble coloured pasta. Serve as a side dish, or sprinkle with freshly grated Parmesan cheese for a light appetizer or vegetarian main course. Flavoured oils, such as garlic (used here), herbs or chilli, are widely available and are a quick way of adding flavour to pasta.

Serves 4
2 large courgettes (zucchini)
2 large carrots
250g/9oz fresh egg tagliatelle

From the storecupboard
60ml/4 tbsp garlic-flavoured olive oil
salt and ground black pepper

1 With a vegetable peeler, cut the courgettes and carrots into long thin ribbons. Bring a large pan of salted water to the boil, then add the courgette and carrot ribbons. Bring the water back to the boil and boil for 30 seconds, drain and set aside.

2 Cook the tagliatelle according to the instructions on the packet. Drain the pasta and return it to the pan. Add the vegetable ribbons, garlic-flavoured oil and seasoning and toss over a medium to high heat until the pasta and vegetables are glistening with oil. Serve the pasta immediately.

Cook's Tip
To make your own herb oils, half fill a jar with washed and dried fresh herbs. Pour over olive oil to cover, then seal the jar and store in cool, dark place for 3 days. Strain the oil into a clean jar and discard the herbs.

Variation
Other types of long pasta are suitable for this dish: try the slightly narrower fettucine, or pappardelle, the broad ribbon noodles with wavy edges.

Spaghetti with Raw Tomato and Ricotta Sauce

This wonderfully simple uncooked sauce goes well with many different kinds of freshly cooked pasta, both long strands such as spaghetti, tagliatelle or linguine, and short shapes such as macaroni, rigatoni or penne. It is always at its best in summer when made with rich, sweet plum tomatoes that have ripened on the vine in the sun and have their fullest flavour.

Serves 4
500g/1¼lb ripe Italian plum tomatoes
350g/12oz dried spaghetti or pasta of your choice
115g/4oz ricotta salata cheese, diced

From the storecupboard
75ml/5 tbsp garlic-flavoured olive oil
salt and ground black pepper

1 Coarsely chop the plum tomatoes, removing the cores and as many of the seeds as you can.

2 Put the tomatoes and oil in a bowl, adding salt and pepper to taste, and stir well. Cover and leave at room temperature for 1–2 hours to let the flavours mingle.

3 Cook the spaghetti or your chosen pasta according to the packet instructions, then drain well.

4 Taste the sauce to check the seasoning before tossing it with the hot pasta. Sprinkle with the cheese and serve immediately.

Cook's Tips
• *The Italian cheese, ricotta salata, is a salted and dried version of ricotta cheese. If it is not available, you can substitute it with the ubiquitous feta cheese in this dish.*
• *Add some plump and juicy black olives, not only are they delicious, but they help to reduce cholesterol and thereby reduce the risk of heart attack.*

Tagliatelle: Energy 397kcal/1663kJ; Protein 11.5g; Carbohydrate 52.4g, of which sugars 8.3g; Fat 17.1g, of which saturates 3.3g; Cholesterol 19mg; Calcium 80mg; Fibre 4.8g; Sodium 127mg.
Spaghetti and Ricotta: Energy 496kcal/2087kJ; Protein 14g; Carbohydrate 69.6g, of which sugars 7.7g; Fat 19.9g, of which saturates 4.9g; Cholesterol 12mg; Calcium 31mg; Fibre 3.8g; Sodium 14mg.

Spaghetti with Bottarga

Although this may seem an unusual recipe, with bottarga (salted and air-dried mullet or tuna roe) as the principal ingredient, it is very well known in Sardinia, Sicily and parts of southern Italy. It is simplicity itself to make and tastes excellent. Bottarga can be bought from Italian delicatessens.

Serves 4
350g/12oz dried spaghetti
2–3 garlic cloves, peeled
60–90ml/4–6 tbsp bottarga

From the storecupboard
about 60ml/4 tbsp olive oil
ground black pepper

1 Cook the pasta in lightly salted water according to the instructions on the packet.

2 Meanwhile, heat half the olive oil in a large pan. Add the garlic and cook gently, stirring, for a few minutes. Remove the pan from the heat, scoop out the garlic with a slotted spoon and discard, leaving the garlic-flavoured oil in the bottom. (You could simply use garlic-infused oil instead.)

3 Drain the pasta very well. Return the pan of oil to the heat and add the drained pasta. Toss well to get a good coating of oil, season with ground pepper and moisten with the remaining oil, or add more to taste.

4 Divide the pasta among four warmed bowls, sprinkle the grated bottarga over the top and serve immediately.

Linguine with Anchovies and Capers

This is a fantastic storecupboard recipe. Use salted capers if you can find them, as they have a better flavour than the ones bottled in brine, but remember that you need to rinse them thoroughly before using. Be sure to chop the anchovies finely so that they literally 'melt' into the sauce.

Serves 4
450g/1lb dried linguine
8 anchovy fillets, drained
30ml/2 tbsp salted capers, thoroughly rinsed and drained

From the storecupboard
75ml/5 tbsp garlic-infused olive oil
salt and ground black pepper

1 Cook the linguine in plenty of salted, boiling water according to the instructions on the packet.

2 Meanwhile, finely chop the anchovy fillets and place in a small pan with the oil and a little black pepper. Heat very gently for 5 minutes, stirring occasionally, until the anchovies start to disintegrate.

3 Drain the pasta thoroughly and toss with the anchovies, oil and capers. Season with a little salt and plenty of ground black pepper to taste. Divide between warmed bowls and serve immediately.

Linguine with Rocket

This fashionable first course is very quick and easy to make. Rocket has an excellent peppery flavour which combines beautifully with the rich, creamy tang of fresh Parmesan cheese. Parmesan keeps well in the refrigerator for up to a month – the dried variety is a very poor substitute and bears little resemblance to the real thing.

Serves 4
350g/12oz fresh or dried linguine
1 large bunch rocket (arugula), about 150g/5oz, stalks removed, shredded or torn
75g/3oz/1 cup freshly grated Parmesan cheese

From the storecupboard
120ml/4fl oz/½ cup extra virgin olive oil
salt and ground black pepper

1 Cook the pasta in a large pan of boiling water according to the instructions on the packet, then drain thoroughly.

2 Gently heat about 60ml/4 tbsp of the olive oil in the pasta pan, then add the drained pasta, followed by the rocket. Toss thoroughly, to get a good coating of oil, over a medium to high heat for 1–2 minutes, or until the rocket is just wilted, then remove the pan from the heat.

3 Transfer the pasta and rocket into a large, warmed bowl. Add half of the freshly grated Parmesan and the remaining olive oil. Add a little salt and black pepper to taste.

4 Toss the mixture quickly to mix. Serve immediately, sprinkled with the remaining Parmesan.

Cook's Tip
Rocket (arugula) has a strong peppery flavour when raw, which is even more robust in wild rocket. When steamed or wilted, the flavour is slightly milder, but equally delicious. Rocket is actually classified as a herb, but is a popular addition to salad. It is often served as an appetizer, simply with shavings of Parmesan cheese and a generous drizzle of olive oil.

Spaghetti Bottarga: Energy 419kcal/1769kJ; Protein 12.7g; Carbohydrate 66.1g, of which sugars 3g; Fat 13.4g, of which saturates 1.9g; Cholesterol 43mg; Calcium 25mg; Fibre 2.9g; Sodium 321mg.
Anchovy Linguine: Energy 516kcal/2176kJ; Protein 14.5g; Carbohydrate 83.4g, of which sugars 3.7g; Fat 16.1g, of which saturates 2.3g; Cholesterol 2mg; Calcium 40mg; Fibre 3.3g; Sodium 151mg.
Rocket Linguine: Energy 632kcal/2647kJ; Protein 28.8g; Carbohydrate 71.1g, of which sugars 8.7g; Fat 27.6g, of which saturates 6.8g; Cholesterol 19mg; Calcium 910mg; Fibre 10.7g; Sodium 753mg.

Farfalle with Tuna

Ready-made tomato sauce and canned tuna are endlessly versatile for making weekday suppers. A variety of herbs can be added to simple pasta dishes like this one – choose from basil, marjoram or oregano – and use fresh herbs, as the short cooking time does not allow the flavour of dried herbs to develop fully. Add a garnish of fresh oregano to this dish if you have some.

Serves 4

400g/14oz/3½ cups dried farfalle
600ml/1 pint/2½ cups tomato sauce
175g/6oz can tuna in olive oil
8–10 pitted black olives, sliced into rings

From the storecupboard

salt and ground black pepper

1 Cook the pasta in a large pan of lightly salted, boiling water according to the instructions on the packet. Meanwhile, heat the tomato sauce in a separate pan and add the olives.

2 Drain the canned tuna and flake it with a fork. Add the tuna to the sauce with about 60ml/4 tbsp of the hot water used for cooking the pasta. Taste and adjust the seasoning.

3 Drain the pasta thoroughly and transfer it into a large, warmed serving bowl. Pour the tuna sauce over the top and toss lightly to mix. Serve immediately.

Cook's Tip

If you have 20 minutes, you can make a fresh tomato sauce out of storecupboard ingredients. Simply heat 15ml/1 tbsp olive oil in a pan, add 1 chopped onion and fry for 3–4 minutes until soft. Add 1 chopped garlic clove and cook for about 1 minute more. Pour in 400g/14oz chopped tomatoes and stir in 15ml/1 tbsp tomato purée (paste). Add 30ml/2 tbsp dried oregano and simmer for about 15 minutes, until thickened. Season with salt and pepper. You can store home-made tomato sauce in the freezer for up to 1 month.

Penne with Cream and Smoked Salmon

This modern way of serving pasta is popular all over Italy and in many Italian restaurants. The three essential ingredients combine perfectly, and the butter and herbs complement them beautifully. This dish is very quick and easy to make.

Serves 4

350g/12oz/3 cups dried penne
115g/4oz thinly sliced smoked salmon
2–3 fresh thyme sprigs
150ml/¼ pint/⅔ cup extra-thick single (light) cream

From the storecupboard

25g/1oz/2 tbsp butter
salt and ground black pepper

1 Cook the pasta in a pan of salted, boiling water according to the instructions on the packet.

2 Meanwhile, using kitchen scissors, cut the smoked salmon into thin strips, about 5mm/¼in wide. Remove the leaves from the thyme sprigs.

3 Melt the butter in a large pan. Stir in the cream with about a quarter of the salmon and thyme leaves, then season with pepper. Heat gently for 3–4 minutes, stirring all the time. Do not allow to boil. Taste the sauce for seasoning.

4 Drain the pasta and toss it in the cream and salmon sauce. Divide among four warmed bowls and top with the remaining salmon and thyme leaves. Serve immediately.

Variations

- *For a low-fat version of this dish, drop the butter from the recipe and replace the single (light) cream with low-fat crème fraîche. It has a slightly sharp taste, but works well in this dish with the rich flavour of smoked salmon.*
- *As an alternative to smoked salmon, smoked trout could be used in this recipe.*

Farfalle with Tuna: Energy 459kcal/1949kJ; Protein 25.2g; Carbohydrate 78.6g, of which sugars 7.8g; Fat 7.1g, of which saturates 1.1g; Cholesterol 22mg; Calcium 53mg; Fibre 4.2g; Sodium 756mg.
Penne with Salmon: Energy 459kcal/1936kJ; Protein 19.1g; Carbohydrate 65.7g, of which sugars 3.8g; Fat 15.2g, of which saturates 8.2g; Cholesterol 44mg; Calcium 62mg; Fibre 2.6g; Sodium 592mg.

Tagliatelle with Prosciutto and Parmesan

Consisting of a few prime Italian ingredients, this pasta dish is simplicity itself to make yet tastes wonderful. Serve with a fresh salad and chunks of warm ciabatta bread for lunch.

Serves 4

115g/4oz prosciutto
400g/14oz fresh or dried tagliatelle
50g/2oz/⅔ cup freshly grated Parmesan cheese
a few fresh sage leaves, to garnish

From the storecupboard

75g/3oz/6 tbsp butter
salt and ground black pepper

1 Cut the prosciutto into strips the same width as the tagliatelle. Bring a pan of lightly salted water to the boil, add the pasta and cook until *al dente*.

2 Meanwhile, melt the butter gently in a pan, stir in the prosciutto strips and heat through over very gentle heat, being careful not to let them colour.

3 Drain the tagliatelle through a colander and pile into a warmed serving dish.

4 Sprinkle the Parmesan cheese over the pasta and pour the buttery prosciutto on the top. Season well with black pepper and garnish with the sage leaves.

Cook's Tip

Both fresh and dried tagliatelle taste very good with this sauce. The flat ribbons are usually 1cm/½in wide. Dried tagliatelle is often sold folded into nests, which begin to unravel as they cook. To ring the changes, use different coloured tagliatelle: green pasta is flavoured and coloured with spinach, while the pink variety has tomato added to it. The pasta can also be flavoured with mushrooms, beetroot (beets) and saffron.

Meatballs in Tomato Sauce

Cook meatballs in their sauce, rather than frying them first, because this helps keep them nice and moist. Serve this comforting dish in the traditional way with spaghetti and shavings of Parmesan cheese.

Serves 4

225g/8oz/1 cup minced (ground) beef
4 Sicilian-style sausages
2 x 400g/14oz cans pomodorino tomatoes

From the storecupboard

salt and ground black pepper

1 Put the minced beef in a bowl and season with salt and pepper. Remove the sausages from their skins and mix thoroughly into the beef.

2 Shape the mixture into balls about the size of large walnuts and arrange in a single layer in a shallow baking dish. Cover and chill for 30 minutes.

3 Preheat the oven to 180°C/350°F/Gas 4. Process the tomatoes in a food processor until just smooth, and season. Pour over the meatballs, making sure they are all covered.

4 Bake the meatballs for 40 minutes, stirring once or twice until they are cooked through, then serve.

Variations

Meatballs can be made with any minced (ground) meat you have available. They are particularly good made from pork or lamb. The meatballs in this recipe get their flavouring from the Sicilian-style sausage meat, but if you want to make them with fresh ingredients, it doesn't take too long. You need some finely chopped or grated onion or shallots, some chopped fresh herbs, such as, sage or flat leaf parsley, some breadcrumbs and a beaten egg to bind the ingredients together. You can also add spices, such as paprika or cumin, for a change. Meatballs can be frozen in an airtight container for 3–4 months. Make sure that you separate them so that they don't all stick together.

Tagliatelle: Energy 569kcal/2394kJ; Protein 22.3g; Carbohydrate 74.5g, of which sugars 3.7g; Fat 22.3g, of which saturates 12.9g; Cholesterol 69mg; Calcium 181mg; Fibre 2.9g; Sodium 598mg.
Meatballs: Energy 475kcal/1972kJ; Protein 28.5g; Carbohydrate 15.8g, of which sugars 5.1g; Fat 33.2g, of which saturates 10.7g; Cholesterol 123mg; Calcium 58mg; Fibre 2g; Sodium 131mg.

Steamed Rice

Rice is such a staple food in China, that 'Have you had rice?' is a synonym for 'Have you eaten?' Stick to the amounts given in this recipe for perfectly cooked rice every time.

Serves 4
225g/8oz/generous 1 cup long grain rice, rinsed and drained

From the storecupboard
a pinch of salt

1 Put the rice into a heavy pan or clay pot. Add 600ml/1 pint/2½ cups water to cover the rice by 2.5cm/1in. Add the salt, and then bring the water to the boil. Reduce the heat, cover the pan and cook gently for about 20 minutes, or until all the water has been absorbed.

2 Remove the pan from the heat and leave to steam, covered, for a further 5–10 minutes. Fluff up with a fork, and serve.

Fragrant Coconut Rice

Originally from India and Thailand, coconut rice is popular throughout Asia. Rich and nourishing, it is often served with a tangy fruit and vegetable salad, and complements some of the spicier curries from the continent. The pandanus provides the fragrance.

Serves 4
1 litre/1¾ pints/4 cups coconut milk
450g/1lb/2¼ cups short grain rice, washed and drained
1 pandanus (screwpine) leaf, tied in a loose knot

From the storecupboard
salt

1 Heat the coconut milk in a heavy pan and stir in the rice with a little salt. Add the pandanus leaf and bring the liquid to the boil. Simmer until the liquid has been absorbed.

2 Turn off the heat and cover with a clean dish towel, then replace the lid. Steam for a further 15–20 minutes. Fluff up the rice and serve.

Steamed Sticky Rice

Sticky rice requires a long soak in water before being cooked. The best cooking method is in a bamboo steamer over a wok or pan of boiling water. Sticky rice is used for savoury and sweet dishes, especially rice cakes, and is available in Chinese and Asian stores, and can also be found in some large supermarkets.

Serves 4
350g/12oz/1¾ cups sticky rice

1 Put the rice into a large bowl and fill the bowl with cold water. Leave the rice to soak for at least 6 hours, then drain, rinse thoroughly, and drain again.

2 Fill a wok or heavy pan one-third full with water. Place a bamboo steamer, with the lid on, over the wok or pan and bring the water to the boil.

3 Uncover the steamer and place a dampened piece of muslin (cheesecloth) over the rack. Transfer the rice into the middle and spread it out to form an even layer. Fold the muslin over the rice, re-cover with the lid and steam for 25 minutes until the rice is tender but firm.

Cook's Tip
The measured quantity of rice grains doubles when cooked, which is a useful point to remember when planning to cook sticky rice for a meal. The grains clump together when cooked, making this type of rice ideal for moulding. It is fairly bulky, so is often served with a dipping sauce.

Variation
Sticky rice can be enjoyed as a sweet, filling snack with sugar and coconut milk.

Steamed Rice: Energy 202kcal/845kJ; Protein 4.2g; Carbohydrate 44.9g, of which sugars 0g; Fat 0.3g, of which saturates 0g; Cholesterol 0mg; Calcium 11mg; Fibre 0g; Sodium 0mg.
Fragrant Coconut Rice: Energy 459kcal/1927kJ; Protein 9.1g; Carbohydrate 102g, of which sugars 12.3g; Fat 1.3g, of which saturates 0.5g; Cholesterol 0mg; Calcium 94mg; Fibre 0g; Sodium 275mg.
Steamed Sticky Rice: Energy 314kcal/1314kJ; Protein 6.5g; Carbohydrate 69.8g, of which sugars 0g; Fat 0.5g, of which saturates 0g; Cholesterol 0mg; Calcium 17mg; Fibre 0g; Sodium 0mg.

Rice Cakes with Dipping Sauce

Easy to make, these rice cakes will keep almost indefinitely in an airtight container. Start making them at least a day before you plan to serve them, so the rice can dry out overnight.

Serves 4–6
175g/6oz/1 cup Thai jasmine rice
dipping sauce, for serving

From the storecupboard
oil, for deep-frying and greasing

1 Preheat the oven to the lowest setting. Grease a baking sheet. Wash the rice in several changes of water. Put it in a pan, add 350ml/12fl oz/1½ cups water and cover tightly. Bring to the boil, reduce the heat and simmer gently for about 15 minutes.

2 Remove the lid and fluff up the rice. Spoon it on to the baking sheet and press it down with the back of a spoon. Leave in the oven to dry out overnight.

3 Break the rice into bitesize pieces. Heat the oil in a wok or deep-fryer to 190°C/375°F, or until a cube of bread, added to the oil, browns in 40 seconds. Deep-fry the rice cakes, in batches, for about 1 minute, until they puff up but are not browned. Remove and drain well. Serve with the dipping sauce.

Cook's Tip
For a spicy meat-based dipping sauce to serve with the rice cakes, soak 6 dried red chillies in warm water, drain, then grind to a paste with 2 chopped shallots, 2.5ml/½ tsp salt, 2 chopped garlic cloves, 4 chopped coriander (cilantro) roots and 10 white peppercorns. Heat 250ml/8fl oz/1 cup coconut milk. When it starts to separate, stir in the chilli paste and cook for 3 minutes. Add 15ml/1 tbsp shrimp paste and 115g/4oz minced (ground) pork. Cook, stirring, for 10 minutes, then stir in 4 chopped cherry tomatoes, 15ml/1 tbsp each fish sauce and brown sugar, 30ml/2 tbsp each tamarind juice and chopped roasted peanuts, and 2 chopped spring onions (scallions). Cook until thick, then pour into a bowl and cool.

Savoury Ground Rice

This rice dish is often served as an accompaniment to soups and stews in West Africa. Cooked with milk and fresh parsley, it makes a creamy dish that would go well with plump herby grilled sausages.

Serves 4
300ml/½ pint/1¼ cups milk
15ml/1 tbsp chopped fresh parsley
275g/10oz/1⅔ cups ground rice

From the storecupboard
25g/1oz/2 tbsp butter or margarine
salt

1 Place 300ml/½ pint/1¼ water in a pan. Pour in the milk, bring to the boil and add the salt and parsley.

2 Add the butter or margarine and the ground rice, stirring with a wooden spoon to prevent the rice from becoming lumpy.

3 Cover the pan and cook over a low heat for about 15 minutes, beating the mixture every 2 minutes to prevent the formation of lumps.

4 To test if the rice is cooked, rub a pinch of the mixture between your fingers: if it feels smooth and fairly dry, it is ready. Serve hot.

Cook's Tip
Ground rice is a creamy white colour, with a grainy texture. Although often used in sweet dishes, it is a tasty grain to serve with savoury dishes, too. The addition of extra milk gives a creamier flavour, if you prefer.

Variation
Instead of adding water to this recipe you could replace it with the same quantity of vegetable stock.

Rice Cakes: Energy 180kcal/750kJ; Protein 2.3g; Carbohydrate 25.7g, of which sugars 2.3g; Fat 7.5g, of which saturates 0.9g; Cholesterol 0mg; Calcium 7mg; Fibre 0.1g; Sodium 136mg.
Ground Rice: Energy 329kcal/1375kJ; Protein 7.8g; Carbohydrate 58.6g, of which sugars 3.6g; Fat 6.8g, of which saturates 4.1g; Cholesterol 18mg; Calcium 109mg; Fibre 0.1g; Sodium 317mg.

Oven-baked Porcini Risotto

This risotto is easy to make because you don't have to stand over it stirring constantly as it cooks, as you do with a traditional risotto. There are several types of risotto rice: both arborio and carnaroli are suitable for this dish and are widely available. Serve with Parmesan shavings.

Serves 4
25g/1oz/½ cup dried porcini mushrooms
1 onion, finely chopped
225g/8oz/generous 1 cup risotto rice

From the storecupboard
30ml/2 tbsp garlic-infused olive oil
salt and ground black pepper

1 Put the mushrooms in a heatproof bowl and pour over 750ml/1¼ pints/3 cups boiling water. Leave to soak for 30 minutes. Drain the mushrooms through a sieve (strainer) lined with kitchen paper, reserving the soaking liquor. Rinse the mushrooms thoroughly under running water to remove any grit, and dry on kitchen paper.

2 Preheat the oven to 180°C/350°F/Gas 4. Heat the oil in a roasting pan on the stove and add the onion. Cook for 2–3 minutes, or until softened but not coloured.

3 Add the rice and stir for 1–2 minutes, then add the mushrooms and stir. Pour in the mushroom liquor and mix well. Season with salt and pepper, and cover with foil.

4 Bake in the oven for 30 minutes, stirring occasionally, until all the stock has been absorbed and the rice is tender. Divide between warm serving bowls and serve immediately.

Variation
You can stir in a knob (pat) of butter and some freshly grated Parmesan cheese to intensify the richness of this comforting dish. A sprinkling of chopped fresh flat leaf parsley makes a colourful and appetizing garnish. Serve this dish with a crisp green salad.

Persian Baked Rice

In this Persian-style dish, rice is cooked slowly over a low heat so that a crust forms on the bottom. The mild flavours of saffron and almonds go perfectly together. This dish is an ideal accompaniment for lamb as a main course.

Serves 4
450g/1lb/2¼ cups basmati rice
a good pinch of saffron strands
50g/2oz/½ cup flaked (sliced) almonds

From the storecupboard
50g/2oz/¼ cup butter
salt and ground black pepper

1 Cook the rice in a pan of boiling, salted water for 5 minutes, then drain thoroughly. Meanwhile, put the saffron in a small bowl with 30ml/2 tbsp warm water and leave to infuse (steep) for at least 5 minutes.

2 Heat the butter in a large flameproof pan and add the almonds. Cook over a medium heat for 2–3 minutes, or until golden, stirring occasionally. Add the rice and stir well, then stir in the saffron and its liquid, plus 1 litre/1¾ pints/4 cups water. Season and cover with a tight-fitting lid.

3 Cook over a very low heat for 30 minutes, or until the rice is tender and a crust has formed on the bottom of the pan. Fork up the rice to mix in the crust before serving.

Cook's Tip
This delicately flavoured rice dish is the perfect foil for some robustly flavoured lamb chops marinated in onion, garlic, chillies, and ginger spiced with cardamom, nutmeg and ground fennel. Alternatively, it would make an excellent accompaniment to a vegetable chilli dish.

Variation
Although basmati rice is traditional in this dish, you could use any long grain rice, or brown rice, if you prefer.

Porcini Risotto: Energy 260kcal/1085kJ; Protein 4.8g; Carbohydrate 46.2g, of which sugars 0.9g; Fat 5.9g, of which saturates 0.8g; Cholesterol 0mg; Calcium 16mg; Fibre 0.5g; Sodium 2mg.
Persian Rice: Energy 314kcal/1310kJ; Protein 6.5g; Carbohydrate 60.2g, of which sugars 0.2g; Fat 4.8g, of which saturates 1.5g; Cholesterol 5mg; Calcium 25mg; Fibre 0.3g; Sodium 16mg.

Risotto with Asparagus

Fresh farm asparagus only has a short season, so make the most of it with this elegant risotto.

Serves 3–4

225g/8oz fresh asparagus
750ml/1¼ pints/3 cups vegetable or chicken stock
1 small onion, finely chopped
275g/10oz/1½ cups risotto rice, such as arborio or carnaroli
75g/3oz/1 cup freshly grated Parmesan cheese, to serve

From the storecupboard

65g/2½oz/5 tbsp butter
salt and ground black pepper

1 Bring a pan of water to the boil. Cut off any woody pieces on the ends of the asparagus stalks, peel the lower portions, then cook in the water for 5 minutes. Drain the asparagus, reserving the cooking water, refresh under cold water and drain again. Cut the asparagus diagonally into 4cm/1¼in pieces. Keep the tip and next-highest sections separate from the stalks.

2 Place the stock in a pan and add 450ml/¾ pint/scant 2 cups of the asparagus cooking water. Heat to simmering point and keep it hot.

3 Melt two-thirds of the butter in a large, heavy pan or deep frying pan. Add the onion and fry until it is soft and golden. Stir in all the asparagus except the top two sections. Cook for 2–3 minutes. Add the rice and cook for 1–2 minutes, mixing well to coat it with butter.

4 Stir in a ladleful of the hot liquid. Using a wooden spoon, stir until the stock has been absorbed. Gradually add the remaining stock, a little at a time, allowing the rice to absorb the liquid before adding more, and stirring all the time.

5 After 10 minutes, add the remaining asparagus sections. Continue to cook as before, for about 15 minutes, until the rice is *al dente* and the risotto is creamy.

6 Off the heat, stir in the remaining butter and the Parmesan, if using. Season and serve.

Sultan's Chickpea Pilaff

A classic buttery pilaff, fit for a sultan according to Turkish legend, this dish is a perfect accompaniment to almost any meat or fish dish.

Serves 4

50g/2oz/⅓ cup dried chickpeas, soaked in cold water overnight
1 onion, chopped
225g/8oz/generous 1 cup long grain rice, well rinsed and drained
600ml/1 pint/2½ cups chicken stock or water

From the storecupboard

30ml/2 tbsp butter
15ml/1 tbsp olive or sunflower oil
salt and ground black pepper

1 Drain the chickpeas, transfer them into a pan and fill the pan with plenty of cold water. Bring to the boil and boil for 1 minute, then lower the heat and partially cover the pan. Simmer the chickpeas for about 45 minutes, or until tender. Drain, rinse well under cold running water and remove any loose skins.

2 Melt the butter with the oil in a heavy pan, stir in the onion and cook until it softens. Add the rice and chickpeas and cover with the water or stock. Season with salt and pepper and bring to the boil. Lower the heat, partially cover the pan and simmer for 10–12 minutes, until almost all of the water has been absorbed.

3 Turn off the heat, cover the pan with a dish towel and put the lid tightly on top. Leave the rice to steam for 10 minutes, then fluff up with a fork before serving.

Cook's Tip

To make chicken stock, put 1.2kg/3lb chicken carcass into a large pan with 2 peeled and quartered onions, 2 halved carrots and 2 roughly chopped celery sticks, 1 bouquet garni, 1 peeled garlic clove and 5 black peppercorns. Cover with 1.2 litres/2 pints/5 cups cold water and bring to the boil. Reduce the heat, cover and simmer for 4–5 hours, regularly skimming off any scum from the surface. Strain through a sieve (strainer) lined with kitchen paper and leave to cool. Freeze in batches for up to 2 months.

Asparagus Risotto: Energy 467kcal/1940kJ; Protein 14.2g; Carbohydrate 56.1g, of which sugars 1.2g; Fat 20.2g, of which saturates 12.4g; Cholesterol 53mg; Calcium 256mg; Fibre 1g; Sodium 304mg.
Chickpea Pilaff: Energy 328kcal/1368kJ; Protein 7.1g; Carbohydrate 52.3g, of which sugars 1.2g; Fat 9.9g, of which saturates 4.4g; Cholesterol 16mg; Calcium 36mg; Fibre 1.6g; Sodium 51mg.

Sour Cherry Pilaff

This is a popular summer pilaff made with small, sour cherries rather than the plump, sweet ones. With its refreshing bursts of cherry, it goes with most vegetable, meat and fish dishes.

Serves 3–4

225g/8oz fresh sour cherries, such as morello, pitted
5–10ml/1–2 tsp sugar
5ml/1 tsp caraway seeds
225g/8oz/generous 1 cup long grain rice, well rinsed and drained

From the storecupboard

30ml/2 tbsp butter
salt and ground black pepper

1 Melt the butter in a heavy pan. Set a handful of the cherries aside, and toss the rest in the butter with the sugar and caraway seeds. Cook for a few minutes, then add the rice and 600ml/1 pint/2½ cups water. Season with salt and pepper.

2 Bring to the boil, lower the heat and partially cover the pan. Simmer for 10–12 minutes, until most of the water has been absorbed. Turn off the heat, cover with a dish towel, and put the lid tightly on top. Leave for 20 minutes.

3 Fluff up the rice with a fork, transfer on to a serving dish and garnish with the reserved cherries.

Cook's Tip

Due to their acidity, sour cherries are often consumed cooked or poached with sugar in sorbets, jam, bread pudding, cakes, and in a pretty compôte that is traditionally spooned over rice or yogurt. If fresh sour cherries are not available, dried cherries soaked in water can be substituted for this recipe.

Variation

Fennel seeds can be used in place of caraway seeds.

Mussel Risotto

The addition of freshly cooked mussels, aromatic coriander and a little cream to a packet of instant risotto transforms simple ingredients into a decadent treat. Serve with a side salad for a splendid supper. Other cooked shellfish, such as clams or prawns, can be used instead of mussels.

Serves 3–4

900g/2lb fresh mussels
275g/10oz packet risotto
30ml/2 tbsp chopped fresh coriander (cilantro)
30ml/2 tbsp double (heavy) cream

From the storecupboard

salt and ground black pepper

1 Scrub the mussels, discarding any that do not close when sharply tapped. Place in a large pan. Add 120ml/4fl oz/½ cup water and seasoning, then bring to the boil. Cover the pan and cook the mussels, shaking the pan occasionally, for 4–5 minutes, until they have opened. Drain, reserving the liquid and discarding any that have not opened. Shell most of the mussels, reserving a few in their shells for garnish. Strain the mussel liquid.

2 Make up the packet risotto according to the instructions, using the cooking liquid from the mussels and making it up to the required volume with water.

3 When the risotto is about three-quarters cooked, add the mussels to the pan. Add the coriander and re-cover the pan without stirring in these ingredients.

4 Remove the risotto from the heat, stir in the cream, cover and leave to rest for a few minutes. Spoon into a warmed serving dish, garnish with the reserved mussels in their shells, and serve.

Cook's Tip

For a super-quick mussel risotto, use cooked mussels in their shells – the type sold vacuum packed ready to reheat. Just reheat them according to the packet instructions and add to the made risotto with the coriander and cream.

Sour Cherry Pilaff: Energy 295kcal/1231kJ; Protein 4.7g; Carbohydrate 54g, of which sugars 9.1g; Fat 6.5g, of which saturates 3.9g; Cholesterol 16mg; Calcium 21mg; Fibre 0.5g; Sodium 46mg.
Mussel Risotto: Energy 439kcal/1833kJ; Protein 17.2g; Carbohydrate 56.6g, of which sugars 1.4g; Fat 11.3g, of which saturates 3.5g; Cholesterol 37mg; Calcium 159mg; Fibre 0.2g; Sodium 146mg.

Rosemary Risotto with Borlotti Beans

Select a high-quality risotto with a subtle flavour as the base for this recipe. The savoury beans, heady rosemary and creamy mascarpone will transform a simple product into a feast. For an even more authentic risotto flavour, substitute half the water with dry white wine. Serve with a simple salad of rocket and Parmesan shavings dressed with balsamic vinegar and plenty of ground black pepper.

Serves 3–4
400g/14oz can borlotti beans
275g/10oz packet vegetable or chicken risotto
60ml/4 tbsp mascarpone cheese
5ml/1 tsp finely chopped fresh rosemary

1 Drain the beans, rinse under cold water and drain again. Process about two-thirds of the beans to a fairly coarse purée in a food processor or blender. Set the remaining beans aside.

2 Make up the risotto according to the packet instructions, using the suggested quantity of water.

3 Immediately the rice is cooked, stir in the bean purée. Add the reserved beans, with the mascarpone and rosemary. Stir thoroughly, then cover and leave to stand for about 5 minutes so that the risotto absorbs the flavours fully.

Pancetta and Broad Bean Risotto

This moist risotto makes a satisfying, balanced meal, especially when served with cooked fresh seasonal vegetables or a mixed green salad. Add some chopped fresh herbs and Parmesan shavings as a garnish, if you like. Pancetta is dry cured pork and is the Italian equivalent of streaky bacon – either can be used in this recipe.

Serves 4
175g/6oz smoked pancetta, diced
350g/12oz/1¾ cups risotto rice
1.5 litres/2½ pints/6¼ cups simmering herb stock
225g/8oz/2 cups frozen baby broad (fava) beans

From the storecupboard
salt and ground black pepper

1 Place the pancetta in a non-stick or heavy pan and cook gently, stirring occasionally, for about 5 minutes, until the fat runs.

2 Add the risotto rice to the pan and cook for 1 minute, stirring constantly. Add a ladleful of the simmering stock and cook, stirring constantly, until the liquid has been absorbed.

3 Continue adding the simmering stock, a ladleful at a time, until the rice is tender, and almost all the liquid has been absorbed. This will take 30–35 minutes.

4 Meanwhile, cook the broad beans in a pan of lightly salted, boiling water for about 3 minutes, until tender. Drain well and stir into the risotto. Season to taste. Spoon into a bowl and serve.

Crab Risotto

This simple risotto has a subtle flavour that makes the most of the delicate crab meat. It serves as a tempting main course or appetizer. It is important to use a good quality risotto rice, which will give a deliciously creamy result, but the cooked grains are still firm to the bite.

Serves 3–4
2 large cooked crabs
275g/10oz/1½ cups risotto rice
1.2 litres/2 pints/5 cups simmering fish stock
30ml/2 tbsp mixed finely chopped fresh herbs such as chives, tarragon and parsley

From the storecupboard
salt and ground black pepper

1 One at a time, hold the crabs and hit the underside with the heel of your hand. This should loosen the shell from the body. Using your thumbs, push against the body and pull away from the shell. Remove and discard the intestines and the grey gills.

2 Break off the claws and legs, then use a hammer or crackers to break them open. Using a pick, remove the meat from the claws and legs. Place the meat on a plate.

3 Using a skewer, pick out the white meat from the body cavities and place with the claw and leg meat, reserving a little white meat to garnish. Scoop out the brown meat from the shell and add to the rest of the crab meat.

4 Place the rice in a pan and add one-quarter of the stock. Bring to the boil and cook, stirring continuously, until the liquid has been absorbed. Adding a ladleful of stock at a time, continue stirring until about two-thirds of the stock has been absorbed. Then stir in the crab meat and the finely chopped herbs, and continue cooking, adding the remaining stock a ladleful at a time.

5 When the rice is almost cooked, remove it from the heat and adjust the seasoning. Cover with a dish towel and leave to stand for 3 minutes. Serve garnished with the reserved white crab meat.

Rosemary Risotto: Energy 419kcal/1752kJ; Protein 15.1g; Carbohydrate 68.8g, of which sugars 3.9g; Fat 6.2g, of which saturates 2.7g; Cholesterol 12mg; Calcium 198mg; Fibre 4.5g; Sodium 412mg.
Pancetta Risotto: Energy 511kcal/2132kJ; Protein 18g; Carbohydrate 77.6g, of which sugars 1.6g; Fat 13.9g, of which saturates 4g; Cholesterol 28mg; Calcium 55mg; Fibre 3.9g; Sodium 556mg.
Crab Risotto: Energy 496kcal/2060kJ; Protein 14.1g; Carbohydrate 56.4g, of which sugars 1.1g; Fat 18.7g, of which saturates 8.9g; Cholesterol 65mg; Calcium 25mg; Fibre 0.2g; Sodium 229mg.

Wild Mushroom and Fontina Tart

Use any types of wild mushrooms you like in this tart – chanterelles, morels, horns of plenty and ceps all have wonderful flavours. It makes an impressive vegetarian main course, served with a green salad tossed in an orange and tarragon dressing.

Serves 6
225g/8oz ready-made shortcrust pastry, thawed if frozen
350g/12oz/5 cups mixed wild mushrooms, sliced if large
150g/5oz Fontina cheese, sliced

From the storecupboard
50g/2oz/¼ cup butter
salt and ground black pepper

1 Preheat the oven to 190°C/375°F/Gas 5. Roll out the pastry and use to a line a 23cm/9in loose-bottomed flan tin (tart pan). Chill the pastry for 30 minutes, then bake blind for 15 minutes. Set aside.

2 Heat the butter in a large frying pan until foaming. Add the mushrooms and season with salt and ground black pepper. Cook over a medium heat for 4–5 minutes, moving the mushrooms about and turning them occasionally with a wooden spoon, until golden.

3 Arrange the mushrooms in the cooked pastry case with the Fontina. Return the tart to the oven for 10 minutes, or until the cheese is golden and bubbling. Serve hot.

Cook's Tip
Fontina is a deep golden yellow Italian cheese with a pale brown rind. It has lots of little holes permeating the cheese. It melts well, making it a perfect topping for this mushroom tart.

Variation
If wild mushrooms are out of season, use chestnut mushrooms, which have a more intense flavour than cultivated varieties. Shiitake mushrooms are also full of flavour.

Mushroom Stroganoff

This creamy mixed mushroom sauce is ideal for a dinner party. Serve it with toasted buckwheat, brown rice or a mixture of wild rices and garnish with chopped chives. For best results, choose a variety of different mushrooms – wild mushrooms such as chanterelles, ceps and morels add a delicious flavour and texture to the stroganoff, as well as adding colour and producing a decorative appearance.

Serves 4
900g/2lb mixed mushrooms, cut into bitesize pieces, including ⅔ button (white) mushrooms and ⅓ assorted wild or unusual mushrooms
350ml/12fl oz/1½ cups white wine sauce
250ml/8fl oz/1 cup sour cream

From the storecupboard
25g/1oz/2 tbsp butter
salt and ground black pepper

1 Melt the butter in a pan and quickly cook the mushrooms, in batches, over a high heat, until brown. Transfer the mushrooms to a bowl after cooking each batch.

2 Add the sauce to the juices remaining in the pan and bring to the boil, stirring. Reduce the heat and replace the mushrooms with any juices from the bowl. Stir well and heat for a few seconds, then remove from the heat.

3 Stir the sour cream into the cooked mushroom mixture and season to taste with salt and lots of ground black pepper. Heat through gently for a few seconds, if necessary, then transfer to warm plates and serve immediately.

Cook's Tips
- *Wild mushrooms can be found growing in shady areas during late summer, autumn and winter. Take care if you pick your own as certain varieties are poisonous.*
- *You can use crème fraîche in place of sour cream for a smooth taste in this recipe.*

Mushroom Tart: Energy 409kcal/1702kJ; Protein 10.2g; Carbohydrate 21.9g, of which sugars 2.3g; Fat 31g, of which saturates 13.4g; Cholesterol 143mg; Calcium 121mg; Fibre 2.3g; Sodium 199mg.
Mushroom Stroganoff: Energy 408kcal/1685kJ; Protein 6.5g; Carbohydrate 14.3g, of which sugars 6.3g; Fat 34.4g, of which saturates 22.4g; Cholesterol 92mg; Calcium 81mg; Fibre 3.4g; Sodium 88mg.

Mushroom Polenta

This simple recipe uses freshly made polenta, but for an even easier version you can substitute ready-made polenta and slice it straight into the dish, ready for baking. The cheesy mushroom topping is also delicious on toasted herb or sun-dried tomato bread as a light lunch or supper. Any combination of mushrooms will work – try a mixture of button and wild mushrooms as an alternative.

Serves 4
250g/9oz/1½ cups quick-cook polenta
400g/14oz chestnut mushrooms, sliced
175g/6oz/1½ cups grated Gruyère cheese

From the storecupboard
50g/2oz/¼ cup butter
salt and ground black pepper

1 Line a 28 x 18cm/11 x 7in shallow baking tin (pan) with baking parchment. Bring 1 litre/1¾ pints/4 cups water with 5ml/1 tsp salt to the boil in a large pan. Add the polenta in a steady stream, stirring constantly. Bring back to the boil, stirring, and cook for approximately 5 minutes, until the polenta is thick and smooth.

2 Turn the polenta into the prepared tin and spread it out into an even layer. Leave to cool.

3 Preheat the oven to 200°C/400°F/Gas 6. Melt the butter in a frying pan and cook the mushrooms for 3–5 minutes, until golden. Season with salt and lots of ground black pepper.

4 Turn out the polenta on to a chopping board. Peel away the baking parchment and cut into large squares.

5 Pile the squares into a shallow, ovenproof dish. Sprinkle with half the cheese, then pile the mushrooms on top and pour over their buttery juices. Sprinkle with the remaining cheese and bake for about 20 minutes, until the cheese is melting and pale golden.

Classic Margherita Pizza

Bought pizza base mixes are a great storecupboard stand-by. A margherita pizza makes a lovely simple supper, but of course you can add any extra toppings you like. Prosciutto and rocket make a great addition – just add them to the pizza after it is cooked.

Serves 2
half a 300g/11oz packet pizza base mix, or ready-made base
45ml/3 tbsp ready-made tomato and basil sauce
150g/5oz mozzarella, sliced

From the storecupboard
15ml/1 tbsp herb-infused olive oil
salt and ground black pepper

1 Make the pizza base mix (if using) according to the instructions on the packet. Brush the base with a little of the olive oil and spread over the tomato and basil sauce, not quite to the edges.

2 Arrange the slices of mozzarella on top of the pizza and bake for 25–30 minutes, or until golden.

3 Drizzle the remaining oil on top of the pizza, season with salt and black pepper and serve immediately, garnished with fresh basil leaves.

Variations

There are endless possibilities for vegetarian pizza toppings. Here are a few to get you started:

- *Fiorentina comprises spinach, thin slices of red onion, an egg and some Gruyère cheese added to the basic margherita.*
- *Quattro formaggi uses four cheeses – Dolcelatte, mozzarella, Gruyère and Parmesan – with some thinly sliced red onion straight on to the pizza base.*
- *Roasted vegetables, such as aubergine (eggplant), red and yellow (bell) peppers, courgette (zucchini) and red onion are delicious on top of a margherita pizza and even better with some goat's cheese crumbled on top.*
- *Black olives give a simple twist to a classic pizza.*

Polenta: Energy 518kcal/2155kJ; Protein 18.9g; Carbohydrate 46.2g, of which sugars 0.3g; Fat 27.2g, of which saturates 16.1g; Cholesterol 69mg; Calcium 334mg; Fibre 2.5g; Sodium 397mg.
Margherita Pizza: Energy 420kcal/1761kJ; Protein 7.6g; Carbohydrate 49.8g, of which sugars 7.8g; Fat 22.6g, of which saturates 2.2g; Cholesterol 2mg; Calcium 133mg; Fibre 3.4g; Sodium 130mg.

Baked Leek and Potato Gratin

Potatoes baked in a creamy cheese sauce make the ultimate comfort dish, whether served as an accompaniment to pork or fish dishes or, as here, with plenty of leeks and melted cheese as a main course. When preparing leeks, separate the leaves and rinse them thoroughly under cold running water for a few minutes, as soil and grit often get caught between the layers.

Serves 4–6
900g/2lb medium potatoes, thinly sliced
2 large leeks, trimmed
200g/7oz ripe Brie or Camembert cheese, sliced
450ml/¾ pint/scant 2 cups single (light) cream

From the storecupboard
salt and ground black pepper

1 Preheat the oven to 180°C/350°F/Gas 4. Cook the potatoes in plenty of lightly salted, boiling water for 3 minutes, until slightly softened, then drain. Cut the leeks into 1cm/½in lengths and blanch them in boiling water for 1 minute, until softened, then drain.

2 Turn half the potatoes into a shallow, ovenproof dish and spread them out to the edge. Cover with two-thirds of the leeks, then add the remaining potatoes. Tuck the slices of cheese and the remaining leeks in among the top layer of potatoes. Season and pour the cream over.

3 Bake for 1 hour, until tender and golden. Cover with foil if the top starts to overbrown before the potatoes are tender.

Cook's Tip
Brie and Camembert can vary enormously in strength. Some are very mild and others extremely strong. Bear this in mind when selecting a cheese for this dish. A blue cheese, such as Gorgonzola, would bring a rich piquancy to the baked leeks and potatoes, whereas Parmesan would offer a sweet-salt flavour.

Potato and Onion Tortilla

This deep-set omelette with sliced potatoes and onions is the best-known Spanish tortilla and makes a deliciously simple meal when served with a leafy salad and crusty bread. Tortilla are often made with a variety of ingredients – chopped red or yellow peppers, cooked peas, corn, or grated cheese can all be added to the mixture.

Serves 4–6
800g/1¾ lb medium potatoes
2 onions, thinly sliced
6 eggs

From the storecupboard
100ml/3½fl oz/scant ½ cup extra virgin olive oil
salt and ground black pepper

1 Thinly slice the potatoes. Heat 75ml/5 tbsp of the oil in a frying pan and cook the potatoes, turning frequently, for 10 minutes. Add the onions and seasoning, and continue to cook for a further 10 minutes, until the vegetables are tender.

2 Meanwhile, beat the eggs in a large bowl with a little seasoning. Transfer the potatoes and onions into the eggs and mix gently. Leave to stand for 10 minutes.

3 Wipe out the pan with kitchen paper and heat the remaining oil in it. Pour the egg mixture into the pan and spread it out in an even layer. Cover and cook over a very gentle heat for 20 minutes, until the eggs are just set. Serve cut into wedges.

Variation
For a fresh and tasty twist on the classic potato and onion tortilla, try adding broad (fava) beans and some chopped fresh herbs to the omelette. Gently cook the potato and onion as you normally would for about 20 minutes in all, without letting it brown. Meanwhile, cook the broad beans in boiling salted water and drain well. When cool enough, remove the broad bean skins, then add the beans to the pan along with 60ml/4 tbsp of chopped fresh herbs.

Leek and Potato: Energy 383kcal/1597kJ; Protein 13.1g; Carbohydrate 28.2g, of which sugars 5.4g; Fat 24.2g, of which saturates 15.4g; Cholesterol 72mg; Calcium 181mg; Fibre 3.3g; Sodium 225mg.
Potato Tortilla: Energy 163kcal/681kJ; Protein 5.8g; Carbohydrate 14.7g, of which sugars 2.9g; Fat 9.5g, of which saturates 1.9g; Cholesterol 127mg; Calcium 32mg; Fibre 1.2g; Sodium 56mg.

Cheesy Leek and Couscous Cake

The tangy flavour of mature Cheddar cheese goes perfectly with the sweet taste of gently fried leeks. The cheese melts into the couscous and helps it stick together, making a firm cake that's easy to cut into wedges. Serve with a crisp green salad.

Serves 4
300g/11oz/1⅔ cups couscous
2 leeks, sliced
200g/7oz/1¾ cups mature (sharp) Cheddar or Monterey Jack, grated

From the storecupboard
45ml/3 tbsp olive oil
salt and ground black pepper

1 Put the couscous in a large heatproof bowl and pour over 450ml/¾ pint/scant 2 cups boiling water. Cover and set aside for about 15 minutes, or until all the water has been absorbed.

2 Heat 15ml/1 tbsp of the oil in a 23cm/9in non-stick frying pan. Add the leeks and cook over a medium heat for 4–5 minutes, stirring occasionally, until tender and golden.

3 Remove the leeks with a slotted spoon and stir them into the couscous. Add the grated cheese and some salt and pepper and stir through.

4 Heat the remaining oil in the pan and add the couscous and leek mixture. Pat down firmly to form a cake and cook over a fairly gentle heat for 15 minutes, or until the underside is crisp and golden.

5 Slide the couscous cake on to a plate, then invert it back into the pan to cook the other side. Cook for a further 5–8 minutes, or until golden, then remove from the heat. Slide on to a board and serve cut into wedges.

Variation
There are endless variations on this tangy cake, but use a good melting cheese to bind the cake together. Try using blue cheese and caramelized onions in place of the leeks and Cheddar.

Red Onion and Goat's Cheese Tartlets

These attractive little pastries couldn't be easier to make. Garnish them with fresh thyme sprigs and serve with a selection of salad leaves and a tomato and basil salad for a light lunch or quick supper. A wide variety of different types of goat's cheeses are available – the creamy log-shaped types without a rind are most suitable for these tasty tartlets.

Serves 4
450g/1lb red onions, sliced
425g/15oz packet ready-rolled puff pastry
115g/4oz/1 cup goat's cheese, cubed

From the storecupboard
15ml/1 tbsp olive oil
salt and ground black pepper

1 Heat the oil in a large, heavy frying pan, add the onions and cook over a gentle heat for 10 minutes, or until softened, stirring occasionally to prevent them from browning. Add seasoning to taste and cook for a further 2 minutes. Remove the pan from the heat and leave to cool.

2 Preheat the oven to 220°C/425°F/Gas 7. Unroll the puff pastry and using a 15cm/6in plate as a guide, cut out four rounds.

3 Place the pastry rounds on a dampened baking sheet and, using the point of a sharp knife, score a border, 2cm/¾ in inside the edge of each pastry round.

4 Divide the onions among the pastry rounds and top with the goat's cheese. Bake for 25–30 minutes until golden brown.

Variation
To make richer-flavoured pastries, ring the changes by spreading the pastry base with red or green pesto, sun-dried tomato paste or tapenade before you top with the goat's cheese and cooked onions.

Cheesy Leek Cake: Energy 475kcal/1973kJ; Protein 18.6g; Carbohydrate 41.4g, of which sugars 2.3g; Fat 25.9g, of which saturates 12.1g; Cholesterol 49mg; Calcium 408mg; Fibre 2.2g; Sodium 364mg.
Red Onion Tartlets: Energy 554kcal/2308kJ; Protein 13.5g; Carbohydrate 48.5g, of which sugars 8g; Fat 36.4g, of which saturates 5.6g; Cholesterol 27mg; Calcium 128mg; Fibre 1.6g; Sodium 506mg.

Roasted Peppers with Halloumi and Pine Nuts

Halloumi cheese is creamy-tasting and has a firm texture and salty flavour that contrasts well with the succulent sweet peppers. This is a good dish to assemble in advance ready to just put in the oven. Halloumi is usually served cooked and lends itself well to barbecuing, frying or grilling. When heated the exterior hardens while the interior softens – similar to mozzarella cheese.

Serves 4

4 red and 2 orange or yellow (bell) peppers
250g/9oz halloumi cheese
50g/2oz/½ cup pine nuts

From the storecupboard

60ml/4 tbsp garlic-infused or herb-infused olive oil
salt and ground black pepper

1 Preheat the oven to 220°C/425°F/Gas 7. Halve the red peppers, leaving the stalks intact, and discard the seeds. Seed and coarsely chop the orange or yellow peppers.

2 Place the red pepper halves on a baking sheet and fill with the chopped peppers. Drizzle with half the garlic-infused or herb-infused olive oil and bake for 25 minutes, until the edges of the peppers are beginning to char.

3 Dice the cheese and tuck in among the chopped peppers. Sprinkle with the pine nuts and drizzle with the remaining oil. Bake for a further 15 minutes, until well browned. Serve warm with some crusty bread and a green salad.

Cook's Tip

Make your own herb-infused oils by half filling a jar with washed dried fresh herbs. Pour over enough olive oil to cover, then seal the jar and leave in a cool, dark place for 3 days. Strain into a clean jar and discard the herbs.

Tofu and Pepper Kebabs

A simple coating of ground, dry-roasted peanuts pressed on to cubed tofu provides plenty of additional flavour along with the peppers. Use metal or bamboo skewers for the kebabs – if you use bamboo, then soak them in cold water for 30 minutes before using to prevent them from scorching during cooking. The kebabs can also be cooked on a barbecue, if you prefer.

Serves 4

250g/9oz firm tofu
50g/2oz/½ cup dry-roasted peanuts
2 red and 2 green (bell) peppers
60ml/4 tbsp sweet chilli dipping sauce

From the storecupboard

salt and ground black pepper

1 Pat the tofu dry on kitchen paper and then cut it into small cubes. Grind the peanuts in a blender or food processor and transfer to a plate. Turn the tofu cubes over in the ground nuts to coat on all sides.

2 Preheat the grill (broiler) to moderate. Halve and seed the peppers, and cut them into large chunks. Thread the chunks of pepper on to four large skewers with the tofu cubes and place on a foil-lined grill rack.

3 Grill (broil) the kebabs, turning frequently, for 10–12 minutes, or until the peppers and peanuts are beginning to brown. Transfer the kebabs to plates and serve with the dipping sauce.

Cook's Tip

Tofu, or beancurd, is made from soya milk in a similar way to soft cheese. It is extremely rich in high-quality protein, containing all eight amino acids that are vital for renewal of cells and tissues in the human body. Tofu can be kept in the refrigerator in an airtight container for up to 1 week. Firm tofu, used in this recipe, should be covered in water, which should be changed regularly to keep completely fresh.

Roasted Peppers: Energy 506kcal/2099kJ; Protein 18.4g; Carbohydrate 32.5g, of which sugars 31g; Fat 34.3g, of which saturates 11.3g; Cholesterol 36mg; Calcium 268mg; Fibre 8.3g; Sodium 267mg.
Tofu Kebabs: Energy 187kcal/778kJ; Protein 10.2g; Carbohydrate 16.8g, of which sugars 15.1g; Fat 9.1g, of which saturates 1.6g; Cholesterol 0mg; Calcium 342mg; Fibre 3.7g; Sodium 214mg.

Tomato and Tapenade Tarts

These delicious individual tarts look and taste fantastic, despite the fact that they demand very little time or effort. The mascarpone cheese topping melts as it cooks to make a smooth, creamy sauce. Cherry tomatoes have a delicious sweet flavour with a low acidity, but plum tomatoes or vine-ripened tomatoes are also suitable for these tarts and will give delicious results. Red pesto can be used instead of the tapenade if you prefer a subtler flavour.

Serves 4
500g/1¼lb puff pastry, thawed if frozen
60ml/4 tbsp black or green olive tapenade
500g/1¼lb cherry tomatoes
90g/3½oz/scant ½ cup mascarpone cheese

From the storecupboard
salt and ground black pepper

1 Preheat the oven to 220°C/425°F/Gas 7. Lightly grease a large baking sheet and sprinkle it with water. Roll out the pastry on a lightly floured surface and cut out four 16cm/6½in rounds, using a bowl or small plate as a guide.

2 Transfer the pastry rounds to the prepared baking sheet. Using the tip of a sharp knife, mark a shallow cut 1cm/½in in from the edge of each round to form a rim.

3 Reserve half the tapenade and spread the rest over the pastry rounds, keeping the paste inside the marked rim. Cut half the tomatoes in half. Pile all the tomatoes, whole and halved, on the pastry, again keeping them inside the rim. Season lightly.

4 Bake for 20 minutes, until the pastry is well risen and golden. Dot with the remaining tapenade. Spoon a little mascarpone on the centre of the tomatoes and season with black pepper. Bake for a further 10 minutes, until the mascarpone has melted to make a sauce. Serve the tarts warm.

Cheese and Tomato Soufflés

Using a ready-made cheese sauce takes the effort out of soufflé making. The key to success when making soufflés is to whisk the egg whites thoroughly to incorporate as much air as possible. During the cooking time don't open the oven door – the cold draught could cause the delicate mixture to collapse.

Serves 6
350g/12oz tub fresh cheese sauce
50g/2oz sun-dried tomatoes in olive oil, drained, plus 10ml/2 tsp of the oil
130g/4½oz/1⅓ cups grated Parmesan cheese
4 large (US extra large) eggs, separated

From the storecupboard
salt and ground black pepper

1 Preheat the oven to 200°C/400°F/Gas 6. Turn the cheese sauce into a bowl. Thinly slice the sun-dried tomatoes and add to the bowl with 90g/3½oz/generous 1 cup of the Parmesan, the egg yolks and seasoning. Stir until well combined.

2 Brush the base and sides of six 200ml/7fl oz/scant 1 cup ramekins with the oil and then coat the insides of the dishes with half the remaining cheese, tilting them until evenly covered.

3 Whisk the egg whites in a clean bowl until stiff. Use a large metal spoon to stir one-quarter of the egg whites into the sauce, then fold in the remainder. Spoon the mixture into the prepared dishes and sprinkle with the remaining Parmesan cheese. Place on a baking sheet and bake for 15–18 minutes, until well risen and golden. Serve the soufflés as soon as you remove them from the oven.

Cook's Tip
To make a cheese sauce, melt 25g/1oz/2 tbsp butter in a pan and stir in 25g/1oz/¼ cup plain (all-purpose) flour. Remove from the heat, then gradually add 200ml/7fl oz/scant 1 cup milk. Stir, return to heat and bring to the boil stirring. Take off the heat and add 115g/4oz/1 cup grated Cheddar cheese.

Tomato Tarts: Energy 543kcal/2269kJ; Protein 10.2g; Carbohydrate 50.8g, of which sugars 6.2g; Fat 35.9g, of which saturates 2.4g; Cholesterol 9mg; Calcium 91mg; Fibre 1.7g; Sodium 736mg.
Cheese Soufflés: Energy 328kcal/1364kJ; Protein 20g; Carbohydrate 6.2g, of which sugars 3g; Fat 24.7g, of which saturates 13.6g; Cholesterol 184mg; Calcium 497mg; Fibre 0.2g; Sodium 473mg.

Mixed Bean and Tomato Chilli

Here, mixed beans, fiery red chilli and plenty of freshly chopped coriander are simmered in a tomato sauce to make a delicious vegetarian chilli. Always a popular dish for a quick and easy lunch, chilli can be served with a variety of accompaniments – choose from baked potatoes, baked rice, crusty bread or tortillas. Garnish with slices of tomato, chopped celery or sweet pepper and top with natural yogurt.

Serves 4
400g/14oz jar ready-made tomato and herb sauce
2 x 400g/14oz cans mixed beans, drained and rinsed
1 fresh red chilli
large handful of fresh coriander (cilantro)

From the storecupboard
salt and ground black pepper

1 Pour the ready-made tomato sauce and mixed beans into a pan. Seed and thinly slice the chilli, then add it to the pan. Reserve a little of the coriander, chop the remainder and add it to the pan.

2 Bring the mixture to the boil, reduce the heat, cover and simmer gently for 10 minutes. Stir the mixture occasionally and add a dash of water if the sauce starts to dry out.

3 Ladle the chilli into warmed individual serving bowls and top with a spoonful of yogurt to serve.

Cook's Tip
To make a tomato and herb sauce, heat 15ml/1 tbsp olive oil in a pan, add 1 chopped onion and fry for 3–4 minutes until soft. Add 1 chopped garlic clove and cook for about 1 minute more. Pour in 400g/14oz chopped tomatoes and stir in 15ml/1 tbsp tomato purée (paste). Add 30ml/2 tbsp dried oregano or dried mixed herbs and simmer for about 15 minutes, until thickened. Season with salt and pepper.

Spicy Chickpea Samosas

A blend of crushed chickpeas and coriander sauce makes an interesting alternative to the more familiar meat or vegetable fillings in these little pastries. Garnish with fresh coriander leaves and finely sliced onion and serve with a simple, but delicious, dip made from Greek yogurt and chopped fresh mint leaves.

Makes 18
2 x 400g/14oz cans chickpeas, drained and rinsed
120ml/4fl oz/½ cup hara masala or coriander (cilantro) sauce
275g/10oz filo pastry

From the storecupboard
60ml/4 tbsp chilli-and-garlic flavoured oil
salt and ground black pepper

1 Preheat the oven to 220°C/425°F/Gas 7. Process half the chickpeas to a paste in a food processor. Put the paste into a bowl and add the whole chickpeas, the hara masala or coriander sauce, and a little salt. Mix until well combined.

2 Lay a sheet of filo pastry on a work surface and cut into three strips. Brush the strips with a little of the oil. Place a dessertspoon of the filling at one end of a strip. Turn one corner diagonally over the filling to meet the long edge. Continue folding the filling and the pastry along the length of the strip, keeping the triangular shape. Transfer to a baking sheet and repeat with the remaining filling and pastry.

3 Brush the pastries with any remaining oil and bake for 15 minutes, until the pastry is golden. Cool before serving.

Cook's Tip
To make chilli oil, add several dried chillis to a bottle of olive oil and leave to infuse (steep) for about 2 weeks before checking. If the flavour hasn't infused sufficiently, leave for a further week before using. The chillies can be left in the bottle as they give a decorative effect. Garlic oil is made in the same way with peeled garlic cloves, but remove the cloves once infused.

Bean Chilli: Energy 309kcal/1302kJ; Protein 16.7g; Carbohydrate 43.7g, of which sugars 14.1g; Fat 8.7g, of which saturates 4.2g; Cholesterol 18mg; Calcium 193mg; Fibre 12.4g; Sodium 1202mg.
Chickpea Samosas: Energy 119kcal/499kJ; Protein 4.1g; Carbohydrate 13.7g, of which sugars 0.4g; Fat 5.7g, of which saturates 0.8g; Cholesterol 0mg; Calcium 36mg; Fibre 2.2g; Sodium 99mg

Creamy Red Lentil Dhal

This makes a tasty and satisfying winter supper for vegetarians and meat eaters alike. Serve with naan bread, coconut cream and fresh coriander leaves. The coconut cream gives this dish a really rich taste.

Serves 4
500g/1¼lb/2 cups red lentils
15ml/1 tbsp hot curry paste

From the storecupboard
15ml/1 tbsp sunflower oil
salt and ground black pepper

1 Heat the oil in a large pan and add the lentils. Fry for 1–2 minutes, stirring continuously, then stir in the curry paste and 600ml/1 pint/2½ cups boiling water.

2 Bring the mixture to the boil, then reduce the heat to a gentle simmer. Cover the pan and cook for 15 minutes, stirring occasionally, until the lentils are tender and the mixture has thickened.

3 Season the dhal with plenty of salt and ground black pepper to taste, and serve piping hot.

Cook's Tip
The orange-coloured red split lentils are the most familiar variety. They cook in just 20 minutes, eventually forming a thick purée. They are very low in fat and have an impressive range of health benefits, including the reduction of cholesterol and aiding bowel function. They are richer in protein than most pulses, too.

Variation
The Indian naan bread is easy to find in supermarkets and is available plain or flavoured with herbs and spices, such as garlic and coriander (cilantro). You can also buy the delicious Peshwari naan filled with coconut and sultanas (golden raisins). The flatbread chapati is less heavy and would make a good alternative.

Spiced Lentils

The combination of Puy lentils, tomatoes and cheese is widely used in Mediterranean cooking. The tang of feta cheese complements the slightly earthy flavour of the attractive dark lentils wonderfully. Serve this richly comforting dish with a big hunk of crusty bread.

Serves 4
250g/9oz/1½ cups Puy lentils
200g/7oz feta cheese
75ml/5 tbsp sun-dried tomato purée (paste)
small handful of fresh chervil or flat leaf parsley, chopped, plus extra to garnish

From the storecupboard
salt and ground black pepper

1 Place the lentils in a heavy pan with 600ml/1 pint/2½ cups water. Bring to the boil, reduce the heat and cover the pan. Simmer gently for at least 20 minutes, until the lentils are just tender and most of the water has been absorbed.

2 Crumble half the feta cheese into the pan. Add the sun-dried tomato purée, chopped chervil or flat leaf parsley and a little salt and ground black pepper. Heat through for 1 minute.

3 Transfer the lentil mixture and juices to warmed plates or bowls. Crumble the remaining feta cheese on top and sprinkle with the fresh herbs to garnish. Serve hot.

Cook's Tip
True Puy lentils come from the region of France, Le Puy, which has a unique climate and volcanic soil in which they thrive.

Variations
- *Any of the more robust fresh herbs could be used with this dish. Try basil, oregano, marjoram or thyme.*
- *You could also vary the cheese. Ricotta salata, the Italian salted ricotta, would be an option.*
- *Really spice this dish up with a little chilli powder or paprika.*

Creamy Lentil Dhal: Energy 455kcal/1929kJ; Protein 30.1g; Carbohydrate 71.3g, of which sugars 3g; Fat 7.5g, of which saturates 1g; Cholesterol 0mg; Calcium 86mg; Fibre 6.9g; Sodium 61mg.
Spiced Lentils: Energy 339kcal/1427kJ; Protein 23.7g; Carbohydrate 38.6g, of which sugars 4.9g; Fat 11g, of which saturates 7g; Cholesterol 35mg; Calcium 221mg; Fibre 3.7g; Sodium 788mg.

Roast Acorn Squash with Spinach and Gorgonzola

Roasting squash brings out its sweetness, here offset by tangy cheese. Acorn squash has been used here, but any type of squash will give delicious results.

Serves 4
4 acorn squash
250g/9oz baby spinach leaves, washed
200g/7oz Gorgonzola cheese, sliced

From the storecupboard
45ml/3 tbsp garlic-infused olive oil
salt and ground black pepper

1 Preheat the oven to 190°C/375°F/Gas 5. Cut the tops off the squash, and scoop out and discard the seeds. Place the squash, cut side up, in a roasting pan and drizzle with 30ml/ 2 tbsp of the oil. Season with salt and pepper and bake for 30–40 minutes, or until tender.

2 Heat the remaining oil in a large frying pan and add the spinach leaves. Cook over a medium heat for 2–3 minutes, until the leaves are just wilted. Season with salt and pepper and divide between the squash halves.

3 Top with the Gorgonzola and return to the oven for 10 minutes, or until the cheese has melted. Season with ground black pepper and serve.

Cook's Tip
There are many different types of squash, coming in all different shapes and sizes. They have a rich sweet flesh that can be used in both sweet and savoury dishes. Acorn squash has a slightly dry texture and a large seed cavity perfect for stuffing. Squash contain high levels of antioxidant, which are believed to reduce the risk of certain cancers. You could use a pumpkin in place of acorn squash, but be sure to choose a small one as they have the sweetest, less fibrous flesh.

Stuffed Baby Squash

It is worth making the most of baby squash while they are in season. Use any varieties you can find and do not worry too much about choosing vegetables of uniform size, as an assortment of different types and sizes looks attractive. The baked vegetables can easily be shared out at the table. Serve with warm sun-dried tomato bread and a ready-made spicy tomato sauce for a hearty autumn supper.

Serves 4
4 small squash, each about 350g/12oz
200g/7oz/1 cup mixed wild and basmati rice
150g/5oz/1¼ cups grated Gruyère cheese

From the storecupboard
60ml/4 tbsp chilli and garlic oil
salt and ground black pepper

1 Preheat the oven to 190°C/375°F/Gas 5. Pierce the squash in several places with the tip of a knife. Bake for 30 minutes, until the squash are tender. Leave until cool enough to handle.

2 Meanwhile, cook the rice in salted, boiling water for 12 minutes, until tender, then drain. Slice a lid off the top of each squash and scoop out and discard the seeds. Scoop out and chop the flesh.

3 Heat the oil in a frying pan and cook the chopped squash for 5 minutes. Reserve 60ml/4 tbsp of the cheese, add the remainder to the pan with the rice and a little salt. Mix well.

4 Pile the mixture into the squash shells and place in a dish. Sprinkle with the remaining cheese and bake for 20 minutes.

Cook's Tip
Serve this warming autumn dish for supper with some crusty white bread and a spicy tomato sauce or home-made chutney.

Acorn Squash: Energy 310kcal/1285kJ; Protein 14.6g; Carbohydrate 9.3g, of which sugars 7.3g; Fat 24g, of which saturates 11.2g; Cholesterol 38mg; Calcium 459mg; Fibre 5.1g; Sodium 698mg.
Stuffed Squash: Energy 483kcal/2011kJ; Protein 15.9g; Carbohydrate 48.2g, of which sugars 6.4g; Fat 24.3g, of which saturates 10.1g; Cholesterol 36mg; Calcium 396mg; Fibre 3.8g; Sodium 271mg.

Aubergines with Cheese Sauce

This wonderfully simple dish of aubergines in cheese sauce is delicious hot and the perfect dish to assemble ahead of time ready for baking at the last minute. Kashkaval cheese is particularly good in this recipe – it is a hard yellow cheese made from sheep's milk and is originally from the Balkans. Serve with lots of crusty bread to mop up the delicious aubergine-flavoured cheese sauce.

Serves 4–6

2 large aubergines (eggplants), cut into 5mm/¼in thick slices

400g/14oz/3½ cups grated cheese, such as kashkaval, Gruyère, or a mixture of Parmesan and Cheddar

600ml/1 pint/2½ cups savoury white sauce or béchamel sauce

From the storecupboard

about 60ml/4 tbsp olive oil

salt and ground black pepper

1 Layer the aubergine slices in a bowl or colander, sprinkling each layer with salt, and leave to drain for at least 30 minutes. Rinse well, then pat dry with kitchen paper.

2 Heat the oil in a frying pan, then cook the aubergine slices until golden brown on both sides. Remove from the pan and set aside.

3 Preheat the oven to 180°C/350°F/Gas 4. Mix most of the grated cheese into the savoury white or béchamel sauce, reserving a little to sprinkle on top of the finished dish.

4 Arrange a layer of the aubergines in an ovenproof dish, then pour over some sauce. Repeat, ending with sauce. Sprinkle with the reserved cheese. Bake for 35–40 minutes until golden.

Cook's Tip

Serve this dish with a nice leafy green salad and plenty of crusty white bread. The chewy Italian olive oil bread, ciabatta, would make a good choice.

Tomato and Aubergine Gratin

This colourful dish from the Mediterranean makes the perfect partner to grilled, pan-fried or baked meat or poultry. If you prefer, thinly sliced courgettes can be used in this dish instead of the aubergines. Grill the courgettes for 10–15 minutes. Choose plum tomatoes if you can – they have fewer seeds than most round tomatoes, so are less watery and are ideal for cooking.

Serves 4–6

2 medium aubergines (eggplants), about 500g/1¼lb

400g/14oz ripe tomatoes, sliced

40g/1½oz/½ cup freshly grated Parmesan cheese

From the storecupboard

90ml/6 tbsp olive oil

salt and ground black pepper

1 Preheat the grill (broiler) to medium-high. Thinly slice the aubergines and arrange them in a single layer on a foil-lined grill rack.

2 Brush the aubergine slices with some of the oil and grill (broil) for 15–20 minutes, turning once, until golden on both sides. Brush the second side with more oil after turning the slices.

3 Preheat the oven to 200°C/400°F/Gas 6. Toss the aubergine and tomato slices together in a bowl with a little seasoning, then pile them into a shallow, ovenproof dish. Drizzle with any remaining olive oil and then sprinkle with the grated Parmesan cheese.

4 Bake for 20 minutes, until the cheese is golden and the vegetables are hot. Serve the gratin immediately.

Variation

Instead of using fresh tomatoes in this recipe, you can layer the aubergine and Parmesan with passata (bottled strained tomatoes) and artichoke hearts.

Aubergines: Energy 535kcal/2219kJ; Protein 24.3g; Carbohydrate 13.9g, of which sugars 7.5g; Fat 41.3g, of which saturates 19.8g; Cholesterol 78mg; Calcium 705mg; Fibre 2.1g; Sodium 957mg.
Tomato Gratin: Energy 101kcal/420kJ; Protein 3.7g; Carbohydrate 3.5g, of which sugars 3.4g; Fat 8.1g, of which saturates 2.3g; Cholesterol 7mg; Calcium 91mg; Fibre 2g; Sodium 80mg.

Japanese-style Spinach with Toasted Sesame Seeds

In this Japanese speciality seasonal green vegetables are simply blanched and cooled and formed into little towers. With a little help from soy sauce and sesame seeds, they reveal their true flavour. Japanese spinach, the long-leaf type with the stalk and pink root intact, is best, but ordinary spinach will suffice, or any soft, deep-green salad leaves. Serve the spinach towers with simply cooked chicken, or fish such as salmon or tuna.

Serves 4

450g/1lb fresh young spinach
30ml/2 tbsp shoyu
15ml/1 tbsp sesame seeds

1 Blanch the spinach leaves in boiling water for 15 seconds. For Japanese-type spinach, hold the leafy part and slip the stems into the pan. After 15 seconds, drop in the leaves and cook for 20 seconds.

2 Drain immediately and place the spinach under running water. Squeeze out all the excess water by hand. Now what looked like a large amount of spinach has become a ball, roughly the size of an orange. Mix the shoyu and 30ml/2 tbsp water, then pour on to the spinach. Mix well and leave to cool.

3 Meanwhile, put the sesame seeds in a dry frying pan and stir or toss until they start to pop. Remove from the heat and leave to cool.

4 Drain the spinach and squeeze out the excess sauce with your hands. Form the spinach into a log shape of about 4cm/1½in in diameter on a chopping board. Squeeze again to make it firm. With a sharp knife, cut it across into four cylinders.

5 Place the spinach cylinders on a large plate or individual dishes. Sprinkle with the toasted sesame seeds and serve.

Braised Lettuce and Peas with Spring Onions

This light vegetable dish is based on the classic French method of braising peas with lettuce and spring onions in butter, and is delicious served with simply grilled fish, or roast or grilled duck. A sprinkling of chopped fresh mint makes a fresh, flavoursome and extremely pretty garnish. Other legumes such as broad beans, mangetouts and sugar snap peas can be used instead of peas to create a delicious variation.

Serves 4

4 Little Gem (Bibb) lettuces, halved lengthways
2 bunches spring onions (scallions), trimmed
400g/14oz shelled peas (about 1kg/2¼lb in pods)

From the storecupboard

50g/2oz/¼ cup butter
salt and ground black pepper

1 Melt half the butter in a wide, heavy pan over a low heat. Add the lettuces and spring onions.

2 Turn the vegetables in the butter, then sprinkle in salt and plenty of ground black pepper. Cover, and cook the vegetables very gently for 5 minutes, stirring once.

3 Add the peas and turn them in the buttery juices. Pour in 120ml/4fl oz/½ cup water, then cover and cook over a gentle heat for a further 5 minutes. Uncover and increase the heat to reduce the liquid to a few tablespoons.

4 Stir in the remaining butter and adjust the seasoning. Transfer to a warmed serving dish and serve immediately.

Variation

Braise about 250g/9oz baby carrots with the lettuce.

Spinach with Sesame Seeds: Energy 54kcal/222kJ; Protein 4.1g; Carbohydrate 2.5g, of which sugars 2.3g; Fat 3.1g, of which saturates 0.4g; Cholesterol 0mg; Calcium 218mg; Fibre 2.7g; Sodium 692mg.
Lettuce and Peas: Energy 161kcal/670kJ; Protein 9.1g; Carbohydrate 15.9g, of which sugars 6.8g; Fat 7.4g, of which saturates 3.7g; Cholesterol 13mg; Calcium 73mg; Fibre 6.5g; Sodium 47mg.

Braised Swiss Chard

Swiss chard (also known as spinach beet) is less well known than spinach. It makes two tasty meals: on the first day, cook the leaves; the next day cook the stalks in the same way as asparagus and serve with cream or a white sauce. Or you can serve both together, with the green leaves heaped up in the middle of a serving dish and the stems around them.

Serves 4
900g/2lb Swiss chard or spinach
a little freshly grated nutmeg

From the storecupboard
15g/½ oz/1 tbsp butter
sea salt and ground black pepper

1 Remove the stalks from the Swiss chard or spinach (and reserve the chard stalks, if you like – see Cook's Tip). Wash the leaves well and lift straight into a lightly greased heavy pan; the water clinging to the leaves will be all that is needed for cooking.

2 Cover with a tight-fitting lid and cook over a medium heat for about 3–5 minutes, or until the leaves are just tender, shaking the pan occasionally.

3 Drain well, add the butter and nutmeg, and season to taste. When the butter has melted, toss it into the Swiss chard and serve immediately.

Cook's Tip
To cook the stalks of Swiss chard, trim the bases, wash them well and tie in bundles like asparagus. Place in a pan of boiling water, with a squeeze of lemon juice added, and cook for about 20 minutes, or until tender but still slightly crisp. Drain and serve the chard stalks with a white sauce or simply pour over 30ml/2 tbsp fresh single (light) cream, heat through gently, season and serve.

Crispy Cabbage

This quick side dish makes a crunchy base for slices of boiled ham or bacon. The crinkly Savoy cabbage is especially pretty cooked this way, as it keeps its verdant colour beautifully.

Serves 4–6
1 medium green or small white cabbage

From the storecupbaord
30–45ml/2–3 tbsp oil
salt and ground black pepper

1 Remove any coarse outside leaves from the cabbage and also the central rib from the larger leaves. Shred the remaining leaves finely. Wash well under cold running water, shake well and pat with kitchen paper to dry.

2 Heat a wok or wide-based flameproof casserole over a fairly high heat. Heat the oil and add the cabbage. Stir-fry for 2–3 minutes, or until it is just cooked but still crunchy. Season and serve immediately.

Cook's Tip
Take care not to overcook the cabbage as not only will it lose its crunchy texture and bright green colour (in the case of Savoy), but it will also lose some of the health-giving properties. Studies show that, when eaten more than once a week, cabbage can reduce colon cancer in men by about 65 per cent.

Variation
For cabbage with a bacon dressing, fry 225g/8oz diced streaky (fatty) bacon in a pan. Set aside while cooking the cabbage. Remove the cabbage from the pan and keep warm with the bacon. Boil 15ml/1 tbsp wine or cider vinegar with the juices remaining in the pan. Bring to the boil and season with ground black pepper. Pour over the cabbage and bacon. This makes a versatile side dish, and is especially good with chicken.

Braised Swiss Chard: Energy 84kcal/347kJ; Protein 6.3g; Carbohydrate 3.6g, of which sugars 3.4g; Fat 4.9g, of which saturates 2.2g; Cholesterol 8mg; Calcium 383mg; Fibre 4.7g; Sodium 338mg.
Crispy Cabbage: Energy 54kcal/224kJ; Protein 1.9g; Carbohydrate 4.6g, of which sugars 4.5g; Fat 3.2g, of which saturates 0.5g; Cholesterol 0mg; Calcium 59mg; Fibre 2.7g; Sodium 6mg.

Colcannon

This traditional Irish dish is especially associated with Hallowe'en, when it is likely to be made with curly kale and would have a ring hidden in it – predicting marriage during the coming year for the person who found it. However, it is also served throughout the winter, and green cabbage is more often used.

Serves 3–4 as a main dish, 6–8 as an accompaniment

450g/1lb potatoes, peeled and boiled
450g/1lb curly kale or cabbage, cooked
milk, if necessary
1 large onion, finely chopped

From the storecupboard

50g/2oz/2 tbsp butter, plus extra for serving
salt and ground black pepper

1 Mash the boiled potatoes. Chop the cooked kale or cabbage, add it to the potatoes and mix. Stir in a little milk if the mash is too stiff.

2 Melt a little butter in a frying pan over a medium heat and add the onion. Cook until softened. Remove and mix well with the potato and kale or cabbage.

3 Add the remainder of the butter to the hot pan. When very hot, turn the potato mixture into the pan and spread it out. Fry until brown, then cut it roughly into pieces and continue frying until they are crisp and brown.

4 Serve in bowls or as a side dish, with plenty of butter.

Cook's Tips

- *Although it is often eaten as a dish in its own right, colcannon also makes an excellent accompaniment to many dishes, for example, boiled ham or bacon.*
- *Other ingredients may be added to the colcannon to ring the changes, such as cream instead of milk, leeks, chives or wild garlic in place of onion and even bacon or ham may be added for a one-pot meal.*

Tomato with Marinated Peppers and Oregano

The Portuguese usually prepare this refreshing appetizer with home-grown tomatoes for maximum flavour and sweetness. They combine superbly with marinated peppers, which, because they have been well roasted before soaking, are sweeter and more digestible than raw ones.

Serves 4–6

2 marinated (bell) peppers, drained
6 ripe tomatoes, sliced
15ml/1 tbsp chopped fresh oregano
30ml/2 tbsp white wine vinegar

From the storecupboard

75ml/5 tbsp olive oil
sea salt

1 If the marinated peppers are in large pieces, cut them into strips. Arrange the tomato slices and pepper strips on a serving dish, sprinkle with the oregano and season to taste with sea salt.

2 Whisk together the olive oil and vinegar in a jug (pitcher) and pour the dressing over the salad. Serve immediately or cover and chill in the refrigerator until required.

Cook's Tips

- *Marinated (bell) peppers are widely available in jars, often labelled as pimentos. However, they are much tastier when prepared yourself. To do this, wrap one green and one red pepper in foil and place on a baking sheet. Cook in a preheated oven at 180°C/350°F/Gas 4, or under a preheated grill (broiler), turning occasionally, for 20–30 minutes, until tender. Unwrap and when cool, peel the peppers, then halve and seed. Cut the flesh into strips and pack into a screw-top jar. Add olive oil to cover, close and store in the refrigerator for up to 6 days.*
- *You can preserve marinated peppers by cooking them in a closed jar in boiling water for about 30 minutes. They can then be kept for approximately 6 weeks.*

Colcannon: Energy 306kcal/1281kJ; Protein 5.4g; Carbohydrate 40.6g, of which sugars 13.6g; Fat 14.6g, of which saturates 8.8g; Cholesterol 36mg; Calcium 104mg; Fibre 5.9g; Sodium 127mg.
Tomatoes and Peppers: Energy 119kcal/494kJ; Protein 1.4g; Carbohydrate 6.9g, of which sugars 6.7g; Fat 9.7g, of which saturates 1.5g; Cholesterol 0mg; Calcium 17mg; Fibre 2.1g; Sodium 12mg.

Roast Mushroom Caps

Hunting for edible wild mushrooms is one of the Italians' great passions. The most prized are porcini, which grow in forests and are sometimes available here fresh in the autumn.

Serves 4
4 large mushroom caps
2 garlic cloves, chopped
45ml/3 tbsp chopped fresh parsley

From the storecupboard
extra virgin olive oil, for drizzling
salt and ground black pepper

1 Preheat the oven to 190C°/375°F/Gas 5. Carefully wipe the mushrooms clean with a damp cloth or kitchen paper. Cut off the stems. (Save them for soup if they are not too woody). Oil a baking dish large enough to hold the mushrooms in one layer.

2 Place the mushroom caps in the dish, smooth side down. Mix together the chopped garlic and parsley and sprinkle the mixture over the mushroom caps.

3 Season the mushrooms with salt and pepper, then sprinkle with oil. Bake for 20–25 minutes until cooked through.

Aromatic Stewed Mushrooms

In this traditional recipe, from North-west Italy, the garlic is used to transform a simple dish of mushrooms into something that is quite memorable.

Serves 6
750g/1½lb fresh mushrooms, a mixture of wild and cultivated
2 garlic cloves, finely chopped
45ml/3 tbsp chopped fresh parsley

From the storecupboard
90ml/6 tbsp olive oil
salt and ground black pepper

1 Clean the mushrooms carefully by wiping them with a damp cloth or kitchen paper.

2 Cut off the woody tips of the stems and discard. Slice the stems and caps fairly thickly.

3 Heat the oil in a large frying pan. Stir in the garlic and cook for about 1 minute. Add the mushrooms and cook for 8–10 minutes, stirring occasionally.

4 Season with salt and pepper and stir in the parsley. Cook for a further 5 minutes, then transfer to a warmed serving dish and serve immediately.

Cook's Tip
Ideally you should use a combination of both wild and cultivated mushrooms for this dish to give a nicely balanced flavour. A good mixture of mushroom varieties would be chanterelles and chestnut mushrooms: both are now sold in good supermarkets.

Slow-cooked Shiitake with Shoyu

Shiitake mushrooms cooked slowly are so rich and filling, that some people call them 'vegetarian steak'. This is a useful side dish which also makes a flavoursome addition to other dishes.

Serves 4
20 dried shiitake mushrooms
30ml/2 tbsp shoyu
5ml/1 tsp toasted sesame oil

From the storecupboard
30ml/2 tbsp vegetable oil

1 Start soaking the dried shiitake the day before. Put them in a large bowl almost full of water. Cover the shiitake with a plate or lid to stop them floating to the surface of the water. Leave to soak overnight.

2 Remove the shiitake from the soaking water and gently squeeze out the water with your fingers.

3 Measure 120ml/4fl oz/½ cup of the liquid in the bowl and set aside.

4 Heat the oil in a wok or a large frying pan. Stir-fry the shiitake over a high heat for 5 minutes, stirring continuously.

5 Reduce the heat to the lowest setting, then stir in the reserved soaking liquid and the shoyu.

6 Cook the mushrooms until there is almost no moisture left, stirring frequently. Sprinkle with the toasted sesame oil and remove from the heat.

7 Leave to cool, then slice and arrange the shiitake on a large plate and serve.

Variation
Cut the slow-cooked shiitake into thin strips. Mix with 600g/1⅓lb/5¼ cups cooked brown rice and 15ml/1 tbsp finely chopped chives. Sprinkle with toasted sesame seeds for a delicious rice.

Roast Mushroom Caps: Energy 104kcal/429kJ; Protein 3.2g; Carbohydrate 2.8g, of which sugars 0.7g; Fat 9g, of which saturates 1.3g; Cholesterol 0mg; Calcium 34mg; Fibre 2.2g; Sodium 10mg.
Stewed Mushrooms: Energy 122kcal/502kJ; Protein 2.7g; Carbohydrate 1.5g, of which sugars 0.5g; Fat 11.7g, of which saturates 1.7g; Cholesterol 0mg; Calcium 23mg; Fibre 1.9g; Sodium 9mg.
Shiitake with Shoyu: Energy 16kcal/69kJ; Protein 2g; Carbohydrate 1g, of which sugars 0.8g; Fat 0.5g, of which saturates 0.1g; Cholesterol 0mg; Calcium 7mg; Fibre 1.1g; Sodium 539mg.

Grilled Radicchio and Courgettes

Radicchio is often grilled or barbecued in Italian cooking to give it a special flavour. Combined with courgettes, it makes a quick and tasty side dish.

Serves 4
2–3 firm heads radicchio, round or long type, rinsed
4 courgettes (zucchini)

From the storecupboard
90ml/6 tbsp olive oil
salt and ground black pepper

1 Preheat the grill, cut the radicchio in half through the root section or base. Cut the courgettes into 1cm/½in diagonal slices.

2 When ready to cook, brush the vegetables with the olive oil and add salt and pepper. Cook for 4–5 minutes on each side.

Baked Courgettes with Cheese

This easy dish makes a great accompaniment to a wide range of main courses, or it can be served with some fresh crusty bread as a light lunch or supper dish for one or two. A piquant hard cheese, such as Desmond or Gabriel, made in West Cork, will give the courgettes character, or you could use a mature farmhouse Cheddar.

Serves 4
4 courgettes (zucchini)
30ml/2 tbsp grated hard farmhouse cheese, such as Gabriel or Desmond, or mature (sharp) farmhouse Cheddar

From the storecupboard
about 25g/1oz/2 tbsp butter
salt and ground black pepper

1 Preheat the oven to 180°C/350°F/Gas 4. Slice the courgettes in half, lengthways. Butter a shallow baking dish and arrange the courgettes, cut side up, inside the dish.

2 Sprinkle the cheese over the courgettes, and top with a few knobs (pats) of butter.

3 Bake in the preheated oven for about 20 minutes, or until the courgettes are tender and the cheese is bubbling and golden brown. Serve immediately.

Variation
The concentrated sweet flavour of sun-dried tomatoes complements courgettes (zucchini) well. Try the following dish which puts these two together in a colourful and mouthwatering way. Slice the 10 sun-dried tomatoes into thin strips. Place in a bowl with 175g/6fl oz/¾ cup warm water. Allow to stand for 20 minutes. Heat some oil in a large frying pan and stir in 1 large sliced onion. Cook gently to soften but do not allow to brown. Stir in 2 finely chopped garlic cloves and 1kg/2lb courgettes cut into thin strips. Cook for about 5 minutes, stirring. Stir in the tomatoes and their liquid. Season with salt and pepper. Increase the heat; cook until the courgettes are tender.

Marinated Courgettes

This is a simple low-fat vegetable dish that is prepared all over Italy using the best of the season's courgettes. It has a light and fresh flavour. It can be eaten hot or cold and is a delicious accompaniment to a main course.

Serves 6
4 courgettes (zucchini)
30ml/2 tbsp chopped fresh mint, plus whole leaves, to garnish
30ml/2 tbsp white wine vinegar

From the storecupboard
30ml/2 tbsp extra virgin olive oil
salt and ground black pepper

1 Cut the courgettes into thin slices using a sharp knife. Heat 15ml/1 tbsp of the oil in a large non-stick frying pan.

2 Fry the courgette slices in batches, for 4–6 minutes, or until tender and brown around the edges. Transfer to a bowl. Season.

3 Heat the remaining oil in the pan, then add the chopped mint and vinegar and let it bubble for a few seconds. Stir into the courgettes. Set aside to marinate for 1 hour, then serve garnished with mint leaves.

Courgettes with Cheese: Energy 96kcal/395kJ; Protein 3.8g; Carbohydrate 1.9g, of which sugars 1.8g; Fat 8g, of which saturates 5g; Cholesterol 21mg; Calcium 82mg; Fibre 0.9g; Sodium 93mg.
Radicchio and Courgettes: Energy 195kcal/802kJ; Protein 4.2g; Carbohydrate 4.9g, of which sugars 4.7g; Fat 17.7g, of which saturates 2.6g; Cholesterol 0mg; Calcium 71mg; Fibre 2.5g; Sodium 4mg.
Marinated Courgettes: Energy 60kcal/248kJ; Protein 2.7g; Carbohydrate 2.8g, of which sugars 2.3g; Fat 4.3g, of which saturates 0.7g; Cholesterol 0mg; Calcium 49mg; Fibre 1.2g; Sodium 3mg.

Caramelized Shallots

Sweet, golden shallots are good with all sorts of main dishes, including poultry or meat. Shallots have a less distinctive aroma than common onions and a milder flavour; they are also considered to be easier to digest. These caramelized shallots are also excellent with braised or roasted chestnuts, carrots or chunks of butternut squash. You may like to garnish the shallots with sprigs of fresh thyme before serving.

Serves 4–6

500g/1¼lb shallots or small onions, peeled, with root ends intact
15ml/1 tbsp golden caster (superfine) sugar
30ml/2 tbsp red or white wine or port

From the storecupboard

50g/2oz/¼ cup butter or 60ml/4 tbsp olive oil
salt and ground black pepper

1 Heat the butter or oil in a large frying pan and add the shallots or onions in a single layer. Cook gently, turning occasionally, until they are lightly browned.

2 Sprinkle the sugar over the shallots and cook gently, turning the shallots in the juices, until the sugar begins to caramelize. Add the wine or port and let the mixture bubble for 4–5 minutes.

3 Add 150ml/¼ pint/⅔ cup water and seasoning. Cover and cook for 5 minutes, then remove the lid and cook until the liquid evaporates and the shallots are tender and glazed. Adjust the seasoning before serving.

Variation

A delicious alternative is shallots with chestnuts and pancetta. Cook the shallots in butter or bacon fat with 90g/3½oz pancetta, then add 175ml/6fl oz/¾ cup water. Toss in 250–350g/9–12oz part-cooked chestnuts. Cook for 5–10 minutes, then serve with chopped flat leaf parsley.

Baked Onions

One of the oldest and most widely used flavouring vegetables, the onion, also deserves to be used more as a vegetable in its own right. Onions become sweet and mildly flavoured when slowly boiled or baked, and can be cooked very conveniently in the oven when baking potatoes or roasting parsnips. Not only do they make a tasty accompaniment to many dishes, but they also have a range of health benefits.

Serves 4

4 large even-sized onions

1 Preheat the oven to 180°C/350°F/Gas 4. Put a little cold water into a medium roasting pan, and arrange the unpeeled onions in it.

2 Bake in the preheated oven for about 1 hour, or until the onions feel soft when squeezed at the sides. Peel the skins and serve immediately.

Cook's Tip

These onions are baked in their skins, but you could peel them, if preferred, before baking. The peeled onions are best baked in a covered casserole dish instead of a roasting pan.

Variation

Sweet-sour roasted onions are a delicious variation on the onion theme. Cut 4 large onions into wedges, leaving them attached at the root end. Preheat the oven to 200°C/400°F/Gas 6. Put the onions in a roasting pan and pour over 60ml/4 tbsp olive oil. Sprinkle over 10ml/2 tsp crushed coriander seeds and mix thoroughly. Season, then roast for 20 minutes. Mix 15ml/1 tbsp honey with 30ml/2 tbsp pomegranate molasses, 15ml/1 tbsp sherry vinegar and 15ml/1 tbsp water. Drizzle over and stir. Reduce heat to 180°C/350°F/Gas 4 and cook for another 20–30 minutes.

Caramelized Shallots: Energy 96kcal/399kJ; Protein 1.3g; Carbohydrate 5.4g, of which sugars 5.4g; Fat 7.5g, of which saturates 1.1g; Cholesterol 0mg; Calcium 22mg; Fibre 1.2g; Sodium 9mg.
Baked Onions: Energy 90kcal/375kJ; Protein 3g; Carbohydrate 19.8g, of which sugars 14g; Fat 0.5g, of which saturates 0g; Cholesterol 0mg; Calcium 63mg; Fibre 3.5g; Sodium 8mg.

Leek Fritters

These crispy fried morsels are best served at room temperature, with a good squeeze of lemon juice and a sprinkling of salt and freshly grated nutmeg. Matzo meal, a traditional Jewish ingredient, is used in these fritters: it is made from crumbled matzo, an unleavened bread, similar to water biscuits. Matzo meal is used in a similar way to breadcrumbs, which can also be used to make these tasty fritters.

Serves 4

4 large leeks, total weight about 1kg/2¼lb, thickly sliced
120–175ml/4–6fl oz/½–¾ cup coarse matzo meal
2 eggs, lightly beaten

From the storecupboard

olive or vegetable oil, for shallow frying
salt and ground black pepper

1 Cook the leeks in salted boiling water for 5 minutes, or until just tender and bright green. Drain well and leave to cool.

2 Chop the leeks coarsely. Put in a bowl and combine with the matzo meal, eggs and seasoning.

3 Heat 5mm/¼in oil in a frying pan. Using two tablespoons, carefully spoon the leek mixture into the hot oil. Cook over a medium-high heat until golden brown on the underside, then turn and cook the second side.

4 Drain on kitchen paper. Add more oil if needed and heat before cooking more mixture.

Variation

You can prepare other vegetables in the same way to wonderful effect. Try mushrooms, red (bell) pepper strips or carrots cut into thin batons, cooked briefly and combined, when cool, with either matzo meal or breadcrumbs and beaten egg, then lightly shallow fried.

Cheesy Creamy Leeks

This is quite a rich accompaniment that could easily be served as a meal in itself with brown rice or couscous. Cheddar cheese has been used here for a slightly stronger flavour, but you could use a milder Swiss cheese, such as Gruyère, if you like.

Serves 4

4 large leeks or 12 baby leeks, trimmed and washed
150ml/¼ pint/⅔ cup double (heavy) cream
75g/3oz/¾ cup Cheddar or Monterey Jack cheese, grated

From the storecupboard

15ml/1 tbsp olive oil
salt and ground black pepper

1 Preheat the grill (broiler) to high. If using large leeks, slice them lengthways. Heat the oil in a large frying pan and add the leeks. Season with salt and pepper and cook for about 4 minutes, stirring occasionally, until starting to turn golden.

2 Pour the cream into the pan and stir until well combined. Allow to bubble gently for a few minutes.

3 Preheat the grill (broiler). Transfer the creamy leeks to a shallow ovenproof dish and sprinkle with the cheese. Grill (broil) for 4–5 minutes, or until the cheese is golden brown and bubbling and serve immediately.

Variation

For a less rich alternative you could simply grill (broil) baby leeks. However, they will need blanching in boiling water for 2–3 minutes prior to grilling to soften the skins slightly. Once drained allow to cool a little, then gently squeeze out any excess water. Leave whole. Dry on a clean dish towel or on kitchen paper. Brush with oil, season with salt and pepper to taste, then grill, preferably in a griddle pan, for 3–4 minutes each side. The grilled leeks can be served hot, warm or cold. They are particularly delicious with a simple dressing of oil, vinegar, mustard and tarragon. Larger leeks can be used, but they will need longer blanching and grilling time.

Leek Fritters: Energy 227kcal/945kJ; Protein 5.8g; Carbohydrate 22.6g, of which sugars 2.7g; Fat 13.2g, of which saturates 1.8g; Cholesterol 48mg; Calcium 78mg; Fibre 3g; Sodium 18mg.
Cheesy Leeks: Energy 322kcal/1330kJ; Protein 7.8g; Carbohydrate 5g, of which sugars 4g; Fat 29.8g, of which saturates 17.1g; Cholesterol 70mg; Calcium 193mg; Fibre 3.3g; Sodium 147mg.

Roasted Jerusalem Artichokes

Jerusalem artichokes, now widely available, conceal a deliciously sweet white flesh inside their knobbly brown exterior. While they are best known for soups, their natural sweetness enables them to glaze easily and they make a delicious side vegetable with many foods, but have a special affinity with game.

Serves 6
675g/1½ lb Jerusalem artichokes
15ml/1 tbsp lemon juice or vinegar
seasoned flour, for dusting

From the storecupboard
50g/2oz/¼ cup unsalted (sweet) butter
salt

1 Peel the artichokes, dropping them straight into a bowl of water acidulated with lemon juice or vinegar to prevent browning. Cut up the artichokes so that the pieces are matched for size, otherwise they will cook unevenly.

2 Preheat the oven to 180°C/350°F/Gas 4. Bring a pan of salted water to the boil, drain the artichokes from the acidulated water and boil them for 5 minutes, or until just tender. Watch them carefully, as they have a tendency to break up easily.

3 Melt the butter in a roasting pan, coat the artichokes in the seasoned flour and roll them around in the butter in the pan.

4 Cook the butter and flour coated artichokes in the preheated oven for 20–30 minutes, or until golden brown. Serve immediately.

Variation
Puréeing is a useful fall-back if the artichokes break up during cooking: simply blend or mash the drained boiled artichokes with salt and ground black pepper to taste and a little single (light) cream, if you like. Puréed artichokes are especially good served with game, which tends to be dry.

Deep-fried Artichokes

The artichokes are baked, then pressed to open them and plunged into hot oil, where their leaves twist and brown, turning the artichokes into crispy flowers. Serve with lamb or pork steaks.

Serves 4
2–3 lemons, halved
4–8 small young globe artichokes

From the storecupboard
olive or vegetable oil, for deep-frying

1 Fill a large bowl with cold water and stir in the juice of one or two of the lemons. Trim and discard the stems of the artichokes, then trim off their tough ends and remove all the tough outer leaves until you reach the pale pointed centre. Carefully open the leaves of one of the artichokes by pressing it against the table or poking them open. Trim the tops if they are sharp.

2 If there is any choke inside the artichoke, remove it with a melon baller or small pointed spoon. Put in the acidulated water and prepare the remaining artichokes in the same way.

3 Put the artichokes in a large pan and pour over water to cover. Bring to the boil, reduce the heat and simmer for 10–15 minutes, or until partly cooked. If they are small, cook them for only 10 minutes. Drain the artichokes and leave upside down until cool enough to handle. Press them open gently, being careful not to break them apart.

4 Fill a pan with oil to a depth of 5–7.5cm/2–3in and heat. Add one or two artichokes at a time, with the leaves uppermost, and press down with a spoon to open up the leaves. Fry for 5–8 minutes, turning, until golden and crisp. Remove from the pan and drain on kitchen paper. Serve immediately, with the remaining lemon cut into wedges.

Cook's Tip
Select immature artichokes, before their chokes have formed. Prepare and boil them ahead and deep-fry just before serving.

Jerusalem Artichokes: Energy 101kcal/419kJ; Protein 0.7g; Carbohydrate 8.9g, of which sugars 8.4g; Fat 7.2g, of which saturates 4.5g; Cholesterol 18mg; Calcium 30mg; Fibre 2.7g; Sodium 242mg.
Deep-fried Artichokes: Energy 132kcal/546kJ; Protein 0.6g; Carbohydrate 1.1g, of which sugars 1.1g; Fat 14g, of which saturates 1.6g; Cholesterol 0mg; Calcium 51mg; Fibre 1.4g; Sodium 75mg.

Broad Bean Purée

Peeling broad beans leaves them tender and sweet, producing a tasty, colourful purée, perfect for serving alongside a selection of Italian meats.

Serves 4

1kg/2lb fresh broad (fava) beans in their pods, or 400g/14oz shelled broad (fava) beans, thawed if frozen
1 onion, finely chopped
2 small potatoes, peeled and diced
50g/2oz/¼ cup prosciutto crudo

From the storecupboard
15ml/1 tbsp extra virgin olive oil
salt and ground black pepper

1 Remove the beans from their pods, if using fresh beans. Place the shelled beans in a pan and cover with water. Bring to the boil and cook for 5 minutes. Drain thoroughly. When they are cool enough to handle, remove the skins from the beans.

2 Place the peeled beans in a pan with the onion and potatoes. Add enough water just to cover the vegetables. Bring to the boil. Lower the heat slightly, cover and simmer for 15–20 minutes, until the vegetables are very soft. Check occasionally that all the water has not evaporated: if necessary add a few tablespoons more.

3 Chop the prosciutto ham into very small dice. Heat the oil and sauté until the ham is golden.

4 Mash or purée the bean mixture. Return to the pan. If the mixture is very moist, cook it over medium heat until it reduces slightly. Stir in the oil with the ham. Season to taste and cook for 2 minutes. Serve immediately.

Cook's Tip
When skinning the broad (fava) beans, hold the hot beans under cold running water for a while; you'll find the skins will slip off quite easily.

Spiced Asparagus Kale

Kale is a very important part of Scottish tradition. 'Kailyards' was the word used to describe the kitchen garden, and even the midday meal was often referred to as 'kail'. Use the more widely available curly kale if you find it hard to get the asparagus variety.

Serves 4
175g/6oz asparagus kale
10ml/2 tsp butter
25g/1 oz piece fresh root ginger, grated
15ml/1 tbsp soy sauce

From the storecupboard
salt and ground black pepper

1 Prepare the kale by removing the centre stalk and ripping the leaves into smallish pieces.

2 Heat a pan over a high heat and add the butter. As it melts, quickly add the kale and toss rapidly to allow the heat to cook it.

3 Grate the ginger into the pan and stir in thoroughly. Then add the soy sauce and mix well. When the kale has wilted, it is ready to serve.

Cook's Tip
Sea kale is a tasty variety which is commonly available between January and March. Its pale green fronds have a slightly nutty taste. It doesn't need cooking but should be washed and drained thoroughly before eating.

Variation
Kale with mustard dressing is traditionally made with sea kale, but any kale or dark green cabbage can be substituted. If using alternatives, boil the leaves for a few minutes before chilling. Whisk 45ml/3 tbsp of olive oil into 5ml/1 tsp wholegrain mustard. Next, whisk in 15ml/1 tbsp white wine vinegar. When it thickens, season with a pinch of caster sugar, salt and ground black pepper. Toss the kale in the dressing and serve at once.

Broad Bean Purée: Energy 142kcal/599kJ; Protein 10.8g; Carbohydrate 17g, of which sugars 2.6g; Fat 3.9g, of which saturates 0.7g; Cholesterol 7mg; Calcium 62mg; Fibre 7g; Sodium 161mg.
Spiced Asparagus Kale: Energy 35kcal/145kJ; Protein 1.6g; Carbohydrate 0.9g, of which sugars 0.9g; Fat 2.8g, of which saturates 1.4g; Cholesterol 5mg; Calcium 58mg; Fibre 1.4g; Sodium 301mg.

Green Beans Tempura

This crispy Japanese dish is distinguished by the green beans, which are coated in a light tempura batter.

Serves 4
400g/14oz green beans
100g/3¾oz/scant 1 cup plain (all-purpose) flour
1 egg

From the storecupboard
vegetable oil, for deep-frying
salt

1 Trim the beans and blanch in a large pan of boiling water for 1 minute. Drain and refresh in iced water, then drain again well.

2 Sift the flour into a bowl and stir in enough cold water to make a paste. Add the egg and beat well, then season with salt.

3 Heat the oil in a large pan or deep-fryer to 170°C/340°F. Dip the beans in the batter, add to the hot oil and deep-fry until golden brown. Drain on kitchen paper and serve.

Green Beans with Almond Butter

A perfect accompaniment for baked or grilled oily fish.

Serves 4
350g/12oz green beans, trimmed
50g/2oz/⅓ cup whole blanched almonds
grated rind and juice of 1 unwaxed lemon

From the storecupboard
50g/2oz/¼ cup butter
salt and ground black pepper

1 Cook the beans in a pan of salted, boiling water for about 3 minutes, or until just tender. Drain well. Meanwhile, melt the butter in a large non-stick pan until foamy.

2 Add the almonds to the pan and cook, stirring occasionally, for 2–3 minutes, or until golden. Remove from the heat and toss with the beans, lemon rind and juice. Season.

Cauliflower with Garlic Crumbs

This simple dish makes a great accompaniment to any meat or fish dish. When buying cauliflower look for creamy white coloured florets with the inner green leaves curled round the flower. Discard cauliflowers with discoloured patches or yellow leaves. As an alternative, try using broccoli florets instead of the cauliflower. Broccoli should have a fresh appearance: avoid yellowing specimens and those that feel soft or are wilting.

Serves 4–6
1 large cauliflower, cut into bitesize florets
130g/4½ oz/2¼ cups dry white or wholemeal (whole-wheat) breadcrumbs
3–5 garlic cloves, thinly sliced or chopped

From the storecupboard
90–120ml/6–8 tbsp olive or vegetable oil
salt and ground black pepper

1 Steam or boil the cauliflower in salted water until just tender. Drain and leave to cool.

2 Heat 60–75ml/4–5 tbsp of the olive or vegetable oil in a pan, add the breadcrumbs and cook over a medium heat, tossing and turning, until browned and crisp. Add the garlic, turn once or twice, then remove from the pan and set aside.

3 Heat the remaining oil in the pan, then add the cauliflower, mashing and breaking it up a little as it lightly browns in the oil. (Do not overcook but just cook until lightly browned.)

4 Add the garlic breadcrumbs to the pan and cook, stirring, until well combined, with some of the cauliflower still holding its shape. Season and serve hot or warm.

Cook's Tip
Serve this garlicky cauliflower dish as they do in Italy, with cooked pasta, such as spaghetti.

Beans Tempura: Energy 227kcal/945kJ; Protein 5.8g; Carbohydrate 22.6g, of which sugars 2.7g; Fat 13.2g, of which saturates 1.8g; Cholesterol 48mg; Calcium 78mg; Fibre 3g; Sodium 18mg.
Green Beans: Energy 191kcal/786kJ; Protein 4.4g; Carbohydrate 3.7g, of which sugars 2.6g; Fat 17.7g, of which saturates 7.2g; Cholesterol 27mg; Calcium 64mg; Fibre 2.9g; Sodium 78mg.
Cauliflower: Energy 244kcal/1016kJ; Protein 8.9g; Carbohydrate 18.8g, of which sugars 2.2g; Fat 15.3g, of which saturates 3.8g; Cholesterol 10mg; Calcium 162mg; Fibre 1.7g; Sodium 280mg.

Gingered Carrot Salad

This fresh and zesty salad is ideal served as an accompaniment to simple grilled chicken or fish. Some food processors have an attachment that can be used to cut the carrots into batons, which makes quick work of the preparation, but even cutting them by hand doesn't take too long. Fresh root ginger goes perfectly with sweet carrots, and the tiny black poppy seeds not only add taste and texture, but also look stunning against the bright orange of the carrots.

Serves 4

350g/12oz carrots, peeled and cut into fine matchsticks
2.5cm/1in piece of fresh root ginger, peeled and grated
15ml/1 tbsp poppy seeds

From the storecupboard

30ml/2 tbsp garlic-infused olive oil
salt and ground black pepper

1 Put the carrots in a bowl and stir in the oil and grated ginger. Cover and chill for a minium of 30 minutes, to allow the flavours to develop.

2 Season the salad with salt and pepper to taste. Stir in the poppy seeds just before serving.

Variation

To make a parsnip and sesame seed salad, replace the carrots with parsnips and blanch in boiling salted water for 1 minute before combining with the oil and ginger. Replace the poppy seeds with the same quantity of sesame seeds.

Cook's Tip

The sweetness of carrots can be heightened by adding Marsala wine and sugar – a traditional Sicilian dish. Cut carrots into sticks, melt butter, add sugar and salt, then stir in a small amount of Marsala. Just cover with water and cook until tender with a lid on. Uncover and reduce the liquid down.

Broccoli with Oil and Garlic

This is a very simple way of transforming steamed or blanched broccoli into a succulent Mediterranean dish. Peeling the broccoli stalks is easy and allows for even cooking.

Serves 6

1kg/2lb fresh broccoli
2–3 garlic cloves, finely chopped

From the storecupboard

90ml/6 tbsp olive oil
salt and ground black pepper

1 Wash the broccoli. Cut off any woody parts at the base of the stems. Using a small sharp knife, peel the broccoli stems. Cut any very long or wide stalks in half.

2 If steaming the broccoli, place water in the bottom of a pan equipped with a steamer and bring to the boil. Put the broccoli in the steamer, cover tightly and cook for 8–12 minutes, or until the stems are just tender when pierced with the point of a knife. Remove from the heat.

3 If blanching the broccoli, bring a large pan of water to the boil, drop the broccoli into the pan of boiling water and blanch for 5–6 minutes, until just tender. Drain.

4 In a frying pan large enough to hold all the broccoli pieces, gently heat the oil with the garlic.

5 When the garlic is light golden (do not let it brown or it will be bitter) add the broccoli and cook over medium heat for 3–4 minutes, turning carefully to coat it with the hot oil. Season with salt and pepper. Serve hot or cold.

Variation

To turn the dish into a vegetarian topping for pasta, add about 25g/1oz each fresh breadcrumbs and pine nuts to the garlic at the beginning of step 4 and cook until golden. Then add the broccoli with 25g/1oz sultanas (golden raisins) and some chopped fresh parsley. Toss into cooked pasta and serve with roasted tomatoes.

Gingered Carrot Salad: Energy 103kcal/424kJ; Protein 1.2g; Carbohydrate 7g, of which sugars 6.5g; Fat 7.9g, of which saturates 1.2g; Cholesterol 0mg; Calcium 47mg; Fibre 2.4g; Sodium 23mg.
Broccoli with Garlic: Energy 159kcal/657kJ; Protein 7.7g; Carbohydrate 3.8g, of which sugars 2.6g; Fat 12.5g, of which saturates 1.9g; Cholesterol 0mg; Calcium 94mg; Fibre 4.5g; Sodium 14mg.

Broccoli with Soy Sauce

A wonderfully simple dish that you will want to make again and again. The broccoli cooks in next to no time, so don't start cooking until you are almost ready to eat.

Serves 4
450g/1lb broccoli
2 garlic cloves, crushed
30ml/2 tbsp light soy sauce
fried garlic slices, to garnish

From the storecupboard
15ml/1 tbsp vegetable oil
salt

1 Cut the thick stems from the broccoli; cut off any particularly woody bits, then cut the stems lengthways into thin slices. Separate the head of the broccoli into large florets.

2 Bring a pan of lightly salted water to the boil. Add the broccoli and cook for 3–4 minutes until tender but still crisp.

3 Transfer the broccoli into a colander, drain thoroughly and arrange in a heated serving dish.

4 Heat the oil in a small pan. Fry the garlic for 2 minutes to release the flavour, then remove it with a slotted spoon. Pour the oil carefully over the broccoli, taking care as it will splatter. Drizzle the soy sauce over the broccoli, sprinkle over the fried garlic and serve.

Cook's Tip
Fried garlic slices make a good garnish but take care that the oil used does not get too hot; if the garlic burns, it will taste unpleasantly bitter.

Variation
Most leafy vegetables taste delicious prepared this way. Try blanched cos or romaine lettuce and you may be surprised at how crisp and clean the taste is.

Stir-fried Broccoli with Soy Sauce and Sesame Seeds

Purple sprouting broccoli has been used for this recipe, but when it is not available an alternative variety of broccoli, such as calabrese, will also work very well.

Serves 2
225g/8oz purple sprouting broccoli
15ml/1 tbsp soy sauce
15ml/1 tbsp toasted sesame seeds

From the storecupboard
15ml/1 tbsp olive oil
salt and ground black pepper

1 Using a sharp knife, cut off and discard any thick stems from the broccoli and cut the broccoli into long, thin florets.

2 Heat the olive oil in a wok or large frying pan and add the broccoli. Stir-fry for 3–4 minutes, or until tender, adding a splash of water if the pan becomes too dry.

3 Add the soy sauce to the broccoli, then season with salt and ground black pepper to taste. Add sesame seeds, toss to combine and serve immediately.

Cook's Tip
Other vegetables from the brassica family could be substituted for broccoli, such as cauliflower, which can be prepared in the same way. Alternatively, try some shredded cabbage or pak choi (bok choy) or brussel sprouts.

Variation
An essential part of the Asian diet for centuries, seaweed is now acknowledged in other parts of the world for its amazing health benefits. Try making this recipe with shredded nori, laver or arame.

Broccoli with Soy Sauce: Energy 65kcal/271kJ; Protein 5.2g; Carbohydrate 2.7g, of which sugars 2.2g; Fat 3.8g, of which saturates 0.6g; Cholesterol 0mg; Calcium 64mg; Fibre 2.9g; Sodium 543mg.
Broccoli and Sesame: Energy 135kcal/558kJ; Protein 6.6g; Carbohydrate 2.7g, of which sugars 2.3g; Fat 10.9g, of which saturates 1.7g; Cholesterol 0mg; Calcium 115mg; Fibre 3.5g; Sodium 545mg.

Noodles with Sesame Spring Onions

You can use any kind of noodles for this Asian-style dish. Rice noodles look and taste particularly good, but egg noodles work just as well. This dish can be served hot, or chilled as a salad. It is excellent with fish and chicken dishes.

Serves 4
1 bunch of spring onions (scallions), trimmed
225g/8oz flat rice noodles
30ml/2 tbsp oyster sauce

From the storecupboard
30ml/2 tbsp sesame oil
salt and ground black pepper

1 Preheat the oven to 200°C/400°F/Gas 6. Cut the spring onions into three pieces, then put them in a small roasting pan and season with salt and pepper.

2 Drizzle the sesame oil over the spring onions and roast for 10 minutes, until they are slightly charred and tender. Set aside.

3 Cook the noodles according to the instructions on the packet and drain thoroughly. Toss with the spring onions and oyster sauce, and season with ground black pepper. Serve immediately.

Cook's Tips
These noodles are equally good made with soy, instead of oyster sauce, and toasted sesame seeds.

Variation
Spicy peanut noodles are a tasty alternative side dish. Cook a 250g/9oz packet of egg noodles according to the instructions. Drain. Then heat 15ml/1 tbsp sunflower oil in a wok and add 30ml/2 tbsp crunchy peanut butter. Add a splash of cold water and a dash of soy sauce and stir the mixture over a gentle heat until thoroughly combined. Add the noodles to the pan and toss to coat in the peanut mixture. Sprinkle with fresh coriander (cilantro) to serve.

Creamy Polenta with Dolcelatte

Soft-cooked polenta, which is made from cornmeal, is a tasty accompaniment to meat dishes and makes a delicious change from the usual potatoes or rice. It can also be enjoyed on its own as a hearty snack.

Serves 4–6
900ml/1½ pints/3¾ cups milk
115g/4oz/1 cup instant polenta
115g/4oz Dolcelatte cheese

From the storecupboard
60ml/4 tbsp extra virgin olive oil
salt and ground black pepper

1 Pour the milk into a large pan and bring to the boil, then add a good pinch of salt. Remove the pan from the heat and pour in the polenta in a slow, steady stream, stirring constantly to combine.

2 Return the pan to a low heat and simmer gently, stirring constantly, for 5 minutes. Remove the pan from the heat and stir in the olive oil.

3 Spoon the polenta into a serving dish and crumble the cheese over the top. Season with more ground black pepper and serve immediately.

Variation
In place of Dolcelatte cheese, you can stir in the same quantity of grated mature (sharp) Cheddar or freshly grated Parmesan. To this you can add a handful of chopped fresh herbs, such as sage, oregano or thyme.

Cook's Tip
There are a variety of ways to serve polenta besides the soft cooked method, such as grilling (broiling) and frying. Pour the cooked polenta into an oiled tray to about 1cm/½in thick, allow to set and then chill for 20 minutes. Turn out on to a chopping board and cut into squares or triangles, then grill or fry until golden brown and add the topping of your choice.

Noodles with Sesame: Energy 266kcal/1111kJ; Protein 3.4g; Carbohydrate 48.8g, of which sugars 2.8g; Fat 5.7g, of which saturates 0.8g; Cholesterol 0mg; Calcium 18mg; Fibre 0.5g; Sodium 131mg.
Creamy Polenta: Energy 271kcal/1131kJ; Protein 10.8g; Carbohydrate 21.1g, of which sugars 7.1g; Fat 16.1g, of which saturates 6.3g; Cholesterol 23mg; Calcium 274mg; Fibre 0.4g; Sodium 298mg.

Soft Fried Noodles

This is a great dish for times when you are feeling a little peckish and fancy something simple but satisfying. Drain the cooked noodles and ladle them into the wok a few at a time, swirling them with the onions, so they don't all clump together on contact with the hot oil.

Serves 4–6

6–8 spring onions (scallions), cut into shreds
350g/12oz dried egg noodles, cooked and drained
soy sauce and coriander, to taste

From the storecupboard

30ml/2 tbsp vegetable oil
salt and ground black pepper

1 Heat the oil in a wok and fry the spring onions for about 30 seconds. Add the noodles and separate the strands. Fry the noodles until they are heated through, lightly browned and crisp on the outside, but still soft inside. Season with soy sauce, chopped coriander, and salt and pepper. Serve immediately.

Bocconcini with Fennel and Basil

These tiny balls of mozzarella are best when they're perfectly fresh. They should be milky and soft when you cut into them. Buy them from an Italian delicatessen or a good cheese shop. If you can't get hold of them, cut a ball of mozzarella into bitesizes.

Serves 6

450g/1lb bocconcini mozzarella
5ml/1 tsp fennel seeds, lightly crushed
a small bunch of fresh basil leaves, roughly torn

From the storecupboard

45ml/3 tbsp extra virgin olive oil
salt and ground black pepper

1 Drain the bocconcini well and place in a bowl. Stir in the olive oil, fennel seeds and basil, and season with salt and pepper. Cover and chill for 1 hour.

2 Remove the bowl from the refrigerator and leave to stand for about 30 minutes for the cheese to return to room temperature before serving.

Okra with Tomatoes and Coriander

This is a favourite Middle Eastern way to prepare okra. Add wedges of lemon as a garnish so that their juice can be squeezed over the vegetables to taste. Okra, also known as lady's fingers, are narrow green lantern-shaped pods. They contain a row of seeds that ooze a viscous liquid when cooked. This liquid acts as a natural thickener in a variety of curries and soups.

Serves 4–6

400g/14oz can chopped tomatoes with onions and garlic
generous pinch each of ground cinnamon, cumin and cloves
90ml/6 tbsp chopped fresh coriander (cilantro) leaves
800g/1¾lb okra

From the storecupboard

salt and ground black pepper

1 Heat the tomatoes and the cinnamon, cumin and cloves with half the coriander in a pan, then season to taste with salt and ground black pepper and bring to the boil.

2 Add the okra and cook, stirring constantly, for 1–2 minutes. Reduce the heat to low, then simmer, stirring occasionally, for 20–30 minutes, until the okra is tender.

3 Taste for spicing and seasoning, and adjust if necessary, adding more of any one spice, salt or pepper to taste. Stir in the remaining coriander. Serve hot, warm or cold.

Cook's Tip

Fresh okra is widely available from most supermarkets and Asian stores. Choose firm, green specimens and avoid any that are limp or turning brown.

Variation

Okra can be stir-fried with chilli and spices, then sprinkled with freshly grated coconut for an exotic twist.

Soft Fried Noodles: Energy 262kcal/1107kJ; Protein 7.2g; Carbohydrate 42g, of which sugars 1.3g; Fat 8.5g, of which saturates 1.8g; Cholesterol 18mg; Calcium 18mg; Fibre 1.8g; Sodium 105mg.
Bocconcini: Energy 245kcal/1015kJ; Protein 14.2g; Carbohydrate 0.2g, of which sugars 0.2g; Fat 20.8g, of which saturates 11.1g; Cholesterol 44mg; Calcium 288mg; Fibre 0.4g; Sodium 299mg.
Okra with Tomatoes: Energy 56kcal/234kJ; Protein 4.5g; Carbohydrate 6.3g, of which sugars 5.6g; Fat 1.6g, of which saturates 0.5g; Cholesterol 0mg; Calcium 235mg; Fibre 6.4g; Sodium 20mg.

Baked Winter Squash with Tomatoes

Acorn, butternut or Hubbard squash can all be used in this simple recipe. Serve the squash as a side dish for grilled meat or poultry, or as a light main course, with warm crusty bread. Canned chopped tomatoes with herbs are used in this recipe. A variety of flavoured canned tomatoes are now available including garlic, onion and olive – they are ideal for adding a combination of flavours when time is short.

Serves 4–6

1kg/2¼lb pumpkin or orange winter squash, peeled and sliced
2 x 400g/14oz cans chopped tomatoes with herbs
2–3 rosemary sprigs, stems removed and leaves chopped

From the storecupboard

45ml/3 tbsp garlic-flavoured olive oil
salt and ground black pepper

1 Preheat the oven to 160°C/325°F/Gas 3. Heat the oil in a pan and cook the pumpkin or squash slices, in batches, until golden brown, removing them from the pan as soon as they are cooked.

2 Add the tomatoes and cook over a medium-high heat until the mixture is of a sauce consistency. Stir in the rosemary and season to taste with salt and pepper.

3 Layer the pumpkin slices and tomatoes alternately in an ovenproof dish, finishing with a layer of tomatoes. Bake for 35 minutes, or until the top layer is lightly glazed and is beginning to turn golden brown, and the pumpkin is tender. Serve immediately.

Cook's Tip

This dish can be blended in a food processor to make a tasty purée, fantastic with rice or couscous, or transformed into a soup with a little added stock or milk for a more subtle creamier result.

Summer Squash and Baby New Potatoes in Warm Dill Sour Cream

Fresh vegetables and fragrant dill are delicious tossed in a simple sour cream or yogurt sauce. Choose small squash with bright skins that are free from blemishes and bruises. To make a simpler potato salad, pour the dill sour cream over warm cooked potatoes. Serve either version of the potato salad with poached salmon or chargrilled chicken.

Serves 4

400g/14oz mixed squash, such as yellow and green courgettes (zucchini), and green patty pan
400g/14oz baby new potatoes
1 large handful mixed fresh dill and chives, finely chopped
300ml/½ pint/1¼ cups sour cream or Greek (US strained plain) yogurt

From the storecupboard

salt and ground black pepper

1 Cut the squash into pieces about the same size as the potatoes. Put the potatoes in a pan and add water to cover and a pinch of salt. Bring to the boil, then simmer for about 10 minutes, until almost tender. Add the squash and continue to cook until the vegetables are just tender, then drain.

2 Put the vegetables into a wide, shallow pan and gently stir in the finely chopped fresh dill and chives.

3 Remove the pan from the heat and stir in the sour cream or yogurt. Return to the heat and heat gently until warm. Season and serve.

Cook's Tip

Summer squash are picked when still young and the skins are tender and edible. Included in this group are patty pan, courgettes (zucchini), marrows and cucumber. Summer squash do not keep well, so should only be stored in the refrigerator for a few days, unlike winter squash, which can be kept for several weeks in a cool dark place.

Baked Winter Squash: Energy 94kcal/392kJ; Protein 2.1g; Carbohydrate 7.8g, of which sugars 7g; Fat 6.2g, of which saturates 1.1g; Cholesterol 0mg; Calcium 58mg; Fibre 3g; Sodium 12mg.
Summer Squash: Energy 317kcal/1317kJ; Protein 5.8g; Carbohydrate 21g, of which sugars 6.1g; Fat 23.9g, of which saturates 14.8g; Cholesterol 66mg; Calcium 105mg; Fibre 2g; Sodium 104mg.

Spicy Potato Wedges

Serve on their own with a dip or as an accompaniment to meat or fish dishes.

Serves 4
675g/1½lb floury potatoes, such as Maris Piper
10ml/2 tsp paprika
5ml/1 tsp ground cumin

From the storecupboard
45ml/3 tbsp olive oil
salt and ground black pepper

1 Preheat the oven to 190°C/375°F/Gas 5. Using a sharp knife, cut the potatoes into chunky wedges and put in a roasting pan.

2 In a small bowl, combine the olive oil with the paprika and cumin and season well. Pour the mixture over the potatoes and toss well to coat thoroughly. Spread the potatoes out in the roasting pan and bake for 30–40 minutes, or until golden brown. Serve immediately.

Garlicky Roasties

Potatoes roasted in their skins retain a deep, earthy taste (and absorb less fat) while the garlic mellows on cooking to give a pungent but not overly-strong taste to serve alongside or squeezed over as a garnish.

Serves 4
1kg/2¼lb small floury potatoes
10ml/2 tsp walnut oil
2 whole garlic bulbs, unpeeled

From the storecupboard
60–75ml/4–5 tbsp sunflower oil
salt and ground black pepper

1 Preheat the oven to 240°C/475°F/Gas 9. Place the potatoes in a pan of cold water and bring to the boil. Drain.

2 Combine the oils in a roasting tin and place in the oven to get really hot. Add the potatoes and garlic and coat in oil.

3 Sprinkle with salt and roast for 10 minutes. Reduce the heat to 200°C/400°F/Gas 6. Continue roasting, basting occasionally, for 30–40 minutes. Serve each portion with some garlic cloves.

Crisp and Golden Roast Potatoes

Goose fat gives the best flavour to roast potatoes and is now widely available in cans in supermarkets. However, if you can't find goose fat, or you want to make a vegetarian version of these potatoes, use a large knob of butter or 15ml/1 tbsp olive oil instead. If you like, add a couple of bay leaves to the potatoes before roasting; they impart a lovely flavour.

Serves 4
675g/1½lb floury potatoes, such as Maris Piper, peeled
30ml/2 tbsp goose fat
12 garlic cloves, unpeeled

From the storecupboard
salt and ground black pepper

1 Preheat the oven to 190°C/375°F/Gas 5. Cut the potatoes into large chunks and cook in a pan of salted, boiling water for 5 minutes. Drain well and give the colander a good shake to fluff up the edges of the potatoes.

2 Return the potatoes to the pan and place it over a low heat for 1 minute to steam off any excess water.

3 Meanwhile, spoon the goose fat into a roasting pan and place in the oven until hot, about 5 minutes.

4 Add the potatoes to the pan with the garlic and turn to coat in the fat.

5 Season well with salt and ground black pepper and roast for 40–50 minutes, turning occasionally, until the potatoes are golden and tender.

Cook's Tip
Goose fat is very high in calories and rich in saturated fat. These tasty potatoes should be reserved as a treat to cook on special occasions.

Spicy Wedges: Energy 200kcal/838kJ; Protein 3.3g; Carbohydrate 28.1g, of which sugars 2.2g; Fat 9.1g, of which saturates 1.4g; Cholesterol 0mg; Calcium 15mg; Fibre 1.7g; Sodium 20mg.
Garlicky Roasties: Energy 312kcal/1310kJ; Protein 6.2g; Carbohydrate 44.3g, of which sugars 3.7g; Fat 13.4g, of which saturates 1.7g; Cholesterol 0mg; Calcium 20mg; Fibre 3.5g; Sodium 29mg.
Crisp Roast Potatoes: Energy 185kcal/778kJ; Protein 2.9g; Carbohydrate 27.2g, of which sugars 2.2g; Fat 7.9g, of which saturates 3.2g; Cholesterol 7mg; Calcium 10mg; Fibre 1.7g; Sodium 19mg.

Fennel, Potato and Garlic Mash

This flavoursome mash of potato, fennel and garlic goes well with practically all main dishes, whether fish, poultry or meat. Floury varieties of potato, such as Pentland Squire, King Edward or Marfona, are best for mashing as they produce a light fluffy result. Waxy potatoes are more suitable for baking, or for salads, as they produce a dense, rather starchy mash.

Serves 4
800g/1¾lb floury potatoes, cut into chunks
2 large fennel bulbs
120–150ml/4–5fl oz/½–⅔ cup milk or single (light) cream

From the storecupboard
90ml/6 tbsp garlic-flavoured olive oil
salt and ground black pepper

1 Boil the potatoes in water for 20 minutes, until tender.

2 Meanwhile, trim and chop the fennel, reserving any feathery tops. Chop the tops and set them aside.

3 Heat 30ml/2 tbsp of the oil in a pan. Add the fennel, cover and cook over a low heat for 20–30 minutes, until soft but not browned.

4 Drain and mash the potatoes. Purée the fennel in a food mill or blender and beat it into the potato with the remaining oil.

5 Warm the milk or cream and beat sufficient into the potato and fennel to make a creamy, light mixture. Season to taste and reheat gently, then beat in any chopped fennel tops. Serve immediately.

Cook's Tip
Cooking fennel tempers its aniseed flavour and brings out the delicious sweetness of the vegetable. Fennel is at its best when eaten fresh, so it should be kept in the refrigerator for a few days and eaten as soon as possible.

Champ

This traditional Irish dish of potatoes and green or spring onions is enriched with a wickedly indulgent amount of butter – for complete indulgence, replace 60ml/4 tbsp of the milk with crème fraîche or buttermilk. Serve the champ as an accompaniment to beef or lamb stew for a warming and hearty winter meal.

Serves 4
1kg/2¼lb potatoes, cut into chunks
300ml/½ pint/1¼ cups milk
1 bunch spring onions (scallions), thinly sliced, plus extra to garnish

From the storecupboard
115g/4oz/½ cup salted butter
salt and ground black pepper

1 Boil the potatoes in lightly salted water for 20–25 minutes, or until they are tender. Drain and mash the potatoes with a fork until smooth.

2 Place the milk, spring onions and half the butter in a small pan and set over a low heat until just simmering. Cook for 2–3 minutes, until the butter has melted and the spring onions have softened.

3 Beat the milk mixture into the mashed potato using a wooden spoon until the mixture is light and fluffy. Reheat gently, adding seasoning to taste.

4 Turn the potato into a warmed serving dish and make a well in the centre with a spoon. Place the remaining butter in the well and let it melt. Serve immediately, sprinkled with extra spring onion.

Variation
To make a traditional bubble and squeak, follow the main recipe, using half the butter. Cook about 500g/1¼lb finely shredded green cabbage or kale in a little water until just tender, drain thoroughly and then beat into the creamed potato. Fry in a hot buttered pan and then brown under the grill (broiler). Bubble and squeak is delicious served with sausages and grilled (broiled) ham or bacon.

Fennel/Potato Mash: Energy 144kcal/608kJ; Protein 4g; Carbohydrate 24.4g, of which sugars 4.6g; Fat 4.1g, of which saturates 2.3g; Cholesterol 10mg; Calcium 60mg; Fibre 4g; Sodium 61mg.
Champ: Energy 334kcal/1415kJ; Protein 13.2g; Carbohydrate 66.6g, of which sugars 10.5g; Fat 3.5g, of which saturates 1.7g; Cholesterol 9mg; Calcium 217mg; Fibre 5.2g; Sodium 92mg.

Griddle Potatoes

This attractive dish has traditionally been cooked with leftover cooked potatoes that have been boiled in their skins. It makes a tasty accompaniment to grilled meat, poultry or fish. It makes a substantial supper with gammon, a fried egg and a glass of beer.

Serves 4–6
2 onions, peeled and chopped
450–675g/1lb–1½ lb whole cooked potatoes, boiled in their skins

From the storecupboard
a mixture of butter and oil, for shallow frying
salt and ground black pepper

1 Put the onions in a large pan and scald them briefly in boiling water. Refresh under cold water and drain well. Peel and slice the potatoes.

2 Put a mixture of butter and oil into a large, heavy frying pan and heat well.

3 When the fat is hot, fry the onion until tender. Add the potato slices and brown them together, turning the potato slices to brown as evenly as possible on both sides.

4 Transfer to a warmed serving dish and season with salt and pepper. Serve very hot.

Cook's Tip
Cook the potatoes for a little longer to get a really crispy, crunchy coating. Serve them with a garlic mayonnaise dip for pure indulgence.

Variation
Try these potatoes spiced up with fresh chopped garlic and thinly sliced chilli, or tossed in chilli powder or paprika, for a fiery alternative.

Roasted Beetroot with Garlic Sauce

Beetroot has a lovely sweet and earthy flavour that is most pronounced when it is roasted. In Greece it is often served with a piquant garlic sauce, which contrasts beautifully with the sweetness of the beetroot.

Serves 4
675g/1½ lb medium or small beetroot (beets)

From the storecupboard
75–90ml/5–6 tbsp extra virgin olive oil
salt

For the garlic sauce (optional)
4 medium slices of bread, crusts removed, soaked in water for 10 minutes
2–3 garlic cloves, chopped
15ml/1 tbsp white wine vinegar
60ml/4 tbsp extra virgin olive oil

1 To make the garlic sauce, squeeze most of the water out of the bread, but leave it quite moist. Place it in a blender or food processor. Add the garlic and vinegar, with salt to taste, and blend until smooth.

2 While the blender or processor is running, drizzle in the olive oil through the lid or feeder tube. The sauce should be runny. Spoon it into a serving bowl and set it aside.

3 Prepare the barbecue. Rinse the beetroot under running water to remove any grit, but be careful not to pierce the skin or the colour will run.

4 Wrap the beetroot in groups of three or four in a double thickness of heavy-duty foil and leave the tops open. Drizzle over a little of the oil and sprinkle lightly with salt.

5 Close up the parcels and arrange them among the coals heated to medium-high. Bake for about 1½ hours until perfectly soft.

6 Remove the beetroot from the foil parcels. When they are just cool enough to handle, peel them. Slice them in thin round slices and serve with the remaining oil drizzled all over.

7 To serve, either spread a thin layer of garlic sauce on top, or hand it around separately. Serve with fresh bread, if you like.

Griddle Potatoes: Energy 163kcal/681kJ; Protein 3.4g; Carbohydrate 26.4g, of which sugars 5g; Fat 5.5g, of which saturates 3.3g; Cholesterol 13mg; Calcium 26mg; Fibre 2.6g; Sodium 49mg.
Beetroot with Garlic: Energy 344kcal/1435kJ; Protein 5.1g; Carbohydrate 25.7g, of which sugars 12.5g; Fat 25.4g, of which saturates 3.6g; Cholesterol 0mg; Calcium 62mg; Fibre 3.6g; Sodium 247mg.

Asparagus with Lemon Sauce

Sometimes less is more: here a simple egg and lemon dressing brings out the best in asparagus. Serve this asparagus dish as an accompaniment to fish or chicken. Alternatively, enjoy it for a light supper, with crusty bread and butter to mop up the delicious lemony juices.

Serves 4
675g/1½lb asparagus, tough ends removed, and tied in a bundle
15ml/1 tbsp cornflour (cornstarch)
2 egg yolks
juice of 1½ lemons

From the storecupboard
salt and ground black pepper

1 Cook the bundle of asparagus in a tall pan of lightly salted, boiling water for 7–10 minutes.

2 Drain well and arrange the asparagus in a serving dish. Reserve 200ml/7fl oz/scant 1 cup of the cooking liquid.

3 Blend the cornflour with the cooled, reserved cooking liquid and place in a pan. Bring to the boil, stirring constantly, and cook over a gentle heat until the sauce thickens slightly. Remove the pan from the heat and leave to cool.

4 Beat the egg yolks with the lemon juice and stir into the cooled sauce. Cook over a low heat, stirring constantly, until the sauce is thick. Be careful not to overheat the sauce or it may curdle. As soon as the sauce has thickened, remove the pan from the heat and continue stirring for 1 minute. Taste and season with salt. Leave the sauce to cool slightly.

5 Stir the cooled lemon sauce, then pour a little over the cooked asparagus. Cover and chill in the refrigerator for at least 2 hours before serving with the rest of the sauce.

Cook's Tip
For a slightly less tangy sauce, add a little caster (superfine) sugar with the salt in step 4.

Asparagus with Crispy Prosciutto

Choose tender, fine asparagus for this recipe, as it cooks through quickly in the oven without losing its flavour or texture.

Serves 4
350g/12oz fine asparagus spears, trimmed
1 small handful of fresh basil leaves
4 prosciutto slices

From the storecupboard
30ml/2 tbsp olive oil
salt and ground black pepper

1 Preheat the oven to 190°C/375°F/Gas 5. Put the asparagus in a roasting pan and drizzle with the olive oil.

2 Sprinkle over the basil and season with salt and ground black pepper. Gently stir to coat in the oil, then spread the asparagus in a single layer.

3 Lay the slices of prosciutto on top of the asparagus and cook for 10–15 minutes, or until the prosciutto is crisp and the asparagus is just tender. Serve immediately.

Cook's Tip
When buying asparagus, look for bright-coloured firm spears with tight buds; avoid the ones with tough woody stems, or remove these before cooking. Always choose roughly uniform-sized spears so that they cook at an even speed. Asparagus itself is low in calories and contains no fat or cholesterol.

Variation
Other cured meats, such as the Italian salami or the Spanish jamon serrano could, equally be used in this dish. It could also be cooked in a griddle pan or on a barbecue by wrapping a slice of ham around each stem of asparagus and tucking a basil leaf inside as you do so.

Asparagus with Lemon: Energy 96kcal/399kJ; Protein 6.4g; Carbohydrate 9.4g, of which sugars 5.8g; Fat 3.8g, of which saturates 1g; Cholesterol 101mg; Calcium 59mg; Fibre 2.9g; Sodium 8mg.
Asparagus with Prosciutto: Energy 82kcal/339kJ; Protein 4.4g; Carbohydrate 1.9g, of which sugars 1.8g; Fat 6.4g, of which saturates 1g; Cholesterol 6mg; Calcium 24mg; Fibre 0.5g; Sodium 121mg.

Figs with Prosciutto and Roquefort

Fresh figs are a delicious treat, whether you choose dark purple, yellowy green or green-skinned varieties. When they are ripe, you can split them open with your fingers to reveal the soft, sweet flesh full of edible seeds. In this easy, stylish dish figs and honey balance the richness of the ham and cheese. Serve with warm bread for a simple appetizer before any rich main course.

Serves 4
8 fresh figs
75g/3oz prosciutto
45ml/3 tbsp clear honey
75g/3oz Roquefort cheese

From the storecupboard
ground black pepper

1 Preheat the grill (broiler). Quarter the figs and place on a foil-lined grill rack.

2 Tear each slice of prosciutto into two or three pieces and crumple them up on the foil beside the figs. Brush the figs with 15ml/1 tbsp of the clear honey and cook under the grill until lightly browned.

3 Crumble the Roquefort cheese and divide among four plates, setting it to one side.

4 Add the honey-grilled figs and ham and pour over any cooking juices caught on the foil. Drizzle the remaining honey over the figs, ham and cheese, and serve seasoned with plenty of ground black pepper.

Cook's Tip
Although commonly thought of as a fruit, the fig is in fact the flower of the fig tree. It is very high in calcium and a well-known laxative. When buying figs, choose unbruised ripe fruits that yield to gentle pressure and eat on the day you purchase them for the best flavour.

Stir-fried Brussels Sprouts with Bacon and Caraway Seeds

This is a great way of cooking Brussels sprouts, helping to retain their sweet flavour and crunchy texture. Stir-frying guarantees that there will not be a single soggy sprout in sight, which is often what puts people off these fabulous vegetables.

Serves 4
450g/1lb Brussels sprouts, trimmed and washed
2 streaky (fatty) bacon rashers (strips), finely chopped
10ml/2 tsp caraway seeds, lightly crushed

From the storecupboard
30ml/2 tbsp sunflower oil
salt and ground black pepper

1 Using a sharp knife, cut the Brussels sprouts into fine shreds and set aside. Heat the oil in a wok or large frying pan and add the bacon. Cook for 1–2 minutes, or until the bacon is beginning to turn golden.

2 Add the shredded sprouts to the wok or pan and stir-fry for 1–2 minutes, or until lightly cooked.

3 Season the sprouts with salt and ground black pepper to taste and stir in the caraway seeds. Cook for a further 30 seconds, then serve immediately.

Variations
- *Substitute the bacon with peeled chopped chestnuts for a more low-fat option.*
- *A delicious alternative way with this much maligned vegetable is to stir-fry Brussels sprouts and add crème fraîche. To make, heat 15ml/1 tbsp sunflower oil in a wok or large frying pan. Add 1 chopped garlic clove and stir-fry for about 30 seconds. Shred 450g/1lb Brussels sprouts and add to the pan. Stir-fry for 3–4 minutes, until just tender. Season with salt and pepper and stir in 30ml/2 tbsp crème fraîche. Warm through for 1 minute before serving.*

Figs with Prosciutto: Energy 326kcal/1378kJ; Protein 10.7g; Carbohydrate 57.4g, of which sugars 57.4g; Fat 7.5g, of which saturates 3.8g; Cholesterol 25mg; Calcium 324mg; Fibre 6.9g; Sodium 512mg.
Brussels Sprouts: Energy 131kcal/545kJ; Protein 5.9g; Carbohydrate 4.6g, of which sugars 3.5g; Fat 10g, of which saturates 2g; Cholesterol 8mg; Calcium 30mg; Fibre 4.6g; Sodium 164mg.

Sweet Cucumber Cooler

This sweet dipping sauce is good served with Thai bites.

Makes 120ml/4fl oz/½ cup
¼ small cucumber, thinly sliced
30ml/2 tbsp sugar
15ml/1 tbsp rice or white wine vinegar
2 shallots or 1 small red onion, thinly sliced

From the storecupboard
2.5ml/½ tsp salt

1 With a sharp knife, cut the cucumber slices into quarters.

2 Measure 75ml/5 tbsp water, the sugar, salt and vinegar into a stainless-steel or enamel pan, bring to the boil and simmer for less than 1 minute until the sugar has dissolved. Allow to cool. Add the cucumber and shallots. Serve at room temperature.

Sour Cucumber with Fresh Dill

This is half pickle, half salad, and totally delicious served with pumpernickel or other coarse, dark, full-flavoured bread. Choose smooth-skinned, smallish cucumbers as larger ones tend to be less tender, with tough skins and bitter seeds. If you can only buy a large cucumber, peel it before slicing.

Serves 4
2 small cucumbers, thinly sliced
3 onions, thinly sliced
75–90ml/5–6 tbsp cider vinegar
30–45ml/2–3 tbsp chopped fresh dill

From the storecupboard
salt and ground black pepper

1 Combine together the thinly sliced cucumbers and the thinly sliced onions. Season and toss together until thoroughly combined. Leave to stand in a cool place for 5–10 minutes.

2 Add the cider vinegar, 30–45ml/2–3 tbsp water and the chopped fresh dill to the cucumber and onion mixture. Toss all the ingredients together until well combined, then chill in the refrigerator for a few hours, or until ready to serve.

Jicama, Chilli and Lime Salad

A very tasty, crisp vegetable, the jicama is sometimes called the Mexican potato. Unlike potato, however, it can be eaten raw and here it is transformed into a zingy salad appetizer to serve with drinks.

Serves 4
1 jicama
2 fresh serrano chillies
2 limes

From the storecupboard
2.5ml/½ tsp salt

1 Peel the jicama with a potato peeler or knife, then cut it into 2cm/¾in cubes. Put the cubes in a large bowl, add the salt and toss well to coat.

2 Cut the serrano chillies in half, scrape out the seeds with a sharp knife, then cut the flesh into fine strips, taking care not to burn yourself with the chilli flesh. Grate the rind of one of the limes thinly, removing only the coloured part of the skin, then cut the lime in half and squeeze the juice.

3 Add the chillies, lime rind and juice to the jicama and mix thoroughly to ensure that all the jicama cubes are coated. Cut the other lime into wedges.

4 Cover the salad and chill for at least 1 hour before serving garnished with lime wedges. If the salad is to be served as an appetizer with drinks, transfer the jicama cubes to little bowls and offer them with cocktail sticks (toothpicks) for spearing.

Cook's Tips

- *Look for jicama in Asian supermarkets, as it is widely used in Chinese cooking. It goes by several names and you may find it labelled as either yam bean or Chinese turnip.*
- *Take care when handling fresh chillies as the juice can burn sensitive skin. Wear rubber gloves to protect your hands or wash your hands very thoroughly after preparation. Be careful also not to touch your eyes when preparing chillies as the juices can cause unpleasant stinging.*

Cucumber Cooler: Energy 147kcal/624kJ; Protein 1.4g; Carbohydrate 37.2g, of which sugars 35.8g; Fat 0.2g, of which saturates 0g; Cholesterol 0mg; Calcium 44mg; Fibre 1.3g; Sodium 6mg
Sour Cucumber and Dill: Energy 59kcal/243kJ; Protein 2.5g; Carbohydrate 11.7g, of which sugars 8.7g; Fat 0.5g, of which saturates 0g; Cholesterol 0mg; Calcium 72mg; Fibre 2.9g; Sodium 11mg.
Jicama, Chilli and Lime: Energy 73kcal/308kJ; Protein 2.1g; Carbohydrate 16.2g, of which sugars 1.4g; Fat 0.4g, of which saturates 0.1g; Cholesterol 0mg; Calcium 10mg; Fibre 1g; Sodium 12mg.

Beetroot with Fresh Mint

This simple and decorative beetroot salad can be served as part of a selection of salads, as an appetizer, or as an accompaniment to grilled or roasted pork or lamb. Balsamic vinegar is a rich, dark vinegar with a mellow, deep flavour. It can be used to dress a variety of salad ingredients and is particularly good drizzled over a fresh tomato and basil salad.

Serves 4

4–6 cooked beetroot (beet)
15–30ml/1–2 tbsp balsamic vinegar
1 bunch fresh mint, leaves stripped and thinly shredded

From the storecupboard

30ml/2 tbsp olive oil
salt and ground black pepper

1 Slice the beetroot or cut into even dice with a sharp knife. Put the beetroot in a bowl. Add the balsamic vinegar, olive oil and a pinch of salt and pepper and toss together to combine.

2 Add half the thinly shredded fresh mint to the salad and toss lightly until thoroughly combined.

3 Place the salad in the refrigerator and chill for about 1 hour. Serve garnished with the remaining thinly shredded mint leaves.

Cook's Tip

Beetroot is well known for its medicinal qualities. It can be used to treat disorders of the blood, including anaemia. It is also an effective detoxifier and, because of its high fibre content, it also relieves constipation.

Variation

To make Tunisian beetroot, add a little harissa to taste and substitute chopped fresh coriander (cilantro) for the shredded mint.

Grated Beetroot and Yogurt Salad

With its beneficial nutritional properties, yogurt makes a tasty dip combined with mashed or grated ingredients, and mixed with a little vinegar or lemon juice it is good spooned as a sauce over grilled or fried vegetables. The most famous of the yogurt dips is the one with smoked aubergine, but there are a few other gems that get little mention, such as this one made with grated beetroot. Spiked with garlic and a pretty shade of pink, it is very moreish scooped on to flatbread or chunks of a warm, crusty loaf.

Serves 4

4 raw beetroot (beets), washed and trimmed
500g/1¼lb/2¼ cups thick and creamy natural (plain) yogurt
2 garlic cloves, crushed
a few fresh mint leaves, shredded, to garnish

From the storecupboard

salt and ground black pepper

1 Boil the beetroot in plenty of water for 35–40 minutes until tender, but not mushy or soft. Drain and refresh under cold running water, then peel off the skins and grate the beetroot on to a plate. Squeeze it lightly with your fingers to drain off excess water.

2 In a bowl, beat the yogurt with the garlic and season with salt and pepper. Add the beetroot, reserving a little to garnish the top, and mix well. Garnish with mint leaves.

Variations

- *In some households, the beetroot is diced and stir-fried with coriander seeds, sugar and a splash of apple vinegar. Then it is served warm with the cooling garlic-flavoured yogurt and garnished with dill.*
- *Cut four carrots into chunks and steam for about 15 minutes, until they are tender but still with some bite, then grate and mix with the yogurt and garlic. Season with salt and pepper and garnish with mint or dill.*

Beetroot with Fresh Mint: Energy 90kcal/378kJ; Protein 1.7g; Carbohydrate 8.9g, of which sugars 8.3g; Fat 5.6g, of which saturates 0.8g; Cholesterol 0mg; Calcium 21mg; Fibre 1.9g; Sodium 66mg.
Beetroot and Yogurt: Energy 95kcal/403kJ; Protein 7.8g; Carbohydrate 14.4g, of which sugars 13g; Fat 1.4g, of which saturates 0.6g; Cholesterol 2mg; Calcium 249mg; Fibre 1.3g; Sodium 137mg.

Globe Artichokes with Green Beans and Garlic Dressing

Piquant garlic dressing or creamy aioli go perfectly with these lightly cooked vegetables. Serve lemon wedges with the artichokes so that their juice may be squeezed over to taste. The vegetables can also be garnished with finely shredded lemon rind.

Serves 4–6

225g/8oz green beans
3 small globe artichokes
250ml/8fl oz/1 cup garlic dressing or aioli

From the storecupboard

15ml/1 tbsp lemon-flavoured olive oil
salt and ground black pepper

1 Cook the beans in boiling water for 1–2 minutes, until slightly softened. Drain well.

2 Trim the artichoke stalks close to the base. Cook them in a large pan of salted water for about 30 minutes, or until you can easily pull away a leaf from the base. Drain well.

3 Using a sharp knife, halve them lengthways and ease out their chokes using a teaspoon.

4 Arrange the artichokes and green beans on serving plates and drizzle with the oil. Season with coarse salt and a little pepper. Spoon the garlic dressing or aioli into the hearts and serve warm.

5 To eat the artichokes, pull the leaves from the base one at a time and use to scoop a little of the dressing. It is only the fleshy end of each leaf that is eaten as well as the base, bottom or 'fond'.

Cook's Tip

Artichokes should feel heavy for their size. When selecting make sure that the inner leaves are wrapped tightly round the choke and the heart inside.

Halloumi and Grape Salad

Firm and salty halloumi cheese is a great standby ingredient for turning a simple salad into a special dish. In this recipe it is tossed with sweet, juicy grapes, which complement its flavour and texture. Fresh young thyme leaves and dill taste especially good mixed with the salad. Serve with a crusty walnut or sun-dried tomato bread for a light lunch.

Serves 4

150g/5oz mixed salad leaves and tender fresh herb sprigs
175g/6oz mixed seedless green and black grapes
250g/9oz halloumi cheese
75ml/5 tbsp oil and lemon juice or vinegar dressing

1 Toss together the salad leaves and fresh herb sprigs and the green and black grapes, then transfer to a large serving plate.

2 Thinly slice the halloumi cheese. Heat a large non-stick frying pan. Add the sliced halloumi cheese and cook briefly until it just starts to turn golden brown on the underside.

3 Turn the cheese with a fish slice or metal spatula and cook the other side until it is golden brown.

4 Arrange the fried cheese over the salad on the serving plate. Pour over the oil and lemon juice, or vinegar, dressing and serve immediately while the cheese is still hot with some warm crusty bread.

Variation

Make this halloumi and grape salad really special with a fresh and tangy orange and tarragon dressing. In a small bowl, whisk together the rind and juice of 1 large orange with 45ml/3 tbsp olive oil and 15ml/1 tbsp chopped fresh tarragon. Season with salt and plenty of ground black pepper to taste.

Globe Artichokes: Energy 299kcal/1232kJ; Protein 1.1g; Carbohydrate 1.7g, of which sugars 1.4g; Fat 22.7g, of which saturates 4.5g; Cholesterol 0mg; Calcium 39mg; Fibre 1.4g; Sodium 418mg.
Halloumi and Grape: Energy 235kcal/974kJ; Protein 8g; Carbohydrate 2.8g, of which sugars 2.8g; Fat 21.4g, of which saturates 7.6g; Cholesterol 24mg; Calcium 160mg; Fibre 0.3g; Sodium 166mg.

Watercress Salad with Pear and Blue Cheese Dressing

A refreshing light salad, this dish combines lovely peppery watercress, soft juicy pears and a tart dressing. Dunsyre Blue cheese from Lanarkshire, Scotland, has a wonderfully sharp flavour with a crumbly texture, but other blue cheeses can be substituted.

Serves 4
25g/1oz Dunsyre Blue cheese
15ml/1 tbsp lemon juice
2 bunches watercress, thoroughly washed and trimmed
2 ripe pears

From the storecupboard
30ml/2 tbsp walnut oil
salt and ground black pepper

1 Crumble the Dunsyre Blue into a bowl, then mash into the walnut oil, using a fork.

2 Whisk in the lemon juice to create a thickish mixture. If you need to thicken it further, add a little more cheese. Season to taste with salt and ground black pepper.

3 Arrange a pile of watercress on the sides of four plates.

4 Peel and slice the two pears, then place the pear slices to the side of the watercress, allowing half a pear per person. Drizzle the dressing over the salad. The salad is best served immediately at room temperature.

Cook's Tips
- *Choose ripe Comice or similar pears that are soft and juicy.*
- *If you want to get things ready in advance, peel and slice the pears, then rub with some lemon juice; this will stop them discolouring so quickly.*

Variation
For a milder, tangy dressing use Dolcelatte cheese instead.

Orange and Chicory Salad with Walnuts

Chicory and oranges are both winter ingredients, so this salad is perfect as a light accompaniment to hearty winter meat dishes. The fresh flavours also go well with seafood dishes.

Serves 6
2 chicory (Belgian endive) heads
2 oranges
25g/1oz/2 tbsp walnut halves, roughly chopped

From the storecupboard
30ml/2 tbsp extra-virgin olive oil
salt and ground black pepper

1 Trim off the bottom of each chicory head and separate the leaves. Arrange on a serving platter.

2 Place one of the oranges on a chopping board and slice off the top and bottom to expose the flesh. Place the orange upright and, using a small sharp knife, slice down between the skin and the flesh. Do this all the way around to remove all peel and pith. Repeat with the remaining orange, reserving any juice.

3 Holding one orange over a bowl to catch the juices, cut between the membrane to release the segments. Repeat with the second orange. Arrange the orange segments on the platter with the chicory.

4 Whisk the oil with any juice from the oranges, and season with salt and pepper to taste. Sprinkle the walnuts over the salad, drizzle over the dressing and serve immediately.

Cook's Tip
Blood oranges look especially attractive served in this dish.

Variation
Use young spinach leaves or rocket (arugula) instead of chicory.

Watercress and Blue Cheese: Energy 106kcal/442kJ; Protein 2.3g; Carbohydrate 7.6g, of which sugars 7.6g; Fat 7.6g, of which saturates 1.8g; Cholesterol 5mg; Calcium 81mg; Fibre 2g; Sodium 91mg.
Orange and Chicory: Energy 81kcal/335kJ; Protein 1.2g; Carbohydrate 4.6g, of which sugars 3.9g; Fat 6.8g, of which saturates 0.8g; Cholesterol 0mg; Calcium 31mg; Fibre 1.2g; Sodium 3mg.

Watermelon and Feta Salad

The combination of sweet watermelon with salty feta cheese is inspired by Turkish tradition. The salad may be served plain and light, on a leafy base, or with a herbed vinaigrette dressing drizzled over. It is perfect served as an appetizer. Feta cheese is salty because it is preserved in brine – but the salt is not supposed to overpower the taste of the cheese.

Serves 4
4 slices watermelon, chilled
130g/4½oz feta cheese, preferably sheep's milk feta, cut into bitesize pieces
handful of mixed seeds, such as lightly toasted pumpkin seeds and sunflower seeds
10–15 black olives

1 Cut the rind off the watermelon and remove as many seeds as possible. Cut the flesh into triangular-shaped chunks.

2 Mix the watermelon, feta cheese, mixed seeds and black olives. Cover and chill the salad for 30 minutes before serving.

Cook's Tips
• *The best choice of olives for this recipe are plump black Mediterranean ones, such as kalamata. Alternatively, use any other shiny, brined varieties or dry-cured black olives.*
• *The nutty flavour and crunchy texture of toasted seeds gives an instant healthy boost to this dish. Sunflower seeds are rich in Vitamin E and pumpkin seeds are high in iron and zinc.*

Variations
• *Exchange watermelon for juicy ripe figs in this recipe.*
• *An alternative equally refreshing way with the appetizing feta cheese is in a classic Greek salad. This distinctive salad is served with juicy ripe tomatoes, crunchy cucumber, onion and plump olives.*

Tomato, Bean and Fried Basil Salad

Infusing basil in hot oil brings out its wonderful, aromatic flavour, which works so well in almost any tomato dish. Various canned beans or chickpeas can be used instead of mixed beans in this simple dish, as they all taste good and make a wholesome salad to serve as an accompaniment or a satisfying snack with some warm, grainy bread.

Serves 4
15g/½oz/½ cup fresh basil leaves
300g/11oz cherry tomatoes, halved
400g/14oz can mixed beans, drained and rinsed

From the storecupboard
75ml/5 tbsp extra virgin olive oil
salt and ground black pepper

1 Reserve one-third of the basil leaves for garnish, then tear the remainder into pieces. Pour the olive oil into a small pan. Add the torn basil and heat gently for 1 minute, until the basil sizzles and begins to colour.

2 Place the halved cherry tomatoes and beans in a bowl. Pour in the basil oil and add a little salt and plenty of ground black pepper. Toss the ingredients together gently, cover and leave to marinate at room temperature for at least 30 minutes. Serve the salad sprinkled with the remaining basil leaves.

Pink Grapefruit and Avocado Salad

Smooth, creamy avocado and zesty citrus fruit are perfect partners in an attractive, refreshing salad. Pink grapefruit are tangy but not too sharp, or use large oranges for a sweeter flavour. Avocados turn brown quickly when exposed to the air: the acidic grapefruit juice will prevent this, so combine the ingredients as soon as the avocados have been sliced.

Serves 4
2 pink grapefruit
2 ripe avocados
90g/3½oz rocket (arugula)

From the storecupboard
30ml/2 tbsp chilli oil
salt and ground black pepper

1 Slice the top and bottom off a grapefruit, then cut off all the peel and pith from around the side. Working over a small bowl to catch the juices, cut out the segments from between the membranes and place them in a separate bowl. Squeeze any juices remaining in the membranes into the bowl, then discard them. Repeat with the remaining grapefruit.

2 Halve, stone (pit) and peel the avocados. Slice the flesh and add it to the grapefruit segments. Whisk a little salt and then the chilli oil into the grapefruit juice.

3 Pile the rocket leaves on to four serving plates and top with the grapefruit segments and avocado. Pour over the dressing and serve.

Watermelon and Feta: Energy 256kcal/1066kJ; Protein 7.7g; Carbohydrate 12.9g, of which sugars 11.6g; Fat 19.7g, of which saturates 6.2g; Cholesterol 23mg; Calcium 165mg; Fibre 1.4g; Sodium 616mg.
Tomato and Basil: Energy 404kcal/1701kJ; Protein 22.8g; Carbohydrate 46.5g, of which sugars 4.9g; Fat 15.4g, of which saturates 2.3g; Cholesterol 0mg; Calcium 113mg; Fibre 16.7g; Sodium 26mg.
Pink Grapefruit and Avocado: Energy 151kcal/625kJ; Protein 1.1g; Carbohydrate 5.6g, of which sugars 5.2g; Fat 13.9g, of which saturates 2.4g; Cholesterol 0mg; Calcium 24mg; Fibre 1.9g; Sodium 13mg.

Date, Orange and Carrot Salad

Take exotic fresh dates and marry them with everyday ingredients, such as carrots and oranges, to make this deliciously different salad. The salad looks really pretty arranged on a base of sweet Little Gem lettuce leaves. This fruity salad is excellent served with chargrilled lamb steaks, or with skewered lamb.

Serves 4
3 carrots
3 oranges
115g/4oz/scant ¾ cup fresh dates, stoned (pitted) and cut lengthways into eighths
25g/1oz/¼ cup toasted whole almonds, chopped

From the storecupboard
salt and ground black pepper

1 Grate the carrots and place in a mound in a serving dish, or on four individual plates.

2 Peel and segment two of the oranges and arrange the orange segments around the carrot. Season with salt and ground black pepper. Pile the dates on top, then sprinkle with the chopped, toasted almonds.

3 Squeeze the juice from the remaining orange and sprinkle it over the salad. Chill in the refrigerator for an hour before serving.

Cook's Tips
- *Dates should be plump and glossy, Medjool dates have a wrinkly skin, but most other varieties are smooth. They can be stored in the refrigerator for up to a week.*
- *There are two types of almond: sweet and bitter. The best sweet varieties come from Spain – they are the flat and slender Jodan almonds and the heart-shaped Valencia almonds, which are also grown in Portugal – and the flatter Californian almonds. For the best flavour, buy the almonds shelled, but still in their skins. Then blanch them yourself by covering with boiling water, leaving for a few minutes, then draining and slipping off the skins.*

Moroccan Carrot Salad

In this intriguing salad from North Africa, the carrots are lightly cooked before being tossed in a cumin and coriander vinaigrette. Cumin is widely used in Indian and Mexican cooking, as well as North African cuisines. It has a strong and spicy aroma and a warm pungent flavour that goes particularly well with root vegetables. This salad is a perfect accompaniment for both everyday or special meals.

Serves 4–6
3–4 carrots, thinly sliced
1.5ml/¼ tsp ground cumin, or to taste
60ml/4 tbsp garlic-flavoured oil and vinegar dressing
30ml/2 tbsp chopped fresh coriander (cilantro) leaves or a mixture of coriander and parsley

From the storecupboard
salt and ground black pepper

1 Cook the thinly sliced carrots by either steaming or boiling in lightly salted water until they are just tender but not soft. Drain the carrots, leave for a few minutes to dry and cool, then put into a mixing bowl.

2 Add the cumin, garlic dressing and herbs. Season to taste and chill well before serving. Check the seasoning just before serving and add more ground cumin, salt or black pepper, if required.

Variation
Raw young tender turnips have a tangy, slightly peppery flavour and make another excellent side salad. Serve as an accompaniment for grilled poultry or meat. It is also delicious as a light appetizer, garnished with parsley and paprika, and served with warmed flatbreads such as pitta or naan. To make, thinly slice or coarsely grate 2–4 young turnips. Alternatively, thinly slice half the turnips and grate the remaining half. Put in a bowl. Add ¼–½ a finely chopped onion and 2–3 drops white wine vinegar and season to taste. Toss together, then stir in 60–90ml/4–6 tbsp sour cream. Chill well before serving.

Date, Orange and Carrot: Energy 138kcal/582kJ; Protein 3.6g; Carbohydrate 21.8g, of which sugars 21.4g; Fat 4.7g, of which saturates 0.4g; Cholesterol 0mg; Calcium 90mg; Fibre 3.9g; Sodium 18mg.
Moroccan Carrot: Energy 53kcal/220kJ; Protein 0.6g; Carbohydrate 4.2g, of which sugars 3.9g; Fat 3.9g, of which saturates 0.6g; Cholesterol 0mg; Calcium 29mg; Fibre 1.6g; Sodium 15mg.

Potato and Olive Salad

This delicious salad is simple and zesty – the perfect choice for lunch, as an accompaniment, or as an appetizer. Similar in appearance to flat leaf parsley, fresh coriander has a distinctive pungent, almost spicy flavour. It is widely used in India, the Middle and Far East and in eastern Mediterranean countries. This potato salad is particularly good served as part of a brunch.

Serves 4
8 large new potatoes
45–60ml/3–4 tbsp garlic-flavoured oil and vinegar dressing
60–90ml/4–6 tbsp chopped fresh herbs, such as coriander (cilantro) and chives
10–15 dry-fleshed black Mediterranean olives

From the storecupboard
salt and ground black pepper

1 Peel the new potatoes and cut them into chunks. Put them in a pan, pour in water to cover and season. Bring to the boil, then reduce the heat and cook gently for about 10 minutes, or until the potatoes are just tender.

2 Drain well and leave in a colander to dry thoroughly and cool slightly.

3 When they are cool enough to handle, chop the potatoes and put them in a serving bowl.

4 Drizzle the garlic dressing over the potatoes. Toss well and sprinkle with the coriander and chives, and black olives. Chill in the refrigerator for at least 1 hour before serving.

Variation
Add a pinch of ground cumin or a sprinkling of roasted whole cumin seeds to give a fragrant warmth to the dish, or a good pinch of smoked paprika to really spice up the salad and give it a vibrant appearance. These earthy flavours give a pleasing contrast to the fresh coriander (cilantro).

Anchovy and Roasted Pepper Salad

Sweet peppers, salty anchovies and plenty of garlic make an intensely flavoured salad that is delicious with meat, poultry or cheese. It also makes a tasty lunch with olive bread. If you find that canned anchovies are too salty for your liking, you can reduce their saltiness by soaking them in milk for 20 minutes. Drain off the oil first and after soaking drain and rinse them in cold water.

Serves 4
2 red, 2 orange and 2 yellow (bell) peppers, halved and seeded
50g/2oz can anchovies in olive oil
2 garlic cloves
45ml/3 tbsp balsamic vinegar

From the storecupboard
salt and ground black pepper

1 Preheat the oven to 200°C/400°F/Gas 6. Place the peppers, cut side down, in a roasting pan. Roast for 30–40 minutes, until the skins are charred.

2 Transfer the peppers to a bowl, cover with clear film (plastic wrap) and leave for 15 minutes.

3 Peel the peppers, then cut them into chunky strips. Drain the anchovies and halve the fillets lengthways.

4 Slice the garlic as thinly as possible and place it in a large bowl. Stir in the olive oil, vinegar and a little pepper. Add the peppers and anchovies and use a spoon and fork to fold the ingredients together. Cover and chill until ready to serve.

Variation
For a less intense flavour, replace the balsamic vinegar with freshly squeezed lemon juice. This will cut through the oiliness and leave a more refreshing sensation on the palate. Serve the salad on a bed of crispy lettuce leaves for a crunchy contrast in texture.

Potato and Olive: Energy 132kcal/548kJ; Protein 1.9g; Carbohydrate 12.4g, of which sugars 1.2g; Fat 8.6g, of which saturates 1.3g; Cholesterol 0mg; Calcium 42mg; Fibre 2g; Sodium 575mg.
Anchovy and Pepper: Energy 108kcal/453kJ; Protein 6g; Carbohydrate 16.4g, of which sugars 15.5g; Fat 2.4g, of which saturates 0.5g; Cholesterol 8mg; Calcium 83mg; Fibre 4.6g; Sodium 506mg.

Warm Chorizo and Spinach Salad

Spanish chorizo sausage contributes an intense spiciness to any ingredient with which it is combined. In this hearty warm salad, spinach has sufficient flavour to compete with the chorizo. Watercress or rocket could be used instead of the spinach, if you prefer. For an added dimension, use a flavoured olive oil – rosemary, garlic or chilli oil would work perfectly. Serve the salad with warm crusty bread to soak up all the delicious cooking juices.

Serves 4
225g/8oz baby spinach leaves
150g/5oz chorizo sausage, very thinly sliced
30ml/2 tbsp sherry vinegar

From the storecupboard
90ml/6 tbsp olive oil
salt and ground black pepper

1 Wash the spinach and discard any tough stalks. Pour the oil into a large frying pan and add the chorizo sausage. Cook gently for 3 minutes, until the sausage slices start to shrivel slightly and colour.

2 Add the spinach leaves and remove the pan from the heat. Toss the spinach in the warm oil until it just starts to wilt.

3 Add the sherry vinegar and a little seasoning. Toss the ingredients briefly, then serve immediately, while still warm.

Variations
- *If you don't have any sherry vinegar, you can replace it with balsamic vinegar, which has a similar sweet and mellow quality, but a slightly darker colour and richer flavour.*
- *Chorizo sausage can be replaced by other spicy cured sausages, such as the Italian salamis, Napoli or Toscana, or the Portuguese sausage, Longaniza.*

Asparagus, Bacon and Leaf Salad

This excellent salad turns a plain roast chicken or simple grilled fish into an interesting meal, especially when served with buttered new potatoes. It also makes an appetizing first course or light lunch. A wide range of different salad leaves are readily available – frisée has feathery, curly, slightly bitter tasting leaves and is a member of the chicory family. Frisée leaves range in colour from yellow-white to yellow-green.

Serves 4
500g/1¼ lb medium asparagus spears
130g/4½ oz thin-cut smoked back bacon
250g/9oz frisée lettuce leaves or mixed leaf salad
100ml/3½ fl oz/scant ½ cup French dressing

From the storecupboard
salt and ground black pepper

1 Trim off any tough stalk ends from the asparagus and cut the spears into three, setting the tender tips aside.

2 Heat a 1cm/½ in depth of water in a frying pan until simmering. Reserve the asparagus tips and cook the remainder of the spears in the water for about 3 minutes, until almost tender. Add the tips and cook for 1 minute more. Drain and refresh under cold, running water.

3 Dry-fry the bacon until crisp and then set it aside to cool. Use kitchen scissors to snip it into bitesize pieces.

4 Place the frisée or mixed leaf salad in a serving bowl and add the bacon.

5 Add the asparagus and a little black pepper to the salad. Pour the dressing over and toss the salad lightly, then serve.

Cook's Tip
Buy asparagus with bright-coloured, firm spears and tight buds.

Chorizo and Spinach: Energy 300kcal/1238kJ; Protein 5.6g; Carbohydrate 4.5g, of which sugars 1.4g; Fat 29g, of which saturates 7g; Cholesterol 18mg; Calcium 111mg; Fibre 1.4g; Sodium 364mg.
Asparagus and Bacon: Energy 259kcal/1068kJ; Protein 9.5g; Carbohydrate 3.6g, of which sugars 3.5g; Fat 23g, of which saturates 4.6g; Cholesterol 17mg; Calcium 53mg; Fibre 2.7g; Sodium 519mg.

Hot Avocado Halves

If you make the basil oil in advance, or buy a ready prepared basil oil, this is an ultra-simple dish. It makes an eye-catching first course and is an excellent appetite teaser to serve while the rest of the food is on the barbecue.

Serves 6
3 ready-to-eat avocados, preferably Hass for flavour
105ml/7 tbsp balsamic vinegar

For the basil oil
40g/1½oz/1½ cups fresh basil leaves, stalks removed
200ml/7fl oz/scant 1 cup olive oil

1 To make the basil oil, place the leaves in a bowl and pour boiling water over. Leave for 30 seconds. Drain, refresh under cold water and drain again. Squeeze dry and pat with kitchen paper to remove as much moisture as possible.

2 Place in a food processor with the oil and process to a purée. Put into a bowl, cover and chill overnight.

3 Next day, line a sieve (strainer) with muslin (cheesecloth), set it over a deep bowl and pour in the basil purée. Leave undisturbed for 1 hour, or until all the oil has filtered into the bowl. Discard the solids and pour into a bottle, then chill until ready to cook.

4 Prepare the barbecue. Cut each avocado in half and prise out the stone (pit). Brush with a little of the basil oil.

5 Heat the balsamic vinegar gently in a pan, on the stove or on the barbecue. When it starts to boil, simmer for 1 minute, or until it is just beginning to turn slightly syrupy.

6 Heat the griddle on the grill rack over hot coals. (Remember it is ready to use when a few drops of water sprinkled on the surface evaporate instantly.) Lower the heat a little and place the avocado halves cut side down on the griddle.

7 Cook for 30–60 seconds, until branded with grill marks. (Move the avocados around carefully with tongs to create a chequered effect.) Serve hot with the vinegar and extra oil.

Grilled Corn on the Cob

Keeping the husks on the corn protects the corn kernels and encloses the butter, so the flavours are contained. Fresh corn with husks intact are perfect, but banana leaves or a double layer of foil are also suitable for cooking corn on the barbecue.

Serves 6
3 dried chipotle chillies
7.5ml/1½ tsp lemon juice
45ml/3 tbsp chopped fresh flat leaf parsley
6 corn on the cob, with husks intact

From the storecupboard
250g/9oz/generous 1 cup butter softened
salt and ground black pepper

1 Heat a frying pan. Add the dried chillies and roast them by stirring them for 1 minute without letting them scorch. Put them in a bowl with almost boiling water to cover. Use a saucer to keep them submerged, and leave them to rehydrate for up to 1 hour.

2 Drain, remove the seeds and chop the chillies finely. Place the butter in a bowl and add the chillies, lemon juice and parsley. Season to taste and mix well.

3 Peel back the husks from each cob without tearing them. Remove the silk. Smear about 30ml/2 tbsp of the chilli butter over each cob. Pull the husks back over the cobs, ensuring that the butter is well hidden.

4 Put the rest of the butter in a pot, smooth the top and chill to use later. Place the cobs in a bowl of cold water and leave in a cool place for 1–3 hours or longer if it suits you better.

5 Prepare the barbecue. Remove the corn cobs from the water and wrap in pairs in foil. Once the flames have died down, position a lightly oiled grill rack over the coals to heat. When the coals are medium-hot, or have a moderate coating of ash, grill the corn for 15–20 minutes. Remove the foil and cook them for about 5 minutes more, turning them often to char the husks a little. Serve hot, with the rest of the butter.

Hot Avocado Halves: Energy 222kcal/916kJ; Protein 1g; Carbohydrate 1g, of which sugars 0.3g; Fat 23.8g, of which saturates 4.1g; Cholesterol 0mg; Calcium 6mg; Fibre 1.7g; Sodium 3mg.
Grilled Corn: Energy 435kcal/1805kJ; Protein 3.4g; Carbohydrate 27.1g, of which sugars 10g; Fat 35.6g, of which saturates 21.9g; Cholesterol 89mg; Calcium 28mg; Fibre 1.8g; Sodium 525mg.

Butter Bean, Tomato and Red Onion Salad

Serve this salad with toasted pitta bread for a fresh summer lunch, or as an accompaniment to meat cooked on a barbecue. For extra flavour and colour, stir in a handful of pitted black olives and a handful of chopped fresh parsley.

Serves 4

2 x 400g/14oz cans butter (lima) beans, rinsed and drained
4 plum tomatoes, roughly chopped
1 red onion, finely sliced

From the storecupboard

45ml/3 tbsp herb-infused olive oil
salt and ground black pepper

1 Mix together the beans, tomatoes and onion in a large bowl. Season with salt and pepper, and stir in the oil.

2 Cover the bowl with clear film (plastic wrap) and chill for 20 minutes before serving.

Variations

- *To make a tasty and nutritious tuna salad, drain a 200g/7oz can tuna, flake the tuna flesh and stir into the bean salad to combine thoroughly.*
- *To make a wholesome version of the Italian salad panzanella, tear half a loaf of ciabatta into bitesize pieces and stir into the salad. Leave to stand for 20 minutes before serving.*

Potato, Caraway Seed and Parsley Salad

Leaving the potatoes to cool in garlic-infused oil with the caraway seeds helps them to absorb plenty of flavour.

Serves 4–6

675g/1½lb new potatoes, scrubbed
15ml/1 tbsp caraway seeds, lightly crushed
45ml/3 tbsp chopped fresh parsley

From the storecupboard

45ml/3 tbsp garlic-infused olive oil
salt and ground black pepper

1 Cook the potatoes in salted, boiling water for about 10 minutes, or until just tender. Drain thoroughly and transfer to a large bowl.

2 Stir the oil, caraway seeds and some salt and pepper into the hot potatoes, then set aside to cool. When the potatoes are almost cold, stir in the parsley and serve.

Variation

This recipe is also delicious made with sweet potatoes instead of new potatoes. Peel and roughly chop the sweet potatoes, then follow the recipe as before.

Aubergines with Feta and Coriander

Aubergines take on a lovely smoky flavour when grilled on a barbecue, which contrasts beautifully with the sharpness of the feta cheese. Choose a good quality Greek feta cheese for the best flavour.

Serves 6

3 medium aubergines (eggplants)
400g/14oz feta cheese
a small bunch of coriander (cilantro), roughly chopped

From the storecupboard

60ml/4 tbsp extra virgin olive oil
salt and ground black pepper

1 Prepare a barbecue. Cook the aubergines for 20 minutes, turning occasionally, until charred and soft. Remove from the barbecue and cut in half lengthways.

2 Carefully scoop the aubergine flesh into a bowl, reserving the skins. Mash the flesh roughly with a fork.

3 Crumble the feta cheese, then stir into the mashed aubergine with the chopped coriander and olive oil. Season with salt and ground black pepper to taste.

4 Spoon the aubergine and feta mixture back into the skins and return to the barbecue for 5 minutes to warm through. Serve immediately.

Cook's Tip

When buying aubergines, look for small- to medium-sized vegetables, which have sweet tender flesh. They can be stored in the refrigerator for up to two weeks.

Variation

Other chopped fresh herbs are equally good in this dish. Why not try mint or basil, or flat leaf parsley. Serve with some sliced ripe beef tomatoes drizzled with olive oil for a delicious al fresco lunch.

Butter Bean and Tomato: Energy 156kcal/658kJ; Protein 8.7g; Carbohydrate 21.4g, of which sugars 4.9g; Fat 4.6g, of which saturates 0.7g; Cholesterol 0mg; Calcium 31mg; Fibre 7.2g; Sodium 567mg.
Potato, Caraway and Parsley: Energy 131kcal/549kJ; Protein 2.1g; Carbohydrate 18.3g, of which sugars 1.6g; Fat 5.9g, of which saturates 0.9g; Cholesterol 0mg; Calcium 22mg; Fibre 1.5g; Sodium 15mg.
Aubergines with Feta: Energy 257kcal/1066kJ; Protein 12g; Carbohydrate 4.2g, of which sugars 3.9g; Fat 21.5g, of which saturates 10.3g; Cholesterol 47mg; Calcium 286mg; Fibre 3.3g; Sodium 968mg.

Grilled Baby Artichokes

This is an enjoyable way to eat artichokes. Just hold the skewer with the artichoke in one hand, tear off a leaf with the other and dip that into the hot melted butter.

Serves 6
12 baby artichokes with stalks, about 1.3kg/3lb total weight
1 lemon, halved
2 garlic cloves, crushed with a pinch of salt
15ml/1 tbsp chopped fresh flat leaf parsley

From the storecupboard
200g/7oz/scant 1 cup butter
salt and ground black pepper

1 Soak 12 wooden skewers in cold water for 30 minutes. Drain, then skewer a baby artichoke on to each one. Bring a large pan of salted water to the boil. Squeeze the juice of one lemon half, and add it, with the lemon shell, to the pan.

2 Place the artichokes head first into the pan and boil for 5–8 minutes, or until just tender. Drain well. Set aside for up to 1 hour or use immediately.

3 Prepare the barbecue. Put the butter, garlic and parsley into a small pan and squeeze in the juice of the remaining half-lemon.

4 Position a lightly oiled grill rack over the coals to heat over medium heat. If the artichokes have been allowed to cool, wrap the heads in foil and place them on the grill for 3 minutes, then unwrap and return to the heat for 1 minute, turning frequently. If they are still hot, grill without the foil for 4 minutes, turning often.

5 When the artichokes are almost ready, melt the butter sauce in the pan on the barbecue. Either transfer the sauce to six small serving bowls or pour a little on to each plate. Serve it with the artichokes on their skewers.

Cook's Tip
Have plenty of napkins on hand to catch any stray drops of butter sauce.

Roasted Red Peppers with Feta, Capers and Preserved Lemons

Red peppers, particularly the long, slim, horn-shaped variety, feature widely in the cooking of North Africa and the Middle East. Roasting them really brings out their smoky flavour and they taste wonderful with crumbled white cheese. Feta is suggested here, but you can use any salty crumbly cheese. This dish makes a great mezze and also tastes good with kebabs.

Serves 4
4 fleshy red (bell) peppers
200g/7oz feta cheese, crumbled
30ml/2 tbsp capers, drained
peel of 1 preserved lemon, cut into small pieces

From the storecupboard
30–45ml/2–3 tbsp olive oil or argan oil
salt

1 Preheat the grill (broiler) on the hottest setting. Roast the red peppers under the grill, turning frequently, until they soften and their skins begin to blacken. (Alternatively, spear the peppers, one at a time, on long metal skewers and turn them over a gas flame, or roast them in a very hot oven.)

2 Place the peppers in a plastic bag, seal and leave them to stand for 15 minutes. Peel the peppers, remove and discard the stalks and seeds and then slice the flesh and arrange on a plate.

3 Add the crumbled feta and pour over the olive or argan oil. Scatter the capers and preserved lemon over the top and sprinkle with a little salt, if required (this depends on whether the feta is salty or not). Serve with chunks of bread to mop up the delicious, oil-rich juices.

Cook's Tip
Argan oil originates in Morocco and is made from the fruit of the argan tree. It has a distinctive nutty flavour, so if you can't find it, use another nutty oil.

Grilled Baby Artichokes 263kcal/1084kJ; Protein 1.4g; Carbohydrate 2.5g, of which sugars 1.2g; Fat 27.7g, of which saturates 17.4g; Cholesterol 71mg; Calcium 49mg; Fibre 1.4g; Sodium 262mg.
Peppers with Feta: Energy 255kcal/1058kJ; Protein 9.6g; Carbohydrate 12g, of which sugars 11.4g; Fat 19.1g, of which saturates 8.2g; Cholesterol 35mg; Calcium 194mg; Fibre 2.8g; Sodium 727mg.

Warm Halloumi and Fennel Salad

The firm rubbery texture of halloumi cheese makes it perfect for the barbecue, as it keeps its shape very well. It is widely available in most large supermarkets and Greek delicatessens.

Serves 4
200g/7oz halloumi cheese, thickly sliced
2 fennel bulbs, trimmed and thinly sliced
30ml/2 tbsp roughly chopped fresh oregano

From the storecupboard
45ml/3 tbsp lemon-infused olive oil
salt and ground black pepper

1 Put the halloumi, fennel and oregano in a bowl and drizzle over the lemon-infused oil. Season with salt and black pepper to taste. (Halloumi is a fairly salty cheese, so be very careful when adding extra salt.)

2 Cover the bowl with clear film (plastic wrap) and chill for about 2 hours to allow the flavours to develop.

3 Place the halloumi and fennel on a griddle pan or over the barbecue, reserving the marinade, and cook for about 3 minutes on each side, until charred.

4 Divide the halloumi and fennel among four serving plates and drizzle over the reserved marinade. Serve immediately.

Cook's Tips

- *To make your own lemon-flavoured oil, finely pare the rind from 1 lemon, place on kitchen paper, and leave to dry for 1 day. Add the dried rind to a bottle of olive oil and leave to infuse (steep) for up to 3 days. Strain into a clean bottle and discard the rind.*
- *Other flavoured oils would work well in this dish, such as herb oils, but take care with chilli or garlic which can be overpowering.*

Pear and Blue Cheese Salad

A juicy variety of pear, such as a Williams, is just perfect in this dish. You can use any other blue cheese, such as Stilton or Gorgonzola, in place of the Roquefort, if you prefer.

Serves 4
4 ripe pears
115g/4oz Roquefort cheese
15ml/1 tbsp balsamic vinegar

From the storecupboard
30ml/2 tbsp olive oil
salt and ground black pepper

1 Cut the pears into quarters and remove the cores. Thinly slice each pear quarter and arrange on a serving platter.

2 Slice the Roquefort as thinly as possible and place over the pears. Mix the oil and vinegar together and drizzle over the pears. Season with salt and pepper and serve.

Cook's Tip

Rich, dark balsamic vinegar has an intense yet mellow flavour. It is produced in Modena in the north of Italy and is widely available in most supermarkets. Sherry vinegar could be used as a substitute, it is mellow but slightly less intense.

Variations

- *Try substituting soft ripe juicy figs for the pears in this salad dish and use walnut oil to replace the olive oil. The combination of exotic flavoured figs and tangy blue cheese with a hint of nuttiness is exquisite.*
- *Add 115g/4oz/1 cup shelled walnut halves to the recipe to give a great crunch. Make it into a more complete meal with a bed of soft mixed salad leaves.*
- *Alternatively, boil some dried pasta shapes, such as penne, according to the packet instructions, drain well and cool. Place some salad leaves in a bowl, pile the pasta on top of the salad, sprinkle over crumbled Roquefort, pour over a dressing and add some walnut halves. Toss and serve.*

Halloumi and Fennel: Energy 215kcal/889kJ; Protein 10.2g; Carbohydrate 1.8g, of which sugars 1.7g; Fat 18.6g, of which saturates 8.1g; Cholesterol 29mg; Calcium 205mg; Fibre 2.4g; Sodium 209mg.
Pear and Blue Cheese: Energy 208kcal/865kJ; Protein 6.4g; Carbohydrate 15g, of which sugars 15g; Fat 14g, of which saturates 6.3g; Cholesterol 22mg; Calcium 157mg; Fibre 3.3g; Sodium 355mg.

Corn Tortillas

These delicious and versatile Mexican specialities cook very quickly. Griddle them over the barbecue and have a clean dish towel on hand to keep the hot stacks warm.

Makes about 14
275g/10oz/2½ cups masa harina

1 Prepare the barbecue. Put the masa harina into a bowl and stir in 250ml/8fl oz/1 cup of water, mixing it to a soft dough that just holds together. If it is too dry, add a little more water. Cover the bowl with a cloth and set aside for 15 minutes.

2 Knead the dough lightly then divide into 14 pieces, and shape into balls.

3 Using a rolling pin, roll out each ball between sheets of clear film (plastic wrap) until you have a thin round of dough measuring about 15cm/6in in diameter.

4 Put a griddle over the hot coals and griddle the first tortilla for 1 minute. Turn it over and cook for a minute more. Wrap in a clean dish towel and keep warm. Repeat for the other tortillas.

Cook's Tips

- *When making tortillas, it is important to get the dough texture right. If it is too dry and crumbly, add a little water; if it is too wet, add more masa harina. If you do not manage to flatten the ball of dough into a neat circle the first time, just re-roll it and try again.*
- *An alternative to rolling out rounds of tortilla dough with a rolling pin is to use a tortilla press. Open the press and line both sides with sheets of clear film (plastic wrap). Shape the tortilla dough into balls, put one ball on the press and bring the top down firmly to flatten it into a neat round. Open the press, peel off the top layer of clear film and, using the bottom layer, lift the tortilla out of the press. Peel off this layer of clear film and repeat the process with the other dough balls.*

Flour Tortillas

Home-made tortillas taste so good filled with barbecued vegetables and thinly sliced chicken or meat. You can make them in advance and then reheat them to serve.

Makes about 14
225g/8oz/2 cups plain (all-purpose) flour

From the storecupboard
5ml/1 tsp salt
15ml/1 tbsp lard or white cooking fat

1 Sift the flour and salt into a large mixing bowl. Gradually rub in the lard or white cooking fat, using your fingertips, until the mixture resembles coarse breadcrumbs.

2 Gradually add 120ml/4fl oz/½ cup water and mix to a soft dough. Knead lightly, form into a ball, cover with a cloth and leave to rest for 15 minutes. Prepare the barbecue.

3 Carefully divide the dough into about 14 portions and form these portions into small balls. One by one, roll out each ball of dough on a lightly floured wooden board to a round measuring about 15cm/6in. Trim the rounds if necessary.

4 Heat an ungreased flat griddle or frying pan over a medium heat. Cook the tortillas for about 1½–2 minutes on each side. Turn over with a palette knife or metal spatula when the bottom begins to brown. Wrap in a clean dish towel to keep warm until ready to serve.

Cook's Tips

- *Make flour tortillas whenever masa harina is difficult to find. To keep them soft and pliable, make sure they are kept warm until ready to serve, and eat as soon as possible.*
- *These flour tortillas can also be cooked in the oven at 150°C/300°F/Gas 2.*
- *For a beef filling, simply fry some minced (ground) beef in oil with ½ chopped onion, 1 small red chilli, finely chopped, 1 crushed garlic clove, ground black pepper and fresh thyme.*

Corn Tortillas: Energy 92kcal/385kJ; Protein 2.4g; Carbohydrate 18.3g, of which sugars 0g; Fat 0.8g, of which saturates 0g; Cholesterol 0mg; Calcium 1mg; Fibre 0.6g; Sodium 0mg.
Flour Tortillas: Energy 254kcal/1074kJ; Protein 5.9g; Carbohydrate 48.6g, of which sugars 0.9g; Fat 5.4g, of which saturates 2g; Cholesterol 4mg; Calcium 88mg; Fibre 1.9g; Sodium 2mg.

Corn Griddle Cakes

Known as arepas, these griddle cakes are a staple bread in several Latin American countries. They are delicious filled with soft white cheese, as in this recipe, or simply eaten plain as an accompaniment. With their crisp crust and chewy interior, arepas make an unusual and tasty snack or accompaniment to a barbecue meal.

Makes 15
200g/7oz/1¾ cups masarepa (or masa harina)
200g/7oz fresh white cheese, such as queso fresco or mozzarella, roughly chopped

From the storecupboard
15ml/1 tbsp oil
2.5ml/½ tsp salt

1 Combine the masarepa or masa harina and salt in a bowl. Gradually stir in the 300ml/½ pint/1¼ cups water to make a soft dough, then set aside for about 20 minutes.

2 Divide the dough into 15 equal-sized balls, then, using your fingers, flatten each ball into a circle, approximately 1cm/½in thick. Prepare the barbecue.

3 Heat a large, heavy frying pan or flat griddle over a medium heat and add 5ml/1 tsp oil. Using kitchen paper, gently wipe the surface of the frying pan, leaving it just lightly greased.

4 Place five of the arepas in the frying pan or on the griddle. Cook for approximately 4 minutes, then flip over and cook for a further 4 minutes. The arepas should be lightly blistered on both sides.

5 Open the arepas and fill each with a few small pieces of fresh white cheese. Return to the pan to cook until the cheese begins to melt. Remove from the heat and keep warm.

6 Cook the remaining ten arepas in the same way, oiling the pan and wiping with kitchen paper in between batches, to ensure it is always lightly greased. Serve the arepas while still warm so that the melted cheese is soft and runny.

Roast Shallot Tart with Thyme

Tarts are perfect for a summer lunch or picnic, and sheets of ready-rolled puff pastry turn a potentially arduous task into an incredibly easy one.

Serves 4
450g/1lb shallots, peeled and halved
30ml/2 tbsp fresh thyme leaves
375g/13oz packet ready-rolled puff pastry, thawed if frozen

From the storecupboard
25g/1oz/2 tbsp butter
salt and ground black pepper

1 Preheat the oven to 190°C/375°F/Gas 5. Heat the butter in a large frying pan until foaming, then add the shallots. Season with salt and pepper and cook over a gentle heat for 10–15 minutes, stirring occasionally, until golden. Stir in the thyme, then remove from the heat and set aside.

2 Unroll the puff pastry on to a large baking sheet. Using a small, sharp knife, score a border all the way around, about 2.5cm/1in from the edge, without cutting all the way through the pastry.

3 Spread the shallots over the pastry, inside the border. Bake for 20–25 minutes, or until the pastry is golden and risen around the edges. Cut into squares and serve hot or warm.

Cook's Tip
Red onions or even regular white onions could be used in this recipe. They will need to be quartered or possibly cut into smaller wedges if very large.

Variations
- *Try this tart with some chopped cooked sausage added, such as French Toulouse sausages or another flavoursome variety.*
- *Add some roasted garlic to the shallots.*

Corn Griddle Cakes: Energy 86kcal/363kJ; Protein 3.7g; Carbohydrate 10.4g, of which sugars 0.2g; Fat 3.6g, of which saturates 2g; Cholesterol 8mg; Calcium 67mg; Fibre 0.4g; Sodium 53mg.
Roast Shallot Tart: Energy 419kcal/1749kJ; Protein 7.1g; Carbohydrate 38.5g, of which sugars 5g; Fat 28.3g, of which saturates 3.3g; Cholesterol 13mg; Calcium 83mg; Fibre 1.6g; Sodium 340mg.

Sardines with Orange and Parsley

Sardines are ideal for the barbecue – the meaty flesh holds together, the skin crisps nicely and there are no lingering indoor cooking smells. Serve them with a selection of salads.

Serves 6
6 whole sardines, gutted
1 orange, sliced
a small bunch of fresh flat leaf parsley, chopped

From the storecupboard
60ml/4 tbsp extra virgin olive oil
salt and ground black pepper

1 Arrange the sardines and orange slices in a single layer in a shallow, non-metallic dish. Sprinkle over the chopped parsley and season with salt and pepper.

2 Drizzle the olive oil over the sardines and orange slices and gently stir to coat well. Cover the dish with clear film (plastic wrap) and chill for 2 hours.

3 Meanwhile, prepare the barbecue. Remove the sardines and orange slices from the marinade and cook the fish over the barbecue for 7–8 minutes on each side, until cooked through. Serve immediately.

Chilli Prawn Skewers

Choose very fresh prawns for this sweet and spicy barbecue classic.

Serves 4
16 giant raw prawns (shrimp), shelled with the tail section left intact
1 lime, cut into 8 wedges
60ml/4 tbsp sweet chilli sauce, for dipping

1 Using eight soaked bamboo skewers, thread each with a prawn, then a lime wedge, then another prawn. Brush the sweet chilli sauce over. Barbecue until cooked through. Serve immediately with more chilli sauce for dipping.

Iced Oysters with Merguez Sausages

Although it seems an unusual barbecue recipe, these two complement each other perfectly. Munch on a little chilli-spiced sausage, then quell the burning sensation with the clean, cool texture of an ice-cold oyster.

Serves 6
675g/1½ lb merguez sausages
crushed ice for serving
24 oysters
2 lemons, cut into wedges

1 Prepare the barbecue. Position a lightly oiled grill rack over the coals to heat. Place the sausages on the grill rack over medium-high heat. Grill them for 8 minutes, or until cooked through and golden, turning often.

2 Meanwhile, spread out some crushed ice on a platter and keep it chilled while you prepare the oysters. Scrub the oyster shells with a stiff brush to remove any sand. Make sure all the oysters are tightly closed, and discard any that aren't.

3 Place them on the grill rack, a few at a time, with the deep-side down, so that as they open the juices will be retained in the lower shell. They will begin to ease open after 3–5 minutes and must be removed from the heat immediately, so that they don't start to cook.

4 Lay the oysters on the ice. When they have all eased open, get to work with a sharp knife, opening them fully if need be. Remove the oysters from the flat side of the shell and place them with the juices on the deep half shells. Discard any oysters that fail to open. Serve with the hot, cooked sausages, and lemon wedges for squeezing.

Cook's Tip
Do not buy oysters in the summer breeding season (May to August in the northern hemisphere) as their flesh becomes soft and milky and rather unpleasant.

Sardines with Orange: Energy 156kcal/649kJ; Protein 13.1g; Carbohydrate 1.7g, of which sugars 1.7g; Fat 10.8g, of which saturates 2.3g; Cholesterol 0mg; Calcium 73mg; Fibre 0.3g; Sodium 72mg.
Chilli Prawn Skewers: Energy 59kcal/247kJ; Protein 11.3g; Carbohydrate 2.6g, of which sugars 2.5g; Fat 0.4g, of which saturates 0.1g; Cholesterol 122mg; Calcium 61mg; Fibre 0.1g; Sodium 242mg.
Oysters with Sausages: Energy 439kcal/1820kJ; Protein 16.3g; Carbohydrate 11.8g, of which sugars 1.6g; Fat 36.6g, of which saturates 13.8g; Cholesterol 76mg; Calcium 102mg; Fibre 0.6g; Sodium 1059mg.

Chicken Wings with Blood Oranges

This is a great recipe for the barbecue – it is quick and easy, and best eaten with the fingers. The oranges can be cooked separately or with the chicken wings. Harissa is a North African spice mix made of chillies, garlic and spices. When mixed into a paste, it will give a fiery kick to any meat or oily fish.

Serves 4
60ml/4 tbsp fiery harissa
16–20 chicken wings
4 blood oranges, quartered
icing (confectioners') sugar
a small bunch of fresh coriander (cilantro), chopped, to garnish

From the storecupboard
30ml/2 tbsp olive oil
salt

1 Mix the harissa powder with the olive oil in a small bowl, or, if using home-made harissa, simply measure the required amount into a bowl. Add a little salt and stir to combine.

2 Brush this mixture over the chicken wings so that they are well coated. Cook the wings on a hot barbecue or under a hot grill (broiler) for 5 minutes on each side.

3 Once the chicken wings begin to cook, dip the orange quarters lightly in icing sugar and grill (broil) them for a few minutes, until they are slightly burnt but not blackened. If you thread them on to skewers, it will be easier to turn them under the heat.

4 Serve the chicken wings immediately with the oranges, sprinkled with a little chopped fresh coriander and plenty of napkins for the sticky fingers.

Cook's Tip
Try making your own harissa if you have a blender. You will need 6–8 dried red chillies, 2 crushed garlic cloves, 2.5ml/½ tsp salt, 5ml/1 tsp ground cumin, 2.5ml/½ tsp ground coriander and 120ml/4fl oz/1 cup olive oil. Blend to a paste. To store, spoon into a jar and cover with olive oil. It will keep for 1 month.

Glazed Duck Breasts

In this Cajun recipe, sliced and barbecued sweet potatoes go particularly well with duck breasts that have been brushed with a sweet and sour glaze. The dish is quick to prepare and cook, making it ideal for a fuss-free barbecue.

Serves 2
2 duck breast portions
1 sweet potato, about 400g/14oz
30ml/2 tbsp red (bell) pepper jelly
15ml/1 tbsp sherry vinegar

From the storecupboard
50g/2oz/4 tbsp butter, melted
coarse sea salt and ground black pepper

1 Prepare the barbecue. Position a lightly oiled grill rack over the hot coals. Slash the skin of the duck breast portions diagonally at 2.5cm/1in intervals and rub plenty of salt and pepper over the skin and into the cuts.

2 Scrub the sweet potato and cut into 1cm/½in slices, discarding the ends.

3 Cook the duck breasts over medium heat, skin side down, for 5 minutes. Turn and cook for a further 8–10 minutes.

4 Meanwhile, brush the sweet potato slices with melted butter and sprinkle with coarse sea salt. Cook on the hottest part of the barbecue for 8–10 minutes until soft, brushing regularly with more butter and sprinkling liberally with salt and pepper every time you turn them. Keep an eye on them so that they do not char.

5 Warm the red pepper jelly and sherry vinegar together in a bowl set over a pan of hot water, stirring to mix them as the jelly melts. Brush the skin of the duck with the jelly and return to the barbecue, skin side down, for 2–3 minutes to caramelize it. Slice and serve with the sweet potatoes.

Cook's Tip
Choose cylindrical sweet potatoes for the neatest slices.

Chicken Wings: Energy 658kcal/2758kJ; Protein 61.9g; Carbohydrate 21.8g, of which sugars 20.7g; Fat 36.7g, of which saturates 10.1g; Cholesterol 264mg; Calcium 163mg; Fibre 2.6g; Sodium 866mg.
Duck Breasts: Energy 643kcal/2702kJ; Protein 42.1g; Carbohydrate 53.1g, of which sugars 21.9g; Fat 34.2g, of which saturates 15.8g; Cholesterol 273mg; Calcium 79mg; Fibre 4.8g; Sodium 456mg.

Steak and Blue Cheese Sandwiches

Many people like their rib eye steaks cooked quite rare in the centre, but how you like yours is up to you. Add a couple of minutes to the cooking time if you prefer them more well done.

Serves 2
1 ready-to-bake ciabatta bread
2 rib eye steaks, about 200g/7oz each
115g/4oz Gorgonzola cheese, sliced

From the storecupboard
15ml/1 tbsp olive oil
salt and ground black pepper

1 Bake the ciabatta, either according to the instructions on the packet, or warming in foil on a barbecue. Remove from the heat and leave to rest for a few minutes. Cut the loaf in half and split each half horizontally.

2 Heat the barbecue, or a griddle pan, until hot. Brush the steaks with the olive oil and lay them on the griddle pan. Cook for 2–3 minutes on each side (for medium rare steaks), depending on the thickness of the steaks and how well cooked you like them.

3 Remove the steaks from the pan and set aside to rest for a few minutes. Cut them in half and place in the sandwiches with the cheese. Season with salt and pepper, and serve.

Cook's Tips

- *Steaks are quick to cook over the barbecue, but don't be tempted to partially precook any meat and then to finish it off on the barbecue, as this will encourage bacteria to grow.*
- *Remember that if you are not cooking at home you will need to transport meat in a cooler bag or box and take out what you need as and when you need it to avoid it becoming warm before it is cooked.*
- *Always pack the cooler with the foods you are going to cook first on the top and close the cooler completely each time you take an item of food out.*

The Gaucho Barbecue

This delicious traditional pampas beef dish consists of short ribs and rump steak accompanied by pork sausages. It involves no marinating, but the meat is brushed with brine during cooking to keep it moist. Serve each meat as it is cooked, accompanied by a selection of salads and salsas.

Serves 6
6 pork sausages
1kg/2¼lb beef short ribs
1kg/2¼lb rump (round) steak, in one piece
salads, salsas and breads, to serve

From the storecupboard
50g/2oz/¼ cup coarse sea salt

1 Dissolve the sea salt in 200ml/7fl oz/scant 1 cup warm water water in a bowl. Leave to cool.

2 Prepare the barbecue. Position a lightly oiled grill rack over the hot coals.

3 Start by cooking the sausages, which should take 15–20 minutes over medium heat, depending on their size.

4 Once cooked on all sides, slice the sausages thickly and arrange them on a plate. Let guests help themselves while you cook the remaining meats.

5 Place the short ribs bony side down on the grill rack. Cook for 15 minutes, turn, brush the cooked side of each rib with brine and grill for a further 25–30 minutes, basting from time to time. Slice the meat and transfer to a plate for guests to help themselves.

6 Place the whole rump steak on the grill rack and cook for 5 minutes, then turn over and baste the browned side with brine.

7 Continue turning and basting in this way for 20–25 minutes in total, until the meat is cooked to your liking. Allow the meat to rest for 5 minutes under tented heavy-duty foil, then slice thinly and serve with salads, salsa and bread.

Steak Sandwiches: Energy 767kcal/3221kJ; Protein 66g; Carbohydrate 52g, of which sugars 3.1g; Fat 34.2g, of which saturates 15.8g; Cholesterol 161mg; Calcium 410mg; Fibre 2.3g; Sodium 1360mg.
Gaucho Barbecue: Energy 785kcal/3283kJ; Protein 97.5g; Carbohydrate 4.8g, of which sugars 0.7g; Fat 41.9g, of which saturates 17.4g; Cholesterol 257mg; Calcium 42mg; Fibre 0.3g; Sodium 575mg.

Barbecue Roast Beef

'Mopping' is big in the south-western states of the USA, where the technique is often used to keep large pieces of meat moist and succulent during the long, slow cooking process. For this recipe, the technique has been adapted. Once seared, mop the meat constantly.

Serves 4
800g/1¾lb beef fillet (tenderloin)
30ml/2 tbsp bottled grated horseradish
120ml/4fl oz/½ cup Chimay beer

From the storecupboard
30ml/2 tbsp olive oil
salt and ground black pepper

1 Pat the beef dry with kitchen paper and place it in a dish. Rub it all over with 5ml/1 tsp of the horseradish and the olive oil. Cover and leave to marinate for 2 hours in a cool place.

2 If spit roasting, skewer the meat with a long spit. Prepare the barbecue. Mix the remaining horseradish with the beer in a deep bowl.

3 Season the meat well. Position a lightly oiled grill rack over the coals to heat. Cook the beef over high heat for about 2 minutes on each side, so that the outside sears and acquires a good colour.

4 Set the spit turning over the coals. Dip a large basting brush in the horseradish and beer mixture and generously mop the meat all over with it. Continue to mop, as the meat turns, for a total grilling time of 11 minutes. Use all of the basting mixture.

5 Rest the meat in a warm place under tented foil for about 10 minutes before slicing thickly. This dish is great served hot, with roasted vegetables, or left to go cold and eaten with thick slices of country-style bread and horseradish-flavoured mayonnaise.

Variation
Chimay is a naturally brewed beer from Belgium, which could be substituted with any other good-quality beer you fancy. Non-alcoholic beers are also fine, or even soda water, if you want.

Cumin- and Coriander-rubbed Lamb

Rubs are quick and easy to prepare and can transform everyday cuts of meat such as chops into exciting and more unusual meals. Serve with a chunky tomato salad.

Serves 4
30ml/2 tbsp ground cumin
30ml/2 tbsp ground coriander
8 lamb chops

From the storecupboard
30ml/2 tbsp olive oil
salt and ground black pepper

1 Mix together the cumin, coriander and oil, and season with salt and pepper. Rub the mixture all over the lamb chops, then cover and chill for 1 hour.

2 Prepare a barbecue. Cook the chops for 5 minutes on each side, until lightly charred but still pink in the centre.

Harissa-spiced Koftas

Serve these spicy koftas in pitta breads with sliced tomatoes, cucumber and mint leaves, with a drizzle of natural yogurt.

Serves 4
450g/1lb/2 cups minced (ground) lamb
1 small onion, finely chopped
10ml/2 tsp harissa paste

From the storecupboard
salt and ground black pepper

1 Place eight wooden skewers in a bowl of cold water and leave to soak for at least 10 minutes. Put the lamb in a large bowl and add the onion and harissa. Mix well to combine, and season with plenty of salt and ground black pepper.

2 Using wet hands, divide the mixture into eight equal pieces and press on to the skewers in a sausage shape to make the koftas. Prepare a barbecue. Cook the skewered koftas for about 10 minutes, turning occasionally, until cooked through.

Barbecue Roast Beef: Energy 409kcal/1701kJ; Protein 45.5g; Carbohydrate 0.8g, of which sugars 0.8g; Fat 24.1g, of which saturates 8.4g; Cholesterol 116mg; Calcium 12mg; Fibre 0g; Sodium 130mg.
Cumin-Coriander Lamb: Energy 494kcal/2059kJ; Protein 55.6g; Carbohydrate 0g, of which sugars 0g; Fat 30.1g, of which saturates 12.6g; Cholesterol 220mg; Calcium 18mg; Fibre 0g; Sodium 150mg.
Harissa-spiced Koftas: Energy 233kcal/972kJ; Protein 22.1g; Carbohydrate 2.1g, of which sugars 0.9g; Fat 15.3g, of which saturates 7g; Cholesterol 87mg; Calcium 28mg; Fibre 0.2g; Sodium 79mg.

Grilled Strawberries and Marshmallows

It is always a treat to have permission to eat marshmallows. After cooking, dredge these little kebabs with loads of icing sugar, some of which will melt into the strawberry juice. The grill has to be very hot to sear the marshmallows quickly before they melt.

Serves 4
16 mixed pink and white marshmallows, chilled
16 strawberries
icing (confectioners') sugar for dusting
8 short lengths of cherry wood or metal skewers

1 Prepare the barbecue. If you are using cherry wood skewers, soak them in water for 30 minutes. Position a lightly oiled grill rack just above the hot coals to heat.

2 Spike two marshmallows and two strawberries on each drained cherry wood or metal skewer and grill over the hot coals for 20 seconds on each side. If nice grill marks don't appear easily, don't persist for too long or the marshmallows may burn – cook until they are warm to the touch and only just beginning to melt.

3 Transfer the skewered strawberries and marshmallows to individual dessert plates or a large platter, dust generously with icing sugar and serve.

Cook's Tip
By chilling the marshmallows for at least half an hour, they will be firmer and easier to thread on to the skewers.

Variation
For pure indulgence, serve these skewers with a chocolate fondue. Combine plain (semisweet) chocolate, cream and alcohol (optional) in a fondue pan and heat until melted.

Honey-seared Melon

This fabulously simple dessert can be made with melon that is slightly underripe, because the honeycomb will sweeten it up beautifully.

Serves 6
1.3kg/3lb melon, preferably Charentais
200g/7oz honeycomb
a bunch of lavender, plus extra flowers for decoration
300g/11oz/2 cups raspberries

1 Prepare the barbecue. Cut the melon in half, scoop out the seeds, then cut each half into three slices. Put a third of the honeycomb in a bowl and dilute by stirring in 5ml/1 tsp water. Make a brush with the lavender and dip it into the honey.

2 Heat a griddle on the grill rack over hot coals. Lightly brush the melon with the honey mixture. Grill for 30 seconds on each side. Serve hot, sprinkled with the raspberries and remaining lavender flowers, and topped with the remaining honeycomb.

Melon with Grilled Strawberries

Sprinkling the strawberries with a little sugar, then grilling them, helps bring out their flavour. Serve with ice cream or lemon sorbet.

Serves 4
115g/4oz/1 cup strawberries
15ml/1 tbsp icing (confectioners') sugar, plus extra for dusting
½ cantaloupe melon

1 Soak four wooden skewers in water. Meanwhile, scoop out the seeds from the half melon. Using a sharp knife, remove the skin, then cut the flesh into wedges and arrange on a plate.

2 Preheat the grill (broiler). Hull the strawberries and cut in half, arrange cut side up on a baking sheet and dust with icing sugar.

3 Thread the strawberry halves on to skewers, place on a grill rack and grill (broil) on high for 3–4 minutes or until the sugar starts to bubble and turn golden. Remove from the skewers and sprinkle over the melon slices, dusting with the remaining icing sugar.

Strawberries and Marshmallows: Energy 110kcal/466kJ; Protein 1.4g; Carbohydrate 27.6g, of which sugars 22.9g; Fat 0.1g, of which saturates 0g; Cholesterol 0mg; Calcium 11mg; Fibre 0.5g; Sodium 10mg.
Honey-seared Melon: Energy 113kcal/480kJ; Protein 1.9g; Carbohydrate 27.2g, of which sugars 27.2g; Fat 0.4g, of which saturates 0.1g; Cholesterol 0mg; Calcium 42mg; Fibre 2.1g; Sodium 71mg.
Melon with Strawberries: Energy 46kcal/197kJ; Protein 1g; Carbohydrate 10.9g, of which sugars 10.9g; Fat 0.2g, of which saturates 0g; Cholesterol 0mg; Calcium 32mg; Fibre 1.6g; Sodium 12mg.

Calvados-flamed Bananas

Soft and creamy baked bananas, flamed with calvados, are delicious served with a rich butterscotch sauce. The sauce can be made in advance and the bananas are quickly cooked. Have a sensible person ignite the calvados, which makes a spectacular end to a meal.

Serves 6
115g/4oz/generous ½ cup sugar
150ml/¼ pint/⅔ cup double (heavy) cream
6 large slightly underripe bananas
90ml/6 tbsp calvados

From the storecupboard
25g/1oz/2 tbsp butter

1 Place the sugar and 150ml/¼ pint/⅔ cup water in a large pan and heat gently until the sugar has dissolved. Increase the heat and boil until the mixture turns a rich golden caramel colour.

2 Remove from the heat and carefully add the butter and cream; the mixture will foam up in the pan. Replace it over a gentle heat and stir to a smooth sauce, then pour into a bowl and leave to cool. Cover and chill until needed.

3 Prepare the barbecue. Wrap the bananas individually in foil. Position a grill rack over the hot coals. Grill the wrapped bananas over high heat for 10 minutes.

4 Transfer the bananas to a tray, open up the parcels and slit the upper side of each banana skin.

5 Meanwhile, gently warm the calvados in a small pan, then pour some into each banana. Put them back on the barbecue and wait for a few seconds before carefully igniting the calvados with a long match. Serve with the sauce as soon as the flames die down.

Cook's Tip
These bananas can be cooked indoors using a grill (broiler) or by baking them in a hot oven.

Baked Bananas with Ice Cream and Toffee Sauce

Bananas make one of the easiest of all desserts, just as welcome as a comforting winter treat as they are to follow a barbecue. For an extra sweet finishing touch, grate some plain chocolate on the bananas, over the sauce, just before serving. If baking on a barbecue, turn the bananas occasionally to ensure even cooking.

Serves 4
4 large bananas
75g/3oz/scant ½ cup light muscovado (brown) sugar
75ml/5 tbsp double (heavy) cream
4 scoops good-quality vanilla ice cream

1 Preheat the oven to 180°C/350°F/Gas 4. Put the unpeeled bananas in an ovenproof dish and bake for 15–20 minutes, until the skins are very dark and the flesh feels soft when squeezed.

2 Meanwhile, heat the light muscovado sugar in a small, heavy pan with 75ml/5 tbsp water until dissolved. Bring to the boil and add the double cream. Cook for 5 minutes, until the sauce has thickened and is toffee coloured. Remove from the heat.

3 Transfer the baked bananas in their skins to serving plates and split them lengthways to reveal the flesh. Pour some of the sauce over the bananas and top with scoops of vanilla ice cream. Serve any remaining sauce separately.

Variation
A spicy vanilla butter adds a luxurious finish to this dessert. To make, split 6 green cardamom pods and remove seeds, crush lightly. Split a vanilla pod lenghtways and scrape out the tiny seeds. Mix with cardamom seeds, finely grated rind and juice of small orange and 45ml/3 tbsp butter into a thick paste. Place a spoonful inside each baked banana.

Calvados Bananas: Energy 359kcal/1501kJ; Protein 1.7g; Carbohydrate 43.7g, of which sugars 41.4g; Fat 17.2g, of which saturates 10.6g; Cholesterol 43mg; Calcium 29mg; Fibre 1.1g; Sodium 33mg.
Bananas/Ice Cream: Energy 455kcal/1910kJ; Protein 6.9g; Carbohydrate 63.2g, of which sugars 56.6g; Fat 21.1g, of which saturates 12.6g; Cholesterol 53mg; Calcium 215mg; Fibre 0.6g; Sodium 178mg.

Baked Apples with Marsala

The Marsala cooks down with the juice from the apples and the butter to make a rich, sticky sauce. Serve these delicious apples with a spoonful of extra-thick cream.

Serves 6
4 medium cooking apples
50g/2oz/⅓ cup ready-to-eat dried figs
150ml/¼ pint/⅔ cup Marsala

From the storecupboard
50g/2oz/¼ cup butter, softened

1 Preheat the oven to 180°C/350°F/Gas 4. Using an apple corer, remove the cores from the apples and discard.

2 Place the apples in a small, shallow baking pan and stuff the figs into the holes in the centre of each apple.

3 Top each apple with a quarter of the butter and pour over the Marsala. Cover the pan tightly with foil and bake for about 30 minutes.

4 Remove the foil from the apples and bake for a further 10 minutes, or until the apples are tender and the juices have reduced slightly. Serve immediately with any remaining pan juices drizzled over the top.

Cook's Tip
Marsala is an Italian fortified wine used to flavour desserts, including the infamous tiramisu. If you are unable to find Marsala, you could use a sweet sherry, such as Manzanilla, or Madeira wine. You could even use port, which would give an attractive pink colour to the dish.

Variation
Instead of dried figs, use raisins, sultanas (golden raisins), dried ready-to-eat apricots or cherries. For a crunchy version, add chopped hazelnuts or almonds.

Passion Fruit Soufflés

These simplified soufflés are so easy and work beautifully. The passion fruit adds a tropical note to a favourite classic. The soufflés look very pretty sprinkled with icing sugar.

Serves 4
200ml/7fl oz/scant 1 cup ready-made fresh custard
3 passion fruits, halved
2 egg whites

From the storecupboard
knob (pat) of softened butter, for greasing

1 Preheat the oven to 200°C/400°F/Gas 6. Grease four 200ml/7fl oz/scant 1 cup ramekin dishes with the butter.

2 Pour the custard into a large mixing bowl. Scrape out the seeds and juice from the halved passion fruit and stir into the custard until well combined.

3 Whisk the egg whites until stiff, and fold a quarter of them into the custard. Carefully fold in the remaining egg whites, then spoon the mixture into the ramekin dishes.

4 Place the dishes on a baking sheet and bake in the oven for 8–10 minutes, or until the soufflés are well risen. Serve immediately.

Cook's Tip
Despite their reputation, soufflés are not difficult to cook. Proper preparation of the cooking dishes is key to the success. If the dish is well greased, the soufflé will rise up the sides better.

Variation
Add a crunchy contrast to the soufflé by adding a layer of coarsely crushed biscuits (cookies) in the middle of the mixture before cooking. Italian amaretti would add a hint of almond, whereas crushed ginger biscuits would give a touch of spice.

Baked Apples/Marsala: Energy 134kcal/560kJ; Protein 0.5g; Carbohydrate 11.1g, of which sugars 11.1g; Fat 7g, of which saturates 4.3g; Cholesterol 18mg; Calcium 24mg; Fibre 1.3g; Sodium 57mg.
Passion Fruit Soufflés: Energy 59kcal/249kJ; Protein 3.1g; Carbohydrate 8.8g, of which sugars 7.1g; Fat 1g, of which saturates 0g; Cholesterol 1mg; Calcium 48mg; Fibre 0.4g; Sodium 53mg.

Grilled Peaches with Meringues

Ripe peaches take on a fabulous scented fruitiness when grilled with brown sugar, and mini meringues are the perfect accompaniment. Serve with crème fraîche flavoured with a little grated orange rind. When buying peaches or nectarines, choose fruit with an attractive rosy bloom, avoiding any that have a green-tinged skin or feel hard. Nectarines have a smoother skin than the furry peaches.

Serves 6
2 egg whites
115g/4oz/½ cup soft light brown sugar, reserving 5ml/1 tsp for the peaches
pinch of ground cinnamon
6 ripe peaches, or nectarines

1 Preheat the oven to 140°C/275°F/Gas 1. Line two large baking sheets with baking parchment.

2 Whisk the egg whites until they form stiff peaks. Gradually whisk in the sugar and ground cinnamon until the mixture is stiff and glossy. Pipe 18 very small meringues on to the trays and bake for 40 minutes. Leave in the oven to cool.

3 Meanwhile, halve and stone (pit) the peaches or nectarines, sprinkling each half with a little sugar as it is cut. Grill (broil) for 4–5 minutes, until just beginning to caramelize.

4 Arrange the grilled peaches on serving plates with the meringues and serve immediately.

Cook's Tip
Use leftover egg whites to make these little cinnamon-flavoured meringues. The meringues can be stored in an airtight container for about 2 weeks. Serve them after dinner with coffee or with desserts in place of biscuits (cookies).

Roast Peaches with Amaretto

This is an excellent dessert to serve in summer, when peaches are at their juiciest and most fragrant. The apricot and almond flavour of the amaretto liqueur subtly enhances the sweetness of the ripe peaches. Serve with a spoonful of crème fraîche or whipped cream.

Serves 4
4 ripe peaches
45ml/3 tbsp Amaretto di Sarone liqueur
45ml/3 tbsp clear honey

1 Preheat the oven 190°C/375°F/Gas 5. Cut the peaches in half and prise out the stones (pits) with the point of the knife.

2 Place the peaches cut side up in a roasting pan. In a small bowl, mix the amaretto liqueur with the honey, and drizzle over the halved peaches, covering them evenly.

3 Bake the peaches for 20–25 minutes, or until tender. Place two peach halves on each serving plate and drizzle with the pan juices. Serve immediately.

Cook's Tip
You can cook these peaches over a barbecue. Place them on sheets of foil, drizzle over liqueur, then scrunch the foil around them to seal. Cook for 15–20 minutes.

Variations
- *Nectarines can be used in place of peaches for this recipe.*
- *Replace the Amaretto and honey with ground almonds and muscovado (brown) sugar, which will caramelize when roasted.*
- *Put a small cube of marzipan in the centre where the stone (pit) was and sprinkle with muscovado sugar.*
- *Serve with ice cream or Greek (US strained plain) yogurt.*

Peaches with Meringues: Energy 107kcal/457kJ; Protein 1.9g; Carbohydrate 26.4g, of which sugars 26.4g; Fat 0.1g, of which saturates 0g; Cholesterol 0mg; Calcium 17mg; Fibre 1.3g; Sodium 22mg.
Peaches with Amaretto: Energy 91kcal/387kJ; Protein 1.1g; Carbohydrate 16.4g, of which sugars 16.4g; Fat 0.1g, of which saturates 0g; Cholesterol 0mg; Calcium 8mg; Fibre 1.5g; Sodium 2mg.

Summer Berries in Sabayon Glaze

This luxurious combination of summer berries under a light and fluffy liqueur sauce is lightly grilled to form a crisp, caramelized topping. Fresh or frozen berries can be used in this dessert. If you use frozen berries, defrost them in a sieve over a bowl to allow the juices to drip. Pour a little juice over the fruit before dividing among the dishes.

Serves 4

450g/1lb/4 cups mixed summer berries, or soft fruit
4 egg yolks
50g/2oz/¼ cup vanilla sugar or caster (superfine) sugar
120ml/4fl oz/½ cup liqueur, such as Cointreau or Kirsch, or a white dessert wine

1 Arrange the mixed summer berries or soft fruit in four individual flameproof dishes. Preheat the grill (broiler).

2 Whisk the yolks in a large bowl with the sugar and liqueur or wine. Place over a pan of hot water and whisk constantly until the mixture is thick, fluffy and pale. You should be able to form peaks in the sauce that hold their shape.

3 Pour equal quantities of the yolk mixture into each dish. Place under the grill for 1–2 minutes, until just turning brown. Add an extra splash of liqueur, if you like, and serve immediately.

Cook's Tip

To separate eggs, gently prise the two halves apart with your thumbs. Keep the yolk in one half and allow the white to drop into a bowl below. Slip the yolk from one to the other.

Variation

If you prefer, you can make a non-alcoholic version of this dish using cranberry juice or pomegranate, or any other full-flavoured fruit juice.

Baked Ricotta Cakes with Red Sauce

These honey-flavoured desserts take only minutes to make from a few ingredients. The fragrant fruity sauce provides a contrast of both colour and flavour. The red berry sauce can be made a day in advance and chilled until ready to use. Frozen fruit doesn't need extra water, as it usually yields its juice easily on thawing.

Serves 4

250g/9oz/generous 1 cup ricotta cheese
2 egg whites, beaten
60ml/4 tbsp scented honey, plus extra to taste
450g/1lb/4 cups mixed fresh or frozen fruit, such as strawberries, raspberries, blackberries and cherries

1 Preheat the oven to 180°C/350°F/Gas 4. Place the ricotta cheese in a bowl and break it up with a wooden spoon. Add the beaten egg whites and honey, and mix thoroughly until smooth and well combined.

2 Lightly grease four ramekins. Spoon the ricotta mixture into the prepared ramekins and level the tops. Bake for 20 minutes, or until the ricotta cakes are risen and golden.

3 Meanwhile, make the fruit sauce. Reserve about one-quarter of the fruit for decoration. Place the rest of the fruit in a pan, with a little water if the fruit is fresh, and heat gently until softened. Leave to cool slightly and remove any pits if using cherries.

4 Press the fruit through a sieve (strainer), then taste and sweeten with honey if it is too tart. Serve the sauce, warm or cold, with the ricotta cakes. Decorate with the reserved berries.

Variation

You could other soft cheeses for this recipe. Mascarpone would be a good choice, but you could use any fresh, creamy, slightly sweet soft cheese.

Summer Berries: Energy 219kcal/919kJ; Protein 3.9g; Carbohydrate 29.7g, of which sugars 29.7g; Fat 5.6g, of which saturates 1.6g; Cholesterol 202mg; Calcium 50mg; Fibre 1.2g; Sodium 20mg.
Baked Ricotta Cakes: Energy 161kcal/674kJ; Protein 8.1g; Carbohydrate 11.5g, of which sugars 11.5g; Fat 9.6g, of which saturates 5.9g; Cholesterol 26mg; Calcium 23mg; Fibre 0.6g; Sodium 63mg.

Deep-fried Cherries

Fresh fruit coated with a simple batter and then deep-fried is delicious and makes an unusual dessert. These succulent cherries are perfect sprinkled with sugar and cinnamon and served with a classic vanilla ice cream.

Serves 4–6

450g/1lb ripe red cherries, on their stalks
225g/8oz batter mix
1 egg

From the storecupboard
vegetable oil, for deep-frying

1 Gently wash the cherries and pat dry with kitchen paper. Tie the stalks together with fine string to form clusters of four or five cherries.

2 Make up the batter mix according to the instructions on the packet, beating in the egg. Pour the vegetable oil into a deep-fat fryer or large, heavy pan and heat to 190°C/375°F.

3 Working in batches, half-dip each cherry cluster into the batter and then carefully drop the cluster into the hot oil. Fry for 3–4 minutes, or until golden. Remove the deep-fried cherries with a wire-mesh skimmer or slotted spoon and drain on a wire rack placed over crumpled kitchen paper, and serve immediately.

Cook's Tip
To check that the oil has come to the required temperature, drop a cube of day-old bread in the oil, if it turns golden brown and crispy in 20 seconds, the oil is hot enough.

Variation
Other fruits can be deep-fried in batter with delicious results. Bananas work well, especially with a little coconut milk in the batter mix. Ready-to-eat stoned (pitted) prunes, dates or figs can also be used in this recipe

Hot Blackberry and Apple Soufflé

The deliciously tart flavours of blackberry and apple complement each other perfectly to make a light, mouthwatering and surprisingly low-fat, hot dessert. Running a table knife around the inside edge of the soufflé dishes before baking helps the soufflés to rise evenly without sticking to the rim of the dish. Make this dish in early autumn, when there are plentiful supplies of blackberries.

Makes 6

350g/12oz/3 cups blackberries
1 large cooking apple, peeled and finely diced
3 egg whites
150g/5oz/¾ cup caster (superfine) sugar, plus extra caster or icing (confectioners') sugar for dusting

1 Preheat the oven to 200°C/400°F/Gas 6. Put a baking sheet in the oven to heat. Cook the blackberries and apple in a pan for 10 minutes, or until the juice runs from the blackberries and the apple has pulped down well. Press through a sieve (strainer) into a bowl. Stir in 50g/2oz/¼ cup caster sugar. Set aside to cool.

2 Put a spoonful of the fruit purée into each of six 150ml/¼ pint/⅔ cup greased and sugared individual soufflé dishes and smooth the surface. Set the dishes aside.

3 Whisk the egg whites in a large bowl until they form stiff peaks. Gradually whisk in the remaining caster sugar. Fold in the remaining fruit purée and spoon the flavoured meringue into the prepared dishes. Level the tops with a metal spatula and run a table knife around the edge of each dish.

4 Place the dishes on the hot baking sheet and bake for 10–15 minutes, until the soufflés have risen well and are lightly browned. Dust the tops with sugar and serve immediately.

Cook's Tip
If you collect blackberries from the hedgerows, wash thoroughly.

Deep-fried Cherries: Energy 201kcal/840kJ; Protein 3.7g; Carbohydrate 25.7g, of which sugars 7.3g; Fat 10g, of which saturates 1.3g; Cholesterol 26mg; Calcium 46mg; Fibre 1.3g; Sodium 11mg.
Blackberry/Apple Soufflé: Energy 123kcal/522kJ; Protein 2.1g; Carbohydrate 30.1g, of which sugars 30.1g; Fat 0.1g, of which saturates 0g; Cholesterol 0mg; Calcium 38mg; Fibre 2g; Sodium 33mg.

Apricot and Ginger Gratin

Made with tangy fresh apricots, this quick and easy dessert has a comforting, baked cheesecake-like flavour. For an even easier version of this delicious gratin, use 400g/14oz canned apricots in juice. Use juice from the can to beat into the cream cheese.

Serves 4
500g/1¼lb apricots, halved and stoned (pitted)
75g/3oz/scant ½ cup caster (superfine) sugar
200g/7oz/scant 1 cup cream cheese
75g/3oz/1½ cups gingernut biscuits (gingersnaps), crushed to crumbs

1 Put the apricots in a pan with the sugar. Pour in 75ml/5 tbsp water and heat until barely simmering. Cover and cook very gently for 8–10 minutes, until they are tender but still holding their shape.

2 Preheat the oven to 200°C/400°F/Gas 6. Drain the apricots, reserving the syrup, and place in a large dish or divide among four individual ovenproof dishes. Set aside 90ml/6 tbsp of the syrup and spoon the remainder over the fruit.

3 Beat the cream cheese until softened, then gradually beat in the reserved syrup until smooth. Spoon the cheese mixture over the apricots. Sprinkle the biscuit crumbs over the cream cheese and juice mixture. Bake for 10 minutes, until the crumb topping is beginning to darken and the filling has warmed through. Serve immediately.

Cook's Tip
If you used canned apricots, there is no need to poach them in water. Merely drain the fruit, reserving the liquid to combine with the cream cheese.

Variation
Peaches or nectarines would be equally good in this dessert.

Tapioca with Banana and Coconut

This is the type of dessert that everybody's mother or grandmother makes. Sweet and nourishing, the tapioca pearls are cooked in coconut milk and sweetened with bananas and sugar.

Serves 4
40g/1½oz tapioca pearls
550ml/18fl oz/2½ cups coconut milk
90g/3½oz/½ cup sugar
3 ripe bananas, diced

From the storecupboard
salt

1 Pour 550ml/18fl oz/2½ cups water into a pan and bring it to the boil. Stir in the tapioca pearls, reduce the heat and simmer for about 20 minutes, until the tapioca is translucent and most of the water is absorbed.

2 Pour in the coconut milk, then add the sugar and a pinch of salt. Cook gently for 30 minutes.

3 Stir in the diced bananas and cook them for 5–10 minutes until soft. Spoon into individual warmed bowls and serve immediately while still hot.

Cook's Tip
A pinch of salt added to this recipe enhances the flavour of the coconut milk and counterbalances the sweetness. You can also make the recipe with sweet potato, taro root, yellow corn or rice.

Variations
Instead of adding the diced bananas to the warm tapioca mixture, try one of the following, adjusting the cooking time as needed so that the fruit is fully cooked:
- *sliced rhubarb*
- *small apple or pear, cut into wedges*
- *nectarine or mango slices*

Apricot/Ginger: Energy 414kcal/1732kJ; Protein 3.8g; Carbohydrate 43.4g, of which sugars 35.3g; Fat 26.3g, of which saturates 16g; Cholesterol 48mg; Calcium 102mg; Fibre 2.4g; Sodium 216mg.
Tapioca with Banana: Energy 226kcal/964kJ; Protein 1.5g; Carbohydrate 57.2g, of which sugars 45.9g; Fat 0.7g, of which saturates 0.4g; Cholesterol 0mg; Calcium 57mg; Fibre 0.9g; Sodium 154mg.

Mango Slices with Lime Sorbet

If you can locate them, use Alphonso mangoes for this dish. Mainly cultivated in India, they have a heady scent and gloriously sensual, silky texture. The scored flesh and diamond branding make a visually appealing dessert.

Serves 6
250g/9oz/1¼ cups sugar
juice of 6 limes
3 star anise
6 small or 3 medium to large mangoes

From the storecupboard
groundnut (peanut) oil, for brushing

1 Place the sugar in a heavy pan and add 250ml/8fl oz/1 cup water. Heat gently until the sugar has dissolved. Increase the heat and boil for 5 minutes. Cool completely. Add the lime juice and any pulp that has collected. Strain the mixture and reserve 200ml/7fl oz/scant 1 cup in a bowl with the star anise.

2 Pour the remaining liquid into a measuring jug or cup and make up to 600ml/1 pint/2½ cups with cold water. Mix well and pour into a freezerproof container. Freeze for 1½ hours, stir well and return to the freezer until set.

3 Transfer the sorbet mixture to a processor and pulse to a smooth icy purée. Freeze for another hour. Alternatively, use an ice cream maker; it will take about 20 minutes, and should then be frozen for at least 30 minutes before serving.

4 Prepare the barbecue. Pour the reserved syrup into a pan and boil for 2–3 minutes, or until thickened a little. Leave to cool. Cut the cheeks from either side of the stone (pit) on each unpeeled mango, and score the flesh on each in a diamond pattern. Brush with a little oil. Heat a griddle on the grill rack over hot coals. Lower the heat a little and grill the mango halves, cut side down, for 30–60 seconds until branded with golden grill marks.

5 Invert the mango cheeks on individual plates and serve hot or cold with the syrup drizzled over and a scoop or two of the sorbet. Decorate with star anise.

Papayas in Jasmine Flower Syrup

The fragrant syrup can be prepared in advance, using fresh jasmine flowers from a house plant or the garden. It tastes fabulous with papayas, but it is also good with all sorts of desserts. Try it with ice cream or spooned over lychees or mangoes.

Serves 2
45ml/3 tbsp soft light brown sugar
20–30 jasmine flowers, plus a few extra, to decorate (optional)
2 ripe papayas
juice of 1 lime

1 Place 105ml/7 tbsp water and sugar in a small pan. Heat gently, stirring occasionally, until the sugar has dissolved, then simmer, without stirring, over a low heat for 4 minutes.

2 Pour into a bowl, leave to cool slightly, then add the jasmine flowers. Leave to steep for at least 20 minutes.

3 Peel the papayas and slice in half lengthways. Scoop out and discard the seeds. Place the papayas on serving plates and squeeze over the lime.

4 Strain the syrup into a clean bowl, discarding the flowers. Spoon the syrup over the papayas. If you like, decorate with a few fresh jasmine flowers.

Cook's Tip
Although scented white jasmine flowers are perfectly safe to eat, it is important to be sure that they have not been sprayed with pesticides or other harmful chemicals. Washing them may not remove all the residue.

Variation
If you don't have access to jasmine flowers, flavour the syrup with ginger, vanilla (steep a vanilla pod or bean in the syrup), or use star anise.

Mango with Lime : Energy 250kcal/1068kJ; Protein 1.3g; Carbohydrate 64.7g, of which sugars 64.2g; Fat 0.3g, of which saturates 0.2g; Cholesterol 0mg; Calcium 40mg; Fibre 3.9g; Sodium 6mg.
Papayas in Flower Syrup: Energy 197kcal/837kJ; Protein 1.6g; Carbohydrate 49.9g, of which sugars 49.9g; Fat 0.3g, of which saturates 0g; Cholesterol 0mg; Calcium 81mg; Fibre 6.6g; Sodium 17mg.

Zabaglione

Light as air and wonderfully heady, this warm, wine egg custard is a much-loved Italian dessert. Traditionally made with Sicilian Marsala, other fortified wines such as Madeira or sweet sherry can be used.

Serves 4
4 egg yolks
50g/2oz/¼ cup caster (superfine) sugar
60ml/4 tbsp Marsala, Madeira or sweet sherry
amaretti, to serve

1 Place the egg yolks and sugar in a large heatproof bowl and whisk with an electric beater until the mixture is pale and thick.

2 Gradually add the Marsala, Madeira or sweet sherry to the egg mixture, 15ml/1 tbsp at a time, whisking well after each addition.

3 Place the bowl over a pan of gently simmering water and whisk for 5–7 minutes, until thick: when the beaters are lifted, they should leave a thick trail on the surface of the mixture. Do not be tempted to give up when beating the mixture, as the zabaglione will be too runny and will be likely to separate if it is underbeaten.

4 Pour into four warmed, stemmed glasses and serve immediately, with amaretti for dipping.

Variation
Marinate chopped strawberries in a little extra Marsala, Madeira or sweet sherry for an hour or so. Sweeten with sugar, if you like, and spoon into the glasses before you add the zabaglione.

Cook's Tip
Serve as a sauce over poached pears, grilled peaches or baked bananas to create a really special dessert.

Grilled Pineapple and Rum Cream

The sweeter and juicier the pineapple, the more delicious the pan juices will be in this tropical dessert. To test whether the pineapple is ripe, gently pull the green spiky leaves at the top of the fruit. If they come away easily, the fruit is ripe and ready to use.

Serves 4
115g/4oz pineapple, roughly chopped
45ml/3 tbsp dark rum
300ml/½ pint/1¼ cups double (heavy) cream

From the storecupboard
25g/1oz/2 tbsp butter

1 Heat the butter in a frying pan and add the pineapple. Cook over a moderate to high heat until the pineapple is starting to turn golden. Turn the pieces carefully, so that they brown on both sides.

2 Add the rum and allow to bubble for 1–2 minutes. Remove the pan from the heat and set aside to cool completely.

3 Whip the cream until it is soft but not stiff. Fold the pineapple and rum mixture evenly through the cream, then divide it between four glasses and serve.

Cook's Tip
If you don't have any dark rum, substitute gold, or white rum. You could even use Malibu to add a hint of coconut, enhancing the tropical flavour of this dessert.

Variation
- *A range of tropical fruits can be used in this dessert. Try grilled mangoes, papayas, or bananas to ring the changes.*
- *Alternatively you could top this with a light and fluffy meringue. Place a spoonful on top of the dessert, in ovenproof ramekins, and bake in the oven at a medium-high temperature for 8–10 minutes.*

Zabaglione: Energy 131kcal/548kJ; Protein 3g; Carbohydrate 14.1g, of which sugars 14.1g; Fat 5.5g, of which saturates 1.6g; Cholesterol 202mg; Calcium 31mg; Fibre 0g; Sodium 12mg.
Pineapple/Rum Cream: Energy 203kcal/853kJ; Protein 3.7g; Carbohydrate 23g, of which sugars 23g; Fat 9.6g, of which saturates 4.4g; Cholesterol 162mg; Calcium 51mg; Fibre 1.8g; Sodium 63mg.

Hot Chocolate Rum Soufflés

Light as air, melt-in-the-mouth soufflés are always impressive, yet they are often based on the simplest storecupboard ingredients. Serve them as soon as they are cooked for a fantastic finale to a special dinner party. For an extra indulgent touch, serve the soufflés with whipped cream flavoured with dark rum and grated orange rind.

Serves 6

50g/2oz/½ cup unsweetened cocoa powder
65g/2½ oz/5 tbsp caster (superfine) sugar, plus extra caster or icing (confectioners') sugar for dusting
30ml/2 tbsp dark rum
6 egg whites

1 Preheat the oven to 190°C/375°F/Gas 3. Place a baking sheet in the oven to heat up.

2 Mix 15ml/1 tbsp of the cocoa with 15ml/1 tbsp of the sugar in a bowl. Grease six 250ml/8fl oz/1 cup ramekins. Pour the cocoa and sugar mixture into each of the dishes in turn, rotating them so that they are evenly coated.

3 Mix the remaining cocoa powder with the dark rum.

4 Whisk the egg whites in a clean, grease-free bowl until they form stiff peaks. Whisk in the remaining sugar. Stir a generous spoonful of the whites into the cocoa mixture to lighten it, then fold in the remaining whites.

5 Divide the mixture among the dishes. Place on the hot baking sheet, and bake for 13–15 minutes, or until well risen. Dust with caster or icing sugar before serving.

Cook's Tip

When serving the soufflés at the end of a dinner party, prepare them just before the meal is served. Put them in the oven when the main course is finished and serve steaming hot.

Warm Chocolate Zabaglione

Once you've tasted this sensuous dessert, you'll never regard cocoa in quite the same way again. The zabaglione can be dusted with icing sugar instead of extra cocoa, if you like. Serve with mini amaretti or other small, crisp biscuits.

Serves 6

6 egg yolks
150g/5oz/¾ cup caster (superfine) sugar
45ml/3 tbsp unsweetened cocoa powder, plus extra for dusting
200ml/7fl oz/scant 1 cup Marsala

1 Prepare a pan of simmering water and a heatproof bowl to fit on top to make a bain-marie. Place the egg yolks and sugar in the bowl and whisk, off the heat, until the mixture is pale and all the sugar has dissolved.

2 Add the cocoa and Marsala, then place the bowl over the simmering water. Beat with a hand-held electric mixer until the mixture is smooth, thick and foamy.

3 Pour quickly into tall glasses, dust lightly with cocoa and serve immediately, with amaretti or other dessert biscuits (cookies), if you like.

Cook's Tip

Serve with crisp chocolate cinnamon tuiles. To make, preheat the oven to 200°C/400°F/Gas 6. Grease two large baking sheets. Whisk 1 egg white into soft peaks. Gradually whisk in 50g/2oz/¼ cup caster (superfine) sugar to a smooth, glossy mixture. Sift 30ml/2 tbsp plain (all-purpose) flour over the meringue and fold in. Stir in 40g/1½oz/3 tbsp melted butter. Transfer about 45ml/3 tbsp of the mixture to a small bowl and set aside. Mix together 15ml/1 tbsp cocoa powder and 2.5ml/½ tsp cinnamon and stir into the mixture. Drop spoonfuls on to prepared baking sheets and spread with a metal spatula. Swirl the reserved mixture over for a marbled effect. Bake for 4–6 minutes until just set. Drape over a rolling pin to curve as they harden.

Chocolate Soufflés: Energy 91kcal/386kJ; Protein 4.5g; Carbohydrate 12.3g, of which sugars 11.3g; Fat 1.8g, of which saturates 1.1g; Cholesterol 0mg; Calcium 18mg; Fibre 1g; Sodium 141mg.
Chocolate Zabaglione: Energy 233kcal/979kJ; Protein 4.8g; Carbohydrate 29.5g, of which sugars 28.4g; Fat 7.5g, of which saturates 2.7g; Cholesterol 202mg; Calcium 51mg; Fibre 1.1g; Sodium 100mg.

Peach Pie

Fruit pies do not have to be restricted to the chunky, deep-dish variety. Here, juicy, ripe peaches are encased in crisp pastry to make a glorious puffed dome – simple but delicious. For a really crispy crust, glaze the pie with beaten egg yolk thinned with a little water before sprinkling with sugar. Serve the pie with good quality vanilla ice cream or clotted cream.

Serves 8

6 large, firm ripe peaches
75g/3oz/6 tbsp caster (superfine) sugar, plus extra for glazing
450g/1lb puff pastry

From the storecupboard
40g/1½oz/3 tbsp butter

1 Blanch the peaches for 30 seconds. Drain, refresh in cold water, then peel. Halve, stone (pit) and slice the peaches.

2 Melt the butter in a large frying pan. Add the peach slices, then sprinkle with 15ml/1 tbsp water and the sugar. Cook for about 4 minutes, shaking the pan frequently, or until the sugar has dissolved and the peaches are tender. Set the pan aside to cool.

3 Cut the pastry into two pieces, one slightly larger than the other. Roll out on a lightly floured surface and, using plates as a guide, cut a 30cm/12in round and a 28cm/11in round. Place the pastry rounds on baking sheets lined with baking parchment, cover with clear film (plastic wrap) and chill for 30 minutes.

4 Preheat the oven to 200°C/400°F/Gas 6. Remove the clear film from the pastry rounds. Spoon the peaches into the middle of the larger round and spread them out to within 5cm/2in of the edge. Place the smaller pastry round on top. Brush the edge of the larger pastry round with water, then fold this over the top round and press to seal. Twist the edges together.

5 Lightly brush the pastry with water and sprinkle evenly with a little sugar. Make five or six small crescent-shape slashes on the top of the pastry. Bake the pie for about 45 minutes and serve warm.

Treacle Tart

The best chilled commercial shortcrust pastry makes light work of this old-fashioned favourite, with its sticky filling and twisted lattice topping. Smooth creamy custard is the classic accompaniment, but it is also delicious served with cream or ice cream. For a more textured filling, use wholemeal (whole-wheat) breadcrumbs or crushed cornflakes instead of the white breadcrumbs.

Serves 4–6

350g/12oz (unsweetened) shortcrust pastry
260g/9½oz/generous ¾ cup golden (light corn) syrup
1 lemon
75g/3oz/1½ cups fresh white breadcrumbs

1 On a lightly floured surface, roll out three-quarters of the pastry to a thickness of 3mm/⅛in. Transfer to a 20cm/8in fluted flan tin (quiche pan) and trim off the overhang. Chill the pastry case (pie shell) for 20 minutes. Reserve the pastry trimmings.

2 Put a baking sheet in the oven and preheat to 200°C/400°F/Gas 6. To make the filling, warm the syrup in a pan until it melts. Grate the lemon rind and squeeze the juice.

3 Remove the syrup from the heat and stir in the breadcrumbs and lemon rind. Leave to stand for 10 minutes, then add more crumbs if the mixture is too thin and moist. Stir in 30ml/2 tbsp of the lemon juice, then spread the mixture evenly in the pastry case.

4 Roll out the reserved pastry and cut into 10–12 thin strips. Twist the strips into spirals, then lay half of them on the filling. Arrange the remaining strips at right angles to form a lattice. Press the ends on to the rim.

5 Place the tart on the hot baking sheet and bake for 10 minutes. Lower the oven temperature to 190°C/375°F/Gas 5. Bake for 15 minutes more, until golden. Serve warm with some smooth creamy custard, or alternatively, a generous spoonful of clotted cream or ice cream.

Peach Pie: Energy 309kcal/1293kJ; Protein 4g; Carbohydrate 36.3g, of which sugars 16.3g; Fat 18g, of which saturates 2.6g; Cholesterol 11mg; Calcium 44mg; Fibre 1.1g; Sodium 206mg.
Treacle Tart: Energy 420kcal/1764kJ; Protein 4.1g; Carbohydrate 63.5g, of which sugars 35.1g; Fat 18.4g, of which saturates 11.3g; Cholesterol 46mg; Calcium 62mg; Fibre 1.1g; Sodium 344mg.

Plum and Almond Tart

To transform this tart into an extravagant dessert, dust with a little icing (confectioners') sugar and serve with a dollop of crème fraîche.

Serves 4

375g/13oz ready-rolled puff pastry, thawed if frozen
115g/4oz marzipan
6–8 plums, stoned (pitted) and sliced

1 Preheat the oven to 190°C/375°F/Gas 5. Unroll the pastry on to a large baking sheet. Using a small, sharp knife, score a border 5cm/2in from the edge of the pastry, without cutting all the way through.

2 Roll out the marzipan into a rectangle, to fit just within the pastry border, then lay it on top of the pastry, pressing down lightly with the tips of your fingers.

3 Sprinkle the sliced plums on top of the marzipan in an even layer and bake for 20–25 minutes, or until the pastry is risen and golden brown.

4 Carefully transfer the tart to a wire rack to cool slightly, then cut into squares or wedges and serve.

Blueberry and Almond Tart

This is a cheat's version of a sweet almond tart and the result is superb. Whisked egg whites and grated marzipan cook to form a light sponge under a tangy topping of contrasting blueberries. When whisking the egg whites for the filling, ensure all traces of yolk are removed – otherwise you won't be able to whisk them to their maximum volume. Serve with crème fraîche.

Serves 6

250g/9oz (unsweetened) shortcrust pastry
175g/6oz/generous 1 cup white marzipan
4 large (US extra large) egg whites
130g/4½ oz/generous 1 cup blueberries

1 Preheat the oven to 200°C/400°F/Gas 6. Roll out the pastry and use to line a 23cm/9in round, loose-based flan tin (quiche pan). Line with baking parchment and fill with baking beans, then bake for 15 minutes.

2 Remove the beans and baking parchment and bake for a further 5 minutes. Reduce the oven temperature to 180°C/350°F/Gas 4.

3 Grate the marzipan. Whisk the egg whites until stiff. Sprinkle half the marzipan over them and fold in. Then fold in the rest.

4 Turn the mixture into the pastry case (pie shell) and spread it evenly. Sprinkle the blueberries over the top and bake for 20–25 minutes, until golden and just set. Leave to cool for 10 minutes before serving.

Caramelized Upside-down Pear Pie

In this gloriously sticky dessert, which is similar to the French classic tarte tatin, the pastry is baked on top of the fruit, which gives it a crisp and flaky texture. When inverted, the pie looks wonderful. Look for good-quality chilled pastry that you can freeze for future use. Serve warm with cream or ice cream.

Serves 8

5–6 firm, ripe pears
175g/6oz/scant 1 cup caster (superfine) sugar
225g/8oz (unsweetened) shortcrust pastry

From the storecupboard

115g/4oz/½ cup butter

1 Peel, quarter and core the pears. Toss with some of the sugar in a bowl.

2 Melt the butter in a 27cm/10½in heavy, ovenproof omelette pan. Add the remaining sugar. When it changes colour, arrange the pears in the pan.

3 Continue cooking, uncovered, for 20 minutes, or until the fruit has completely caramelized.

4 Leave the fruit to cool in the pan. Preheat the oven to 200°C/400°F/Gas 6. Meanwhile, on a lightly floured surface, roll out the pastry to a round that is slightly larger than the diameter of the pan. Lay the pastry on top of the pears and then carefully tuck it in around the edge.

5 Bake for 15 minutes, then lower the oven temperature to 180°C/350°F/Gas 4. Bake for a further 15 minutes, or until the pastry is golden.

6 Let the pie cool in the pan for a few minutes. To unmould, run a knife around the pan's edge, then, using oven gloves, invert a plate over the pan and quickly turn the two over together.

7 If any pears stick to the pan, remove them gently with a metal spatula and replace them on the pie.

Plum/Almond Tart: Energy 478kcal/2003kJ; Protein 7.1g; Carbohydrate 58.1g, of which sugars 24.6g; Fat 26.7g, of which saturates 0.3g; Cholesterol 0mg; Calcium 79mg; Fibre 1.3g; Sodium 297mg.
Blueberry/Almond Tart: Energy 321kcal/1347kJ; Protein 6g; Carbohydrate 42.3g, of which sugars 22.3g; Fat 15.4g, of which saturates 4g; Cholesterol 6mg; Calcium 56mg; Fibre 1.8g; Sodium 212mg.
Upside-down Pear Pie: Energy 365kcal/1528kJ; Protein 2.1g; Carbohydrate 47.4g, of which sugars 34.5g; Fat 19.8g, of which saturates 10g; Cholesterol 35mg; Calcium 51mg; Fibre 3g; Sodium 204mg.

Pumpkin Poached in Syrup

In winter, Turkish markets and streets are alive with busy pumpkin stalls selling pumpkin flesh, prepared especially for this exquisite dish. Serve on its own or with chilled clotted cream or crème fraîche.

Serves 4–6
450g/1lb sugar
juice of 1 lemon
6 cloves
1kg/2¼lb peeled and deseeded pumpkin flesh, cut into cubes or rectangular blocks

1 Put the sugar into a deep, wide, heavy pan and pour in 250ml/8fl oz/1 cup water. Bring to the boil, stirring continuously, until the sugar has dissolved, then boil gently for 2–3 minutes.

2 Lower the heat and stir in the lemon juice and cloves, then slip in the pumpkin pieces and bring the liquid back to the boil. Lower the heat and put the lid on the pan.

3 Poach the pumpkin gently, turning the pieces over from time to time, until they are tender and a rich, gleaming orange colour. This may take 1½–2 hours, depending on the size of the pumpkin pieces.

4 Leave the pumpkin to cool in the pan, then lift the pieces out of the syrup and place them in a serving dish.

5 Spoon most, or all, of the syrup over the pumpkin pieces and serve at room temperature or chilled.

Variation
This dessert can be varied infinitely by changing the fruit and the syrup flavouring. Another classic Turkish combination uses dried apricots, soaked in water overnight, and lemon juice and orange blossom water to scent the syrup. In this recipe the poached and cooled fruits are filled with Kaymak, a cream made from water buffalo milk, but you could use crème fraîche or clotted cream instead.

Tropical Scented Fruit Salad

With its special colour and exotic flavour, this fresh fruit salad is perfect after a rich, heavy meal. For fabulous flavour and colour, try using three small blood oranges and three ordinary oranges. Other fruit that can be added include pears, kiwi fruit and bananas. Serve this tropical fruit salad with whipping cream flavoured with 15g/½oz finely chopped drained preserved stem ginger.

Serves 4–6
350–400g/12–14oz/3–3½ cups strawberries, hulled and halved
6 oranges, peeled and segmented
1–2 passion fruit
120ml/4fl oz/½ cup medium dry or sweet white wine

1 Put the hulled and halved strawberries and peeled and segmented oranges into a serving bowl. Halve the passion fruit and, using a teaspoon, scoop the flesh into the bowl.

2 Pour the wine over the fruit and toss gently. Cover and chill in the refrigerator until ready to serve.

Cook's Tip
To prepare the oranges, place on a chopping board and slice off the top and bottom to expose the flesh. Stand upright and, using a small sharp knife, slice down between the skin and the flesh. Do this all the way around to remove all the peel and pith. Repeat with the remaining oranges, reserving any juice. Holding one orange over a bowl to catch the juices, cut between the membrane to release the segments. Repeat. Pour any reserved juice over the fruit salad.

Variation
Combine any sweet and tart fruits with contrasting colours.

Pumpkin in Syrup: Energy 317kcal/1353kJ; Protein 1.6g; Carbohydrate 82.1g, of which sugars 81.2g; Fat 0.3g, of which saturates 0.2g; Cholesterol 0mg; Calcium 88mg; Fibre 1.7g; Sodium 5mg.
Tropical Scented Fruit: Energy 81kcal/342kJ; Protein 2g; Carbohydrate 15.6g, of which sugars 15.6g; Fat 0.2g, of which saturates 0g; Cholesterol 0mg; Calcium 75mg; Fibre 3g; Sodium 13mg.

Fresh Fig Compôte with Vanilla and Coffee

A vanilla and coffee syrup brings out the wonderful flavour of figs in this compôte. Serve Greek yogurt or vanilla ice cream with the poached fruit. A wide selection of different honey is available – its aroma and flavour will be subtly scented by the plants surrounding the hives. Orange blossom honey works particularly well in this recipe, although any clear variety is suitable.

Serves 4–6

400ml/14fl oz/1⅔ cups fresh brewed coffee
115g/4oz/½ cup clear honey
1 vanilla pod (bean)
12 slightly underripe fresh figs

1 Choose a frying pan with a lid, large enough to hold the figs in a single layer. Pour in the coffee and add the honey.

2 Split the vanilla pod lengthways and scrape the seeds into the pan. Add the vanilla pod, then bring to a rapid boil and cook until the liquid has reduced to about 175ml/6fl oz/¾ cup.

3 Wash the figs and pierce the skins several times with a sharp skewer. Cut in half and add to the syrup. Reduce the heat, cover and simmer for 5 minutes. Remove the figs from the syrup with a slotted spoon and set aside to cool.

4 Strain the syrup over the figs. Allow to stand at room temperature for 1 hour before serving with Greek (US strained plain) yogurt or vanilla ice cream.

Cook's Tip
Figs come in three main varieties – red, white and black – and all three are suitable for cooking. They are sweet and succulent, and complement the stronger, more pervasive flavours of coffee and vanilla very well.

Oranges in Coffee Syrup

This recipe works well with most citrus fruits – for example, try pink grapefruit or sweet, perfumed clementines, which have been peeled but left whole. Serve the oranges with 300ml/½ pint/1¼ cups whipped cream flavoured with 5ml/1 tsp ground cinnamon or 5ml/1 tsp ground nutmeg, or simply with a spoonful of Greek yogurt.

Serves 6

6 medium oranges
200g/7oz/1 cup sugar
100ml/3½ fl oz/scant ½ cup fresh strong brewed coffee
50g/2oz/½ cup pistachio nuts, chopped (optional)

1 Finely pare, shred and reserve the rind from one orange. Peel the remaining oranges. Cut each one crossways into slices, then re-form them, with a cocktail stick (toothpick) through the centre.

2 Put the sugar in a heavy pan and add 50ml/2fl oz/¼ cup water. Heat gently until the sugar dissolves, then bring to the boil and cook until the syrup turns pale gold.

3 Remove from the heat and carefully pour 100ml/3½fl oz/scant ½ cup freshly boiling water into the pan. Return to the heat until the syrup has dissolved in the water. Stir in the coffee.

4 Add the oranges and the rind to the coffee syrup. Simmer for 15–20 minutes, turning the oranges once during cooking. Leave to cool, then chill. Serve the oranges and syrup in individual bowls and sprinkle with pistachio nuts, if using.

Cook's Tip
Choose a pan in which the oranges will just fit in a single layer – use a deep frying pan if you don't have a pan that is large enough.

Fresh Fig Compôte: Energy 147kcal/628kJ; Protein 1.7g; Carbohydrate 36g, of which sugars 35.8g; Fat 0.6g, of which saturates 0g; Cholesterol 0mg; Calcium 103mg; Fibre 3g; Sodium 27mg.
Oranges in Syrup: Energy 191kcal/815kJ; Protein 2g; Carbohydrate 48.5g, of which sugars 48.5g; Fat 0.2g, of which saturates 0g; Cholesterol 0mg; Calcium 93mg; Fibre 2.7g; Sodium 10mg.

Pistachio and Rose Water Oranges

This light and citrusy dessert is perfect to serve after a heavy main course, such as a hearty meat stew or a leg of roast lamb. Combining three favourite Middle Eastern ingredients, it is delightfully fragrant and refreshing. If you don't have pistachio nuts, use hazelnuts instead.

Serves 4
4 large oranges
30ml/2 tbsp rose water
30ml/2 tbsp shelled pistachio nuts, roughly chopped

1 Slice the top and bottom off one of the oranges to expose the flesh. Using a small serrated knife, slice down between the pith and the flesh, working round the orange, to remove all the peel and pith. Slice the orange into six rounds, reserving any juice. Repeat with the remaining oranges.

2 Arrange the orange rounds on a serving dish. Mix the reserved juice with the rose water and drizzle the liquid over the oranges.

3 Cover the dish with clear film (plastic wrap) and chill for about 30 minutes. Sprinkle the chopped pistachio nuts over the oranges to serve.

Cook's Tip
Rose-scented sugar is delicious sprinkled over fresh fruit salads. Wash and thoroughly dry a handful of rose petals and place in a sealed container filled with caster (superfine) sugar for 2–3 days. Remove the petals before using the sugar.

Variation
Almonds could be used instead of pistachio nuts for this dish and orange blossom water could replace rose water.

Juniper-scented Pears in Red Wine

More often used in savoury dishes than sweet, juniper berries have a dark blue, almost black colour with a distinct gin-like flavour. In this fruity winter dessert crushed juniper berries give the classic partnership of pears and red wine a slightly aromatic flavour. These pears are particularly good sprinkled with toasted almonds and whipped cream.

Serves 4
30ml/2 tbsp juniper berries
50g/2oz/¼ cup caster (superfine) sugar
600ml/1 pint/2½ cups red wine
4 large or 8 small firm pears, stalks intact

1 Lightly crush the juniper berries using a pestle and mortar or with the end of a rolling pin. Put the berries in a pan with the sugar and wine and heat gently until the sugar dissolves.

2 Meanwhile, peel the pears carefully, leaving them whole and with the stalks left on. Add them to the wine and heat until just simmering. Cover the pan and cook gently for about 25 minutes, until the pears are tender. Turn the pears once or twice to make sure they cook evenly.

3 Use a slotted spoon to remove the pears. Boil the syrup hard for a few minutes, until it is slightly reduced and thickened. If serving the pears hot, reheat them gently in the syrup, otherwise arrange them in a serving dish and spoon the syrup over.

Variations
• *Use ruby port or Madeira wine instead of red wine for a sweeter more intense flavour.*
• *Substitute other fruits depending on the season. For example, in late summer you could use ripe plums, apples or blackberries.*

Pistachio Oranges: Energy 101kcal/424kJ; Protein 3g; Carbohydrate 13.4g, of which sugars 13.2g; Fat 4.3g, of which saturates 0.6g; Cholesterol 0mg; Calcium 79mg; Fibre 3g; Sodium 47mg.
Juniper-scented Pears: Energy 378kcal/1595kJ; Protein 1g; Carbohydrate 65.7g, of which sugars 65.7g; Fat 0.2g, of which saturates 0g; Cholesterol 0mg; Calcium 53mg; Fibre 3.9g; Sodium 22mg.

Gooseberry Fool

This quickly made dessert never fails to impress. Blackberries, raspberries, blackcurrants or rhubarb work well in place of gooseberries. When using young pink rhubarb there is no need to sieve the cooked fruit. Serve in pretty glasses with small crisp biscuits to provide a contrast in texture.

Serves 4
450g/1lb chopped gooseberries
125g/4½oz/¼ cup caster (superfine) sugar, or to taste
300ml/½ pint/1¼ cups double (heavy) cream

1 Put the gooseberries into a pan with 30ml/2 tbsp water. Cover and cook gently for about 10 minutes, until the fruit is soft. Stir in the sugar to taste.

2 Transfer the fruit into a nylon sieve (strainer) and press through. Leave the purée to cool.

3 Whip the cream until stiff enough to hold soft peaks. Stir in the gooseberry purée without over-mixing (it looks pretty with some streaks).

4 Spoon the mixture into serving glasses and refrigerate until you are ready to eat.

Mango and Lime Fool

Canned mangoes are used here for convenience, but this zesty, tropical fruit fool tastes even better if made with the superior fresh ones. Choose a variety with a good flavour, such as the fragrant Alphonso mango.

Serves 4
400g/14oz can sliced mango, plus extra to garnish (optional)
grated rind of 1 lime, plus juice of ½ lime
150ml/¼ pint/⅔ cup double (heavy) cream
90ml/6 tbsp Greek (US strained plain) yogurt

1 Drain the canned mango slices and put them in a food processor, then add the grated lime rind and lime juice. Process until the mixture forms a smooth purée.

2 Alternatively, place the mango slices in a bowl and mash with a potato masher, then press through a sieve (strainer) into a bowl with the back of a wooden spoon. Stir in the lime rind and juice.

3 Pour the cream into a bowl and add the yogurt. Whisk until the mixture is thick and then quickly whisk in the mango mixture.

4 Spoon the fool into four tall cups or glasses and chill for at least 1 hour. Just before serving, decorate each glass with fresh mango slices, if you like. Serve with small crunchy biscuits (cookies) for a contrasting texture.

Rhubarb and Ginger Jellies

Made with bright pink, young rhubarb, these softly set jellies get the taste buds tingling. They are spiced with plenty of fresh ginger, which gives just a hint of zesty warmth. Pour the jelly into pretty glasses and serve it as it is or top it with spoonfuls of lightly whipped cream.

Serves 5–6
1kg/2¼lb young rhubarb
200g/7oz/1 cup caster (superfine) sugar
50g/2oz fresh root ginger, finely chopped
15ml/1 tbsp powdered gelatine

1 Cut the rhubarb into 2cm/¾in chunks and place in a pan with the sugar and ginger.

2 Pour in 450ml/¾ pint/scant 2 cups water and bring to the boil. Reduce the heat, cover and simmer gently for 10 minutes, until the rhubarb is very soft and pulpy.

3 Meanwhile, sprinkle the gelatine over 30ml/2 tbsp cold water in a small heatproof bowl. Leave to stand, without stirring, for 5 minutes, until the gelatine has become sponge-like in texture.

4 Set the bowl over a small pan of hot water and simmer, stirring occasionally, until the gelatine has dissolved completely into a clear liquid. Remove from the heat.

5 Strain the cooked rhubarb through a fine sieve (strainer) into a bowl. Stir in the dissolved gelatine until thoroughly mixed. Leave to cool slightly before pouring into serving glasses. Chill for at least 4 hours or overnight, until set.

Variation
There are endless possibilities on the theme of fruit jellies. A classic English combination is raspberry and white wine, but you could equally use clementines and grape juice or just about any other combination. You can make your life really easy by simply using a carton of juice and gelatine.

Gooseberry Fool: Energy 517kcal/2147kJ; Protein 2.6g; Carbohydrate 37.3g, of which sugars 37.3g; Fat 40.7g, of which saturates 25.1g; Cholesterol 103mg; Calcium 85mg; Fibre 2.7g; Sodium 21mg.
Mango Fool: Energy 269kcal/1118kJ; Protein 2.8g; Carbohydrate 15.2g, of which sugars 14.9g; Fat 22.6g, of which saturates 13.8g; Cholesterol 51mg; Calcium 64mg; Fibre 2.6g; Sodium 26mg.
Rhubarb Jellies: Energy 152kcal/652kJ; Protein 3.8g; Carbohydrate 36.2g, of which sugars 36.2g; Fat 0.2g, of which saturates 0g; Cholesterol 0mg; Calcium 176mg; Fibre 2.4g; Sodium 12mg.

Rhubarb and Ginger Trifles

Choose a good quality jar of rhubarb compôte for this recipe; try to find one with large, chunky pieces of fruit. Alternatively, make your own by poaching in sugar and water.

Serves 4
12 gingernut biscuits (gingersnaps)
50ml/2fl oz/¼ cup rhubarb compôte
450ml/¾ pint/scant 2 cups extra thick double (heavy) cream

1 Put the ginger biscuits in a plastic bag and seal. Bash the biscuits with a rolling pin until roughly crushed.

2 Set aside two tablespoons of crushed biscuits and divide the rest among four glasses.

3 Spoon the rhubarb compôte on top of the crushed biscuits, then top with the cream. Place in the refrigerator and chill for about 30 minutes.

4 To serve, sprinkle the reserved crushed biscuits over the trifles and serve immediately.

Cook's Tip
To make a rhubarb compôte, take 450g/1lb rhubarb, trimmed, cut into pieces and wash thoroughly. Put in a pan with 75g/3oz/½ cup soft light brown sugar (and a little ginger wine if desired) and place over a low heat for about 10 minutes.

Variation
You can make many versions of this dessert by varying the fruit, the type of biscuit (cookie) and the topping. Stewed plums or peaches would make a good choice. Alternatively, use a summer fruits or apricot compôte. Any type of crunchy biscuit can be used, but amaretti would be excellent. In place of the extra thick double (heavy) cream use Greek (US strained plain) yogurt or crème fraîche.

Crispy Mango Stacks with Raspberry Coulis

This makes a very healthy yet stunning dessert – it is low in fat and contains no added sugar. However, if the raspberries are a little sharp, you may prefer to add a pinch of sugar to the purée.

Serves 4
3 filo pastry sheets, thawed if frozen
2 small ripe mangoes
115g/4oz/⅔ raspberries, thawed if frozen

From the storecupboard
50g/2oz/¼ cup butter, melted

1 Preheat the oven to 200°C/400°F/Gas 6. Lay the filo sheets on a clean work surface and cut out four 10cm/4in rounds from each.

2 Brush each round with the melted butter and lay the rounds on two baking sheets. Bake for 5 minutes, or until crisp and golden. Place on wire racks to cool.

3 Peel the mangoes, remove the stones (pits) and cut the flesh into thin slices.

4 Put the raspberries in a food processor with 45ml/3 tbsp water and process to a purée. Place a pastry round on each of four serving plates.

5 Top with a quarter of the mango and drizzle with a little of the raspberry purée. Repeat until all the ingredients have been used, finishing with a layer of mango and a drizzle of raspberry purée.

Variation
This dessert could be made with many fruit combinations. The main things to consider are the complementary colours and the contrast of sweetness and sharpness in the fruit. Peach and strawberry is just one example.

Rhubarb Trifles: Energy 695kcal/2874kJ; Protein 3.6g; Carbohydrate 27.1g, of which sugars 14.1g; Fat 64.3g, of which saturates 39.4g; Cholesterol 154mg; Calcium 98mg; Fibre 0.6g; Sodium 124mg.
Mango Stacks: Energy 186kcal/779kJ; Protein 2.2g; Carbohydrate 21.7g, of which sugars 11.9g; Fat 10.7g, of which saturates 6.7g; Cholesterol 27mg; Calcium 36mg; Fibre 3.1g; Sodium 79mg.

Tangy Raspberry and Lemon Tartlets

Fresh raspberries teamed with a sharp lemon curd create colourful and tangy tartlets. Choose a top quality lemon curd for the best result.

Serves 4

175g/6oz ready-made short-crust pastry, thawed if frozen
120ml/8 tbsp good quality lemon curd
115g/4oz/⅔ cup fresh raspberries

1 Preheat the oven to 190°C/375°F/Gas 5. Roll out the pastry and use to line four 9cm/3½in tartlet tins (muffin pans). Line each tin with a circle of baking parchment and fill with baking beans or uncooked rice.

2 Bake for 15–20 minutes, or until golden and cooked through. Remove the baking beans or rice and paper and take the pastry cases out of the tins. Leave them to cool completely on a wire rack.

3 Set aside 12 raspberries for decoration and fold the remaining ones into the lemon curd. Spoon the mixture into the pastry cases and top with the reserved raspberries. Serve immediately.

Cook's Tips

• *To save on last-minute preparation time, you can make the pastry cases (pie shells) for these little tartlets in advance and store them in an airtight container until ready to serve.*
• *For an attractive finish, dust the tartlets with sifted icing (confectioners') sugar and decorate with mint sprigs.*

Variation

Stir a little whipped cream or crème fraîche into the lemon curd for a creamy, luxurious finish, or serve with whipped cream on the side.

Strawberry Cream Shortbreads

Simple to assemble, these pretty strawberry desserts are always popular. Serve them as soon as they are ready because the shortbread biscuits will lose their lovely crisp texture if left to stand.

Serves 3

150g/5oz/ generous 1 cup strawberries
450ml/¾ pint/scant 2 cups double (heavy) cream
6 round shortbread biscuits (cookies)
fresh mint sprigs, to decorate (optional)

1 Reserve three strawberries for decoration. Hull the remaining strawberries and cut them in half.

2 Put the halved strawberries in a bowl and gently crush using the back of a fork. (Only crush the berries lightly; they should not be reduced to a purée.)

3 Put the cream in a large, clean bowl and whip to form soft peaks. Add the crushed strawberries and gently fold in to combine. (Do not overmix.)

4 Halve the reserved strawberries, then spoon the strawberry and cream mixture on top of the shortbread biscuits. Decorate each one with half a strawberry and serve immediately.

Cook's Tip

To decorate, you can use whole strawberries and give them a pretty frosted effect by painting them with egg white and dipping in caster (superfine) sugar. Leave them to dry before using and add a mint sprig.

Variation

You can use any other berry you like for this dessert – try raspberries or blueberries. Two ripe, peeled peaches will also give great results.

Raspberry Tartlets: Energy 289kcal/1214kJ; Protein 3.1g; Carbohydrate 40.6g, of which sugars 13.8g; Fat 13.9g, of which saturates 4.3g; Cholesterol 13mg; Calcium 47mg; Fibre 1.6g; Sodium 195mg.
Shortbreads: Energy 976kcal/4035kJ; Protein 5.7g; Carbohydrate 34.6g, of which sugars 16.8g; Fat 90.8g, of which saturates 50.1g; Cholesterol 206mg; Calcium 122mg; Fibre 1.3g; Sodium 204mg.

Baby Summer Puddings

This classic English dessert is always a favourite, and serving it in individual portions with spoonfuls of clotted cream makes it extra special. White bread that is more than a day old actually works better than fresh bread. Slices of brioche make an extra special alternative to white bread.

Serves 4

6 slices one-day-old white bread, crusts removed
450g/1lb/4 cups summer fruits
75g/3oz/6 tbsp caster (superfine) sugar

1 Cut out four rounds from the bread slices, large enough to fit in the bottom of four 175ml/6fl oz/¾ cup dariole moulds.

2 Line the moulds with clear film (plastic wrap) and place a bread round in the base of each mould. Reserve two slices of bread and cut the remaining bread into slices and use to line the sides of the moulds, pressing to fit.

3 Put the summer fruits in a pan with the sugar and heat gently until the sugar has dissolved. Bring to the boil, then simmer gently for 2–3 minutes. Remove from the heat and leave to cool slightly, then spoon into the moulds.

4 Cut four rounds out of the remaining slices of bread to fit the top of the dariole moulds. Place the bread rounds on the fruit and push down to fit. Cover each dariole mould loosely with clear film and place a small weight on top.

5 Chill the desserts overnight, then turn out on to serving plates. Remove the clear film lining and serve immediately.

Cook's Tip
You can enjoy this lovely dessert even in the winter. Use frozen summer fruits, which are available in supermarkets all year round. Simply thaw the fruits, then cook as if using fresh fruits.

Raspberry Brûlée

Cracking through the caramelized sugary top of a crème brûlée to reveal the creamy custard underneath is always so satisfying. This version has the added bonus of a deliciously rich, fruity custard packed with crushed raspberries.

Serves 4

115g/4oz/⅔ cup fresh raspberries
300ml/½ pint/1¼ cups ready-made fresh custard
75g/3oz/6 tbsp caster (superfine) sugar

1 Put the raspberries into a large bowl and crush with a fork. Add the custard and gently fold in until combined.

2 Divide the mixture between four 120ml/4fl oz/½ cup ramekin dishes. Cover each one with clear film (plastic wrap) and chill in the refrigerator for 2–3 hours.

3 Preheat the grill (broiler) to high. Remove the clear film from the ramekin dishes and place them on a baking sheet. Sprinkle the sugar over the custards and grill (broil) for 3–4 minutes, or until the sugar has caramelized.

4 Remove the custards from the grill and set aside for a few minutes to allow the sugar to harden, then serve.

Cook's Tip
You can now buy little gas blow torches for use in the kitchen. They make quick work of caramelizing the sugar on top of the brûlées – and are also fun to use.

Variation
Besides the classic vanilla crème brûlée, you could make an indulgent chocolate one by adding melted chocolate to the custard. Combined with the exotic taste of mangoes, this is a heavenly variation.

Summer Puddings: Energy 347kcal/1455kJ; Protein 4.5g; Carbohydrate 50.4g, of which sugars 43.1g; Fat 14.3g, of which saturates 8.3g; Cholesterol 0mg; Calcium 86mg; Fibre 0.6g; Sodium 165mg.
Raspberry Brûlée: Energy 155kcal/657kJ; Protein 2.5g; Carbohydrate 33.2g, of which sugars 30.5g; Fat 1.4g, of which saturates 0g; Cholesterol 2mg; Calcium 86mg; Fibre 0.8g; Sodium 33mg.

Steamed Ginger Custards

Delicate and warming, ginger custard is a favourite among the Chinese. These individual custards are often served warm, straight from the steamer, and enjoyed as a mid-afternoon snack. They work just as well served as a chilled dessert, however.

Serves 4

115g/4oz/⅔ cup fresh root ginger, chopped
400ml/14fl oz/1⅔ cups coconut milk
60ml/4 tbsp sugar
2 egg whites

1 Using a mortar and pestle or food processor, grind the ginger to a fine paste. Press the ginger paste through a fine sieve (strainer) set over a bowl, or twist it in a piece of muslin (cheesecloth), to extract the juice.

2 Fill a wok one-third of the way up with water. Place a bamboo steamer in the wok, bring the water to the boil and reduce the heat to low.

3 In a bowl, whisk the coconut milk, sugar and egg whites with the ginger juice until the mixture is smooth and the sugar has dissolved.

4 Pour the mixture into four individual heatproof bowls and place them in the steamer. Cover and steam for 15–20 minutes, until the mixture sets.

5 Remove the bowls from the steamer and leave to cool. Cover them with clear film (plastic wrap) and place in the refrigerator overnight. Serve the custards chilled or at room temperature, as desired.

Variation
For an alternative way, slice about six pieces of preserved (stem) ginger and add them to the coconut mixture before pouring into bowls for steaming. It will intensify the spicy flavour of this sweet custard dessert.

Portuguese Custard Tarts

Called pastéis de nata in Portugal, these tarts are traditionally served with a small strong coffee as a sweet breakfast dish, but they are equally delicious served as a dessert, or with coffee at the end of a meal.

Makes 12

225g/8oz ready-made puff pastry, thawed if frozen
175ml/6fl oz/¾ cup fresh ready-made custard
30ml/2 tbsp icing (confectioners') sugar

1 Preheat the oven to 200°C/400°F/Gas 6. Roll out the pastry and cut out twelve 13cm/5in rounds.

2 Line a 12-hole muffin tin (pan) with the pastry rounds. Line each pastry round with a circle of baking parchment and some baking beans or uncooked rice.

3 Bake the tarts for 10–15 minutes, or until the pastry is cooked through and golden. Remove the paper and baking beans or rice and set aside to cool.

4 Spoon the custard into the pastry cases and dust with the icing sugar. Place the tarts under a preheated hot grill (broiler) and cook until the sugar caramelizes. Remove the tarts from the heat and leave to cool before serving.

Cook's Tip
Make your own fresh custard for these gorgeous little tarts – the end result will reward your endeavours. Heat 450ml/¾ pint/scant 2 cups milk with a few drops of vanilla extract and remove from the heat just as the milk comes to the boil. Whisk 2 eggs and 1 extra yolk in a bowl with 15–30ml/1–2 tbsp caster (superfine) sugar. Blend together 15ml/1 tbsp cornflour (cornstarch) with 30ml/2 tbsp water and mix with the eggs. Whisk in the hot milk, strain the egg and milk mixture back into the pan and heat gently, stirring continuously until the custard thickens enough to coat the back of a spoon. Cover the surface with clear film (plastic wrap) to stop a skin forming.

Ginger Custards: Energy 89kcal/380kJ; Protein 2g; Carbohydrate 20.8g, of which sugars 20.8g; Fat 0.4g, of which saturates 0.2g; Cholesterol 0mg; Calcium 50mg; Fibre 0.3g; Sodium 159mg.
Portuguese Custard Tarts: Energy 94kcal/395kJ; Protein 1.5g; Carbohydrate 11.9g, of which sugars 4.7g; Fat 4.9g, of which saturates 0g; Cholesterol 0mg; Calcium 26mg; Fibre 0g; Sodium 64mg.

Baked Custard with Burnt Sugar

This delicious egg custard or crème brûlée is a rich indulgent dessert that can be prepared well in advance. You can buy vanilla sugar or make your own by placing a split vanilla pod in a jar of caster sugar – the sugar will be ready to use after a couple of days.

Serves 6

1 litre/1¾ pints/4 cups double (heavy) cream
6 egg yolks
90g/3½ oz/½ cup vanilla sugar
75g/3oz/⅓ cup soft light brown sugar

1 Preheat the oven to 150°C/300°F/Gas 2. Place six 120ml/4fl oz/½ cup ramekins in a roasting pan or ovenproof dish and set aside while you prepare the vanilla custard.

2 Heat the double cream in a heavy pan over a gentle heat until it is very hot, but not boiling.

3 In a bowl, whisk the egg yolks and vanilla sugar until well blended. Whisk in the hot cream and strain into a large jug (pitcher). Divide the custard equally among the ramekins.

4 Pour enough boiling water into the roasting pan to come about halfway up the sides of the ramekins. Cover the pan with foil and bake for about 30 minutes, until the custards are just set. (Push the point of a knife into the centre of one; if it comes out completely clean, the custards are cooked.) Remove from the pan, cool, then chill.

5 Preheat the grill (broiler). Sprinkle the sugar evenly over the surface of the custards and grill (broil) for 30–60 seconds, until the sugar melts and caramelizes, taking care not to let it burn. Place in the refrigerator to chill and set the crust.

Cook's Tip

It is best to make the custards the day before you wish to eat them and chill overnight, so that they are really cold and firm.

Baked Caramel Custard

Many countries have their own version of this classic dessert. Known as crème caramel in France and flan in Spain, this chilled baked custard has a rich caramel flavour. The custard is cooked very gently to prevent the eggs from curdling.

Serves 6–8

250g/9oz/1¼ cups vanilla sugar
5 large (US extra large) eggs, plus 2 extra yolks
450ml/¾ pint/scant 2 cups double (heavy) cream

1 Put 175g/6oz/generous ¾ cup of sugar in a small pan with just enough water to moisten. Bring to the boil, swirling the pan until the sugar has dissolved completely. Boil for about 5 minutes, without stirring, until the syrup turns a dark caramel colour.

2 Quickly pour the caramel into a 1 litre/1¾ pint/4 cup soufflé dish. Holding the dish with oven gloves, carefully swirl it to coat the base and sides with the caramel mixture. Set aside to cool.

3 Preheat the oven to 160°C/325°F/Gas 3. In a bowl, whisk the eggs and egg yolks with the remaining sugar for 2–3 minutes, until smooth and creamy.

4 Heat the cream in a heavy pan until hot, but not boiling. Whisk the hot cream into the egg mixture and carefully strain the mixture into the caramel-lined dish. Cover tightly with foil.

5 Place the dish in a deep pan and pour in boiling water to halfway up the dish. Bake for 40–45 minutes, until just set. Test whether set by inserting a knife about 5cm/2in from the edge; if the blade comes out clean, the custard should be ready.

6 Remove the soufflé dish from the pan and leave to cool for at least 30 minutes, then put in refrigerator and chill overnight.

7 To turn out, run a knife around the edge of the dish to loosen. Cover the dish with a serving plate and, holding them together tightly, invert, allowing the custard to drop on to the plate.

Baked Custard: Energy 996kcal/4116kJ; Protein 5.7g; Carbohydrate 31.6g, of which sugars 31.6g; Fat 95g, of which saturates 57.2g; Cholesterol 430mg; Calcium 120mg; Fibre 0g; Sodium 47mg.
Caramel Custard: Energy 233kcal/983kJ; Protein 11g; Carbohydrate 30.8g, of which sugars 30.8g; Fat 8.4g, of which saturates 2.9g; Cholesterol 234mg; Calcium 168mg; Fibre 0g; Sodium 129mg.

Chocolate Banana Fools

This de luxe version of banana custard looks great served in glasses. It can be made a few hours in advance and chilled until ready to serve.

Serves 4

115g/4oz plain (semisweet) chocolate, chopped
300ml/½ pint/1¼ cups fresh custard
2 bananas

1 Put the chocolate in a heatproof bowl and melt in the microwave on high power for 1–2 minutes. Stir, then set aside to cool. (Alternatively, put the chocolate in a heatproof bowl and place it over a pan of gently simmering water and leave until melted, stirring frequently.)

2 Pour the custard into a bowl and gently fold in the melted chocolate to make a rippled effect.

3 Peel and slice the bananas and stir these into the chocolate and custard mixture. Spoon into four glasses and chill for 30 minutes–1 hour before serving.

Lemon Posset

This simple creamy dessert has distant origins, dating back to the Middle Ages. It is perfect for warm summer evenings and is particularly good served with crisp shortbread cookies.

Serves 4

600ml/1 pint/2½ cups double (heavy) cream
175g/6oz/scant 1 cup caster (superfine) sugar
grated rind and juice of 2 unwaxed lemons

1 Gently heat the cream and sugar together in a pan until the sugar has dissolved completely, then bring to the boil, stirring constantly. Add the lemon juice and rind and stir until the cream mixture thickens.

2 Pour the mixture into four heatproof serving glasses and chill until just set, then serve.

Passion Fruit Creams

These delicately perfumed creams are light with a fresh flavour from the passion fruit. When halved, the fragrant, sweet juicy flesh with small edible black seeds are revealed. These creams can be decorated with mint or geranium leaves and served with cream.

Serves 5–6

600ml/1 pint/2½ cups double (heavy) cream, or a mixture of single (light) and double (heavy) cream
6 passion fruits
30–45ml/2–3 tbsp vanilla sugar
5 eggs

1 Preheat the oven to 180°C/350°F/Gas 4. Line the bases of six 120ml/4fl oz/½ cup ramekins with rounds of baking parchment and place them in a roasting pan.

2 Heat the cream to just below boiling point, then remove the pan from the heat.

3 Sieve (strain) the flesh of four passion fruits and beat together with the sugar and eggs. Whisk in the hot cream and then ladle into the ramekins.

4 Half fill the roasting pan with boiling water. Bake the creams for 25–30 minutes, or until set, then leave to cool before chilling in the refrigerator.

5 Run a knife around the insides of the ramekins, then invert them on to serving plates, tapping the bases firmly and allowing the creams to drop on to the plates.

6 Carefully peel off the baking parchment and chill in the refrigerator until ready to serve. Spoon on a little passion fruit flesh just before serving.

Cook's Tip
Ripe passion fruit should look purple and wrinkled – choose fruit that feel heavy for their size.

Chocolate Fools: Energy 268kcal/1127kJ; Protein 4.1g; Carbohydrate 42.1g, of which sugars 38.1g; Fat 9.6g, of which saturates 4.9g; Cholesterol 3mg; Calcium 81mg; Fibre 1.4g; Sodium 33mg.
Lemon Posset: Energy 917kcal/3801kJ; Protein 2.7g; Carbohydrate 48.5g, of which sugars 48.5g; Fat 80.6g, of which saturates 50.1g; Cholesterol 206mg; Calcium 98mg; Fibre 0g; Sodium 36mg.
Passion Fruit Creams: Energy 585kcal/2414kJ; Protein 7.2g; Carbohydrate 8.5g, of which sugars 8.5g; Fat 58.4g, of which saturates 34.7g; Cholesterol 296mg; Calcium 77mg; Fibre 0.5g; Sodium 84mg.

Chocolate and Espresso Mousse

Heady, aromatic espresso coffee adds a distinctive flavour to this smooth, rich mousse. For a special occasion, serve the mousse in stylish chocolate cups decorated with sprigs of mint, and a spoonful of mascarpone or clotted cream on the side.

Serves 4
450g/1lb plain (semisweet) chocolate
45ml/3 tbsp freshly brewed espresso
4 eggs, separated

From the storecupboard
25g/1oz/2 tbsp unsalted (sweet) butter

1 For each chocolate cup, cut a double thickness 15cm/6in square of foil. Mould it around a small orange, leaving the edges and corners loose to make a cup shape. Remove the orange and press the bottom of the foil case gently on a surface to make a flat base. Repeat to make four foil cups.

2 Break half the chocolate into small pieces and place in a bowl set over a pan of very hot water. Stir occasionally until the chocolate has completely melted.

3 Spoon the chocolate into the foil cups, spreading it up the sides with the back of a spoon to give a ragged edge. Chill for 30 minutes in the refrigerator, or until set hard. Gently peel away the foil, starting at the top edge.

4 To make the chocolate mousse, put the remaining chocolate and espresso into a bowl and set over a pan of hot water and melt as before, until smooth and liquid. Stir in the butter, a little at a time. Remove the pan from the heat and then stir in the egg yolks.

5 Whisk the egg whites in a bowl until they form stiff peaks, but are not dry, then fold them into the chocolate mixture.

6 Pour into a bowl and chill for at least 3 hours, or until the mousse is set. Scoop the chilled mousse into the chocolate cups just before serving.

Meringue Pyramid with Chocolate Mascarpone

This impressive cake makes a perfect centrepiece for a celebration buffet. Sprinkle a little sieved icing sugar and a few rose petals over the pyramid for simple, but stunning, presentation.

Serves about 10
200g/7oz plain (semisweet) chocolate
4 egg whites
150g/5oz/¾ cup caster (superfine) sugar
115g/4oz/¾ cup mascarpone cheese

1 Preheat the oven to 150°C/300°F/Gas 2. Line two large baking sheets with baking parchment. Grate 75g/3oz of the chocolate into a bowl.

2 Whisk the egg whites in a clean, grease-free bowl until they form stiff peaks. Gradually whisk in half the sugar, then add the rest and whisk until the meringue is very stiff and glossy. Add the grated chocolate and whisk lightly to mix.

3 Draw a 20cm/8in circle on the lining paper on one of the baking sheets, turn it upside down, and spread the marked circle evenly with about half the meringue.

4 Spoon the remaining meringue in 28–30 teaspoonfuls on both baking sheets. Bake the meringue for 1–1½ hours, or until crisp and completely dried out.

5 Make the filling. Melt the remaining chocolate in a heatproof bowl over hot water. Cool slightly, then stir in the mascarpone. Cool the mixture until firm.

6 Spoon the chocolate mixture into a large piping (pastry) bag and use to sandwich the meringues together in pairs, reserving a small amount of filling for the pyramid.

7 Arrange the filled meringues on a serving platter, piling them up in a pyramid and keeping them in position with a few well-placed dabs of the reserved filling.

Chocolate Mousse: Energy 694kcal/2901kJ; Protein 11.9g; Carbohydrate 71.5g, of which sugars 70.5g; Fat 42.2g, of which saturates 23.7g; Cholesterol 210mg; Calcium 67mg; Fibre 2.8g; Sodium 115mg.
Meringue Pyramid: Energy 701kcal/2941kJ; Protein 8.2g; Carbohydrate 94.2g, of which sugars 93.1g; Fat 35g, of which saturates 21g; Cholesterol 12mg; Calcium 49mg; Fibre 3g; Sodium 31mg.

Cherry Chocolate Brownies

This is a modern version of the classic Black Forest gateau. Choose really good-quality bottled fruits because this will make all the difference to the end result. Other types of fruit will work equally well – try slices of orange preserved in liqueur or pears bottled in brandy.

Serves 4
4 chocolate brownies
300ml/½ pint/1¼ cups double (heavy) cream
20–24 bottled cherries in Kirsch

1 Using a sharp knife, carefully cut the brownies in half crossways to make two thin slices. Place one brownie square on each of four serving plates.

2 Pour the cream into a large bowl and whip until soft but not stiff, then divide half the whipped cream between the four brownie squares.

3 Divide half the cherries among the cream-topped brownies, then place the remaining brownie halves on top of the cherries to form a stack. Press down lightly.

4 Spoon the remaining cream on top of the brownies, then top each one with more cherries and serve immediately.

Coffee Mascarpone Creams

For the best results, use good quality coffee beans and make the coffee as strong as possible. These little desserts are very rich so you need a really robust shot of coffee to give the desired result. They are particularly good served with a glass of liqueur or a cup of espresso and a crunchy amaretti.

Serves 4
115g/4oz/½ cup mascarpone cheese
45ml/3 tbsp strong espresso coffee
45ml/3 tbsp icing (confectioners') sugar

1 Put the mascarpone in a bowl and add the coffee. Mix well until smooth and creamy. Sift in the icing sugar and beat until thoroughly combined.

2 Spoon the mixture into little china pots or ramekin dishes and chill for 30 minutes before serving.

Variation
You can flavour mascarpone cheese with almost anything you like to make a quick but elegant dessert. Try replacing the coffee with the same quantity of orange juice, Marsala wine or Kirsch.

Classic Chocolate Roulade

This rich, squidgy chocolate roll should be made at least eight hours before serving to allow it to soften. Expect the roulade to crack a little when you roll it up, and sprinkle with a little grated chocolate, if you like, as a final decoration.

Serves 8
200g/7oz plain (semisweet) chocolate
200g/7oz/1 cup caster (superfine) sugar, plus extra caster or icing (confectioners') sugar to dust
7 eggs, separated
300ml/½ pint/1¼ cups double (heavy) cream

1 Preheat the oven to 180°C/350°F/Gas 4 then grease and line a 33 x 23cm/13 x 9in Swiss roll tin (jelly roll pan) with baking parchment.

2 Break the chocolate into squares and melt in a bowl over a pan of barely simmering water. Remove from the heat and leave to cool for about 5 minutes.

3 In a large bowl, whisk the sugar and egg yolks until they become light and fluffy. Stir in the melted chocolate. Whisk the egg whites until stiff, but not dry, and then gently fold into the chocolate mixture.

4 Pour the chocolate mixture into the prepared tin, spreading it level with a metal spatula. Bake for about 25 minutes, or until firm. Leave the cake in the tin and cover with a cooling rack, making sure that it does not touch the cake.

5 Cover the rack with a damp dish towel, then wrap in clear film (plastic wrap). Leave in a cool place for at least 8 hours.

6 Dust a sheet of baking parchment with caster or icing sugar and turn out the roulade on to it. Peel off the lining paper.

7 To make the filling, whip the double cream until soft peaks form. Spread over the roulade. Starting from one of the short ends, carefully roll it up, using the paper to help. Place seam side down, on to a serving plate and dust generously with more caster or icing sugar before serving.

Brownies: Energy 632kcal/2619kJ; Protein 5g; Carbohydrate 31.1g, of which sugars 20.3g; Fat 53.5g, of which saturates 25.1g; Cholesterol 103mg; Calcium 78mg; Fibre 0.2g; Sodium 234mg.
Coffee Creams: Energy 96kcal/403kJ; Protein 2.7g; Carbohydrate 12.7g, of which sugars 12.7g; Fat 4.2g, of which saturates 2.6g; Cholesterol 12mg; Calcium 6mg; Fibre 0g; Sodium 1mg.
Chocolate Roulade: Energy 476kcal/1988kJ; Protein 7.4g; Carbohydrate 42.6g, of which sugars 42.4g; Fat 32g, of which saturates 18.1g; Cholesterol 219mg; Calcium 65mg; Fibre 0.6g; Sodium 73mg.

Lychee and Elderflower Sorbet

The flavour of elderflowers is famous for bringing out the essence of gooseberries, but what is less well known is how wonderfully it complements lychees.

Serves 4
175g/6oz/¾ cup caster (superfine) sugar
500g/1¼lb fresh lychees, peeled and stoned (pitted)
15ml/1 tbsp elderflower cordial
dessert biscuits (cookies), to serve

1 Place the sugar and 400ml/14fl oz/1⅔ cups water in a pan and heat gently until the sugar has dissolved. Increase the heat and boil for 5 minutes, then add the lychees. Lower the heat and simmer for 7 minutes. Remove from the heat and allow to cool.

2 Purée the fruit and syrup in a blender or food processor. Place a sieve (strainer) over a bowl and pour the purée into it. Press through as much of the purée as possible with a spoon. Stir the elderflower cordial into the strained purée, then pour the mixture into a freezerproof container. Freeze for 2 hours, until ice crystals start to form around the edges.

3 Remove the sorbet from the freezer and process briefly in a food processor or blender to break up the crystals. Repeat this process twice more, then freeze until firm. Transfer to the refrigerator for 10 minutes to soften slightly before serving in scoops, with dessert biscuits.

Cook's Tip
Switch the freezer to the coldest setting before making the sorbet – the faster the mixture freezes, the smaller the ice crystals that form and the better the final texture will be.

Variation
Use other cordials to vary this delicately flavoured sorbet, but ensure it doesn't overpower the lychee: lemon would be good.

Blackcurrant Sorbet

Wonderfully sharp and bursting with flavour, blackcurrants make a really fabulous sorbet. Blackcurrants are more acidic than white or redcurrants and are very rarely eaten raw. Taste the mixture after adding the syrup, and if you find it a little too tart, add more sugar before freezing.

Serves 6
500g/1¼lb/5 cups blackcurrants, trimmed, plus extra to decorate
150g/5oz/¾ cup caster (superfine) sugar
1 egg white

1 Put the blackcurrants in a pan and add 150ml/¼ pint/⅔ cup water. Cover the pan and simmer for 5 minutes, or until the fruit is soft. Cool, then process to a purée in a food processor or blender.

2 Set a large sieve (strainer) over a bowl, pour the purée into the sieve, then press it through the mesh with the back of a spoon to form a smooth liquid.

3 Pour 200ml/7fl oz/scant 1 cup water into a clean pan. Add the sugar and bring to the boil, stirring until the sugar has dissolved. Pour the syrup into a bowl. Cool, then chill.

4 Mix the blackcurrant purée and sugar syrup together. Spoon into a freezerproof container and freeze until mushy. (To ensure rapid freezing, use a metal container and place directly on the freezer shelf.)

5 Lightly whisk the egg white until just frothy. Process the sorbet in a food processor until smooth, then return it to the container and stir in the egg white. Freeze for 4 hours, or until firm.

6 Transfer the sorbet to the refrigerator about 15 minutes before serving. Serve in scoops, decorated with the blackcurrant sprigs.

Lychee and Elderflower: Energy 249kcal/1064kJ; Protein 1.4g; Carbohydrate 64.7g, of which sugars 64.7g; Fat 0.1g, of which saturates 0g; Cholesterol 0mg; Calcium 31mg; Fibre 0.9g; Sodium 4mg.
Blackcurrant Sorbet: Energy 84kcal/361kJ; Protein 1.3g; Carbohydrate 21.2g, of which sugars 21.2g; Fat 0g, of which saturates 0g; Cholesterol 0mg; Calcium 58mg; Fibre 3g; Sodium 14mg.

Lemon Sorbet

This tangy sorbet creates a light and refreshing dessert that can be served alone or to accompany fresh fruit. If you have cooked a rich meal, this clean-tasting dessert might be the perfect choice to end with.

Serves 6
200g/7oz/1 cup caster (superfine) sugar
4 lemons
1 large (US extra large) egg white
a little granulated (white) sugar, for sprinkling

1 Put the caster sugar and 300ml/½ pint/1¼ cups water into a heavy pan and bring slowly to the boil, stirring occasionally, until the sugar has just dissolved.

2 Using a vegetable peeler, pare the rind thinly from two of the lemons directly into the pan. Simmer for about 2 minutes without stirring, then remove the pan from the heat. Leave the syrup to cool, then chill.

3 Squeeze the juice from all the lemons and carefully strain it into the syrup, making sure all the pips (seeds) are removed. Take the lemon rind out of the syrup and set it aside.

4 If you have an ice cream maker, strain the syrup into the machine tub and churn for 10 minutes, or until thickening. If working by hand, strain the syrup into a shallow freezerproof container and freeze for 4 hours, or until the mixture is mushy.

5 In a bowl, lightly whisk the egg white with a fork, then pour it into the tub. Continue to churn for 10–15 minutes, or until firm enough to scoop. If you are not using an ice cream maker, scoop the mushy mixture into a blender or food processor and process until smooth. Whisk the egg white with a fork until it is just frothy. Spoon the sorbet back into its container; beat in the egg white. Freeze for 1 hour.

6 To make the sugared rind decoration, use the blanched rind set aside earlier. Cut into very thin strips and sprinkle with granulated sugar on a plate. Scoop the sorbet into bowls or glasses and decorate with the sugared lemon rind.

Strawberry and Lavender Sorbet

A hint of lavender transforms a familiar strawberry sorbet into a perfumed dinner-party dessert. When buying strawberries, look for plump, shiny fruit without any signs of staining or leakage at the bottom of the punnet – this suggests that the fruit at the bottom has been squashed. To hull strawberries, prise out the leafy top with a sharp knife or a specially designed strawberry huller.

Serves 6
150g/5oz/¾ cup caster (superfine) sugar
6 fresh lavender flowers, plus extra to decorate
500g/1¼lb/5 cups strawberries, hulled
1 egg white

1 Place the sugar in a pan and pour in 300ml/½ pint/1¼ cups water. Bring to the boil, stirring until the sugar has dissolved.

2 Take the pan off the heat, add the lavender flowers and leave to infuse (steep) for 1 hour. If time permits, chill the syrup in the refrigerator before using.

3 Process the strawberries in a food processor or blender, then press the purée through a large sieve (strainer) into a bowl.

4 Pour the purée into a freezerproof container, strain in the syrup and freeze for 4 hours, or until mushy. Transfer to a food processor and process until smooth.

5 Whisk the egg white until frothy, and stir into the sorbet. Spoon the sorbet back into the container and freeze until firm. Serve in scoops, piled into tall glasses, and decorate with sprigs of lavender flowers.

Cook's Tip
Check the flavour of the cooled lavender syrup. If you think the flavour is too mild, add two or three more flowers, reheat and cool again before using.

Lemon Sorbet: Energy 133kcal/569kJ; Protein 0.7g; Carbohydrate 34.8g, of which sugars 34.8g; Fat 0g, of which saturates 0g; Cholesterol 0mg; Calcium 18mg; Fibre 0g; Sodium 12mg.
Strawberry Sorbet: Energy 123kcal/523kJ; Protein 1.3g; Carbohydrate 31.1g, of which sugars 31.1g; Fat 0.1g, of which saturates 0g; Cholesterol 0mg; Calcium 27mg; Fibre 0.9g; Sodium 17mg.

Damson Water Ice

Perfectly ripe damsons are sharp and full of flavour – if you can't find damsons, use another deep-red variety of plum or extra-juicy Victoria plums. To add an extra, nutty flavour to this mouthwatering ice, serve sprinkled with finely chopped toasted almonds.

Serves 6
500g/1¼lb ripe damsons, washed
150g/5oz/¾ cup caster (superfine) sugar

1 Put the damsons into a pan and add 150ml/¼ pint/⅔ cup water. Cover and simmer gently for 10 minutes, or until the damsons are tender.

2 Pour 300ml/½ pint/1¼ cups water into a second pan. Add the sugar and bring to the boil, stirring until the sugar has dissolved. Pour the syrup into a bowl, leave to cool, then chill.

3 Break up the cooked damsons in the pan with a wooden spoon and scoop out any free stones (pits). Pour the fruit and juices into a large sieve (strainer) set over a bowl. Press the fruit through the sieve and discard the skins and any remaining stones from the sieve.

4 Pour the damson purée into a shallow plastic container. Stir in the syrup and freeze for 6 hours, beating once or twice to break up the ice crystals.

5 Spoon into tall serving glasses or dishes and serve the water ice with wafers.

Variation
Apricot water ice can be made in exactly the same way. Flavour the water ice with a little lemon or orange rind or add a broken cinnamon stick to the pan when poaching the fruit. Serve garnished with sprigs of mint or nasturtium flowers.

Peach and Cardamom Yogurt Ice

Make the most of spices that are familiar in savoury cooking by discovering their potential for sweet dishes. Cardamom, often used in Indian cooking, has a warm pungent aroma and a subtle lemon flavour. Although it is made with yogurt rather than cream, this ice cream has a luxurious velvety texture and it is a healthy choice, too.

Serves 4
8 cardamom pods
6 peaches, total weight about 500g/1¼lb, halved and stoned (pitted)
75g/3oz/6 tbsp caster (superfine) sugar
200ml/7fl oz/scant 1 cup natural (plain) yogurt

1 Place the cardamom pods on a board and crush them with the base of a ramekin, or use a mortar and pestle.

2 Chop the peaches coarsely and put them in a pan. Add the crushed cardamom pods, with their black seeds, the sugar and 30ml/2 tbsp water. Cover and simmer for 10 minutes, or until the fruit is tender. Leave to cool.

3 Process the peach mixture in a food processor or blender until smooth, then press through a sieve (strainer) placed over a bowl.

4 Mix the yogurt into the sieved purée and pour into a freezerproof container. Freeze for 5–6 hours, until firm, beating once or twice with a fork, electric whisk, or in a processor to break up the ice crystals.

5 Scoop the ice cream on to a large platter, or into individual glasses or dishes, and serve.

Variation
There are endless combinations of fruit and spice yogurt ice – a good one to try is rhubarb and ginger.

Damson Water Ice: Energy 130kcal/555kJ; Protein 0.6g; Carbohydrate 34.1g, of which sugars 34.1g; Fat 0g, of which saturates 0g; Cholesterol 0mg; Calcium 33mg; Fibre 1.5g; Sodium 3mg.
Peach Yogurt Ice: Energy 69kcal/296kJ; Protein 3.8g; Carbohydrate 13.3g, of which sugars 13.3g; Fat 0.6g, of which saturates 0.3g; Cholesterol 1mg; Calcium 104mg; Fibre 1.9g; Sodium 43mg.

Summer Berry Freeze

Any combination of summer fruits will work for this dish, as long as they are frozen, because this helps to create a chunky texture. Whole fresh or frozen berries make an attractive decoration.

Serves 6
350g/12oz/3 cups frozen summer fruits
200g/7oz/scant 1 cup Greek (US strained plain) yogurt
25g/1oz icing (confectioners') sugar

1 Put all the ingredients into a food processor and process until combined but still quite chunky. Spoon the mixture into six 150ml/¼ pint/⅔ cup ramekin dishes.

2 Cover each dish with clear film (plastic wrap) and place in the freezer for about 2 hours, or until firm.

3 To turn out the frozen yogurts, dip the dishes briefly in hot water and invert them on to small serving plates. Tap the base of the dishes and the yogurts should come out quite easily. Serve immediately.

Cook's Tip
Serve a scoop of this colourful berry frozen yogurt with a meringue nest and a dollop of whipped cream for an iced version of summer berry pavlova. Alternatively, make one large meringue, pile the scoops of frozen yogurt in the middle and decorate with glistening frosted berries for a really impressive dessert.

Variation
To make a rich and creamy ice cream, use double (heavy) cream in place of the yogurt. It's a lot less healthy but the heavenly taste is irresistible. Other substitutes for yogurt include the creamy, slightly sweet, mascarpone cheese, which makes a perfectly smooth base for ices. A low-fat alternative can be made with virtually fat-free fromage frais.

Rose Petal Sorbet

Clear fragranced rose water is much prized in Middle Eastern households. It is splashed on the face and hands to freshen up before or after a meal, and it is used to scent many sweet dishes – milk puddings, syrupy pastries, fragrant jams, sherbet drinks, fruit salads and, of course, Turkish delight. This sorbet looks lovely served in frosted glasses or fine glass bowls, decorated with fresh or crystallized rose petals – these are easy to make by brushing the petals with whisked egg white, dipping them in sugar and leaving to dry until crisp.

Serves 3–4
fresh petals of 2 gloriously scented red or pink roses, free from pesticides
225g/8oz/generous 1 cup caster (superfine) sugar
juice of 1 lemon
15ml/1 tbsp rose water

1 Wash the rose petals and cut off the white bases. Place in a pan with 600ml/1 pint/2½ cups water and bring to the boil. Turn off the heat, cover the pan and leave the petals to steep for 10 minutes.

2 Strain off the water and reserve the petals. Pour the water back into the pan, add the sugar and bring to the boil, stirring, until the sugar has dissolved.

3 Boil for 1–2 minutes, then lower the heat and simmer for 5–10 minutes, until the syrup thickens a little. Stir in the lemon juice, rose water and reserved petals, turn off the heat and leave the mixture to cool in the pan.

4 Pour into a freezer container and place in the freezer until beginning to set. Take out of the freezer at 2–3 hour intervals and whisk to disperse the ice crystals. Alternatively, freeze in an electric sorbetière. Before serving, take the sorbet out of the freezer for 5–10 minutes, so that it softens enough to scoop.

Summer Berry Freeze: Energy 51kcal/215kJ; Protein 2.2g; Carbohydrate 10.4g, of which sugars 10.4g; Fat 0.4g, of which saturates 0.2g; Cholesterol 0mg; Calcium 75mg; Fibre 0.7g; Sodium 32mg.
Rose Petal Sorbet: Energy 222kcal/946kJ; Protein 0.3g; Carbohydrate 58.8g, of which sugars 58.8g; Fat 0g, of which saturates 0g; Cholesterol 0mg; Calcium 30mg; Fibre 0g; Sodium 4mg.

Raspberry Sherbet

Traditional sherbets are made in a similar way to sorbets but with added milk. This low-fat version is made from raspberry purée blended with sugar syrup and virtually fat-free fromage frais or yogurt.

Serves 6

175g/6oz/scant 1 cup caster (superfine) sugar
500g/1¼lb/3½ cups raspberries, plus extra, to serve
500ml/17fl oz/2¼ cups virtually fat-free fromage frais or yogurt

1 Put the sugar in a small pan with 150ml/¼ pint/⅔ cup water and bring to the boil, stirring until the sugar has dissolved completely. Pour into a jug (pitcher) and cool.

2 Put 350g/12oz/2½ cups of the raspberries in a food processor and blend to a purée. Press through a sieve (strainer) into a large bowl and discard the seeds. Stir the sugar syrup into the raspberry purée and chill until very cold.

3 Add the fromage frais or yogurt to the chilled purée and whisk until smooth. Using an ice cream maker, churn the mixture until it is thick but too soft to scoop. Scrape into a freezerproof container, then crush the remaining raspberries between your fingers and add to the ice cream. Mix lightly, then freeze for 2–3 hours until firm. Scoop the ice cream into dishes and serve with extra raspberries.

Cook's Tip
To make the sherbet by hand, pour the raspberry purée into a freezerproof container and freeze for 4 hours, beating once with a fork, electric whisk or in a food processor to break up the ice crystals. Freeze, then beat again.

Variation
Use virtually any fruit: soft fruits can be blended and sieved (strained), whereas firmer fruits need poaching in sugar and water first.

Watermelon Ice

This simple, refreshing dessert is perfect after a hot, spicy meal. The aromatic flavour of kaffir lime leaves goes perfectly with watermelon.

Serves 4–6

90ml/6 tbsp caster (superfine) sugar
4 kaffir lime leaves, torn into small pieces
500g/1¼lb watermelon

1 Put the sugar and kaffir lime leaves in a pan with 105ml/7 tbsp water. Heat gently until the sugar has dissolved, then pour into a large bowl and set aside to cool.

2 Slice the watermelon into wedges with a large knife. Cut the flesh from the rind, remove the bitter seeds carefully and chop the flesh.

3 Place the flesh in a food processor and process to a slush, then mix in the sugar syrup. Chill for 3–4 hours.

4 Strain the chilled mixture into a freezer container and freeze for 2 hours, then beat with a fork to break up the ice crystals.

5 Return to the freezer and freeze for 3 hours more, beating at half-hourly intervals, then freeze until firm. Transfer the ice to the refrigerator about 30 minutes before serving. Serve in elegant dishes or glasses with a wedge of watermelon.

Cook's Tip
Work quickly when you are beating the frozen watermelon mixture. If you take too long, it will melt completely before you return it to the freezer.

Variation
Watermelon has a beautiful pink colour, but other varieties of melon can be just as delicious. Try cantaloupe or charentais melon for a delicate orange effect.

Raspberry Sorbet: Energy 276kcal/1181kJ; Protein 11.6g; Carbohydrate 60g, of which sugars 60g; Fat 0.6g, of which saturates 0.3g; Cholesterol 1mg; Calcium 163mg; Fibre 3.1g; Sodium 48mg.
Watermelon Ice: Energy 85kcal/363kJ; Protein 0.5g; Carbohydrate 21.6g, of which sugars 21.6g; Fat 0.3g, of which saturates 0.1g; Cholesterol 0mg; Calcium 14mg; Fibre 0.1g; Sodium 3mg.

Watermelon Sorbet

A slice of this refreshing fruit sorbet is the perfect way to cool down on a hot sunny day. This pretty pink frozen dish also makes a mouthwatering summer appetizer with a difference or a sophisticated palate cleanser between courses.

Serves 6

½ small watermelon, weighing about 1kg/2¼lb
75g/3oz/½ cup caster (superfine) sugar
60ml/4 tbsp cranberry juice or water
30ml/2 tbsp lemon juice
fresh mint sprigs, to decorate

1 Using a sharp knife, cut the watermelon cleanly into six even wedges. Scoop out or cut away the pink flesh from each wedge, carefully removing the seeds. Put the shell to one side.

2 Line a freezerproof bowl, about the same size as the melon, with clear film (plastic wrap). Arrange the melon skins in the bowl to re-form the shell, fitting them together snugly so that there are no gaps. Put in the freezer.

3 Put the sugar and cranberry juice or water in a pan and stir over low heat until the sugar has dissolved. Bring to the boil, then reduce the heat and simmer for 5 minutes. Remove the pan from the heat and set aside to cool.

4 Put the melon flesh and lemon juice in a blender or food processor and process to a smooth purée. Pour into a bowl, stir in the sugar syrup, then pour into a freezer container. Freeze the mixture for 3–3½ hours, or until slushy.

5 Turn the sorbet into a chilled freezerproof bowl and whisk well to break up the ice crystals. Return to the freezer for a further 30 minutes. Whisk again, then turn into the melon shell and freeze until solid.

6 Remove the sorbet from the freezer and leave to stand at room temperature for 15 minutes. Take the melon out of the bowl and cut into wedges with a warmed sharp knife. Serve decorated with fresh mint sprigs.

Iced Oranges

A colourful dessert that often features on menus in Italian eateries, this sorbet is not only totally refreshing, but also virtually fat-free.

Serves 8

150g/5oz/⅔ cup caster (superfine) sugar
juice of 1 lemon
14 oranges, extra orange or orange juice if necessary
8 fresh bay leaves, to decorate

1 Put the sugar in a heavy pan. Add half the lemon juice, then add 120ml/4fl oz/½ cup water. Cook over low heat, stirring until the sugar has dissolved. Bring to the boil and boil for 2–3 minutes, until the syrup is clear. Remove the pan from the heat and set aside.

2 Slice the tops off eight of the oranges to make lids. Scoop out the flesh of the oranges and reserve. Freeze the empty orange shells and lids until required.

3 Finely grate the rind of the remaining oranges and stir into the syrup. Squeeze the juice from the oranges and from the reserved flesh. There should be about 750ml/1¼ pints/3 cups of juice. If necessary, to make up to the correct quantity, squeeze another orange or add bought unsweetened orange juice.

4 Stir the orange juice and remaining lemon juice with 90ml/6 tbsp water into the syrup. Taste, adding more lemon juice or sugar as desired. Pour the mixture into a shallow freezer container and freeze for 3 hours.

5 Turn the orange sorbet mixture into a chilled bowl and whisk thoroughly to break up the ice crystals. Return to the container and freeze for a further 4 hours, until firm, but not solid.

6 Pack the frozen mixture into the hollowed-out orange shells, and set the lids on top. Freeze the sorbet-filled shells until ready to serve. Just before serving, push a skewer into the tops of the lids and push in a bay leaf, to decorate. Leave to stand for 15 minutes to allow the sorbet to soften slightly before serving.

Watermelon Sorbet: Energy 101kcal/432kJ; Protein 0.9g; Carbohydrate 24.9g, of which sugars 24.9g; Fat 0.5g, of which saturates 0.2g; Cholesterol 0mg; Calcium 18mg; Fibre 0.2g; Sodium 4mg.
Iced Oranges: Energy 210kcal/896kJ; Protein 4.1g; Carbohydrate 50.8g, of which sugars 50.8g; Fat 0.4g, of which saturates 0g; Cholesterol 0mg; Calcium 183mg; Fibre 6.3g; Sodium 20mg.

Star Anise Ice Cream

This syrup-based ice cream is flavoured with the clean, warming taste of star anise and is the perfect exotic treat to cleanse the palate.

Serves 6–8

500ml/17fl oz/2¼ cups double (heavy) cream
8 whole star anise
90g/3½ oz/½ cup caster (superfine) sugar
4 large (US extra large) egg yolks
ground star anise, to decorate

1 In a heavy pan, heat the cream with the star anise to just below boiling point, then remove from the heat and leave to infuse (steep) until cool.

2 In another pan, dissolve the sugar in 150ml/¼ pint/⅔ cup water, stirring constantly. Bring to the boil for a few minutes to form a light syrup, then leave to cool for 1 minute.

3 Whisk the egg yolks in a bowl. Trickle in the hot syrup, whisking constantly, until the mixture becomes mousse-like. Pour in the infused cream through a sieve (strainer), and continue to whisk until well mixed.

4 Pour the mixture into a freezerproof container and freeze for 4 hours, beating twice with a fork or whisking with an electric mixer to break up the ice crystals. To serve, dust with a little ground star anise.

Cook's Tip
You can use an ice cream maker, if you have one. Simply pour in the mixture at the start of step 3 and churn until smooth.

Variation
Spices play an important role in many traditional Asian ice creams, with their lively tastes of cinnamon, clove, star anise and pandanus (screwpine) leaf also proving popular.

Green Tea Ice Cream

In the past, the Japanese did not follow a meal with dessert, apart from some fruit. This custom is slowly changing and now many Japanese restaurants offer light desserts such as sorbet or ice cream. Here, ice cream is flavoured with matcha – the finest green powdered tea available.

Serves 4

500ml/17fl oz carton good-quality vanilla ice cream
15ml/1 tbsp matcha (powdered green tea)
seeds from ¼ pomegranate (optional)

1 Soften the ice cream by transferring it to the refrigerator for 20–30 minutes. Do not allow it to melt.

2 Mix the matcha powder and 15ml/1 tbsp lukewarm water from the kettle in a cup and stir well to make a smooth paste.

3 Put half the ice cream into a mixing bowl. Add the matcha liquid and mix thoroughly with a rubber spatula, then add the rest of the ice cream. You can stop mixing when the ice cream is streaked with dark green and white for a marbled effect, or continue mixing until the ice cream is a uniform pale green colour. Cover with clear film (plastic wrap) and put the bowl into the freezer.

4 After 1 hour, the ice cream will be ready to serve. Scoop into individual glass cups and, if you like, decorate with pomegranate seeds.

Cook's Tips
• *Matcha is the tea used in the Tea Ceremony, a special tea-making ritual integral to Japanese culture.*
• *Sweet azuki beans and French sweet chestnut purée can be used to make other Japanese-style ice creams. Use 30ml/2 tbsp soft cooked sweet azuki beans or 20ml/4 tsp chestnut purée per 100ml/3fl oz/scant ½ cup good-quality vanilla ice cream.*

Star Anise: Energy 380kcal/1570kJ; Protein 2.3g; Carbohydrate 12.8g, of which sugars 12.8g; Fat 35.9g, of which saturates 21.5g; Cholesterol 170mg; Calcium 46mg; Fibre 0g; Sodium 18mg.
Green Tea: Energy 269kcal/1120kJ; Protein 4.9g; Carbohydrate 21.1g, of which sugars 21g; Fat 18.9g, of which saturates 11.3g; Cholesterol 0mg; Calcium 126mg; Fibre 0g; Sodium 75mg.

Custard Ice Cream

Capture the divine experience of fine Italian ice cream with this classic recipe. The ice cream is soft in consistency and not too sweet, making it truly melt-in-the-mouth.

Serves 6
750ml/1¼ pints/3½ cups milk
2.5ml/½ tsp grated lemon rind
6 egg yolks
150g/5oz/¾ cup granulated (white) sugar

1 To make the custard, heat the milk with the lemon rind in a small pan. Remove the pan from the heat as soon as small bubbles start to form on the surface. Do not let it boil.

2 Beat the egg yolks with a wire whisk or electric mixer. Gradually incorporate the sugar and continue beating for about 5 minutes, until the mixture is pale yellow. Strain the infused milk, then slowly beat it into the egg mixture drop by drop, making sure it is well incorporated.

3 When all the milk has been added, pour the mixture into the top of a double boiler or into a heatproof bowl placed over a pan of simmering water. Stir over medium heat, until the water in the pan is boiling and the custard thickens enough to lightly coat the back of a spoon. Remove from the heat and allow the custard to cool.

4 Freeze in an ice cream maker, following the manufacturer's instructions. The ice cream is ready when it is firm but still soft.

5 If you do not have an ice cream maker, pour the mixture into a metal or plastic freezer container and freeze for about 3 hours until set. Remove from the container and chop roughly into 7.5in/3in pieces. Place in the bowl of a food processor and process until smooth. Return to the freezer container, and freeze again until firm. Repeat the freezing-chopping process two or three times, until a smooth consistency is reached.

6 Allow the ice cream to soften slightly before scooping into individual glass dishes. Serve with some crunchy amaretti for a true taste of Italy.

Chocolate Ice Cream

Nothing beats a good chocolate ice cream as a refreshing finish to a meal. Use good quality plain or cooking chocolate for the best flavour.

Serves 6
750ml/1¼ pints/3½ cups milk infused with vanilla
4 egg yolks
150g/5oz/¾ cup granulated (white) sugar
225g/8oz cooking chocolate

1 To make the custard, heat the milk in a small pan. Remove the pan from the heat as soon as small bubbles start to form on the surface. Do not let it boil.

2 Beat the egg yolks with a wire whisk or electric mixer. Gradually incorporate the sugar and continue beating for about 5 minutes, until the mixture is pale yellow. Strain the infused milk, then slowly beat it into the egg mixture drop by drop, making sure it is well incorporated.

3 Meanwhile, melt the chocolate in the top of a double boiler or in a heatproof bowl set over a pan of hot water.

4 Pour the custard into the top of the double boiler or bowl containing the melted chocolate. Stir over medium heat, until the custard thickens enough to lightly coat the back of a spoon. Remove from the heat and allow to cool.

5 Freeze in an ice cream maker, following the manufacturer's instructions. The ice cream is ready when it is firm but still soft.

6 If you do not have an ice cream maker, pour the mixture into a metal or plastic freezer container and freeze for about 3 hours until set. Remove from the container and chop roughly into 7.5in/3in pieces. Place in the bowl of a food processor and process until smooth. Return to the freezer container and freeze again until firm. Repeat the freezing-chopping process two or three times, until a smooth consistency is reached.

7 Serve the ice cream in scoops in individual glass dishes or in good quality cones.

Custard Ice Cream: Energy 238kcal/1008kJ; Protein 6.5g; Carbohydrate 39.5g, of which sugars 39.5g; Fat 7.2g, of which saturates 2.6g; Cholesterol 208mg; Calcium 161mg; Fibre 0g; Sodium 54mg.
Chocolate Ice Cream: Energy 296kcal/1244kJ; Protein 7.1g; Carbohydrate 36.3g, of which sugars 36g; Fat 14.7g, of which saturates 7.7g; Cholesterol 142mg; Calcium 152mg; Fibre 0.8g; Sodium 52mg.

Hazelnut Ice Cream

This popular flavour goes very well with scoops of chocolate and custard ice cream. Serve with wafers for an Italian iced treat.

Serves 4–6
75g/3oz/½ cup hazelnuts
475ml/16fl oz/2 cups fresh ready-made custard
25g/1oz/2 tbsp granulated (white) sugar

1 Spread the hazelnuts out on a baking tray and place under a grill (broiler) for about 5 minutes, shaking the pan frequently to toast the nuts evenly.

2 Cool the nuts slightly, then place on a clean dish towel and rub to remove the dark outer skin. Chop very finely, or grind in a food processor with 25g/1oz/2 tbsp sugar.

3 Put the custard in a large bowl, add the ground hazelnuts and stir thoroughly to combine.

4 Transfer the mixture into an ice cream maker, following the manufacturer's instructions to freeze. The ice cream is ready when it is firm but still soft.

5 If you do not have an ice cream maker, pour the mixture into a freezer container and freeze for about 3 hours, until set. Remove and chop roughly into 7.5in/3in pieces. Place in a food processor and process until smooth. Return to the container, and freeze again until firm. Repeat the freezing-chopping process two or three times, until smooth.

6 Serve scooped into bowls.

Cook's Tip
For easy freezing, the individual ingredients should be well chilled before they are mixed together at step 3. So if time allows, it's always a good idea to set the freezer to its coldest setting several hours earlier (or overnight) and then leave the mixed ingredients in the refrigerator to chill.

Bara Brith Ice Cream

Bara brith means 'speckled bread'. This delicious ice-cream recipe combines a teabread version of bara brith with cream, custard and brandy. It is simple to make and thoroughly decadent. You can either make it by hand or use an ice cream machine.

Serves 6–8
300ml/½ pint/1¼ cups double (heavy) cream, chilled
500g/1lb 2oz carton ready-made custard, chilled
30ml/2 tbsp brandy or whisky
225g/8oz/2 cups bara brith (teabread version) or similar teabread

1 Switch your freezer to its very coldest setting. Put the cream, custard and whisky into a large plastic bowl or freezer box and, with a whisk, stir well.

2 Cover and freeze for 1½–2 hours. Every 30 minutes or so take the box out of the freezer and stir well to move the ice crystals from around the edges to the centre of the bowl.

3 Meanwhile, crumble or chop the bara brith or teabread into very small pieces.

4 When the mixture is slushy, break up the ice crystals with a fork, electric hand-mixer or food processor, and quickly return it to the freezer for about 1 hour.

5 Each time the mixture thickens and becomes slushy, repeat the mashing procedure once or twice more until the ice cream is thick and creamy.

6 Stir in the crumbled or chopped bara brith, cover and freeze the ice cream until required.

Variation
Replace the brandy or whisky with a flavoured liqueur such as the Welsh Black Mountain, made with blackcurrants and apples, or any other fruit-based liqueur.

Hazelnut Ice Cream: Energy 223kcal/930kJ; Protein 6.9g; Carbohydrate 15g, of which sugars 14.6g; Fat 15.5g, of which saturates 2.6g; Cholesterol 139mg; Calcium 134mg; Fibre 1.1g; Sodium 40mg.
Bara Brith: Energy 340kcal/1415kJ; Protein 4.5g; Carbohydrate 25.6g, of which sugars 13.1g; Fat 22.8g, of which saturates 13.1g; Cholesterol 53mg; Calcium 106mg; Fibre 0.7g; Sodium 123mg.

Blackberry Ice Cream

There could scarcely be fewer ingredients in this delicious, vibrant ice cream, which is simple to make and ideal as a prepare-ahead dessert. Serve the ice cream with shortbread or almond biscuits, to provide a delicious contrast in taste and texture.

Serves 4–6

500g/1¼lb/5 cups blackberries, hulled, plus extra to decorate
75g/3oz/6 tbsp caster (superfine) sugar
300ml/½ pint/1¼ cups whipping cream
crisp dessert biscuits (cookies), to serve

1 Put the blackberries into a pan, add 30ml/2 tbsp water and the sugar. Cover and simmer for 5 minutes, until just soft.

2 Transfer the fruit into a sieve (strainer) placed over a bowl and press it through the mesh, using the back of a spoon. Put the blackberry purée to one side and leave to cool, then chill in the refrigerator.

3 Whip the cream until it is just thick but still soft enough to fall from a spoon, then mix it with the chilled fruit purée. Pour the mixture into a freezerproof container and freeze for 2 hours, or until it is part frozen.

4 Mash the mixture with a fork or process it in a food processor to break up the ice crystals. Return it to the freezer for 4 hours more, mashing or processing the mixture again after 2 hours.

5 Scoop the ice cream into dishes and decorate with extra blackberries. Serve with crisp dessert biscuits.

Cook's Tip
Frozen blackberries can be used instead of fresh ones. You will need to increase the cooking time to 10 minutes and stir occasionally.

Coffee Ice Cream

This classic ice cream is always a favourite and, despite its simplicity, has an air of sophistication and elegance about it. If you have an ice cream maker, simply pour the mixture into it and churn until firm.

Serves 8

600ml/1 pint/2½ cups fresh ready-made custard
150ml/¼ pint/⅔ cup strong black coffee
300ml/½ pint/1¼ cups double (heavy) cream

1 Using chilled ingredients straight from the refrigerator, put the custard in a large bowl and stir in the coffee. In a separate bowl, whip the cream until soft but not stiff and fold evenly into the coffee and custard mixture.

2 Pour the mixture into a freezerproof container and cover with a tight-fitting lid or clear film (plastic wrap) and freeze for about 2 hours.

3 Remove the ice cream from the freezer and beat with a fork to break up the ice crystals.

4 Return the ice cream to the freezer, freeze for a further 2 hours, then beat again. Return it to the freezer until completely frozen, then serve.

Cook's Tip
To brew fresh coffee, place 75g/3oz/6 tbsp fine coffee grounds in a coffee press and pour in 250ml/8 fl oz/1 cup boiling water. Let it cool, then strain and chill.

Variation
For a dinner party or special occasions, add 30ml/2 tbsp of Kahlúa or any other coffee-based liqueur. To decorate, sprinkle some whole coffee beans over the scoops of ice cream, or for a really luxurious treat use chocolate-coated coffee beans.

Blackberry Ice Cream: Energy 261kcal/1081kJ; Protein 1.8g; Carbohydrate 18.7g, of which sugars 18.7g; Fat 20.3g, of which saturates 12.6g; Cholesterol 52mg; Calcium 70mg; Fibre 2.6g; Sodium 15mg.
Coffee Ice Cream: Energy 260kcal/1076kJ; Protein 2.6g; Carbohydrate 12.9g, of which sugars 10.2g; Fat 21.5g, of which saturates 12.5g; Cholesterol 53mg; Calcium 87mg; Fibre 0.1g; Sodium 39mg.

Kulfi

This favourite Indian ice cream is traditionally made by carefully boiling milk until it has reduced to about one-third of its original quantity. Although you can save time by using condensed milk, nothing beats the luscious result achieved by using the authentic method. When they are available, rose petals are a stylish decoration to complement the pistachio nuts.

Serves 4

1.5 litres/2½ pints/6¼ cups full-fat (whole) milk
3 cardamom pods
25g/1oz/2 tbsp caster (superfine) sugar
50g/2oz/½ cup pistachio nuts, skinned

1 Pour the milk into a large, heavy pan. Bring to the boil, reduce the heat and simmer gently for 1 hour, remembering to stir occasionally.

2 Put the cardamom pods in a mortar and crush them with a pestle. Add the pods and the seeds to the milk and continue to simmer, stirring frequently, for 1–1½ hours, or until the milk has reduced to about 475ml/16fl oz/2 cups. Strain the milk into a jug (pitcher), stir in the sugar and leave to cool.

3 Finely grind half the pistachio nuts in a blender or nut grinder. Cut the remaining pistachios into thin slivers and put them to one side to use as decoration. Stir the ground nuts into the milk mixture.

4 Pour the milk and pistachio mixture into four kulfi or lolly (popsicle) moulds. Freeze the mixture overnight or until firm.

5 To unmould the kulfi, half fill a plastic container or bowl with very hot water, stand the moulds in the water and count to ten. Immediately lift out the moulds and invert them on a baking sheet. Transfer the ice creams to individual plates and sprinkle sliced pistachios over the top.

Coconut Ice Cream

The creamy taste and texture of this ice cream comes from the natural fat content of coconut as the mixture contains neither cream nor egg and is very refreshing. The lime adds a delicious tangy flavour as well as pretty green specks to the finished ice. Decorate with toasted coconut shavings or toasted desiccated coconut (this browns very quickly, so watch it constantly to avoid this happening).

Serves 4–6

115g/4oz/generous ¼ cup caster (superfine) sugar
2 limes
400ml/14fl oz can coconut milk
toasted coconut shavings, to decorate (optional)

1 Pour 150ml/¼ pint/⅔ cup water into a small pan. Add in the caster sugar and bring to the boil, stirring constantly until the sugar has completely dissolved. Remove the pan from the heat and leave the syrup to cool, then chill well.

2 Grate the rind from the limes finely, taking care to avoid the bitter pith. Squeeze out their juice and add to the pan of syrup with the rind. Add the coconut milk.

3 Pour the mixture into a freezerproof container and freeze for 5–6 hours, or until firm. Beat twice with a fork or electric whisk, or process in a food processor to break up the crystals. Scoop into dishes and decorate with toasted coconut shavings, if you like.

Cook's Tip

To make toasted coconut shavings, rinse the flesh from a coconut under cold water. Shave slices using a vegetable peeler, then toast under a moderate grill (broiler) until they are curled and the edges have turned golden.

Kulfi: Energy 347kcal/1443kJ; Protein 14.7g; Carbohydrate 24.4g, of which sugars 24.1g; Fat 21.6g, of which saturates 10.3g; Cholesterol 53mg; Calcium 460mg; Fibre 0.8g; Sodium 228mg.
Coconut Ice Cream: Energy 158kcal/668kJ; Protein 3.9g; Carbohydrate 26.9g, of which sugars 26.9g; Fat 4.6g, of which saturates 2.9g; Cholesterol 16mg; Calcium 142mg; Fibre 0g; Sodium 199mg.

Gingered Semi-freddo

This delicious Italian ice cream is made with a boiled sugar syrup rather than a traditional egg custard, and generously speckled with chopped stem ginger, it will remain soft when frozen. For a really impressive dinner party dessert, serve the semi-freddo in plain chocolate cases.

Serves 6

115g/4oz/generous ½ cup caster (superfine) sugar
4 egg yolks
300ml/½ pint/1¼ cups double (heavy) cream
115g/4oz/⅔ cup drained stem (preserved) ginger, finely chopped, plus extra slices, to decorate

1 Mix the sugar and 120ml/4fl oz/½ cup cold water in a pan and heat gently, stirring occasionally, until the sugar has dissolved. Increase the heat and boil for 4–5 minutes, without stirring, until the syrup registers 119°C/238°F on a sugar thermometer. Alternatively, test by dropping a little of the syrup into a cup of cold water. Pour the water away and you should be able to mould the syrup into a small ball.

2 Put the egg yolks in a large heatproof bowl and whisk until frothy. Place the bowl over a pan of simmering water and whisk in the sugar syrup. Continue whisking until the mixture is very thick. Remove from the heat and whisk until cool.

3 Whip the cream and lightly fold it into the egg yolk mixture with the chopped stem ginger. Pour into a freezerproof container and freeze for 1 hour.

4 Stir thoroughly, then return it to the freezer for 5–6 hours, until firm. Scoop into dishes or chocolate cases. Decorate with slices of ginger and serve.

Cook's Tip

To make the cases, pour melted chocolate over squares of baking parchment and drape them over upturned glasses. Peel off the baking parchment when set.

Miniature Choc-ices

These little chocolate-coated ice creams make a fun alternative to the more familiar after-dinner chocolates, especially on hot summer evenings – although they need to be eaten quickly. Serve the choc-ices in fluted paper sweet cases. If you can, buy gold cases as they will contrast very prettily with the dark chocolate coating.

Makes about 25

750ml/1¼ pints/3 cups vanilla, chocolate or coffee ice cream
200g/7oz plain (semisweet) chocolate, broken into pieces
25g/1oz milk chocolate, broken into pieces
25g/1oz/¼ cup chopped hazelnuts, lightly toasted

1 Put a large baking sheet in the freezer for 10 minutes. Using a melon baller, scoop balls of ice cream and place these on the baking sheet. Freeze for at least 1 hour or until firm.

2 Line a second baking sheet with baking parchment and place in the freezer for 15 minutes. Melt the plain chocolate in a heatproof bowl set over a pan of gently simmering water. Melt the milk chocolate in a separate bowl.

3 Using a metal spatula, transfer the ice cream scoops to the parchment-lined sheet. Spoon a little plain chocolate over one scoop so that most of it is coated. If the melted chocolate is very runny, set it aside for a few minutes to thicken up slightly before spooning on to the ice cream scoops.

4 Sprinkle the miniature choc-ices immediately with chopped nuts, before the chocolate sets. Coat half the remaining scoops in the same way, sprinkling each one with nuts before the chocolate sets. Spoon the remaining plain chocolate over all the remaining scoops.

5 Using a teaspoon, drizzle the milk chocolate over the choc-ices that are not topped with nuts. Alternatively, pipe over using a piping (pastry) bag fitted with a writing nozzle. Freeze again until ready to serve.

Semi-freddo: Energy 371kcal/1540kJ; Protein 2.9g; Carbohydrate 22.6g, of which sugars 22.6g; Fat 30.5g, of which saturates 17.7g; Cholesterol 203mg; Calcium 51mg; Fibre 0.3g; Sodium 19mg.
Miniature Choc-ices: Energy 117kcal/488kJ; Protein 1.8g; Carbohydrate 10.7g, of which sugars 10.6g; Fat 7.7g, of which saturates 4.3g; Cholesterol 1mg; Calcium 36mg; Fibre 0.3g; Sodium 19mg.

White Chocolate Castles

With a little ingenuity, good-quality bought ice cream can masquerade as a culinary masterpiece – it's down to perfect presentation. For a professional finish, dust the castles and plates with a hint of cocoa powder or icing sugar.

Serves 6
225g/8oz white chocolate, broken into pieces
250ml/8fl oz/1 cup white chocolate ice cream
250ml/8fl oz/1 cup dark (bittersweet) chocolate ice cream
115g/4oz/1 cup berries

1 Put the white chocolate in a heatproof bowl, set it over a pan of gently simmering water and leave until melted. Line a baking sheet with baking parchment. Cut out six 30 x 13cm/12 x 5in strips of baking parchment, then fold each in half lengthways.

2 Stand a 7.5cm/3in pastry (cookie) cutter on the baking sheet. Roll one strip of paper into a circle and fit inside the cutter with the folded edge on the base paper. Stick the edges together with tape.

3 Remove the cutter and shape more paper collars in the same way, leaving the pastry cutter in place around the final collar.

4 Spoon a little of the melted chocolate into the base of the collar supported by the cutter. Using a teaspoon, spread the chocolate over the base and up the sides of the collar, making the top edge uneven. Carefully lift away the cutter.

5 Make five more chocolate cases in the same way, using the cutter for extra support each time. Leave the cases in a cool place or in the refrigerator to set.

6 Carefully peel away the paper from the sides of the chocolate cases, then lift the cases off the base. Transfer to serving plates.

7 Using a large melon baller or teaspoon, scoop the white and dark chocolate ice creams into the cases and decorate with berries. Serve immediately.

Caramel and Pecan Terrine

Frozen or long-life cream is a useful ingredient for making impressive desserts. Caramel and nuts transform cream to parfait in this recipe. Take care that the syrup does not become too dark, or the ice cream will taste bitter.

Serves 6
115g/4oz/generous ½ cup sugar
450ml/¾ pint/scant 2 cups double (heavy) cream
30ml/2 tbsp icing (confectioners') sugar
75g/3oz/¾ cup pecan nuts, toasted

1 Heat the sugar and 75ml/5 tbsp water in a small, heavy pan until the sugar dissolves. Boil rapidly until the sugar has turned pale golden. Remove the pan from the heat and leave to stand until the syrup turns a rich brown colour.

2 Pour 90ml/6 tbsp of the cream over the caramel. Heat to make a smooth sauce. Leave to cool.

3 Rinse a 450g/1lb loaf tin (pan), then line the base and sides with clear film (plastic wrap). Whip a further 150ml/¼ pint/⅔ cup of the cream with the icing sugar until it forms soft peaks. Whip the remaining cream separately and stir in the caramel sauce and the toasted pecan nuts.

4 Spoon one-third of the caramel cream into the prepared tin and spread with half the plain whipped cream. Repeat. Finally, add the remaining caramel cream and level the surface. Freeze for 6 hours.

5 To serve, dip the tin in very hot water for 2 seconds, invert it on to a serving plate and peel away the film. Serve sliced.

Cook's Tip
Watch the caramel syrup closely after removing it from the heat. If it starts to turn too dark, dip the base of the pan in cold water. If the syrup remains very pale, return the pan to the heat and cook it for a little longer.

Chocolate Castles: Energy 351kcal/1463kJ; Protein 6g; Carbohydrate 34.3g, of which sugars 34.2g; Fat 22g, of which saturates 13.1g; Cholesterol 0mg; Calcium 182mg; Fibre 1.2g; Sodium 84mg.
Caramel Terrine: Energy 553kcal/2292kJ; Protein 2.5g; Carbohydrate 27.3g, of which sugars 27.1g; Fat 49g, of which saturates 25.8g; Cholesterol 103mg; Calcium 57mg; Fibre 0.6g; Sodium 18mg.

White Chocolate and Brownie Torte

This delicious dessert is easy to make and guaranteed to appeal to just about everyone. If you can't buy good quality brownies, use a moist chocolate sponge or make your own. For extra decoration, put a few fresh summer berries such as strawberries or raspberries around the edge or on the centre of the torte.

Serves 10

300g/11oz white chocolate, broken into pieces
600ml/1 pint/2½ cups double (heavy) cream
250g/9oz rich chocolate brownies
unsweetened cocoa powder, for dusting

1 Dampen the sides of a 20cm/8in springform tin (pan) and line with a strip of baking parchment. Put the chocolate in a small pan. Add 150ml/¼ pint/⅔ cup of the cream and heat very gently until the chocolate has melted. Stir until smooth, then pour into a bowl and leave to cool.

2 Break the chocolate brownies into chunky pieces and sprinkle these over the base of the tin. Pack them down lightly to make a fairly dense base.

3 Whip the remaining cream until it forms peaks, then fold in the white chocolate mixture. Spoon into the tin to cover the layer of brownies, then tap the tin gently on the work surface to level the chocolate mixture. Cover and freeze overnight.

4 Transfer the torte to the refrigerator about 45 minutes before serving to soften slightly. Decorate with a light dusting of cocoa powder just before serving.

Cook's Tip

Serve with a fresh fruit salad as a foil to the richness. A simple mix of summer fruit topped with a purée made from lightly cooked raspberries is the perfect partner. Alternatively, try tropical fruits in a ginger syrup.

Soft Fruit and Meringue Gateau

This recipe takes only five minutes to prepare but looks and tastes as though a lot of preparation went into it. The trick is to use really good vanilla ice cream. For a dinner party, slice the gateau and place on individual plates, spoon ready-made strawberry or raspberry coulis around each slice and garnish with whole strawberries or raspberries.

Serves 6

400g/14oz/3½ cups mixed small strawberries, raspberries and/or redcurrants
30ml/2 tbsp icing (confectioners') sugar
750ml/1¼ pints/3 cups vanilla ice cream
6 meringue nests or 115g/4oz meringue

1 Dampen a 900g/2lb loaf tin (pan) and line it with clear film (plastic wrap). If using strawberries, chop them into small pieces. Put them in a bowl and add the raspberries or redcurrants and icing sugar. Toss until the fruit is beginning to break up, but do not let it become mushy.

2 Put the vanilla ice cream in a large bowl and break it up with a fork. Crumble the meringues into the bowl and then add the soft fruit mixture.

3 Fold all the ingredients together until evenly combined and lightly marbled. Pack into the prepared tin and press down gently to level. Cover and freeze overnight.

4 Transfer to the refrigerator about 30 minutes before serving. To serve, turn out on to a plate, peel away the clear film and cut into slices.

Cook's Tip

To make your own meringues, whisk 2 egg whites until stiff. Gradually whisk in 90g/3½oz/½ cup caster (superfine) sugar, then put spoonfuls on to lined baking sheets and cook in the oven, preheated to 150°C/300°F/Gas 2, for 1 hour or until dry.

Chocolate Torte: Energy 570kcal/2365kJ; Protein 5.2g; Carbohydrate 31.1g, of which sugars 25.7g; Fat 48.1g, of which saturates 25.6g; Cholesterol 82mg; Calcium 129mg; Fibre 0g; Sodium 154mg.
Soft Fruit Gateau: Energy 332kcal/1397kJ; Protein 6.1g; Carbohydrate 52.4g, of which sugars 51g; Fat 10.8g, of which saturates 7.6g; Cholesterol 30mg; Calcium 141mg; Fibre 0.7g; Sodium 102mg.

All Butter Cookies

Crisp, buttery cookies are perfect with strawberries and cream or any creamy dessert or fruit compôte. The dough for these biscuits or cookies is chilled until it is firm enough to cut neatly into thin biscuits. However, the dough can also be frozen and when thawed enough to slice, can be freshly baked, but you will need to allow a little extra cooking time.

Makes 28–30
275g/10oz/2½ cups plain (all-purpose) flour
90g/3½ oz/scant 1 cup icing (confectioners') sugar, plus extra for dusting
10ml/2 tsp vanilla extract

From the storecupboard
200g/7oz/scant 1 cup unsalted (sweet) butter

1 Put the flour in a food processor. Add the butter and process until the mixture resembles coarse breadcrumbs. Add the icing sugar and vanilla, and process until the mixture comes together to form a dough.

2 Knead lightly and shape into a thick sausage or log shape, 30cm/12in long and 5cm/2in in diameter. Wrap and chill for at least 1 hour, until firm.

3 Preheat the oven to 200°C/400°F/Gas 6. Grease two baking sheets. Using a sharp knife, cut 5mm/¼ in thick slices from the dough and space them slightly apart on the baking sheet.

4 Bake for 8–10 minutes, alternating the position of the baking sheets in the oven halfway through cooking, if necessary, until the biscuits are cooked evenly and have just turned pale golden around the edges. Leave for 5 minutes, then transfer to a wire rack to cool. Serve dusted with icing sugar.

Cook's Tip
A sharp knife is important when cutting the dough roll into cookies for a neat and precise finish.

Almond Cookies

These short, light cookies have a melt-in-the-mouth texture. Their simplicity means they are endlessly versatile – irresistible with mid-morning coffee or afternoon tea and equally stylish with special desserts sprinkled with some toasted almond halves.

Makes about 24
115g/4oz/1 cup plain (all-purpose) flour
175g/6oz/1½ cups icing (confectioners') sugar, plus extra for dusting
50g/2oz/½ cup chopped almonds, plus halved almonds to decorate

From the storecupboard
115g/4oz/½ cup unsalted (sweet) butter, softened

1 Preheat the oven to 180°C/350°F/Gas 4. Combine the flour, sugar and chopped almonds in a bowl.

2 Put the softened unsalted butter in the centre of the flour and nut mixture and use a blunt knife or your fingertips to draw the dry ingredients into the butter until a dough is formed. Shape the dough into a ball.

3 Place the dough on a lightly floured surface and roll it out to a thickness of about 3mm/⅛ in. Using a 7.5cm/3in cookie cutter, cut out about 24 rounds, re-rolling the dough as necessary. Place the cookie rounds on baking sheets, leaving a little space between them. Bake the cookies for about 25 minutes, until pale golden.

4 Leave the cookies on the baking sheet for 10 minutes, then transfer to wire racks to cool. Dust thickly with sifted icing sugar before serving, decorated with halved almonds.

Cook's Tip
Use different-shaped cutters to make these cookies look even more interesting. Hearts, stars and crescents are just three shapes that you might like to try.

All Butter Cookies: Energy 84kcal/350kJ; Protein 0.8g; Carbohydrate 9.6g, of which sugars 3.3g; Fat 4.9g, of which saturates 3.1g; Cholesterol 12mg; Calcium 14mg; Fibre 0.3g; Sodium 36mg.
Almond Cookies: Energy 204kcal/858kJ; Protein 3.6g; Carbohydrate 26.8g, of which sugars 26.4g; Fat 9.9g, of which saturates 0.8g; Cholesterol 0mg; Calcium 47mg; Fibre 1.2g; Sodium 17mg.

Chewy Flapjacks

Flapjacks are popular with adults and children alike and they are so quick and easy to make. For alternative versions of the basic recipe, stir in 50g/2oz/¼ cup finely chopped ready-to-eat dried apricots or sultanas. To make a really decadent treat, you can dip the cooled flapjack fingers into melted chocolate, to coat one half.

Makes 12
50g/2oz/¼ cup caster (superfine) sugar
150g/5oz/generous ⅓ cup golden (light corn) syrup
250g/9oz/2¾ cups rolled oats

From the storecupboard
175g/6oz/¾ cup unsalted (sweet) butter

1 Preheat the oven to 180°C/350°F/Gas 4. Line the base and sides of a 20cm/8in square cake tin (pan) with baking parchment.

2 Mix the butter, sugar and syrup in a pan and heat gently until the butter has melted. Add the oats and stir until all the ingredients are combined. Turn the mixture into the tin and level the surface.

3 Bake the flapjacks for 15–20 minutes, until just beginning to turn golden-brown. Leave them to cool slightly, then cut into fingers and remove from the tin. Store the flapjacks in an airtight container.

Cook's Tip
Don't be tempted to overcook the flapjacks; they will turn crisp and dry and lose their lovely chewy texture.

Variation
Any dried fruit and chopped nuts, such as pecan or walnuts, can be added to the flapjacks to transform these bars into a really tempting treat.

Creamed Coconut Macaroons

These coconut cookies have a wonderfully rich creaminess. Cooking the gooey mixture on baking parchment makes sure that the cookies are easily removed from the baking sheet. Make mini versions and coat them in chocolate for a more luxuriant after-dinner treat.

Makes 16–18
50g/2oz creamed coconut, chilled
2 large (US extra large) egg whites
90g/3½ oz/½ cup caster (superfine) sugar
75g/3oz/1 cup desiccated (dry unsweetened shredded) coconut

1 Preheat the oven to 180°C/350°F/Gas 4. Line a large baking sheet with baking parchment. Finely grate the creamed coconut.

2 Use an electric beater to whisk the egg whites in a large bowl until stiff. Whisk in the sugar, a little at a time, to make a stiff and glossy meringue.

3 Fold in the grated coconut and desiccated coconut, using a large, metal spoon.

4 Place dessertspoonfuls of the mixture, spaced slightly apart, on the baking sheet. Bake for 15–20 minutes, until slightly risen and golden brown. Leave to cool on the parchment, then transfer to an airtight container.

Cook's Tip
The cooked macaroons can be stored in an airtight container for up to one week.

Variation
For a tangy flavour, add the grated rind of one lime to the mixture along with the coconut and fold in. You can also coat the cooked macaroons in melted plain (semisweet) chocolate.

Chewy Flapjacks: Energy 241kcal/1008kJ; Protein 2.7g; Carbohydrate 29.5g, of which sugars 14.3g; Fat 13.2g, of which saturates 7.2g; Cholesterol 30mg; Calcium 18mg; Fibre 1.4g; Sodium 125mg.
Coconut Macaroons: Energy 65kcal/270kJ; Protein 0.7g; Carbohydrate 5.7g, of which sugars 5.7g; Fat 4.5g, of which saturates 3.9g; Cholesterol 0mg; Calcium 4mg; Fibre 0.6g; Sodium 9mg.

Cinnamon Pinwheels

These impressive sweet pastries go well with tea or coffee for a late breakfast. If you find they turn soft during storage, re-crisp them briefly in the oven. Cinnamon is widely used in both sweet and savoury cooking: here ground cinnamon is used but it is also available as woody sticks. It has a delicious fragrant aroma and gives these simple-to-make pinwheels a warm spicy flavour.

Makes 20–24
50g/2oz/¼ cup caster (superfine) sugar, plus a little extra for sprinkling
10ml/2 tsp ground cinnamon
250g/9oz puff pastry
beaten egg, to glaze

1 Preheat the oven to 220°C/425°F/Gas 7. Grease a large baking sheet. Mix the sugar with the cinnamon in a small bowl.

2 Roll out the pastry on a lightly floured surface to a 20cm/8in square and sprinkle with half the sugar mixture. Roll out the pastry again, extending it to a 25cm/10in square so that the sugar is pressed into it.

3 Brush with the beaten egg and then sprinkle with the remaining sugar mixture. Loosely roll up the pastry into a log, brushing the end of the pastry with a little more egg to secure the edge in place.

4 Using a sharp knife, cut the log into thin slices and transfer them to the prepared baking sheet. Bake for 10 minutes, until golden and crisp. Sprinkle with more sugar and transfer to a wire rack to cool.

Cook's Tip
Serve these pastries with ice cream and other creamy desserts.

Coconut Ice

A great favourite with both adults and children, the ice is always sweet and juicy. However, if you've only ever eaten sweets made with dried coconut, you are about to experience a taste explosion.

Makes 16 squares each 5cm/2in
1 coconut
450g/1lb sugar
120ml/4fl oz/½ cup coconut milk
red food colouring

From the storecupboard
25g/1oz butter
flavourless oil, for greasing

1 Grease a 20cm/8in square cake tin (pan) or brush with a little flavourless oil.

2 Crack the coconut and drain off the milk into a bowl. Break open the shell, remove the flesh and grate it.

3 Put the sugar, reserved coconut milk and butter into a pan and bring to the boil over a low heat, stirring frequently, until the sugar has dissolved and the butter has melted. Gradually stir in the grated coconut and continue to boil, stirring constantly, for 10 minutes, until thickened. Remove the pan from the heat.

4 Divide the mixture between two bowls. Add a few drops of red food colouring to one batch and mix well to colour it pink. Leave the second batch uncoloured.

5 Firmly press the uncoloured coconut mixture into the prepared tin in an even layer. Cover with the pink, pressing it down evenly. Leave to set, then cut into squares with a sharp knife. These can be wrapped in individual cellophane parcels.

Cook's Tip
To crack a coconut, hold it firmly in one hand and pierce the eyes with a skewer. Pour the milk into a bowl. Hit the coconut all around the centre with a hammer and lever apart. Scoop out the flesh with a small knife and peel off the skin.

Cinnamon Pinwheels: Energy 47kcal/197kJ; Protein 0.6g; Carbohydrate 6g, of which sugars 2.3g; Fat 2.6g, of which saturates 0g; Cholesterol 0mg; Calcium 12mg; Fibre 0g; Sodium 33mg.
Coconut Ice: Energy 162kcal/683kJ; Protein 0.5g; Carbohydrate 30.2g, of which sugars 30.2g; Fat 5.2g, of which saturates 4.2g; Cholesterol 3mg; Calcium 19mg; Fibre 0.9g; Sodium 21mg.

Golden Ginger Macaroons

Macaroons are classic no-fuss biscuits – easy to whisk up in minutes from the minimum ingredients and always acceptable. A hint of ginger makes this recipe that bit different. For a darker colour and slightly richer flavour, use soft dark brown sugar instead. Bake these biscuits on non-stick baking trays or on a baking tray lined with baking parchment to stop them sticking.

Makes 18–20

1 egg white
75g/3oz/scant ½ cup soft light brown sugar
115g/4oz/1 cup ground almonds
5ml/1 tsp ground ginger

1 Preheat the oven to 180°C/350°F/Gas 4. In a large, grease-free bowl, whisk the egg white until stiff and standing in peaks, but not dry and crumbly, then whisk in the brown sugar.

2 Sprinkle the ground almonds and ginger over the whisked egg white and gently fold them together.

3 Using two teaspoons, place spoonfuls of the mixture on non-stick baking trays, leaving plenty of space between each. Bake for about 20 minutes, until golden brown and just turning crisp.

4 Leave to cool slightly on the baking trays before transferring to a wire rack to cool completely.

Nutty Nougat

Nougat is an almost magical sweetmeat that emerges from honey-flavoured meringue made with boiled syrup. Since any other nuts or candied fruits can be used instead of almonds, as long as you have eggs, sugar and honey, you have the potential for making an impromptu gift or dinner-party treat.

Makes about 500g/1¼lb

225g/8oz/generous 1 cup granulated (white) sugar
225g/8oz/1 cup clear honey or golden (light corn) syrup
1 large (US extra large) egg white
115g/4oz/1 cup flaked (sliced) almonds or chopped pistachio nuts, roasted

1 Line an 18cm/7in square cake tin (pan) with rice paper. Place the sugar, honey or syrup and 60ml/4 tbsp water in a large, heavy pan and heat gently, stirring frequently, until the sugar has completely dissolved.

2 Bring the syrup to the boil and boil gently to the soft crack stage (when the syrup dropped into cold water separates into hard but not brittle threads) or 151°C/304°F on a sugar thermometer.

3 Meanwhile, whisk the egg white until very stiff, but not crumbly, then slowly drizzle in the syrup while whisking constantly.

4 Quickly stir in the nuts and pour the mixture into the prepared tin. Leave to cool but, before the nougat becomes too hard, cut it into squares. Store in an airtight container.

Anglesey Shortbread

Originating on the island of Anglesey, these Welsh biscuits were decorated with a shell motif depicting the sign of pilgrims on their way to a holy site. They are moulded by pressing the dough into a queen scallop shell prior to baking.

Makes 12

50g/2oz/¼ cup caster (superfine) sugar, plus extra for sprinkling
150g/5½ oz/1¼ cups plain (all-purpose) flour

From the storecupboard

90g/3½ oz/7 tbsp butter, softened

1 Preheat the oven to 200°C/400°F/Gas 6. Then line a baking sheet with baking parchment.

2 Put the butter and sugar into a bowl and beat until light and fluffy. Sift the flour over and stir it in until the mixture can be gathered into a ball of soft dough.

3 Work the dough so that the warmth of your hand keeps the dough soft and pliable. Divide and shape it into 12 balls.

4 Sprinkle the inside of a scallop shell with sugar, gently press a ball of dough into it, spreading it evenly so the shell is filled. Invert on to the paper-lined sheet, pressing down to flatten the base and to mark it with the impression of the shell. Lift the shell off, carefully prising out the dough. Alternatively, press or roll the dough balls into plain biscuits (cookies).

5 Put into the hot oven and cook for about 10 minutes until set. Traditionally, they should not be allowed to brown, but they look very attractive and taste delicious with crisp golden edges.

6 Sprinkle with a little extra sugar, transfer to a wire rack and leave to cool completely.

Cook's Tip

Although moulding the first biscuit (cookie) may be tricky, the shell will become coated with sugar and the rest will slip out easily.

Ginger Macaroons: Energy 51kcal/211kJ; Protein 1.4g; Carbohydrate 4.3g, of which sugars 4.2g; Fat 3.2g, of which saturates 0.3g; Cholesterol 0mg; Calcium 16mg; Fibre 0.4g; Sodium 4mg.
Nutty Nougat: Energy 1177kcal/4907kJ; Protein 29.9g; Carbohydrate 85g, of which sugars 83.4g; Fat 82.2g, of which saturates 38.9g; Cholesterol 163mg; Calcium 799mg; Fibre 4.6g; Sodium 483mg.
Anglesey Shortbread: Energy 121kcal/506kJ; Protein 1.2g; Carbohydrate 14.1g, of which sugars 4.6g; Fat 7g, of which saturates 4.4g; Cholesterol 18mg; Calcium 21mg; Fibre 0.4g; Sodium 51mg.

Rich Chocolate Brownies

These brownies are packed with both milk and plain chocolate instead of adding sugar to the mixture. Serve them in small squares as they are very rich. When buying plain chocolate, bear in mind that the higher the percentage of cocoa solids, the higher the quality of the chocolate, and the less sugar it contains. The best quality has at least 70 per cent cocoa solids.

Makes 16
300g/11oz each plain (semisweet) and milk chocolate
75g/3oz/⅔ cup self-raising (self-rising) flour
3 large (US extra large) eggs

From the storecupboard
175g/6oz/¾ cup unsalted (sweet) butter

1 Preheat the oven to 180°C/350°F/Gas 4. Line the base and sides of a 20cm/8in square cake tin (pan) with baking parchment.

2 Break the plain chocolate and 90g/3½ oz of the milk chocolate into pieces and put in a heatproof bowl with the butter. Melt over a pan of barely simmering water, stirring frequently.

3 Chop the remaining milk chocolate into chunky pieces. Stir the flour and eggs into the melted chocolate until combined. Stir in half the chopped milk chocolate and turn the mixture into the prepared tin, spreading it into the corners. Sprinkle with the remaining chopped chocolate.

4 Bake the brownies for 30–35 minutes, until risen and just firm to the touch. Leave to cool in the tin, then cut the mixture into squares. Store the brownies in an airtight container.

Cook's Tip
Chocolate and butter can be softened in a microwave on high for a few seconds. Take care not to burn by leaving too long.

Rich Chocolate Biscuit Slice

This dark chocolate refrigerator cake is packed with crisp biscuit pieces and chunks of white chocolate for colour and flavour contrast. The slice is perfect served with strong coffee, either as a tea-time treat or in place of dessert. Once set, cut the cake into slices and store in an airtight container in the refrigerator until ready to serve.

Serves 8–10
275g/10oz fruit and nut plain (semisweet) chocolate
90g/3½ oz digestive biscuits (graham crackers)
90g/3½ oz white chocolate

From the storecupboard
130g/4½ oz/9 tbsp unsalted (sweet) butter

1 Grease and line the base and sides of a 450g/1lb loaf tin (pan) with baking parchment.

2 Break the fruit and nut chocolate into pieces and place in a heatproof bowl with the butter. Place the bowl over a pan of barely simmering water and stir the chocolate gently until it is melted and smooth. Remove the bowl from the pan and leave to cool for 20 minutes.

3 Break the biscuits into small pieces. Finely chop the white chocolate. Stir the biscuits and white chocolate into the melted mixture until evenly combined.

4 Turn the mixture into the prepared tin and pack down gently. Chill for about 2 hours, or until set. Turn out on to a chopping board. Cut the mixture into slices and store in an airtight container.

Variation
You can vary this ever-popular tea-time treat by using different flavoured chocolate, such as ginger, hazelnut, spice, honey and almond, raisin, peanut or mocha, or any other flavour you find that appeals.

Chocolate Brownies: Energy 285kcal/1190kJ; Protein 3.1g; Carbohydrate 29.6g, of which sugars 25.9g; Fat 18g, of which saturates 10.7g; Cholesterol 61mg; Calcium 37mg; Fibre 0.9g; Sodium 98mg.
Rich Biscuit Slice: Energy 326kcal/1361kJ; Protein 2.7g; Carbohydrate 29g, of which sugars 23.8g; Fat 23g, of which saturates 13.9g; Cholesterol 33mg; Calcium 44mg; Fibre 0.9g; Sodium 144mg.

Chocolate and Prune Refrigerator Bars

Wickedly self-indulgent and very easy to make, these fruity chocolate bars will keep for 2–3 days in the refrigerator – if they don't all get eaten beforehand, that is. Although the children will love them, try and reserve a few for an after-dinner treat with a glass of wine or a brandy.

Makes 12 bars

250g/9oz good quality milk chocolate
115g/4oz digestive biscuits (graham crackers)
115g/4oz/½ cup ready-to-eat prunes

From the storecupboard

50g/2oz/¼ cup unsalted (sweet) butter

1 Break the chocolate into small pieces and place in a heatproof bowl. Add the butter and melt in the microwave on high for 1–2 minutes. Stir to mix and set aside. (Alternatively, place the bowl over a pan of gently simmering water and leave until melted, stirring frequently.)

2 Put the biscuits in a plastic bag and seal, then bash into small pieces with a rolling pin. Roughly chop the prunes and stir into the melted chocolate with the biscuits.

3 Spoon the chocolate and prune mixture into a 20cm/8in square cake tin (pan) and chill for 1–2 hours until set. Remove the cake from the refrigerator and turn out on to a chopping board. Then, using a sharp knife, cut into 12 bars.

Cook's Tip

Serve these mouthwatering slices in pretty paper cases after dinner, with a glass of brandy for a special occasion.

Variation

Other dried fruits are just as good in these indulgent little bars. Try ready-to-eat apricots, figs, raisins or sultanas (golden raisins) for a fruity flavour.

Blueberry Cake

Cake mixes can make life very easy and are available in most supermarkets. For a professional finish, lightly dust with icing sugar and serve with cream for a tasty, simple dessert.

Serves 6–8

220g/8oz packet sponge cake mix
1 egg, if needed
115g/4oz/1 cup blueberries

1 Preheat the oven to 190°C/375°F/Gas 5. Grease a 20cm/8in cake tin (pan). Make up the sponge cake mix according to the instructions on the packet, using the egg if required. Spoon the mixture into the prepared cake tin.

2 Bake the cake according to the instructions on the packet. Ten minutes before the end of the cooking time, sprinkle the blueberries over the top of the cake. (Work quickly so that the cake is out of the oven for as short a time as possible, or it may sink in the middle.) Return the cake to the oven.

3 Once cooked, remove from the oven and leave the cake to cool in the tin for 2–3 minutes, then carefully remove from the tin and transfer to a wire rack. Leave to cool completely before serving.

Cook's Tip

Serve a slice of cake with a dollop of Marsala mascarpone for an impressive, but deceptively easy, dinner party dessert. To make, spoon 200g/7oz/scant 1 cup mascarpone into a large bowl and add 30ml/2 tbsp icing (confectioners') sugar and add 45ml/3 tbsp Marsala wine. Beat well until smooth and thoroughly combined.

Variation

You can make this light fruity cake with other soft fruits, such as raspberries, strawberries or blackberries.

Refrigerator Bars: Energy 197kcal/826kJ; Protein 2.5g; Carbohydrate 21.7g, of which sugars 16.4g; Fat 11.8g, of which saturates 6.8g; Cholesterol 18mg; Calcium 59mg; Fibre 0.9g; Sodium 102mg.
Blueberry Cake: Energy 167kcal/698kJ; Protein 2.3g; Carbohydrate 19g, of which sugars 11.3g; Fat 9.6g, of which saturates 2g; Cholesterol 39mg; Calcium 29mg; Fibre 0.7g; Sodium 115mg.

Orange Shortbread Fingers

These delicately scented cookies are a real tea-time treat and they would be the perfect choice for a leisurely summer afternoon sitting in the shade in the garden.

Makes 18

50g/2oz/4 tbsp caster (superfine) sugar, plus extra for sprinkling
finely grated rind of 2 oranges
175g/6oz/1½ cups plain (all-purpose) flour

From the storecupboard

115g/4oz/½ cup unsalted (sweet) butter at room temperature, diced

1 Preheat the oven to 190°C/375°F/Gas 5. Grease a large baking sheet. Beat together the butter and sugar until soft and creamy. Beat in the orange rind.

2 Gradually add the flour and gently pull the dough together to form a soft ball. Roll out the dough on a lightly floured surface to about 1cm/½ in thick.

3 Cut into narrow bars, sprinkle over a little extra caster sugar and place on the baking sheet.

4 Prick the surface with a fork and bake for about 20 minutes, until the cookies are a light golden colour. Transfer the cookies to a wire rack and leave to cool.

Cook's Tip

Store the cookies in plastic bags or an airtight container for up to 2 weeks.

Variation

Use the rind of 1 or 2 lemons in place of the orange rind. Remember to use unwaxed fruit and wash thoroughly before use.

Sweet Peanut Wafers

Delicate wafers filled with a sweet, peanut-flavoured buttercream make a fun, no-bake recipe that kids of any age can help with. Just remember to chill the wafer sandwiches after they have been assembled, otherwise they will be almost impossible to cut.

Makes 12

65g/2½ oz/generous ½ cup icing (confectioners') sugar
115g/4oz/½ cup crunchy peanut butter
12 fan-shaped wafers
50g/2oz plain (semisweet) chocolate

From the storecupboard

65g/2½ oz/5 tbsp unsalted (sweet) butter, at room temperature, diced

1 Put the butter and sugar in a bowl and beat with a wooden spoon, or a hand-held electric whisk, until very light and creamy. Beat in the peanut butter.

2 Using a small metal spatula, spread a thick layer of the mixture on to a wafer and spread to the edges. Place another wafer on top of the peanut buttercream and press it down very gently. Spread the top wafer with more buttercream, then place another wafer on top and press down gently.

3 Use the remaining buttercream and wafers to assemble three more fans in the same way. Spread any leftover buttercream around the sides of the fans. Chill for at least 30 minutes until firm.

4 Using a serrated knife, carefully slice each fan into three equal wedges and arrange in a single layer on a small tray.

5 Break the chocolate into pieces and put in a heatproof bowl placed over a pan of gently simmering water. Stir frequently until melted. Remove the bowl from the heat and leave to stand for a few minutes to cool slightly.

6 Drizzle lines of chocolate over the wafers, then leave to set in a cool place for at least 1 hour.

Orange Shortbread: Energy 92kcal/383kJ; Protein 1g; Carbohydrate 10.5g, of which sugars 3.1g; Fat 5.4g, of which saturates 3.4g; Cholesterol 14mg; Calcium 16mg; Fibre 0.3g; Sodium 39mg.
Peanut Wafers: Energy 184kcal/769kJ; Protein 3.7g; Carbohydrate 19.4g, of which sugars 9.1g; Fat 10.7g, of which saturates 4.8g; Cholesterol 12mg; Calcium 30mg; Fibre 0.6g; Sodium 79mg.

Almond Cigars

These simple, Moroccan-inspired pastries can be prepared in minutes. They are perfect served with strong black coffee or black tea at any time of day, or as an after-dinner treat. They are also delicious served with traditional sweet Moroccan mint tea. To serve, sprinkle with a little icing sugar as a pretty, yet simple, finishing touch.

Makes 8–12
250g/9oz marzipan
1 egg, lightly beaten
8–12 sheets filo pastry

From the storecupboard
melted butter, for brushing

1 Knead the marzipan until soft and pliable, then put it in a mixing bowl and mix in the lightly beaten egg. Chill in the refrigerator for 1–2 hours.

2 Preheat the oven to 190°C/375°F/Gas 5. Lightly grease a baking sheet. Place a sheet of filo pastry on a piece of baking parchment, keeping the remaining pastry covered with a damp cloth, and brush with the melted butter.

3 Shape 30–45ml/2–3 tbsp of the almond paste into a cylinder and place at one end of the pastry. Fold the pastry over to enclose the ends of the paste, then roll up to form a cigar shape. Place on the baking sheet and make 7–11 more cigars in the same way.

4 Bake the pastries in the preheated oven for about 15 minutes, or until golden brown in colour. Transfer to a wire rack to cool before serving.

Variation
Coat in syrup and sesame seeds after baking. Make the syrup by dissolving 150g/5oz/¾ cup sugar in 300ml/½ pint/1¼ cups water, add 15ml/1 tbsp lemon juice and bring to the boil.

Marshmallow Crispie Cakes

This is a delicious variation of a perennially popular childhood cookie, which even very young children will love to help make. The marshmallows make them wonderfully sticky.

Makes 45
250g/9oz bag of toffees
45ml/3 tbsp milk
115g/4oz/1 cup marshmallows
175g/6oz/6 cups crisped rice cereal

From the storecupboard
50g/2oz/¼ cup butter

1 Lightly brush a 20 x 33cm/8 x 13in roasting pan with a little oil. Put the toffees, butter and milk in a pan and heat gently, stirring until the toffees have melted.

2 Add the marshmallows and crisped rice cereal and stir until well mixed and the marshmallows have melted.

3 Spoon the mixture into the prepared roasting pan, level the surface and leave to set.

4 When cool and hard, cut into squares, remove from the pan, and put into paper cases to serve.

Cook's Tip
These crispy cakes can be made just as well with cornflakes, rather than crisped rice cereal. Simply put the required amount in a plastic bag and crush lightly with a rolling pin to break them up into smaller pieces.

Variation
Instead of using toffees, try using plain (semisweet) chocolate. Melt the chocolate by putting it into a heatproof bowl set over a pan of hot water on a low heat. Do not allow the water to touch the base of the bowl otherwise the chocolate may become too hot.

Almond Cigars: Energy 109kcal/458kJ; Protein 2.2g; Carbohydrate 18.9g, of which sugars 14.2g; Fat 3.2g, of which saturates 0.4g; Cholesterol 16mg; Calcium 25mg; Fibre 0.6g; Sodium 10mg.
Marshmallow Crispie Cakes: Energy 56kcal/235kJ; Protein 0.7g; Carbohydrate 9g, of which sugars 4.4g; Fat 2.2g, of which saturates 1.1g; Cholesterol 3mg; Calcium 39mg; Fibre 0g; Sodium 28mg.

Chocolate Truffles

Luxurious truffles are expensive to buy but very easy and fun to make. These rich, melt-in-the-mouth treats are flavoured with coffee liqueur, but you could use whisky or brandy instead. The mixture can be rolled in cocoa powder or icing sugar instead of being dipped in melted chocolate. Remember to store the fresh-cream truffles in the refrigerator.

Makes 24

350g/12oz plain (semisweet) chocolate
75ml/5 tbsp double (heavy) cream
30ml/2 tbsp coffee liqueur, such as Tia Maria, Kahlúa or Toussaint
225g/8oz good quality white or milk dessert chocolate

1 Melt 225g/8oz of the plain chocolate in a heatproof bowl set over a pan of barely simmering water. Stir in the cream and liqueur, then chill the mixture for 4 hours, until firm.

2 Divide the mixture into 24 equal pieces and quickly roll each into a ball. Chill for about 1 hour, or until the truffles are firm again.

3 Melt the remaining plain, white or milk chocolate in separate small bowls. Using two forks, carefully dip eight of the truffles, one at a time, into the melted plain chocolate.

4 Repeat to cover the remaining 16 truffles with the melted white or milk chocolate. Place the truffles on a board or tray, covered with baking parchment or foil. Leave to set before placing in mini paper cases or transferring to a serving dish.

Variations

Ring the changes by adding one of the following to the mixture:

- *Stir in 40g/1½oz/¼ cup chopped crystallized (candied) ginger.*
- *Stir in 50g/2oz/⅓ cup finely chopped crystallized fruit, such as pineapple and orange.*
- *Stir in 25g/1oz/¼ cup chopped skinned pistachio nuts.*
- *Roll each ball of chilled truffle mixture around a whole skinned hazelnut.*

Chocolate Petit Four Cookies

Make these dainty cookies as stylish after-dinner snacks. If you do not have any amaretto liqueur, they will work well without it. Alternatively, you can substitute the same quantity of brandy or rum.

Serves 8

350g/12oz carton chocolate chip cookie dough
115g/4oz plain (semisweet) chocolate
30ml/2 tbsp Amaretto di Sarone liqueur

From the storecupboard

50g/2oz/¼ cup butter

1 Preheat the oven according to the instructions on the cookie dough packet. Roll out the cookie dough on a floured surface to 1cm/½in thick. Using a 2.5cm/1in cutter, stamp out as many rounds from the dough as possible and transfer them to a lightly greased baking sheet. Bake for about 8 minutes, or until cooked through. Transfer to a wire rack to cool completely.

2 To make the filling, break the chocolate into small pieces and place in a heatproof bowl with the butter and Amaretto liqueur. Sit the bowl over a pan of gently simmering water and stir occasionally, until the chocolate has melted. Remove from the heat and set aside to cool.

3 Spread a small amount of the filling on the flat bottom of one of the cookies and sandwich together with another. Repeat until all the cookies have been used.

Praline Chocolate Bites

These delicate, mouthwatering little bites never fail to impress guests, but are quite simple to make. They are perfect for serving with coffee after dinner. Dust with icing sugar for a decorative finish.

Serves 4

115g/4oz/1 cup caster (superfine) sugar
115g/4oz/⅔ cup whole blanched almonds
200g/7oz plain (semisweet) chocolate

1 Put the sugar in a heavy pan with 90ml/6 tbsp water. Stir over a gentle heat until the sugar has dissolved. Bring the syrup to the boil and cook for about 5 minutes, without stirring, until the mixture is golden and caramelized.

2 Remove the pan from the heat and add in the almonds, swirling the pan to immerse them in the caramel. Transfer the mixture on to a lightly oiled baking sheet and set aside for 10–15 minutes, or until hardened. Meanwhile, melt the chocolate in a heatproof bowl set over a pan of simmering water.

3 Cover the hardened caramel mixture with clear film (plastic wrap) and break up with a rolling pin, then place in a food processor. Process until finely chopped, then stir into the melted chocolate. Chill until set enough to roll into balls. Roll the mixture into 16 balls and place in mini gold or silver paper cases to serve.

Chocolate Truffles: Energy 101kcal/421kJ; Protein 0.6g; Carbohydrate 6g, of which sugars 5.9g; Fat 8.1g, of which saturates 5g; Cholesterol 15mg; Calcium 7mg; Fibre 0.2g; Sodium 10mg.
Petit Four Cookies: Energy 317kcal/1327kJ; Protein 3.3g; Carbohydrate 37.7g, of which sugars 22.8g; Fat 17.1g, of which saturates 9g; Cholesterol 9mg; Calcium 42mg; Fibre 1.2g; Sodium 177mg.
Praline Bites: Energy 544kcal/2280kJ; Protein 8.7g; Carbohydrate 63.8g, of which sugars 62.6g; Fat 30.1g, of which saturates 9.7g; Cholesterol 3mg; Calcium 101mg; Fibre 3.4g; Sodium 9mg.

Stuffed Prunes

Prunes and plain chocolate are delectable partners, especially when the dried fruit is soaked in Armagnac. Serve these sophisticated sweetmeats dusted with cocoa powder as a dinner-party treat with coffee.

Makes about 30
225g/8oz/1 cup unpitted prunes
50ml/2fl oz/¼ cup Armagnac
150ml/¼ pint/⅔ cup double (heavy) cream
350g/12oz plain (semisweet) chocolate, broken into squares

1 Put the prunes in a bowl and pour the Armagnac over. Stir, then cover with clear film (plastic wrap) and set aside for 2 hours, or until the prunes have absorbed the liquid.

2 Make a slit along each prune to remove the pit, making a hollow for the filling, but leaving the fruit intact.

3 Heat the cream in a pan almost to boiling point. Put 115g/4oz of the chocolate in a bowl and pour over the hot cream.

4 Stir until the chocolate has melted and the mixture becomes smooth. Leave to cool, until the mixture has the consistency of softened butter.

5 Fill a piping (pastry) bag with a small plain nozzle with the chocolate mixture. Pipe into the cavities of the prunes. Chill for about 20 minutes.

6 Melt the remaining chocolate in a heatproof bowl set over a pan of barely simmering water. Using a fork, dip the prunes, one at a time, into the chocolate to coat them generously. Place on baking parchment to set.

Cook's Tip
Armagnac is a type of French brandy produced in the Gascogne region in the south-west of the country. It has a pale colour and a biscuity aroma. Other types of brandy can be used in this recipe.

Vanilla Fudge

Perennially popular, home-made fudge ends a meal beautifully when served as a petit four. This meltingly good vanilla version is sure to become a favourite.

Makes about 60 pieces
900g/2lb/4 cups soft light brown sugar
400g/14oz can condensed milk
2.5ml/½ tsp vanilla extract, or to taste

From the storecupboard
175g/6oz/¾ cup butter

1 Butter a shallow tin (pan), about 18 x 28cm/7 x 11in. Put the butter and 150ml/¼ pint/⅔ cup water into a large, heavy pan and warm very gently over a low heat until the butter melts.

2 Add the sugar and stir over a low heat until it has completely dissolved. Raise the heat and bring the mixture to the boil. Boil hard until it reaches hard crack stage (168°C/336°F on a sugar thermometer). Test by pouring a small amount into a saucer of cold water to form strands that can be cracked.

3 Remove from the heat and beat in the condensed milk with a wooden spoon. Return to a medium heat, stirring, for a few minutes.

4 Remove from the heat again, add the vanilla extract, and beat again with a spoon until glossy. Pour the mixture into the tin. Leave to cool.

5 Cut the fudge into cubes and store in an airtight container until required. Place in petits fours cases to serve.

Variations
- *For Coffee Fudge, add 30ml/2 tbsp coffee extract.*
- *For Almond and Raisin Fudge, omit the vanilla and add 2.5ml/½ tsp natural almond extract with 50g/2oz/½ cup chopped almonds and 50g/2oz/scant ½ cup chopped seedless raisins.*

Stuffed Prunes: Energy 100kcal/419kJ; Protein 0.9g; Carbohydrate 10.1g, of which sugars 9.9g; Fat 6.3g, of which saturates 3.8g; Cholesterol 8mg; Calcium 10mg; Fibre 0.8g; Sodium 7mg.
Vanilla Fudge: Energy 103Kcal/435kJ; Protein 0.7g; Carbohydrate 19.4g, of which sugars 19.4g; Fat 3.1g, of which saturates 1.9g; Cholesterol 9mg; Calcium 28mg; Fibre 0g; Sodium 28mg.

Brown Soda Breakfast Scones

These unusually light scones are virtually fat-free, so they must be eaten very fresh – warm from the oven if possible, but definitely on the day of baking. Serve with fresh, high-quality butter.

Makes about 16
225g/8oz/2 cups plain (all-purpose) flour
2.5ml/½ tsp bicarbonate of soda (baking soda)
225g/8oz/2 cups wholemeal (whole-wheat) flour
about 350ml/12fl oz/1½ cups buttermilk or sour cream and milk mixed
topping (optional): egg wash (1 egg yolk mixed with 15ml/1 tbsp water) or a little grated cheese

From the storecupboard
2.5ml/½ tsp salt
oil for greasing

1 Preheat the oven to 220°C/425°F/Gas 7. Oil and flour a baking tray. Sift the flour, bicarbonate of soda and salt in a bowl, add the wholemeal flour and mix.

2 Make a well in the centre, pour in almost all the liquid and mix, adding the remaining liquid as needed to make a soft, moist dough. Do not overmix.

3 Lightly dust a work surface with flour, turn out the dough and dust the top with flour; press out evenly to a thickness of 4cm/1½in. Cut out about 16 scones with a 5cm/2in fluted pastry (cookie) cutter.

4 Place on the baking tray and then brush the tops with egg wash, or sprinkle with a little grated cheese, if using.

5 Bake for about 12 minutes until well risen and golden brown.

Variation
For a more traditional scone mixture that keeps longer, rub 50g/2oz/¼ cup butter into the dry ingredients. Increase the proportion of the soda to 5ml/1 tsp if you like, as the scones will not be as light.

Chive and Potato Scones

These little scones should be fairly thin, soft inside and crisp on the outside. Traditionally served for what was once known as high tea, they are also excellent for breakfast.

Makes about 20
450g/1lb potatoes
115g/4oz/1 cup plain (all-purpose) flour
30ml/2 tbsp chopped fresh chives

From the storecupboard
30ml/2 tbsp olive oil, plus extra for greasing
salt and ground pepper

1 Peel the potatoes, chop into even chunks and cook in a pan of lightly salted, boiling water for about 20 minutes, until tender, then drain thoroughly.

2 Return the potatoes to the clean pan and mash them with a masher or fork. Preheat a griddle or heavy frying pan.

3 Add the flour, olive oil and chives to the mashed potato. Season to taste with salt and pepper. Mix to a soft dough.

4 Roll out the dough on a well-floured surface to a thickness of about 5mm/¼in and stamp out rounds with a floured 5cm/2in plain biscuit (cookie) cutter. Lightly grease the griddle or frying pan with a little olive oil.

5 Cook the scones in batches for about 10 minutes, turning once halfway through cooking.

Cook's Tip
Cook over a low heat to avoid burning the outsides before the insides are cooked.

Variation
If chives are not available, use softened onions instead.

Brown Soda Scones: Energy 117Kcal/493kJ; Protein 3.8g; Carbohydrate 20.9g, of which sugars 1.5g; Fat 2.6g, of which saturates 1.4g; Cholesterol 6mg; Calcium 49mg; Fibre 1.7g; Sodium 72mg
Chive and Potato Scones: Energy 46kcal/193kJ; Protein 1g; Carbohydrate 8.1g, of which sugars 0.4g; Fat 1.3g, of which saturates 0.2g; Cholesterol 0mg; Calcium 12mg; Fibre 0.5g; Sodium 3mg.

Tea Time Scones

Although the great British institution of tea time is fast becoming a memory, there are occasions when reviving the tradition is worthwhile – and serving these scones is one of them.

Makes 16
225g/8oz/2 cups plain (all-purpose) flour
2.5ml/½ tsp bicarbonate of soda (baking soda)
5ml/1 tsp cream of tartar
about 150ml/¼ pint/⅔ cup milk

From the storecupboard
25g/1oz/2 tbsp butter
pinch of salt

1 Preheat the oven to 220°C/425°F/Gas 7. Flour a baking sheet. Sift the flour, salt, bicarbonate of soda and cream of tartar together into a large bowl.

2 Rub in the butter until the mixture resembles breadcrumbs. Gradually stir in just enough milk to make a light spongy dough.

3 Turn out the dough on to a lightly floured surface and knead until smooth. Roll to 2.5cm/1in thick. Stamp out rounds with a floured 5cm/2in plain biscuit (cookie) cutter.

4 Place the scones on the prepared baking sheet and brush the tops with a little milk. Bake for 7–10 minutes, until the scones are well risen and golden brown.

Cook's Tip
The easiest way to keep cooked scones warm is to tuck them into a folded dish towel.

Variation
Replace the milk with buttermilk for a light and creamy taste. Serve fresh from the oven with home-made jam and clotted cream for a bite of heaven.

Orange and Pecan Scones

Serve these nutty orange scones with satiny lemon or orange curd or, for a simple, unsweetened snack, fresh and warm with unsalted butter. Scones are best served on the day they are made, or they can be frozen, if you prefer. To freeze, place in an airtight container. To thaw, remove from the freezer and thaw at room temperature for an hour.

Makes 10
225g/8oz/2 cups self-raising (self-rising) flour
grated rind and juice of 1 orange
115g/4oz/1 cup pecan nuts, coarsely chopped

From the storecupboard
50g/2oz/¼ cup unsalted (sweet) butter, chilled and diced
salt

1 Preheat the oven to 220°C/425°F/Gas 7. Grease a baking sheet. Put the flour in a food processor with a pinch of salt and add the butter. Process the mixture until it resembles coarse breadcrumbs.

2 Add the orange rind. Reserve 30ml/2 tbsp of the orange juice and make the remainder up to 120ml/4fl oz/½ cup with water. Add the nuts and the juice mixture to the processor, process very briefly to a firm dough, adding a little water if the dough feels dry.

3 Turn the dough out on to a floured surface and roll out to 2cm/¾ in thick. Cut out scones using a round cutter and transfer them to the baking sheet. Re-roll the trimmings and cut more scones. Brush the scones with the reserved juice and bake for 15–20 minutes. Transfer to a wire rack to cool.

Variations
- *To make wheatmeal scones, use half white and half fine wholemeal (whole-wheat) flour.*
- *For sultana (golden raisin) scones, replace pecans with 50–115g/2–4oz/⅓–⅔ cup sultanas with the sugar.*

Tea Time Scones: Energy 68kcal/288kJ; Protein 2g; Carbohydrate 11.8g, of which sugars 1.1g; Fat 1.8g, of which saturates 1g; Cholesterol 4mg; Calcium 43mg; Fibre 0.4g; Sodium 18mg.
Orange/Pecan Scones: Energy 191kcal/797kJ; Protein 3.1g; Carbohydrate 17.7g, of which sugars 0.8g; Fat 12.4g, of which saturates 3.3g; Cholesterol 11mg; Calcium 87mg; Fibre 1.2g; Sodium 11mg.

Crumpets

These yeast pancakes can be served hot and buttered, or with sweet or savoury accompaniments. Try them for breakfast, American style, with crispy bacon and a thin drizzle of clear honey or maple syrup. The best results come from using strong bread flour, though ordinary plain flour works well too.

Makes 8–10

225g/8oz/2 cups strong white bread flour or plain (all-purpose) flour
6.25ml/1¼ tsp quick or easy-bake yeast
150ml/¼ pint/⅔ cup milk
1 egg

From the storecupboard

2.5ml/½ tsp fine sea salt
15g/½ oz/1 tbsp butter
melted butter, for brushing

1 Sift the flour and salt into a large jug (pitcher) or bowl and stir in the yeast. Combine the milk with 150ml/¼ pint/⅔ cup water and add the butter. Warm gently (on the stove or in the microwave) until the liquid is lukewarm when tested with your little finger. With a whisk, beat in the egg. Still with the whisk, stir the liquid into the flour to make a thick smooth batter. Cover and leave to stand at room temperature for about 1 hour to allow the yeast to start working.

2 Preheat a bakestone or heavy frying pan over medium to medium-low heat. Brush melted butter on the inside of three or four metal rings (each measuring about 9cm/3½in) and lightly butter the hot bakestone or pan.

3 Place the metal rings on the hot surface. Pour a large spoonful of batter into each one. Alternatively, drop generous spoonfuls of batter on to the hot buttered surface to make pancakes about 9cm/3½in in diameter, allowing some space between each one for the spreading of the batter.

4 Cook for a minute or two until the underside is golden brown, bubbles have burst on the surface and the top is just set. Carefully remove the metal rings and gently turn the crumpets over. Cook the second side until light golden brown. Lift off and keep warm. Repeat with the remaining batter.

English Muffins

Perfect served warm, split open and buttered for breakfast or afternoon tea, these muffins are the ultimate comfort food, especially with a large spoonful of strawberry jam. Try these all-time favourites toasted, split and topped with ham and eggs for lunch.

Makes 9

450g/1lb/4 cups unbleached strong white bread flour, plus extra for dusting
350–375ml/12–13fl oz/1½–1⅔ cups lukewarm milk
2.5ml/½ tsp caster (superfine) sugar
15g/½oz fresh yeast

From the storecupboard

7.5ml/1½ tsp salt
15ml/1 tbsp melted butter or olive oil

1 Generously flour a non-stick baking sheet. Very lightly grease a griddle. Sift the flour and salt together into a large bowl and make a well in the centre. Blend 150ml/¼ pint/⅔ cup of the milk, sugar and yeast together. Now, stir in the remaining milk and butter or oil.

2 Add the yeast mixture to the centre of the flour and beat for 4–5 minutes, until smooth and elastic. The dough will be soft but just hold its shape. Cover with lightly oiled clear film (plastic wrap) and leave to rise, in a warm place, for 45–60 minutes, or until doubled in bulk.

3 Turn out the dough on a well floured surface and knock back. Roll out to about 1cm/½ in thick. Using a floured 7.5cm/3in plain cutter, cut out nine rounds.

4 Dust with rice flour or semolina and place on the prepared baking sheet. Cover and leave to rise, in a warm place, for about 20–30 minutes.

5 Warm the griddle over a medium heat. Carefully transfer the muffins in batches to the griddle. Cook slowly for about 7 minutes on each side, or until golden brown. Transfer to a wire rack to cool.

Crumpets: Energy 102kcal/432kJ; Protein 3.3g; Carbohydrate 18.2g, of which sugars 1.1g; Fat 2.3g, of which saturates 1.1g; Cholesterol 23mg; Calcium 53mg; Fibre 0.7g; Sodium 23mg.
English Muffins: Energy 60kcal/254kJ; Protein 1.5g; Carbohydrate 12.8g, of which sugars 6g; Fat 0.6g, of which saturates 0.2g; Cholesterol 14mg; Calcium 25mg; Fibre 0.3g; Sodium 8mg.

Quick and Easy Teabread

This succulent, fruity teabread can be served just as it is, or spread with a little butter. The loaf can be stored, tightly wrapped in foil or in an airtight container, for up to five days. A great way to get children to eat some fruit, this teabread is ideal for packed lunches, picnics, or simply served with a cup of tea for afternoon tea.

Serves 8

350g/12oz/2 cups luxury mixed dried fruit
75g/3oz/scant ⅓ cup demerara (raw) sugar, plus 15ml/1 tbsp
1 large (US extra large) egg
175g/6oz/1½ cups self-raising (self-rising) flour

1 Put the fruit in a bowl. Add 150ml/¼ pint/⅔ cup boiling water and leave to stand for 30 minutes.

2 Preheat the oven to 180°C/350°F/Gas 4. Grease and line the base and long sides of a 450g/1lb loaf tin (pan).

3 Beat the main quantity of sugar and the egg into the fruit. Sift the flour into the bowl and stir until combined.

4 Turn into the prepared tin and level the surface. Sprinkle with the remaining sugar.

5 Bake the teabread for about 50 minutes, until risen and firm to the touch. When the bread is cooked, a skewer inserted into the centre will come out without any sticky mixture on it. Leave the loaf in the tin for 10 minutes before turning out on to a wire rack to cool.

Variation

You can make a moist version of this simple teabread by adding 5ml/1 tsp mixed (apple pie) spice and a cup of 225ml/8fl oz/1 cup hot strong tea to the quick and easy teabread ingredients.

Sultana and Walnut Bread

This versatile bread is delicious with savoury dishes, but also tastes good with lashings of jam.

Makes 1 loaf

300g/11oz/2¾ cups strong white flour, plus extra for dusting
7.5ml/1½ tsp easy-blend (rapid-rise) dried yeast
115g/4oz/scant 1 cup sultanas (golden raisins)
75g/3oz/½ cup walnuts, roughly chopped

From the storecupboard

2.5ml/½ tsp salt
15ml/1 tbsp butter, plus melted butter, for brushing

1 Sift the flour and salt into a bowl, cut in the butter with a knife, then stir in the yeast.

2 Gradually add 175ml/6fl oz/¾ cup warm water to the flour mixture, stirring with a spoon at first, then forming the dough with your hands.

3 Turn the dough out on to a floured surface and knead for about 10 minutes until smooth and elastic. Knead the sultanas and walnuts into the dough until they are evenly distributed. Shape into a rough oval, place on a lightly oiled baking sheet and cover with oiled clear film (plastic wrap).

4 Leave to rise in a warm place for 1–2 hours, or until doubled in size. Preheat the oven to 220°C/425°F/Gas 7.

5 Uncover the loaf and bake in the oven for 10 minutes, then reduce the oven temperature to 190°C/375°F/Gas 5 and bake for a further 20–25 minutes. When cooked, transfer to a wire rack, brush with melted butter and cover with a dish towel. Cool before slicing.

Cook's Tip

Easy-blend dried yeast is sold in sachets at most supermarkets. It is a real boon for the busy cook because it cuts out the need to let the dough rise before shaping.

Teabread: Energy 236kcal/1004kJ; Protein 3.8g; Carbohydrate 56.1g, of which sugars 39.9g; Fat 1.1g, of which saturates 0.2g; Cholesterol 24mg; Calcium 117mg; Fibre 1.6g; Sodium 109mg.
Sultana Bread: Energy 1967kcal/8283kJ; Protein 42.4g; Carbohydrate 315.5g, of which sugars 86.4g; Fat 68.1g, of which saturates 12.6g; Cholesterol 32mg; Calcium 567mg; Fibre 14.2g; Sodium 1110mg.

Bakestone Bread

A loaf of bread that is cooked on the hob – watch it rise and marvel. The finished article has a distinctive appearance with a soft texture and scorched crust. If you have a bread machine, do use it on a short programme to make the dough and then continue from step 3. Make sure to use ordinary plain flour and not strong bread flour.

Makes 1 loaf
500g/1lb 2oz/4¼ cups plain (all-purpose) flour
5ml/1 tsp sugar
7.5ml/1½ tsp easy-blend (rapid-rise) yeast
150ml/¼ pint milk

From the storecupboard
5ml/1 tsp fine sea salt
15g/½ oz/1 tbsp butter, cut into small pieces
5ml/1 tsp oil

1 Put the flour into a large bowl and add the salt, sugar and yeast. Combine the milk with 150ml/¼ pint/⅔ cup water and add the butter. Heat gently until the liquid is lukewarm. Stir the liquid into the flour, then gather together to make a dough ball.

2 Transfer the dough on to a lightly floured surface and knead it until smooth, firm and elastic. Then put the oil in a large bowl and turn the dough in it until it is lightly coated. Cover the dough with clear film (plastic wrap) or a damp dish towel and leave to rise for about 1½ hours, or until just about doubled in size.

3 Turn out the dough on to a lightly floured surface and knead (gently this time) just until the dough becomes soft and stretchy. On the same floured surface, and using your hands or a rolling pin, press the dough into a rough circle measuring about 20cm/8in in diameter and 2cm/¾ in thick. Leave to stand for 15 minutes to allow the dough to relax.

4 Meanwhile, heat a bakestone or heavy frying pan over a medium heat. Using a wide spatula and your hands, lift the dough on to the warm surface and leave it to cook gently for 20 minutes. Turn the bread over – it may sink, but will soon start rising again. Gently cook the second side for about 20 minutes. The top and bottom should be firm and browned while the sides remain pale. Leave to cool on a wire rack.

Morning Rolls

These soft, spongy bread rolls are irresistible while still warm and aromatic. Made with milk, rather than the more usual water, they have a rich flavour. In Scotland they are a firm favourite for breakfast with fried eggs and bacon. To speed up the rising time, place the rolls in the airing cupboard or on the top of the preheated oven.

Makes 10 rolls
450g/1lb/4 cups unbleached strong white bread flour, plus extra for dusting
20g/¾ oz fresh yeast
150ml/¼ pint/⅔ cup lukewarm milk, plus extra for glazing

From the storecupboard
10ml/2 tsp salt

1 Grease two baking sheets. Sift the flour and salt together into a large bowl and make a well in the centre. Mix the yeast with the milk, then mix in 150ml/¼ pint/⅔ cup lukewarm water. Add to the centre of the flour and mix together to form a soft dough.

2 Knead the dough lightly in the bowl, then cover with lightly oiled clear film (plastic wrap) and leave to rise in a warm place for 1 hour, or until doubled in bulk. Turn the dough out on to a lightly floured surface and knock back (punch down).

3 Divide the dough into ten equal pieces. Knead lightly and, using a rolling pin, shape each piece of dough into a flat oval 10 x 7.5cm/4 x 3in, or a flat round 9cm/3½ in.

4 Transfer to the prepared baking sheets, spaced well apart, and cover the rolls with oiled clear film. Leave to rise, in a warm place, for about 30 minutes.

5 Meanwhile, preheat the oven to 200°C/400°F/Gas 6. Press each roll in the centre with the three middle fingers to equalize the air bubbles and to help prevent blistering. Brush with milk and dust with flour. Bake for 15–20 minutes, or until lightly browned. Dust with more flour and cool slightly on a wire rack. Serve warm.

Bakestone: Energy 1928kcal/8179kJ; Protein 52.2g; Carbohydrate 399.8g, of which sugars 18.8g; Fat 24.4g, of which saturates 10.8g; Cholesterol 41mg; Calcium 885mg; Fibre 15.5g; Sodium 2136mg.
Scottish Morning Rolls: Energy 160kcal/682kJ; Protein 4.7g; Carbohydrate 35.7g, of which sugars 1.4g; Fat 0.8g, of which saturates 0.3g; Cholesterol 1mg; Calcium 81mg; Fibre 1.4g; Sodium 401mg.

Split Tin Loaf

The deep centre split down this loaf gives it its name. The split tin loaf slices well for making thick-cut sandwiches, or for serving hearty chunks of bread to accompany robust cheese with a generous spoonful of pickle or relish.

Makes 1 loaf
500g/1¼lb/5 cups unbleached strong white bread flour, plus extra for dusting
15g/½oz fresh yeast
60ml/4 tbsp lukewarm milk

From the storecupboard
10ml/2 tsp salt

1 Grease a 900g/2lb loaf tin (pan). Sift the flour and salt into a bowl and make a well in the centre. Mix the yeast with 150ml/¼ pint/⅔ cup lukewarm water. Stir in another 150ml/¼ pint/⅔ cup lukewarm water. Pour the yeast mixture into the centre of the flour and using your fingers, mix in a little flour to form a smooth batter.

2 Sprinkle a little more flour from around the edge over the batter and leave in a warm place for about 20 minutes to 'sponge'. Add the milk and remaining flour; mix to a firm dough.

3 Lay the dough on a lightly floured surface and knead for about 10 minutes, until smooth and elastic. Place it in a lightly oiled bowl, cover with lightly oiled clear film (plastic wrap) and leave to rise in a warm place for 1–1¼ hours, or until nearly doubled in bulk.

4 Knock back (punch down) the dough and turn out on to a lightly floured surface. Shape it into a rectangle, the length of the prepared tin. Roll the dough up lengthways, tuck the ends under and place, seam side down, in the tin. Cover the loaf and leave to rise in a warm place for about 20–30 minutes.

5 Using a sharp knife, make one deep central slash. Dust the top of the loaf with a little sifted flour. Leave for 10–15 minutes. Meanwhile, preheat the oven to 230°C/450°F/Gas 8. Bake for 15 minutes, then reduce the oven temperature to 200°C/400°F/Gas 6. Bake for 20–25 minutes, until golden and it sounds hollow when tapped on the base. Cool on a wire rack.

Cottage Loaf

Create a culinary masterpiece from a few basic ingredients and experience the satisfaction of traditional baking. Serve this classic-shaped loaf to accompany home-made soup.

Makes 1 large round loaf
675g/1½lb/6 cups unbleached strong white bread flour
20g/¾oz fresh yeast

From the storecupboard
10ml/2 tsp salt

1 Lightly grease two baking sheets. Sift the flour and salt together into a large bowl and make a well in the centre.

2 Mix the yeast in 150ml/¼ pint/⅔ cup lukewarm water until dissolved. Pour into the centre of the flour and add a further 250ml/8fl oz/1 cup lukewarm water, then mix to a firm dough.

3 Knead the dough on a lightly floured surface for 10 minutes, until it is smooth and elastic. Place in a lightly oiled bowl, cover with lightly oiled clear film (plastic wrap) and leave to rise in a warm place for about 1 hour.

4 Turn out on to a lightly floured surface and knock back (punch down). Knead for 2–3 minutes, then divide the dough into two-thirds and one-third and shape each piece into a ball. Place the balls of dough on the prepared baking sheets. Cover with inverted bowls and leave to rise in a warm place for 30 minutes.

5 Gently flatten the top of the larger round of dough and cut a cross in the centre, about 4cm/1½in across. Brush with a little water and place the smaller round on top. Carefully press a hole through the middle of the top ball, down into the lower part, using your thumb and first two fingers. Cover with lightly oiled clear film and leave to rest in a warm place for about 10 minutes.

6 Preheat the oven to 220°C/425°F/Gas 7 and place the bread on the lower shelf of the oven. Bake for 35–40 minutes, or until a rich golden brown colour. Cool on a wire rack before serving.

Split Tin Loaf: Energy 1733kcal/7367kJ; Protein 49g; Carbohydrate 391.3g, of which sugars 10.3g; Fat 7.5g, of which saturates 1.6g; Cholesterol 4mg; Calcium 773mg; Fibre 15.5g; Sodium 3971mg.
Cottage Loaf: Energy 2302kcal/9788kJ; Protein 63.5g; Carbohydrate 524.5g, of which sugars 10.1g; Fat 8.8g, of which saturates 1.4g; Cholesterol 0mg; Calcium 946mg; Fibre 20.9g; Sodium 3950mg.

Granary Cob

Mixing and shaping a simple round loaf is one of the most satisfying kitchen activities. This bread is made with fresh yeast – it is a similar colour and texture to putty and should crumble easily when broken. For best results, buy fresh yeast in small quantities as required: it will keep for up to one month in the refrigerator.

Makes 1 round loaf
450g/1lb/4 cups Granary (multigrain) or malthouse flour
15g/½ oz fresh yeast
wheat flakes or cracked wheat, for sprinkling

From the storecupboard
12.5ml/2½ tsp salt

1 Lightly flour a baking sheet. Mix the flour and 10ml/2 tsp of the salt together in a large bowl and make a well in the centre. Place in a very low oven for 5 minutes to warm.

2 Measure 300ml/½ pint/1¼ cups lukewarm water. Mix the yeast with a little of the water, then blend in the rest. Pour the yeast mixture into the centre of the flour and mix to a dough.

3 Turn out on to a lightly floured surface and knead for about 10 minutes, until smooth and elastic. Place in a lightly oiled bowl, cover with lightly oiled clear film (plastic wrap) and leave to rise in a warm place for 1¼ hours, or until doubled in bulk.

4 Turn dough out on to a lightly floured surface and knock back (punch down). Knead for 2–3 minutes, then roll into a ball. Place in centre of the prepared baking sheet. Cover with an inverted bowl and leave to rise in a warm place for 30–45 minutes.

5 Preheat the oven to 230°C/450°F/Gas 8 towards the end of the rising time. Mix 30ml/2 tbsp water with the remaining salt and brush evenly over the bread. Sprinkle the loaf with wheat flakes or cracked wheat. Bake the bread for 15 minutes, then reduce the oven temperature to 200°C/400°F/Gas 6 and bake for a further 20 minutes, or until the loaf is firm to the touch and sounds hollow when tapped on the base. Remove from the oven and cool on a wire rack.

Grant Loaves

This quick and easy recipe was created by a baker called Doris Grant and was published in the 1940s. It is a dream for busy cooks as the dough requires no kneading and takes only a minute to mix. Nowadays we can make the recipe even quicker by using easy-blend yeast, which is added directly to the dry ingredients. Now there really is no excuse not to get baking.

Makes 3 loaves
1.3kg/3lb/12 cups wholemeal (whole-wheat) bread flour
15ml/1 tbsp easy-blend (rapid-rise) dried yeast
15ml/1 tbsp muscovado (molasses) sugar

From the storecupboard
15ml/1 tbsp salt
30ml/2 tbsp vegetable oil

1 Thoroughly grease three loaf tins (pans), each 21 x 11 x 6cm/ 8½ x 4½ x 2½in and set aside in a warm place.

2 Sift the flour and salt together in a large bowl and warm slightly to take off the chill.

3 Sprinkle the dried yeast over 150ml/¼ pint/⅔ cup lukewarm water. After a couple of minutes, stir in the muscovado sugar. Leave the mixture for 10 minutes.

4 Make a well in the centre of the flour. Pour in the yeast mixture and add a further 900ml/1½ pints/3¾ cups lukewarm water. Stir to form a slippery dough. Mix for about 1 minute, working the dry ingredients from the sides into the middle.

5 Divide among the prepared tins, cover with oiled clear film (plastic wrap) and leave to rise in a warm place for 30 minutes, or until the dough has risen by about one-third to within 1cm/ ½in of the top of the tins.

6 Meanwhile, preheat the oven to 200°C/400°F/Gas 6. Bake for 40 minutes, or until the loaves are crisp and sound hollow when tapped on the base. Turn out on to a wire rack to cool.

Granary Cob: Energy 1395kcal/5931kJ; Protein 57.1g; Carbohydrate 287.6g, of which sugars 9.4g; Fat 9.9g, of which saturates 1.4g; Cholesterol 0mg; Calcium 172mg; Fibre 40.5g; Sodium 4926mg.
Grant Loaves: Energy 1363kcal/5795kJ; Protein 55.1g; Carbohydrate 282.1g, of which sugars 14.3g; Fat 9.5g, of which saturates 1.3g; Cholesterol 0mg; Calcium 168mg; Fibre 39g; Sodium 1978mg.

Panini all'Olio

Italian-style dough enriched and flavoured with extra virgin olive oil is versatile for making decorative rolls. Children will love helping to make and shape these rolls. The rolls are sure to disappear as soon as they are cool enough to eat.

Makes 16 rolls
450g/1lb/4 cups unbleached strong white bread flour
15g/½ oz fresh yeast

From the storecupboard
10ml/2 tsp salt
60ml/4 tbsp extra virgin olive oil

1 Lightly oil three baking sheets. Sift the flour and salt together in a large bowl and make a well in the centre. Measure 250ml/8fl oz/1 cup lukewarm water. Cream the yeast with half the water, then stir in remainder. Pour into the well with the oil and mix to a dough.

2 Turn the dough out on to a lightly floured surface and knead for 8–10 minutes, until smooth and elastic. Place in a lightly oiled bowl and cover with lightly oiled clear film (plastic wrap). Leave to rise in a warm place for about 1 hour, or until nearly doubled in bulk.

3 Turn the dough on to a lightly floured surface and knock back (punch down). Divide into 12 and shape into rolls. To make twists, roll each piece of dough into a strip 30cm/12in long and 4cm/1½ in wide. Twist each strip into a loose spiral and join the ends together to make a circle. Place on the baking sheets. Brush lightly with olive oil, cover with lightly oiled clear film and leave to rise in a warm place for 20–30 minutes.

4 To make artichoke-shapes, shape each piece of dough into a ball and space well apart on the baking sheets. Brush with oil, cover with lightly oiled clear film and leave to rise in a warm place for 20–30 minutes. Using scissors, snip 5mm/¼ in deep cuts in a circle on the top of each ball, then make five larger horizontal cuts around the sides.

5 Preheat the oven to 200°C/400°F/Gas 6. Bake the rolls for 15 minutes.

Tuscany Bread

This Tuscan bread is made without salt and probably originates from the days when salt was heavily taxed in Italy. To compensate for the lack of salt, serve it with salty foods, such as olives, feta cheese, anchovies or salami.

Makes 1 loaf
500g/1¼ lb/4½ cups unbleached strong white bread flour, plus extra for dusting
15g/½ oz fresh yeast

1 Sift 175g/6oz/1½ cups of the flour into a large bowl. Pour over 350ml/12fl oz/1½ cups boiling water, leave for a couple of minutes, then mix well. Cover the bowl with a damp dish towel. Leave to stand for 10 hours or overnight.

2 Lightly flour a baking sheet and set aside. In a bowl, cream the yeast with 60ml/4 tbsp lukewarm water. Mix well into the flour mixture. Gradually add the remaining flour and mix to form a dough. Turn out on to a lightly floured surface and knead for 5–8 minutes, until smooth and elastic.

3 Place in a lightly oiled bowl, cover with lightly oiled clear film (plastic wrap) and leave to rise in a warm place for 1–1½ hours, or until doubled in bulk.

4 Turn the dough out on to a lightly floured surface, knock back (punch down) and shape into a round. Fold the sides of the round into the centre and seal. Place seam side up on the prepared baking sheet. Cover with oiled clear film and leave to rise in a warm place for 30–45 minutes, or until doubled in bulk.

5 Flatten the loaf to about half its risen height and flip over. Cover with a large upturned bowl and leave to rise again in a warm place for 30 minutes.

6 Meanwhile, preheat the oven to 220°C/425°F/Gas 7. Slash the top of the loaf, using a sharp knife, if you wish. Bake for 30–35 minutes, or until golden. Transfer to a wire rack to cool. Serve in slices or wedges.

Panini all'Olio: Energy 121kcal/509kJ; Protein 2.6g; Carbohydrate 21.9g, of which sugars 0.4g; Fat 3.1g, of which saturates 0.5g; Cholesterol 0mg; Calcium 39mg; Fibre 0.9g; Sodium 246mg.
Tuscany Bread: Energy 1713kcal/7286kJ; Protein 48.8g; Carbohydrate 388.7g, of which sugars 7.5g; Fat 6.6g, of which saturates 1g; Cholesterol 0mg; Calcium 704mg; Fibre 15.5g; Sodium 17mg.

Rosemary Focaccia

This simple dimple-topped Italian flatbread is punctuated with olive oil and the aromatic flavour of rosemary. Other herbs, such as oregano, sage or basil can also be used. Sprinkle the loaves with finely chopped garlic or chopped black olives, if you prefer.

Makes 2 loaves
675g/1½lb/4 cups strong white bread flour
15ml/1 tbsp easy-blend (rapid-rise) dried yeast
45ml/3 tbsp chopped fresh rosemary

From the storecupboard
75ml/5 tbsp olive oil
5 ml/1tsp salt

1 Put the flour and yeast in a large bowl with the salt. Stir in 45ml/3 tbsp of the oil and 450ml/¾ pint/scant 2 cups lukewarm water. Mix with a round-bladed knife, then by hand to a soft dough, adding a little more lukewarm water if the dough feels dry.

2 Turn the dough out on to a lightly floured surface and knead for 10 minutes, until smooth and elastic. Put in a lightly oiled bowl and cover with oiled clear film (plastic wrap). Leave in a warm place for about 1 hour, until doubled in size.

3 Preheat the oven to 200°C/400°F/Gas 6. Turn out the dough on to a floured surface and cut in half. Roll out each half into a 25cm/10in round. Transfer to greased baking sheets, cover with lightly oiled clear film, and leave for 20 minutes, until risen.

4 Press your fingers into the dough to make deep holes all over it about 3cm/1¼in apart. Leave for a further 5 minutes. Sprinkle with the rosemary and plenty of sea salt. Sprinkle with water to keep the crust moist and bake for 25 minutes, until pale golden. Remove from the oven and drizzle with the remaining olive oil. Transfer to a wire rack to cool.

Cook's Tip
If you do not need both loaves, freeze one for another time and warm it in the oven before serving.

French Baguettes

Fine French flour is available from French delicatessens and superior supermarkets. If you can't find it, use plain flour instead. Baguettes can be filled, sliced and toasted to serve with soup, or cut into chunks, buttered, and served with cheese.

Makes 3 loaves
500g/1¼lb/4½ cups unbleached strong white bread flour
115g/4oz/1 cup fine French plain (all-purpose) flour
15g/½oz fresh yeast

From the storecupboard
30ml/2 tbsp olive oil
10ml/2 tsp salt

1 Sift the flours and salt into a bowl. Add the yeast to 550ml/18fl oz/2½ cups lukewarm water in another bowl and stir. Gradually beat in half the flour mixture to form a batter. Cover with clear film (plastic wrap) and leave for about 3 hours, or until nearly trebled in size.

2 Add the remaining flour a little at a time, beating with your hand. Turn out on to a floured surface and knead to form a moist dough. Place in a lightly oiled bowl, cover with lightly oiled clear film and leave to rise, in a warm place, for 1 hour.

3 Knock back (punch down) dough, turn out on to a floured surface and divide into three equal pieces. Shape each into a ball and then into a 15 x 7.5cm/6 x 3in rectangle. Fold the bottom third up lengthways and the top third down and press. Seal the edges. Repeat two or three more times until each loaf is oblong. Leave to rest between folding for a few minutes.

4 Gently stretch each piece of dough into a 33–35cm/13–14in long loaf. Pleat a floured dish towel on a baking sheet to make three moulds for the loaves. Place the loaves between the pleats, cover with lightly oiled clear film and leave to rise in a warm place for 45–60 minutes.

5 Preheat the oven to maximum, at least 230°C/450°F/Gas 8. Roll the loaves on to a baking sheet, spaced well apart. Slash the top of each loaf diagonally several times. Place at the top of oven, spray the inside of the oven with water and bake for 20–25 minutes. Cool on wire racks.

Focaccia: Energy 1001kcal/4225kJ; Protein 22.4g; Carbohydrate 177.7g, of which sugars 6.2g; Fat 27.2g, of which saturates 4g; Cholesterol 0mg; Calcium 334mg; Fibre 8.1g; Sodium 505mg.
Baguettes: Energy 699kcal/2973kJ; Protein 19.3g; Carbohydrate 159.3g, of which sugars 3.1g; Fat 2.7g, of which saturates 0.4g; Cholesterol 0mg; Calcium 287mg; Fibre 6.4g; Sodium 1316mg.

Poppy-seeded Bloomer

This long, crusty loaf gets its fabulous flavour from poppy seeds. A variety of seeds can be used to add flavour, colour and texture to this loaf – sunflower, pumpkin and sesame seeds are all good alternatives. Brushing the loaf with the salted water before baking helps to give it a crisp finish. Cut into thick slices, the bread is perfect for mopping up the cooking juices of hearty stews, or for absorbing good dressing on summery salads.

Makes 1 large loaf
675g/1½lb/6 cups unbleached strong white bread flour
15g/½oz fresh yeast
poppy seeds, for sprinkling

From the storecupboard
30ml/2 tbsp olive oil
12.5ml/2½ tsp salt

1 Lightly grease a baking sheet. Sift the flour and 10ml/2 tsp salt into a large bowl and make a well in the centre.

2 Measure 450ml/¾ pint/scant 2 cups lukewarm water and stir a third into the yeast. Stir in remaining water and pour into the flour well. Mix, gradually incorporating the flour, to a firm dough.

3 Turn out on to a lightly floured surface and knead the dough well, for at least 10 minutes, until smooth and elastic. Place in a lightly oiled bowl, cover with clear film (plastic wrap) and leave to rise, at cool room temperature (about 15–18°C/60–65°F), for 5–6 hours, or until doubled in bulk.

4 Knock back (punch down) the dough, turn out on to a lightly floured surface and knead it thoroughly for about 5 minutes. Return the dough to the bowl and re-cover. Leave to rise, at cool room temperature, for a further 2 hours or slightly longer.

5 Knock back again and repeat the thorough kneading. Leave the dough to rest for 5 minutes, then roll out on a lightly floured surface into a rectangle 2.5cm/1in thick. Roll the dough up from one long side and shape it into a square-ended, thick baton shape about 33 x 13cm/13 x 5in.

6 Place the loaf, seam side up, on a lightly floured baking sheet. Cover with lightly oiled clear film and leave to rest for 15 minutes. Turn the loaf over and place on the greased baking sheet. Plump the loaf up by tucking the dough under the sides and ends. Using a sharp knife, cut six diagonal slashes on the top.

7 Leave to rest, covered, in a warm place, for 10 minutes. Meanwhile, preheat the oven to 230°C/450°F/Gas 8.

8 Mix the remaining salt with 30ml/2 tbsp water and brush this glaze over the bread. Sprinkle with poppy seeds.

9 Spray the oven with water, bake the bread immediately for 20 minutes, then reduce the oven temperature to 200°C/400°F/Gas 6. Bake for 25 minutes more, or until golden and it sounds hollow when tapped on the base. Transfer to a wire rack to cool.

Brown Soda Bread

Soda bread is best eaten on the day of baking, but it slices better if left to cool and 'set' for several hours. It is delicious with good butter, farmhouse cheese and some crisp sticks of celery or a bowl of home-made soup.

Makes 1 loaf
450g/1lb/4 cups wholemeal (whole-wheat) flour
175g/6oz/1½ cups plain (all-purpose) flour
7.5ml/1½ tsp bicarbonate of soda (baking soda)
about 450ml/¾ pint/scant 2 cups buttermilk

From the storecupboard
30ml/2 tbsp olive oil
5ml/1 tsp salt
sea salt

1 Preheat the oven to 200°C/400°F/Gas 6, and grease a baking sheet. Combine the dry ingredients in a mixing bowl and stir in enough buttermilk to make a soft dough. Turn on to a work surface dusted with wholemeal flour and knead until smooth.

2 Form the dough into a circle, about 4cm/1½in thick. Lay on the baking sheet and mark a deep cross in the top with a floured knife.

3 Bake for about 45 minutes, or until the bread is browned and sounds hollow when tapped on the base. Cool on a wire rack. If a soft crust is preferred, wrap the loaf in a clean dish towel while cooling.

Cook's Tip
Buttermilk can be cultured easily at home, using a 'buttermilk plant'. Cream 25g/1oz fresh yeast, 25g/1oz sugar and 950ml/2 pints/4 cups of tepid milk gradually. Pour the mixture into a well sterilized jug (pitcher). Cover and put in warm place to ferment. Leave until it smells like buttermilk, strain off the liquid and use. Pour tepid water over the lumps in the strainer to wash. Return to the jug and add more milk or milk and water to make more buttermilk.

Bloomer: Energy 2302kcal/9787kJ; Protein 63.5g; Carbohydrate 524.5g, of which sugars 10.1g; Fat 8.8g, of which saturates 1.3g; Cholesterol 0mg; Calcium 946mg; Fibre 20.9g; Sodium 3950mg.
Soda Bread: Energy 2262kcal/9643kJ; Protein 88.5g; Carbohydrate 465.4g, of which sugars 31.4g; Fat 18.9g, of which saturates 6.5g; Cholesterol 27mg; Calcium 1.37g; Fibre 34.2g; Sodium 2.18g.

Spring Onion Flatbreads

Use these flavoured flatbreads to wrap around barbecue-cooked meat and chunky vegetable salads, or serve with tasty dips such as hummus. They taste best if eaten as soon as they're cooked.

Makes 16
450g/1lb/4 cups strong white bread flour, plus extra for dusting
7g/¼ oz packet easy-blend (rapid-rise) dried yeast
4 spring onions (scallions), finely chopped

From the storecupboard
5ml/1 tsp salt

1 Place the flour in a large mixing bowl and stir in the salt, yeast and spring onions. Make a well in the centre and pour in 300ml/½ pint/1¼ cups hand hot water. Mix to form a soft, but not sticky, dough.

2 Turn out the dough on to a floured work surface and knead for about 5 minutes, until smooth. Put the dough back in the bowl, cover with a damp dish towel and leave in a warm place until doubled in size.

3 Knock back (punch down) the dough to get rid of any excess air and turn out on to a floured work surface. Divide the dough into 16 pieces and roll each piece into a smooth ball. Roll out each ball to a 13cm/5in round.

4 Heat a large frying pan until hot. Dust off any excess flour from one dough round and place in the frying pan. Cook for about 1 minute, then flip over and cook the other side for a further 30 seconds. Repeat with the remaining dough rounds until all are cooked.

Variation
To make garlic flatbreads, use 2 finely chopped garlic cloves in place of the chopped spring onions. To add extra bite, mix in 1 finely chopped fresh red chilli as well.

West Indian Flatbreads

Eclectic Caribbean food is influenced by a wide range of international cultures. It is the Anglo-Indian connection that brought the Indian flatbread called roti to Trinidad in the West Indies. Serve these simple-to-make breads straight from the pan to accompany spicy seafood chowders, curries, or any other dish that has plenty of sauce for mopping up.

Makes 8 rotis
450g/1lb/4 cups atta or fine wholemeal (whole-wheat) flour
5ml/1 tsp baking powder

From the storecupboard
30ml/2 tbsp vegetable oil
115–150g/4–5oz/8–10 tbsp clarified butter or ghee, melted
5ml/1 tsp salt

1 Mix the flour, baking powder and salt together in a large bowl and make a well in the centre. Gradually mix in 300ml/½ pint/1¼ cups water to make a firm dough.

2 Knead on a lightly floured surface until smooth. Place in a lightly oiled bowl, cover with lightly oiled clear film (plastic wrap). Leave to stand for 20 minutes.

3 Divide the dough into eight equal pieces and roll each one on a lightly floured surface into an 18cm/7in round. Brush the surface of each round with a little of the clarified butter or ghee, fold in half and half again. Cover the folded rounds with lightly oiled clear film and leave to rest for 10 minutes.

4 Take one roti and roll out on a lightly floured surface into a round about 20–23cm/8–9in in diameter. Brush both sides with some clarified butter or ghee.

5 Heat a griddle or heavy frying pan, add one roti at a time and cook for about 1 minute on the first side. Turn over and cook for 2 minutes, then turn over again and cook for 1 minute. Wrap the cooked rotis in a clean dish towel to keep warm while cooking the remaining ones. Serve warm with chowder or curry.

Onion Flatbreads: Energy 97kcal/410kJ; Protein 2.7g; Carbohydrate 21.9g, of which sugars 0.5g; Fat 0.4g, of which saturates 0.1g; Cholesterol 0mg; Calcium 40mg; Fibre 0.9g; Sodium 124mg.
West Indian Flatbreads: Energy 303kcal/1270kJ; Protein 7.1g; Carbohydrate 36g, of which sugars 1.2g; Fat 15.5g, of which saturates 7.1g; Cholesterol 0mg; Calcium 21mg; Fibre 5.1g; Sodium 2mg.

Tandoori Rotis

Indian flatbreads are fun to make at home: these may not be strictly authentic in terms of cooking method, but they taste fantastic. There are numerous varieties of bread in India, most unleavened. This bread would normally be baked in a tandoor, a clay oven that is heated with charcoal or wood. The oven becomes extremely hot, cooking the bread in minutes.

Makes 6 rotis

350g/12oz/3 cups atta or fine wholemeal (whole-wheat) flour

From the storecupboard

30ml/2 tbsp vegetable oil

30–45ml/2–3 tbsp melted ghee or butter, for brushing

5ml/1 tsp salt

1 Sift the flour and salt into a large bowl. Add 250ml/8fl oz/1 cup water and mix to a soft dough.

2 Knead on a lightly floured surface for 3–4 minutes, until smooth. Place the dough in a lightly oiled mixing bowl, cover with lightly oiled clear film (plastic wrap) and leave to rest for 1 hour.

3 Turn out the dough on to a lightly floured surface. Divide the dough into six pieces and shape each piece into a ball. Press out into a larger round with the palm of your hand, cover with lightly oiled clear film and leave to rest for 10 minutes.

4 Meanwhile, preheat the oven to 230°C/450°F/Gas 8. Place three baking sheets in the oven to heat. Roll the rotis out into six 15cm/6in rounds, place two on each baking sheet and bake for 8–10 minutes. Brush with ghee or butter and serve while still warm.

Cook's Tip

The rotis are ready when light brown bubbles begin to appear on the surface.

Pitta Bread

Soft, slightly bubbly pitta bread is a pleasure to make. It can be eaten in a variety of ways, such as Mediterranean-style filled with salad or little chunks of meat cooked on the barbecue, or it can be torn into pieces and dipped in savoury dips such as hummus or tzatziki.

Makes 12

500g/1¼lb/5 cups strong white bread flour, or half white and half wholemeal (whole-wheat)

12.5ml/2½ tsp easy-blend (rapid-rise) dried yeast

From the storecupboard

15ml/1 tbsp olive oil

15ml/1 tbsp salt

30ml/2 tbsp vegetable oil

1 Combine the flour, yeast and salt. Combine the oil and 250ml/8fl oz/1 cup water, then add half of the flour mixture, stirring in the same direction, until the dough is stiff. Knead in the remaining flour. Place the dough in a clean bowl, cover with a clean dish towel and leave in a warm place for at least 30 minutes and up to 2 hours.

2 Knead the dough for 10 minutes, or until smooth. Lightly oil the bowl, place the dough in it, cover again and leave to rise in a warm place for about 1 hour, or until doubled in size.

3 Divide the dough into 12 equal pieces. With lightly floured hands, flatten each piece, then roll out into a round measuring about 20cm/8in and about 4mm–1cm/¼–½in thick. Keep the rolled breads covered while you make the remaining pittas.

4 Heat a heavy frying pan over a medium-high heat. When hot, lay one piece of flattened dough in the pan and cook for 15–20 seconds. Turn over and cook for about 1 minute.

5 When large bubbles start to form on the bread, turn it over again. It should puff up. Using a clean dish towel, gently press on the bread where the bubbles have formed. Cook for a total of 3 minutes, then remove the pitta from the pan. Repeat with the remaining dough. Wrap the pitta breads in a clean dish towel, stacking them as each one is cooked. Serve the pittas hot while they are soft and moist.

Tandoori Rotis: Energy 226kcal/953kJ; Protein 7.4g; Carbohydrate 37.3g, of which sugars 1.2g; Fat 6.3g, of which saturates 2.6g; Cholesterol 0mg; Calcium 22mg; Fibre 5.3g; Sodium 329mg.
Pitta Bread: Energy 150kcal/638kJ; Protein 3.9g; Carbohydrate 32.4g, of which sugars 0.6g; Fat 1.5g, of which saturates 0.2g; Cholesterol 0mg; Calcium 58mg; Fibre 1.3g; Sodium 493mg.

Chilli Pooris

Pooris are small discs of dough that when fried, puff up into light airy breads. They will melt in your mouth.

Makes 12 Pooris
115g/4oz/1 cup unbleached plain (all-purpose) flour
115g/4oz/1 cup wholemeal (whole-wheat) flour
2.5ml/½ tsp chilli powder (optional)

From the storecupboard
2.5ml/½ tsp salt
30ml/2 tbsp vegetable oil
oil, for frying and oiling

1 Sift the flours, salt and chilli powder, if using, into a large bowl. Add the vegetable oil, then add about 100ml/3½fl oz/scant 1 cup water to mix to a dough. Turn out on to a lightly floured surface and knead for 8–10 minutes until smooth.

2 Place in a lightly oiled bowl and cover with lightly oiled clear film (plastic wrap). Leave to rest for 30 minutes.

3 Turn out on to a lightly floured surface. Divide the dough into 12 equal pieces. Keeping the rest of the dough covered, roll one piece into a 13cm/5in round. Repeat with the remaining dough. Stack the pooris, layered between clear film to keep moist.

4 Heat oil to a depth of 2.5cm/1in in a deep frying pan to 180°C/350°F. Using a metal spatula, lift one poori and gently slide it into the oil; it will sink but return to the surface and begin to sizzle. Gently press the poori into the oil. It will puff up. Turn over after a few seconds and cook for 20–30 seconds.

5 Remove the poori from the pan and drain on kitchen paper. Keep warm in a low oven while cooking the remaining pooris. Serve warm.

Variation
To make spinach-flavoured pooris, thaw 50g/2oz frozen chopped spinach, drain it well and add it to the dough with a little grated fresh ginger root and 2.5ml/½ tsp ground cumin.

Yemeni Sponge Flatbreads

These flatbreads, known as lahuhs and made from a batter, are bubbly and soft. They are eaten with soups but are also good with salads, dips or cheese.

Serves 4
15ml/1 tbsp active dried yeast
350g/12oz/3 cups plain (all-purpose) flour

From the storecupboard
50g/2oz/¼ cup butter, melted, or 60ml/4 tbsp vegetable oil
5ml/1 tsp salt

1 Measure 500ml/17fl oz/generous 2 cups lukewarm water. In a bowl, dissolve the dried yeast in about 75ml/5 tbsp of the water. Leave in a warm place for about 10 minutes, or until frothy.

2 Stir the remaining water, the flour, salt and melted butter or vegetable oil into the yeast mixture and mix until it forms a smooth batter. Cover with a clean dish towel, then leave in a warm place for about 1 hour, until doubled in size.

3 Stir the thick, frothy batter and, if it seems too thick to ladle out, add a little extra water. Cover and leave the batter to stand in a warm place for about 1 hour.

4 Cook the flatbreads in a non-stick frying pan. Ladle 45–60ml/3–4 tbsp of batter (or less for smaller breads) into the pan and cook over a low heat until the top is bubbling and the colour has changed. (Traditionally these breads are cooked on only one side, but they can be turned over and the second side cooked for just a moment, if you like.)

5 Remove the cooked flatbread from the frying pan with a spatula and keep warm in a clean dish towel. Continue cooking until you have used up all the remaining batter.

Cook's Tip
Use several frying pans at the same time so that the flatbreads are ready together and can be eaten piping hot.

Chilli Pooris: Energy 128kcal/536kJ; Protein 2.1g; Carbohydrate 13.6g, of which sugars 0.3g; Fat 7.7g, of which saturates 0.9g; Cholesterol 0mg; Calcium 17mg; Fibre 1.2g; Sodium 82mg.
Yemeni Flatbreads: Energy 392kcal/1651kJ; Protein 8.3g; Carbohydrate 68.1g, of which sugars 1.4g; Fat 11.4g, of which saturates 6.7g; Cholesterol 27mg; Calcium 125mg; Fibre 2.7g; Sodium 570mg.

Chilli and Herb Crackers

These spicy, crisp little crackers are very low in fat and ideal for serving as a nibble with drinks. They would also make an interesting alternative to bread or rolls served with a seafood appetizer.

Makes 12
50g/2oz/½ cup plain (all-purpose) flour
5ml/1 tsp curry powder
1.5ml/¼ tsp chilli powder
15ml/1 tbsp chopped fresh coriander (cilantro)

From the storecupboard
pinch of salt

1 Preheat the oven to 180°C/350°F/Gas 4. Sift the flour and salt into a mixing bowl, then add the curry powder and chilli powder and mix well.

2 Make a well in the centre and add the chopped fresh coriander and 30ml/2 tbsp water. Gradually incorporate the flour and mix to a firm dough.

3 Turn the dough out on to a lightly floured surface, knead until smooth, then cover and leave to rest for about 5 minutes.

4 Cut the dough into 12 even pieces and knead each one into a small ball. Roll each ball out very thinly to a 10cm/4in round, sprinkling more flour over the dough if necessary to prevent it from sticking to the rolling pin.

5 Arrange the dough rounds on two ungreased baking sheets, making sure there is plenty of space between them, then bake for 15 minutes, turning the crackers over once during cooking. Using a metal spatula, transfer the rounds to a wire rack to cool.

Variation
Omit the curry and chilli powders and replace with 15ml/1 tbsp caraway, fennel or mustard seeds for an aromatic but less spicy alternative.

Prosciutto Loaf

This savoury bread from Parma is spiked with the local dried ham.

Makes 1 loaf
350g/12oz/3 cups unbleached strong white bread flour, plus extra for dusting
15g/½ oz fresh yeast
40g/1½ oz prosciutto, torn into small pieces

From the storecupboard
7.5ml/1½ tsp salt
30ml/2 tbsp olive oil
5ml/1 tsp ground black pepper

1 Lightly grease a baking sheet and set aside. Measure out 250ml/8fl oz/1 cup lukewarm water. Sift the flour and salt into a bowl and make a well in the centre. In a small bowl, cream the yeast with 30ml/2 tbsp of the water, then gradually mix in the rest. Pour into the centre of the flour.

2 Gradually beat in most of the flour to make a batter. When most of the flour is incorporated, mix in the rest with your hand to form a moist dough. Knead on a lightly floured surface for 5 minutes until smooth and elastic. Place in an oiled bowl, cover with lightly oiled clear film (plastic wrap) and leave to rise in a warm place for 1½ hours, or until doubled in bulk.

3 Turn the dough out on to a lightly floured surface, knock back and knead for 1 minute. Flatten to a round, then sprinkle with half the prosciutto and pepper. Fold in half and repeat with the remaining ham and pepper. Roll up, tucking in the sides.

4 Place on the baking sheet, cover with oiled clear film. Leave to rise in a warm place for 30 minutes. Turn out on to a lightly floured surface, roll into an oval, fold in half and seal the edges. Flatten and fold again. Seal and fold again to make a long loaf.

5 Roll into a stubby long loaf. Draw out the edges by rolling the dough under the palms of your hands. Place back on the prepared baking sheet, cover with oiled clear film and leave to rise in a warm place for 45 minutes, or until the loaf has doubled in bulk. Preheat the oven to 200°C/400°F/Gas 6. Make 3–4 slashes in the top and bake for 30 minutes, or until golden. Transfer to a wire rack to cool. Serve in slices.

Chilli and Herb Crackers: Energy 16kcal/69kJ; Protein 0.5g; Carbohydrate 3.5g, of which sugars 0.1g; Fat 0.1g, of which saturates 0g; Cholesterol 0mg; Calcium 9mg; Fibre 0.2g; Sodium 1mg.
Prosciutto Loaf: Energy 1236kcal/5255kJ; Protein 40.3g; Carbohydrate 272.3g, of which sugars 5.7g; Fat 5.9g, of which saturates 1.1g; Cholesterol 23mg; Calcium 493mg; Fibre 10.8g; Sodium 490mg.

Pink Grapefruit and Cranberry Marmalade

Cranberries give this glorious marmalade an extra tartness and a full fruit flavour, as well as an inimitable vibrant colour. The resulting preserve makes a lively choice for breakfast or a brilliant accompaniment for cold roast turkey during the festive season.

Makes about 2.25kg/5lb

675g/1½lb pink grapefruit
2 lemons
225g/8oz/2 cups cranberries, fresh or frozen
1.3kg/3lb/6½ cups granulated (white) sugar, warmed

1 Wash and quarter the grapefruit, then slice them thinly, reserving the pips (seeds) and any juice that runs out. Juice the lemons, reserving the pips.

2 Tie the grapefruit and lemon pips in a muslin (cheesecloth) bag and place in a large pan with the grapefruit slices and lemon juice.

3 Add 900ml/1½ pints/3¾ cups water and bring to the boil. Cover and simmer gently for 1½–2 hours, or until the grapefruit rind is tender. Remove the muslin bag, leave to cool, then squeeze over the pan.

4 Add the cranberries, then bring to the boil. Simmer for 15–20 minutes, or until the berries have popped and softened.

5 Add the sugar to the pan and stir over a low heat until the sugar has completely dissolved. Bring to the boil and boil rapidly for about 10 minutes, or until setting point is reached (105°C/220°F).

6 Remove the pan from the heat and skim off any scum from the surface using a slotted spoon. Leave to cool for 5–10 minutes, then stir and pour into warmed sterilized jars. Seal, then label when the marmalade is cold.

Ruby Red Grapefruit Marmalade

If you like a really tangy marmalade, grapefruit is the perfect choice. To achieve a wonderfully red-blushed preserve, look for the red variety rather than pink. They have a wonderful flavour and make a sweet, jewel-coloured preserve.

Makes about 1.8kg/4lb

900g/2lb ruby red grapefruit
1 lemon
1.3kg/3lb/6½ cups granulated (white) sugar, warmed

1 Wash the grapefruit and lemon and remove the rind in thick pieces using a vegetable peeler. Cut the fruit in half and squeeze the juice into a preserving pan, reserving all the pips (seeds).

2 Put the pips and membranes from the fruit in a muslin (cheesecloth) bag and add to the pan. Discard the grapefruit and lemon shells.

3 Using a sharp knife, cut the grapefruit and lemon rind into thin or coarse shreds, as preferred, and place in the pan.

4 Add 1.2 litres/2 pints/5 cups water and bring to the boil. Cover and simmer for 2 hours, or until the rind is very tender.

5 Remove the muslin bag from the pan, leave to cool, then squeeze it over the pan. Add the sugar and stir over a low heat until it has dissolved. Bring to the boil, then boil rapidly for 10–15 minutes, or to setting point (105°C/220°F).

6 Remove the pan from the heat and skim off any scum using a slotted spoon. Leave to cool for about 10 minutes, then stir and pour into warmed sterilized jars. Seal, then label when cold.

Cook's Tip

Although you can use yellow grapefruit to make this marmalade, it tends to give a very pale result with more tang than the ruby red variety, but a much less fruity flavour.

Grapefruit and Cranberry: Energy 5403kcal/23,043kJ; Protein 12.6g; Carbohydrate 1424.4g, of which sugars 1424.4g; Fat 0.9g, of which saturates 0g; Cholesterol 0mg; Calcium 853mg; Fibre 12.4g; Sodium 103mg.
Ruby Red Grapefruit: Energy 5392kcal/22,987kJ; Protein 13.7g; Carbohydrate 1419.7g, of which sugars 1419.7g; Fat 0.9g, of which saturates 0g; Cholesterol 0mg; Calcium 896mg; Fibre 11.7g; Sodium 105mg.

Oxford Marmalade

The characteristic caramel colour and the intensely rich flavour of a traditional Oxford marmalade is obtained by cutting the fruit coarsely and cooking it for several hours before adding the sugar.

Makes about 2.25kg/5lb
900g/2lb Seville (Temple) oranges
1.3kg/3lb/6½ cups granulated (white) sugar, warmed

1 Scrub the orange skins, then remove the rind using a vegetable peeler. Thickly slice the rind and put in a large pan.

2 Chop the fruit, reserving the pips (seeds), and add to the rind in the pan, along with 1.75 litres/3 pints/7½ cups water. Tie the orange pips (seeds) in a piece of muslin (cheesecloth) and add to the pan. Bring to the boil, then cover and simmer for 2 hours. Add more water during cooking to maintain the same volume. Remove from the heat and leave overnight.

3 The next day, remove the muslin bag from the oranges, squeezing well, and return the pan to the heat. Bring to the boil, then cover and simmer for 1 hour.

4 Add the warmed sugar to the pan, then slowly bring the mixture to the boil, stirring until the sugar has dissolved completely. Increase the heat and boil rapidly for about 15 minutes, or until setting point is reached (105°C/220°F).

5 Remove the pan from the heat and skim off any scum from the surface. Leave to cool for about 5 minutes, stir, then pour into warmed sterilized jars and seal. When cold, label, then store in a cool, dark place.

Cook's Tip
Traditionalists say that only bitter oranges such as Seville (Temple) should be used to make marmalade. Although this isn't always true, it is certainly the case when making Oxford marmalade.

St Clement's Marmalade

This classic preserve made from oranges and lemons has a lovely citrus tang. It has a light, refreshing flavour and is perfect for serving for breakfast, spread on freshly toasted bread.

Makes about 2.25kg/5lb
450g/1lb Seville (Temple) oranges
450g/1lb clementines
4 lemons
1.2kg/2½lb/5½ cups granulated (white) sugar, warmed

1 Wash the oranges and lemons, then halve and squeeze the juice into a large pan. Tie the pips (seeds) and membranes in a muslin (cheesecloth) bag, shred the orange and lemon rind and add to the pan.

2 Add 1.5 litres/2½ pints/6¼ cups water to the pan, bring to the boil, then cover and simmer for 2 hours. Remove the muslin bag, leave to cool, then squeeze any liquid back into the pan.

3 Add the warmed sugar to the pan and stir over a low heat until completely dissolved. Bring to the boil and boil rapidly for about 15 minutes, or until the marmalade reaches setting point (105°C/220°F).

4 Remove the pan from the heat and skim off any scum from the surface. Leave to cool for about 5 minutes, stir, then pour into warmed sterilized jars and seal. When cold, label, then store in a cool, dark place.

Cook's Tip
Any member of the mandarin family can be used to make this preserve, but clementines tend to give the best result.

Variation
Add 60ml/4 tbsp of Grand Marnier or Cointreau to give the marmalade a potent kick. Serve it, mixed with natural (plain) yogurt, on pancakes for a special breakfast treat.

Oxford: Energy 5455kcal/23,275kJ; Protein 16.4g; Carbohydrate 1435g, of which sugars 1435g; Fat 0.9g, of which saturates 0g; Cholesterol 0mg; Calcium 1112mg; Fibre 15.3g; Sodium 123mg.
St Clement's: Energy 5061kcal/21,594kJ; Protein 15.9g; Carbohydrate 1330.5g, of which sugars 1330.5g; Fat 0.9g, of which saturates 0g; Cholesterol 0mg; Calcium 1059mg; Fibre 15.3g; Sodium 117mg.

Three-fruit Marmalade

Seville oranges have a powerful flavour and plenty of setting power to make an excellent preserve. These bitter oranges are usually only available for a short time in January – but sweet oranges can be used.

Makes 2.25kg/5lb

2 Seville (Temple) oranges
2 lemons
1 grapefruit
1.5kg/3lb 6oz/6¾ cups granulated (white) sugar

1 Wash the fruit, halve, and squeeze their juice. Pour into a large heavy pan or preserving pan. Place the pips (seeds) and pulp into a square of muslin (cheesecloth), gather the sides into a bag and tie the neck. Tie the bag to the pan handle so that it dangles in the juice.

2 Remove and discard the membranes and pith from the citrus skins and cut the rinds into slivers. Add to the pan with 1.75 litres/3 pints/7½ cups water. Heat until simmering, then cook gently for 2 hours, or until the rinds are soft and tender.

3 Remove the muslin bag, squeezing the juice into the pan. Discard the bag. Stir the sugar into the pan and heat very gently, stirring occasionally, until the sugar has dissolved.

4 Bring the mixture to the boil and boil for 10–15 minutes, or until the marmalade registers 105°C/220°F on a sugar thermometer. Alternatively, test the marmalade for setting by pouring a small amount on to a chilled saucer. Chill for 3 minutes, then push the marmalade with your finger: if wrinkles form on the surface, it is ready. Cool for 15 minutes.

5 Stir the marmalade and pour it into warm, sterilized jars. Cover with waxed paper discs. Seal and label when cold.

Cook's Tip

Allow the marmalade to cool slightly before potting so that it is thick enough to stop the fruit from sinking in the jars.

Spiced Poached Kumquats

Warm cinnamon and star anise make a heady combination with the full citrus flavour of kumquats. Star anise is an attractive spice: it is an eight-pointed star that contains tiny aniseed-flavoured, amber coloured seeds. The kumquats go well with rich meats, such as roast pork or baked ham, or with punchy goat's milk cheese. They are also good with desserts and ice creams.

Serves 6

450g/1lb/4 cups kumquats
115g/4oz/½ cup caster (superfine) sugar
1 small cinnamon stick
1 star anise

1 Cut the kumquats in half and discard the pips (seeds). Place the kumquats in a pan with the caster sugar, 150ml/¼ pint/⅔ cup water and the cinnamon stick and star anise. Cook over a gentle heat, stirring until the sugar has dissolved.

2 Increase the heat, cover the pan and boil the mixture for about 8–10 minutes, until the kumquats are tender. To bottle the kumquats, spoon them into warm, sterilized jars, seal and label.

3 If you want to serve the spiced kumquats soon after making them, let the mixture cool, then chill it.

Cook's Tips

- *Use half the quantity of kumquats and half of limequats – their green coloured-cousins – in this recipe for a highly decorative preserve.*
- *Kumquats (and limequats) are unusual among the citrus family because they can be eaten whole and do not need to be peeled, although it is advisable to cook or preserve them first. Their thin skins have a pleasantly bitter flavour.*

Marmalade: Energy 6106kcal/26,049kJ; Protein 13.2g; Carbohydrate 1612.4g, of which sugars 1612.4g; Fat 0.6g, of which saturates 0g; Cholesterol 0mg; Calcium 1020mg; Fibre 8.9g; Sodium 115mg.
Spiced Kumquats: Energy 103kcal/441kJ; Protein 0.8g; Carbohydrate 26.6g, of which sugars 26.6g; Fat 0.1g, of which saturates 0g; Cholesterol 0mg; Calcium 33mg; Fibre 0.9g; Sodium 4mg.

Blueberry and Lime Jam

The subtle yet fragrant flavour of blueberries can be elusive on its own. Adding a generous quantity of tangy lime juice enhances their flavour and gives this jam a wonderful zesty taste.

Makes about 1.3kg/3lb

1.3kg/3lb/12 cups blueberries
finely pared rind and juice of 4 limes
1kg/2¼lb/5 cups preserving sugar with pectin

1 Put the blueberries, lime juice and half the sugar in a large, non-metallic bowl and lightly crush the berries using a potato masher. Set aside for about 4 hours.

2 Transfer the crushed berry mixture into a pan and stir in the finely pared lime rind together with the remaining preserving sugar. Heat slowly, stirring continuously, until the sugar has completely dissolved.

3 Increase the heat and bring to the boil. Boil rapidly for about 4 minutes, or until the jam reaches setting point (105°C/220°F).

4 Remove the pan from the heat and set aside for 5 minutes. Stir the jam gently, then pour into warmed sterilized jars. Seal the jars, then label when completely cool. Store in a cool, dark place.

Cook's Tip
Blueberries are not naturally high in pectin, so extra pectin is needed for a good set. If you prefer, use granulated (white) sugar and add pectin according to the instruction on the packet in place of the preserving sugar with pectin.

Variation
You can replace the lime juice with lemon juice or the juice of sharp oranges, such as Seville (Temple) oranges, to give a citrusy zing.

Strawberry Jam

This is the classic fragrant preserve for English afternoon tea, served with freshly baked scones and clotted cream. It is also extremely good stirred into plain yogurt for breakfast. When selecting strawberries for making jam, choose undamaged, slightly under-ripe fruit if possible – the pectin content will be high and ensure a good set.

Makes about 1.3kg/3lb

1kg/2¼lb/8 cups small strawberries
900g/2lb/4 cups granulated (white) sugar
juice of 2 lemons

1 Layer the strawberries and sugar in a large bowl. Cover and leave overnight.

2 The next day, scrape the strawberries and their juice into a large, heavy pan. Add the lemon juice. Gradually bring to the boil over a low heat, stirring until the sugar has dissolved.

3 Boil steadily for 10–15 minutes, or until the jam registers 105°C/220°F on a sugar thermometer. Alternatively, test for setting by spooning a small amount on to a chilled saucer. Chill for 3 minutes, then push the jam with your finger: if wrinkles form on the surface, it is ready. Cool for 10 minutes.

4 Stir the jam before pouring it into warm sterilized jars, filling them right to the top. Cover with waxed paper discs immediately, but do not seal with lids until the jam is completely cold.

Cook's Tip
For best results when making jam, avoid washing the strawberries unless absolutely necessary. Instead, brush off any dirt, or wipe the strawberries with a damp cloth. If you have to wash any, pat them dry and then spread them out on a clean dish towel to dry.

Blueberry Jam: Energy 4265kcal/18,162kJ; Protein 16.7g; Carbohydrate 1111.3g, of which sugars 1111.3g; Fat 2.6g, of which saturates 0g; Cholesterol 0mg; Calcium 1063mg; Fibre 40.3g; Sodium 86mg.
Strawberry Jam: Energy 3816kcal/16,259kJ; Protein 12.5g; Carbohydrate 1000.5g, of which sugars 1000.5g; Fat 1g, of which saturates 0g; Cholesterol 0mg; Calcium 637mg; Fibre 11g; Sodium 114mg.

Greengage and Almond Jam

This is the perfect preserve to make when greengages are readily available in stores, or if you find you have a glut of the fruit. It has a gloriously rich, golden honey colour and a smooth texture that contrasts wonderfully with the little slivers of almond.

Makes about 1.3kg/3lb
1.3kg/3lb greengages, stoned (pitted)
juice of 1 lemon
50g/2oz/½ cup blanched almonds, cut into thin slivers
1.3kg/3lb/6½ cups granulated (white) sugar, warmed

1 Put the greengages and 350ml/12fl oz/1½ cups water in a preserving pan with the lemon juice and almond slivers. Bring to the boil, then cover and simmer for 15–20 minutes, or until the greengages are really soft.

2 Add the sugar to the pan and stir over a low heat until the sugar has dissolved. Bring to the boil and cook for 10–15 minutes, or until the jam reaches setting point (105°C/220°F).

3 Remove the pan from the heat and skim off any scum from the surface using a slotted spoon.

4 Leave to cool for 10 minutes, then stir gently and pour into warmed sterilized jars. Seal, then leave to cool completely before labelling. Store in a cool place.

Cook's Tip
Greengages look like unripened plums. However, despite their appearance, they have a wonderfully aromatic flavour that is captured perfectly in this delicious jam.

Variation
Almonds, coarsely chopped, work well with dried apricots to make a deliciously rich jam.

Lemon Curd

This classic tangy, creamy curd is still one of the most popular of all the curds. It is delicious spread thickly over freshly baked white bread or served with American-style pancakes, and also makes a wonderfully rich, zesty sauce spooned over fresh fruit tarts.

Makes about 450g/1lb
3 unwaxed lemons
200g/7oz/1 cup caster (superfine) sugar
2 large (US extra large) eggs
2 large (US extra large) egg yolks

From the storecupboard
115g/4oz/½ cup unsalted (sweet) butter, diced

1 Wash the lemons, then finely grate the rind and place in a large heatproof bowl. Using a sharp knife, halve the lemons and squeeze the juice into the bowl. Set over a pan of gently simmering water and add the sugar and butter. Stir until the sugar has dissolved and the butter melted.

2 Put the eggs and yolks in a bowl and beat together with a fork. Pour the eggs through a sieve (strainer) into the lemon mixture, and whisk well until thoroughly combined.

3 Stir the mixture constantly in the bowl over the pan of simmering water until the lemon curd thickens and lightly coats the back of a wooden spoon.

4 Remove the pan from the heat and pour the curd into small, warmed sterilized jars. Cover, seal and label. Store in a cool, dark place, ideally in the refrigerator. Use within 3 months. (Once opened, store in the refrigerator.)

Cook's Tip
If you are really impatient when it comes to cooking, it is possible to cook the curd in a heavy pan directly over a low heat. However, you really need to watch it like a hawk to avoid the mixture curdling. If the curd looks as though it's beginning to curdle, plunge the base of the pan in cold water and beat vigorously.

Greengage Jam: Energy 5896kcal/25,135kJ; Protein 24.9g; Carbohydrate 1476.3g, of which sugars 1475g; Fat 29.2g, of which saturates 2.2g; Cholesterol 0mg; Calcium 978mg; Fibre 24.5g; Sodium 111mg.
Lemon Curd: Energy 1927kcal/8056kJ; Protein 20.7g; Carbohydrate 212.1g, of which sugars 212.1g; Fat 116.8g, of which saturates 66.2g; Cholesterol 1029mg; Calcium 294mg; Fibre 0g; Sodium 871mg.

Damson Jam

Dark, plump damsons used only to be found growing in the wild, but today they are available commercially. They produce a deeply coloured and richly flavoured jam that makes a delicious treat spread on toasted English muffins or warm crumpets at tea time.

Makes about 2kg/4½lb

1kg/2¼lb damsons or wild plums
1kg/2¼lb/5 cups preserving or granulated (white) sugar, warmed

1 Put the damsons in a preserving pan and pour in 1.4 litres/2¼ pints/6 cups water. Bring to the boil. Reduce the heat and simmer gently until the damsons are soft, then stir in the sugar.

2 Bring the mixture to the boil, skimming off stones as they rise. Boil to setting point (105°C/220°F). Leave to cool for 10 minutes, then pour into jars. Seal, then label when cool. Store in a cool dark place.

Cook's Tip
It is important to seal the jars as soon as you have filled them to ensure the jam remains sterile. However, you should then leave the jars to cool completely before labelling and storing them to avoid the risk of burns.

Blackcurrant Jam

This jam has a rich, fruity flavour and a wonderfully deep colour. It is punchy and delicious with scones for tea or spread on croissants for a continental-style breakfast. The perfect comforting jam on a slice of toast.

Makes about 1.3kg/3lb

1.3kg/3lb/12 cups blackcurrants
grated rind and juice of 1 orange
1.3kg/3lb/6½ cups granulated (white) sugar, warmed
30ml/2 tbsp cassis (optional)

1 Place the blackcurrants, orange rind and juice and 475ml/16fl oz/2 cups water in a large heavy pan. Bring to the boil, reduce the heat and simmer for 30 minutes.

2 Add the warmed sugar to the pan and stir over a low heat until the sugar has dissolved.

3 Bring the mixture to the boil and cook for about 8 minutes, or until the jam reaches setting point (105°C/220°F).

4 Remove the pan from the heat and skim off any scum from the surface using a slotted spoon. Leave to cool for 5 minutes, then stir in the cassis, if using.

5 Pour the jam into warmed sterilized jars and seal. Leave the jars to cool completely, then label and store in a cool, dark place.

Gooseberry and Elderflower Jam

Pale green gooseberries and fragrant elderflowers make perfect partners in this sharp, aromatic, intensely flavoured jam. The jam turns a pretty, but unexpected, pink colour during cooking.

Makes about 2kg/4½lb

1.3kg/3lb/12 cups firm gooseberries, topped and tailed
1.3kg/3lb/6½ cups granulated (white) sugar, warmed
juice of 1 lemon
2 handfuls of elderflowers removed from their stalks

1 Put the gooseberries into a large preserving pan, add 300ml/½ pint/1¼ cups water and bring the mixture to the boil.

2 Cover the pan with a lid and simmer gently for 20 minutes until the fruit is soft. Using a potato masher, gently mash the fruit to crush it lightly.

3 Add the sugar, lemon juice and elderflowers to the pan and stir over a low heat until the sugar has dissolved.

4 Boil for 10 minutes, or to setting point (105°C/220°F). Remove from the heat, skim off any scum and cool for 5 minutes, then stir. Pour into pots and seal, then leave to cool before labelling.

Cook's Tip
The time taken to reach setting point will vary depending on the ripeness of the gooseberries. The amount of pectin in gooseberries diminishes as the fruit ripens. The riper the fruit, the longer the jam will take to reach setting point.

Variation
Poach the gooseberries and elderflowers with a little sugar and sieve (strain) the resulting mixture to form a purée, then mix it with whipped cream to make a perfect, muscat-flavoured gooseberry and elderflower fool.

Damson Jam: Energy 4320kcal/18,430kJ; Protein 10g; Carbohydrate 1141g, of which sugars 1141g; Fat 0g, of which saturates 0g; Cholesterol 0mg; Calcium 770mg; Fibre 18g; Sodium 80mg.
Blackcurrant Jam: Energy 5504kcal/23,503kJ; Protein 18.4g; Carbohydrate 1448.7g, of which sugars 1448.7g; Fat 0.1g, of which saturates 0g; Cholesterol 0mg; Calcium 1474mg; Fibre 46.9g; Sodium 122mg.
Gooseberry Jam: Energy 5369kcal/22,906kJ; Protein 20.8g; Carbohydrate 1397.5g, of which sugars 1397.5g; Fat 5.2g, of which saturates 0g; Cholesterol 0mg; Calcium 1053mg; Fibre 31.2g; Sodium 104mg.

Orange Spoon Preserve

Spoon preserves are made with various types of fruit in a luscious syrup. Make orange peel preserve in late autumn with navel oranges and in winter use Seville oranges. Orange peel preserve is the easiest type to make and will happily keep for one or two years.

Makes about 30 pieces

8–9 thick-skinned oranges, total weight about 1kg/2¼lb, rinsed and dried
1kg/2¼lb/4½ cups caster (superfine) sugar
juice of 1 lemon

1 Grate the oranges lightly and discard the zest. Slice each one vertically into 4–6 pieces (depending on the size), remove the peel from each segment, keeping it in one piece, and drop it into a bowl of cold water. Use the flesh for another recipe.

2 Have ready a tapestry needle threaded with strong cotton string. Roll up a piece of peel and thread the needle through it. Continue this process until there are 10–12 pieces on the string, then tie the ends together. String the remaining peel in the same way. Put strings in a bowl of cold water and leave for 24 hours, changing the water 3–4 times.

3 Next day, drain the strings of peel and put them in a large pan. Pour in about 2.8 litres/4½ pints/11 cups water. Bring to the boil, partially cover the pan and continue to boil for 15 minutes. Drain. Return the peel to the pan, cover with same amount of water and boil for 10 minutes until the peel feels soft. Transfer into a colander and leave to drain for at least 1 hour.

4 Put the sugar in a large heavy pan and add 150ml/¼ pint/⅔ cup water. Stir over a gentle heat until the sugar dissolves, then boil gently without stirring for about 4 minutes until a thick syrup forms. Remove the fruit from the threads. Simmer for 5 minutes, then take off the heat and leave to stand overnight.

5 Next day, boil the syrup very gently for 4–5 minutes, until it starts to set. Stir in the lemon juice, take the pan off the heat and cool. Pack into sterilized jars. Seal and label when cool.

Plum Tomato and Almond Jam

In the style of a conserve, you will only ever come across this jam in a Turkish home, as it is not made commercially like the well-known Turkish varieties made with rose petals, green figs, sour cherries or quince. A summer jam, made with slightly unripe or firm plum tomatoes, it is syrupy in consistency, and spooned, rather than spread, on to bread.

Makes 900g/2lb

1kg/2¼lb firm plum tomatoes
500g/1¼lb/2½ cups sugar
115g/4oz/1 cup whole blanched almonds
8–10 whole cloves

1 Skin the tomatoes. Submerge them for a few seconds in boiling water, then plunge them straight away into a bowl of cold water. Remove them from the water one at a time and peel off the skins.

2 Place the skinned tomatoes in a heavy pan and cover with the sugar. Leave them to sit for a few hours, or if possible overnight, to draw out some of the sweet red juices, then stir in 150ml/¼ pint/⅔ cup water. The consistency of the tomatoes should be quite juicy – if not, stir in more water, you may need up to 300ml/½ pint/1¼ cups.

3 Place the pan over the heat and stir gently until the sugar has completely dissolved. Bring the syrup to the boil and boil for a few minutes, skimming off any froth, then lower the heat and stir in the almonds and cloves. Simmer gently for about 25 minutes, stirring from time to time.

4 Turn off the heat and leave the jam to cool in the pan before spooning into sterilized jars and sealing.

5 Stored in a cool, dry place, it will keep for several months, but you will probably find that you eat it almost as soon as you've made it.

Orange Spoon Preserve: Energy 131kcal/560kJ; Protein 0.3g; Carbohydrate 34.8g, of which sugars 34.8g; Fat 0g, of which saturates 0g; Cholesterol 0mg; Calcium 31mg; Fibre 0g; Sodium 3mg.
Tomato and Almond: Energy 948kcal/4016kJ; Protein 11.3g; Carbohydrate 187.1g, of which sugars 186.1g; Fat 22.4g, of which saturates 2g; Cholesterol 0mg; Calcium 204mg; Fibre 6.2g; Sodium 45mg.

Cranberry and Claret Jelly

The slight sharpness of cranberries makes this a superb jelly for serving with rich meats such as lamb or game. Together with claret, the cranberries give the jelly a beautiful deep red colour.

Makes about 1.2kg/2½lb

900g/2lb/8 cups fresh or frozen cranberries
about 900g/2lb/4½ cups preserving or granulated (white) sugar
250ml/8fl oz/1 cup claret

1 Wash the cranberries, if fresh, and put them in a large heavy pan with 350ml/12fl oz/1½ cups water. Cover the pan and bring to the boil.

2 Reduce the heat under the pan and simmer for about 20 minutes, or until the cranberries are soft.

3 Pour the fruit and juices into a sterilized jelly bag suspended over a large bowl. Leave to drain for at least 3 hours or overnight, until the juices stop dripping.

4 Measure the juice and wine into the cleaned preserving pan, adding 400g/14oz/2 cups preserving or granulated sugar for every 600ml/1 pint/2½ cups liquid.

5 Heat the mixture gently, stirring occasionally, until the sugar has dissolved, then bring to the boil and boil rapidly for 10 minutes until the jelly reaches setting point (105°C/220°F). Remove the pan from the heat.

6 Skim any scum from the surface using a slotted spoon and pour the jelly into warmed sterilized jars. Cover and seal. Store in a cool, dark place and use within 2 years. Once opened, keep the jelly in the refrigerator and eat within 3 months.

Cook's Tip
When simmering the cranberries, keep the pan covered until they stop 'popping', as they can occasionally explode and jump out of the pan.

Guava Jelly

Fragrant guava makes an aromatic, pale rust-coloured jelly with a soft set and a slightly sweet-sour flavour that is enhanced by lime juice. Guava jelly goes well with goat's cheese.

Makes about 900g/2lb

900g/2lb guavas
juice of 2–3 limes
about 500g/1¼lb/2½ cups preserving or granulated (white) sugar

1 Thinly peel and halve the guavas. Using a spoon, scoop out the seeds (pips) from the centre of the fruit and discard them.

2 Place the halved guavas in a large heavy pan with 15ml/1 tbsp lime juice and 600ml/1 pint/2½ cups cold water – there should be just enough to cover the fruit. Bring the mixture to the boil, then reduce the heat, cover with a lid and simmer for about 30 minutes, or until the fruit is tender.

3 Pour the fruit and juices into a sterilized jelly bag suspended over a large bowl. Leave to drain for at least 3 hours.

4 Measure the juice into the cleaned preserving pan, adding 400g/14oz/2 cups sugar and 15ml/1 tbsp lime juice for every 600ml/1 pint/2½ cups guava juice.

5 Heat gently, stirring occasionally, until the sugar has dissolved. Boil rapidly for about 10 minutes. When the jelly reaches setting point, remove the pan from the heat.

6 Skim any scum from the surface of the jelly using a slotted spoon, then pour the jelly into sterilized jars. Cover and seal.

7 Store the jelly in a cool, dark place and consume within 1 year. Once opened, keep in the refrigerator and eat within 3 months.

Cook's Tip
Do not be tempted to squeeze the jelly bag while the fruit juices are draining from it; this will result in a cloudy jelly.

Cranberry Jelly: Energy 3821kcal/16,290kJ; Protein 5.7g; Carbohydrate 967.7g, of which sugars 967.7g; Fat 0.3g, of which saturates 0g; Cholesterol 0mg; Calcium 506mg; Fibre 4.8g; Sodium 78mg.
Guava Jelly: Energy 2090kcal/8912kJ; Protein 3.4g; Carbohydrate 552.5g, of which sugars 552.5g; Fat 0.3g, of which saturates 0g; Cholesterol 0mg; Calcium 298mg; Fibre 6.6g; Sodium 39mg.

Plum and Apple Jelly

Use dark red cooking plums, damsons or wild plums such as bullaces to offset the sweetness of this deep-coloured jelly. Its flavour complements rich roast meats such as lamb and pork.

Makes about 1.3kg/3lb
900g/2lb plums
450g/1lb tart cooking apples
150ml/¼ pint/⅔ cup cider vinegar
about 675g/1½lb/scant 3½ cups preserving or granulated (white) sugar

1 Cut the plums in half along the crease, twist apart, then remove the stones (pits) and roughly chop the flesh. Chop the apples, including the cores and skins. Put the fruit in a large heavy pan with the vinegar and 750ml/1¼ pints/3 cups water.

2 Bring the mixture to the boil, reduce the heat, cover and simmer for 30 minutes, or until the fruit is soft and pulpy.

3 Pour the fruit and juices into a sterilized jelly bag suspended over a large bowl. Leave to drain for at least 3 hours, or until the fruit juices stop dripping.

4 Measure the juice into the cleaned pan, adding 450g/1lb/2¼ cups sugar for every 600ml/1 pint/2½ cups juice.

5 Bring the mixture to the boil, stirring occasionally, until the sugar has dissolved, then boil rapidly for about 10 minutes, or until the jelly reaches setting point (105°C/220°F). Remove the pan from the heat.

6 Skim any scum from the surface, then pour the jelly into warmed sterilized jars. Cover and seal while hot. Store in a cool, dark place and use within 2 years.

Cook's Tip
This jelly can be stored for up to 2 years. However, once opened, it should be stored in the refrigerator and eaten within 3 months.

Rosehip and Apple Jelly

This economical jelly is made with windfall apples and wild rosehips. It is rich in vitamin C, full of flavour, and excellent spread on freshly toasted crumpets or scones.

Makes about 2kg/4½lb
1kg/2¼lb windfall apples, trimmed and quartered
450g/1lb firm, ripe rosehips
about 1.3kg/3lb/6½ cups preserving or granulated (white) sugar, warmed

1 Place the quartered apples in a large pan with just enough water to cover, plus 300ml/½ pint/1¼ cups of extra water.

2 Bring the mixture to the boil and cook gently until the apples soften and turn to a pulp. Meanwhile, chop the rosehips coarsely. Add the rosehips to the pan with the apple and simmer for 10 minutes.

3 Remove from the heat and stand for 10 minutes, then pour the mixture into a scalded jelly bag suspended over a non-metallic bowl and leave to drain overnight.

4 Measure the juice into a preserving pan and bring to the boil. Add 400g/14oz/2 cups warmed sugar for each 600ml/1 pint/2½ cups of liquid. Stir until the sugar has completely dissolved. Boil to setting point (105°C/220°F).

5 Pour the jelly into warmed, sterilized jars and seal. Label and store when completely cold.

Cook's Tip
There is no need to remove all the peel from the apples: simply cut out any bruised, damaged or bad areas.

Variation
Add 900g/2lb/6 cups muscat grapes, same quantity sugar, 2 lemons, 30ml/2 tbsp elderflower cordial for grape jelly.

Plum Jelly: Energy 2803kcal/11,963kJ; Protein 5.5g; Carbohydrate 740.7g, of which sugars 740.7g; Fat 0.4g, of which saturates 0g; Cholesterol 0mg; Calcium 401mg; Fibre 6.4g; Sodium 49mg.
Rosehip Jelly: Energy 5684kcal/24,259kJ; Protein 8.4g; Carbohydrate 1505.7g, of which sugars 1505.7g; Fat 0.5g, of which saturates 0g; Cholesterol 0mg; Calcium 761mg; Fibre 7.7g; Sodium 94mg.

Rhubarb and Mint Jelly

This delicious jelly is very pretty, speckled with tiny pieces of chopped fresh mint. It has a sharp, tangy flavour and is fabulous spread on toast or crumpets at tea time.

Makes about 2kg/4½lb
1kg/2¼lb rhubarb
about 1.3kg/3lb/6½ cups preserving or granulated (white) sugar, warmed
large bunch fresh mint
30ml/2 tbsp finely chopped fresh mint

1 Using a sharp knife, cut the rhubarb into chunks and place in a large, heavy pan. Pour in just enough water to cover, cover the pan with a lid and cook until the rhubarb is soft.

2 Remove the pan from the heat and leave the stewed fruit and juices to cool slightly before pouring into a scalded jelly bag. Suspend the jelly bag over a non-metallic bowl and leave to drain overnight.

3 Measure the strained juice into a preserving pan and add 450g/1lb/2¼ cups warmed sugar for each 600ml/1 pint/2½ cups strained juice.

4 Add the bunch of mint to the pan. Bring to the boil, stirring until the sugar has dissolved. Boil to setting point (105°C/220°F). Remove the mint.

5 Leave to stand for 10 minutes, stir in the chopped mint, then pour into jars and seal. Label when completely cold. Store in a cool dark place.

Cook's Tips
- *This recipe is a good way to use up older dark red or green-stemmed rhubarb, which is usually too tough to use for desserts.*
- *As well as serving as a delightful sweet preserve, this jelly is also very good served with fatty roast meats such as lamb and goose.*

Pineapple and Passion Fruit Jelly

This exotic jelly has a wonderful warming glow to its taste and appearance. For the best-flavoured jelly, use a tart-tasting, not too ripe pineapple rather than a very ripe, sweet one.

Makes about 900g/2lb
1 large pineapple, peeled, topped and tailed and coarsely chopped
4 passion fruit, halved, with seeds and pulp scooped out
about 900g/2lb/4½ cups preserving or granulated (white) sugar, warmed

1 Place the pineapple and the passion fruit seeds and pulp in a large pan with 900ml/1½ pints/3¾ cups water.

2 Bring the mixture to the boil, cover and simmer for 1½ hours. Remove from the heat and leave to cool slightly. Transfer the fruit to a food processor and process briefly.

3 Transfer the fruit pulp and any juices from the pan into a sterilized jelly bag suspended over a non-metallic bowl and leave to drain overnight.

4 Measure the strained juice into a preserving pan and add 450g/1lb/2¼ cups warmed sugar for every 600ml/1 pint/2½ cups juice.

5 Heat gently, stirring, until the sugar has dissolved. Increase the heat and boil rapidly, without stirring, for 10–15 minutes, or to setting point (105°C/220°F).

6 Remove the pan from the heat and skim off any scum using a slotted spoon. Ladle the jelly into warmed sterilized jars, cover and seal. When cool, label and store in a cool, dark place.

Cook's Tip
For the best tropical exotic flavour, choose passion fruit with dark purple, wrinkled skins. When cut in half their heady perfume will permeate the room.

Rhubarb Jelly: Energy 6260kcal/26,715kJ; Protein 13.5g; Carbohydrate 1652.8g, of which sugars 1649.6g; Fat 0.8g, of which saturates 0g; Cholesterol 0mg; Calcium 1301mg; Fibre 5.1g; Sodium 115mg.
Pineapple Jelly: Energy 3633kcal/15,504kJ; Protein 5.7g; Carbohydrate 961.6g, of which sugars 961.6g; Fat 0.5g, of which saturates 0g; Cholesterol 0mg; Calcium 515mg; Fibre 2.9g; Sodium 61mg.

Forest Berries in Kirsch

Late summer in a bottle, this preserve captures the essence of the season in its rich, dark colour and flavour. Adding the sweet cherry liqueur Kirsch to the syrup intensifies the flavour of the bottled fruit.

Makes about 1.3kg/3lb

1.3kg/3lb/12 cups mixed prepared summer berries, such as blackberries, raspberries, strawberries, redcurrants and cherries

225g/8oz/generous 1 cup granulated (white) sugar

120ml/4fl oz/½ cup Kirsch

1 Preheat the oven to 120°C/250°F/Gas ½. Pack the prepared fruit loosely into sterilized jars. Cover the jars without sealing and place in the oven for 50–60 minutes, or until the juices start to run.

2 Meanwhile, put the sugar and 600ml/1 pint/2½ cups water in a large pan and heat gently, stirring, until the sugar has dissolved. Increase the heat, bring to the boil and boil for 5 minutes. Stir in the Kirsch and set aside.

3 Carefully remove the jars from the oven and place on a dish towel. Use the fruit from one of the jars to top up the rest.

4 Pour the boiling syrup into each jar, twisting and tapping each one to ensure that no air bubbles have been trapped. Seal, allow to cool, then label. Store in a cool, dark place.

Cook's Tip

Be careful not to overcook the fruits because they will lose their beautiful colour and fresh flavour.

Variation

You can make aromatic blueberries in gin syrup in much the same way, using 1.3kg/3lb/12 cups blueberries, 120ml/4fl oz/½ cup gin and the same quantities of sugar and water.

Cherries in Eau de Vie

These potent cherries should be consumed with respect as they pack quite an alcoholic punch. Serve them with rich, dark chocolate torte or as a wicked topping for creamy rice pudding.

Makes about 1.3kg/3lb

450g/1lb/generous 3 cups ripe cherries

8 blanched almonds

75g/3oz/6 tbsp granulated (white) sugar

500ml/17fl oz/scant 2¼ cups eau de vie

1 Wash and pit the cherries, then pack them into a sterilized, wide-necked bottle along with the blanched almonds.

2 Spoon the sugar over the fruit, then pour in the eau de vie to cover and seal tightly.

3 Store for at least 1 month before serving, shaking the bottle now and then to help dissolve the sugar.

Cook's Tip

Eau de vie actually refers to all spirits distilled from fermented fruits. It is in fact a fruit brandy. Eau de vie is always colourless, with a high alcohol content (sometimes 45% ABV) and a clean, pure scent and the flavour of the founding fruit. This is due to the fast fermenting process used. Popular eaux de vie are made from cherries and strawberries, which go perfectly with the luscious ripe cherries used in this recipe, producing a heady aroma of summer fruit.

Variation

Strawberries, raspberries and blackcurrants are all excellent preserved in eau de vie. They will all produce fine fruity liqueurs and macerated fruit. Orchard fruits, such as apples, pears and plums, are also used to make eau de vie. Use one of these as a base for a preserve of the same type of fruit. The resulting fruit liqueurs, strained, make fabulous champagne cocktails.

Berries in Kirsch: Energy 1517kcal/6487kJ; Protein 19.3g; Carbohydrate 334.1g, of which sugars 334.1g; Fat 3.9g, of which saturates 1.3g; Cholesterol 0mg; Calcium 444mg; Fibre 32.5g; Sodium 52mg.
Cherries in Eau de Vie: Energy 1479kcal/6142kJ; Protein 9.3g; Carbohydrate 53.5g, of which sugars 52.8g; Fat 14.4g, of which saturates 1.1g; Cholesterol 0mg; Calcium 119mg; Fibre 5.9g; Sodium 8mg.

Preserved Lemons

These richly flavoured fruits are widely used in Middle Eastern cooking. Only the rind, which contains the essential flavour of the lemon, is used in recipes. Traditionally, whole lemons are preserved, but this recipe uses wedges, which can be packed into jars more easily.

Makes about 2 jars
10 unwaxed lemons
about 200ml/7fl oz/scant 1 cup fresh lemon juice or a combination of fresh and preserved juice

From the storecupboard
sea salt

1 Wash the lemons well and cut each into six to eight wedges. Press a generous amount of salt on to the cut surface of each wedge.

2 Pack the salted lemon wedges into two 1.2 litre/2 pint/5 cup warmed sterilized jars. To each jar, add 30–45ml/2–3 tbsp sea salt and half the lemon juice, then top up with boiling water to cover the lemon wedges. Seal the jars and leave to stand for 2–4 weeks before using.

3 To use, rinse the preserved lemons well to remove some of the salty flavour, then pull off and discard the flesh. Cut the lemon rind into strips or leave in chunks and use as desired.

Cook's Tip
The salty, well-flavoured juice that is used to preserve the lemons can be used to flavour salad dressings or added to hot sauces.

Variation
Other acidic citrus fruits can be preserved in a similar way. Try it with vibrant green limes or the smaller relations, such as kumquats and limequats.

Middle Eastern Pickle

Beetroot brings an attractive colour and its inimitable sweet, slightly earthy flavour to this Middle Eastern speciality. The pale baby turnips take on a rich red hue in their beetroot-spiked brine. The deep red colour looks gorgeous when the jars are stacked up on shelves in the storecupboard. This pickle is delicious served with falafel or cold roast beef.

Makes 4 jars
1kg/2¼lb young turnips
3–4 raw beetroot (beets)
juice of 1 lemon

From the storecupboard
about 45ml/3 tbsp kosher salt or coarse sea salt

1 Wash, but do not peel the turnips and beetroot. Then cut them into slices about 5mm/¼in thick.

2 Put the salt in a bowl with about 1.5 litres/2½ pints/6¼ cups water, stir and leave on one side until the salt has completely dissolved.

3 Sprinkle the beetroot with lemon juice and divide among four 1.2 litre/2 pint/5 cup sterilized jars. Top with the sliced turnips, packing them in very tightly. Pour over the brine, making sure that the vegetables are completely covered.

4 Seal the jars and leave in a cool place for seven days for the flavours to develop before serving.

Cook's Tip
When buying beetroot, choose firm, unblemished, small- to medium-sized specimens. If you buy beetroot with green tops, you can reserve the tops and cook them in the same way as you would spinach for a tasty vegetable accompaniment to any meal.

Preserved Lemons: Energy 48kcal/198kJ; Protein 2.5g; Carbohydrate 8g, of which sugars 8g; Fat 0.8g, of which saturates 0.3g; Cholesterol 0mg; Calcium 213mg; Fibre 0g; Sodium 13mg.
Middle Eastern Pickle: Energy 94kcal/399kJ; Protein 4g; Carbohydrate 19.4g, of which sugars 18.3g; Fat 0.9g, of which saturates 0g; Cholesterol 0mg; Calcium 141mg; Fibre 7.9g; Sodium 4525mg.

Horseradish and Beetroot Sauce

This is a traditional Jewish speciality. Known as chrain, it is often eaten at the Passover meal, for which horseradish is one of the traditional bitter flavours. However, it complements a variety of foods and dishes of many different cooking styles, including roast meats and grilled fish.

Serves about 8
150g/5oz grated fresh horseradish
2 cooked beetroot (beets), grated
15ml/1 tbsp sugar
15–30ml/1–2 tbsp red wine vinegar

From the storecupboard
salt

1 Put the horseradish and beetroot in a bowl and mix together, then season with sugar, vinegar and salt to taste.

2 Spoon the sauce into a sterilized jar. Pack it down firmly before sealing the jar. Store in the refrigerator, where it will keep for up to 2 weeks.

Cook's Tip
Fresh horseradish has very potent fumes and should be handled with care as it can make the skin burn as well as the eyes run. Wear fine rubber gloves to protect your hands and keep the root submerged in water while you peel it. Use a food processor to do the fine chopping or grating, and avert your head when removing the lid.

Variation
To make a traditional British horseradish sauce to go with roast beef or smoked salmon, combine 45ml/3 tbsp freshly grated horseradish with 15ml/1 tbsp white wine vinegar, 5ml/1 tsp sugar and a pinch of salt in a bowl. Pour the mixture into a sterilized jar and store in the refrigerator for up to 6 months. A few hours before you want to serve the sauce, stir in 150ml/¼ pint/⅔ cup thick double (heavy) cream and leave to infuse (steep).

Mint Sauce

In England, mint sauce is the traditional and inseparable accompaniment to roast lamb. Its fresh, tart, astringent flavour is the perfect foil to rich, sumptuous roasted lamb. It is extremely simple to make and is infinitely preferable to the ready-made varieties.

Makes about 250ml/8fl oz/1 cup
1 large bunch mint
150ml/¼ pint/⅔ cup wine vinegar
30ml/2 tbsp granulated (white) sugar

1 Using a sharp knife, or a herb mill, chop the mint very finely and place it in a 600ml/1 pint/2½ cup jug (pitcher). Pour 105ml/7 tbsp boiling water over the mint and leave to infuse (steep) for about 10 minutes.

2 When the mint infusion has cooled and is lukewarm, stir in the wine vinegar and sugar. Continue stirring (but do not mash up the mint leaves) until the sugar has dissolved completely.

3 Pour the mint sauce into a sterilized bottle or jar, seal and store in the refrigerator.

Cook's Tips
- *Traditional mint sauce has the consistency of double (heavy) cream because the herbs are chopped so finely, but you can make it to your own preference.*
- *This mint sauce can keep for up to 6 months stored in the refrigerator, but is best used within 3 weeks.*

Variation
Add mint sauce to natural (plain) yogurt, as a replacement for fresh mint, and combine with grated cucumber to make a version of raita, the Indian yogurt sauce.

Horseradish Sauce: Energy 18kcal/76kJ; Protein 0.5g; Carbohydrate 4g, of which sugars 3.9g; Fat 0.1g, of which saturates 0g; Cholesterol 0mg; Calcium 14mg; Fibre 0.7g; Sodium 28mg.
Mint Sauce: Energy 161kcal/685kJ; Protein 3.9g; Carbohydrate 36.6g, of which sugars 31.3g; Fat 0.7g, of which saturates 0g; Cholesterol 0mg; Calcium 226mg; Fibre 0g; Sodium 17mg.

Shallots in Balsamic Vinegar

These whole shallots cooked in balsamic vinegar and herbs are a modern variation on pickled onions, but they have a much more gentle, smooth flavour. They are delicious served with cold pies, meats and cheese. A combination of bay leaves and thyme are used here but rosemary, oregano or marjoram sprigs would work just as well.

Serves 6

500g/1¼lb shallots
30ml/2 tbsp muscovado (molasses) sugar
several bay leaves or fresh thyme sprigs
300ml/½ pint/1¼ cups balsamic vinegar

1 Put the unpeeled shallots in a bowl, cover with boiling water and leave for 2 minutes for the skins to loosen. Drain and peel the shallots, leaving them whole.

2 Put the sugar, bay leaves or thyme and vinegar in a heavy pan and bring to the boil. Add the shallots, cover and simmer gently for about 40 minutes, until the shallots are just tender.

3 Transfer the mixture to a sterilized jar, seal and label, then store in a cool, dark place. Alternatively, drain and transfer to a serving dish. Leave to cool, then chill until ready to serve.

Cook's Tip

For sterilizing, stand clean, rinsed jars (with rubber seals removed) upside down on a rack or a baking sheet and place in the oven at 180°C/350°F/Gas 4 for 20 minutes.

Variation

Various herbs and spices can be used to flavour onions. The stronger the onion the stronger the flavourings you can add. Try mustard or coriander seeds, peppercorns, chillies and cloves.

Pickled Ginger

The Chinese love cooking with ginger. Warming, good for the heart, and believed to aid digestion, it finds its way into salads, soups, stir-fries and puddings. Pickled ginger is an immensely useful condiment, easy to prepare and often served with noodles and rice.

Serves 4–6

225g/8oz fresh young root ginger, peeled
200ml/7fl oz/1 cup white rice vinegar
50g/2oz/¼ cup sugar

From the storecupboard

10ml/2 tsp salt

1 Place the ginger in a bowl and sprinkle with salt. Cover and place in the refrigerator for 24 hours.

2 Drain off any excess liquid and pat the ginger dry with a clean dish towel.

3 Slice each knob of ginger very finely along the grain, to create thin slivers of pale pink that should resemble rose petals, and place them in a clean bowl or a sterilized jar suitable for storing.

4 In a small bowl, beat the vinegar and 50ml/2fl oz/¼ cup water with the sugar, until it has dissolved. Pour the pickling liquid over the ginger and cover or seal. Store in the refrigerator or a cool place for about a week.

Cook's Tips

- *Juicy and tender with a pinkish-yellow skin, young ginger is less fibrous than the mature rhizome. When pickled in vinegar, the flesh turns pale pink.*
- *Aside from its obvious application in Chinese cookery, pickled ginger is also served with sushi. It can also enliven less exotic dishes such as a pear and walnut salad, a few slices of cold roast duck, or even something as simple as a ham sandwich. It is valued for the way in which it cuts through oily flavours, so this pickle also tastes good with smoked mackerel.*

Shallots in Balsamic Vinegar: Energy 50kcal/209kJ; Protein 1g; Carbohydrate 11.8g, of which sugars 9.9g; Fat 0.2g, of which saturates 0g; Cholesterol 0mg; Calcium 24mg; Fibre 1.2g; Sodium 3mg.
Pickled Ginger: Energy 36kcal/151kJ; Protein 0.2g; Carbohydrate 9.1g, of which sugars 9.1g; Fat 0.1g, of which saturates 0g; Cholesterol 0mg; Calcium 20mg; Fibre 0.4g; Sodium 678mg.

Orange, Tomato and Chive Salsa

Fresh chives and sweet oranges provide a very cheerful combination of flavours. This fruity salsa is very good served alongside other salads.

Serves 4
2 large, sweet oranges
1 beefsteak tomato, or 2 plum tomatoes
bunch of fresh chives
1 garlic clove

From the storecupboard
30ml/2 tbsp extra-virgin olive oil or grapeseed oil
sea salt

1 Slice the base off one orange so that it will stand firmly on a chopping board. Using a sharp knife, remove the peel by slicing from the top to the bottom of the orange. Repeat with the second orange.

2 Working over a bowl to catch the juice, cut the segments away from the membranes in each orange: slice towards the middle of the fruit, and slightly to one side of a segment, and then gently twist the knife to release the orange segment. Squeeze any juice from the remaining membrane.

3 Roughly chop the segments and add them to the bowl with the collected juice. Halve the tomato and use a teaspoon to scoop the seeds into the bowl. With a sharp knife, finely dice the tomato flesh and add to the oranges and juice in the bowl.

4 Hold the bunch of chives neatly together and use a pair of kitchen scissors to snip them into the bowl.

5 Thinly slice the garlic and stir it into the orange mixture. Pour the olive oil over the salad, season with sea salt and stir well to mix. Serve the salsa within 2 hours.

Variation
Add a sprinkling of chopped pistachios or toasted pine nuts.

Chilli Strips with Lime

This fresh, tangy relish is ideal for serving with stews, rice dishes or bean dishes. The oregano adds a sweet note and the absence of sugar or oil makes this a very healthy choice.

Makes about 60ml/4 tbsp
10 fresh green chillies
½ white onion
4 limes
2.5ml/½ tsp dried oregano

From the storecupboard
salt

1 Roast the chillies in a griddle pan over a medium heat until the skins are charred and blistered. The flesh should not be allowed to blacken as this might make the salsa bitter. Place the roasted chillies in a strong plastic bag and tie the top to keep the steam in. Set aside for 20 minutes.

2 Meanwhile, slice the onion very thinly and put it in a large bowl. Squeeze the limes over a sieve (strainer) and add the juice to the bowl, with any pulp that gathers in the sieve. The lime juice will soften the onion. Stir in the oregano.

3 Remove the chillies from the bag and peel off the skins. Slit them, scrape out the seeds with a small sharp knife, then cut the chillies into long strips, which are called 'rajas'.

4 Add the chilli strips to the onion mixture and season with salt. Cover the bowl and chill for at least 1 day before serving, to allow the flavours to develop.

Cook's Tips
- *This method of roasting chillies in a griddle pan is ideal if you need more than one or two chillies, or if you do not have a gas burner. If you prefer to roast the chillies over a burner, spear the chillies, four or five at a time, on a long-handled metal skewer and hold them over the flame until the skins begin to blister. Take care not to let them burn.*
- *This salsa will keep for up to 2 weeks in a covered bowl in the refrigerator. Use to add fiery flavour to a meal.*

Orange and Tomato Salsa: Energy 91kcal/380kJ; Protein 1.3g; Carbohydrate 9.3g, of which sugars 9.3g; Fat 5.7g, of which saturates 0.8g; Cholesterol 0mg; Calcium 49mg; Fibre 2g; Sodium 7mg.
Chilli Strips with Lime: Energy 49kcal/204kJ; Protein 3.9g; Carbohydrate 7g, of which sugars 5.7g; Fat 0.7g, of which saturates 0g; Cholesterol 0mg; Calcium 52mg; Fibre 0.9g; Sodium 10mg.

Yellow Pepper and Coriander Relish

Relishes are quick and easy to make and they are delicious with cold meats, cheese and biscuits, or as a sandwich filler. The ingredients are lightly cooked, then processed to a chunky consistency. Red or orange peppers will work just as well as yellow as they all have a sweet flavour. Don't use green peppers as they are bitter.

Serves 4–6
3 large yellow (bell) peppers
1 large mild fresh red chilli
small handful of fresh coriander (cilantro)

From the storecupboard
45ml/3 tbsp sesame oil
salt

1 Seed and coarsely chop the peppers. Heat the oil in a frying pan and gently cook the peppers, stirring frequently, for 8–10 minutes, until lightly coloured.

2 Meanwhile, seed the chilli and slice it as thinly as possible. Transfer the peppers and cooking juices to a food processor and process lightly until chopped. Transfer half the peppers to a bowl. Using a sharp knife, chop the fresh coriander, then add to the food processor and process briefly.

3 Transfer the contents of the food processor into the bowl with the rest of the peppers and add the chilli and salt. Mix well, cover and chill until ready to serve.

Cook's Tip
The relish can be stored in an airtight container in the refrigerator for several days.

Variation
Other flavoured oils, such as lemon- or garlic-infused oil, can be used in place of the sesame oil.

Hot Mango Salsa

For sweet, tangy results, select a really juicy, ripe mango for this salsa – it is not worth making the salsa with a firm, unripe mango as it will not offer the beautifully perfumed, succulent result that it should. Keep an unripe mango in the fruit bowl for a few days until it has ripened. This fruity salsa is a delicious accompaniment to chargrilled or barbecued chicken or fish.

Serves 4–6
1 medium ripe mango
1 lime
1 large mild fresh red chilli
½ small red onion

From the storecupboard
salt

1 To prepare the mango, cut the flesh off on either side of the flat stone (pit). Peel and finely dice the mango halves and cut off and chop the flesh that still clings to the stone.

2 Finely grate the lime rind and squeeze the juice. Seed and finely shred the fresh red chilli.

3 Finely chop the onion and mix it in a bowl with the mango, lime rind, 15ml/1 tbsp lime juice, the chilli and a little salt. Cover and chill until ready to serve.

Cook's Tip
Take care when handling fresh chilli as the juice can burn your skin. Wear gloves or wash your hands straight afterwards.

Variation
For a milder version of this mango salsa, replace the chilli and red onion with diced radish and use lemon juice in place of lime.

Pepper Relish: Energy 91kcal/374kJ; Protein 0.8g; Carbohydrate 2.9g, of which sugars 2.8g; Fat 8.5g, of which saturates 1.3g; Cholesterol 0mg; Calcium 8mg; Fibre 0.7g; Sodium 3mg.
Hot Mango Salsa: Energy 18kcal/76kJ; Protein 0.3g; Carbohydrate 4.3g, of which sugars 4g; Fat 0.1g, of which saturates 0g; Cholesterol 0mg; Calcium 6mg; Fibre 0.8g; Sodium 1mg.

Roasted Garlic Sauce

A roasted garlic sauce has plenty of robust flavour without the harshness of some uncooked garlic sauces, such as aioli. This one keeps well in the refrigerator for several days. Serve it as an accompaniment to potato wedges, burgers, sausages, grilled steaks, lamb or pork chops – the possibilities are endless.

Serves 6–8
6 large heads of garlic
2 slices white bread, about 90g/3½oz
30–45ml/2–3 tbsp lemon juice

From the storecupboard
120ml/4fl oz/½ cup olive oil
salt and ground black pepper

1 Preheat the oven to 200°C/400°F/Gas 6. Slice the tops off the garlic and place the bulbs on a sheet of foil. Spoon over 30ml/2 tbsp of the oil and sprinkle with salt. Wrap the foil over the garlic and bake for 1 hour, until soft. When cooked, open out the foil and leave the garlic to cool.

2 Discard the crusts from the bread. Soak the bread in water for 1 minute, then squeeze dry and place in a food processor. Squeeze the garlic flesh from each clove into the processor. Process to a smooth paste.

3 Add 30ml/2 tbsp lemon juice with a little salt and pepper. With the machine running, gradually add the remaining oil in a thin stream to make a smooth paste. Check the seasoning, adding more lemon juice if needed. Turn into a bowl, cover and chill until required.

Variation
To make aioli, pound 4 large peeled garlic cloves with a pinch of salt to a smooth paste in a mortar. Transfer to a bowl, add 2 egg yolks, and whisk for about 30 seconds, until creamy. Whisk in 250ml/8fl oz/1 cup extra virgin olive oil, drop by drop, until the mixture begins to thicken, then add in a slow drizzle until thick and creamy. Beat in 15ml/1 tbsp lemon juice and season.

Watercress Sauce

This pretty green sauce is refreshingly tart and peppery. It is delicious served as an accompaniment to poached fish, or as a dip for simply grilled prawns. Do not prepare the sauce more than a few hours ahead of serving, as the watercress will discolour the sauce. Peppery rocket leaves make an equally good alternative to watercress, if you prefer.

Serves 6–8
200g/7oz watercress leaves
300g/11oz/1½ cups mayonnaise
15–30ml/1–2 tbsp freshly squeezed lemon juice

From the storecupboard
200g/7oz/scant 1 cup unsalted (sweet) butter
salt and ground black pepper

1 Remove the tough stems from the watercress and finely chop the leaves by hand or in a food processor.

2 Add the mayonnaise and the freshly squeezed lemon juice and process to mix.

3 Melt the unsalted butter, then add to the watercress mixture, a little at a time, processing or whisking in a bowl until the butter has been fully incorporated and the sauce is thick and smooth.

4 Season to taste with salt and pepper, then cover and chill in the refrigerator for at least an hour before serving.

Variations
- *Garlic makes a delicious addition to this sauce. Peel and finely chop 1–2 garlic cloves and combine with the chopped watercress leaves, mayonnaise and lemon juice, before adding the melted butter.*
- *Try replacing the watercress with rocket (arugula) leaves for a similarly peppery result.*

Roated Garlic Sauce: Energy 141kcal/585kJ; Protein 2.9g; Carbohydrate 9.6g, of which sugars 0.7g; Fat 10.4g, of which saturates 1.5g; Cholesterol 0mg; Calcium 17mg; Fibre 1.2g; Sodium 60mg.
Watercress Sauce: Energy 451kcal/1854kJ; Protein 1.3g; Carbohydrate 0.9g, of which sugars 0.7g; Fat 49.2g, of which saturates 17.4g; Cholesterol 81mg; Calcium 50mg; Fibre 0.4g; Sodium 333mg.

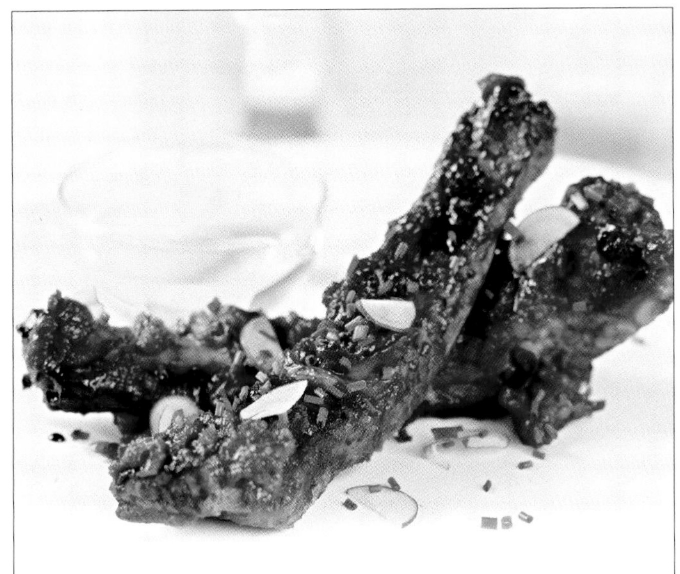

Barbecue Sauce

A wide selection of ready-made barbecue sauces are available in the supermarkets, but they really don't compare with the home-made variety. This 10-minute version can be used to transform baked or grilled chicken, sausages or fish into an interesting meal that needs no more than a mixed salad and baked potatoes alongside.

Serves 4–6
2 x 400g/14oz cans chopped tomatoes with herbs or garlic
1 onion, finely chopped
15ml/1 tbsp black treacle (molasses)
45ml/3 tbsp Worcestershire sauce

From the storecupboard
salt and ground black pepper

1 Empty the cans of chopped tomatoes with herbs or garlic into a medium, heavy pan and add the finely chopped onion, black treacle and Worcestershire sauce.

2 Bring to the boil and cook, uncovered, until the mixture is thickened and pulpy, stirring frequently with a wooden spoon to stop the sauce catching on the base of the pan.

3 Season lightly with salt and plenty of ground black pepper and transfer to a serving dish or jug (pitcher). Serve the sauce warm or cold.

Cook's Tip
The barbecue sauce will keep in an airtight container in the refrigerator for up to 3 days, or longer if poured into a sterilized jar and sealed.

Variation
For a more spicy barbecue sauce, add 2.5ml/½ tsp of chilli powder (choose mild or hot depending on the level of heat you want) or add a seeded and chopped small red chilli.

Mixed Herb and Peppercorn Sauce

This lovely, refreshing sauce relies on absolutely fresh herbs (any combination will do) and good-quality olive oil for its fabulous flavour. Make it a day in advance, to allow the flavours to mingle. Serve the sauce with simply cooked fish such as salmon, cod or monkfish, with chicken or, alternatively, with grilled beef or lamb steaks.

Serves 4–6
10ml/2 tsp cumin seeds
15ml/1 tbsp pink or green peppercorns in brine, drained and rinsed
25g/1oz/1 cup fresh mixed herbs, such as parsley, mint, chives and coriander (cilantro)

From the storecupboard
45ml/3 tbsp lemon-infused olive oil
salt

1 Crush the cumin seeds using a mortar and pestle. Alternatively, put the seeds in a small bowl and pound them with the end of a rolling pin. Add the pink or green peppercorns and pound a little to break them up slightly.

2 Remove any tough stalks from the herbs. Put the herbs in a food processor with the cumin seeds, peppercorns, oil and salt and process until the herbs are finely chopped, scraping the sauce down from the sides of the bowl if necessary.

3 Turn the sauce into a small serving dish, cover with clear film (plastic wrap) and chill until ready to serve.

Cook's Tip
Extra virgin olive oil, the cold-pressed oil, is far superior to the ordinary olive oil, which contains some refined oil.

Variation
If you don't have any lemon-infused oil, you could use ordinary olive oil and add the grated zest and juice of one lemon to the sauce for a really tangy result.

Barbecue Sauce: Energy 94kcal/393kJ; Protein 1g; Carbohydrate 14.1g, of which sugars 13.7g; Fat 4.1g, of which saturates 0.6g; Cholesterol 0mg; Calcium 21mg; Fibre 1.5g; Sodium 66mg.
Mixed Herb Sauce: Energy 56kcal/229kJ; Protein 0.4g; Carbohydrate 0.7g, of which sugars 0.1g; Fat 5.8g, of which saturates 0.8g; Cholesterol 0mg; Calcium 11mg; Fibre 0.2g; Sodium 2mg.

Tomato and Cucumber Juice with Basil

Basil is an excellent herb for juicing, keeping its distinctive fresh fragrance. It makes the perfect partner for mild, refreshing cucumber and the sweetest, juiciest tomatoes you can find – use cherry tomatoes for an extra sweet flavour.

Serves 1–2
½ cucumber, peeled
a handful of fresh basil
350g/12oz tomatoes

1 Quarter the cucumber lengthways. There's no need to remove the seeds. Push it through a juicer with the basil, then do the same with the tomatoes.

2 Pour the tomato, basil and cucumber juice over ice cubes in one tall or two short glasses and echo the herb flavour by adding a few basil sprigs for decoration.

Beetroot, Ginger and Orange Juice

Despite its firmness, beetroot can be juiced raw and its intense flavour goes perfectly with tangy citrus fruits and fresh root ginger.

Serves 1
200g/7oz raw beetroot (beets)
1cm/½ in piece fresh root ginger, peeled
1 large orange

1 Scrub the beetroot, then trim them and slice them into quarters. Push half the beetroot through a vegetable juicer, followed by the ginger and the remaining beetroot and pour the juice into a jug (pitcher).

2 Squeeze the juice from the orange, using a citrus juicer or by hand, and pour into the beetroot juice. Stir to combine.

3 Pour the juice over ice cubes in a glass and serve immediately to enjoy the full benefit of all the nutrients. (Do not let the ice cubes melt into the juice or they will dilute its flavour.)

Carrot Revitalizer

This vibrant combination of vegetables and fruit makes a lively, health-giving drink. Carrots yield generous quantities of sweet juice, which goes perfectly with the sharp flavour of pear and the zesty taste of orange. This powerful drink will nourish and stimulate the system.

Serves 1
3 carrots
2 apples
1 orange

1 Scrub and trim the carrots and quarter the apples. Peel the orange and cut into rough segments.

2 Using a juice extractor, juice the carrots and fruit, pour into a glass and serve immediately.

Purple Pep

Jewel-coloured beetroot juice is well known for its detoxifying properties, so this juice makes the perfect choice when you've been over-doing it, offering an excellent supply of valuable essential nutrients.

Serves 1
3 carrots
115g/4oz beetroot (beet)
25g/1oz baby spinach, washed and dried
2 celery sticks

1 Scrub and trim the carrots and beetroot. Using a sharp knife, cut the beetroot into large chunks.

2 Using a juice extractor, juice the carrots, beetroot, spinach and celery, then pour into a glass and serve immediately.

Cook's Tip
Beetroot has the highest sugar content of any vegetable and makes a delicious juice with a rich but refreshing taste.

Tomato Juice: Energy 40kcal/168kJ; Protein 1.9g; Carbohydrate 7g, of which sugars 6.8g; Fat 0.7g, of which saturates 0.2g; Cholesterol 0mg; Calcium 31mg; Fibre 2.4g; Sodium 19mg.
Beetroot Juice: Energy 116kcal/498kJ; Protein 4.7g; Carbohydrate 25.4g, of which sugars 24.2g; Fat 0.3g, of which saturates 0g; Cholesterol 0mg; Calcium 96mg; Fibre 5.8g; Sodium 138mg.
Carrot Revitalizer: Energy 160kcal/678kJ; Protein 2.9g; Carbohydrate 37.6g, of which sugars 36.6g; Fat 0.8g, of which saturates 0.2g; Cholesterol 0mg; Calcium 112mg; Fibre 8.9g; Sodium 59mg.
Purple Pep: Energy 122kcal/513kJ; Protein 4.2g; Carbohydrate 25.5g, of which sugars 23.8g; Fat 1g, of which saturates 0.2g; Cholesterol 0mg; Calcium 140mg; Fibre 8.2g; Sodium 197mg.

Leafy Apple Lift-off

This delicious blend of fruit and fresh green leaves is refreshing and healthy. The leaves are robustly flavoured and have a peppery, pungent taste. To prepare the leaves, discard any damaged and discoloured ones and rinse thoroughly in cold water to remove any grit. To prevent the juice from being watery, dry the leaves in a salad spinner or on kitchen paper before juicing.

Serves 1

1 eating apple
150g/5oz white grapes
25g/1oz watercress, rocket (arugula) or spinach
15ml/1 tbsp lime juice

1 Quarter the apple. Using a juice extractor, juice the fruit and watercress, rocket or spinach.

2 Add the lime juice to the apple, grape and leaf mixture and stir thoroughly to blend all the ingredients together. Pour the juice into a tall glass and serve immediately.

Fennel Fusion

The hearty combination of raw vegetables and apples makes a surprisingly delicious juice that is packed with natural goodness and is a truly wonderful pick-me-up for those times when you are depleted of energy.

Serves 1

½ small red cabbage
½ fennel bulb
2 eating apples
15ml/1 tbsp lemon juice

1 Coarsely slice the red cabbage and the fennel bulb and quarter the eating apples. Using a juice extractor, juice the vegetables and fruit.

2 Add the lemon juice to the red cabbage, fennel and apple mixture and stir thoroughly to blend all the ingredients together. Pour into a glass and serve immediately.

Melon Pick-me-up

Spicy fresh root ginger is delicious with melon and pear in this reviving and invigorating concoction. Charentais or Galia melon can be used instead of the cantaloupe melon. To enjoy fresh root ginger at its best, keep in a cool, dry place for up to a week.

Serves 1

½ cantaloupe melon
2 pears
2.5cm/1in piece of fresh root ginger

1 Quarter the cantaloupe melon, remove the seeds, and carefully slice the flesh away from the skin, reserving any juice. Quarter the pears and reserve any juice.

2 Using a juice extractor, juice the melon flesh and juice, quartered pears and juice and the fresh root ginger. Pour the juice into a tall glass and serve immediately.

Apple Shiner

This refreshing fusion of sweet apple, honeydew melon, red grapes and lemon provides a reviving burst of energy and a feel-good sensation. Serve as a drink or use to pour over muesli for a quick and healthy breakfast.

Serves 1

1 eating apple
½ honeydew melon
90g/3½ oz red grapes
15ml/1 tbsp lemon juice

1 Quarter the apple and remove the core. Cut the melon into quarters, remove the seeds and slice the flesh away from the skin.

2 Using a juice extractor, juice the apple, melon and grapes. Alternatively, process the fruit in a food processor or blender for 2–3 minutes, until smooth. Pour the juice into a long, tall glass, stir in the lemon juice and serve immediately.

Leafy Apple Lift-off: Energy 120kcal/512kJ; Protein 1.5g; Carbohydrate 29.5g, of which sugars 29.4g; Fat 0.4g, of which saturates 0g; Cholesterol 0mg; Calcium 65mg; Fibre 2.6g; Sodium 39mg.
Fennel Fusion: Energy 142kcal/600kJ; Protein 5.5g; Carbohydrate 29.3g, of which sugars 28.9g; Fat 0.9g, of which saturates 0g; Cholesterol 0mg; Calcium 177mg; Fibre 10.9g; Sodium 35mg.
Melon Pick-me-up: Energy 240kcal/1017kJ; Protein 3.4g; Carbohydrate 58g, of which sugars 58g; Fat 0.8g, of which saturates 0g; Cholesterol 0mg; Calcium 98mg; Fibre 8.6g; Sodium 164mg.
Apple Shiner: Energy 197kcal/842kJ; Protein 3.1g; Carbohydrate 47.8g, of which sugars 47.8g; Fat 0.7g, of which saturates 0g; Cholesterol 0mg; Calcium 79mg; Fibre 3.7g; Sodium 158mg.

Citrus Sparkle

Pink grapefruit have a sweeter flavour than the yellow varieties – in fact, the pinker they are, the sweeter they are likely to be.

Serves 1
1 pink grapefruit
1 orange
30ml/2 tbsp freshly squeezed lemon juice

1 Cut the pink grapefruit and orange in half and squeeze out the juice using a citrus fruit squeezer. Pour the juice into a glass, stir in 15ml/1 tbsp lemon juice, add the remaining lemon juice if required and serve.

Cranberry and Spice Spritzer

Partially freezing fruit juice gives it a refreshingly slushy texture. The combination of cranberry and apple juice is tart and clean. Add a few fresh or frozen cranberries to decorate each glass, if you like.

Serves 4
600ml/1 pint/2½ cups chilled cranberry juice
150ml/¼ pint/⅔ cup clear apple juice
4 cinnamon sticks
about 400ml/14fl oz/1⅔ cups chilled ginger ale

1 Pour the cranberry juice into a shallow freezerproof container and freeze for about 2 hours, or until a thick layer of ice crystals has formed around the edges. Mash the semi-frozen juice with a fork, then return the mixture to the freezer for 2–3 hours, until almost solid.

2 Pour the apple juice into a small pan, add two cinnamon sticks and bring to just below boiling point. Pour into a jug (pitcher) and leave to cool, then remove the cinnamon sticks and set them aside. Cool, then chill the juice.

3 Spoon the cranberry ice into a food processor or blender. Add the cinnamon-flavoured apple juice and process briefly until slushy. Pile the mixture into cocktail glasses, top up with chilled ginger ale, decorate with cinnamon sticks and serve.

Blue Lagoon

Blackcurrants are not only an excellent source of betacarotene and vitamin C, but they are also rich in flavonoids, which help to cleanse the system. Mixed with other dark red fruits, such as blackberries and grapes, they make a highly nutritious and extremely delicious blend that can be refrigerated and enjoyed throughout the day.

Serves 1
90g/3½ oz/scant 1 cup blackcurrants or blackberries
150g/5oz red grapes
130g/4½ oz/generous 1 cup blueberries

1 If you are using blackcurrants, gently pull the stalks through the tines of a fork to remove the fruit. Next remove the stalks from the grapes.

2 Push all the fruits through a juicer, saving a few for decoration. Place some ice in a medium glass and pour over the juice. Decorate with the reserved fruit and serve.

Hum-zinger

Aromatic tropical fruits make a drink that is bursting with flavour and energy. Enjoy a glass first thing in the morning to kick-start your day.

Serves 1
½ pineapple, peeled
1 small mango, peeled and stoned (pitted)
½ small papaya, seeded and peeled

1 Remove any 'eyes' left in the pineapple, then cut all the fruit into fairly coarse chunks.

2 Using a juice extractor, juice the fruit. Alternatively, use a food processor or blender and process for about 2–3 minutes until smooth. Pour into a glass and serve immediately.

Citrus Sparkle: Energy 92kcal/391kJ; Protein 2.6g; Carbohydrate 21.1g, of which sugars 21.1g; Fat 0.3g, of which saturates 0g; Cholesterol 0mg; Calcium 93mg; Fibre 4.1g; Sodium 11mg.
Cranberry and Spice: Energy 86kcal/370kJ; Protein 0.2g; Carbohydrate 22.5g, of which sugars 22.5g; Fat 0.2g, of which saturates 0g; Cholesterol 0mg; Calcium 13mg; Fibre 0g; Sodium 4mg.
Blue Lagoon: Energy 189kcal/805kJ; Protein 2.7g; Carbohydrate 47.2g, of which sugars 42g; Fat 0.2g, of which saturates 0g; Cholesterol 0mg; Calcium 74mg; Fibre 6.9g; Sodium 6mg.
Hum-zinger: Energy 322kcal/1378kJ; Protein 3.7g; Carbohydrate 79.1g, of which sugars 78.7g; Fat 1.3g, of which saturates 0.1g; Cholesterol 0mg; Calcium 136mg; Fibre 13.1g; Sodium 21mg.

Raspberry and Orange Smoothie

Sharp-sweet raspberries and zesty oranges taste fabulous combined with the light creaminess of yogurt. This smoothie takes just minutes to prepare, making it perfect for breakfast.

Serves 2–3

250g/9oz/1½ cups fresh raspberries, chilled
200ml/7fl oz/scant 1 cup natural (plain) yogurt, chilled
300ml/½ pint/1¼ cups freshly squeezed orange juice, chilled

1 Place the raspberries and yogurt in a food processor or blender and process for about 1 minute, until smooth.

2 Add the orange juice to the raspberry and yogurt mixture and process for about 30 seconds, or until thoroughly combined. Pour into tall glasses and serve immediately.

Strawberry and Banana Smoothie

The blend of perfectly ripe bananas and strawberries creates a drink that is both fruity and creamy, with a luscious texture. Papaya, mango or pineapple can be used instead of strawberries for a tropical drink. Popular with adults and children alike, this is a great way to get children to enjoy fruit – much healthier than commercial milkshakes, too.

Serves 4

200g/7oz/1¾ cups strawberries, plus extra, sliced, to decorate
2 ripe bananas
300ml/½ pint/1¼ cups skimmed milk
10 ice cubes

1 Hull the strawberries. Peel the bananas and chop them into fairly large chunks.

2 Place the fruit in a food processor or blender. Process to a thick, coarse purée, scraping down the sides of the goblet as necessary.

3 Add the skimmed milk and ice cubes, crushing the ice first unless you have a heavy-duty processor. Process until smooth and thick. Pour into tall glasses and top each with strawberry slices to decorate. Serve immediately.

Cook's Tip

For a super-chilled version, use frozen strawberries or a combination of frozen summer berries, such as raspberries, redcurrants and blueberries instead of fresh. You may need to blend the strawberries and milk slightly longer for a really smooth result.

Variation

For a rich and velvety drink, add 120ml/4fl oz/½ cup coconut milk and process as above. Reduce the volume of milk to 175ml/6fl oz/¾ cup.

Peppermint Candy Crush

The next time you see peppermint candy canes that are on sale at Christmas time, buy a few sticks and make this fun kid's drink.

Serves 4

90g/3½ oz pink peppermint candy canes, plus four extra to serve
750ml/1¼ pints/3 cups milk
a few drops of pink food colouring (optional)

1 Break the candy canes (inside wrappers) into small bits using a rolling pin. (If unwrapped, put the candy in a bag before you crush it.) Transfer the pieces into a food processor or blender.

2 Pour the milk over the candy and add a few drops of pink food colouring, if using. Process until the cane is broken into tiny pieces, then pour the mixture into a shallow freezer container and freeze for 2 hours, until frozen around the edges.

3 Beat the mixture with a fork, breaking up the semi-frozen areas and stirring them into the centre. Re-freeze and repeat once or twice more until the mixture is slushy. Spoon into tall glasses and serve with candy cane stirrers.

Strawberry Smoothie: Energy 165kcal/695kJ; Protein 8.4g; Carbohydrate 30.2g, of which sugars 23.6g; Fat 2.1g, of which saturates 0.7g; Cholesterol 2mg; Calcium 255mg; Fibre 1.8g; Sodium 111mg.
Raspberry Smoothie: Energy 94kcal/401kJ; Protein 5.1g; Carbohydrate 17.6g, of which sugars 17.6g; Fat 1g, of which saturates 0.4g; Cholesterol 1mg; Calcium 158mg; Fibre 2.2g; Sodium 68mg.
Peppermint Crush: Energy 175kcal/743kJ; Protein 6.5g; Carbohydrate 31.9g, of which sugars 31.9g; Fat 3.4g, of which saturates 2g; Cholesterol 11mg; Calcium 227mg; Fibre 0g; Sodium 83mg.

New York Egg Cream

No one knows precisely why this legendary drink is called egg cream, but some say it was an ironic way of describing its richness at a time when no one could afford to put both expensive eggs and cream together in a drink.

Serves 1
45–60ml/3–4 tbsp good quality chocolate syrup
120ml/4fl oz/½ cup chilled milk
175ml/6fl oz/¾ cup chilled sparkling mineral water
unsweetened cocoa powder, to decorate

1 Carefully pour the chocolate syrup into the bottom of a tall glass, avoiding dripping any on the inside of the glass.

2 Pour the chilled milk into the glass on to the chocolate syrup.

3 Gradually pour the chilled sparkling mineral water into the glass, sip up any foam that rises to the top of the glass and carefully continue to add the remaining chilled sparkling mineral water. Stir well and sprinkle with cocoa powder before drinking.

Chocolate Brownie Milkshake

This truly indulgent drink is so simple, yet utterly luxurious, so take a quiet moment to sit back, relax and enjoy. For an even more indulgent treat, add whipped cream and sprinkle with grated chocolate to serve.

Serves 1
40g/1½ oz chocolate brownies
200ml/7fl oz/scant 1 cup full cream (whole) milk
2 scoops vanilla ice cream

1 Crumble the chocolate brownies into a food processor or blender and add the milk. Blend until the mixture is smooth.

2 Add the ice cream to the chocolate milk mixture and blend until the shake is really smooth and frothy. Pour into a tall glass and serve immediately.

Banana and Maple Flip

This satisfying drink is packed with so much goodness that it makes a complete breakfast in a glass – great for when you're in a hurry. Be sure to use a really fresh, free-range egg. The glass can be decorated with a slice of orange or lime to serve.

Serves 1
1 small banana, peeled and halved
50ml/2fl oz/¼ cup thick Greek (US strained plain) yogurt
1 egg
30ml/2 tbsp maple syrup

1 Put the peeled and halved banana, thick Greek yogurt, egg and maple syrup in a food processor or blender. Add 30ml/ 2 tbsp chilled water.

2 Process the ingredients constantly for about 2 minutes, or until the mixture turns a really pale, creamy colour and has a nice frothy texture.

3 Pour the banana and maple flip into a tall, chilled glass and serve immediately. Decorate the glass with an orange or lime slice, if you like.

Cook's Tips
• *To chill the drinking glass quickly, place it in the freezer while you are preparing the drink.*
• *If you don't have a heavy-duty food processor or blender, crush the ice before adding it.*

Variations
• *For a more exotic tropical fruit flavour, substitute a small, very ripe, peeled and stoned mango for the banana.*
• *For a hint of sharpness, add 5ml/1 tsp lemon or lime juice or use a slightly tangy yogurt.*
• *Use a fat-free natural (plain) yogurt for a low-fat version.*

New York Cream: Energy 302kcal/1266kJ; Protein 6.9g; Carbohydrate 32.9g, of which sugars 32.5g; Fat 16.9g, of which saturates 5.8g; Cholesterol 8mg; Calcium 202mg; Fibre 0.4g; Sodium 74mg.
Chocolate Milkshake: Energy 637kcal/2652kJ; Protein 15.4g; Carbohydrate 54.4g, of which sugars 45.5g; Fat 41g, of which saturates 18.6g; Cholesterol 28mg; Calcium 416mg; Fibre 0g; Sodium 348mg.
Banana and Maple Flip: Energy 296kcal/1248kJ; Protein 10.5g; Carbohydrate 43.3g, of which sugars 41.4g; Fat 10.9g, of which saturates 4.2g; Cholesterol 190mg; Calcium 113mg; Fibre 0.9g; Sodium 187mg.

Barley Water

Like lemonade, barley water has been widely enjoyed as a refreshing summer drink for centuries and, until a generation ago, it would always have been home-made. Barley water is usually served chilled, but it also makes a delicious hot drink.

Makes about 10 glasses
50g/2oz/⅓ cup pearl barley
1 lemon
sugar, to taste
ice cubes and mint sprigs, to serve

1 Wash the pearl barley, then put it into a large stainless steel pan and cover with cold water. Bring to the boil and simmer gently for two minutes, then strain the liquid. Return the barley to the rinsed pan.

2 Wash the lemon and pare the rind from it with a vegetable peeler. Squeeze the juice and set aside.

3 Add the lemon rind and 600ml/1 pint/2½ cups cold water to the pan containing the barley. Bring to the boil over a medium heat, then simmer the mixture very gently for 1½–2 hours, stirring occasionally.

4 Strain the liquid into a jug (pitcher), add the reserved lemon juice, and sweeten to taste. Then leave to cool. Once cooled, pour the liquid into a bottle and keep in the refrigerator to use as required.

5 To serve, dilute to taste with cold water, and add ice cubes or crushed ice and a sprig of mint, if you like.

Variations
- *The barley water can also be used with milk, in which case omit the lemon juice as it would curdle the milk.*
- *Make up the barley water with hot water to be drunk as a cold remedy.*

Lemonade

Fresh lemonade has been a traditional country drink for many generations, drunk on farms to refresh the workers during harvest. Now, although still popular in rural areas, it is just as likely to be on the menu in a smart contemporary café.

Serves 4–6
3 lemons
115g/4oz/generous ½ cup sugar

1 Pare the skin from the lemons with a vegetable peeler and squeeze the juice from the lemons.

2 Put the lemon rind and sugar into a bowl, add 900ml/1½ pints/3¾ cups boiling water and stir well until the sugar has dissolved. Cover and leave until cold.

3 Add the lemon juice, mix well and strain into a jug (pitcher). Place in the refrigerator to chill.

4 Serve with plenty of ice.

Cook's Tips
- *Old-fashioned cloudy lemonade made with freshly squeezed lemons is a far cry from the clear carbonated commercial varieties. If you want to add some fizz, it can be topped up with soda water.*
- *Home-made lemonade will keep for up to 2 weeks in the refrigerator, if stored in bottle with a well fitting cap.*

Variation
For the ultimate thirst-quenching cooler on a hot summer's day, place 4 scoops of lemon sorbet in a tall chilled glass, tuck some slices of lemon and lime down the sides, add crushed ice and top up with home-made lemonade. Garnish with fresh mint.

Lemonade: Energy 115Kcal/489kJ; Protein 0.2g; Carbohydrate 30.4g, of which sugars 30.4g; Fat 0g, of which saturates 0g; Cholesterol 0mg; Calcium 17mg; Fibre 0g; Sodium 2mg.
Barley Water: Energy 37.9Kcal/161.6kJ; Protein 0.43g; Carbohydrate 9.44g, of which sugars 5.26g; Fat 0.08g, of which saturates 0g; Cholesterol 0mg; Calcium 3.8mg; Fibre 0g; Sodium 0.5mg

Lemon Vodka

Very similar to the deliciously moreish Italian liqueur, Limoncello, this lemon vodka should be drunk in small quantities due to its hefty alcoholic punch. Blend the sugar, lemons and vodka and keep in a bottle in the refrigerator, ready for pouring over crushed ice, or topping up with soda or sparkling water.

Serves 12–15
10 large lemons
275g/10oz/generous 1¼ cups caster (superfine) sugar
250ml/8fl oz/1 cup vodka

1 Squeeze the lemons using a citrus juicer. Pour the juice into a jug (pitcher), add the sugar and whisk well until all the sugar has dissolved.

2 Strain the sweetened lemon juice into a clean bottle or narrow-necked jar and add the vodka. Shake the mixture well to combine and chill for up to 2 weeks.

3 To serve, fill small glasses with ice and pour over the lemon vodka or pour into larger, ice-filled glasses and top up with chilled soda water (club soda).

Variation
Try using flavoured vodkas to make different classic vodka cocktails. The traditional Bloody Mary can be made using chilli-flavoured vodka, which can easily be made at home by putting a fresh red chilli in a bottle of vodka and leaving to infuse (steep). Quater-fill four tall glasses with a handful of ice cubes and pour a double measure of chilli vodka in each. If the chilli is in the bottle, make sure you don't pour it out. Top up with tomato juice and add a shake of celery salt and a pinch of ground black pepper. Stir well to combine and serve with a stick of fresh celery in each glass.

Tropical Fruit Royale

Based on the Kir Royale, a blend of champagne and crème de cassis, this elegant cocktail is made with tropical fruits and sparkling wine. So delight your guests with this appetizing drink on a balmy summer evening for a taste of the tropics.

Serves 6
2 large mangoes
6 passion fruit
sparkling wine

1 Peel the mangoes, cut the flesh off the stone (pit), then put the flesh in a food processor or blender. Process until smooth, scraping the mixture down from the sides of the bowl.

2 Fill an ice cube tray with a good half of the mango purée and freeze for 2 hours until solid.

3 Cut six wedges from one or two of the passion fruits and scoop the pulp from the rest into the remaining mango purée. Process until well blended.

4 Spoon the mixture into six stemmed glasses. Divide the mango ice cubes among the glasses, top up with sparkling wine and add the passion fruit wedges. Serve with stirrers.

Cook's Tip
Remember to blend the fruits ahead of time to give the mango ice cubes time to freeze.

Variation
Make a blackcurrant version of this drink, by freezing blackcurrants, washed and stripped from their stems. Half fill each section of the ice cube tray with blackcurrants and top up with water. Put a blackcurrant ice cube in a glass, add some blackcurrant flavoured syrup and top up with sparkling wine.

Lemon Vodka: Energy 110kcal/464kJ; Protein 0.1g; Carbohydrate 19.3g, of which sugars 19.3g; Fat 0g, of which saturates 0g; Cholesterol 0mg; Calcium 10mg; Fibre 0g; Sodium 1mg.
Tropical Fruit Royale: Energy 136kcal/570kJ; Protein 1.2g; Carbohydrate 16.7g, of which sugars 16.5g; Fat 0.2g, of which saturates 0.1g; Cholesterol 0mg; Calcium 21mg; Fibre 2.2g; Sodium 11mg.

Hot Whiskey, or Whiskey Punch

Also known as a 'hot toddy', this traditional 'cure' for colds is more often drunk as a pleasant, warming nightcap, particularly to round off a day's winter sporting activities, and it is a great drink to hold and sip on cold, damp winter evenings.

Serves 1
4–6 whole cloves
60ml/4 tbsp Irish whiskey
1 thick slice of lemon, halved
5–10ml/1–2 tsp demerara (raw) sugar, to taste

1 Stick the cloves into the lemon slice, and put it into a large stemmed glass (or one with a handle) with the whiskey and the sugar.

2 Put a teaspoon in the glass, to prevent the hot water from cracking it, then top it up with boiling water. Stir well to dissolve the sugar and serve.

Cook's Tip
There are three types of Irish whiskey: single malt, pure pot stilled and a column-and-pot still blend of grain and malt. All are distilled three times and matured in oak barrels.

Variation
Irish Chocolate Velvet is another whiskey-based hot drink, perfect to round off a day in the cold winter air, whether walking through the mountains or skiing down the slopes. To make four, whip half of 250ml/8fl oz/1 cup double (heavy) cream until it begins to hold its shape. Place 400ml/14fl oz/1⅔ cups milk and 115g/4oz milk chocolate, broken into small pieces, in a pan and heat gently until the chocolate has melted. Whisk in 30ml/2 tbsp unsweetened cocoa powder and bring to the boil. Remove from the heat and stir in the remaining cream and 60ml/4 tbsp Irish whiskey. Pour into mugs and top with whipped cream.

Apple-spiced Beer

Light beer takes on a whole new dimension in this fruity cooler. Diluted with freshly juiced apple and flavoured with ginger and star anise, it is a refreshing drink and less alcoholic than normal beer.

Makes 8–10 tall glasses
8 eating apples
25g/1oz fresh root ginger
6 whole star anise
800ml/1⅓ pints/3½ cups light beer
crushed ice

1 Quarter and core the apples and, using a small, sharp knife, cut the flesh into pieces small enough to fit through a juicer. Roughly chop the ginger. Push half the apples through the juicer, then juice the ginger and the remaining apples.

2 Put 105ml/7 tbsp of the juice in a small pan with the star anise and heat gently until almost boiling. Add to the remaining juice in a large jug (pitcher) and chill for at least 1 hour.

3 Add the light beer to the juice and stir gently until the froth has dispersed a little. Pour the spiced beer over crushed ice in tall glasses, allow to settle again and serve immediately.

Cuba Libre

Rum and coke takes on a much livelier, citrus flavour in this vibrant Caribbean cocktail that's sure to put you in a party mood.

Serves 8
9 limes
250ml/8fl oz/1 cup dark rum
800ml/1⅓ pints/3½ cups cola drink

1 Thinly slice one lime, then squeeze the juice from the others into a suitable container.

2 Put plenty of ice cubes into a large glass jug (pitcher), tucking the lime slices around them, then pour in the lime juice.

3 Pour the rum into the jug and stir well with a long-handled spoon. Top up with cola and serve immediately in tall glasses.

Hot Whiskey: Energy 153kcal/635kJ; Protein 0g; Carbohydrate 5.2g, of which sugars 5.2g; Fat 0g, of which saturates 0g; Cholesterol 0mg; Calcium 3mg; Fibre 0g; Sodium 0mg.
Apple-spiced Beer: Energy 42kcal/178kJ; Protein 0.4g; Carbohydrate 4.8g, of which sugars 4.8g; Fat 0.1g, of which saturates 0g; Cholesterol 0mg; Calcium 6mg; Fibre 0.9g; Sodium 7mg.
Cuba Libre: Energy 110kcal/461kJ; Protein 0g; Carbohydrate 10.9g, of which sugars 10.9g; Fat 0g, of which saturates 0g; Cholesterol 0mg; Calcium 6mg; Fibre 0g; Sodium 5mg.

Hot Claret

A hot wine cup is now unlikely to be made with claret, but the name dates back hundreds of years to the time when it was plentiful, and probably not very special.

Makes about 10 glasses

1 bottle red wine
175g/6oz/scant 1 cup sugar, or to taste
1 lemon
5cm/2in piece of cinnamon stick
lemon slices, to decorate (optional)

1 Put the red wine, 300ml/½ pint/1¼ cups water and the sugar into a large stainless steel pan.

2 Peel the lemon thinly with a vegetable peeler and add the peel to the pan with the cinnamon stick. Slowly heat this mixture over a low heat, stirring to dissolve the sugar, until almost boiling.

3 Remove from the heat, cover and leave for 10 minutes to infuse (steep). Strain into a heated jug (pitcher) and pour the hot mulled wine into warmed glasses, each garnished with a half-slice of lemon, if you like.

Sea Breeze

One of today's most requested cocktails, Sea Breeze was one of the first popular cocktails to use cranberry juice. Ocean Spray is one of the most famous brands, but the supermarkets nearly all have a proprietary version.

Serves 1

2 measures/3 tbsp vodka
2 measures/3 tbsp grapefruit juice
3 measures/4½ tbsp cranberry juice
lime wedges and cranberries, to decorate

1 Shake all the ingredients well with plenty of ice, and pour everything into a chilled highball glass.

2 Add a wedge of lime and a few cranberries.

Sloe Gin

The small, purple sloes grow widely in the hedgerows everywhere and are not much used except, perhaps, for sloe gin, which is drunk as a liqueur. Remember to allow at least three months for it to mature – sloes picked in September will make a special drink at Christmas time.

Makes 2–3 bottles

450g/1lb/4 cups ripe sloes (black plums)
225g/8oz/generous 1 cup caster (superfine) sugar
1 litre/1¾ pint/4 cups Dry Gin

1 Check through the sloes and discard any damaged or unsound fruit. Rinse the sloes and remove the stalks.

2 Prick each sloe with a silver or stainless steel fork or use a cocktail stick (toothpick).

3 Select several wide-necked screw-top or easy to seal sterilized jars and arrange alternate layers of fruit and sugar in them. Top up the jars with gin, and close them tightly. Store for at least 3 months in a cool, dark place.

4 Shake the jars gently every now and then to help extract and distribute the flavour evenly. When ready, strain into a jug (pitcher) and then pour into sterilized bottles and store for another 3 months, if possible.

Cook's Tip
Sloes are the fruit of the wild blackthorn bush.

Variation
Sloe gin is best served alone at room temperature, but you could add some to a glass of sparkling wine or champagne to make a royale.

Hot Claret: Energy 120kcal/506kJ; Protein 0.2g; Carbohydrate 18.4g, of which sugars 18.4g; Fat 0g, of which saturates 0g; Cholesterol 0mg; Calcium 15mg; Fibre 0g; Sodium 6mg.
Sea Breeze: Energy 133kcal/554kJ; Protein 0.2g; Carbohydrate 8.4g, of which sugars 8.4g; Fat 0.1g, of which saturates 0g; Cholesterol 0mg; Calcium 8mg; Fibre 0g; Sodium 3mg.
Sloe Gin: Energy 1554kcal/6486kJ; Protein 0.6g; Carbohydrate 117.6g, of which sugars 117.6g; Fat 0g, of which saturates 0g; Cholesterol 0mg; Calcium 60mg; Fibre 0g; Sodium 7mg.

Black Velvet

This modern classic always provokes a vicious debate. If you subscribe to the side of the argument that believe this drink is a waste of good champagne, why not substitute it with sparkling wine for a bubbly, but inexpensive version.

Serves 8

1 bottle of champagne, chilled
about 750ml/1¼ pints Guinness, or to taste

1 Mix the champagne with an equal quantity of Guinness, or to taste, in eight tall glasses.

2 Drink immediately, while very bubbly.

Brandy Alexander

One of the greatest cocktails of them all, Brandy Alexander can be served at the end of a grand dinner with coffee, or as an aperitif at a cocktail party, since the cream in it helps to line the stomach. It was possibly originally made with gin rather than brandy, and the cream was sweetened, but the formula below is undoubtedly the best of all possible worlds.

Serves 1

1 measure/1½ tbsp cognac
1 measure/1½ tbsp brown crème de cacao
1 measure/1½ tbsp double (heavy) cream
ground nutmeg or grated dark (bittersweet) chocolate, to decorate

1 Shake the ingredients thoroughly with ice, and strain into a cocktail glass.

2 Sprinkle ground nutmeg, or grate a little whole nutmeg, on top. Alternatively, sprinkle with grated dark chocolate.

Gaelic Coffee

A good Gaelic coffee, also called Irish coffee, is an exercise in contrast and a rare treat indeed – and often taken as an alternative to dessert.

Serves 1

25ml/1½ tbsp Irish whiskey
about 150ml/¼ pint/⅔ cup hot strong black coffee
demerara (raw) sugar, to taste
about 50ml/2fl oz/¼ cup lightly whipped chilled cream

1 Measure the whiskey into a stemmed glass, or one with a handle. Pour in enough freshly made strong black coffee to come to about 1cm/½in from the top.

2 Sweeten to taste and stir vigorously to dissolve the sugar and create a small whirlpool in the glass.

3 Top the coffee with the lightly whipped cream, poured over the back of the teaspoon. It will settle on the top to make a distinct layer in creamy contrast to the dark coffee underneath. (It is important that the coffee should be very hot to contrast with the chilled cream.) Serve immediately and do not stir in the cream.

Cook's Tip

If you are trying to avoid caffeine in your drinks, make this Irish coffee with decaffeinated ground or instant coffee. Products are much improved in recent years and now the only agent used in the process is carbonated water.

Variation

A simple cup of normal espresso coffee laced with a liqueur or alcoholic spirit is often the chosen way to end a meal in Italy. Sometimes a little sugar and even lemon zest can be added to it. The list of spirits is endless, but as a starting point, you can choose from: brandy, rum, whisky, eau de vie, Grand Marnier, Amaretto, Tia Maria, Drambuie or Cointreau.

Black Velvet: Energy 98kcal/406kJ; Protein 0.7g; Carbohydrate 6.2g, of which sugars 6.2g; Fat 0g, of which saturates 0g; Cholesterol 0mg; Calcium 12mg; Fibre 0g; Sodium 10mg.
Brandy Alexander: Energy 288kcal/1190kJ; Protein 0.6g; Carbohydrate 6.3g, of which sugars 6.3g; Fat 22.7g, of which saturates 11.7g; Cholesterol 48mg; Calcium 22mg; Fibre 0g; Sodium 30mg.
Gaelic Coffee: Energy 262kcal/1081kJ; Protein 1g; Carbohydrate 5.5g, of which sugars 5.5g; Fat 20.1g, of which saturates 12.6g; Cholesterol 53mg; Calcium 31mg; Fibre 0g; Sodium 13mg.

Index